Y0-ARP-886

PUBLIC REGULATION OF BUSINESS

THE IRWIN SERIES IN ECONOMICS

Consulting Editor
LLOYD G. REYNOLDS
Yale University

AMES *Soviet Economic Processes*
ANDERSON, GITLOW, & DIAMOND (eds.) *General Economics: A Book of Readings* rev. ed.
BALASSA *The Theory of Economic Integration*
BEAL & WICKERSHAM *The Practice of Collective Bargaining* 3d ed.
BLAUG *Economic Theory in Retrospect* rev. ed.
BORNSTEIN (ed.) *Comparative Economic Systems: Models and Cases* rev. ed.
BORNSTEIN & FUSFELD (eds.) *The Soviet Economy: A Book of Readings* rev. ed.
BUCHANAN *The Public Finances* rev. ed.
CARTTER *Theory of Wages and Employment*
CARTTER & MARSHALL *Labor Economics: Wages, Employment, and Trade Unionism*
DAVIDSON, SMITH, & WILEY *Economics: An Analytical Approach* rev. ed.
DAVIS, HUGHES, & MCDOUGALL *American Economic History: The Development of a National Economy* 3d ed.
DOLL, RHODES, & WEST *Economics of Agricultural Production, Markets, and Policy*
DRUMMOND *The Canadian Economy: Organization and Development*
DUE *Government Finance: Economics of the Public Sector* 4th ed.
DUE & CLOWER *Intermediate Economic Analysis* 5th ed.
FELLNER *Probability and Profit: A Study of Economic Behavior along Bayesian Lines*
FERGUSON *Microeconomic Theory* rev. ed.

GAMBS & KOMISAR *Economics and Man* 3d ed.
GORDON *The Investment Financing and Valuation of the Corporation*
GRAMPP & WEILER (eds.) *Economic Policy: Readings in Political Economy* 3d ed.
GROSSMAN, HANSEN, HENDRIKSEN, MCALLISTER, OKUDA, & WOLMAN (eds.) *Readings in Current Economics* rev. ed.
GUTHRIE *Statistical Methods in Economics*
GUTHRIE & WALLACE *Economics* 4th ed.
HAGEN *The Economics of Development*
HARRISS *The American Economy: Principles, Practices, and Policies* 6th ed.
HERBER *Modern Public Finance*
HIGGINS *United Nations and U.S. Foreign Economic Policy*
JOME *Principles of Money and Banking*
KINDLEBERGER *International Economics* 4th ed.
KUHLMAN & SKINNER *The Economic System* rev. ed.
LEE *Macroeconomics: Fluctuations, Growth, and Stability* 4th ed.
LLOYD *Microeconomic Analysis*
LOCKLIN *Economics of Transportation* 6th ed.
MEYERS *Economics of Labor Relations*
PEGRUM *Public Regulation of Business* rev. ed.
PEGRUM *Transportation: Economics and Public Policy* rev. ed.
PETERSON & GRAY *Economic Development of the United States*
PHILLIPS *The Economics of Regulation: Theory and Practice in the Transportation and Public Utility Industries*
REYNOLDS *Economics: A General Introduction* 3d ed.
RIMA *Development of Economic Analysis*
SCITOVSKY *Welfare and Competition: The Economics of a Fully Employed Economy*
SIEGEL *Aggregate Economics and Public Policy* rev. ed.
SIRKIN *Introduction to Macroeconomic Theory* rev. ed.
SMITH & TEIGEN (eds.) *Readings in Money, National Income, and Stabilization Policy*
SNIDER *Introduction to International Economics* 4th ed.
SPENCER *Managerial Economics: Text, Problems, and Short Cases* 3d ed.
VANEK *International Trade: Theory and Economic Policy*
WILCOX *Public Policies toward Business* 3d ed.

PUBLIC REGULATION OF BUSINESS

BY **DUDLEY F. PEGRUM** PH.D.

PROFESSOR OF ECONOMICS

UNIVERSITY OF CALIFORNIA, LOS ANGELES

REVISED EDITION

1965

RICHARD D. IRWIN, INC.

HOMEWOOD, ILLINOIS

REVISED EDITION

First Printing, May, 1965

Second Printing, September, 1967

Third Printing, July, 1968

Fourth Printing, April, 1969

Fifth Printing February, 1971

PRINTED IN THE UNITED STATES OF AMERICA

Library of Congress Catalogue Card No. 65-20527

TO MARION, MY WIFE

PREFACE

TO THE FIRST EDITION

Public regulation of business enterprise may be approached from a number of different points of view and may be dealt with by a number of different disciplines, each with its own particular emphasis and techniques. The formulation and administration of public policy by courts, commissions, and legislatures must comprehend and utilize all these varied disciplines, even though those who are charged with developing and carrying out the policies are specialists in only one, or perhaps even none of them. The businessman is faced with the task of managing economic enterprise in an environment to which he must adjust his activities, at the same time that he is shaping that very environment by his own decisions and actions. The citizen, by his reactions to managerial behavior and public policy and by his response through the medium of the ballot box, exercises an influence that is vital, even crucial, to the functioning and development of the society in which he lives and wants to live.

The task of an author who endeavors to bring the diverse threads together into a comprehensive treatment of public regulation is a formidable one. At the outset, he is faced with a vast array of material from which he must make a selection of the facts and issues which seem to him to be important for the purpose at hand. If he is to be objective, he must select and present them in a way that will make it possible for the reader to form his own judgment, independent of that which the author may hold. At the same time, the latter, in approaching the subject from the viewpoint of his own discipline, must endeavor to utilize all the relevant tools that are available without turning the presentation into a technical exercise. The author is also faced with the task of bringing his discipline to bear on the interpretation of the facts and the analysis of the issues so as to provide standards for decision making and bases for the formulation of judgments on critical questions. This author has endeavored to meet these criteria by bringing economic analysis to bear on every phase of the subject matter dealt with, at the same time that he has drawn heavily on other disciplines, particularly law, history, and political science. He has avoided, however, usurping the specialist's role in those other fields.

The book is divided into five sections, each of which stands alone. They form a continuous whole, however, in that what is developed in one section is antecedent and essential to that which follows. Part I is designed to set forth the basic facts of institutional and governmental arrangements, within which regulation in this country takes place; the organizational structure of business; and the development of modern business enterprise from which the current problems of regulation emerge.

Part II develops what the author believes to be the basic economic principles that bear upon regulation. Attention is centered on the pricing process and the factors which have to be considered in the making of decisions with regard to prices, because these are the focuses of the problem of an efficient allocation and utilization of economic resources and the subject of most discussion and controversy in the economic aspects of regulation.

Part III deals with the antitrust laws and their administration. One reason for a somewhat more detailed attention to regulation in this area is that antitrust forms the basic approach in the United States, to government regulation of private business. It embodies the underlying philosophy of this country on the public control of business activity; and all organized economic activity is subject to antitrust insofar as the federal government is concerned, unless exemption is provided by specific legislation or constitutional protection. Somewhat extensive treatment is accorded to court decisions because there does not seem to be any other way of portraying satisfactorily the present state of regulation in this area and the critical issues of administration on the current scene.

Part IV deals with transportation and public utilities. No attempt has been made to set forth the myriad details of legislation or administrative action in these two fields. The main issues of public policy and the economic principles applicable to them have been portrayed, however. This section has been included because it is in these two areas that our most extensive experience in detailed regulation has been obtained.

Part V, which consists of a single chapter, aims to bring out the relationships of economic policy on the one hand to political and social objectives on the other. Any program of public regulation, and all policies dealing with economic considerations, must of necessity, explicitly or implicitly, be based on a theory of the state and of the economic functions of the state. In this chapter, the author sets forth his own views on this, together with a brief appraisal of alternatives and their relation to individual freedom and action.

The author has specifically avoided any attempt to make the book an encyclopedia of government and business. Instead, he has confined his attention to the institutional, organizational, and economic considerations essential to the understanding and development of regulation of business enterprise in this country. These considerations are then applied to the regulation of business in general through the antitrust laws, and the special regulation of transportation and public utilities under the unique and more restrictive laws which apply to these industries. As a consequence, labor, money and banking, public finance, agriculture, and so forth, have not been covered. Inclusion of them would have stretched an already long book to inordinate size; in addition, issues other than those centering on regulation occupy such a large part of these fields that inclusion could have resulted only in superficial and rather uninformative treatment. It is the author's belief that a more intensive analysis of a more restricted, but still very large, area of economic policy provides a better basis for an understanding of the economic problems of public control.

The approach to regulation is necessarily through the organization of the productive activity of economic life under private enterprise, because regulation has meaning only under such circumstances; or at least, it has meaning only in a society where the management of production is in the hands of those who are independent of the state, and in which the government acts as a third party between consumers and producers. Because regulation must assume that industry is organized separately and independently of the government, it is not necessary to justify the private-enterprise point of view in the discussion. It must be taken for granted that the prime responsibility of public regulation is to assist in the successful functioning of a private-enterprise system. An explanation of the reason for the private-enterprise approach could stop at this point. The author makes no apologies, however, for the fact that he espouses private enterprise, and regards departures therefrom as exceptions, the adoption of which should be scrutinized with extreme care, and acceded to only when there is no tolerably operationally practicable way of dispensing with government operation. Democracy and economic freedom are possessions too precious to be bartered away for fancied benefits to be derived from the political management of the productive processes. No one has yet demonstrated that total ownership and management of the productive resources of a country by the government are compatible with democracy and individual freedom. Theory and experience so far provide convincing evidence to the contrary. It is therefore essential that all of those who are interested in economic policy and public regulation be fully aware of the political and social arrangements through which our ideas of democracy and individual freedom are able to express themselves, of the impact of economic policy on those arrangements, and the limitations which the latter impose on that policy. The present book undertakes to set forth the economic problems of public regulation so as to provide the basis for developing policies in keeping with the heritage which the people of this country enjoy, and presumably wish to pass on to their heirs.

The present book is not a revision of the author's previous work, *The Regulation of Industry*—it is a new book. The author has drawn on the experience gained in writing the previous book and necessarily has utilized such material as was pertinent to the present treatment. Every endeavor has been made to make this book an analysis of the economic aspects of public regulation. In scope, the subject matter has been extended to include all that the author believes is generally comprehended by the term "public regulation of business." In approach, the activities of public agencies and the problems faced by them, as well as the aspects of business decision making which come within the sope of public scrutiny, have been subject to economic analysis. Because of this, the author has endeavored to avoid the development of any economic principles for their own sake, but instead has tried to shape the relevant ones to the purpose of policy making and policy evaluation.

The author wishes to acknowledge his indebtedness to the scholars and writers, whose numbers are legion, who have made contributions to the subject matter covered by this book. He has drawn so heavily on them that it is often difficult for him to know which ideas are theirs and which are his. He has given extensive recognition to them in footnotes and in references which are to be found at the end of each chapter. Many, however, will not find their names in either place and for this omission the author offers his apologies. Only the names of those whose works were directly and specifically drawn upon, or whose writings constitute a convenient starting point for those who wish to pursue further the study of any particular topic have been included, and only the names appearing in the text material or in the footnotes are contained in the index.

Special recognition for direct assistance in developing the subject matter of the book should go to the author's colleagues in his own department and to a number of his friends in other departments throughout the country, with whom he has discussed many of the topics and issues. Particular thanks are due to Professors Warren C. Scoville and Robert Baldwin of the Department of Economics of the University of California, Los Angeles, for assistance in resolving certain technical questions, and to Mrs. Gratia C. Bell who worked untiringly in collecting the vast amount of material on the law and its administration. The book owes far more to her assistance than any mere acknowledgment in a preface can portray. Finally, to my wife must go that recognition for assistance, encouragement, and self-denial, without which this book would never have been completed.

PREFACE

TO THE REVISED EDITION

Since the first edition of this book was completed almost seven years ago considerable change has taken place in the economic and industrial structure of the United States. The influence of almost continuous prosperity, inflation, and international developments has given us a "new era" of big business, mergers, and conglomerate combinations. Possibly of greater significance has been what appears to be a revitalization of the antitrust laws, especially as a result of the Supreme Court's decisions in cases arising under the Celler–Kefauver amendment to the Clayton Act. The strict interpretation and application of this law now offers some prospect even of being carried over to the Sherman Act. Furthermore, the application of the rule of reason seems to be less concerned with considerations of what is good for public policy than of carrying out what the Court believes to be the will of Congress, even though the impact of political forces on the point of view of the Court seems to be very pronounced. Finally, there has been a shift toward a more competitively oriented transportation policy as evidenced by the emphasis on this in the Message to Congress of the late President Kennedy in April, 1962.

This revised edition endeavors to place these developments in their historical perspective. It brings the factual materials up to date in the hope that the reader will be able to place his own evaluation on them, while at the same time it tries to interpret them in light of the goals and requisites of a private enterprise system and a free society.

The basic structure of the previous edition has been retained. A few major changes, however, have been made partly as a result of suggestions, generously given, by many scholars interested in resolving the difficulties of synthesizing the legal and economic approaches to regulation, and partly as a result of the author's own endeavors to make economics more useful for public policy, and to make economists more aware of the need to understand the legal and institutional environment with which they must work. The last chapter of the previous edition, "The State and Economic Life," has been moved to the front of the book at the suggestion of many readers in the hope that it will provide a broad setting within which regulation takes place and must be appraised.

The major change is in the section on the antitrust laws. The presentation of these and their enforcement have been completely reorganized on what, it is hoped, is a more logical and unified basis from the standpoint of economics. The basic case approach has been retained because it is felt that economists are concerned with the impact of antitrust on enterprises as a whole, in contrast to the lawyer's approach of special points of pleading and violation of the law. A completely new chapter on Section 7 of the Clayton Act has been added. Enforcement of the Clayton Act by the Federal Trade Commission has been integrated with that of the Justice Department.

Reading references have been removed from the end of each chapter and have been placed in a bibliography for further study in Appendix II. Selections from the antitrust laws of what seem to be the most relevant sections for the purpose of this book are given in Appendix I. This is done to give the reader immediate reference to the wording of the laws which play so prominent a part in the interpretation of them.

Once again I wish to acknowledge the assistance of all those readers who have offered suggestions for eliminating errors and improving presentation. Particularly do I wish to accord special thanks to Mrs. Gratia C. Bell for her continued assistance in collecting material on the law and its administration. Finally to my wife, Marion, must go that recognition for assistance, encouragement and self-denial, too often taken for granted, without which this revision would not have been undertaken.

DUDLEY F. PEGRUM

UNIVERSITY OF CALIFORNIA, LOS ANGELES
April, 1965

TABLE OF CONTENTS

PART I: PROLOGUE

PART II: INSTITUTIONAL AND ORGANIZATIONAL ARRANGEMENTS

PART V: THE REGULATION OF TRANSPORTATION AND PUBLIC UTILITIES

PART I

Prologue

Chapter 1 THE STATE AND ECONOMIC LIFE

REGULATION AND THE THEORY OF THE STATE

Need for a Theory of the State

Public regulation of business enterprise is based upon assumptions regarding the functions of the state in economic life. Those assumptions may be explicitly set forth or merely implicitly contained in the policies that are pursued. The analysis in this book is in terms of an economy based primarily on private ownership; in other words, a private enterprise economy. The evaluation of policies and proposals for dealing with various issues is based on the premise that the continued development of such an economy is a desirable objective, and that it is necessary if the democratic heritage of this country is to be preserved. The subject could be developed on the assumption that so long as the goal of a free society is maintained, policies will be shaped to that end. The matter is not that simple, however, because the means that are adopted will affect the ends; and unless the implications of the means are understood, the end result may be vastly different from that which was envisaged. One cannot draw up a blueprint of the economic order for a free society, because the economic life of such a society is but a part of the sum total of all of its activities. The role which the state is called upon to play in the economic life of the people therefore involves the rest of their social behavior, and must be considered in conjunction with it.

Economic policy, to have any realism, must be developed in an institutional setting. It is, consequently, appropriate to examine briefly the role of the state in economic life and to set forth the functions of the state which the evaluation and appraisal of policies assume. Without this setting the proposals are largely academic because they depend upon the validity of the primary assumptions and cannot be adopted without them. Furthermore, the fundamental issues are insoluble unless—and until—we analyze with greater care the political and social implications of the proposals and programs that are now being advanced to deal with current problems. The regulation or control of industry is meaningless outside of a particular political setting, and to assume that democracy is independent of the type of solution that may be developed for economic problems is to fly in the face of facts. A national policy for the regulation of business enterprise must be in keeping with the demands of adjustment to a rapidly changing technology in a strife-torn world, but the plans for the latter must be focused on the primary objective of economic policies essential to the maintenance of a liberal society. This necessitates an understanding of the basic tenets of such a society and the policy implications of them.[1]

Theories of the State

The location of responsibility for directing and controlling economic activity is the core of the problem of the relation of the state to economic life. The issues that are involved are not unique to the present day, nor are the basic questions that are posed confined to economic matters alone. They are fundamental to the whole problem of freedom versus authority and an understanding of the meaning of each of these terms. Today, one frequently meets with forthright challenge if he suggests that there are limitations on the power of the state to control or regulate economic life. Yet, strangely enough, he is not likely to be faced with the same sort of challenge if he asserts that there are definite limitations to the authority that it can exert over religion. These are not different problems, however. They are simply different aspects of the same one; but because of the emphasis today on economic affairs, and because of the prominence of these in everyday life, we seem to think that they are quite distinct.

Theories of the scope of the powers that the state enjoys, or should enjoy, over the various activities of men are associated with what appear, at particular times, to be the most immediately pressing needs. These theories are commonly connected with ideas, implied or stated, of the origins or bases of the state. Many explanations of the forces which have molded the development of organized political life have been advanced at one time or another. Some have found the origin of the state in the family, with the father as the head of the family. This is patriarchal theory. A similar hypothesis, which, however, traces the origin to the maternal side of the family, is the basis for the matriarchal theory. Another explanation that has played a very important part in the history of political thought traces the beginning of the state to a social contract. This theory proceeded from the assumption that the past history of mankind might be divided into two periods, the first of which was antecedent to the institution of government, the second being subsequent to it. From the first "natural" state, man formed a union by covenant with his fellows. Human law was substituted for natural law; and the individual, in submitting to social duties, was clothed with social rights. In the course

[1]For an excellent discussion of this whole matter, see W. A. Orton, *The Liberal Tradition* (New Haven: Yale University Press, 1945); H. C. Simons, *Economic Policy for a Free Society* (Chicago: University of Chicago Press, 1948); Lionel Robbins, *The Theory of Economic Policy* (London: Macmillan & Co., Ltd., 1953).

of development, this theory became a defense for absolutism by some and a basis for popular sovereignty by others.

One of the most influential theories, especially in relation to current developments, finds the origin of the state in the existence of a single or dominant motive power. This theory holds that government is the outcome of human aggression and is thus really a theory of force. Its principal role in political thought has been to justify the assumption of the supreme power of the state, especially on economic matters. The most renowned exponent of the theory was Karl Marx, who attributed the origin of the state to economic exploitation. Political power, he said, is merely the organized power of one class for oppressing another. The state is the product and manifestation of the irreconcilability of class antagonisms. All social organization is determined by economic relationships that are the result of the mode of production. Even man's ideas and ideals spring from economic foundations. Government is simply a dictatorship in the hands of the dominant class of the time and will remain that way until the classless society is reached.

The difficulty with all explanations which trace the origin of the state to a single or primary cause is that they are too simple and place undue emphasis on some one factor. The modern political state is the result of evolution under the impact of a variety of forces that have weighed differently in each particular case. It is impossible to predicate any universal course of development or any necessary institutional arrangements. In any case, however, the modern state has evolved from early obscure origins by a gradual process running throughout the history of mankind. Speaking generally, the growth of the state has been accompanied by a steady increase in the territory occupied by it There has been an increasing fixity and certainty of action, together with a growth of political consciousness. In the most advanced stages of development, politics and religion have been separated, with the state giving up its religious functions. Finally, the most significant feature has been the growth of democratic government. The appeal, real or pretended, to the masses by all the governments of the world is evidence of the potency of the democratic ideal, even though it may be perverted—temporarily, at least—by autocratic leaders to the ends of personal and national power.

The challenge to democracy, today, lies in the endeavors of special groups to use the state to further their interests by compulsion of one kind or another, without regard for the welfare of the nation as a whole. This is not a new story; the progress of democracy has been marked by a continuous struggle against special interests, but the present tendency to organize in order to utilize the state for particular purposes is so widespread that it can lead to state dominance of all walks of life, and will result in it if the present tide does not recede. This tendency to call upon the state exaggerates the functions and power of the state to the point that the latter becomes an end in itself. The all-powerful national state is the outcome. The consequences of this have already been written in the blood, devastation, and demoralization of World War II.

LIBERALISM AND THE THEORY OF THE STATE

The Meaning of Liberalism

Today, practically everyone professes to be a liberal or, at least, "liberal." Used in this way, of course, the term has no meaning; and no content for it covers every shade of political belief. Frequently, "liberal" and "leftist" are contrasted with "conservative" and "rightist," the implication being that all leftist proposals are liberal, and vice versa. This also carries the connotation that liberal programs, especially on economic matters, involve an extension of state authority over the direction and management of the economy, because this is the essence of the "leftist" philosophy. Anyone who opposes this extension is a conservative or reactionary and belongs to the "right." A moment's reflection, however, will indicate the fallacy of this distinction. Nazis and Fascists are condemned in this country as extreme "rightists," but no one exalted the supreme position of the state more than they did. There are those who support public ownership in some industries or instances and yet believe in capitalism and an economy based primarily on private enterprise. They are neither "leftists" nor doctrinaire socialists; nor does recognition of the advantages of public ownership and operation of certain enterprises under appropriate circumstances make them socialists. The distinction lies deeper than that.

Liberalism is not merely an economic philosophy; indeed, it is not an economic philosophy at all. It is a social philosophy, of which its theory of the state, and theory of the economic functions of the state, are an integral and necessary part, but only a part. Much contemporary discussion identifies liberalism with the theory of the economic functions of the state when, in point of fact, the liberal theory of those functions is the result of the concept of the state as an associational device through which liberty and justice are to be achieved and maintained. Contemporary criticism of liberalism proceeds from the assumption that economic considerations are the primary controlling factors in human affairs and that economic organization and planning can be subject to precisely the same type of procedure that has created the marvels of modern technology. It is not without relevance that the models thus created for the economic order, with all their mathematical precision, have not been developed for religious, political, and social life in general. That it has been done for economics on the analogy of the physical sciences is because it has been possible to remove the human being for analytic purposes in a way that is not feasible for political and religious constructs. Economics as a discipline has gained both its strength and its weakness from this fact. Liberalism, however, does not forget that, as applied to public policy, economics is political economy.

The liberal tradition is the great repository of freedom—the goal which seems to appeal to all people, once they get a glimpse of it, but which, in its modern perverted form, has become freedom through sublimation in the state. Liberalism is based upon an optimistic view of man and society. Its proponents believe in the possibilities of beneficent change and in the capacity of rational minds to achieve it. The ideas expressed by liberalism are both progressive and humanitarian—the supreme value in life is human personality, the function of institutional arrangements being to further its development. Liberalism advances the belief in freedom as the basis of progress, but it also maintains that true freedom can be obtained only in society. The basis of a progressive society is the free individual who, however, is an individual in society. Hence, there is institutional emphasis on voluntary associations and group action. Liberalism holds that the progress it postulates can be achieved only through voluntary group action and, in this respect, stands in contrast to extreme individualism, which denies that society has a responsibility for the development of the individual or the furthering of his welfare. Liberalism is willing to use the state as an instrument for creating and maintaining the conditions of freedom, for preventing abuse of power, for establishing equality of opportunity for all, and for insuring toleration of the ideas and beliefs of others (on the necessary assumption that this involves reciprocation).[2]

Liberalism and the Law

Law, under liberalism, is the formal expression of the citizens of a state of what constitutes right and wrong as related to public policy. It emerges from settled convictions as they are embodied in customary procedures; and, in so far as it resorts to compulsion, it involves only recalcitrants. It thus embraces, in a very real sense, the idea of "government by the consent of the governed." Under liberalism, therefore, change or reform comes about through state action only when there is widespread conviction that existing laws do not correspond to the facts or when the desire for a particular innovation is so broad that voluntary

[2]One of the best definitions of liberalism is the one given by Professor Ramsey Muir: "Liberalism is a belief in the value of human personality and a conviction that the source of all progress lies in the free exercise of individual energy; it produces an eagerness to emancipate all individuals or groups so that they may freely exercise their powers so far as this can be done without injury to others; and it therefore involves a readiness to use the power of the state for the purposes of creating the conditions within which individual energy can thrive, of preventing all abuses of power, of affording to every citizen the means of acquiring mastery of his own capacities, and of establishing a real equality for all" ("Liberal Party," *Encyclopaedia Britannica*, Vol. XIII [1940], p. 1000). See also George H. Sabine, *A History of Political Theory* (rev. ed.; New York: Henry Holt and Co., 1950), pp. 740-49.

acceptance by the vast majority will insure its success. If those who do not wish to comply do not thereby harm or infringe upon the rights of others, there is no need to impose coercion on them. This is in distinct contrast to the position of many present-day reformers, who seek to use the state as a means of compelling adherence to their programs, and who —seizing upon moments of enthusiasm or despair to enact them—frequently do so on the idea that "we must do it now while we have the chance, otherwise enthusiasm will wane when conditions change, and then it will be too late."[3] The enactment of laws by a party possessing a bare majority, or even a comfortable margin, in the face of any considerable opposition, should be the result only of long and careful deliberation. The various devices which democratic governments employ to secure adequate and careful consideration, compliance with established procedures, and a thoroughgoing airing of public opinion are the result of the development of the liberal tradition in government.

Because liberalism rests on a widespread consensus of opinion and voluntary compliance with the established ways of doing things, it opposes monopolies and undue concentration of power in whatever hands it may reside. The prohibition against monopolies contained in our laws, or the demand for the strict control of them by the state if they cannot be eliminated, is an expression of this. It recognizes the right of voluntary association and group action—indeed, it rests on these; but it also recognizes the need for imposing curbs on the abuse of monopoly powers. In this respect, the state must be impartial if a liberal structure is to be preserved. Neither industrial leaders nor labor unions can enjoy any specially privileged position in this respect. The individual should have the right to join associations as he sees fit, and to withdraw from them. Moreover, he should not be compelled by law to deal with any particular one but should be free to select among them. Where this, for some reason, is impossible, the state must intervene to curb the monopoly powers.[4]

The liberal point of view, necessarily, insists on a limitation of the powers of the state. The roots of a democratic structure lie in voluntary associations and local government. The reasons for this are that such organizations are much closer to the people than are the central governments and that they are more subject to direct control by the people. This is not to say that liberalism assumes a weak central government. On the contrary, it assumes a strong central government; but it also requires a decentralization of functions among local governments. The central government's functions should be confined to dealing with those matters which transcend local competence and on which there is wide-

[3]"One has to respect personality very much indeed to reject doing good by force" (Orton, *op. cit.*, p. 285).

[4]For a good, short exposition of this, see O. H. Taylor, "Economics versus Politics," *Economics of the Recovery Program* (New York: McGraw-Hill Book Co., Inc., 1934), pp. 160–88.

spread consensus for unanimity of action. Liberalism is, thus, thoroughly in accord with federalism. A federal state has no place under socialism or a totalitarian government.

Freedom of the individual means that he must be able to make his own choices regarding the various activities of his social life, be they religious, economic, or any other kind. The seventeenth- and eighteenth-century English philosophers recognized the interplay and placed as much emphasis on property rights as on political and religious freedom in recognition of the interdependence of these. Monopoly in the hands of the Crown was as abhorrent as monopoly in any one else's possession. Today, we take strong steps to prevent business from using its economic power to intimidate, bribe, or entice employees to vote for particular measures, but government is no less dangerous, to say the least, when it uses the vast resources at its disposal to influence decisions at the polls. Nor can it very well be argued that the government represents the views of all the people on vital issues when the losing side has a large following. Extensive control by government over vast quantities of economic resources can be a potent weapon in the hands of those in power, as has been clearly demonstrated in a large part of the contemporary world. Even political control over religion has not been eschewed by a goodly number of countries. Where this has been most effective it has been implemented through control over church property.

Liberalism and *Laissez Faire*

Nineteenth-century liberalism, in its economic aspects, found expression in the doctrine of *laissez faire*. As a philosophic basis for public policy, it arose in opposition to the prevalent system of state interference known as "mercantilism." The latter meant the state direction of commercial activities for the purpose of furthering national power. *Laissez faire* advocated competition, individual initiative, and free trade. It was a protest aimed at freeing economic enterprise from state direction. It was based on a belief in the harmony of interests (that is, everyone should be left to follow his own interest as he understood it), in the operation of natural laws in human affairs, and in the automatic direction of economic activity by the forces of competition.

This philosophy originated in the age of commercialism, as contrasted with modern industrialism, and at a time when industry itself was small scale. In seeking to free the individual from economic dominance by the state, *laissez faire* was the economic counterpart of political democracy. Its basic tenent was competition; but at the same time, it presupposed a stable and strong political state. It did not mean that there would be no regulation of business. On the contrary, it assumed that there would be state interference for the purpose of creating the conditions necessary to individual competition. It did not, however, regard the state as an important factor in the guidance of economic activity. Government intervention in economics was largely confined to broad questions of the political implications of the operation of natural laws and to the maintenance of justice.[5]

This relatively simple concept of the role of the state in controlling economic activity was inadequate to meet the conditions brought about by the rise of modern industry. The necessity for the more complex and positive types of control that these conditions created led to a decline in the influence of *laissez faire*. It is too easy to jump to the conclusion, however, that the passing of some of the conditions upon which this philosophy was based also meant that competition and private enterprise had been abandoned, or that the force of competition had been lessened. It is evident that the growth of industrialism and large-scale business and the use of the corporate device introduced new complexities into competition and new elements into monopoly. These not only exposed the inadequacy of existing laws and controls but also made it difficult for legislation to keep pace with changes. The resulting problems have led to a discrediting of *laissez faire*. This has taken the form of a vigorous attack on competition and private enterprise, as they have manifested themselves on the modern scene, and has given rise to the belief, in many quarters, that the alternative is to return to extensive direction and management of economic activity by the state. This point of view has been given impetus by the wave of economic nationalism that has swept over the world during the twentieth century and the consequent revival of intervention on the part of the state.

If it is assumed, however, that we wish to continue a private enterprise economy, it is unfortunate that the term *laissez faire* has fallen into such disrepute, since this has led to the tendency to discard everything that it espoused. That the earlier concepts were inadequate to meet modern conditions is obvious; but if private enterprise and the competitive system are to be retained, then the basic requisites, adapted to modern conditions, need to be revived in the period of reconstruction that lies ahead. The evolution of *laissez faire* into a modernized version does not warrant the assumption that the idea and its implementation constituted an excursion into a blind alley, the retreat from which necessitates a return to the earlier forms of state domination of economic life. The development of positive regulation for private enterprise cannot fairly be considered as resulting from the failure of economic liberalism. Legislation designed to maintain competition, eliminate monopoly, dis-

[5]Professor Robbins points out that the system of economic freedom for the classical economists was not something which would come into being if things were just allowed to take their course. They could only come into being if things were *not* left to take their course. "[It] was the central contention of the Classical Economists that, when the market conformed to the conditions which they postulated, then interference with its working was harmful and self-frustrating. They did not conceive the self-acting mechanism to be self-created" (*op. cit.*, p. 57); also see W. H. Hutt, *Keynesianism, Retrospect and Prospect* (Chicago: Henry Regnery Co., 1963), chap. iv.

solve monopolistics combines, extend the idea of unfair methods of competition, etc., constituted a recognition of the objectives that lay at the root of this philosophy. It relied upon the implementation of those objectives by public policy directed to the end of fostering and maintaining freedom of action and initiative. The experience of the nineteenth century demonstrated that social action was required if a private enterprise economy was to succeed.

The fact that *laissez faire* has declined, however, can scarcely be denied. The rise of economic nationalism, with its demands for power and self-sufficiency, drove the world completely away from free trade, especially after the outbreak of World War I. The spread of state-controlled trade in raw materials and the rise of state-planned domestic economies marked the final demise. Today, we are faced with the choice of reconstructing a private enterprise economy or of replacing it with some form of socialism. If the latter is adopted, economic liberalism and the principles of competition and free trade for which it stood will have disappeared. If, on the other hand, the state is not to assume the responsibility for directing and managing the processes of production, it will be necessary to rely on the initiative of private enterprise to do so and to develop controls and policies in keeping with that approach.[6]

FUNCTIONS OF THE LIBERAL STATE

Protection of Liberty

The state is an instrument of organized social life. Although it is merely one of the means by which such organized life is pursued, it is, for people in a given territory, the only agency capable of co-ordinating the multiplicity of activities into peaceful and orderly conduct. This is accomplished through the media of political government and legal processes. In the final analysis, the law simply formalizes the customs and forms of behavior that have become the generally accepted modes of conduct into rules that must be obeyed by all. Where the pattern of conduct is based upon the conception of the primacy of the individual, it is the function of the state to maintain the conditions necessary for individual liberties, to protect those liberties, and to prevent their destruction by the action of others. Within any state, a wide variety of associations and group organizations emerges by virtue of the interests and liberties which individuals have. These relate to many different aspects

[6]"The *laissez-faire* ideal of government, which on the whole has been the dominant American ideal until the New Deal came along, was in its origins precisely the ideal of an all-around renunciation of and binding guarantee against all special interest legislation, and all forms of the struggle for power and advantage over others in economic and political life" (Taylor, *op. cit.*, p. 175). An illustration of the caricaturing of *laissez faire* and the private competitive system for the purpose of building up an argument for national planning, see M. D. Reagan, *The Managed Economy* (New York: Oxford University Press, 1963).

of social life—family, religious, economic, scientific, artistic, literary, etc. Out of these associations and organizations emerge concepts of rights upon which the state cannot and must not encroach.

The Protection of Rights

In any liberal state, a variety of group interests exists; and with groups, rights emerge. Thus, we have rights of labor, minority rights, religious rights, etc.[7] Underlying this notion of rights is recognition of the fact that the state is not the creator of all social activities within its confines but is rather the agency that sanctions all that are not inimical to orderly and organized social and political life. If this were not so, it would not be possible to speak of the rights of any groups within a state.[8] Were the state to be completely dominant in economic life and, more especially, ultimately to be the sole authority for the direction of production, labor would not have any rights. Under such circumstances, there would be no superior authority to which appeal could be made for redress of grievances, because the final arbiter would be the one with which the dispute existed. Nor would labor have the right to strike in an endeavor to force compliance with its demands. Indeed, it would not even have the privilege of changing employers, since there would be no other from whom a position could be obtained. Nor would there be any possibility of escape by entry into one's own business for the same reason.

In a similar fashion, it is not logical to speak of minority rights if no recognition is given to the limitation of the powers of the state. Minorities have rights, presumably, because the state protects them against encroachments by special groups. It may be legal, if sufficient power can be obtained in the government, for majority groups to eliminate the rights of minorities. However, it is only by recognizing the fact that the interference of the state with the life and activities of the individual, and of individuals acting in groups, is limited to the preservation of an organized and orderly society that minority rights can be maintained. In totalitarian countries, nonconformists do not even have the right to leave the country and go elsewhere. That this is a privilege

[7]The extent to which these remarks hold true in dictatorships, of the type of which too many are in evidence today, will not be examined here. In the highly personalized dictatorships exemplified by Nazi Germany and present-day Russia, rights as conceived in the modern liberal state may not exist. They are manifest as mere dispensations of the individual who happens to be the supreme dictator at the time. Even he cannot act or stand entirely alone; but the extent to which this is the result of balancing powerful rivals against each other, or the result of deep-seated institutional arrangements in the social structure is a subject that is worthy of much more careful analysis than it has yet received. Under an omnipotent dictator, however, rights can never be more, vis-à-vis the dictator, than the distribution of his largesse. There is no such thing as a rule of law; it is the rule of one man or of a very small clique.

[8]See E. S. Corwin, *The "Higher Law" Background of American Constitutional Law* (Ithaca: Cornell University Press, 1955).

not lightly to be disregarded is evidenced by the Pilgrims, who were permitted to go to the New World.

What constitutes the appropriate sphere of governmental intervention is a relative matter, conditioned by the objectives of a particular society and by the historical continuity of its institutional development. Because all of the various activities of government are related, it is difficult to separate them, even for analytical purposes. Some of them, however, may be regarded as primarily political and social in nature, while others are predominantly economic. The maintenance of adequate national defense, public works for health and safety, and a police force for law and order may all be regarded as tasks that are chiefly noneconomic in nature, although, of course, they have their economic implications. They are activities that cannot be appraised satisfactorily through the medium of the market and are not amendable to precise valuation in terms of price.

Government and the Economy

In a capitalistic—or private enterprise—economy, the responsibility for directing the economy is primarily in private hands. The role of government is that of regulating business by establishing conditions within which private management is able to exercise its discretion. This does not, however, preclude the government from undertaking production. In general, the dividing line between public and private functions is drawn where the market is to be used as the arbiter of demand and where the pricing process is to be employed to allocate resources. Such a division of functions between government and private industry, nevertheless, leaves a significant area between the two which forms a considerable part of the debatable ground today. Thus, monopolies such as railroads and public utilities either have to be subject to price regulation by public authority or have to be publicly owned, since the market cannot serve as a satisfactory arbiter of the prices for the services. The choice as to which procedure shall be employed in a particular case frequently involves the evaluation of imponderables such that opposite conclusions may be reached, even by those who have the same economic philosophy.[9]

[9]Some students feel that private ownership with government regulation of prices creates an enomalous situation and that the government, therefore, should take over the ownership and management of railroads, public utilities, and all other industries in which it is impossible to maintain competitive conditions effectively. See H. C. Simons, *A Positive Program for Laissez-Faire*, Public Policy Pamphlet No. 15 (Chicago: University of Chicago Press, 1934). The present writer attaches considerable weight to the advantage of having a third party reconcile the conflicting interests of buyer and seller. Under government ownership this is difficult to accomplish. In multiple-use projects, such as Hoover Dam or the Tennessee Valley Authority, government construction and ownership of the facilities seems to be the only feasible arrangement; but the operation of them can be on a strictly business basis in the hands of either public or private enterprise. Hoover Dam illustrates both.

Many activities involving important economic considerations have such significant political and social implications that the presumption is strongly in favor of government performance of the services. Thus, water supply and sanitation are largely matters of public ownership in this country. These could be organized under private enterprise, and their services sold accordingly; but public welfare seems to offer a good reason for public ownership. In some respects, education falls into the same category. The training of people for earning a living would seem to warrant the imposition of some considerable payment on the shoulders of those who are to be the direct recipients of the benefits. The diffused social effects, however, and the widespread necessity of education for successful democratic political life weigh heavily in favor of making public instruction available for all those who wish to accept it.[10] The provision of highways by government, instead of through the private ownership of toll roads, may be justified on the grounds, again, of diffused social benefits and their significance to the community for organized social life, even though the question of how they shall be supported is still debatable. This activity, however, is rapidly reaching an acute stage because of the heavy demands on economic resources and the large amount of use of the highways for commercial purposes. The difficulties arising from the lack of an adequate price gauge for the amount that needs to be devoted to highway construction have not yet been resolved by other indicators. Departure from the discipline of the market mechanism raises serious issues when many of the benefits received from the utilization of resources are of an immediate economic nature.

There are other reasons for the expansion of public participation in production. Many things cannot be provided on a private commercial basis; and yet, they may seem to be desirable for the community. Public parks and public monuments fall into this category. Then, there is the feeling that many services connected with public welfare will not be forthcoming adequately in the desired form within the framework of private enterprise organization. The government provides public medical facilities for the indigent, for example, financing them out of the public treasury. The pressure of political groups upon those holding office may promote the expenditure of public funds in order that those in power may retain office. In some countries, at least, the government has undertaken widespread provision of services in order to create a dependence of a large part of the population upon the state. This seems to have been one of the motivating factors in the social welfare policies of Bismarck.

[10]The threat to private educational institutions, especially colleges and universities, contained in the heavy support of public education by the government needs to be examined with care. Private institutions have a definite function to perform, and it would be desirable to make their services available to others besides the economically well-to-do. To secure the financial independence to accomplish this, to say nothing of the sheer struggle for existence, is a formidable task for the private institution today.

In recent years, the idea that depressions result from oversavings and inadequate consumption or underinvestment has resulted in the extension of public production for the purpose of stimulating investment and consumption. This policy is based upon the theory that such stimulation is necessary to bring about a revival of prosperity and must periodically be repeated to prevent recurring depressions.

One of the compelling motives for public production is to bring about the distribution of the burden of supporting production that is different from the benefits received. One advantage of private enterprise lies in the process by which each individual is able to weigh the particular price against the specific returns received from it and to consume what he wishes if he can afford it, without regard to what other individuals may do. Contrariwise, there is in free, or partly free, public services an inevitable regimentation of expenditure and consumption. The individual's expenditures and consumption are not connected, since his outlays are largely involuntary; and the returns from these outlays are limited to the production of whatever services the public authorities see fit to provide. This gives rise to the problem of evaluating the benefits received against the cost of providing them. Under private enterprise, the services are forthcoming only if the individuals who wish them are willing to pay for them, and there is therefore a presumption that the services are worth the price they command. Under public production, this gauge is largely lost, unless the standards of private production are used; and the benefits received have to be evaluated largely without the advantage of the price calculus. The extent to which the provision of such services should be undertaken will depend upon the amount of compulsion to which the community is willing to submit, together with the cost of providing them. While it may be urged that the results—as in the case of social insurance, for example—will offset the costs, it is difficult to find an adequate means for measuring this. There is real danger that the goal for benefits may be set at a level that cannot be reached, at least not without the sacrifice of other and ultimately more important things.[11] There is the added danger of the growing dependence of the individual on the government—a matter which cannot be dismissed lightly in a democracy.

One of the outstanding developments in the relation of the private sector to the public sector of the economy in the last thirty-five years is the relative as well as the absolute rise of government expenditures. In 1929 the gross national product was $104.4 billion, and government purchases of goods and services amounted to $8.5 billion; in 1940 the amounts were $100.6 billion and $14.1 billion, respectively; in 1962 they were $554.9 billion and $117 billion. The current federal budget as pre-

[11]For a challenging detailing of the economic functions of government in a free society, see Milton Friedman, *Capitalism and Freedom* (Chicago: University of Chicago Press, 1962).

sented to Congress approximates $100 billion, of which approximately $50 billion is for national defense. The impact of the public sector on the operation of the economy is obviously crucial, if not decisive.[12] A considerable part of the public sector operates outside the discipline of the market. Some of this is probably unavoidable. The gauge of the market can be brought to bear on much of it, however, if there is the desire to do so. For example, in transportation the federal government provides free airways and free waterways, and the users of motor vehicles do not cover the full costs of the roadways. The use of the waterways and airways is not subject to any rationing devices, although they constitute economic goods, and the users of most roadway facilities do not make their choice on the basis of payment for services received. As a consequence, economic gauges for efficient investment and utilization are lacking. Numerous other examples of similar situations could be cited. A misallocation of economic resources is unavoidable, and continuous pressure for a perpetuation of this is also unavoidable in the absence of appeal to the market place, or at least as much of it as possible. Services that are free to the user are never economized.

War and the Economy

War inevitably leads to a rapid expansion of governmental functions, and the frontier between private and public production is pushed heavily against private enterprise. The outbreak of hostilities in World War II involved vast expenditures for the conversion of the peacetime economy to a wartime footing. The transfer of economic resources from peace to war purposes, by various kinds of persuasions and compulsions, required a radical overhauling of the whole structure of production. It also meant calling upon all of the nation's resources for their utmost immediate use. The end of the war confronted the country with the expensive problem of reconversion. This could not be carried out without widespread assistance from the government. In fact, the problem was analogous to that of industrial mobilization at the outbreak of war. It was more difficult, however, because of the scarcity of peacetime goods, the dislocations caused by the "demobilization" of men and industry, and the resistance to the continuation of wartime controls. In addition, the international economy was impoverished. Even under the most favorable circumstances, reconstruction would obviously have been a formidable task. Elimination of the severe inflationary pressures, the reversal of deficit financing, and the transference of spending from public to private hands could scarcely have been carried out without some painful

[12]For 1963, the 100 top military contractors for the Department of Defense had total contracts amounting to $25,834 million. The individual contracts ranged all the way from $1,517 million for Lockheed Aircraft to $26.5 million for Phillips Petroleum Co. Five firms had contracts of over $1 billion each (*Los Angeles Times*, February 9, 1964).

consequences. It is too easily forgotten that the costs of the war were not met by production during the period of the conflict; war imposes an enormous forced draft on manpower and material resources that is met, in part, by using up what has been accumulated before the conflict begins.

The sort of public policy that might have been pursued, had it been possible to undertake reconstruction in a relatively peaceful world, will never be known. Unfortunately, it has not been a peaceful world, and reconversion has not yet taken place. So far, we have failed completely to resolve the problems of inflation and deficit spending. Current indications are that the heavy burden of armaments will continue for a long time to come. If this were met within the limits of balanced budgets and noninflationary fiscal policy, the real impact would be felt in a hurry. If resolution of the matter is postponed for political reasons, the effect on the organization of the economy is not easy to foretell. The manipulation of fiscal policy for political purposes can become a form of bribery that can do the integrity of a liberal state and society no good. If economic security, which is so desired, could be maintained by such a procedure, there would at least be the choice of giving up some freedom for it. Unfortunately, experience to date does not warrant any such conclusion; and there is no evidence to demonstrate that the maintenance of the wartime position of a state can offer any guarantee of ecurity in the postwar period.

The impact of forces outside this country on reconversion to a peacetime economy is not confined to the burden of armaments and national rivalries of a military nature. There is probably no other sphere of economic activity in which the economic policies of the state are brought into sharper focus than in international economic relations. It will be pointed out later[13] that a successful antitrust policy also has to be anticartel. This has two implications. In the first place, it means that we must not sanction the participation of American firms in cartel arrangements because of the impact on our domestic economy and policies. In the second place, it means that we cannot follow domestic policies designed to support domestic prices above those which outside markets afford and then, through private or government trading, dispose of the surpluses in other countries. The utilization of foreign trade by the government for national ends is the essence of economic nationalism—the pursuit of economic power for nationalistic purposes—and the consequences are no different whether the policies be directed to securing monopoly prices in foreign markets or using foreign markets as a means of supporting domestic prices. The manifestations of nationalistic policies are found in protective tariffs, subsidies to aid nationals to compete against foreigners, assistance to or recognition of cartels, or outright gov-

[13]Chapter 19.

ernment trading. Unfortunately, much of our foreign aid program falls into this category. The support for it to keep friendly foreign governments in power and to bolster some segments of our domestic economy undoubtedly exceeds the backing it receives for the purpose of rehabilitating foreign countries. Even were this not so, and even though one assumes that investment, both public and private, in other countries will be honored by their meeting the obligations that have been created, the problem of repayment, which reared its head in such ugly fashion after World War I, will have to be faced.

All of this has serious implications. Our present policies, domestic and foreign, are incompatible with the objectives and requirements of a liberal state. In spite of the reciprocal trade agreements program, we are not yet prepared to reconcile our domestic and foreign economic policies. In other words, we have not accepted the logical necessity of reducing trade restrictions and domestic price supports at the same time. If we are to have private enterprise at home, then our foreign trade must be carried on by private enterprise and on a competitive basis. If it is unwise to concentrate economic and political power in the same hands,[14] it is no more manifest than in the field of international economic transactions.

> America's stake in free markets is closely associated with its stake in political democracy. To defend the second and sacrifice the first, in the interests of international harmony, would produce only a deceptive security. The world wants peace but it has had enough of appeasement. If the United States cannot reasonably expect foreign countries to abandon forthwith a collectivist economic philosophy and an authoritative industrial discipline, no more can foreign countries reasonably demand that this country renounce the doctrines of economic and political liberalism that are the warp and woof of the American Proposition—not only in Jefferson's phrase but in current opinion.[15]

ECONOMIC PLANNING

The Meaning of Economic Planning

Economic planning, like liberalism, is a term that is used by people with widely differing points of view. In a world beset with disorder and confusion, it is only natural that people everywhere should seek a formula for stability and orderliness. The word "planning" connotes orderly procedure and, also, a clearly defined pattern of action. It implies a systematic and precisely formulated guidance of economic activity, as contrasted with the "unplanned" approach of the competitive system. To be opposed

[14]Orton, *op. cit.*, p. 286.

[15]G. W. Stocking and M. W. Watkins, *Cartels or Competition?* (New York: Twentieth Century Fund, Inc., 1948), p. 382. It is not possible to examine here the basis upon which trade with a country like Russia might be developed successfully. Suffice it to say that such an undertaking does not require that it take place only through governmental channels. A country whose trade is carried on through the medium of private enterprise is not so devoid of economic and political weapons as to be a hapless victim of the power of state trading.

to economic planning is to invite classification as a "rugged individualist" who objects to any government interference in economic affairs. This distinction, however, is neither useful nor accurate. Everyone plans for the future; and governments have always planned, in the sense that they have participated in the control of economic activity and have formulated policies for the conduct of the economic affairs of nations. What gives economic planning its distinctive characteristics and differentiates it from policy is the type of governmental direction of economic affairs that it proposes or undertakes.

Today, there is a great deal of planning. In the field of industry, we have industrial planning that deals with investment policy, market exploitation, production policy, plant location and layout, etc. In government, the leading development, so far, has been city planning of sewage, water, public utilities, streets, parks, schools, zoning, civic centers, and public buildings. In recent years, the idea has been extended to regional planning, especially in connection with the utilization of water and power resources. During World War II, we undertook very extensive military planning—the direction of the entire life of the country to one supreme end.

Although all of these have their economic implications and can be pursued successfully only after careful consideration of the economic problems that arise, only military planning in a total war entails economic planning or a planned economy. Economic planning, both in origin and concept, means the direction by the central government of the economic life of the nation as a whole, in accordance with a comprehensive and unified plan into which all the various economic activities are fitted for the purpose of achieving the specified objectives. Economic planning during World War II had the single purpose of mobilizing, to the full, the economic resources of this country; and it was to that end that the authorities directed the employment of manpower and materials. Economic planning for peacetime purposes has a very different goal, but it seeks to employ the same sort of authoritative control to attain the goal.

Theory of Socialist Planning

Socialist economic planning necessitates the placing of all resources under the direct control and administration of the planning authority, which would be the state.[16] The state would, therefore, ultimately be the

[16]The following summary of the theory of a planned economy is taken from two articles by F. M. Taylor and O. Lange, reprinted in B. E. Lippincott (ed.), *On the Economic Theory of Socialism* (Minneapolis: University of Minnesota Press, 1938). These two articles constitute the most complete theoretical picture of a planned economy. For a theoretical analysis which reaches opposite conclusions, see F. A. Hayek. *Collectivist Economic Planning* (London: George Routledge & Sons, Ltd., 1935). See also D. F. Pegrum, "Planning and Economic Science," *American Economic Review*, Vol. XXXI, No. 2 (June, 1941), pp. 298–307; and "Economic Planning in a Democratic Society," *Journal of Land and Public Utility Economics*, Vol. XIX, No. 1 (February 1943), pp. 18–27.

sole producer, maintaining exchange relations with its citizens, buying their services with money, and selling to them the goods and services which it produces. A "socially correct"—i.e., state-determined—system of incomes would be established; that is, incomes would be fixed so that they represented that distribution of the total income of the state which is called for in the interests of citizens generally and of the group as an organic whole. Consumers' freedom of choice would be maintained.[17] The preferences of consumers, as expressed by their demand prices, would be the criteria of production policy and of the allocation of resources. Freedom of occupation would be allowed, the allocation of labor being determined by the market price for it. A social dividend would be paid so as to make the income of labor, the sole source of income in such a society, conform to the "socially correct" system of incomes. The rate of capital accumulation would be determined by the planning authority.

The administration of the economy would be in the hands of a central planning board. The problems of economic calculation—that is, the allocating of resources—would be solved by the board in accordance with the principles that govern competitive equilibrium. Thus, the board would perform the functions that the competitive market discharges under capitalism. It would establish the rules necessary to maximize output. One of these rules would require the combination of the agents of production on such a scale that the average cost of production for an industry would be at a minimum. Another rule would require that the marginal cost of an industry be equal to the price of the product.[18] The prices of consumers' goods and the services of labor would be settled by the market, but all other prices would be determined by the board. This would involve what is called the problem of imputation—that is, ascertaining the effective importance in the productive process of each primary factor. This would be essential to the calculation of the resources cost of any commodity, without which it would be impossible to compute the correct selling price. Assuming the stock or income of each primary factor available for the current production period to be a determinate quantity, the administrators would assign provisional prices to the factors of production. By trial and error—that is, by successive approximations—the correct accounting prices would be ascertained and the problem of equilibrium solved.[19] Such, in very brief form, is the theoretical structure of a planned economy.

[17]This would be a very different consumers' freedom of choice, however, from that which characterizes a market economy. Consumers, at best, would have only the freedom to choose among the products offered by a monopoly. They would not have the choice among readily substitutable products offered by rival producers whose discretion is circumscribed by the actions of rivals. Competition on the supply side would necessarily be restricted by the planning authority.

[18]This is based on the theory of marginal cost pricing, on which see Chapters 10 and 27.

[19]The trial and error which would be used would not be that of competition, but that of the monopolistic and the central statistical bureau. It would not even be

Appraisal of Planning

Theory and practice, of course, are very different things, at least, when the theory is simply a model of the things that would have to be done in order that planning could be successful. It is possible to erect a theoretical model of a planned economy by a simplification of conditioning factors beyond any semblance of reality—e.g., by exclusion of all non-economic factors as not being germane to the economic problem,[20] and by assuming, as given or obtainable, whatever economic conditions are basic to the success of the plan. Thus, planning assumes that it is possible for the state to determine a socially correct system of incomes and the rate of capital accumulation, to control the disposition of all physical resources, and to allocate labor solely through market prices. It also assumes that the problems of cost calculation and the estimation of demand could be solved by a central statistical bureau and that production could readily be shifted from one field of endeavor to another.

The enormity of the administrative tasks that a planned economy would involve surely provides good grounds for doubt as to the possibility of success. It is one of the characteristics of such an economy that the geographic area encompassed is of no consequence. It applies equally well to a country like the United States or to one like Holland. Yet, it is just as the scope of the economy increases, either in area or multiplicity of industries, that centralization becomes a more overwhelming task and decentralization a greater necessity. Moreover, it is the inability to control many of the crucial factors that influence the course of our present economy which is at the root of our gravest current difficulties. Merely to assume such control for purposes of building a model is far different from exercising it. The consequences of state authority of such magnitude need to be appraised in the light of the implications on our whole social life.

After what has been said in previous sections of this chapter, it is scarcely necessary to point out the conflict of economic planning with

---

analogous to the trial and error of the competitive system. It would be like running race horses against the clock but never allowing them to run against each other. Not only would each industry be a monopoly, but the whole of a country's productive enterprise would be a single monopoly. If competition were allowed to intrude, that would upset the production plan. Socialist planning and competition among producers are totally incompatible, except in the very generalized sense of competition between such diverse products as electricity and straw hats.

[20]This is precisely what the models of a perfectly competitive system have done. Planners insist that the competitive system does not work as theory indicates it should because the assumptions are not approximated in fact. Yet, they fall into precisely the same error of oversimplification. The difference lies in the fact that the planners assume that they can and will possess the authority necessary to put their plans into effect. See M. A. Copeland, "Institutionalism and Welfare Economics," *American Economic Review*, Vol. XLVIII, No. 1 (March, 1958), pp. 1–17.

liberalism.[21] The basic assumptions of the two are diametrically opposed. Private property in the means of production has no place in central planning, and it may be doubted that private property has any real meaning if it is eliminated from the field of production. Voluntary associations have no part in the scheme of control, labor unions would have no real functions, and collective bargaining could not be tolerated. Freedom of speech, freedom of expression, and freedom of communication would be literally impossible, because the organs of public opinion could not be politically independent if controlled or owned by the state. Freedom of religion would be nothing short of a myth under such circumstances.

A planned economy is a closed economy by the very nature of the assumptions, since the state has complete control over all production. This might be a world economy, or a rigidly national one. The first may be dismissed as being totally out of the question in the present stage of human development. The second merits the fate of condemnation because of the results it has already produced. Free international trade, which presupposes trading—primarily, at least—in the hands of private enterprise, is eliminated by the nature of the assumptions. Trading between nations would, therefore, be trading between sovereign political states and would have to be conducted strictly in accordance with their own domestic plans. Experience to date fails to give any grounds for assuming that international trade under such circumstances would follow any other course than that dictated by political considerations.[22] It is difficult to see how the friction that would be engendered could lead to anything other than armed conflict.

Not all advocates of centralized planning subscribe to compulsion or socialization. Many believe that planning on a voluntary basis can be undertaken in a liberal society. Professor Clark suggests that this should involve no compulsory control over the consumer's choice between spend-

[21]The late Professor Schumpeter held that modern democracy was a product of the capitalist process (J. A. Schumpeter, *Capitalism, Socialism and Democracy* [New York: Harper & Bros., 1942], p. 297). He also took the position that capitalism, by its very success, had destroyed its *raison d'être.* He held no illusions on the survival of democracy under socialism, however; "effective management of the socialist economy means dictatorship not *of* but *over* the proletariat in the factory . . . socialist democracy may eventually turn out to be more of a sham than capitalist democracy ever was" (p. 302). This does not mean that Schumpeter was a liberal. His philosophy, in fact, was precisely the opposite of the liberal philosophy as expressed by Professor Ramsey Muir. "[Whether] favorable or unfavorable, value judgments about capitalist performance are of little interest. For mankind is not free to choose. . . . Things economic and social move by their own momentum and the ensuing situations compel individuals and groups to behave in certain ways whatever they may wish to do, not indeed by destroying their freedom of choice but by shaping the choosing mentalities and by narrowing the list of possibilities from which to choose" (p. 130). Perhaps so, but many of us refuse to subscribe to Schumpeter's fatalism or the process of reasoning upon which it is based.

[22]See Jacob Viner, "International Relations between State-Controlled National Economies," *American Economic Review*, Vol. XXXIV, No. 1, Part 2, Supplement (March, 1944), pp. 315–29.

ing and saving, or any over the producer's choice of how, when, and how much to invest in productive equipment.[23] Planning of this nature means voluntary co-operation in business for the purpose of achieving broad economic objectives, aided by government in acquiring the necessary information and in formulating policies. It would also require consistency and co-ordination in government policy in keeping with the liberal philosophy. Mr. Gerard Swope advanced a "plan" of this nature at the beginning of the 1930's by suggesting that organized industry should exert every effort to stabilize economic activity; and to that end, corporation reports should be standardized, and production and consumption should be co-ordinated on a broader and more intelligent basis.[24] In order to accomplish this, Mr. Swope proposed that trade associations should be formed with a variety of enumerated powers. There were suggestions relative to a workmen's compensation act; life and disability insurance; pensions; and, finally, unemployment insurance, when regularity and continuity of employment proved impracticable. If such arrangements as these could be put into effect without fixing relative prices and determining production quotas, they would deserve wholehearted support. Voluntary planning of this nature is completely in keeping with the liberal tradition. The attempt to put it into practice during the depression of the thirties, however, eliminated too many of the voluntary features. This is likely to be the case as long as planning involves the national mobilization of resources, whether it be to fight a war, fight depression, or fight anything else.

During World War II, our economic activity was planned for war purposes; and as far as winning the war was concerned, it was a success. This very fact, however, created a serious danger. The devices and procedures appropriate to the prosecution of war are not capable of winning the peace. The pursuit of this analogy constitutes one of the greatest threats to freedom in the future. The fundamental problem of reconstruction is that of changing from a war to a peace economy. The need for the withdrawal of the government from the position that it assumed during the war and the restoration of conditions that will make private enterprise once more the foundation of our economy are the crux of the whole issue. In other words, we are now faced with the task of working out a program to "unplan." This is a delicate and difficult assignment that, in the present state of world affairs, will tax our faith and ingenuity for years to come.

Recently, proponents of "voluntary" economic planning have placed considerable emphasis on the success of France in staging a striking economic recovery from the ravages of war, without sacrificing a

[23] J. M. Clark, *Social Control of Business* (2nd ed.; New York: McGraw-Hill Book Co., Inc., 1939), p. 469.

[24] See J. G. Frederick, *Readings in Economic Planning* (New York: Business Bourse, 1932), especially chap. i.

democratic political order. Space does not permit a careful analysis of this development. However, one may note that the voluntary aspects of the centralized planning upon which the French embarked under President de Gaulle in 1946 are provided with the incentive that "Its implementation is assured through the propelling force of public investments and through a whole range of economic stimuli granted by the government (tax exemptions, loans, subsidies)."[25] The democratic process is employed through the discussion of goals before these are voted on by Parliament. As Professor Landauer, who views these developments most favorably, says, "Hence the government needs powers to bring non-compliant entrepreneurs into line. These powers need not involve compulsion; it will be sufficient if the government has the means to make compliance more profitable than non-compliance."[26] The present difficulties France faces with regard to inflation, the resurgence of French nationalism, the position of dictator occupied by President de Gaulle, together with the problem of securing a successor, and the conflicts of French policies with the Common Market, should give pause to those who view French planning with enthusiasm. It certainly is not compatible with liberalism and the concepts of democracy set forth earlier in this chapter.[27]

CONCLUSION

If the regulation of private industry is to fulfill its purpose and competition is to occupy a primary role in our economic structure, extensive substantive and administrative changes in the present laws are imperative. These, however, can only be the formal expression of a reaffirmation of faith in a free society. The success of liberalism depends as much on what the state does not do, or does not have to do, as on what it does. Liberalism must therefore rely heavily on informal controls. Custom, tradition, public opinion, education, and religion are the foundations upon which a free and orderly society is erected. The state, in the final analysis, cannot compel its citizens to do those things that present any fundamental conflict with these foundations, nor can it successfully enforce laws that are not the embodiment of settled convictions which have been translated into action and thus have become part of established procedures. Even though a majority may endorse the general principles upon which legislation is founded, it may still be unwilling to employ the coercive powers of the state against nonconformers if there is no deep-seated conviction that injustice or immorality results from non-

[25] *France and Economic Planning*, Ambassade de France, Service de Presse et d'Information. New York, 1963, p. 5.

[26] Carl Landauer, *Contemporary Economic Systems* (Philadelphia and New York: J. B. Lippincott Co., 1964), p. 282.

[27] A cartoon in the *Los Angeles Times* based on the famous remark of Louis XIV, "Après moi le déluge," depicts President de Gaulle as saying "Après lé deluge Moi." One cannot help but wonder what comes after "Moi."

compliance or resistance. The failure of the prohibition laws is a case in point. Many laws relating to the regulation of business fall into the same category.

Successful regulation, therefore, must deal only with the broad issues that cannot be dealt with by voluntary associations and, even then, only when settled convictions have emerged as to what public policy should be. This is a slow process requiring considerable restraint, especially in times of emergency or rapid change. This is the process, however, by which our laws and institutions have developed. That they have fallen short of perfection is all too obvious; that they have lagged seriously at times is also apparent. The results, however, have surely justified the means, for the "American way of life" and the liberal traditions upon which it is founded constitute the only beacon in a world gravely threatened by autocracy. The Atlantic Charter was a proclamation of hope and freedom to an enslaved Europe. If it is to have any real significance, the principles upon which it was founded and for which it stands must find their fullest expression in the country of its birth.

The realization of these high ideals requires more than a mere proclamation of them. They must be put into action by the community at large. This imposes a heavy responsibility on leaders in all walks of life. If businessmen wish to retain private business, they must be prepared to discharge to the full the social responsibilities that it entails. It will not suffice to maintain the attitude that their sole duty is to their corporation and that as long as they abide by the letter of the law (as it may be stretched by astute lawyers), they are beyond reproach. It is up to them to help make the law what it should be; to insist upon high moral purpose, not merely "a pound of flesh"; and to accept responsibility and assume leadership in developing solutions to grave economic problems and social injustice. If they insist upon calling upon the state to solve all the problems of unemployment, abuse of monopoly power, wasteful exploitation of natural resources, and competition of foreign enterprise, they have only themselves to thank if the state decides that they are incapable of filling the role they have assumed.[28] If they insist on supporting "pork barrels" and participating in the spoils therefrom, they cannot criticize others for doing the same thing; and they should not be surprised at being caught with unclean hands when the inevitable scandals are uncovered.

The same remarks apply to labor unions and other special-interest groups. Labor cannot decry monopoly in industry while it struggles to achieve its own. Present labor union tactics, which rely so heavily on compulsion, are basically contradictory to the liberal society in which labor leaders profess belief. If they really have faith in a democratic order, then

[28]The medical profession has been particularly backward in developing a modernized form of organization for supplying adequate medical facilities and care, although now, somewhat belatedly, it seems to be waking up.

it is high time that they demonstrate how it can work within the unions themselves. If, also, they wish to preserve a private enterprise system, they must offer leadership to that end and not expect the employer or the state to assume the entire task. They must recognize that successful collective bargaining saddles them with a real responsibility for unemployment and retirement benefits. If they insist on using the state alone to solve the problem, they will discover, perhaps too late, that the state will swallow them up. Unless—and until—employers and employees can work together in a spirit of co-operation rather than conflict, and the struggle for power is resolved into a reasonably harmonious industrial commonwealth, our democratic structure will be constantly threatened with supersession by a totalitarian order.

All of this, of course, means that industrial leaders, business, and labor alike need to engage in a little introspection. They need to examine their organizations and their codes of ethics in the light of the aims of society, which are probably their aims, too, except when they are filling their particular job. Private enterprise must rely heavily on self-government, but the self-government of industry (and labor unions) must be something more than a means of self-protection and monopolizing. Indeed, if it contains much of these, it will not last. It must, instead, be a means of governing industry by voluntary methods in the interests of society and must be completely in keeping with the spirit of private enterprise, competition, and the democratic ideal.[29]

It is in periods of crisis that a social structure meets the test of its strength. Whether it survives that test or not depends upon the moral convictions which the challenge awakens. Liberalism and the freedom of Western nations emerged from great moral convictions; for these nations emerged with strong religious ideals, and they developed their educational institutions to further their convictions. In the twentieth century, the forces of education and religion have fallen far short of fulfilling the task for which they alone are fitted. No civilization can hope to survive without an educational system whose prime task is to preserve and pass on the great traditions of the society of which it is a part. In our structure, this means full and free inquiry into all phases of knowledge and preparation of the youth of the nation for the assumption of the responsibilities of citizenship in a free society. No civilization can hope to survive without the deep moral convictions that religion alone can impart. If our religion is gone, the outlook is indeed dark, for we have no substitute to take its place. Only a nation, however, that has lost faith in its past and its heritage, and has forgotten what they stood for, will lose its religious foundations. We have not yet reached that stage of decline, even though the god of materialism has been waging a furious battle.

[29]For a decidedly pessimistic view of these possibilities, see Ben W. Lewis, "Economics by Admonition," *American Economic Review*, Vol. XLIV, No. 2 (May, 1959), pp. 384–98.

The issue, today, is much more than the merely technical one of devising procedures to deal with specific problems. It is the issue of freedom versus authority. The preservation of freedom demands a reaffirmation of the faith of the American people in their heritage and in the capacity of a free people to solve their political and economic problems without sacrificing that freedom.

PART II

Institutional and Organizational Arrangements

Chapter 2 THE PROBLEM AND ITS SETTING

INTRODUCTION

Public regulation of industry is but one phase of the general problem of the relations of government to economic life. An examination of the issues involved in such regulation must be undertaken, therefore, in the general setting of the political and economic framework of the nation. This calls for an understanding of the governmental and economic structure of the country as well as of the social and political objectives of its people. All economic activity is subject to some form of regulation or control in an orderly society, because the latter presupposes arrangements whereby the actions of individuals and organized groups are controlled in such a way as to make group life possible.

In a period of comparative tranquility, assuming adaptive political and social institutions, regulation develops by the more or less gradual processes of adjustment to new situations as they arise. As long as the change is not too rapid, serious distortions do not emerge, because there is time to gain a reasonable grasp of the implications of the change. Moreover, such periods are usually characterized by relatively settled conditions throughout the entire social structure, with the result that the patterns of action are pretty well understood and accepted.

Today, however, we are living in one of those epochs of history in which all phases of human life and activity are seemingly being rocked to their very foundations. It is, perhaps, trite to say that the world will never be the same again, for it is possible to make that statement at any time; but the rate of change today is so rapid that the present generation can scarcely comprehend the environment in which its parents lived as children. This new world is not merely one of different economic arrangements; it is new in every respect, in so far as that phrase can ever be applied. We are groping for new foundations in philosophy, religion, science, art, and music; we are probably witnessing the most phenomenal change in technology that has ever been experienced. This is not to say that the connection with the past has been broken, for historians are constantly unfolding the continuity of processes in human society. In many respects, the present situation is the culmination of the results of Reformation, the rise of the nation-state, and the scientific achievements of Leonardo da Vinci, Copernicus, Francis Bacon, Galileo, and Newton.

It is the accelerated pace at which the unfolding has taken place that has made it so difficult for us to appraise the nature and significance of the changes and to make the necessary adaptations to them in an orderly and intelligent fashion. The implications of recent developments in atomic energy, aeronautics, and space exploration cannot possibly be discerned with any accuracy at this time. It is safe to say, however, that they have not diminished the rate of change; nor have they simplified the social, political, and economic reconstruction facing the world today.

Probably the most outstanding characteristics of the modern world are the development of science and its application to everyday living. On the economic side, this development and application of science have given rise to industrialism. The transformation in our economic life which has resulted, especially since 1870, would, of itself, have placed a great strain on the institutional arrangements of the country and the means of regulation and control that had been developed, even if the opportunity had been afforded to meet the new problems under conditions of external peace. Unfortunately, this has not been the case.

Since 1914, most of the world has moved rapidly from one crisis to another. World War I, with its political disruptions and extensive destruction of physical wealth, was followed by severe economic disturbances, culminating in the disastrous depression of 1929. Full recovery from the depression had not been achieved before World War II broke out. The conflict of political and economic ideologies, of authoritarianism versus political freedom, and of state-directed economies versus capitalism that grew so rapidly between the two world wars has now almost divided the world into two groups which are diametrically opposed. To add to the complications, the division is not only manifest in the international scene; the ideological conflict is also evident within this country. Reconstruction is taking place, therefore, under severe political uncertainty and with pronounced differences of opinion, not only on the specific means to be taken to deal with the economic problems which we face but also on the social objectives themselves. It is safe to assume that the great bulk of the people of this country wish to preserve the political and personal freedoms that characterize our social life, but the lack of reasonable unanimity of opinion on means and the confusion of means and ends are very serious obstacles to a peaceful and orderly solution of the problems we face.

Despite all this—or rather, even more urgently because of it—analysis of the problems of regulation and the proposals for measures to be taken to deal with the issues which have emerged must be undertaken in light of the political and economic structure of the country and the means of control which we have developed over our history. We are in the midst of an economic storm, but we cannot ignore familiar landmarks if we are to sail through it with safety.

SOME BASIC ECONOMIC CONCEPTS

Economizing and Allocation

Economic activity arises from the fact that man must economize. That is to say, in the satisfaction of his wants, he finds that he has to make choices because he cannot satisfy all of his desires. Some of the means which he has for gratifying these desires are scarce; hence, he uses them to meet those wants which are most urgent at the time. The scarce means are economic goods, and they are economic goods because choice has to be exercised in the use of them. If things are so abundant that no choice has to be exercised in the use to which they are to be put, they are not economic goods; they are free goods. Only economic goods, therefore, are scarce; and scarcity refers not to the absolute amount of anything but only to the amount available relative to the uses to which it can be put. All economic goods possess utility or the capacity to satisfy human wants. Because economic goods are scarce, each and every unit of a stock is capable of satisfying a want which will have to be foregone if any unit is taken away. The utility of a unit that satisfies the least important of the wants for which the stock may be used is the marginal utility of that stock. When marginal utility is zero—that is, when no want goes unsatisfied as the result of the loss of a unit of the stock—the goods are free goods. Economic goods, therefore, have marginal utility; free goods have none.

The economic goods and services of a community that are available for use at any time are its economic resources. The process of assigning these resources to different uses is known as the allocation of resources. Economic resources must be allocated because they are scarce. It is the task of efficient allocation to dispose of the use of resources so that they are used in their most valuable way. This is what is meant by economizing.

All economic activity consists of utilizing scarce resources, both human and material, for the purpose of satisfying human wants. One of the most important aspects of this activity is production. Production is undertaken because of the scarcity of the means for satisfying man's wants. Man does not produce those things which are so abundant that he does not have to exercise any choice in acquiring them. If all the goods he desires were as plentiful and as accessible as the air he breathes, there would be no production, no economizing, and no scarcity. We produce because we have to economize. If there were no necessity for economizing, there would be no need for production; indeed, it simply could not take place. As long as there is such a thing as economic goods, therefore, there will have to be production; and for this reason, the problems of production are never solved. We do not live in an economy of abundance, that is, one in which there is no scarcity. If, for any reason, our economy should ever become an economy of abundance, it would no longer be an economy; and there would be no economic problems to bother us.

Production

Production involves the utilization of scarce resources for the creation of goods or services. It may be defined as the creation of time, place, or form utilities. Goods and services are produced when they are made available in the form, at the time, and at the place desired by human beings. The problem of production, therefore, is to allocate scarce resources among their various possible uses so that the greatest possible output is obtained from the limited quantity of productive agents available at any time. What constitutes the greatest possible output depends upon the method employed to determine what shall be produced. In time of war, when every effort is being made to defeat the enemy, the requirements of prosecuting the conflict are the controlling factors; and the decisions as to what shall be produced are made by the governing authorities on the basis of actual or estimated war needs. In a peacetime economy, what shall be produced may be determined, in whole or in part, by public authority, in accordance with some plan which allocates resources to particular uses; or it may be determined by the preference of consumers for the various goods and services, as indicated by the prices they are willing to pay for them. In either case, the problems of production are to allocate the resources among their various uses and to combine them for the creation of specific commodities and services in such a way that these resources would not be more valuable if used in some other way. It is obvious that this ideal utilization can never be obtained in fact. It is the goal, however, which an economic system seeks to achieve.

The process of production requires that decisions be made so that some resources shall be used in one way and some in other ways. In a private enterprise economy, the way in which the available resources are utilized is determined by the decisions of individuals, acting alone or in groups. They decide when and where to work or not to work, when and where to invest or not to invest, and what and how much to produce. These decisions are based on the opportunities which are available and individual reactions to them.

Assumptions of Private Enterprise

An economic system that relies on individual initiative in this fashion is based upon certain explicit or implicit assumptions with regard to the way it operates. It is assumed that the different resources used in production have, for the most part, a relatively high degree of mobility, so that they can readily be turned to new uses or be adapted to new techniques of production. This presupposes a widespread knowledge of the techniques of production available at any time, as well as an opportunity to employ them. There is the assumption that the organizers of business are well informed on the conditions of the market—that is, the opportunities for the sale of goods and services that may be produced—and that they are able to acquire and combine the resources of production in the proportions they decide upon. The owners of resources are assumed to have a knowledge of the alternative possibilities of utilizing or disposing of them and the opportunity of acting accordingly. It is also assumed that producers, acting individually or collectively, do not have, and will be unable to acquire, sufficient control over the supply of any good or service to be able to determine its price. Finally, consumers are assumed to be fully informed of the market opportunities, that is, of the various products available to them and their quantity, quality, and price.

If production is carried on under the conditions set forth in the foregoing assumptions, consumers will express their preference for the goods and services they wish through the prices they are willing to pay for them. Business, seeking to apply the resources at its disposal in the most profitable fashion, will direct its efforts to producing those things which will lead to that result. The owners of productive services and resources will put them to those uses which will yield the most satisfactory rewards. As a result, the agents of production will be allocated to the various possible uses in such a way as to satisfy the most pressing demands, as expressed through price, for goods and services. Business and the owners of productive resources will constantly be seeking new and more profitable outlets for their products. This will lead to shifting of the agents of production to other uses whenever favorable opportunities arise, and new methods of production will be introduced if they are superior to existing ones.

Competition

One of the basic requisites of a private enterprise economy, if it is to fulfill the conditions just discussed, is competition. Competition refers to the market situation among buyers and sellers of goods and services in which no one person, or group of persons acting in concert, is able to exercise any control over the conditions of sale.[1] This could be put in another, and perhaps more general, way by saying that, to the extent a buyer or seller is unable to control sales because of other opportunities available to the other party in the transaction, competition prevails. On the sellers' or producers' side, this means that no one has control over the supply of a commodity sufficient for him to be able to influence the price to his own advantage. If competition is perfect, there will be instantaneous adaptations of supply to changed market situations; each producer will adjust his output so that the cost of producing the last unit of output will just equal the price that can be obtained for it; the average cost of production for him will be the same as the marginal cost; and the average

[1]See Chapter 8 for a more extended discussion.

cost of production will be the lowest he can obtain. Under these circumstances, also, the agents of production will be employed in the most profitable manner; but they will receive only that price which is necessary to attract them to the particular use to which they are put.

Actual markets, however, manifest many imperfections. Consumers and producers rarely have full knowledge of the various opportunities available to them; at best, their knowledge of the market is bound to be incomplete. Secret practices, secret processes, the vast array of goods competing for the consumers' purchasing power, and the variety of markets imperfectly connected with each other make it impossible for the producer to be apprised completely of competitive conditions. The buyer finds it difficult, and very often impossible, to obtain full information on the prices at which he can buy; and differences in style, quality, etc., of rival products do not lend themselves to precise price comparisons. The mobility of many productive resources is impeded by geography, the structure of industry, custom, and legal restrictions. Natural resources such as coal and iron ore are highly localized; as a result, industry becomes heavily concentrated in certain areas and tends to move rather slowly to new areas. Large-scale production with fixed and specialized equipment impedes the entrance or exit of producers; consequently, there may be a serious maladjustment of productive capacity to demand at any particular time or over a very considerable period. Then, too, customary ways of doing things or modes of life may impede adjustments. One of the difficult phases of reconstruction in Great Britain, for example, has arisen from the unwillingness or inability to abandon long-established methods of production. Agriculture presents a somewhat analogous situation in this country because of the importance of farming as a way of life, as well as because of the difficulty of changing from rural to urban occupations. These impediments to the competitive system frequently bring about serious deviations from the competitive norm, with the result that resources are not continuously allocated to their most effective use.

Monopoly

One of the most important problems of public policy that arises with the departure of competition from its assumptions is monopoly. Monopoly is commonly thought of as the exclusive, or nearly exclusive, control over the supply of a commodity by a single seller. This is the idea that seems to be held by the courts. Thus, one court held that the Aluminum Corporation of America was a monopoly, because it controlled the supply of 80-90 per cent of the "virgin" aluminum ingot in this country; but in another case, the Supreme Court said that the United States Steel Corporation was not a monopoly (at least under the law), because it controlled only 48.5 per cent of the supply, which was less than the combined output of its competitors.

This idea of monopoly, however, is not a satisfactory one for economic analysis. It emphasizes restriction of competition rather than control of the market. The economist's emphasis, on the other hand, is on sufficient control of the supply of a product to enable the producer to influence its price to his advantage. Such control may be very slight, or even negligible, in the total market situation. Thus, one manufacturer of pens has a monopoly on "Parker" pens, but his position in the total market situation for fountain pens is such as to confront him with highly competitive conditions. Some producers may enjoy a monopoly in one market and have to meet vigorous competition in others. This seems to be the situation—in part, at least—in steel. It seems more satisfactory, therefore, to define monopoly in terms of control of the market, no matter how large or small that control may be. Some monopoly or control of the market exists whenever a seller, or group of sellers acting by agreement, has sufficient control over the volume of sales to be able to influence the price of the commodity sold, to his advantage. It is more satisfactory, therefore, to speak of a firm as having "monopoly powers" than to designate it as a monopoly.

Control of the market may arise from many factors other than the imperfections which are the result of lack of knowledge, lack of mobility in resources, inertia, and the technological structure of industry. These other factors include organizational devices which may be employed to secure or enhance control of the market; property rights which may confer considerable monopoly power; various types of agreements and understandings that impose limitations on competition; and various kinds of threats, cajolery, outright bludgeoning, and more subtle means of bringing competitors into line. Not all of these arrangements are legal, and none of them can be used legally to extend monopoly or to restrict competition, as understood at law, beyond the privileges granted by public authority. The legal concept of monopoly and restriction of competition, however, is such as to leave a wide range of opportunity for control of the market, a range possibly beyond that which economists think is tolerable or necessary for a private enterprise system to conform to its basic assumptions. Reconciliation of the economic concept of monopoly with legal requirements that demand a tolerable degree of objectivity is one of the most difficult issues in regulation, because it is obviously impossible to eliminate all monopoly, as that term is used in economic analysis.

THE NEED FOR REGULATION

Regulation to Implement Competition

It is too frequently assumed that the need for regulation is the result of the faults of private enterprise and the greed and unscrupulousness of individuals. This is only partially true. The regulation of industry in a private enterprise economy arises, in the first instance, from the necessity of giving legal sanction to private property rights and of providing for redress against infringement of them. Even the most extreme form of individualism and free competition would have to have some such minimum. Competition and private enterprise cannot operate in a legal vacuum. All competition requires rules, for it is only within rules that competition can be said to exist in an orderly society. The conditions of competition must be established, and this is one of the basic functions of regulation, using this term in its broadest sense. If the production of something is not prohibited, then it may be assumed in this country that such production may legitimately take place. It may be profitable for someone to peddle narcotics; and if this were left for competition to decide, one could conclude that there was not sufficient opposition to it to make public prohibition desirable or feasible. Public welfare, however, demands a ban on the indiscriminate sale and use of them. There is also the need for protection against intimidation and fraud, which an orderly society must provide. Regulation of business is necessary, no matter how effectively competition may work.

In a complex industrial society such as exists in the United States today, regulation requires an elaborate set of rules to meet all the varying situations that are encountered. The spread of competition from local to national markets, the wide variety of goods and services offered to consumers, the replacement of personal contact by the more impersonal arrangements of modern marketing, the growth of advertising, and the creation of new ways of appealing to the consumer have necessitated the development of controls designed to protect both competitors and consumers. Public authority has, therefore, been called upon to set up and to assist business in developing standards of conduct that conform to public interest, as well as to eliminate the use of those practices that are undesirable.

Imperfections in Competition

Regulation is also a means whereby public authority endeavors to curb abuses arising from imperfections in the market. It seeks to prevent business practices that are used to harm other businesses or consumers, and it seeks to prevent arrangements that are aimed at controlling the market when such control would not be obtained by productive efficiency. It may even impose limitations on competition which might lead to the elimination of some competitors, if public interest demands such limitations. In addition, it is necessary as a means of reconciling producer and consumer interests where the operation of competition is severely restricted by technological conditions. This is the situation with public utilities. The market can be only a partial arbiter of the conditions of production and sale. Regulation steps in to substitute, as best it can, for competition.

Regulation to Control Monopoly

Regulation is necessary to curb the misuse or abuse of monopoly power. Some element of monopoly is present in most markets. It is not possible to eliminate all of it, nor is all of it harmful to public interest. Monopoly powers conferred by trade-marks, trade names, copyrights, and patents are granted on the assumption that public interest is furthered by the private rights which the grants confer. Monopoly powers also emerge from the technological structure of modern industry. In other words, monopoly is an inescapable part of the structure of modern business. That is not to say, however, that private enterprise should be permitted to use whatever powers it possesses to control the market as it sees fit. In many instances, and especially where giant corporations play a prominent part in production, decisions on business policy impinge so directly on public interest that they cannot be left as a matter of purely private concern, even though the executives making those decisions have no intention of inflicting public injury. The issues involve too many different interests to be left to the judgment of one group.

In addition to this, it cannot be assumed that private and public interests always coincide. The desire to obtain monopoly profits, the endeavor to secure protection against some of the rigors of competition, and the quest for power all may give rise to practices that demand public intervention. When such practices are employed in their more ruthless forms—as they have been by many of the trusts, for example—drastic remedies and penalties are called for.

THE PROBLEM OF REGULATION

Social control, as applied to economic activity, means all of the various ways by which society achieves conformity to generally accepted standards of conduct. The methods by which the conformity is obtained vary widely and may rely upon coercion or voluntary compliance. Some of these controls are expressed in law, many of them are not. Public regulation of economic life or activity refers to those controls which are embodied in the laws of the land and which are administered by designated governmental agencies.

Regulation and Private Enterprise

In its broadest aspects, public regulation refers to all the laws and administrative processes that deal with the country's economic life. In the somewhat narrower but more important aspects, it applies primarily to that part of economic activity that is concerned with production. It is here that the key to the control of the economic processes lies. This is especially true in a democratic society, which assumes, among other things, that the individual can exercise his own choice over what he shall consume with the economic means at his disposal. It is production that creates the wealth of the community that the consumer may use. The way in which production is permitted to respond to the dictates of the consumer will determine the direction of the productive effort. The way to secure the greatest economic wealth for a country is to permit the population to exercise a free choice as consumers and to devise means whereby production is permitted to respond to that choice in a way that conforms as nearly as possible to competitive standards.

Public regulation is the result of the separation of the responsibility for managing and directing the productive processes and resources of the nation, on the one hand, from the responsibility of establishing the conditions under which the managing and directing shall be discharged, on the other. In other words, public regulation emerges from the separation of the functions of government from the functions of managing production. It therefore assumes a private enterprise system or at least one that has the attributes of such a system. Public ownership in a capitalistic setting may satisfy these conditions, but it is unlikely to do so without a predominance of private ownership.[2] Regulation is consequently a term that really has meaning only in a private enterprise economy. Other types of economies will exercise controls, but these controls will not be public regulation.

An analysis of public policy as it applies to regulation must proceed from the assumption of a private enterprise economy. Whatever may be the merits of a private enterprise system versus some other type, appraisal of these merits is not a part of the analysis of the problems of regulation, because these are two separate and distinct issues. Private enterprise is therefore assumed in this presentation, and no discussion of its relation to a free economy or democracy will be undertaken at this time.[3] At this juncture, all that is necessary is a realization of the fact that the assumption of private enterprise is fundamental to a statement of the problem of regulation and to an analysis of the processes by which regulation is carried out in this country.

Competition and Private Enterprise

A private enterprise system is based on the assumption of competition. In the broadest sense, competition is the basis of the economic and economical way of doing things, because it establishes the conditions under which options are made available. It affords the opportunity to choose among them, so that those that are foregone are less important than those that are selected. Competition arises, therefore, because of the opportunity of choice and the necessity of exercising it.

In a private enterprise economy, the management and direction of

[2]See, for example, H. C. Simons, *Economic Policy for a Free Society* (Chicago: University of Chicago Press, 1948), chap. i, pp. 30–31.

[3]See Chapter 1, *supra*, for a discussion of this issue.

production is decentralized in the hands of a great number of persons. It is competition that affords the co-ordinating mechanism for an economical allocation of resources. Reliance is placed on competition for the incentives for exercising initiative and undertaking business ventures, as a condition of survival, and as a means of ascertaining by experimentation what to produce. In so far as man is motivated by economic considerations, economic rewards are a requisite for stimulating enterprise. In any case, economic considerations play a significant part in decision making; and, other things being equal, a person will choose the activity with the larger economic returns in place of the one with the lower returns; and this is the rational and economic action to take. Competition is also a condition of survival, because the producer who cannot dispose of his wares at prices that cover his costs together with the necessary profit will discontinue his endeavors, either because of failure or because of better opportunities elsewhere. The buyer is not forced to buy from a particular producer because of the alternatives that are available. Finally, competition affords a means of experimentation by trial and error whereby consumer wants are ascertained. In point of fact, there is really no other way to discover the wants; and the most comprehensive experimentation will come from a multiplicity of producers striving for the market.

The Basic Problem of Regulation

The basic problem of regulation is that of establishing or maintaining the conditions necessary for the economical utilization of resources under a system of private enterprise. This means that public authority must endeavor to prescribe rules of conduct for business behavior that are designed to promote the operation of a private enterprise economy in at least tolerable conformity to the prime assumptions on which that economy is predicated. Regulation must therefore seek to maintain a competitive environment and carry out its policies with reliance on competitive forces whenever possible.

There are serious difficulties in the way of carrying out such a policy. Technological conditions may be such that some of the important requisites of competition are lacking, or at least partially deficient. Much production requires large and specialized investment that seriously impedes the mobility of some of the resources and restricts the number of competitors to a few. In some instances, such as the supply of electricity, direct competition and readily available substitute products may be lacking. In others, as in transport, a very high degree of competition may exist side by side with limited competitive conditions. Finally, institutional arrangements may offer severe complications. The business corporation, with its literally unlimited capacity for integration of ownership as well as its ability to escape some of the important restrictions of the market, is an illustration. Many corporate enterprises engage in many different lines of production. This diversity of activity is the result of public sanction; it is not the inevitable or inescapable consequence of competition. The extent to which it should be permitted is a matter of considerable controversy.

The difficulties encountered in regulating private enterprise have led many to conclude that the task cannot be accomplished if economic efficiency is to be maintained. Some believe that the very success of capitalism has provided the seeds of its own destruction.[4] Others, however, are convinced that regulation can be successful and that it must be if a free society is to survive. Whatever may be the merits of these different points of view, it is clear that if we wish to maintain a system of private enterprise, public policy must be directed to that end. Regulation must seek to maintain the conditions of competition, not to thwart or destroy them. It must be administered in keeping with our ideas of democracy and in accordance with our concepts of law and justice. These are not simple prescriptions, and they are likely to be carried out in a disconnected and often contradictory manner. It is here that our institutional arrangements and historical development step in to play a primary role and focus attention on basic objectives.

THE INSTITUTIONAL FOUNDATIONS OF CONTROL

Control in human society is expressed through the medium of group action and denotes the various ways by which the activities of those making up the group are co-ordinated. It comprises all the compulsions and sanctions by which group life is carried on. The way in which social control manifests itself and the issues it creates vary from one country to another because of differences in social philosophy, customs, habits, and physical environment. All control, however, is expressed through institutions or procedures, each group having its own distinctive types.

Social Institutions

Every society has its characteristic institutions, and it is largely by these that one society is distinguished from another. The term "institution" has somewhat varied meanings. In a narrow and technical sense, it refers to the established forms or conditions of procedure characteristic of group activity. These forms or conditions are the habitual and crystallized means of guiding and controlling social relationships which have grown up out of custom and tradition. They rely heavily on precedent and are, as a consequence, persistent elements in the life or culture of organized groups. The institutions of a nation or a body politic are surrounded by a large number of legal sanctions and are, therefore, a fundamental and indispensable part of the legal and political framework of a country. Representative government is an institution, because it con-

[4]This is the thesis of the late Professor Schumpeter. He also holds that the disappearance of capitalism will be accompanied by the demise of democracy. See J. A Schumpeter *Capitalism, Socialism and Democracy* (New York: Harper & Bros., 1942).

stitutes the procedure by which government is carried on in this country. Similarly, marriage, private property, and trial by jury are institutions under this definition.

The term "institution" may also be used in a less restrictive fashion to indicate certain broader conceptions than the foregoing. It may connote not only the established or habitual procedures by which group life is carried on but also the specific types of organizations by which these forms are implemented. Frequently, both ideas are included at the same time. Thus, when one speaks of the federal form of government, he may mean the procedure by which the government of the United States is carried on, or he may be thinking of the more technical means through which government functions. Similarly, when the term "corporation" is used, it may indicate a particular arrangement by which group activity for special purposes is implemented; or it may refer to the group as an association of people, thereby emphasizing associational and group aspects. There are good reasons for confining the term "institution" to the first and more technical usage; but is is, nevertheless, convenient at times to use it in its broader sense.

Man, in his social conduct, does not act instinctively but only as the result of learning the forms of behavior of the group of which he is a member. These forms grow out of the experiences of the past. Consequently, man cannot discard familiar institutional arrangements and start anew. If he is temporarily cut off from patterns with which he has been associated, he reverts to them in time simply because he has no other accustomed guide of conduct. If, perchance, he could be completely deprived of any memory of any previous institutional contacts and associations, he would be totally at a loss to know how to carry on his social life. Basic changes in a social structure develop slowly because of this. Even revolutions do not eliminate the fundamental elements of a structure, although they may exterminate outworn forms. This is the reason why the people of a country return to earlier patterns after they have experienced a revolution.

Institutional Basis of Regulation

Man, in his group relations, is subject to various kinds of control. Only in this way is organized life possible, since individuals in their activities as they relate to one another must have common rules by which they can proceed. The word "control" implies compulsion, the requirement to abide by certain modes of behavior on pain of penalty. However, compulsion is only one aspect of control, voluntary co-operation being the other. The compulsory aspect of the idea emphasizes the dominance of the authority exercising the control and restricts the term to those procedures which must be adhered to. The restraints which are imposed may be either positive or negative. The negative restraints prohibit certain actions and impose penalties for engaging in the practices forbidden.

On the positive side, the control may emphasize the things that must be done and provide appropriate penalties for failure to conform. In this country, the bulk of the restraints are of a negative nature.

Control in business means arrangements to secure compliance with established rules of conduct; and the emphasis, generally speaking, is on the compulsory aspects. However, it should be recognized that control also involves consent and that successful control can be exercised only when the established rules give expression to generally accepted standards of conduct. In short, control may involve compulsion; but it cannot succeed if the resistance to particular laws is very strong. Thus, in a broader sense, it relies on voluntary co-operation. This voluntary co-operation not only is essential to the successful enforcement of rules and regulations involving various kinds of compulsion but also applies to a large part of business conduct in which procedures have been adopted by common practice. Many rules of the game have grown up because they facilitate business activity; and they have become part of the pattern of business behavior, even though no particular penalties are imposed for noncompliance. In fact, the regulation of business becomes intelligible only when it is understood that, besides prohibiting certain types of practices, regulation must also formulate rules which will act as guides to business conduct and policy. Whether adherence to the standards agreed upon will be required as a matter of law or whether compliance will be left to individual choice will depend upon the importance of those standards and the effect of noncompliance on the operation of the economic system. Thus, for example, trade associations may be permitted to establish rules for members, conformity to which may be a condition of membership. It may not be necessary to belong to the association in order to do business, and competitors may not find it convenient to follow the rules laid down for members. If those rules, however, are considered essential to the orderly conduct of that kind of business or for the protection of the general public, they may be incorporated into law. In this case, compliance will be required by public authority, and transgressors will suffer whatever penalties the law imposes.

The types of regulation and control that exist in various countries depend upon the institutional arrangements of those countries. To understand the nature of them, cognizance of existing institutions is necessary. The problems of control must also be examined in the light of the same conditions. This is not to say that control of economic activity is a purely institutional issue. Technology exercises considerable influence; and although the means by which control is imposed may vary from country to country, there are many common problems, in spite of institutional differences, because of the technological similarities which create many of the issues.

The way in which these problems are handled, however, is dependent upon the institutional structure of the country in which they arise. Change takes place through institutional arrangements; and hence, this fact must be recognized in the development of regulation and control. The persistence of institutional patterns presents facts to be reckoned with that can be ignored only by those who would inaugurate innovations that do violence to those arrangements. This does not mean that institutions must be taken entirely for granted, for they are constantly changing and being changed. The process, however, is slow; and man has not yet shown an ability to invent a new "order" divorced completely from the past of the people and institutions that comprise it.

THE SIGNIFICANCE OF HISTORICAL DEVELOPMENT

Human beings think and act largely in terms of the past. Indeed, without the experience of the past, we would be worse than a ship without a rudder, for organized life of any kind would be impossible. Paradoxically, man strives only for the future. But he moves from the experiences of the past and the interpretations of them to meet the issues of the future through what is frequently an intolerably, or at least disconcertingly, short present. Even in times of revolution, when all the past appears to be, or is proclaimed as being, cast to one side, man has the peculiar habit of eying wistfully some golden age of a previous period, upon the idealizing of which he proceeds to erect a new era. Unfortunately, when the excesses fail to produce the results expected, reactions set in; and society settles back to patterns even more extreme than those immediately eliminated. From that situation, if at all, comes reconstruction by the process of development and adaptation, which was eschewed or probably impossible when the revolution broke.

The social and industrial structure of the United States is the result of a long period of growth. It is the product of an environment which has so richly endowed us with natural resources; of a genius which has made it possible to utilize those resources with such amazing results; of people, inventions, and ideas from other countries to which we owe so much; and of institutions which, in the balance, have provided the atmosphere and implementation for an economic development unparalleled in the history of the world.

All of this did not just happen. From comparatively restricted and elementary foundations, there began a growth at the opening of the nineteenth century that took on an accelerated pace after the Civil War and rose to the crescendo of the industrialism of the twentieth century, in the throes of which we are now trying to locate our bearings. The beginning of our industrialization, shortly after securing independence, were mostly the result of the importations of inventions adapted to our environment. After the Civil War, however, a large part of the development was indigenous; and today, it is the United States that is in the vanguard of the changing industrial structure of the world.

Industrial growth is dynamic in the sense that it is an unfolding process, emerging cumulatively from the past. As it moves along, it discards many features and takes on new ones; but it does not follow an inexorable path, nor does it change without influence from human beings. To understand the industrial pattern of the present, we must comprehend the forces which have determined its course to date. Without a knowledge of the history of a country, it is impossible to understand that country.

On the strictly technological side, we must seek a knowledge of the technical changes that have taken place, of the forces which brought them about, and of the impact of new techniques on the existing ones. The methods of production which we use are strongly conditioned by habit, and resistances encountered to changing techniques are frequently the result of inability to divorce ourselves from accustomed ways of doing things. In a similar manner, managerial and organizational practices and procedures are the results of accumulation and adaptation. As the technical structure of modern enterprise has emerged, new devices for management and direction have been required. The adaptation has been accomplished by a molding and transforming of existing arrangements into new types of organization which retain many original characteristics even as they take on forms that are far removed from the origin. At the same time, the industrial structure itself exhibits the peculiarity of displaying simultaneously, partly because of its complexity, all of the forms which it has developed historically.

The understanding of industrial behavior follows, then, its development. Man acts first and comprehends afterward. This does not mean that he is completely unable to mold his environment in accordance with his socially expressed desires. On the contrary, he does just that, sometimes more effectively and sometimes more dramatically than at other times. Man is constantly seeking to control the conditions under which he lives. In the broadest sense, he lives in a world which he has created; but the results of his efforts can scarcely be said to conform to a preconceived pattern. Not only does he have to accept at any given time the limiting conditions of the world of nature, but he also has to bow to the inertia and restraining force of historical accumulation. For better or for worse, he is compelled to proceed from the environment he has to one of which he knows nothing. Although he can predict the results of policies within narrow limits, this can usually be done only in broad terms.

Social control of economic life is forced by necessity to work with immediate problems and materials. If it is carried out intelligently, it will be based on broad objectives and a philosophy that embodies all the social values that have come to be cherished because they are indispensable to the civilization we wish to preserve and nourish. This fact precludes the recasting of the economic and social structure in a pattern indicated by some abstract model that does not and cannot comprehend within its framework all of the essential ingredients of the social structure of a virile civilization. The basic institutional arrangements which have conditioned the development of economic life in the United States are the subject of the next chapter.

Chapter 3 INSTITUTIONAL ARRANGEMENTS

It was pointed out in the previous chapter that every society has its own characteristic social institutions through which it carries on its activities. Social control is expressed through these institutional arrangements, and each nation or country has its own distinctive types. This accounts—in part, at least—for the different problems of public control and the different approaches to those problems in the various countries of the world. Those types which are in existence at any particular time have developed through the slow process of history. They are deeply rooted in the social fabric; and although they are constantly being modified, they cannot be discarded suddenly without seriously disrupting, and frequently destroying, orderly social development. Some of these arrangements are more fundamental to the political and economic life of the country than are others. They condition public policy at any particular time because they not only impose limitations on what the government may do but also constitute the primary channels through which it must act. The following treatment deals with those institutions which seem to be most basic to the regulation of industry in this country.

COMMON LAW

The foundation of the legal system of the United States is the common law. It is one of the two great legal systems of the Western world and prevails in England and most English-speaking lands. The other is the civil or modern Roman law system, which is characteristic of continental Europe and the parts of the world colonized therefrom. The distinct features of common law as contrasted with civil law are the reliance on judicial precedent, trial by jury, and the doctrine of the supremacy of the law.

Common Law as a Body of Rules

Common law may refer to that part of the law of the land which has grown up without benefit of legislation and which can be found only in court decisions. As a body of rules, it designates that part of the law, in countries having the common-law system, which is traditional in form. Substantively, it embraces those rules of law which developed out of customs that have been incorporated into court precedent. In this respect, common law is distinct from statute law and may be referred to as the traditional part of the law of the land. When one wishes to ascertain what the law is on a particular topic, he must search through court decisions to determine what the courts have said the law is. Their interpretation depends upon the issues in the particular case and the principles which have been followed in previous similar cases or the customs which have prevailed under such circumstances in the past. When a court decision establishes a rule for a new situation, that rule becomes part of the law of the land, which governs subsequent acts where facts are substantially of the same nature. Changing conditions and changing ideas over periods of time have introduced new concepts into the interpretation of legal relationships and modified the old ones. As a consequence of this development by interpretation, the common law has grown and changed in substance over the centuries and is still in a process of change.

Common Law as a Method of Procedure

The common-law system involves a distinct method of procedure in developing the law of the land. This is accomplished by the continuous process of court interpretation in specific cases of the legal issues which arise, the accumulation of decisions giving meaning to the law. It is the function of the courts to give the authoritative interpretation of the law. When this is done for a particular legal issue, the ruling becomes a precedent for subsequent litigation. It is by adherence to precedent that the law gains its continuity and stability within reasonably predictable limits. This method of developing the law is so deeply ingrained in our political and legal structure that it will probably persist in the United States for the indefinite future. "Two things are likely to make the common law, as a system, an enduring basis for American law . . . ; its technique of finding the law through judicial experience and its conception of rights and duties as involved in or incident to relations."[1]

Common Law and Statute Law

The common law is frequently contrasted with statute law. The contrast is largely one of the ways the formal part of the law comes into being. Statute law is that which is enacted by legislative bodies, whereas common law has no such basis. The courts develop the common law out of custom, but statute law is the result of specific enactment by legislatures. Thus, we go to court decisions to see what the common law is; but on statutory matters, we first look to the statute.

However, the contrast is more apparent than real. Where the common-law system prevails, statutes must be interpreted by the courts; and the meaning of statutory—or for that matter, even constitutional—provisions depends upon the constructions placed upon them by the courts. Furthermore, the interpretation of statutory enactments is made in the

[1]Roscoe Pound, "Common Law," *Encyclopedia of the Social Sciences*, Vol. IV, p. 56.

light of existing law; and unless legal arrangements already in force are specifically set to one side, they are presumed to continue, and statutes will be interpreted accordingly. Thus, common-law concepts permeate all of our statutory law in both substance and procedure.

Common Law and Business

Under the common law, men can engage in any kind of business not specifically prohibited to them. In many respects, the common law may be called a personal law, in that the individual is the focus of attention. It does not create legal entities that are distinct from the individual himself. Hence, individual responsibility is the characteristic of business operations conducted under common-law provisions. As a consequence, liability is personal and unlimited; and in the absence of contractual arrangements to the contrary, each individual is regarded as possessing equal power and responsibility before the law.

Although a large part of the law pertaining to the control of business is statutory in origin, the common-law rules are by no means insignificant. Over the many centuries during which the common law has developed, extensive rules of business conduct have grown up. When they have not been set aside or superseded by statutory enactment, these common-law rules prevail. Even when there has been specific legislation, however, the common-law concepts are still of basic importance because of the incorporation of the terminology of the law into our everyday vocabulary. Terms which have come to receive more or less precise meanings in business and in business practice are, in the absence of specific statutory definition, accorded such meaning when the courts interpret statutes.

The Supremacy of the Law

The doctrine of the supremacy of the law, which is one of the most distinguishing features of the common law, is derived from the origin of the common law in custom and traditional behavior. It means that all agencies of government are bound to act in accordance with general legal principles, and not according to arbitrary will. As a consequence, the acts of agencies of government are constantly subject to scrutiny in ordinary legal proceedings before the regular courts of the land. No one can escape the possibility of being called into court to answer for his actions; and furthermore, if he is a public official, he is bound to discharge the law as it stands. This means that all persons, whether public officials or private citizens, are subject to the rules of law, either statutory or traditional, and that they are required to carry out their responsibilities in accordance with those rules.[2] The traditional and popular

[2]This means the "absolute supremacy or predominance of regular law as opposed to the influence of arbitrary power and excludes the existence of arbitrariness, of prerogatives, or even of wide discretionary authority on the part of the government.

(*Continued on next page*).

origins of this doctrine are given further emphasis by the right of "trial by jury," which is still preserved as a means of safeguarding the individual against arbitrary action. The idea that a man is entitled to be judged by his "peers"—that is, his equals—despite many shortcomings in practice, embodies the fundamental principle that the law must not be permitted to exceed the bounds of customary procedure and popular support.

It is in the common law that our basic concepts regarding individual rights and private property are rooted. This is no mere accident in view of the development of the two together, especially during the last three hundred years. The doctrine of the supremacy of the law has become part and parcel of the guarantee of personal and property rights and to date, at least, has acted as a strong safeguard against the encroachment of public authority upon these. The emergence of the idea of property rights as natural rights in the seventeenth century has further reinforced the position of private property in our system. Because rights in private property came to be regarded as natural—and therefore, to a degree at least, apart from the state—they received protection at common law against encroachment by the state. This does not mean that conceptions of property rights have not changed, but rather that they have changed within the framework of the traditional legal system and, because of their close relationship with our ideas of individual freedom, have changed more slowly than otherwise might have been the case. This seems to be in definite contrast to developments on the continent of Europe, where the civil law prevails. As one writer expresses it:

> Politically, the civil law developing under the absolutist traditions of monarchy and empire has tended to encourage the supremacy of the legislative and administrative rather than the judicial organs of the state and no doctrine of the "rule of law" has entered the legal system as a guarantee of individual freedom. The state has thus tended to maintain a position of supreme competence.[3]

Equity

Another feature of our law which is sometimes treated as quite distinct from the common law is the law of equity. The distinction between equity and the common law is essentially that of rules and procedures.[4] Because of the limitations of relief which common law afforded,

. . . It means equality before the law or the equal subjection of all classes to the ordinary law of the land as administered by the law courts" (A. V. Dicey, *Law of the Constitution* [London: Macmillan & Co., Ltd., 1920], p. 198). For a detailed examination of this subject, see Bernard Schwartz, *American Constitutional Law* (London: The Cambridge University Press, 1955).

[3]J. Declareuil, "Civil Law," *Encyclopedia of the Social Sciences*, Vol. III, p. 507.

[4]"In the federal courts common law and equity are administered by the same court, but the two are kept substantially distinct. . .in equity cases the procedure is prescribed by the Federal Equity Rules adopted by the Supreme Court of the United States in pursuance of a statute of Congress" *Encyclopedia for the Social Sciences*, Vol. V (New York: Macmillan Co., 1931) p. 587. In some states there are separate courts for the administration of law and of equity. See B. A. Arneson, *Elements of Constitutional Law* (New York: Harper & Bros., 1928), pp. 44–45.

equity developed as a means of securing justice when the former was inadequate. The common-law courts can only penalize wrongs. Action can be brought in court and damages secured only after injury has taken place. On the other hand, a court of equity, under appropriate circumstances, can prevent the injury from being committed. Thus, injunctions are sought in courts of equity because the purpose of an injunction is to prevent injury from occurring or injustice from being committed. Although this court may be a different judicial body from a court of law, usually it is the same body sitting and operating under different rules. Certain items such as trusts, wills, and estates are specifically assigned to courts of equity. The significance of equity in the control of business lies largely in the legal differences in procedure from that which obtains at law and in the possibilities of securing court action to protect rights in advance of the application of the law. Suits in equity have played a very prominent part in the administration of the antitrust laws.

PRIVATE PROPERTY AND CONTRACT

Meaning of Private Property

The term "property" as used in everday language designates the things which are owned. These may be tangible or intangible. Tangible property consists of such things as land, buildings, machinery, tools, stocks, bonds, etc., whereas intangible property refers to items such as patents, good will, trade-marks, and trade names. This view of property places emphasis on the thing owned rather than on the rights which the ownership confers. It arose from the fact that the earlier forms of property were land, livestock, and similar things. Even today, the physical aspects of property are usually uppermost in one's mind when he uses the term, whereas "property rights" is used when the benefits to be obtained are the center of attention. It is ownership, however, which is the essence of the concept of property. There is no property if there is no ownership. Ownership, strictly speaking, is the result of sanction and presupposes the existence of authority to guarantee the possession of the property and the legal right to it. Private property is that which is owned by persons, natural or otherwise; and public property is that which is owned by the government, either directly or through agencies created for that purpose.

A broader and more useful concept of property regards it as a bundle of rights and privileges which may be enjoyed as the result of ownership. Only in modern times have we come to recognize that it is what one is allowed to do with the things he owns and the protection which is afforded for the disposition or utilization of them which form the basis of private property. A curtailment or expansion of these powers changes the nature of the property and reduces or enhances what a person possesses. This idea emphasizes the institutional aspect of property, because only when the rights and privileges of ownership are protected by a superior authority can they be said to exist at all. It is these rights and privileges that constitute the essence of private property. They set the legal limits on its use, guarantee protection against encroachment by others, and form the legal basis of its economic value.

Private Property and Public Control

Private property in the means of production is probably the distinguishing characteristic of capitalism. Hence, the private property rights arising therefrom constitute one of the focal points of the regulation of business. Problems of public policy relating to this control in the United States are very largely confined to production processes. Production is a means to an end, the end being the consumption or the use of the results of production to satisfy wants. The way in which a person may satisfy his wants, at least within the choices at his disposal, is largely a matter of individual taste; but the opportunities available for the satisfaction of those wants are primarily matters of production. Hence, the key point of control of economic activity is in the production processes. When these are carried on mainly through the medium of private property, the delineation of private property rights is the cornerstone of the whole structure of social control.

Although these private property rights depend upon the development of public policy on matters of control, public policy is conditioned by existing concepts of these rights. The latter, being largely cumulative and with long historical connotations, are, by and large, subject to relatively slow change. They are also associated with our ideas of freedom and the way in which we carry on our political life, for private property is the economic counterpart of political democracy. Therefore, a change of the relationships existing in current conceptions of property rights has repercussions throughout the entire social and legal structure.

The institution of private property is so thoroughly a part of our political and economic fabric that the introduction of new arrangements or the imposition of new limitations designed to alter radically and rapidly the current rights of property meet with considerable resistance. And therefore, while the process of control is affected by existing institutional concepts, the reverse is also true. When regulatory measures are under consideration, they must be examined in the light of their impact upon our concept of private property. The latter may have to change under pressure of new conditions and objectives. This does not necessarily mean that the rights have to be abolished or even restricted in total. Restrictions may be imposed on the property rights of some people in order to expand those of others. The exercise of the right of eminent domain to condemn property for public use is an illustration of this. Recognition of the system of private property as one of the most important parts of our political constitution carries with it the implications of a gradual development of the ideas of private property and property rights and of the growth of regulation as therefore a comparatively slow process. But this is the essence of the democratic and liberal process.

Contract

Accompanying the institution of private property, and really part and parcel of it, is contract. Without contract, the private property concept is largely devoid of meaning, because one's right to acquire or dispose of property is one of its principal attributes. Strictly speaking, contract denotes an act or set of acts creating obligations. As a legal concept, it connotes the creation of a legal relationship whereby one party may exact a performance of another party in return for certain considerations. The conditions of the contract are enforceable at law. Many arrangements frequently called "contractual" may really be only agreements relying upon moral responsibility for their fulfillment. These, however, lack the essential characteristic of the enforceability of contract, and it seems wise to restrict the latter term to its more precise meaning. This conception of contract involves both the agreement and the entire body of law that has grown up around its interpretation and enforcement. Thus, contract is an institutional arrangement which relies upon an independent authority that is not a party to it for its existence.

Private property and contract require the continuous exercise of public regulation and control. Without a superior legal authority to guarantee the rights and enforce the responsibilities arising from these two arrangements, they could not exist. The question, therefore, is not whether there should be any regulation or control but rather how much and of what kind. Instead of viewing regulation and control primarily as limitations on private property and contract, it is more accurate to recognize that the very existence and survival of these arrangements are dependent upon a body politic to establish and enforce the conditions of their use. When there is no private property and contract, an individual's actions are very severely circumscribed; but when these institutional arrangements do prevail, the state surrenders much of its authority over economic matters to the individual. New rules grow up as the concepts change, but this does not necessarily mean the extension of control at the expense of private property and contract. This, of course, may happen, but it is not an inherent part of control. If the law is designed to assist in bringing about a wider enjoyment of the privileges embodied in these devices, then the result of control is to expand them, not the reverse.

Is Private Property a Natural Right?

A persistent question in social theory in the English-speaking countries is whether private property is a natural right or one created or conferred by the state. Is property a creation of the state or a recognition of arrangements that have already come into existence? It is true that private property is a social concept, and, in that sense, it is certainly a creation of society; but this is not the same thing as saying it is the creation of the state. That depends on the theory of the nature of the state. The natural-law concepts of property and liberty grew up as a protection for the individual against the encroachment of the power of the state. These concepts recognized that the state was not the whole of society and did not create or control all social relations. Nineteenth-century theories of the state leaned to the idea of absolute sovereignty; the natural-law concept gradually waned, and "state" origin of all rights and institutions took its place. But the rise of totalitarianism has led to a re-examination of the role of the state in human affairs. Today, there appears to be some reawakening of the idea that the "natural-rights" philosophy was not all wrong, that there are limitations on the power of the state, and that the state is not the sole creator of social arrangements. This point of view gives private property and contract an independence of the state, even though a state may be necessary to enforce the legal rights pertaining to them. This does not alter the fact that these concepts have meaning only within an established political order; but it does emphasize their traditional foundations and the role of the state as an instrument of society rather than as a dictator, either beneficent or otherwise, of the procedures by which people conduct their affairs.

FEDERAL FORM OF GOVERNMENT

Nature of the Federal Form

The United States is governed by what is known as the "federal" form of government. It is the result of the uniting of a number of more or less independent states into a union in which each member retains a large degree of sovereignty. For the purpose of forming the union, the states give up those powers which are considered to be of significance to the union as a whole and which require unity of action on the part of the members. Thus, there results a central government, with control over those matters which relate to the well-being of the whole country, and a series of state governments, with the latter enjoying, within the limits of the federal structure, sovereign powers.

Because of its origin, the federal form of government necessitates a written constitution. This constitution forms the basic framework of government for the federal union. It sets forth the respective rights of the central and local governments, and provides means whereby the general framework may be modified to meet the needs arising from changing conditions. The written constitution which seems characteristic of and essential to a federal union engenders a fixity of pattern and a tendency toward inertia, in some respects, that is not present under a unitary system. The relative inflexibility arises, however, not so much from the written constitution as from the fact that the relationships of the composite parts of the union involve divergencies that require careful adjustment. There is the tendency among members of the union to insist on retaining individual rights, just as there is among nations. The consequence is that the federal form of government, despite all its advantages, constantly necessitates compromise and adjustment, which complicates the development of uniform policies throughout the entire country.

It should be emphasized that the federal form of government, as such, has nothing to do with the separation of legislative, executive, and judicial powers; nor has it anything to do with the protection of individual rights. These can be a part of any form of government. They have been associated with the federal type in this country because the separation of powers and the incorporation of protection to life, liberty, and property in a written constitution originated in the United States, which was the first example of a federal union.

Problems of Regulation and Control

The federal form of government gives rise to special problems in the control of economic activity. State governments enjoy widespread powers of regulation over economic life because of their jurisdiction over what are considered purely state matters. At the same time, economic activity persistently defies political boundaries. As a consequence, interstate business is ever present. In fact, interstate commerce has grown enormously in significance since the formation of the union and, in many respects, predominates today. Because of the interrelationship of business transactions and activities, it frequently becomes extremely difficult to separate interstate from intrastate commerce. The federal government in this country is given control of commerce among the states, but the Constitution contains no definition of that term. The powers, therefore, which the federal government may exercise, as contrasted with those of the states, are the subject of continuous debate and controversy. In recent years, there has been a strong tendency, especially under the impact of widespread economic dislocation, to extend the authority of the federal government by a broader and more far-reaching concept of interstate commerce. Whatever may be the arguments in favor of this extension, it must be remembered that there is a fundamental problem of reconciliation of the economic powers which the federal government exercises and the preservation of the separate existence of the several states. If the federal form of government is to remain, it will be necessary to recognize that the several states must continue to enjoy extensive control over economic activity.

The problems of control under a federal system are considerably more complicated than under a unitary form of government because of the conflicting powers of the respective sovereignties. The disadvantage of the federal form of government from the standpoint of control of economic activity is the complexity of that government. The advantage which seems considerably to outweigh any disadvantage is that the federal form makes possible the welding of a large number of diverse peoples into a workable union, in lieu of which there probably would be separate nation-states, with resulting conflict and national barriers. The elimination of the complications arising from states' rights can, in the present stage of our history, be accomplished only by eliminating the states themselves, the consequences of which no serious person could contemplate with equanimity.

The Constitution and Regulation

There are two distinct features of the Constitution of the United States which are important in the control of industry. In the first place, the Constitution provides for a framework of government, two aspects of which are significant from the standpoint of this discussion. The federal government is given exclusive control of interstate commerce,[5] and in the event of conflict of powers, the federal power is supreme when such supremacy is necessary for the appropriate exercise of the functions assigned to the federal government. The absence of a definition of interstate commerce in the Constitution has left in the hands of the federal government flexible powers which can be adapted to the changing problems of control. The ever-widening boundaries of everyday business and the increasing interrelationships of various phases of economic activity have made the matter of interstate commerce one of the focal points of public policy. This has had marked repercussions not only on the respective positions of the state and federal governments but also on the relationship of the legislative and executive branches to the judicial branch of our government.

The second aspect of the framework of government which is significant for the analysis of control is the separation of powers. Under the constitutional structure of the United States, the executive, judicial, and legislative branches of the government are co-ordinate. Governmental action, therefore, requires the sanction and co-operation of all three parts. This means that in the matters of control of industry, the legislative, executive, and judicial viewpoints must be in agreement and that each department must act strictly within its own sphere of competence. Because of constantly changing conditions, the adjustment of these three divisions is a continuous process, often very delicately balanced.

The second main feature of the Constitution of the United States which is important from the standpoint of public regulation is the Bill of Rights. Our Constitution contains guarantees for the protection of life, liberty, and property. These guarantees are not necessarily an inherent

[5]"It is substantially correct to say that Congress enjoys exclusive authority to regulate interstate commerce," F. A. Ogg and P. O. Ray, *Essentials of American Government* (6th ed.; New York: Appleton-Century-Crofts, Inc., 1950), p. 381. There is a wide range of concurrent powers, however, in the concept of interstate commerce, and that which is reserved exclusively to Congress is quite narrowly construed.

part of a written constitution or of the federal form of government. The Canadian Constitution, for example, does not include them. Since they are, however, a specific part of the Constitution of the United States, they have become interwoven with the other aspects of our constitutional development. This is the reason why the functions of the courts as an integral part of the federal form of government and of the courts as the protector of liberty and property are so frequently confused. Our Constitution places a special emphasis on the importance of property and individual freedom on economic matters as the basis of liberty. Historically, the reason for this emphasis is that the struggle for liberty in England and in this country involved a contest for the protection of property rights as one of the basic means of maintaining individual liberty. In both countries, it was recognized that, as long as the king had control of the key points of the economic life of the people, personal liberty was imperiled, if not impossible. Thus, the economic foundations of freedom became one of the focal points of the conflict, which finally resulted in the acceptance of the Bill of Rights in England by William of Orange (William III) in 1689. This action and the controversy over taxation with George III led to the incorporation of the Bill of Rights in the Constitution of the United States. Thus, the protection of personal and property rights at the outset of our national development was established as a matter of fundamental law. The historical sanction which this policy has received as a result of a long period of growth makes the maintenance of personal and property rights one of the main duties of the government of the United States.

JUDICIAL REVIEW

Meaning of Judicial Review

One of the distinguishing characteristics of the American system of government is the position occupied by the judiciary. In no other country is the power of the judiciary so pronounced or evident. Indeed, this has developed to such an extent in the United States that on matters of social policy, the question too frequently asked is, "Is the procedure legal?" rather than "Is it socially sound?" If the answer to the legal aspect is a negative one, there is the tendency to drop the issue. If it is positive, there is an equal tendency to assume that the other aspects of the problem are necessarily sound.

The position which the courts have come to occupy in this country has given rise to the American doctrine of judicial review. In its technical sense, this doctrine refers to the procedure whereby the courts review the legislation of the various governments of the country in the light of the constitutions of those governments. When the courts find that the actions of the various parts of the governmental structure violate the written constitutions, they declare those actions invalid. The power to declare legislation unconstitutional has been developed more extensively here than in any other country.

In its broader aspects, the idea of judicial review refers to the power of the courts to interpret laws. Although the courts, for example, in Great Britain do not have the right to set acts of Parliament aside, they nevertheless do have the duty of interpreting whatever legislation Parliament enacts; and the law in England, as in this country, means what the courts say it means. The difference lies in the power of the judiciary in the United States to declare the legislation invalid; this cannot be done in Great Britain. But in both countries, the courts do interpret and enforce the law. Both countries adhere to the common-law tradition of the rule of the law and the development of its meaning by court precedent. In this respect, judicial review has a definite historical basis, for through the interpretation of law by the courts, there has developed a continuity of process and principle that could scarcely have been attained in any other way.

The most important reason, probably, for the rise of judicial review to its supreme significance in this country was the adoption of the federal form of government, which presupposes agreement by equal parties, in the formation of a government, with contractual rights in that government. Various procedures might have been adopted to interpret these rights, but the most obvious was to leave to the courts the matter of giving content to the Constitution and of interpreting legislation in the light of the Constitution. It is difficult to see how the federal form of government could have been successful without the courts occupying a key position.

Contrary to widespread belief, review by the courts is not unique to the United States; a similar situation exists in Canada and the other British dominions. There is one fundamental difference, however, which has colored the whole process of judicial review in the United States and which arose from the incorporation of the Bill of Rights into our Constitution. Not only do the courts in this country occupy a key position in the federal system of government, but they also play a rather decisive role in the protection of life, liberty, and property. Which of the two functions has been the most important in American constitutional history may be a matter of debate. It is, however, highly essential to remember that the protection of life and property has given the courts a sense of importance that has made their place in the government decidedly more prominent than it would have been otherwise.

Judicial Review and Economic Policy

Judicial review, as it has developed in this country, has undoubtedly resulted in a slowness of response at times on the part of government to the demands of the electorate. One is frequently impressed with the more immediate and direct response displayed by Parliament in Great

Britain than by Congress in the United States. This response is partly the result of judicial review and partly the result of the lack of what is known as "responsible" government.[6] However, the limitations of tradition on the British Parliament are probably as great as the limitations of the Constitution on American legislatures. The essential fact seems to be that both countries have developed arrangements whereby change is undertaken gradually only after opportunity for careful deliberation and in accordance with historical tradition. It should be remembered, also, that when court decisions are quite contrary to public opinion, there is always the remedy of constitutional amendment in the United States. The fact that this is cumbersome and slow should not be taken as an argument against its effectiveness; it was made cumbersome and slow deliberately. Ill-advised amendments could easily lead to very unstable government.

The position of the courts in this country as powerful agencies of public policy has given rise to much criticism and has created the feeling that the country is being ruled by judicial rather than by legislative process. There is some basis of support for this position, and economists are prone to be impatient when court decisions exhibit economic reasoning of very dubious validity. The possibility of other arrangements is not inviting, however. The long tradition of procedure and the deep-rooted practice of judicial review indicate that changes in our present methods will come about only gradually and more or less imperceptibly as a result of new problems. The dangers that lurk in proposals to exempt the decisions of administrative commissions, for example, from judicial scrutiny are too great to warrant the experiment.

CAPITALISM

Definition of Capitalism

The term "capitalism" is employed to denote a particular set of institutional arrangements through which the direction of the processes of production is carried out. It refers to an economic system in which there is private property in the means of production, the prime responsibility for the guidance of that production being in the hands of private enterprise. The private owners of the means of production have the function of deciding what shall be produced—and when, where, and how much shall be produced. Capitalism or the capitalistic management of industrial resources presupposes a competitive struggle for trade among businessmen, not only for the purpose of securing profits but also for survival

[6]The term "responsible government" refers to that procedure by which the government is carried on by a chief executive or prime minister who must have the support of the majority of the elected house. If he is unable to secure a majority of the representatives, or if his party is defeated on a major issue, he resigns. This may result in a general election or in an attempt by someone to form a new cabinet which can secure the necessary support. The terms of office of the representatives are fixed as to maximum by statute, but not as to minimum. A general election may be called at any time.

of the enterprise once a business has been undertaken. The profit motive offers the incentive of profits for success and the penalty of losses for failure. It also implies that enterprise must rely on its own results for survival; and any business, either public or private, may be said to operate on the basis of the profit motive if its continued existence depends upon the sale of its own products.

Pure capitalism has never existed in any country. There has always been a mixture involving both public and private ownership of enterprises that are primarily economic in nature. A society may be said to be capitalistic, however, if the predominating form for directing production is that of private ownership. It is in the fields of public utilities and transportation that the most significant exceptions to private ownership and operation are found in the United States today. In these industries, some special political, organizational, and economic considerations place them in a unique category, which is explained later in this book. The conditions under which their activities are carried on, however, are primarily in the capitalistic setting and within capitalistic concepts.

Capitalism is not a static concept or condition. Today, it is something very different from what it was a hundred years ago. Technological developments have changed the conditions of control, and the rules under which capitalism operates have likewise been altered. The emergence of capitalism in its modern aspects was first associated with commercial activities; and as it took on its modern form, the outstanding characteristic of capitalism was the issuance of negotiable shares of stock which represented the ownership of capital in large enterprises. With the coming of what was known as the Industrial Revolution, capitalism became especially identified with industry. Thus, capitalistic organization has gone through many different stages in which its dominant activities have varied from the fields of commerce to banking and finance until, at the present time, the principal manifestation is in industry, with its archetype, the modern giant enterprise engaged in mass production.

Capitalism and Government

The evolution of capitalism has been accompanied by changing relationships between government and industry. Down to the beginning of the nineteenth century, trade, commerce, and industry were, to a very large extent, carried on under government sanction for nationalistic purposes; and the large trading companies were—in part, at least—agencies of government in overseas territories. With the rise of nineteenth-century liberalism and the doctrine of *laissez faire*, the direction of commercial industrial activity for state ends largely disappeared. The regulations and controls for private industry which had prevailed prior to that time were primarily those of a simple economic society in which the state exercised an important role for state purposes. The reaction against those policies was couched in terms of noninterference by the state. Most business was conducted on the basis of the sole proprietorship or partnership, where personal relations and responsibilities were emphasized. Interference by the state was therefore a very personal matter, closely associated with personal liberty. It was in these terms that the concepts of regulation were framed; and for that purpose, they were adequate. Adam Smith, however, clearly discerned the threats which were posed by the joint-stock companies and the emerging structure of modern business.

The development of industrialism in the nineteenth century led to new problems of organization and control. The means of implementation which had theretofore been adequate underwent rather rapid change, with the result that a large amount of legislation gradually emerged for the purpose of maintaining and developing a framework within which private enterprise could operate in an orderly fashion. Although this is continually referred to as an expansion of the functions of government, it would be more accurate to say that it was a change in the nature of the relations of government to business. The rise of industrial enterprises made it necessary to substitute new rules and regulations to guide industry in the altered and enlarged part it was to play. Thus, although there was an enormous growth of private economic activity, there was, at the same time, an increase in the scope and volume of functions performed by the government. Whether it is correct to say that the role of government in the economy has been expanding as a result of all this, with the implication that this has been done at the expense of private enterprise, is debatable; for at the very same time, the functions and scope of private enterprise have also been increasing.

The conditions which have prevailed throughout the world since 1914 have placed an exceedingly severe strain on the institution of capitalism, because private enterprise cannot fight a war; only the government can do that. For the same reason, reconstruction after a war places heavy responsibility on government, and so does the continued threat of war. To date, the expansion of economic activity has provided plenty of room for the growth of both private and government spheres of action, and the growth of one does not necessarily mean the contraction of the other. This point is particularly emphasized in the modern world by the tremendous increase in governmental activities in such things as highways, water supply, public education, etc., which involve not an encroachment upon the field of private enterprise but rather the entry of the government into activities which were heretofore largely nonexistent. The significant question, however, is whether those institutional arrangements which are considered fundamental to orderly society and which are cherished as a national heritage can be retained under the impact of worldwide upheaval. This is the challenge which the people of the United States must meet if the civilization which they prize is to survive.

Capitalism and Democracy

The recognition that capitalism is changing and therefore, in terms of an absolute definition, disappearing, has raised the question as to whether democracy can survive. It is agreed that capitalism and democracy have been closely associated with each other, and it may be questioned whether democracy could possibly have developed to its present stage without capitalism. This, however, must not be interpreted to mean that democracy originated in capitalism and that the disappearance of the latter, as we now know it, will result in the eclipse of the former.

The driving forces in the evolution of political institutions, first in England and then in the English-speaking countries to which her basic political institutions migrated, have been the constant emphasis on the rule of law and the popular origins of that rule. From the earliest known periods, the role of free men and assemblies in the development and administration of the law was a fundamental part of the government of the realm. William the Conqueror was chosen the king by the Witan; and even Henry VIII, the most absolute monarch in English history, constantly consulted Parliament on major problems. His controversy with the Church of Rome made it necessary for him to secure the support of his subjects through the use of age-old procedures. Regardless of the superficiality of his use of traditional arrangements—for his Parliaments were invariably "packed"—the concessions to tradition made to a people for whom the Magna Carta was such a landmark simply reaffirmed what were already regarded as ancient rights and rapidly led to an assertion of independence of action by Parliament. The challenging of this independence cost Charles I his life and James II his throne. These monarchs failed to recognize that the distinguishing characteristic of English political development was the persistence of common-law traditions, with their emphasis on the rights and dignity of the individual. Feudalism, the Reformation, and modern capitalism have all been conditioned by those factors. Hence, in England and the United States, at least, one must seek the democratic foundations of capitalism rather than the reverse. If primacy is to be accorded any single consideration, then it is to the democratic process that one must look for the molding of capitalism. Our form of economic life will undergo many modifications in the future, as it has in the past; but it is not likely to be superseded by economic statism, or what has been euphemistically called "state capitalism," so long as the historical continuity of our institutions persists.[7] Neither the logic nor the history of our basic political institutions warrants the conclusion

[7]Failure to understand the essence of Anglo-Saxon political and legal institutions seems to be the reason why the late Professor Schumpeter foresaw the inevitable disappearance of capitalism and, along with it, democracy. See J. A. Schumpeter, *Capitalism, Socialism and Democracy* (New York: Harper & Bros., 1942), Part IV; David McCord Wright, "Prospects for Capitalism," in Howard Ellis (ed.), *A Survey of Contemporary Economics* (Homewood, Ill.: Richard D. Irwin, Inc., 1952), Vol. I, chap. xiii.

that the economic primacy of the state is probable. Despite the stress of the times, it is difficult to believe that we shall embark upon a course that will destroy our political heritage for merely economic reasons. The belief that we shall have to do so to protect ourselves from the rest of the world is lacking in historical foundation—to date, at least.

Capitalism and Laissez Faire

Capitalism in the modern world has characteristically been associated with the doctrine of *laissez faire*. This formed the philosophic foundations of the relationship of government to economic life in much of the Western world, and especially in England and the United States, in the nineteenth century. Basically, *laissez faire* was a protest against the direction of economic activity by the state for nationalistic ends through the restrictive devices which characterized mercantilism. As a consequence, it came to be used as a bulwark against government interference in economic life, reliance being placed upon the forces of competition and the harmony of interests. The concept of harmony of interests assumed that if a man worked in his own best interests, he also worked for the best interests of society. It should be emphasized, however, that the doctrine also assumed a strong government which was able to maintain law, order, and justice and to protect its citizens in foreign affairs. *Laissez faire*, however, did not regard the state as an important factor in the direction of economic activity. Government intervention in economic life was largely confined to broad questions of the political implications of the operation of natural laws. This was reasonably adequate for the relatively simple economic structure at the time the philosophy was developed, since it required a much simpler approach to control than that which exists today. It should be emphasized that *laissez faire* was a philosophy which supported the idea of private enterprise controlled by competition and operating within the rules of the game.

It is now recognized that control of industry needs more rules established by government for the guidance of private and competitive enterprise than the *laissez-faire* philosophy called for.[8] Effective and adequate control today necessitates government in intervention as a matter of conscious social policy. That policy, however, must give full recognition to our institutional environment and social objectives if political freedom, with all that it implies, is to be retained. The abandonment of the doctrine of *laissez faire*, at least in its extreme nineteenth-century manifestation, does not warrant the conclusion that the end of capitalism and the substitution of government direction and management of industry in its place will result, unless one assumes that private enterprise is impossible except under conditions of extreme *laissez faire*. What the dis-

[8]One of the basic assumptions of *laissez faire* was that monopoly resulted only from deliberate attempts to eliminate competition or from special grants of privilege. Monopoly problems arising from technology were not understood.

carding of that doctrine entails is recognition of the inadequacy of theories of natural law and the harmony of interests, and the necessity of replacing them with the idea that control calls for positive social action and the establishment of rules of the game by conscious public policy.

MARKET ECONOMY

Requisites of a Market Economy

A "market economy" may be defined as one in which buyers and sellers compete with each other for the economic goods and services which are offered for sale. Producers compete with each other for the resources which they need and with the commodities which they sell, and buyers compete with each other to secure the products which are offered for sale. The market economy therefore assumes numerous buyers and sellers, with different wants and different products, expressing their desires and offering their wares through the medium of buying and selling. It requires both numerous producers and numerous purchasers of products; and an effective market economy refers to markets for producers' goods and services, as well as to those for consumers' goods.

The essence of a free market is the absence of power by individuals, groups of individuals, or a government to exercise control so as to influence the market appreciably. Thus, the term "market economy" applies really only to a competitive system. Production is guided by the desires of purchasers, as expressed through their willingness to buy and by the opportunity afforded producers to make profits. In the final analysis, this means that the consumers' demands are the decisive forces. The expression of these demands through the medium of price leads to the allocation of the resources of production to the various activities as indicated by the prospective price for the product. It is essential to the market economy that the pricing process operates so as to give effect to the demands of the various consumers and so as to eliminate—or, at least, thoroughly curb—the exercise of arbitrary power by any person or group of persons.

Free competition presupposes that no one person is able to exercise any decisive influence on the operation of the market, either as a buyer or as a seller. It is thus the economic counterpart of political democracy which has, as its basic assumption, the idea that one person is no more important than another. In political democracy, it is aggregate action that counts; and in a market economy, the same principle applies. The aggregate, however, is the result of diverse activities, not of uniformity. Under the market economy, resources are allocated in accordance with the demands as indicated by the offers of various buyers, and whether resources will be used to produce one thing or another will depend upon the price inducements for the products. This does not provide any moral justification for what is produced, because the market is impartial in that respect.

Need for Regulation

What may be produced or sold will be dependent—in part, at least—upon the rules which are in operation. If the general sale of narcotic drugs is forbidden, then the question of the morality or undesirability of that trade is decided by law, not by the market. In a similar way, the conditions of production may be limited in other respects. Within the general rules laid down by government or by customary standards, the allocation of resources in a market economy will follow price inducements. This is not an entirely mechanistic process, for the utilization of resources for various types of production will depend upon the judgment of those who embark upon that production. Whether operations will prove to be profitable or not will depend upon the soundness of the judgment upon which they are undertaken. Under an effective market economy, an individual decision is insignificant in the direction of economic activity. Hence, the effect of individual misjudgment and arbitrary decisions is minimized.

Because the essence of the market economy is the absence of a dominating position by any individual or group, the problems of monopoly are of especial concern. Historically, the laws of England and this country have paid more attention to the curbing of monopoly than to any other one phase of control. The reasons for this are the effect of monopoly on public welfare and its threat to the institution of the market economy. Monopoly, however, is inherent to some degree in many parts of our current economic structure. The objective of public policy as it relates to monopoly is to reduce the influence of the monopolist to a minimum, so that the forces of competition may operate in such a way as to make the power and discretion of a single producer as insignificant as possible.

Consumers' Freedom of Choice

Closely linked to, and really part of the idea of, a market economy is consumers' freedom of choice. This means that the consumer is free to allocate his purchasing power to any of the various commodities or services offered for sale and to buy any amount he wishes. He is not compelled to purchase certain things, nor is he restricted from buying them by some arbitrary device.

Freedom to allot purchasing power among the commodities offered for sale is only one side of consumers' freedom of choice. It does not indicate the institutional conditions of production essential to its full implementation. To have any real meaning, this freedom of choice must be accompanied by competition in production. In short, it involves not merely the privilege to apportion one's purchasing power to the goods and services which may be bought but also the unrestricted opportunity to choose among various producers of similar or nearly similar goods. If production is monopolized, the consumer is limited in his decision to the goods produced by the monopolist, who may exercise his discretionary powers as he sees fit. Under such circumstances, product differentiation, differences in styles, etc., are less likely to appear. Consumers will have little, if any, opportunity to indicate the variations that they may wish in different products and will be unable to apply pressure on the producer by buying from others who are willing to cater to their wishes. Thus, the full exercise of consumers' freedom of choice depends upon limiting the discretionary power of the producer. Freedom of choice in the market and freedom of the producers to compete to satisfy the choices are really the opposite sides of the same thing. They enhance the freedom of the individual and reduce the possibilities of exercising arbitrary controls over him.

DEMOCRACY

The Democratic Process

"Democracy" means government in accordance with the will of the people, expressed through the selection of those who are to govern by exercise of the free and unhampered choice of the electorate. Although theoretically, at least, democracy depends upon the rule of the majority, it does not mean that minority interests are without rights or privileges in the government. As a matter of fact, the more effective the democracy, the more will steps be taken to safeguard the position of the minorities, so that, while they may lack voting control, they are nevertheless influential in the government of the country and can find ample means for expressing their points of view. It is the essence of democracy that those who govern are held responsible to the laws of the land, can be called upon to answer in the courts for the discharge of their duties under the laws, and are responsive to public opinion.

It is frequently argued that government as developed in the United States, Great Britain, and other capitalistic countries is not qualified to serve as a model for political democracy. The implication is, of course, that pure democracy has not been achieved in any of these countries and that the governmental processes as they now stand are subject to severe limitations. There is some truth in this contention, but it must also be recognized that democracy is a relative term and that it is in a constant process of change. Whatever the shortcomings, the institutional foundations that have been established in the United States and Great Britain offer the best basis so far developed for the continuance of the growth of democracy. At least, it can be said that the evolution of democracy in these two countries has reached the highest and most permanent stage yet achieved.

Democracy and Regulation

A workable program for the control of industry must be related to the structure of government of a country. If the structure is democratic and is to remain such, then the program of control must be based upon that assumption. It is possible, of course, that other objectives may dominate, such as enhancing the power of the state—in which case, the means for exercising control will be quite different. It would seem to be reasonable to assume, however, that in the United States, democracy and freedom are primary goals. This conditions the economic policies which we must follow. If these policies conflict with democratic procedures, they must be modified so as to harmonize with those procedures if the basic assumptions are to be fulfilled. In other words, controls must be envisaged within our basic institutional arrangements; and unless these arrangements are to be changed, the policies of government as they relate to economic life must be directed toward the end of preserving the fundamental ideas and must be in accord with the institutional patterns.

To date, the growth of modern democracy and the development of private enterprise have gone hand in hand. Whereas it may be possible to argue, in the abstract, that democracy is compatible with other forms of organization of economic life, or vice versa, both the historical background and the institutional foundations for any other arrangement are at present lacking; nor is there an absence of logical foundations of the connection between private enterprise and democracy.

Democracy and Economics

The history of political democracy has been the story of the lessening of state control over important aspects of social life, although this has followed anything but an even course. It is difficult to conceive of a democratic state without freedom of religion; and the separation of state and church was a major step in the development of political freedom, for the reason that the exercise of state control over a phase of human activity as vital as religion made it necessary to maintain control over other phases of social life, such as freedom of thought and freedom of speech. The same remarks may be applied to the relationship of the state to economic activity. Comprehensive control and direction, such as envisaged by socialism, for example, may well carry the extension of controls into other aspects of life to an extent that is incompatible with a democracy. This is because of the interrelationship of all phases of social activity. The economic man may be a convenient analytic device, but he is an illusory administrative tool.

Democracy, in the final analysis, is a political concept; but it has its economic implications and social connotations. The implementations of the control of economic life and the significance of the relationship of private property to the development of political liberty were fully grasped by John Locke in England and by the founders of the United States in America. They recognized what has become all too apparent on the continent of Europe—that ownership and management of the means of production, carried to their logical conclusion, give such a powerful weapon to the government that freedom for opposition rests on very tenuous grounds. The idea that such control may be democratic is predicated on an assumption of uniformity of behavior that is markedly at variance with the diversity that emanates from individual freedom. One might as well assert that religious freedom is possible in a state where all churches are state churches and no nonstate places or forms of worship are allowed.

The essence of democracy lies in the diversity of ideas and procedures. This applies to all phases of social life. Furthermore, complexity in all aspects is characteristic and appears to be inevitable. Hence, a multiplicity and diversity of arrangements for control is inescapable if democracy is to be maintained or achieved. Simplification that is obtained by required conformity to preconceived patterns which are developed by centralized control is not conducive to the preservation or development of political freedom. The fact that this control, theoretically, is to be applied to only one phase of social life does not lessen the danger; rather, the reverse is likely to be the case. It is too easy to assume that other phases can remain free. To say the least, historical evidence for this assumption is lacking. The democratic process does not, however, imply the absence of group action. On the contrary, it recognizes the right of groups to organize for various purposes, but with the assurance of freedom for the individual to choose membership in any or no group, as he desires.

Chapter 4 BUSINESS OWNERSHIP ORGANIZATION

INTRODUCTION

The utilization of resources for the purpose of production requires organization in any type of economy. It is the function of management to co-ordinate productive resources and apply them to the creation of goods and services. In a private enterprise economy, this process has two aspects—one relating to the form of ownership of the enterprises, the other to the internal management of those enterprises. The type of ownership organization which is selected will depend upon a number of different conditions. The particular arrangement which is used, however, bears directly on procedures and problems of regulation because of the different privileges and responsibilities which each form of ownership entails. The regulation of industry involves, among other things, control of the various types of ownership organization. This is especially true of the corporation, whose present status and scope of activity have created some of the most important and difficult problems in regulation.

THE OWNERSHIP ORGANIZATION OF BUSINESS

The Legal Form

Business organization is the legal form under which resources are combined for the purpose of producing goods and services for sale. The different types of organization which are in existence in any country will depend upon the legal system which prevails, the historical background, and legislative enactments. In a country where private enterprise predominates, many different types exist side by side. These reflect all the varying conditions—technical, financial, legal, and personal—to which the organizers must give consideration when they embark on a business undertaking. Frequently, enterprises develop through the various kinds of organization in their growth. Thus, many present-day firms started as sole proprietorships and ended up as corporations.

Major Types of Ownership Organization

In the United States, business organizations fall into two broad categories—the common-law type and the statutory type. For some purposes, they may be classified as unincorporated and incorporated. The common-law forms of business organizations are those which may be created as a matter of personal right, no action on the part of the state being necessary for their formation. This is simply one aspect of the general principle of freedom to choose one's occupation, and these types apparently existed before there was any law applicable to them. In other words, the law grew up to deal with the legal problems to which they gave rise—after they had come into operation. As controversy arose, recourse was had to the courts; and the result was the development, out of precedent, of a body of law relating to the types of business organization which grew up without benefit of statute.

In contrast to these are the statutory kinds of organization. They acquire their privileges and are assessed their responsibilities through statutory enactments. The business corporation is the leading illustration of the statutory type; but common-law forms involving more than one person may become statutory forms of conforming to legislative requirements which, in turn, accord them special privileges. There may be, for example, statutory partnerships. In some states, legislation has grown up that has modified the common-law status so as to make it statutory. This is practically the situation with regard to the joint-stock association in New York.

All common-law forms are unincorporated; that is, they are not treated as legal entities. Except where statutes specifically provide to the contrary, they cannot sue or be sued in their own name, or own property. Even though the unincorporated forms do rest in part upon statute, they revert to the common-law type in the event of dispute, if they have failed to conform strictly with the statutes.

The incorporated type of ownership organization, which is exemplified by the business corporation, is a legal entity and is a person in the eyes of the law. It enjoys legal existence only through legislative action and has no status apart from that action.

Modern forms of business organization in this country have their primary origin in the common law. Although other elements, such as concepts of Roman law, have entered into the picture, the chief characteristic of the development of business organizations at common law has been the emergence of various kinds and their subsequent recognition by the law. In the course of time, this procedure has been supplemented, in many instances, by positive action by the legislature. Thus, there has been an evolution from common-law types into statutory types, with the corporation, which is a primary statutory type, marking the major step in the transition.

COMMON-LAW FORMS OF BUSINESS ORGANIZATION

There are four basic common-law types of business organizations. These are the sole proprietorship, the partnership, the joint-stock association, and the Massachusetts or business trust.

The Sole Proprietorship

The sole proprietorship is a form of business organization which is owned and controlled by a single individual, who risks all of his property in the enterprise and receives all of the profits therefrom. This form of organization comes into existence by the simple process of an individual deciding to go into business for himself and devoting his capital thereto. The proprietor is subject to unlimited liability. Not only are the assets which he devotes to the business available to satisfy the claims of creditors, but so is all of the other property which he owns. Furthermore, a sole proprietorship is limited in duration to the life of the owner and, therefore, disappears upon his death or withdrawal from business. It is for this reason that this type of organization cannot engage in certain types of business where continuity of existence is necessary for the protection of others. Life insurance and commercial banking are illustrations of this type of limitation.

The Partnership

The partnership is the most elementary type of business organization in which the idea of association is introduced. Fundamentally, it is an extension of the sole proprietorship resulting from the pooling of resources and abilities by two or more people. It is a form in which two or more individuals associate themselves by means of a contract in the common ownership, management, and control of a business enterprise. At common law, every partner has equal power and responsibility. Each is entitled to an equal share in the profits or losses, regardless of the amount of capital he may have invested. The common-law partnership is not regarded by the law as a legal entity, and all partners are subject to unlimited liability to creditors. The partnership cannot sue or be sued in its own name, nor can it own property.[1]

In general, any person who is competent to make a contract may become a partner, and partnerships may engage in any type of business not specifically prohibited to them by statute. Any partner may act on behalf of the partnership and as the agent of the other members, unless notice is given to outsiders to the contrary. Decisions on management policies may be made by majority vote; but on many important items, unanimous consent is necessary, unless the articles of formation specify otherwise. The withdrawal of any partner from the enterprise terminates its existence. Whenever dissolution takes place, creditors must be fully satisfied, even though the business activity of the previous organization is being continued. This is because a new partnership has emerged.

The common law regards the partnership as being based upon a contract, which may be written or inferred. In the absence of a written

[1]For a more detailed discussion of the partnership as a form of business organization, see C. S. Tippetts and S. Livermore, *Business Organization and Control* (2d ed.; New York: D. Van Nostrand Co. Inc., 1941), chap. iii.

contract or oral agreement concerning the relations of the partners with each other, common-law rules regard their position as equal, except that the amount of capital contributed by a member belongs to him. If it is desired that the common-law rules should be modified—as, for example, in the division of profits or the powers of control of the respective partners—this may be done by contract. By the same means, profits and losses may be apportioned as the partners see fit. However, whenever issues arise on which the contract is silent, the courts will apply the common-law principles governing general partnerships.

The general or common-law partnership is the basic type. There are, however, many modifications. Some of these arise from statutory conditions, and others emerge from special developments to suit certain unique situations. The joint adventure is a form of partnership organized for a single undertaking. It is usually managed by one of the participants. Dissolution does not take place until the adventure is completed. The mining partnership is also a special type of arrangement which has grown up because of the necessity of continuity of life in connection with the exploitation of mining properties. It is not dissolved by the death of a partner. If there are more than two participants, there is free substitution of membership without changing the continuity of the partnership; and no partner is able to act as general agent for the others. Another type that has special characteristics is the underwriting syndicate, which developed for the purpose of distributing securities. This is based upon agreement or contract and has a syndicate manager; also, the liabilities among the members are usually limited by agreement. As in the case of the joint adventure, the underwriting syndicate is established for a single purpose.

The Joint-Stock Association

The joint-stock association is a form of business organization in which a number of individuals associate together on the basis of articles of association, membership being evidenced by transferable shares of stock. The association enjoys a continuity of life apart from any particular member and is managed by a board of directors elected by the shareholders. Thus, the joint-stock association introduces three important modifications of the common-law partnership, in that it has freely transferable proprietary interests, a continuity of existence apart from its membership, and management distinct from ownership.

The joint-stock association has frequently been called a securities-issuing partnership. This description emphasizes the method of formation by articles of association, that is, by contract; the unlimited liability of the owners of shares; and the absence of a legal entity. It cannot sue or be sued in its own name, nor can it own property. The latter is effected by using trustees or some other similar arrangement. The designation of the joint-stock association as a securities-issuing partnership is somewhat misleading, however, because members of a joint-stock association can act only by vote and through the board of directors. Moreover, there is a continuity of life which may extend for an indefinite period; and the free transference of shares makes membership independent of the wishes or control of any other member.

The terms "joint-stock association" and "joint-stock company" are frequently used interchangeably. This has led to confusion regarding two essentially different things. The joint-stock company quite possibly had an earlier origin than the joint-stock association and, in the beginning, was definitely associated with organizations established by special grant from the government for the purpose of carrying out governmental functions in return for trading privileges. The actual transition to the joint-stock company seems to have taken place in Genoa in the fourteenth century,[2] and it is from this origin that the idea of division of stock and transferability of shares has developed. It should be noted, however, that the joint-stock company remained an organization dependent upon a charter and, as such, was not a common-law type but a special creation of the government. The joint-stock association, on the other hand, seems to have developed as a common-law organization in England at quite an early date from an extension of the partnership device.[3]

The Massachusetts Trust

The "Massachusetts trust" is a form of business organization created by contractual arrangement in which the legal ownership and management of the business are vested in one or more individuals who hold and operate the property in trust for the benefit of others. The contract, known as a "trust agreement" or "deed of trust," is drawn up by the creators or settlors, who designate, in the deed of trust, individuals known as "trustees" to manage the business for the benefit of others, known as "beneficiaries." As a result of historical development, courts of equity supervise the execution of all trust agreements.[4]

The trust device, which developed largely as a device for maintaining control over property and bequeathing it, has provided a means for organizing business when the corporation is unusable or unacceptable, but when some method of limiting liability is desirable. The Massachusetts or business trust has fulfilled this function. It is known as an active trust, in which the conditions under which the business is to be conducted are stated in the deed of trust, leaving to the court of equity only the duty of seeing that the terms of the agreement are carried out. Management is strictly divorced from ownership. The trustees are responsible for directing the enterprise in accordance with the trust agreement, and

[2]M. M. Knight, H. E. Barnes, and F. Flügel, *Economic History of Europe* (Boston: Houghton Mifflin Co., 1928), p. 123.

[3]E. Jenks, *A Short History of English Law* (Boston: Little, Brown & Co., 1913), pp. 277–78.

[4]F. W. Maitland, *The Constitutional History of England* (Cambridge, Eng.: Cambridge University Press, 1919), pp. 222–25.

they must adhere rigidly to it. Furthermore, in order to avoid the common-law responsibility of unlimited liability, they must see that the limitation of their liability is stipulated in all contracts. The beneficiaries are the passive recipients of the benefits received and, as such, have only limited liability. In order to retain this privilege, however, they must in no way participate in the management of the enterprise. If the conditions which govern the formation and operation of the trust are not strictly adhered to, it will be adjudged a general partnership by the courts in the event of litigation.

The Massachusetts trust derives its name from the state of Massachusetts, where it came to be used because of the inability of the corporation to own real estate. It was simply an adaptation of a very old procedure to business purposes in order to obtain some of the advantages possessed by the corporation without the onerous burdens imposed by some jurisdictions upon it. Transferable and divided ownership is obtained by issuing certificates of beneficial interest, which give the owner title to the benefits from the enterprise but no say in the management. Although the use of the trust device for many purposes is well established at law, the application of it to the organization of business has raised many legal questions which have not been resolved. The courts seem to have been unwilling or unable to reconcile the duties and responsibilities of trusteeship with the active direction of business enterprise. An appreciable increase in the number of businesses organized along trust lines is unlikely so long as present legal uncertainties remain.

Statutory Modifications

The common-law rules applicable to the various forms of business organization may be modified by statute. As a consequence, the legal status of some forms of organization may be changed considerably. Thus, a number of states have legislation which permits the formation of limited partnerships, in which some of the partners enjoy limited liability. In some states, joint-stock association are subject to statutory enactments which place them virtually in the category of corporations. The Massachusetts trust has been subjected to more legislation governing its operations than the other common-law forms. Whatever the statutory enactments may be, however, the privileges that are granted are available only in the state which enacts the legislation. Furthermore, the privileges obtainable under the statutes are available only by strict adherence to the conditions laid down in the laws. Failure to comply may turn even a Massachusetts trust into a common-law partnership.

Significance of Common-Law Forms

Historically, the sole proprietorship and the partnership are the oldest forms of business organization. In England and in this country, at least, they clearly reflect their common-law foundations in that they are a recognition of the basic right of an individual to use his private property as he sees fit. The highly personalized nature of early business ventures and the force of circumstances which limited them to individuals and families not only obviated the need for more complex types but also had the effect of keeping business activity in the hands of powerful families. The predominance of trade and commerce, at least down to the seventeenth century, made the personal element of paramount significance; and the production of most of the goods which entered into the market by skilled tradesmen, and later by domestic handicraft, kept these activities on a personal basis also. Thus, apart from corporate bodies formed principally for purposes of regulation—that is, for the performance of governmental functions—the common-law types of business organization held complete sway down to the middle of the seventeenth century.

Some encroachment upon this pre-eminence came with the development of trading companies for purely private purposes, during the period of expansion from the middle of the seventeenth century down to the middle of the eighteenth. These, however, were exceptions which were severely curbed in England by the Bubble Act of 1719. The growth of finance and of trading activities and the widening of their geographical scope led to a development of the association idea which had been manifest in the partnership. The joint-stock association appears to have emerged from this under the necessity of providing for continuity of existence and a transfer of proprietary interest which did not impair that existence. Similarly, numerous variations of the general or common-law partnerships, such as the joint venture, grew up to meet the demands of the changing economic structure. As the need arose for larger amounts of capital—and therefore, for participation of more investors in supplying it—the joint-stock principle came into wider use, and the characteristics of the modern corporation began to manifest themselves.

The mutations which took place in the various forms of business organization were the result of the changing conditions which these developments were designed to meet. It was not a case of foresight but rather one of a continuance of old devices, with the new ones gradually emerging to meet situations which the previous types were incapable of filling. Thus, the historical aspect of business organization emphasizes three things: (1) the evolution of more complex arrangements from simpler types as conditions rendered the more elementary forms inadequate for many purposes; (2) the development of these various types as adaptations to meet changing situations, without benefit of legal recognition until some time after they had become thoroughly established; (3) the evolution of business organization under the common law from personal foundations in England and the United States.

Although, historically, growth of the various forms of business organizations progressed from the simple to the more complex, all forms exist side by side at the present time. The common-law types, especially the sole proprietorship and partnership, predominate in agriculture and where personal services are rendered. They are the only ones used in professions such as law, medicine, and accounting and in private banking, where the element of personal responsibility is considered of prime importance. In fact, corporations are forbidden by legislation from engaging in the professions just mentioned.[5] Even at the present time, it is estimated that there are over 4 million business units in the United States, of which approximately 84 per cent are unincorporated.[6] During the depression of the thirties, a substantial number of smaller corporations became partnerships or proprietorships in order to avoid the excess profits tax.[7]

THE BUSINESS CORPORATION

The development of modern industry, after the middle of the eighteenth century, created the definite need for a form of business organization which would make it possible to secure the large amount of investment that was required without imposing upon the suppliers of the funds the unlimited liability characteristic of the common-law forms. The means for meeting this new situation developed slowly, however; and until about 1850, most of the burden of financial and industrial expansion was borne by the common-law types. A rather basic change took place about that date with the widespread adoption of the corporate concept to the purpose of private business. This was an expansion of the idea of association into a more formal arrangement operating under a statutory grant of privilege

Nature of the Corporation

Many attempts have been made to define the corporation, but all encounter difficulties and limitations because of the fact that the nature of the corporation differs somewhat with the purpose for which it is formed. One of the most famous definitions was that given by Chief Justice Marshall: "A corporation is an artificial being, invisible, intangible, and existing only in contemplation of law. Being a mere creature of the law it possesses only those properties which the charter of its creation confers upon it, either expressly or as incidental to its very existence."[8]

[5]In 1953 the New York Stock Exchange changed its rules to allow member organizations to become corporations. Previously, this had been limited to partnerships. Under the 1953 rule the corporations were tightly controlled. The Exchange is now (1964) studying the key question of whether these corporations should be permitted to offer stock and debt securities to the public who are not subject to the Exchange jurisdiction. At present there are 127 member corporations of the NYSE and 534 member partnerships.

[6]National City Bank (New York), *Monthly Letter* (November, 1957), p. 130

[7]M. A. Adelman, "The Measurement of Industrial Concentration," *Review of Economics and Statistics*, Vol. XXXIII, No. 4 (November, 1951), p. 290.

[8]*Dartmouth College* v. *Woodward*, 4 Wheat (U.S.) 518, 636 (1819).

This definition emphasizes the strictly legal aspects and seems to be satisfactory for corporations set up by the government for accomplishing some specific public purpose. It would probably be adequate for a state university created *ab initio* by the legislature.

This concept is not satisfactory when applied to the business corporation, which comes into existence by quite a different process. The business corporation is the result of the association of a group of individuals for a common business purpose. They seek a grant of privilege from the state whereby they can act as a unit through a legal entity which —legally, at least—is distinct from them. A "business corporation" may be defined, therefore, as a voluntary association possessing autonomy and continuity of existence with compulsory unity of action, through a governmental grant of privilege known as a charter.

The corporation, then, is a legal entity and is the only type of business organization that is so recognized universally.[9] It has continuity of existence apart from the life or participation of its individual members, but its length of life depends upon the period of time specified in the charter. Within the limits of the powers granted by the charter, the corporation is an autonomous enterprise; that is, it possesses an independence of action established by the privileges which the charter contains. For the most part, it is regarded as a person at law but not as a citizen. As a person, it receives all of the privileges which the Constitution of the United States affords to those so designated. This means, for example, that the due process clauses of the Constitution are applicable equally to corporations and to natural persons. Because the corporation is not recognized as a citizen, it cannot take advantage of the privileges of its charter and the laws under which it is incorporated when it does business in another state, unless the other state consents. It thus becomes a foreign corporation in any jurisdiction other than that in which it is incorporated. However, the courts have treated it as a citizen in one respect, and that is when provisions of the Constitution of the United States relating to diversity of citizenship are involved.

The Corporate Charter

In order that an organization may be recognized at law as a corporation, it normally must receive a charter, which is a license to carry on stipulated activities granted by a legislative agency. The charter contains a statement of the nature of the business to be conducted; the name of the enterprise; the place and date of incorporation; length of time for which the charter is granted; place of the home office; and the amount,

[9]For discussions of the origin of the business corporation in England, which is the basis of the business corporation in the United States, see W. S. Holdsworth, *A History of English Law* (Boston: Little, Brown & Co., 1926), Vol. III, chap. iv, pp. 469–90; Vol. IX, Part II, chap. vi, pp. 45–71; Jenks, *op. cit.*, p. 289; A. B. DuBois, *The English Business Company after the Bubble Act, 1720–1800* (New York: Commonwealth Fund, 1938), chap. iii.

type, and number of shares of capital stock which may be issued. It also contains the names of the original directors and incorporators, and the number of shares owned by the latter. The corporate charter is the framework of government of the corporation and is really the constitution of the corporation. The details of the governing procedure are set forth in bylaws which are adopted by the stockholders and which can be changed by whatever methods the latter wish to prescribe. The charter of the corporation, on the other hand, can be altered only by permission of the authority which granted it and in accordance with the legal procedure required for the amendment of it.

A corporation can engage only in those activities and legally do only those things which its charter, by stipulation or reasonable implication, allows it to do. If it exceeds these powers, it is guilty of *ultra vires* acts and is subject to the loss of its charter. In effect, what this amounts to is that the association, as a corporation, is entitled to privileges in return for the agreement to adhere to certain conditions. If it fails to abide by them, it loses its corporate rights. The logic for this would seem to call for the treatment of the corporation as a joint-stock association if *ultra vires* acts are committed or if the charter is revoked. To date, the courts, have not seen fit to do this, perhaps because of the persistence—to a certain extent, at least—of the idea that the corporation is a creation of the state.

Normally, all corporations enjoy some kind of limited liability. The nature of this has varied somewhat from time to time in various jurisdictions; but today, the liability of the stockholder is generally limited to his interest in the enterprise. This means that in the event of insolvency, the stockholder stands to lose his equity, but no more.

The rights which stockholders enjoy vary with legislation in different jurisdictions and with the conditions of particular charters. In general, however, stockholders have the right to vote at annual meetings, either in person or by proxy; the right to share in dividends when they are declared by the directors; the right to subscribe to new stock in proportion to holdings; and the right to share in the assets available to stockholders at time of dissolution. The stockholder is also supposed to have the right to inspect the books of the corporation; but in practice, this has virtually disappeared. The right may be exercised, however, if sufficient pressure for it can be brought to bear upon the management or if a court order can be obtained to compel it. The growth of the modern large corporation obviously makes it impracticable to allow stockholders to inspect books at any time they see fit.

Incorporation Laws

Practically all private business corporations come into existence today through the receipt of a charter which is issued under a general incorporation law rather than by a special act of the legislature. General acts of incorporation, by which corporations may be formed as a matter of right by complying with the conditions laid down in the legislation, are of relatively recent origin. The earliest form of corporate enterprise was the result of a special grant of privilege by the sovereign authority. These early organizations, which appear to have had their origins on the continent of Europe and under Roman law, were established principally for the purpose of carrying on functions of government. Certain types of business activities which were associated with these responsibilities also grew up at a very early date. For example, the corporate device was used for collecting taxes or handling public debt through the creation of concerns that were paid for their services by the profits they made on the transactions.

In England, the corporate idea emerged very early in the form of boroughs and trading associations. As such, corporations had definite governmental functions; but in accordance with prevailing governmental practices, they derived their revenues from special privileges, such as the monopoly of some branch of trade. After the middle of the sixteenth century, the use of the corporate device as a means of promoting overseas expansion grew rapidly. The great trading companies of this period were designed for that purpose.

Accompanying the development of the private enterprise aspect of the trading companies was the expansion of the joint-stock idea. Just which corporation was the first one to initiate it seems to be a matter of some doubt; but the real turn came with the decision in 1612 of the East India Company, which had been chartered in 1600, to have one kind of joint stock for the whole of its affairs.[10] The use of the corporate device for trading purposes expanded considerably during the next hundred years, and charters granted by special acts of incorporation multiplied rather rapidly in England. The speculation in stock resulting from overseas expansion culminated in the fiasco of the South Sea Company and led to the Bubble Act of 1719. This legislation, aimed apparently at all enterprises using joint stock, whether incorporated or unincorporated, was designed to curb severely incorporation for business purposes and the use of transferable stock. For the next hundred years, the use of the legally recognized corporate device as a means of conducting business developed very slowly, while its employment as an agency of government was gradually disappearing.

The rapid growth in manufacturing and the increased size of manufacturing enterprises that took place after 1750, and especially in the early part of the nineteenth century, soon led to a recognition of the necessity of adjusting the law to the new situation that had arisen. As a consequence, legislation appeared which laid the foundation for present-day laws on business corporations. In 1825, a statute which was passed in

[10]Jenks, *op. cit.*, p. 287.

England virtually gave the Crown power to establish limited liability in granting charters thereafter. Legislation enacted in 1844–45 definitely distinguished the business corporation from unincorporated enterprises; and ten years later, the principle of limited liability was made a matter of general right.[11]

The developments in the United States paralleled those in England, although the adoption of general acts of incorporation came first in this country, New York State passing its law in 1811. Other states followed in the course of the first half of the century; and by the end of the Civil War, the corporation with limitations on liability[12] had firmly established itself as the prime vehicle of modern large-scale business enterprise.

Along with this, there developed the right of one corporation to own the stock of another. The state of New Jersey, in 1893, passed the first general incorporation law, which allowed corporations to be formed for the sole purpose of owning the stocks of other companies. This laid the legal foundations of the corporations as a holding company. However, it should be noted that there were many prior illustrations of charters which permitted the ownership of the stocks of other companies, and such ownership may always have been possible at common law. The right of a corporation to own property quite possibly carried with it the right to own stock, since free persons have always been able to do that; and the corporation has been recognized as a person at law from the beginning.[13] Nevertheless, the general statutory sanctioning of such ownership removed whatever barriers to intercorporate control through stock ownership may have existed theretofore. The effects of this on the combination movement and the formation of combinations is discussed in the next two chapters.

There are 54 charter-granting bodies in the United States. They are the 50 states, the territories, the insular possessions, and Congress, acting in the dual capacity of the federal government and the government of the District of Columbia. Because of the almost total lack of uniformity of laws, it is well-nigh impossible to make any general statements of the requirements of incorporation imposed by the various legislatures. The general relaxation of requirements for incorporation and the competition among states for the business of granting charters have resulted in the almost total abolition of minimum standards. This has progressed so far in some states, such as Nevada and Delaware, as to make incorporation largely a matter of paying the fee which the state

[11]*Ibid.*, pp. 287–90.

[12]Bank stockholders were usually subject to double liability; and some states, such as California, subjected stockholders to proportional liability. After 1933, the corporate laws of practically all jurisdictions extended limited liability to stockholders of all corporations.

[13]But see L. S. Lyon, M. W. Watkins, and Victor Abramson, *Government and Economic Life* (Washington, D.C.: Brookings Institution, 1939), Vol. I, p. 63.

imposes. The minimum conditions that have to be met vary from one state to another. In some, it is possible to incorporate with only one incorporator; no residence is required of incorporations in others; and in still other states, a corporation may be formed for any lawful business, with no further specification. The minimum amount of capital necessary in some cases is only $500. Stock may have par value or no-par value; and annual reports are not required in many instances, whereas in some other cases, they are so perfunctory as to be meaningless. As a consequence, the choice of a state in which to incorporate will depend upon the particular advantages which that state happens to offer. This does not always mean that the jurisdiction with the most lax laws is the one selected. As a matter of fact, life insurance companies are typically incorporated in the states establishing the severest conditions, because they can then secure entry to do business elsewhere without any restrictions or difficulty. For most lines of business, however, it is the minimum of limiting conditions that is the controlling factor in the selection of a state for incorporation.

The Growth and Importance of the Corporation

Although the corporate device has been used for organization of business activities for many centuries, it was, until the beginning of the nineteenth century, connected primarily with business enterprise which performed some public function. Up to 1800, 335 corporate charters had been issued in the United States, of which 295 were obtained in the last 10 years of the eighteenth century. Of the total, 219 were for highway companies, 36 for local public service, 67 for banking and insurance, and only 13 under the head of strictly private activities.[14]

Corporations prior to the nineteenth century were relatively large in size. The South Sea Company, which was created in 1711, had a nominal capital of £9,000,000. The capital of the Bank of England was originally fixed at £1,200,000 in 1694, and this was raised to £2,000,000 in 1697 and to £5,559,000 in 1710.[15] The Bank of North America, chartered in 1781 and the first modern bank in the United States, had a capital stock fixed at $160,000 in May, 1781, and this was increased to $400,000 in September of the same year.[16] It was not, however, until after the Civil War that the private business corporation became the most important organizational device for manufacturing industries in England or in the United States. In the last half of the nineteenth century, it grew rapidly in terms of the number of enterprises incorporated, the proportion of corporate to noncorporate entities, and the total volume of assets owned by corporations.

[14]Twentieth Century Fund, Inc., *Big Business: Its Growth and Its Place* (New York, 1937), p. 11.

[15]Knight, Barnes, and Flügel, *op. cit.*, p. 326.

[16]W. W. Jennings, *A History of Economic Progress in the United States* (New York: Thomas Y. Crowell Co., 1926), pp. 208–9.

The most spectacular aspect of the growth of corporations in modern business has been in the emergence of a number of gigantic enterprises which are known all over the country—in many cases, over a large part of the world—and which seem to overshadow completely other businesses in the country. In 1901, the United States Steel Corporation was formed as the first billion-dollar concern in the United States. Since that time, many more such firms have risen in other branches of industry. One compilation lists 30 corporations possessing assets of over $1 billion each in 1935.[17] Of these enterprises, 3 were industrials, 6 were public utilities, 9 were railroads, 6 were banks, and 6 were insurance companies—that is, 18 of the 30 corporations were nonfinancial enterprises. *Fortune* magazine lists 40 industrial enterprises with assets of over $1 billion in 1963, one merchandising firm (Sears, Roebuck), 10 railroads, and 17 utilities, for a total of 68 firms.[18] The 5 largest nonfinancial corporate enterprises in the United States in 1935 were the American Telephone and Telegraph Company, with total assets of $3,998,300,000;[19] the Pennsylvania Railroad Company, $2,863,000,000; the New York Central Railroad Company, $2,356,000,000; the Standard Oil Company (New Jersey), $1,894,900,000; and the United States Steel Corporation, $1,822,400,000.[20] In 1963, they were, in order of size, the American Telephone and Telegraph Company, Standard Oil Company (New Jersey). General Motors, Ford Motor Co., and United States Steel.[21]

Size measured in terms of sales is even more impressive than when measured by assets owned. In 1963, 60 nonfinancial corporations had sales of over $1 billion. Forty-nine of these were industrial corporations, 10 were merchandising firms, and one, the American Telephone and Telegraph Company, was a public utility. General Motors headed the list with total sales of $16,494,818,000 followed by Standard Oil of New Jersey, American Telephone and Telegraph Co., Ford Motor Co., and Great Atlantic and Pacific Tea Co.[22]

Although there has been an enormous growth in size of a few corporations, a great increase in the number of corporations in existence in this country has taken place at the same time. As has already been pointed out, only 335 corporate charters were issued in the United States up to the year 1800; and down to the Civil War, the corporation was a relatively unimportant form of business organization. Yet, by the year 1909,

[17]Temporary National Economic Committee, *Final Report and Recommendations* (Washington, D.C.: U.S. Government Printing Office, 1941), p. 676.

[18]The Fortune Directory, August, 1964. The Directory also lists 19 foreign industrial companies with assets of over $1 billion, the largest being Royal Dutch–Shell (Netherlands–Britain) with total assets of $10,651 millions. Of the 200 largest foreign industrial corporations, 53 were in Great Britain.

[19]Assets of $28,274,740,000 in 1963 make American Telephone and Telegraph the largest private corporation of any kind in the world.

[20]National Resources Committee, *The Structure of the American Economy* (Washington, D.C.: U.S. Government Printing Office, 1939), Part I, pp. 274–76.

[21]Fortune Directory. *op. cit.*

[22]Fortune Directory, *op. cit.*

262,490 corporations had been formed in the United States. This number had increased to 430,072 in 1925 and reached a total of 533,631 in 1935.[23]

The position which the corporation occupies in American business life is not easy to describe. In this connection, it should be noted that the corporation is a form of business organization and not a method of doing business. The corporate form is frequently selected for purposes of convenience without altering the structure of the particular enterprise and without presenting any unique questions of public policy. The Ford Motor Car Company came to dominate the automobile industry before it was incorporated, and the change to the corporate form left the ownership and management structure just where it was before. On the other hand, practically all of the present-day business giants have grown up as corporations, and many of them would probably not have achieved their present stature without the corporate device.

The tremendous size of some corporations and the prominent position which they occupy in their particular line of endeavor have focused attention on the amount of wealth and income concentrated in their hands. The Twentieth Century Fund, Inc., found that 594 corporations, each with assets of $50 million or over, out of the 504,080 corporations in the United States in 1933, owned more than half of the total assets of all business corporations. Put in another way, this meant that 95 per cent of all the corporations in the United States owned less than 14 per cent of all the corporate assets. In 1933, the same 594 corporations produced 18.4 per cent of the total national income and 20 per cent of the national income created by profit-seeking business.[24]

The prominent position of the giant corporation is emphasized in another way in a study by the National Resources Committee. In 1933, the 200 largest nonfinancial corporations in the United States controlled 60 per cent of the physical assets of all nonfinancial corporations in the country, about 48 per cent of all industrial wealth, and 20 per cent of the total national wealth.[25] On the other hand, 81 per cent of all economic activity in the United States in 1933 was carried on through the medium-sized or small corporations and by unincorporated enterprise. About 43 per cent of the entire business activity of the country was not in corporate hands at all; whereas unincorporated firms, together with corporations having assets of less than $1 million, accounted for nearly 60 per cent of the national income created by profit-seeking business.[26]

[23]Temporary National Economic Committee, "Economic Prologue," *Hearings*, Part I (Washington, D.C.: U.S. Government Printing Office, 1939), p. 228. Kaplan reports 536,833 corporations submitting balance sheets to the Bureau of Internal Revenue in 1948. See A. D. H. Kaplan, *Big Enterprise in a Competitive System* (Washington, D.C.: Brookings Institution, 1954), p. 114. The current figure is now over the 1,000,000 mark.

[24]Twentieth Century Fund, Inc., *op. cit.*, pp. 96–99.

[25]National Resources Committee, *op. cit.*, pp. 104–6.

[26]These proportions showed no change from 1929 to 1949. See Kaplan, *op. cit.*, pp. 115–20.

The use of the corporate device in business varies widely with the different branches of industry. In 1933, corporations produced 96 per cent of the income in mining and quarrying, 92 per cent in manufacturing, 86 per cent in transportation and public utilities, and 63 per cent in trade. On the other hand, only 6 per cent of the income in agriculture and related industries was produced by corporations in 1933.[27] It is clear that the use of the corporate form is influenced strongly by the technical structure of industry.

The importance attached to the corporate form of business organization in the modern world depends to a considerable extent upon the point to be emphasized. As has already been noted, there are a few corporations in the United States that stand out as gigantic industrial empires. The tremendous economic resources which these giants possess undoubtedly enables them to wield a good deal of power in the economic affairs of the country and even of the world. It makes possible—in many instances, at least—their exercise of a dominating influence in the particular line of activity in which they happen to be engaged.

Whether this modern giant in business could have developed without the corporate device is something that can never be known. That the corporate idea has, however, facilitated the growth of size in firms seems to be quite evident. As a consequence, we come to identify modern large-scale business with the corporation. This identification is useful in so far as it stresses the fact that increasing size may be facilitated by the corporation, and that it may be the direct result of corporate activities and the opportunity for expansion merely through corporate interrelations. Emphasis on the corporate aspect of modern large-scale enterprise, however, tends too frequently to conceal the basic economic factors which have led to this growth in size. The technical conditions which have made possible, and apparently more or less inevitable, the growth of large-scale production and big business enterprises, in a few lines of industry have necessitated the development of a form of business organization which is adequate to implement the scale required by modern technology. The corporate form has fulfilled this need.

Ownership in the Large Corporation

The development of the large business corporation has had a profound influence in another direction. In the first place, ownership in American business corporations is widely dispersed. The exact number of corporate stockholders is not known; the Temporary National Economic Committee estimated it to be between 8 million and 9 million

[27]Twentieth Century Fund, Inc., *op. cit.*, pp. 94–95. Total national income in 1962 originating in business was $374,181 million; corporate business accounted for $244,111 million; sole proprietorships and partnerships, $91,039 million; other private business, $28,651 million; and government enterprises, $5,804 million. *Survey of Current Business* (July, 1962), p. 17.

just before World War II;[28] the Brookings Institution, in a somewhat more precise survey, estimated that as of March 1, 1952, 6,490,000 individuals in the United States were share owners in publicly owned corporations;[29] and the New York Stock Exchange stated that there were over 10 million stockholders at the beginning of 1956.[30] The great bulk of these stockholders own only small amounts of stock, and the dividends they receive represent but a small portion of their total income. The number of share owners in some of the corporate giants is very large. The American Telephone and Telegraph Company reported 2,251,065 stockholders for 1963; for General Motors in 1962 there were 1,059,225; General Electric, 446,919; United States Steel, 363,637; and Atchison, Topeka and Santa Fe Railway, 115,421. In none of these instances did the largest, single stockholding amount to more than 1.5 per cent of the outstanding stock.

Second, although stock ownership is widely dispersed in one respect, it seems to be highly concentrated in another. It is estimated that 10,000 persons own one fourth and 75,000 persons own fully one half of all the corporate stock held by individuals in the United States.[31] The same source stated that on the average, in 1937, the 20 largest shareholdings in each of the 200 largest nonfinancial corporations in the United States accounted for nearly one third of the total market value of all the outstanding stock.[32]

In the same 200 corporations, the average financial stake of the officers and directors appears to be relatively small. In the study made by the Securities and Exchange Commission for the Temporary National Economic Committee, it was estimated that the officers and directors of these enterprises owned only 6 per cent of the common stock outstanding and slightly over 2 per cent of the preferred.[33] One half of the individual officers and directors owned stocks having a market value of less than $20,000 in 1939 for each position held.[34] The average size of holdings, however, was $616,000. There were 245 positions, or 7 per cent of the total, in which the value of the stockholdings was $1 million or more each. These holdings, in total, accounted for $1,892,000,000, or 80 per

[28]Temporary National Economic Committee, Monograph No. 29, *Distribution of Ownership in the 200 Largest Nonfinancial Corporations* (Washington, D.C.: U.S. Government Printing Office, 1940), p. 1.

[29]Lewis H. Kimmel, *Share Ownership in the United States* (Washington, D.C.: Brookings Institution, 1952), p. 89.

[30]Current reports indicate that the present number may be as large as 20 million.

[31]Temporary National Economic Committee, Monograph No. 29, p. 13. See Victor Perlo, " 'People's Capitalism' and Stock-Ownership," *American Economic Review*, Vol. XLVIII, No. 3 (June, 1958), pp. 333–47.

[32]Temporary National Economic Committee, Monograph No. 29, p. 70.

[33]*Ibid.*, p. 57.

[34]*Ibid.*, p. 59. It has been reported that Wm. Lynn Townsend, President of Chrysler Corporation, made a profit of $750,000 in six months in 1963, through the company's stock option plan (*Los Angeles Times*, January 2, 1964).

cent of the value of all management holdings. Finally, the 40 holdings with a value of $10 million or more each had an aggregate value of $1,312,000,000, or slightly over 60 per cent of the total, although they represented only 1 per cent of the number of reported positions of officers and directors.[35]

The available information makes it somewhat difficult to appraise the position of ownership control in the giant corporation. The Securities and Exchange Commission study concluded that about 60—or less than one third—of the 200 corporations were without a visible center of ownership control. In about 140 instances, the blocks of stock in the hands of one interest group were large enough to justify classifying these companies as more or less definitely under ownership control. About 40 companies, or one fifth of all the corporations included in the study, were controlled by one-family interest groups. In only 8 of these, however, was the control absolute, being based on the ownership of a majority of the voting stock. In 12 other companies, control was based on a predominant minority of from 30 to 50 per cent; while in the remainder, control rested on less than 30 per cent voting stock ownership.[36] Another study concluded that the number of instances in which a small compact group actually possesses the power to change the management by virtue of the size of its stockholdings is appreciably less than that estimated by the Securities and Exchange Commission. The number of companies in which any large degree of active leadership results from stock ownership is even smaller. It estimated that not more than one fifth, and perhaps less, of the stock of the giant corporations is owned by those who are in a position to exercise strong influence on the management.[37]

The conclusion that seems to be warranted from these studies is that those who are actively engaged in the leadership and management of the very large corporations own only a small minority of the stock. Minority interests do participate actively in management in a limited number of cases, but it is the corporate executives who are primarily responsible for business leadership in the large corporation today. Management and ownership in these enterprises are therefore largely in separate hands, and the role of ownership is decidedly different from that which the theory of corporate control assumes.[38]

[35]*Ibid.*, p. 60.

[36]*Ibid.*, pp. 103–5.

[37]R. A. Gordon, *Business Leadership in the Large Corporation* (Washington, D.C.: Brookings Institution, 1945), chap. ii, especially pp. 23–45.

[38]The same remarks are undoubtedly true for many corporations much smaller than these giants, but no reliable data on this are available. The remarks have even greater force when applied to mutual life insurance companies. Each policyholder is an owner and has a vote; but obviously, he exercises literally no control over the affairs of the firm. There can be no focus of ownership, and the policyholder has much less chance of leaving the firm if he is dissatisfied than does the stockholder of a nonfinancial enterprise.

The stockholders of the large corporation fall into two more or less extreme categories. At the one end is the great bulk of the shareholders who own only a few shares and who, if they vote at all, vote only by proxy. They know little about the internal affairs of the enterprise and take no part in management or leadership. They are investors; but they are not entrepreneurs in any sense, unless it be in connection with risk bearing and profits. At the other end is a small percentage of large stockholders who, in a few instances, have definite control of some of the corporations and, in a number of other instances, occupy a strong minority position.

The role of the small stockholder—that is, small in number of shares owned, and in total investment—is relatively easy to evaluate. He plays no significant part in the active leadership of the large corporation. As the owner of a considerable share of the equity capital of many of the prominent corporations, he is dependent upon the actions and decisions of management, over which he has no control. This is not to say that he has no rights and that there are no means of protecting them, but the methods that are ordinarily available to him are such as to leave him a completely passive member of the corporation. The possibilities, therefore, of directing the affairs of these corporations to the interest of minority groups and management are very great. Whether these potentialities are more or less realized is another question, but the present means of compelling responsibility to the small stockholder are not adequate to the task.

The role played by the minority groups of stockholders is more difficult to assess. The influence of these groups in corporate management seems to vary widely. In some instances, they participate continuously and actively in the direction of management; in others, they take part only occasionally; while in others, they seem to occupy a passive position. In general, it is safe to say that minority groups do play a definite part in exercising leadership in some of the large corporations and that they stand as a definite check to managerial irresponsibility in others. This does not seem to alter the fact, however, that management and ownership have become largely separated in the modern business giant. Even where minority groups do exercise effective control, there is no guarantee that the interests of the majority of the stockholders are safeguarded, since community of interest and interlocking directorates may encourage practices that are of benefit to management and minority groups but that are inimical to the interests of the stockholders, as such,[39] as well as the general public.

[39]The discontent which has arisen over management compensation in the form of large salaries and huge bonuses in some instances is a case in point. When boards of directors are composed of the executive heads of various enterprises, they are not likely to be too parsimonious in regard to each other's compensation; and there is the

(*Continued on next page*).

The prominent role that the large corporation plays in American economic life today and the position that its management occupies make the problem of leadership and internal control a matter of public concern. A great deal of attention has been focused on the small and "disfranchised" stockholder. The ease with which corporate investors, especially stockholders, were fleeced and the fortunes that were built through highhanded finance called for legislation which was designed to impose limits on the powers conferred by corporate charters and to offer some measure of protection to the investing public by setting up standards for the marketing of securities. Until 1933, legislation dealing with these matters was confined to the states, except in certain special instances, such as railroads. Fraudulent sales and deceptive practices were substantially reduced by these so-called "blue-sky" laws in many instances. There was still ample opportunity for high finance to run rampant, however, as was convincingly demonstrated in the 1920's, especially in the public utility field. The Securities Act of 1933 and the Securities and Exchange Act of 1934 marked the first general steps of the federal government to protect the investing public. The purpose of the Securities Act was to require adequate, uniform, and honest disclosure of all information considered necessary for the protection of the public. To this end, all new offerings coming within the jurisdiction of the Securities and Exchange Commission had to be registered with it; the seller was required to publish an extensive prospectus, which was to be available to all investors; and corporations that failed to comply with the law were subject to severe penalties. The Securities and Exchange Act contained requirements designed to prevent corporate insiders from profiting from information about the corporation which, because of their position, they received in advance of the ordinary stockholder. The law also dealt with proxy solicitation, by requiring that solicited security holders of all listed corporations be given a clear statement of all the important actions to be taken at the stockholders' meeting, the source of the solicitation, and the interest of the solicitor in the proposals.[40]

A further step, aimed in part, at least, at giving additional protection to the stockholder, was taken by bankruptcy legislation passed in 1934 and the Chandler Act of 1938. This not only provided for improved procedure in corporate reorganization, which for too long had frequently been a source of gross exploitation; but the Chandler Act also required that the charter of the reorganized corporation should (1) prohibit the

temptation, in the interests of harmony and co-operation, to allow each management to determine its own reward. According to *U.S. News and World Report* (May 13, 1963), the compensation for the 46 highest paid business executives in the United States in 1962 ranged from $643,975 for F. G. Donner, Chairman of the Board of General Motors, to $250,000 for Robert C. Tyson, Chairman of Finance for the United States Steel Corporation. Of the top 18, eleven were executives of General Motors and seven of the Ford Motor Company. Twenty-one of the top 46 were from these two companies.

[40]For a summary of this legislation, see Lindahl and Carter, *op. cit.*, chaps. 6 and 7.

issuance of nonvoting stock; (2) provide for a fair and equitable distribution of voting power among all classes of stocks; (3) include fair and equitable provisions with respect to the terms, position, rights, and privileges of the various classes of securities; and (4) provide for adequate annual financial reports to security holders.[41]

The protection of the stockholder against the grosser forms of exploitation is an important step toward making management more responsible for its actions or, at least, toward curtailing some of the means by which managerial powers can be abused to the detriment of the interests of the general public. However, this has not done very much to modify the procedures by which management and control function in the large corporation. As matters stand, the organizational structure of the large corporation is essentially oligarchical and bureaucratic, even where business leaders themselves are not sympathetic to it. One reason for this is that, so far, we have been unable to devise a practicable solution to the problem. Greater publicity of corporate affairs, especially on salaries and bonus-sharing arrangements; increased uniformity in accounting practices; more adequate annual reports; and more effective enforcement of the responsibilities of directors, all point in that direction; but they do not go to the heart of the problem. Furthermore, it is difficult to see how the basic issue can be solved by legislation. Perhaps it is not too much to hope that institutional patterns will emerge in time under the pressure of public opinion and with an awareness on the part of corporate executives that a solution will have to be forthcoming, and that they will have to provide the leadership for it, if private enterprise is to remain in that category.[42]

Ownership Control and Capital Formation

The relation of the corporate form of business organization to capital formation has a number of facets. First of all, the corporate form itself has facilitated the accumulation of capital into the large investment units required in much of our modern industrial structure. As has already been noted, the corporation has provided the ownership organizational requisite, without which it is difficult to see how the modern industrial era could have developed. In the second place, the corporate device, as distinct from big business, has been used, on occasion, as a means of restricting competition in various ways. To the extent that this has been so, it has resulted in a less efficient use of resources, with the probable retardation of capital formation and a less efficient use of capital

[41]For a short but comprehensive discussion of public policy on bankruptcy and reorganization, see Lyon, Watkins, and Abramson, *op. cit.*, Vol. I, chap. v.

[42]See, for example, A. A. Berle, Jr., *The Twentieth Century Capitalist Revolution* (New York: Harcourt, Brace & Co., Inc., 1954). It is well to bear in mind that the problem of leadership, which involves making power and responsibility commensurate with each other, is not confined to business. Business seems to have deported itself very well in comparison with the general picture today. That does not, however, alter the problem.

than would have been the case in the absence of restrictions. Discussion of this effect of the corporation will be deferred until after the examination of antitrust policy.[43]

The third facet of the relation of the corporate form to capital formation lies in the effect which the corporate type of ownership, particularly in the large corporation, has on investment decisions. It is estimated that in 1955, the assets of the 100 largest nonfinancial corporations in the United States increased by almost $9.6 billion, of which $3.2 billion went into net property investment. Of this total new investment, $4.6 billion, or 75 per cent, of the new equity capital came from retained earnings. The latter also made up 50 per cent of the total new capital going into these enterprises in 1955.[44] Professor Weston studied the internal financing of 31 large firms from the years prior to World War I (with the exception of Chrysler, which started in 1925) down to 1948 and found that the average increase in total assets from internal financing was 46.3 per cent. U.S. Steel stood at the top, with 87.2 per cent coming from internal financing over the years from 1903 to 1948; R. J. Reynolds Tobacco was at the bottom, with 25.4 per cent from 1913 to 1948.[45] At the same time, there is evidence to indicate that big business devoted a larger percentage of net income to dividends than the smaller corporations and also had sounder financial structures.[46]

The evidence is clear that reinvestment of earnings plays a major role in the expansion of big business in the industrial world.[47] Management makes the decision with regard to the division of earnings between dividends and what is retained. The factors influencing that decision will be numerous and varied. When it is felt that there is need for additional capital, it will undoubtedly be cheaper to raise it by retention of earnings than by going into the market, if the earnings are available. Whether this is good from the standpoint of the stockholder or public policy is another matter. Appraisal by the market and investor judgment has been dispensed with in favor of management decision.[48] It is by no means certain that disbursement of earnings to stockholders, with appeal to the market through new security issues, would bring about the same pattern of expansion as do present policies.

[43]See Chapter 20.

[44]First National City Bank, *Monthly Letter* (September, 1956), p. 107.

[45]J. F. Weston, *The Role of Mergers in the Growth of Large Firms* (Berkeley and Los Angeles: University of California Press, 1953), pp. 24–26.

[46]Twentieth Century Fund, Inc., *How Profitable Is Big Business?* (New York, 1937), p. 162.

[47]These remarks have little application to railroads and public utilities, because of regulatory policies, although there is considerably more reinvestment by public utilities than by railroads. See P. J. Garfield and W. F. Lovejoy, *Public Utility Econom ics* (Englewood Cliffs, N.J.: Prentice-Hall, Inc., 1964) chap. 19.

[48]". . .one may say that 85 per cent of the total internal plus external long-term funds of the corporate sector circumvented the public capital markets" (in 1959). H. G. Vatter, *The U.S. Economy in the 1950's* (New York: W. W. Norton and Co., Inc., 1963), p. 194.

The problems presented to corporate managers are by no means easy to resolve. There is no use undertaking the procedures of disbursement and reinvestment by appeal to the market just for the sake of going through the motions. On the other hand, competitive forces, especially in a private enterprise economy, must be relied upon as fully as possible if an efficient economic system is to be obtained. Management may be able to appraise these forces with sufficient accuracy to get the same results that the market would yield. It is doubtful, however, that the industrial pattern of this country is the same as it would have been had expansion of firms taken place primarily from external rather than internal financing. A competitive, private enterprise economy needs to utilize competition as much as possible, and this means that the market place must be the arbiter whenever possible.[49]

[49]One possible method of dealing with this problem is advanced by Professor Milton Friedman, who proposes that the corporate tax should be abolished and that the corporation should be required to attribute to individual stockholders the earnings which are not distributed as dividends. The stockholder would then have to report these undistributed earnings on his tax return. Milton Friedman, *op. cit.*, p. 132. This procedure would obviously encounter many difficulties, and its practicability may be doubted

Chapter 5 THE COMBINATION MOVEMENT IN THE UNITED STATES

THE NATURE OF THE COMBINATION MOVEMENT

The critical problems of regulation of business in the United States today center around the control of big business. This situation is the result of the emergence of the modern giant enterprise under the impact of the technology of mass production, the development of nationwide markets, and financial integration. The effect of these forces has been twofold. In the first place, they have promoted the expansion of individual enterprises through the process of internal growth, on the one hand, and through external growth by various forms of merger, on the other. In the second place, they have induced the use of a variety of devices and practices aimed at limiting or eliminating competition among producers of rival commodities or services.

Meaning of the Combination Movement

The term "trust" or "combination" movement is the one commonly given to these two aspects of American business development since the Civil War. Sometimes, the term "merger" movement is applied to the same phase of business development; but this designation is more restrictive than trust or combination movement, in that it is confined to the growth of firms through some form of merger or ownership unification, whereas the combination movement also includes arrangements of a restrictive nature among otherwise independent firms. The term "trust movement" includes all of the above, but always carries with it the connotation of restrictive practices and objectives.

A clearer understanding of the combination movement and its bearing on public policy is obtained if it is recognized that it involves two different aspects which are quite distinct analytically, even though they may be difficult to separate in fact. One aspect of the movement has been characterized by the attempts of business to limit competition by the combination of separate firms under single ownership, or by some form of restrictive agreement among previously independent firms. Frequently, the latter was the first step in the process of restriction; but the principal manifestation, and certainly the most complicated, has been the industrial giant resulting from consolidation or merger.

The other aspect is the result of the fact that modern combination movement had its foundation in a technology that compelled large-scale production in many lines of industry. Historically, this meant, in the majority of cases, that production was first undertaken by numerous small and independent units. The pressure of competition and the economies of larger-scale operations brought about the elimination of many of them, either by extinction or by combination. Available markets were not large enough to support all of them operating on an economical scale, and the high degree of localization of many of our natural resources exerted an influence in the same direction. Of course, the technological conditions of modern industry have presented both the opportunity and the incentive for combinations designed to achieve monopolistic power and reap monopoly profits. Predatory practices, speculation, unsatisfactory laws, and inept or misguided administration have all played their part. From the standpoint of public policy, however, the importance of distinguishing between these two sets of forces is that no amount of compulsion can bring about economical production by a large number of producers if the technical conditions are unsuited to that type of structure. If an intelligent public policy is to be developed, the influence of the various factors at work must be recognized in order that legislation and regulation may be directed to the elimination of the undesirable consequences of the combination movement without destroying its beneficial features.

The use of the term "trust" to designate monopolistic combinations, as well as joint action by independent concerns for the purpose of controlling the market, arose from two factors. One was the widespread use of various arrangements by which enterprises combined to secure control of the market and to limit competition. Sometimes, these took the form of agreements of one kind or another among producers of similar products; sometimes, they consisted of outright consolidation of independent enterprises. The second factor was the use of the "trustee" device by the Standard Oil Company of Ohio in 1879. This combine was formed by the transfer of stock of competing oil companies to a group of trustees who exercised the voting power and thus secured unified control. The success of this procedure led to widespread imitation, which aroused public demand for legislation to combat industrial monopoly. The Sherman Antitrust Act of 1890 was the result. This legislation, which marked the beginning of federal regulation in the industrial field, has given the generic term "antitrust laws" to all subsequent laws aimed at curbing monopoly and fostering competition.

Emergence of the Modern Industrial Structure

The end of the Civil War may conveniently be said to mark the inauguration of modern United States. This is not to be taken as indicating that the conflict between the North and the South effected a catastrophic break, technically and industrially, with the previous period but rather that the developments which had been taking place prior to that time assumed their present form at an accelerated pace. Prior to 1860, industrial enterprises were characteristically small, and the period from 1840 to 1860 has frequently been called the "golden age of small industry." In the years immediately following the end of hostilities, industrial expansion rapidly transformed the structure into the modern one of large-scale enterprise. This transformation was the result of a phenomenal application of physical science to the production of goods and services, accompanied by developments in business organization, which readily supplied the necessary implementation.

The railroad introduced the first economical means of providing the vast inland areas of the continent with access to national and international markets. The development of the modern factory system, as the result of the application of power and machine technology, gave the means for producing large quantities of standardized products that merely awaited the markets to reap the advantages of large-scale production. At the same time, these new production techniques made for a great annual increase in the output of wealth that could be used for further production. This created the basis for a rapid growth in the capital necessary for the expansion of modern industry. Accompanying this was the development of financial arrangements and devices needed to make this capital readily available. The rise of savings banks, trust companies, and insurance companies provided the institutions in which large amounts of savings could be accumulated, while the corporation became the organizational vehicle whereby these accumulations could be tapped. The adaptation of the corporate device to the use of private business made it possible to offer various kinds of securities to the investing public with the advantages of limited liability and what may be termed "absentee ownership."

By the end of the Civil War, the patterns and the foundation of future growth had been established—the country had been explored, the framework of the future railroad network erected, and the geographical and industrial pattern of the nation's industries had been built. A national banking system had been set up; the factory system had developed to the point that the United States ranked fourth among the manufacturing nations; the corporation, as the new vehicle of business organization, had exhibited its superiority over other forms; and the increase in population was the greatest any country had experienced in a similar period of time. The United States had become one of the great industrial and political powers of the world. The effects of these factors on the political and economic structure of this country were not manifest, however, until after 1870.

In the next thirty years, all of these developments took on a rapidly accelerated pace and extended their influence into entirely new fields.

The railroad net expanded almost to its present size and provided railroad transport to practically every part of the country. The improvements in transportation led to the concentration of industry in large manufacturing centers—first of all, because they provided an economical means of bringing raw materials and power together and, second, because they gave ready access to markets for the finished product. At the same time, the increased use of power for manufacturing, improved mechanical processes, and the standardization of products resulted in the rapid growth of the size of manufacturing units and the location of them in a relatively limited number of urban centers. Minneapolis, St. Louis, and Chicago became the focal points for the bulk of the milling industry. The invention of the refrigerator car in 1868 led to the rapid growth of the huge meat-packing establishments of the Midwest. The discovery of the Bessemer and open-hearth processes for the production of steel provided the means of supplying cheaply the huge quantities of that material required by the new developments in transportation and industry. Petroleum emerged as one of the great sources of power, with the solving of the problems of storage and transportation. The introduction of the pipe line in 1865 and the tubular tank car in 1870 afforded economical transportation of the raw product to the refining centers, which were located where the finished products were to be used. The need for more adequate means of communication was met by the expansion of the telegraph. This had been established in 1844, with the opening of a line from Baltimore to Washington. In 1851, connections were made with the Pacific Coast; and in 1866, transatlantic service was commenced. As a result, market quotations in the large centers of this country and Europe were available overnight. The first telephone was exhibited in 1876; and thereafter, telephone service expanded rapidly to a national scale. The development of a practical dynamo in 1877 and the erection of the first central power station in 1882 laid the foundations of electricity as a new source of power and light. From 1882 to 1929, the output of central stations almost doubled every 5½ years.

The improvements in mechanized production, together with the vast and readily available resources of the American continent, led to a wave of immigration of population and capital. From 1870 to 1900, the United States experienced the most phenomenal growth of population of any country in the history of the world. The immigrants not only afforded a readily available supply of labor but also a vast domestic market for the products of the field, forest, mine, and factory. The prospects of profits in American industry also attracted large quantities of European capital. Thus, the stage was set for modern finance and the captains of industry. The opportunities for profit, power, and the prestige of industrial leadership required only the development of an effective means of business organization, through which the creation of industrial empires could be achieved. This was soon forthcoming in the rapid adaptation of the corporate device to the needs and desires of the new industrial leaders.

In summary, the period from 1870 to 1900 marked the rise of the United States to the position of the foremost industrial power of the world. This was accompanied by the extension of business, not only to a national but also to an international scale, and the emergence of a vast network of industrial empires no longer adequately amendable to rules which presupposed essentially local economic activity, industrial leadership directly responsible to owners, and absence of widespread monopolistic powers except those which were specially granted or those which were the result of predatory practices. The problems of control of modern business arose with such rapidity that there was little opportunity to keep pace with them.

The transformation of the economic structure was accompanied by significant changes in the relation of government to industry. Prior to 1870, legislation affecting business was confined largely to laws designed to assist, rather than to control, business activity. After that date, statutes aimed at curbing and channeling many business practices emerged in fairly rapid succession. A number of factors foreshadowed this basic change. The railroad had been growing somewhat gradually down to the Civil War and had established its position as the prime means of inland transport by the end of that conflict. It really signalized the beginning of large-scale specialized investment with heavy fixed costs. It was also the first of the group of industries known today as "natural monopolies." These characteristics soon gave rise to ruinous competition, discrimination, and the demand for extensive regulation. The enactment of state legislation to regulate the railroads marked the break between the regulatory policies of the first half of the nineteenth century and those which were to follow after 1870. However, although the Interstate Commerce Act was passed in 1887 to provide for federal regulation of railroads and the Sherman Antitrust Act was passed in 1890, no serious attempt to regulate industry in any form was undertaken by the federal government until after the turn of the century.

FACTORS PROMOTING THE COMBINATION MOVEMENT

The modern industrial structure, with its complex intermixture of competitive and monopoly elements and the preponderance of large-scale mechanized production in so many lines, developed under the influence of a number of factors—technological, economic, and institutional.

Technological Factors

Foremost among these forces were the changing techniques of production, which registered their full impact after 1870 and which do not seem to have lost any of their momentum as yet. Large-scale production was the result of the application of mechanical power to the creation of goods and services. It made possible a continuous repetition of processes with a precision impossible to achieve in any other way; and with this came mass standardized output based upon specialization in equipment, labor, and management. It has also resulted in geographical specialization, with concentration of industry at focal points of natural resources and the transportation of resulting products to points of consumption. The economies of mass production necessitated large plants, large firms, and huge investments. Although large scale was essential to successful competition in many lines because of constant pressure to reduce cost, it also introduced elements of monopoly and incentives to acquire monopoly power. The resulting industrial structure was a mixture of competition and monopoly. Rapid changes in technology constantly created new sources of competition, as, for example, in the development of petroleum and electricity, which led to almost chronic depression in coal. On the other hand, endeavors to preserve investments and to ward off disastrous competition encouraged monopolistic practices of various kinds. The advantages of very wide market areas because of the nature of the product, as illustrated by telephone communications and automobiles, gave an incentive to expansion on a nationwide basis and the reduction of the number of producers. Moreover, the large amount of initial investment required in many instances served to preserve a field, sometimes for a long period, to established firms. Although modern methods of production laid the technical foundations for present-day giant business enterprises, they also intensified competition on a national, and even international, scale. The continuous appearance of alternative commodities and new sources of supply imposed severe limitations on the growth of monopoly and still left competition as the most potent factor in the evolution of the economy.

The Influence of the Corporation

The adaptation of the corporate form of organization to the use of private business was at least as significant as the development of technology in influencing the rise of the modern industrial structure. The corporation introduced a flexibility and unity into business organization previously unknown. Moreover, the fact that it was an impersonal type gave it a continuity that, by and large, had been lacking theretofore. This, coupled with the privilege of limited liability, made it possible to raise capital on a scale commensurate with the requirements of the new technology. Appeal could be made to various groups of investors by issuring different kinds of securities, which were able to tap the many different sources of supply of capital funds. The benefits of financial economies could be obtained by plowing back profits, by having a wider appeal to the financial market, and by being able to secure foreign capital by sale of securities to foreign investors. This was aided by the ease with which the corporation could expand into the large firm by building or owning plants in widely separated areas, setting them up, if necessary or desirable, as separate corporations. The privilege of acquiring other enterprises by stock purchase or exchange facilitated growth, reducing the amount of capital which the expanding firms needed to raise.

The effectiveness of this means of expansion was enhanced by the emergence of the holding company device. Once it came into general use, the obstacles which complete consolidation frequently faced were thereby removed. It was no longer necessary to dissolve, or even absorb, the businesses acquired. All that had to be done was to obtain sufficient stock to control their activity and then let them continue as before, if it was desired. An even simpler procedure was available in the form of ownership of stock by individuals in various corporations, which ownership could then be used to secure interlocking directorates and the promotion of policies beneficial to those in control. These various devices not only made expansion under the impetus of large-scale economies much easier but also offered inducements to bring about limitations on competition and to secure monopoly power. The holding company also made it possible to expand control without encountering the usual technological limitations on size. In addition to that, it was immune to legal attack if it did not combine competing enterprises so as to restrict "competition," as that term was narrowly construed by the courts; and it was frequently and effectively used to evade the restrictions of regulation.

The corporation, in its various manifestations and with its multiplicity of devices, changed the whole complexion of the combination movement. It is impossible to say what the nature of the development would have been without the modern corporation. But the extreme laxity of the law in this country and the consequent almost unlimited adaptability of the corporate device gave an opportunity for growth in the size and scope of activity of the single firm far beyond that which was inherent in the technology of modern industry.

It was this use of the corporation to effect control of large segments of an industry under unified ownership that constituted the distinctive aspect of the combination movement in the United States. In other countries, restriction of competition was achieved largely through various kinds of agreements which left a large amount of independence of action and complete independence of ownership to the participating enterprises. Antitrust legislation prohibited such arrangements here. At the same time, the greater difficulty of incorporation in other countries made control through the medium of a single corporation less inviting. In other words, while modern methods of production laid the technological foundation for large-scale industry, the direction which the development of the organizational structure took was determined by the corporate laws enacted in this country and the opportunity which they afforded for business aggrandizement.

Captains of Industry

The ease with which the corporate device could be used to effect large combinations set the stage for the advent of the captains of industry. Ambitious individuals could control industrial empires with a minimum of responsibility and could bring under their sway activities which would have escaped them had the corporation not proved to be so effective a tool. The opportunity to penetrate into fields of production not technically related to each other made it possible to limit competition and secure the boundaries of the empire, so to speak. The danger inherent in this procedure was that, in the hands of aggressive and unscrupulous individuals, there was no logical stopping place. Expansion for expansion's sake was too often the result. The lack of corporation laws imposing limitations and assessing responsibilities commensurate with the privileges gained frequently resulted in integration and combination inimical to public welfare. The legal privilege of combining enterprises that had no more relation to each other than that arising from stock ownership made any logical policy of industrial control impossible. Much of the difficulty of administering the antitrust laws has arisen from this source.[1]

Growth of Financial Institutions

The tremendous amounts of capital required by modern industry necessitated the development of institutions to perform the function of financing business enterprise. Arrangements for accumulating savings and marketing securities were both essential. The needs were met in a number of ways. Savings associations of various kinds collected the accumulations of individuals and, in turn, invested them in various industrial activities. Life insurance companies, seeking long-term investments for the premiums which they received, supplied business with a large amount of capital. Banks did likewise, and they also served as depositories for the accounts of business. The function of acting as fiscal agents for modern enterprise devolved very largely upon private banking institutions. They assisted in the marketing of securities by acting as underwriters and, in a large number of instances, were the promoters of many of the giant consolidations that took place. Finally, the stock exchanges served as the principal markets for the transfer of securities. Industry not only required a wide market in which to secure its capital but also depended upon financial arrangements whereby people could

[1]The role of captains of industry did not end with the early phases of the combination movement. It seems to have taken on a new lease of life since 1960. Administration of the Celler-Kefauver Act may have blocked the merger road to corporate empires through the merger of competing firms, but it has done nothing to inhibit the growth of the "conglomerate" merger which may be heralding a new development for corporate giants, the empire builder, and the promoter.

readily buy and sell securities. If it had always been necessary for a person to commit his capital permanently to some particular investment, much of that which was available would have been retained in the form of liquid funds. By making these funds accessible to industry, the financial institutions which developed provided an increase in the supply of capital funds and a reduction of the costs of them. The source of the capital itself was the vast increase of wealth arising from the increased productivity of industry from which great accumulations of productive wealth could be made, even while standards of living were rising rapidly. The increased supply of capital funds led to the lowering of costs of capital,[2] which, in turn, encouraged expansion.

The Professional Promoter

The opportunity for making speculative profit by organizing combinations attracted the attention of the professional promoter. The heyday of prewar trust promotion, from 1897 to 1903, is to be attributed to this. Rising prices, unbridled faith in big business, and a general speculative orgy enabled financiers to float huge volumes of securities to finance the mergers. A similar development took place again from 1925 to 1929, especially in the industries which rose to prominence after World War I.[3] This aspect of the combination movement was given additional impetus by the opportunity afforded aggressive and ambitious individuals seeking power and prestige. The industrial world presented new opportunities for adventure—men who in previous times might have been warriors, explorers, or empire builders turned their energies to domination in the industrial world.

Expansion of Markets

Economies of size arising from division of labor, specialization, and mass production are realizable only if there is a market for the product. It was the application of power, especially to land transport and the development of communications, that provided the opportunity for the growth of modern manufacturing. The ability to accumulate raw materials from widely separated sources resulted in the concentration of industry at places where production could be carried on most advantageously. At the same time, reduction in the cost of transportation resulted

[2] *The Annalist* (New York), January 25, 1940, pp. 144–45. See also M. W. Watkins, *Industrial Combinations and Public Policy* (Boston: Houghton Mifflin Co., 1927), pp. 19–22. The tremendous growth of pension and mutual funds among other sources of investment funds, has given new impetus to this development since World War II.

[3] W. I. Thorp, "The Persistence of the Merger Movement," *American Economic Review*, Vol. XXI, No. 1, Supplement (March, 1931), pp. 77–89; also Temporary National Economic Committee, Monograph No. 27, *The Structure of Industry* (Washington, D.C.: U.S. Government Printing Office, 1941), pp. 231–34. For a discussion of the role of promoters in the development of big business, see G. W. Stocking and M. W. Watkins, *Monopoly and Free Enterprise* (New York: The Twentieth Century Fund, 1951).

in the rise of large urban centers. These, in turn, led to expansion of rural areas of population, which were afforded markets for their products. All this led to a rapid growth of economic interdependence within this country and among the nations of the world. Business ceased to be local in nature and instead became national—even international—in scope. The resulting impersonal nature of production led to an enormous increase in the use of advertising and reliance on trade names and special brands to appeal to consumers and to acquire their good will. Enterprises with nationally known products enjoyed a marked advantage in many lines. Competition grew in intensity and scope; and this, in turn, led to the development of various devices to curb it. The increased market opportuntities not only made possible the exploitation of the advantages of large-scale enterprise but also induced such a change in the structure of industry that rules of conduct, previously adequate, no longer sufficed.

Desire for Control of Markets

The desire to acquire monopoly profits was a powerful factor in influencing the development of the combination movement in this country. It was undoubtedly the principal motive leading to the formation of trusts and monopolistic combines. By extending their sway so as to secure an effective control of the products in which they were interested, these organizations were able to stifle competition and influence price to their own advantage. Not all combinations can be traced to the desire to secure monopoly; many of them can be attributed to the advantages to be secured from large-scale production. However, the severe competition which resulted from falling prices down to 1896, the phenomenal industrial expansion which changed the competitive structure so fundamentally, together with the example set by such combines as the Standard Oil trust, the whiskey trust, and the sugar trust, elevated the desire to escape competition to a position of prime importance. Excesses of competition arising from the new industrial expansion, plus the lack of adequate public restraint on business practices, resulted in a variety of devices designed to curb what was felt in many quarters to be disastrous competition. The idea rapidly took hold that unlimited rivalry in large-scale enterprise was ruinous. This was already being recognized by public policy in the field of transportation, and it was easy to foster the idea that the same situation applied to industry in general. Belief in the efficacy of size was encouraged by the success of big business; and furthermore, size itself offered marked advantages in an industrial order almost uninhibited by ethical standards and lacking an effective expression of crystallized public policy. Under such circumstances, monopoly frequently became a defense against monopoly.

Monopolistic combinations also stood to reap special advantages from the establishment of orderly markets. The simple type of competitive market, appropriate to a small-scale enterprise, no longer sufficed. The constant threat of competition and the fear that the value of huge investments would be impaired led to agreements to stabilize the market and eliminate price wars. The technology of present-day industry compels industrial leaders to plan ahead for some considerable time. This is very difficult in the face of price uncertainties and the threat of rapidly shifting competition. Monopolistic control offered promise of removing a large part of this threat. Similarly, the need for large quantities of raw materials led many industries to expand their control to strategic resources. Where it was possible to obtain ownership of highly localized sources of supply, the threat of competition was lessened and the source of raw materials assured.

Combinations and agreements also afforded the opportunity of avoiding the wastes of competition. Competition is both wasteful and irksome to particular enterprises. They may be desirous of securing the advantages of it in the things which they buy, but they do not like to incur the expenses which it entails in the things that they sell, if that can be avoided. Competition is also wasteful to the consuming public when excessive duplication of production facilities is the result. It is the problem of achieving an appropriate balance, which will obtain the advantages of competition without the costs of overexpansion, that makes control so difficult today. It is the endeavor—in part, at least—to meet this situation that lies at the bottom of many attempts of business to control competition. Whatever may be the verdict on many of the arrangements, it has to be admitted that competition always must be subjected to rules; if public policy fails to meet the situation, business will supply its own remedies.

Inadequacies of the Law

Another factor which influenced the direction which the combination movement took in the United States was the inadequacy of the law to deal with the rapidly changing industrial and social conditions brought about by economic expansion. The frontier spirit, lack of deeply rooted business morality, and the consequent slow crystallization of public policy gave unusual scope for economic experimentation, aggression, and exploitation. An almost free rein to these was afforded by the laxity of incorporation laws, resulting from charter-mongering by the states, legislative corruption, legal ingenuity, and a lack of understanding of the dangers inherent in virtually unlimited corporate powers.

To all of this must be added the difficulties of industrial control which the federal form of government entailed. The division of powers between the federal and state governments creates the continuous problem of reconciling conflict and makes for a diversity of policies that are not easy to reconcile. When the combination movement first began, the federal government exercised few powers over interstate commerce. It was not only slow in expanding its authority but met a great deal of resistance in doing so. At the same time, business was developing on a national scale, and an important segment of it was consequently outside the scope of most existing legislation. Furthermore, the effective regulation of business activity by the federal government presented political and administrative obstacles that were very difficult to overcome. The problem of working out co-ordinated policy on national and local levels has given rise to the most difficult issues of government that we have faced. The result has been that public policy has constantly lagged behind business practices. In the meantime, the latter—for good or for ill—have continued to develop. If this had taken place over a relatively long period of time and under conditions of comparative stability, solutions could have been developed and gaps narrowed to insignificance. But this has not been the lot of the United States to date.

PHASES OF THE COMBINATION MOVEMENT

The combination movement in the United States has been characterized by three distinct phases or aspects: (1) the merger movement,[4] (2) growth of large corporations by internal expansion, and (3) various kinds or restrictive arrangements among otherwise independent firms. The relative roles of these three aspects in shaping the structure and conduct of industry in this country is a matter of some considerable difference of opinion, although prime importance seems to belong to the first two. Until comparatively recently, the greatest emphasis has been placed on the influence of the merger movement; but some students feel that the most significant factor in the growth of big business since the beginning of World War I has been internal expansion. The evidence seems to indicate that, quantitatively, this is probably correct but that, qualitatively, mergers have been more important. Certainly, the first period of the merger movement established the foundation for the subsequent developments; and even in the second and third periods, mergers have played a key role in shaping the structures of many of our major industries. It is also safe to say that if the legal restrictions had been less severe, mergers would play and would have played a considerably larger part than they have done.

The Merger Movement

First Period: 1887–1904. Down to 1896, mechanization, the rise of new industries, and the expansion of the market led to a rapid growth in the size of industrial units, either from internal expansion or from the combination of small concerns by outright consolidation into larger enterprises. This was partly the normal result of industrial development

[4]The term "merger" here means any form of fusion or integration of independent companies which brings them under unified control.

and the effect of the economies of size. The intensification of competition under the impact of a falling price level, speculative excesses, and over-expansion were further incentives. A considerable number of combinations were formed, but most of them exercised no monopoly power. The trust movement, however, was foreshadowed by the Standard Oil trust (1879), which used the trustee device; the linseed oil trust (1885); the sugar trust (1887); and a number of others which followed the Standard Oil example. Some large single combines also emerged, among them being the American Tobacco Company (1890), United States Rubber Company (1892), General Electric Company (1892), and the United States Leather Company (1893). Of far more importance at this time, however, was the use of the various kinds of pools and simple price agreements, frequently known as "gentlemen's agreements." These arrangements were used to control output and prices but proved to be rather unstable in the face of the law and in the absence of effective means for compelling adherence to them.

It was after 1896 that the trust movement rose to its full proportions. The principal objective of the new combinations was to secure monopoly control of the market. It has been estimated that 234 monopolistic combines were formed from 1898 to 1903.[5] These included such prominent names as International Silver, United Shoe Machinery, American Can, Eastman Kodak, International Harvester, Corn Products, International Nickel, and United States Steel. The latter was the first billion-dollar corporation to be formed in the history of this country. Many of the restrictive devices that had been used at the beginning of the combination movement had been eliminated by the courts, but they were replaced by new arrangements that had greater stability and were more difficult to attack. The holding company, community of interest, interlocking directorates, and consolidations became the principal means of effecting control.

The major factors contributing to the spectacular rise of trusts during these five years were the discovery of the holding company device, rising prices, speculative fever, and the promoter. Rising prices contributed to business optimism and aided the flotation of the vast quantities of securities needed to finance the combines. This, together with the resulting speculative fever, set the stage for the professional promoter. The usual procedure followed by the promoter was to secure the financial backing of some banking firms for a projected combination. He would then negotiate with a number of enterprises in the industry and reach a purchase price for each firm. A new corporation would be formed, with its capitalization based on the prospective profits of the consolidation. As a rule, the owners of the original firm were paid by the exchange of

[5]Temporary National Economic Committee, Monograph No. 27, p. 231.

their stocks for those of the new corporation, and the promoter and the bankers would obtain the remainder of the new securities. This generally resulted in overcapitalization of the new firm.

The stock market crash of 1903 put an end to this period of high finance. By that time, popular opposition to the trusts had reached considerable proportions, and an aggressive attack on them soon got under way. A number of Supreme Court decisions, commencing with the Northern Securities case of 1904, resulted in the dissolution of some of the most notorious combines. The vigorous antitrust policy inaugurated by President Theodore Roosevelt was reinforced in 1914 by the passage of the Clayton and Federal Trade Commission acts. Thus, by the outbreak of World War I, the first major phase of the combination movement in the United States had come to an end. Many of the most menacing monopolies had been dissolved; there was little incentive to enter into a new period of trustification; and laws had been enacted which gave promise of establishing the foundations of a policy that would preserve and promote competition and prevent the use of industrial power to the detriment of public interest.

Second Period: 1919–30. What the result of this new policy would have been, had it been given the opportunity to develop under peaceful conditions, is impossible to say. The outbreak of World War I marked a new departure in the combination movement. The war itself resulted in a great expansion of production in this country and stimulated the rise of new industries. The electric power, radio, automobile, rubber, airplane, motion-picture, and chemical industries all rose to first rank and offered new fields for combination and large-scale production. The additional impetus of inflation and the belief in a new era of permanent prosperity resulted in the second great merger period, from 1919 to 1930.

The combination movement after 1914 differed, in many respects, from that which had taken place prior to that date. Only a few attempts were made to secure domination in any particular field of endeavor. The earlier period was characterized by efforts to control whole industries by vertical combination, which combined the processes from raw materials to finished product, and by horizontal mergers designed to embrace literally all competitors. Some examples of these appeared after World War I—the Anaconda Copper Mining Company (1922) being an outstanding illustration of the vertical type, and the General Outdoor Advertising Company (1925) of the horizontal. Much more attention was paid, however, to mergers involving noncompetitive products. These were characteristic of the automobile industry, where each of the large producers undertook to manufacture different kinds of cars, even with different names, to complete in the various price classes. International Business Machines Company, Allied Chemical and Dye Corporation, and General Foods Corporation were examples of the same thing in other fields. The chain type of merger or combination was another postwar development, illustrated most prominently by chain stores like Woolworth, Penney, Kresge, and Safeway.

The holding company proved to be especially adaptable to this new development. It provided the means whereby separate and noncompeting enterprises could be combined into single units without the complications of outright consolidation and the disadvantage of dissolution of the component firms. The holding company also afforded the advantage of maintaining separate corporate existence where special charter privileges were worth retaining or where state laws made local incorporation advisable. Bonbright and Means[6] report that of the 97 largest industrial companies in the United States in 1929, 21 were pure holding companies; and of these, only 3—namely, Standard Oil of New Jersey, Eastman Kodak, and United States Steel—were formed prior to 1910; even then, Standard of New Jersey did not become a pure holding company until 1927. Fourteen of the 21 companies were formed after 1922. In contrast, 36 out of 63 of the big operating or primarily operating companies were formed before 1910.

The most spectacular and notorious development of the holding company was in the public utility field. While some of these companies originated before 1920, the phenomenal growth of all of them took place in the decade following the end of World War I. By 1930, the 10 largest gas and electrical holding company groups did approximately 75 per cent of the electric light and power business of the entire nation and accounted for about 45 per cent of the gas output. The American Telephone and Telegraph Company, a parent holding company, supplied over 80 per cent of the telephone service. Through its subsidiary, the Western Electric Company, it produced the overwhelming proportion of telecommunication equipment.

The parent operating company, which carries on operations itself as well as through subsidiaries, has characterized the organization of railroads almost from the beginning. The holding company established primarily for the purpose of forming combinations has played a relatively minor role in railroads. By 1920, only two pure holding companies remained—the Western Pacific Railroad Company and the Atlantic Coast Line Company.[7] In the period of the second merger movement, however, a number were organized principally to effect consolidation outside the control of the Interstate Commerce Commission. Of these, the Alleghany Corporation, organized by the Van Sweringen brothers, was the largest and most notorious.

The second merger movement ended with the stock market crash of October, 1929, and the ensuing period of depression. The general

[6]J. C. Bonbright and G. C. Means, *The Holding Company* (New York: McGraw-Hill Book Co., Inc., 1932), pp. 77–78.

[7]*Ibid.*, pp. 253 f.

consensus seems to be that mergers played a less significant role in shaping the structure of the economy than was the case in the first period, although, in absolute numerical terms, it may have been larger in size.[8] Mergers, however, did play a primary role in the development of public utility enterprises. Except for the case of public utilities, other factors—such as internal growth and co-operative devices exemplified by trade associations and patent pools—appear to have exercised a much more important influence than mergers from 1919 to 1930.

Third Period: 1939 to the Present. The period of the third merger movement, which is continuing at the time of this writing, has been characterized by the rise of new industries, just as were the previous periods. Although most of these industries had their start prior to World War II, it was not until after 1940 that they became really prominent in the economy. The most important of these newer developments have occurred in the fields of electronics, television, natural gas transmission, air transport, motor transport, and atomic energy. What the effects of these on the economy and the structure of industry will be, remains to be seen.

The third merger movement commenced with the outbreak of World War II and maintained a rather steady rate to 1954.[9] From 1939 to 1954, according to the Federal Trade Commission, over 4,000 mergers took place in mining and manufacturing. This is a much smaller number than the 7,000 for the shorter period of 1919 to 1929, which period also witnessed the orgy of mergers in the public utility field. These are not included in the 7,000 figure. The food and kindred products industry accounted for 32 per cent of the mergers from 1940 to 1954; nonelectrical machinery, 22 per cent; fabricated metals, 14.3 per cent; petroleum and coal products, 9.6 per cent.[10] In approximately 30 per cent of the mergers, the acquiring firms had assets of $50 million or over. In other words, about 70 per cent of the mergers involved firms of less than $50 million of assets. The evidence indicated that mergers were a relatively unimportant source of growth, at least quantitatively, of large firms but were a major source of growth of the smaller ones.[11] It seems clear that monopolistic forces which characterized the first period were not a significant factor in the third period. Indeed, the Federal Trade Commission concludes that:

> The forces involved are those which underlie the considered decisions by business executives. These which are basic have to do with the efforts of management to attain the advantages of scale in production and distribution so diversified as to products and as to distribution services performed as to level out peaks and valleys due to seasonal changes, changes in consumer demand, or shifts in the

[8]National Bureau of Economic Research, *Business Concentration and Price Policy* (Princeton: Princeton University Press, 1955), p. 168.

[9]Federal Trade Commission, *Report on Corporate Mergers and Acquisitions* (Washington, D.C.: U.S. Government Printing Office, 1955), p. 21.

[10]*Ibid.*, p. 31.

[11]National Bureau of Economic Research, *op. cit.*, p. 177.

markets for their products. These are the forces which are relied upon to keep a free economy vital and active . . . . Neither the economic objectives nor the methods used in acquisition by even the largest corporations differ appreciably from those which underlie the smallest purchase and sale or exchange of property . . . . The individual retailer who buys out a nearby competitor in order to increase the size of his operations has much in common with the industrialist who buys the facilities of a competitor engaged in the same line of manufacture rather than to build new manufacturing facilities of his own.[12]

Since 1954 there has been a definite acceleration of mergers, the total for 1963 being more than double of that for 1954—1,311 in the former as compared with 617 for the latter year. In the ten-year period, 1954–1963, the Federal Trade Commission recorded just over 10,000 mergers,[13] the overwhelming number being in manufacturing and mining. This recent development has given rise to a vigorous antimerger program on the part of the Department of Justice and the Federal Trade Commission,[14] with emphasis on the effect of it on the growth of concentration in industry—this despite the statement quoted above from the Federal Trade Commission. Just how this aggressive policy will influence the growth of big business remains to be seen, but mergers as the basis for the development of industrial giants in a particular line of activity seem to be improbable. On the other hand, as a basis for diversification into nonrelated lines of production, the recent wave may indicate a new line of development. How successful this may be if capital markets should become less exuberant, remains to be seen.[15]

Internal Growth

The second important phase or aspect of the combination movement has been the growth of large business enterprises resulting either from the plowing-back of profits or from the sale of securities to the general public. Tippetts and Livermore[16] state that between 40 and 45 per cent of the largest industrial firms in existence in the United States since 1925 were originally created during the first merger period. If the successor units of the oil and tobacco combines—which were dissolved—are counted only once, then the proportion drops to approximately one third. At the same time, fewer than 10 per cent of the largest companies are the result of mergers since 1905. From this, they conclude that well over half of the largest industrial companies today are the result of growth by reinvestment of their own profits.

[12] Federal Trade Commission, *op. cit.*, pp. 142–43.

[13] *News Summary*, Federal Trade Commission (April 29, 1964).

[14] See Chapter 15, *infra.*

[15] For an analysis of merger movements down to 1954, see R. L. Nelson, *Merger Movements in American Industry* (Princeton: Princeton University Press, 1959). Integration and diversification are analyzed in M. Gort, *Diversification and Integration in American Industry* (Princeton: Princeton University Press, 1962).

[16] C. S. Tippetts and S. Livermore, *Business Organization and Control* (2d ed.; New York: D. Van Nostrand Co., Inc., 1941), pp. 474–75.

In an analysis of the role of mergers in the growth of large industrial firms, Professor Weston found[17] that 63.7 per cent of the growth of 74 large firms from 1900 to 1948 was from internal sources and 26.3 from acquisitions, if the assets of the initial years are classified as external growth. If the assets of the initial years are used as the base from which subsequent growth is measured, then 77.4 per cent resulted from internal growth. He also found that for 31 large firms, including U.S. Steel, Ford, Chrysler, General Motors, and Standard Oil of New Jersey, 46.3 per cent of the growth was from internal financing. He then concluded that acquisitions have been a negligible portion of total growth of most of the firms in census industries now characterized by a high degree of concentration in output. He also stated that internal expansion has accounted for a relatively small degree of present industrial concentration for most firms and most industries, and that the degree of concentration in American industry is the result of the merger movement at the beginning of the century. Subsequent developments have not changed the relative positions of the firms.

Whatever may be the evaluation of the relative roles of mergers and internal growth in shaping the structure of the American economy and the combination movement, it is obvious that internal expansion has played a major part. Moreover, it has been the most important factor in promoting the phenomenal increase in absolute size of the corporate giants since World War I. The current antimerger policy of the government is unlikely to reverse this trend, but it may stimulate mergers of firms in unrelated lines.

Co-operation and Agreements

The third aspect of the combination movement sprang from various arrangements which frequently resulted in restrictions on competition among otherwise independent firms. In the period preceding the great merger movement, various kinds of pools and simple price agreements, frequently known as gentlemen's agreements, were more important in the combination movement than were mergers. As public checks to monopolistic combines appeared, community-of-interest and trade associations, sometimes called "open-price" associations, emerged as new types of combination. Over the last quarter of a century, in particular, the patent pool has played an especially prominent part.

Combinations resulting from various types of agreement are by no means all harmful. In fact, most of them may be quite harmless or even helpful to the competitive process. On the other hand, they may be used very effectively to limit competitive behavior. Whatever their relative effect may be in their influence on competition and monopoly, it seems

[17] J. F. Weston, *The Role of Mergers in the Growth of Large Firms* (Berkeley and Los Angeles: University of California Press, 1953).

to be clear that they could not play a significant part in the absence of big business, which the other two phases of the combination movement have brought about. The various types of combination and their structure will be discussed in the next chapter.

CONCENTRATION IN AMERICAN INDUSTRY

The spectacular growth of big business in the United States in the latter years of the nineteenth century and the first three decades of the twentieth century has given rise to a voluminous amount of literature on the place of big business in the economy, the concentration of industry, and the growth of concentration. In the last quarter of a century, since the appearance of Berle and Mean's work on the role of the corporation in the business structure,[18] a great deal of attention has been given to these questions. Although the amount of factual information that has been gathered is very large, clear-cut answers to the basic questions have not been obtained. So far, we have not developed a satisfactory measurement of the place of the very largest corporations in the economy; we lack information on the historical development of concentration and deconcentration in specific industries; and we have no very satisfactory meaning of concentration or of indices of the degree of concentration.[19] Definite appraisal of the effect of the combination movement on the structure of American industry is therefore lacking at this date.

Big Business in the Economic Structure

One of the obviously striking features of the American economic scene is the presence of a relatively small number of very large corporations that own a considerable portion of the corporate assets in the country and enjoy a large volume of sales. *Fortune* magazine[20] compiles a list of the 500 largest industrial corporations in the United States, from United States census figures. The sales of these corporations for the year 1963 ranged from $16,494,818 million for General Motors Corporation down to $85,984 million for Permanente Cement Company. The assets of the same 500 ranged from $11,996,691 million for Standard Oil Company of New Jersey to $7,317 million for Needham Packing Company. The sales for the year 1962 of the 100 largest nonfinancial corporations in the United States according to the First National City Bank, New York,[21] ranged from $14,852 million for General Motors to

[18]A. A. Berle, Jr., and G. C. Means, *The Modern Corporation and Private Property* (New York: Macmillan Co., 1933).

[19]See M. Adelman, "The Measurement of Industrial Concentration," *Review of Economics and Statistics*, Vol. XXXIII, No. 4 (November, 1951), p. 295; National Bureau of Economic Research, *op. cit.*, papers by G. Rosenbluth, T. Scitovsky, and J. P. Miller, pp. 57–141; E. S. Mason, *Economic Concentration and the Monopoly Problem* (Cambridge, Mass.: Harvard University Press, 1957), chap. 2.

[20]The Fortune Directory, August, 1964.

[21]*Monthly Letter* (June, 1963), p. 66.

$657 million each for Tidewater Oil Company and American Tobacco Company. (See Table 1.) Of the largest 100 corporations, 76 are manufacturing enterprises, 18 are engaged in trade, and 3 each in public utilities and railroads. The combined revenues of the 100 firms aggregated

TABLE 1

Total Revenues, 100 Largest U.S. Nonfinancial Corporations, as Reported for Year 1962

(In Millions of Dollars)

Manufacturing	
Allied Chemical	$ 873
Aluminum Co. of Amer.	950
American Can	1,181
American Cyanamid	665
American Motors	1,065
American Tobacco	657
Anaconda	695
Armco Steel	939
Armour	1,862
Bendix	797
Bethlehem Steel	2,097
Boeing	1,771
Borden	1,056
Borg-Warner	661
Burlington Industries	1,013
Caterpillar Tractor	827
Chrysler	2,390
Cities Service	1,104
Colgate-Palmolive	674
Continental Can	1,186
Continental Oil	872
Corn Products	807
Douglas Aircraft	757
Dow Chemical	946
E. I. duPont	2,601
Eastman Kodak	1,087
Firestone	1,285
Ford Motor	8,099
General Dynamics	1,901
General Electric	4,843
General Foods	1,216
General Motors	14,852
Gen. Tel. & Electronics	1,328
General Tire	968
B. F. Goodrich	816
Goodyear	1,600
Gulf Oil	2,869
Inland Steel	768
Intl. Business Machines	1,977
International Harvester	1,853
International Paper	1,107
Intl. Tel. & Tel.	1,111
Jones & Laughlin Steel	795
Lockheed Aircraft	1,755
Martin-Marietta	1,202
Minn. Mining & Mfg.	692
Monsanto Chemical	1,075
National Dairy	1,827
National Steel	753
North Amer. Aviation	1,635
Olin Mathieson Chem.	744
Phillips Petroleum	1,261
Pittsburgh Plate Glass	665
Manufacturing (cont'd.)	
Procter & Gamble	$1,632
Radio Corp. of America	1,752
Ralston Purina	686
Republic Steel	1,066
R. J. Reynolds Tobacco	901
Shell Oil	1,970
Sinclair Oil	1,198
Socony Mobil Oil	4,014
Sperry Rand	1,187*
Standard Oil of Calif.	2,313
Standard Oil (Ind.)	2,177
Standard Oil (N. J.)	9,786
Sun Oil	804
Swift	2,498
Texaco	3,465
Tidewater Oil	657
Union Carbide	1,658
United Aircraft	1,166
U. S. Rubber	1,010
U. S. Steel	3,501
Western Electric	2,776
Westinghouse Electric	1,979
Wilson	712
Trade	
Acme Markets	1,082
Allied Stores	771
Anderson, Clayton	751
Federated Dept. Stores	897
First National Stores	711*
Food Fair	925†
W. T. Grant	687
Great A. & P. Tea	5,312
Kroger	1,948
McKesson & Robbins	756
May's Dept. Stores	711
Montgomery Ward	1,425
National Tea	979
J. C. Penney	1,704
Safeway Stores	2,510
Sears, Roebuck	4,642
Winn-Dixie Stores	778
F. W. Woolworth	1,139
Public Utilities	
American Tel. & Tel.	9,148
Con. Edison Co. of N.Y.	725
Pacific Gas & Electric	732
Railroads	
New York Central	720
Pennsylvania	906
Southern Pacific	847

* Fiscal year ending March 31, 1962.

† Fiscal year ending April 30, 1962.

SOURCE: First National City Bank of New York, *Monthly News Letter* (June, 1963).

$178.2 billion, while their total assets amounted to $168.8 billion, or an average of $26,000 investment for each employee (as contrasted to $16,000 in 1955). The total number of persons employed by them was some 6.5 million. Fifty-eight of the companies had sales of over $1 billion, in contrast to only 34 in 1955. Forty-nine of these were in the manufacturing group, eight in trade, and one in public utilities. *Fortune's* corresponding list for 1963 shows 49 industrials, 10 in trade, and one public utility for a total of 60 firms. (In 1954, *Fortune* listed only 21 industrials with sales over $1 billion.)

Concentration in Industry

The term "concentration in industry" is one that has a very indefinite meaning. It may refer to the ownership or control of business enterprise by a relatively limited number of people, or it may refer to the position of a limited number of firms in the economy. Even in the latter sense, the meaning is still indefinite, for the gauge may be sales, assets, or employment. These by no means lead to the same rankings, grouping, or even conclusions. Relatively large sales may be associated with relatively small investment or employment, or vice versa. *Fortune's* list of the 500 largest industrial corporations for 1963 shows sales ranging from $16,494,818 thousand for General Motors to $85,984 thousand for Permanente Cement; assets from $11,996,691 thousand for Standard Oil of New Jersey to $7,317 thousand for Needham Packing Company; and employment from 640,073 for General Motors to 475 for Needham Packing Company. In the first 200 of the list, ranked in terms of sales, Rexall Drug and Chemical was at the bottom for sales, $280,511 thousand; Hygrade Food Products, which ranked 132 in sales, had assets of only $56,042 thousand; and Central Soya Company ranking 160 in sales employed only 3,881 persons. The smallest number of employees for any of the 500 was Needham Packing with 475.

The National Resources Committee, bringing up to date the pioneering study of Berle and Means on concentration, found that, in 1933, the 200 largest nonfinancial corporations in this country controlled 60 per cent of the physical assets of all the nonfinancial corporations, about 48 per cent of the industrial wealth of the country, and 20 per cent of the total national wealth.[22] The Twentieth Century Fund, Inc., found that 594 corporations, approximately one tenth of 1 per cent of the corporations in the United States, each with assets of over $50 million, owned more than half of the total assets of all business corporations, produced 18.4 per cent of the total national income, and accounted for 20 per cent of the national income created by profit-seeking business.[23] Finally, it may

[22]National Resources Committee, *The Structure of the American Economy* (Washington, D.C.: U.S. Government Printing Office, 1939), pp. 104–6.

[23]Twentieth Century Fund, Inc., *Big Business: Its Growth and Its Place* (New York, 1937), pp. 96–99.

TABLE 2

Total Assets, 100 Largest Manufacturing Corporations as Reported in 1919, 1948 and 1963

(Millions of Dollars)

	1919	1948	1963		1919	1948	1963		1919	1948	1963
Allied Chemical	60	339	1,069	Ford Motor	333	1,149	5,949	Pittsburgh Plate Glass		227	768
Allis-Chalmers Mfg.	61	254	522	General Amer. Transp.		148	484	Prairie Oil and Gas	130		
Aluminum Co. of Amer.	133	504	1,464	General Dynamics			626	Procter and Gamble	94	316	1,158
American Agric. Chem.	111			General Electric	277	1,177	3,015	Pullman	171	195	
American Can	135	276	952	General Foods		222	725	Pure Oil	132	271	680
American Car & Foundry	140	190		General Motors	447	2,958	10,785	Quaker Oats	53		
American Cotton Oil	63			General Tire & Rubber			557	Radio Corp. of America		248	1,129
American Cyanamid		212	739	Georgia-Pacific			565	Republic Steel	126	489	1,165
American Linseed	55			B.F. Goodrich	176	267	658	Reynolds Metals			1,028
American Locomotive	93			Goodyear Tire and Rub.	113	425	1,290	R.J. Reynolds Tobacco	103	531	1,038
American Rad. & Std. San.		171		W.R. Grace			723	Richfield Oil		147	470
American Shipbuilding	153			Gulf Oil	143	1,191	4,549	St. Regis Paper		158	604
American Smelt & Ref.	215	290		Hearst Cons. Publ.		161		Schenley Industries		342	
American Sugar Ref.	147			Inland Steel	59	293	888	Shell Oil		641	2,139
American Tobacco	206	687	822	Intl. Business Machines		242	2,374	Sinclair Oil	232	710	1,619
American Viscose		227		Intl. Harvester	267	672	1,561	Singer	140	209	769
American Woolen	133			Intl. Paper	88	323	1,069	Skelly Oil		169	
Anaconda	237	660	1,261	Intl. Tel. & Tel.			1,469	Socony Mobil Oil	300	1,443	4,660
Armco Steel		316	1,023	Jones & Laughlin Steel	120	379	881	Sperry Rand			889
Armour	491	448	455	Kaiser Alum. & Chem.			847	Standard Oil of Calif.	174	1,075	3,545
Associated Oil	69			Kennecott Copper	136	575	847	Standard Oil (Ind.)	155	1,500	3,207
Atlantic Refining	95	383	937	Kimberly-Clark			515	Standard Oil (N.J.)	853	3,526	11,997
Baldwin Locomotive	65			Lackawanna Steel	95			Standard Oil (Ohio)		237	469
Bethlehem Steel	357	1,029	2,344	Libby McNeill & Libby	68			Steel & Tube Co. of Amer.	92		
Boeing			690	Liggett & Myers Tob.	151	425		J.P. Stevens		164	
Borden	55	242	552	Lockheed Aircraft			546	Studebaker	88		
Borg-Warner		151	497	Long-Bell Lumber	56			Submarine Boat	65		
Brunswick			698	P. Lorillard	88			Sun Oil		279	888
Burlington Industries		177	697	Magnolia Petroleum	182			Sunray DX Oil			615
Caterpillar Tractor		147	741	Marathon Oil	82	203	643	Swift	490	523	610
Celanese Corp. of Amer.		257	551	Martin Marietta			542	Texaco	226	1,277	4,455
Central Leather	147			Midvale Steel & Ord.	280			Tidewater Oil	60	288	981
Chrysler	92	541	2,124	Midwest Refining	73			Transcontinental Oil	198		
Cities Service		992	1,587	Minneapolis-Honeywell			468	Union Carbide	200	723	1,832
Coca-Cola		205	483	Minn. Mining and Mfg.			653	Union Oil Co. of Cal.	90	298	853
Colorado Fuel & Iron	83			Monsanto Chemical		227	1,416	United Aircraft		147	574
Continental Can		222	812	Morris and Co.	114			United Fruit	148	450	
Continental Oil		262	1,463	Philip Morris		156		United Shoe Machinery	79		
Corn Products	138		544	Nash-Kelvinator		154		United States Gypsum		151	
Cosden	53			National Biscuit	78	162		U.S. Ind. Alcohol	55		
Crane	65	142		Natl. Cash Register			463	U.S. Smelting, Ref. & Min.	80		
Crown Zellerbach		167	645	National Dairy Prod.		318	797	United States Rubber	320	349	716
Crucible Steel	123			National Distillers		215	633	United States Steel	2,366	2,535	5,139
Cuba Cane Sugar	110			National Lead	88	183		Vacuum Oil	80		
Cuban-American Sugar	54			National Steel		330	940	Virginia-Carolina Chem.	121		
Cudahy Packing	92			New York Shipbuilding	118			Walker-Gooderham & Worts		154	
Curtiss-Wright		156		North Amer. Aviation			672	Western Electric	108	649	1,981
Deere	84	258	689	Olin Mathieson Chem.			916	Westinghouse Electric	160	694	1,543
Dist. Corp.-Seagrams		346	673	Owens-Illinois Glass		180	553	Weyerhaeuser		210	647
Dow Chemical		294	1,069	Packard Motor Car	63			Wheeling Steel		172	
E.I. duPont de Nemours	241	1,189	2,970	Pan-American Pet. & Transp.	82			Willys	58		
Eastman Kodak	89	412	1,171	Phelps Dodge	247	274	455	Willys-Overland	129		
FMC Corp.			522	Phillips Petroleum		579	1,760	Wilson	127	154	
Firestone Tire & Rub.	74	344	1,045	Pierce Oil	60			Youngstown Sh. & Tube	109	312	809
Fisk Rubber	53										

Note: In the few cases where companies did not publish balance sheets for 1919, we used information obtained directly from the companies, estimates by A.D.H. Kaplan of Brookings Institution or 1920-21 financial data. Fiscal years ending nearest to December 31 were used for companies not on a calendar year basis. Companies are indicated by their names at the time of latest appearance on list; three companies on the 1963 list have changed names: Chrysler (Maxwell), Allied (General) Chemical and Marathon (Ohio) Oil. Several old companies have acquired new names since dropping off the list—American Car and Foundry (ACF Industries), American Locomotive (Alco Products), Baldwin Locomotive (Baldwin-Lima-Hamilton), Cuban-American (North American) Sugar and Nash-Kelvinator (American Motors). The remaining companies either retain comparable names or have since merged with other companies, except for Central Leather. Cosden on the 1919 list became Mid-Continent Oil in 1925 and merged with Sunray DX in 1955; Willys Corporation was the predecessor of Electric Auto-lite which merged with Mergenthaler Linotype in 1963 to form Eltra Corp.; Willys-Overland was acquired by Kaiser Industries in 1953; Morris and Company was a meatpacker which merged with Armour in 1923. Total assets exclude reported depreciation reserves.

SOURCE: First National City Bank of New York, *Monthly News Letter* (August, 1964).

be noted that 92.3 per cent of the motor vehicle output was produced by 4 companies in 1948; 61.9 per cent of ingot steel and steel castings, by 4 companies; 81 per cent of the cigarettes, by 5 companies; all of the aluminum, by 3 companies; 84 per cent of rubber tires and tubes, by 4 companies; 83 per cent of tin cans and other tinware, by 4 companies; 47 per cent of cement, by 6 companies; 40 per cent of electrical machinery and equipment, by 2 companies; and 31.7 per cent of meat packing (wholesale), by 4 companies.[24]

Growth of Concentration

The combination movement in the United States, particularly with regard to mergers and internal growth, has provoked much discussion on the question of whether concentration is increasing. Berle and Means, after examining the growth of the 200 largest nonfinancial corporations from 1909 to 1929, concluded that on the basis of gross assets, the large corporations appeared to have been growing two to three times as fast as other nonfinancial corporations; and this conclusion was supported by the figures of corporate income. The industrial wealth controlled by the large corporations had been increasing at a rate even faster than the proportion of corporate wealth controlled by them, and the proportion of national wealth controlled by them had been increasing at a rapid rate. Berle and Means estimated that it would take only 40 years at the 1909–29 rates, or only 30 years at the 1924–29 rates, for all corporate activity and practically all industrial activity to be absorbed by 200 giant companies.[25]

That the rates of growth calculated by Berle and Means have not continued is quite apparent from current evidence. The question remains, however, whether there has been a trend toward concentration in the last quarter of a century, even though the rate may have slackened appreciably. The most careful study of this aspect of the problem that has been made is that of Professor Adelman. He concluded that there was not only no evidence of a trend in concentration in enterprise in the last quarter of a century; there was no evidence of a trend in the American economy since the beginning of the century. There was a rapid growth of concentration from 1870 to 1903, and the latter date seems to have marked the end of the trend. In the manufacturing segment of the economy, which is the key to the story since 1903, no trend appears discernible since the beginning of the century. In light of all the difficulties of handling the data, Adelman concludes: "The odds are better than even that there has actually been some decline in concentration. It is a good bet that there has at least been no actual increase; and the odds do seem high against any substantial increase."[26]

[24]Weston, *op. cit.*, pp. 39–41.

[25]Berle and Means, *op. cit.*, pp. 40–41.

[26]M. Adelman, *op. cit.*, pp. 292–93. These observations seem to be confirmed by A. D. H. Kaplan, *Big Enterprise in a Competitive System* (Washington, D.C.: Brookings

One final point may be noted with regard to concentration and the trend of concentration. The presence of the industrial giant is not necessarily an indication of a high degree of concentration in any particular line of production. Some industries—such as electrical equipment, steel production, aluminum production, automobile manufacture, and agricultural equipment—are characterized by a high degree of concentration in the hands of a very few firms; but the oil and airplane-manufacture industries have only a moderate degree of concentration, despite the presence of very large companies in each. In other lines, such as textiles, printing and publishing, clothing, and retail trade, there is little that can be described as concentration, even though there are many firms in each which operate on a national scale. Thus, there appears to be no simple picture by which one can characterize concentration in American industry.

Concentration and Deconcentration

A study for the Temporary National Economic Committee of the history of concentration of output in seven selected industries[27] concluded that industrial evolution never moves in even and steady stages and, furthermore, that the various industries do not follow any single pattern. The International Harvester Company, as shown by the study, started out with almost a complete monopoly in the manufacture of agricultural implements. In 1902, this firm controlled 85 per cent of the output of harvesting machines; this had dropped to 80 per cent by 1911 and to 64 per cent by 1918. The company increased its share of the national total of most agricultural implements from 1918 to 1929 and then lost ground severely down to 1936. The industry has always had a high degree of concentration, the maximum of which was reached in 1902; but since that time, there has been a considerable decline in the degree of leadership of the International Harvester Company.

Institution, 1954). In a detailed analysis of the Report of the Subcommittee on Antitrust and Monopoly of the United States Senate, Betty Bock concludes "the present Senate subcommittee data appear to show that where there has been large-scale expansion, there has not in general been any serious barrier to entry of new companies; on the other hand, a high proportion of the industries that had major losses in companies and major gains in concentration were industries where shipments were falling off or growing only moderately—or where new products were being explored." Betty Bock, *Concentration Patterns in Manufacturing* (New York: National Industrial Conference Board, 1959), Studies in Business Economics, No. 65, p. 54. For the statistics, see: *Concentration Ratios on Manufacturing Industry*, Report of the Bureau of the Census for the Subcommittee on Antitrust and Monopoly of the Committee on the Judiciary, United States Senate (Washington, D.C.: U.S. Government Printing Office, 1958), 87th Cong., 2d. sess., Parts I and II; and *Concentration in American Industry*, Report of the Subcommittee on Antitrust and Monopoly of the Committee on the Judiciary United States Senate, S.Res. 57 (Washington, D.C.: U.S. Government Printing Office, 1957), 85th Cong., 1st sess.; *Mergers and Superconcentration*, Staff Report of the Committee on Small Business, House of Representatives, 87th Cong. (Washington, D.C.: U.S. Government Printing Office, 1962).

[27]Temporary National Economic Committee, Monograph No. 27, pp. 237–64.

In the automobile industry, the study found that during a period of more than four decades, the industry had shown steadily increasing concentration among the leading producers. After 1925, the changes that occurred were principally in the proportions produced by the "Big Three,"[28] although there was some increase in concentration up to 1935. The most significant alteration the study concluded, was the astonishing decline in the proportion of Ford's production.

In 1925, the new-car registrations by Ford, General Motors, and Chrysler, respectively, were 42.8 per cent, 20 per cent, and 9.1 per cent of the total for the industry, for an aggregate for the 3 companies of 71.9 per cent. By 1930, this aggregate for the 3 companies had increased to 83.3 per cent; in 1935, it was 91.5 per cent; and in 1938, 90.3 per cent. By that year, the proportions of the "Big Three" had changed to 20.5 per cent for Ford, 44.8 per cent for General Motors, and 25 per cent for Chrysler.[29] Further concentration in the hands of these same companies has taken place in recent years, as evidenced by their share of total output for the years 1961 and 1962. The percentage of total passenger cars manufactured in the United States by the "Big Three" was 49.6 and 54.5, respectively, for General Motors; 24.4 and 27 for Ford; and 9.3 and 10.3 for Chrysler. American Motors, the last remaining producer of passenger cars in the United States in 1964, produced 5.3 per cent of the total in 1961 and 6.7 per cent in 1962.[30] Ford has improved its relative position since 1938 and so has General Motors. There seems to be no trend in the relative positions, however, since 1956.

The copper industry showed a high degree of concentration by 1890, when 4 companies held about 75 per cent of the products. From then until the twenties, the concentration declined; but in recent years, it has reached new high levels, exceeding 80 per cent in the hands of the 4 producers. In contrast, a century's record for the cotton textiles shows no period of appreciable concentration. Changes have taken place among the leaders, but the leading 4 have seldom exceeded 10 per cent of the industry's total.

Concentration took place steadily in iron and steel, with the United States Steel Corporation obtaining an overwhelming position by 1901. At that time, it controlled 33 per cent of blast furnace capacity. The 4 largest companies held a total of 44 per cent. The United States Steel Corporation also had 47 per cent of the rolling mill capacity, and the 4 largest companies had 61 per cent. United States Steel's proportion of steel ingot capacity reached its peak in 1908, when it included more than 50 per cent of the industry. It dropped to 40.1 per cent in 1920 and declined to 35.5 per cent in 1938.[31] In the meantime, the next 3 companies, which totaled

[28]That is, Ford, General Motors, and Chrysler.

[29]Temporary National Economic Committee, Monograph No. 27, p. 244.

[30]Computed from figures in Automobile Manufacturers Association, *Automobile Facts and Figures* (43rd ed.; Washington, D.C., 1963).

[31]It is now approximately 33 per cent of the total.

only 11.9 per cent in 1908, increased to 14.4 per cent in 1920, 26.7 per cent in 1930, and 28.5 per cent in 1938.

A more striking illustration of decline in control is provided by the petroleum industry, which was dominated by the Standard Oil Company down to 1906, at which time it controlled 85–90 per cent of the total refined products. By 1926, 11 of the old Standard companies and their affiliates marketed only 44.8 per cent of the total production. The Temporary National Economic Committee study concluded that the 5 largest companies lost position, while the second 5 gained slightly, and the rest of the industry gained even more. All of this was in marked contrast to the dominance attained by the Standard Oil Company prior to 1911.

A somewhat similar situation was found in the rayon industry, which led the authors of the study to conclude: "If this industry responds in the fashion as similarly rapid growing industries have done, whose history in America is older than this recent one, the leaders will continue to receive a smaller share of the market as new competitors are brought into the field by promise of profit now being enjoyed by a popular-product industry."[32]

The field of transportation offers a striking illustration of this generalization. Inland transport, at the beginning of the century, could conveniently be classified as an industry. Today, it is a group of industries, with highly divergent economic characteristics. Even as late as 1920, railroads hauled approximately 84 per cent of the ton-mileage of intercity freight traffic and provided 89 per cent of the intercity passenger-miles. Today, with the enormous increase in total transport, the railroads are hauling about 43 per cent more of freight ton-mileage, but their relative position has declined to 43 per cent of the total intercity freight traffic. In passenger-mileage, their position has declined in absolute terms as well as relative; they now supply a mere 2.3 per cent of intercity passenger movement. There is probably no more decisive illustration of deconcentration than has taken place in transport during this century.[33]

RESULTS OF THE COMBINATION MOVEMENT

Transformation of the Industrial Structure

The outstanding result of the various aspects of the combination movement has been the transformation of the industrial structure of the United States. During the last seventy-five years, the country has changed from one that was primarily agricultural and rural into one that is now

[32]Temporary National Economic Committee, Monograph No. 27, p. 264.

[33]See D. F. Pegrum, "Investment in the Railroad and Other Transportation Industries under Regulation," *American Economic Review*, Vol. XLVII, No. 2 (May, 1957), pp. 416–29. A more extended treatment of the significance of these developments is given in Part V, "The Regulation of Transportation and Public Utilities." Transportation is an inviting area for the study of concentration because of its complexity and also because the nation's transportation bill constitutes about 20 per cent of the gross national product.

dominantly industrial and urban. The mechanization of industry has led to the predominance of large-scale production, especially in such types of business as rail, air, and pipe-line transportation; public utilities; heavy industries, like steel; petroleum and copper; the electrochemical and electrometallurgical industries; automobile production; machinery; and, to a certain extent, even retail marketing.

Integration of Industry

Integration, both vertical and horizontal, has been aided not only by the technical processes of production but also by the use of the corporate device. The ease with which the corporation can be adapted to almost any set of circumstances not only has facilitated integration of closely knit types of business but also has made it possible to spread out into allied products and, on occasion, even to tie together enterprises that have no technical relationship to each other. This has resulted not only in the expansion to national scope of industries producing standardized products but also in an increase of the urge to standardization, as the result of the necessity of creating products that can compete in the national market. It has also led to concentration of production in a few concerns in many different lines of industry. Thus, while concentration and integration emerged on the one hand, competition, specialization, and differentiation of products have expanded on the other. This has afforded the consuming public a variety of choice and an opportunity to exercise preference that was not only not possible prior to these industrial developments but also is greater than that which is available anywhere else in the world.

Growth of National Markets

It was the combination movement that made possible the development of business in the United States on a national scale. In the first instance, this was the result of improvements in transportation, which expanded markets and, at the same time engendered the concentration of industry in areas and centers where resources were most readily available. With the opening-up of nationwide markets, aggressive marketing and extensive advertising became characteristically American. Today, literally hundreds of products are household names all over the nation, and one is able to buy a vast array of the same products in practically every city in the country. The development of the radio and television has added to this intensive penetration of all markets, so that even tooth paste, shaving cream, and aspirin tablets have a national reputation.

All these changes have literally eliminated the local economy at least as a more or less self-contained entity. This is not to say that there is not a great deal of local production and regional specialization but rather that local markets and production are so affected by the competition of goods produced in other regions that competition has become national, rather than local, in scope. The resulting interrelation of markets throughout the entire country has brought about a tremendous reduction in local differences and has led to a rather thoroughgoing integration of the whole national economy.

Growth of the Corporate Giant

The continued growth in size and scope of many firms has accompanied this development. In 1901, the United States Steel Corporation was the first billion-dollar enterprise in this country; in 1963 there were sixty-eight such concerns, not counting financial enterprises. Twenty-seven of these are in railroads and public utilities, but railroad expansion seems to be at an end.[34] It seems to be safe to say that the number of giant enterprises will increase in the future, and many of them will possibly be larger than any we now have. Although the tremendous importance of business giants in the economy of the nation must be recognized, it should be remembered that the products of a large number of them are marketed on a national scale. A few firms may dominate a particular line of industry, but the fact that they compete in all of the markets of the country may result in much more competition than if industry were smaller and confirmed to purely local markets. Thus, for example, if automobiles and radios were produced by independent concerns in all of the various cities in the United States, it is highly improbable that the competition in any of those centers would be nearly as keen as it is today, and there is little doubt that the consumer would be much worse off. The scale of operations compatible with such a situation not only would result in higher prices but also would prevent intermarket competition. Marketing on a national basis necessitates huge size in many lines of production, but it is also the only way in which effective competition is possible in many fields of business.

Changes in Price Competition

Another result of the combination movement has been fundamental changes in price competition and the price structure. Competition has become more complex than it was prior to 1870; and what is more, price is not the only aspect of competition in present-day industry. Price making has become an increasingly intricate process, and price resulting from the simple and direct operation of the market alone is no longer characteristic of the price structure. The production of many varieties of products by single enterprises, the need for long-range production planning, large fixed investment, etc., have all led to the emergence of price policies. This is not an especially new attribute of the marketing of manufactured goods, but the rise in importance of such goods in the whole economy

[34]However, railroad consolidation now in progress will probably increase the number of billion-dollar enterprises in this area.

has meant that price making by industrial enterprises has assumed a far greater significance than it had before the rise of the combination movement.

Price Stabilization

Along with this, there has developed a rather persistent endeavor to stabilize the prices of particular commodities or services. Part of this is the result of monopolistic tendencies and the desire to avoid the effects of disastrous price wars; part is the consequence of the advantage of relatively long-range price stability, especially for both sellers and buyers in heavy industries, because of the need for industrial planning; and a good deal of it, in recent years, has also arisen from the extremely uncertain economic conditions prevailing throughout the world. The general desire to promote economic stability has had a tendency to focus attention on the stabilization of particular prices, in the belief that, if the latter could be achieved, a major step toward general economic stability would result. This has led not only to widespread business attempts at price stabilization but to government policy aimed in the same direction.

The combination movement, by elevating price policies to a role of primary importance, has played a significant part in fostering the belief that price stability is a prime requisite for industrial stability. The fundamental change which has occurred in the process of price making has engendered rather strenuous resistance to price adaptation. This resistance, however, is by no means confined to industry. Labor today vigorously resists wage reductions, and government has stepped into the picture in an endeavor to prevent drastic price changes. Not all of this, however, can be attributed to the growth of modern industry; perhaps the major role must be ascribed to the dislocation of world markets and the extreme uncertainties which have beset all aspects of economic life as the result of world disorder and conflict since 1914.[35]

Growth of Federal Regulation

All of these developments have had their repercussions on the problem of public regulation. In the first place, the problem of control has risen to national importance, in contrast to the almost total absence of federal implications until after 1870. From what was assumed to be a comparatively elementary problem of forbidding restraint of trade, monopoly, or simple methods of unfair competition, the regulation of business has evolved into the complex one of safeguarding the public interest against abuses or the exercise of undue discretion in the administration of price policies by private industry, of limiting the growth of monopoly

[35]For an extended discussion with anything but unanimity in point of view, see *Administered Prices: A Compendium on Public Policy*, Subcommittee on Antitrust and Monopoly of the Committee on the Judiciary, United States Senate, 88th Cong. 1st sess. S.Res. 56 (Washington, D.C.: U.S. Government Printing Office, 1963.)

by concerted action, of curbing the use of monopoly powers in industries where there is also a great deal of competition, and of developing new concepts of unfair methods of competition under conditions which change so rapidly that old methods are quickly rendered obsolete.

The complexity of these phases of the problem has been intensified by other aspects arising from the development of the corporate device. The ramifications and unusual flexibility of this type of business organization have created the necessity of finding means for limiting its scope that were not comprehended as late as 1890. The concentration of a great deal of wealth in the hands of corporations has risen to a problem of major proportions; and the wide dispersion of stock ownership, the opportunity in some instances for a few individuals to exercise control with a comparatively small investment, and the possibilities of exploitation by insiders have resulted in the demand for discovering ways of enforcing responsibility on directors and corporate executive commensurate with the powers they possess. Officials of large industrial enterprises have now become public servants in a way not heretofore recognized. Public regulation has thus become a more complicated task because of the widespread interrelationships in the economic structure and because of the great increase in the interdependence of the activities of the federal and state governments. This is true whether one thinks in terms of more reliance on competition, or more comprehensive regulation by government.

Combinations and Private Enterprise

The rapidity and magnitude of the developments arising from the industrialization of the nation have induced such a transformation in the problems and methods of control as to raise grave doubt of our ability to preserve private industry and the competitive structure. Many feel that the growth of industrialism and the resulting combination movement clearly denote the decline of capitalism and the system of private enterprise. They regard their demise and replacement by a fascist, communist, or socialist order as well-nigh a foregone conclusion.

It can scarcely be denied that the capitalistic system is facing a severe task of reconstruction or at least adjustment to a new environment. It is also evident that other economic orders are more widespread throughout the world. Much of the world has been experiencing violent political transformation for forty years, and the consequence has been the obliteration of old political and economic orders. But revolutionary social upheavals always engender extreme developments and the question may legitimately be raised whether these extremes have in them the necessary elements for permanence. The new foundations have not yet been sufficiently delineated to warrant the conclusion that their permanent outlines are yet discernible. Moreover, many recent developments have resulted in the very dominance of social life by the state that was one of the prime causes of the revolutions in the first place. Presumably, if the original factors which induced the present era of conflict are to be eliminated, a considerable retrenchment of the authority of the state will have to ensue.

When the statement is made that capitalism is declining, the point of reference is usually capitalism as it prevailed in the nineteenth century under *laissez faire* as it existed, or was interpreted, at that time. If such is the point of view, then there is little use in arguing. Capitalism, like other social and political institutions, is in a constant process of change. The crucial question is whether the change is leading to more and more management and direction of economic life by the state; certainly, this has been the tendency since 1914. But this has been a war period and generalizations from it are hazardous to make. Taking the longer-run point of view, the trend seems to have been the reverse, with the state taking less of a direct part in the management of economic affairs. The rules governing economic activity have changed and, in many respects, multiplied. But to say they have multiplied relative to the increasing magnitude and importance of economic life is another matter. Laws relating to human conduct and political life have multiplied enormously, too; yet, political freedom in the United States is probably greater than at any previous time.

Chapter 6 TYPES OF COMBINATIONS

Combinations in the United States have taken on a variety of different forms. They may be conveniently grouped, however, into two main types: (1) those that arise from integration under single ownership or control and (2) those that are the result of some form of agreement or understanding among otherwise independent concerns.

INTEGRATED COMBINATIONS

The Trustee Device

Most of the present-day corporate giants have emerged from the combining of previously independent enterprises under single ownership. In the earlier stages of the combination movement, the trustee device was the commonest method employed to bring about integration. It was used solely, however, as a means of effecting monopoly in a particular field. The example was set by the Standard Oil Company of Ohio, which established a trust in 1879. To this trust, which was administered by nine trustees, the stocks of competing oil companies, which controlled some 90 per cent of the refining capacity of the country, were transferred in return for trust certificates. The success of the Standard Oil trust invited imitation; and in the course of the next ten years, a large number of other combinations were formed on the same basis.[1]

This method of organizing combinations came to an early end as the result of unfavorable court decisions. The sugar trust was dissolved by the decision in *New York* v. *North River Sugar Refining Company* (1890).[2] The New York Court of Appeals held that the trust was in substance and effect a partnership of twenty corporations, and that it was a violation of law for a corporation to enter into a partnership. The Court ordered the forfeiture of the charter and the liquidation of the corporation. This was a common-law decision.

The Standard Oil trust was dissolved by a decision of the Supreme Court of Ohio in *State* v. *Standard Oil Company* (1892).[3] The Court held that the entry into the trust by the corporation was an *ultra vires* action

[1]See Chapter 5, *supra;* and Eliot Jones, *The Trust Problem in the United States* (New York: Macmillan Co., 1921), chap. iii.

[2]121 N.Y. 582 (1890).

[3]49 Ohio 137 (1892).

and that the objective of creating a monopoly was contrary to the policy of the state of Ohio. The Standard Oil Company was ordered to terminate its connections with the trust. This was also a common-law decision.

A more subtle use of the trustee device appeared in the form of the Massachusetts trust, which became a particularly effective arrangement for effecting combination in the public utility field. Used in this way, it became one of the most notorious illustrations of the holding company, which is discussed below.

Consolidation or Outright Fusion

Methods. Combination or integration may also be achieved through a single corporation which acquires the plants and other properties of the firms which are to be united. This may take place in various ways. One method is to consolidate or merge the independent enterprises into one corporation, which may be one of those participating in the consolidation, or it may be a new one set up for the purpose of taking over all the existing ones. Whichever procedure is used, there is a union in one corporate body of two or more existing corporations. A second method is for one corporation to purchase the property of other enterprises. This does not terminate the existence of the selling corporations. Whether the latter disburse the proceeds to their stockholders and go out of existence or merely go out of that line of activity is for the selling corporations to decide. A third method is for one corporation to acquire the stock of another corporation and then proceed through its ownership of that stock to obtain the assets of the corporation over which it has secured control.

Legal Problems. These methods of bringing property previously owned by independent corporations into the hands of a single corporation involve certain legal problems. The first method requires legislative approval; and if the corporations have received charters from different jurisdictions, approval of each jurisdiction is necessary. In addition, the consent of at least a majority of the stockholders is necessary. Under the second method, sanction by the majority of the stockholders is usually adequate, although unanimous consent may have to be obtained under certain circumstances. The third method may be achieved by the acquiring corporation buying up all of the stock of those to be acquired, or by exchanging its stock for that of the others. If the buying corporation acquires all of the stock of the others, it can then proceed to liquidate the acquired enterprises; if it does not possess all of the stock, it must receive unanimous consent of the stockholders to bring about the liquidation.

In the early days of the combination movement, the legal problems of outright fusion constituted a serious obstacle. The amendment by the state of New Jersey of its corporation laws, especially in 1889, initiated the movement toward a general relaxation of corporate legislation. In that year, New Jersey authorized the directors of any company that had been incorporated under the act of 1875 to purchase the stock of companies which owned mining, manufacturing, or producing materials, and to issue stock in payment thereof. The law was further extended in 1893 by a provision which allowed any corporation to acquire the stock of any other corporation and to exercise all the rights of ownership in that stock. Other states soon followed suit and also passed general corporation laws permitting consolidations for lawful purposes. In addition, charter provisions were relaxed, so that consolidation became comparatively easy to accomplish.

Importance. As a result of this legislation, the third method of achieving consolidation was the one that was generally adopted down to 1900. In fact, this was the commonest form of "trust" organization down to that year,[4] the most notable exception to this being Standard Oil of New Jersey, which was organized as a pure holding company in 1899; it did not dissolve the acquired corporations. This third method of consolidation may result in long-delayed action in bringing about outright fusion; in other words, outright fusion does not have to take place at the time the stock is acquired. Thus, both the United States Steel Corporation and General Motors originated as pure holding companies, but have now become almost outright consolidations by the dissolution of the subsidiary corporations. For example, Chevrolet, Oldsmobile, Buick, and Cadillac are now divisions of General Motors, not subsidiary corporations; while Columbia Steel, Consolidated Western Steel, and so forth are divisions of United States Steel.[5] The reasons for this change are both legal and administrative.

The Holding Company

The third means by which integrated combination may be achieved is the holding company.

The Nature of the Holding Company. In the broadest sense, "holding company" may be defined as any form of business organization which is able to control or materially influence the management of one or more other corporations by virtue of ownership of voting stock in the other corporation or corporations.[6] The most usual form, however, is a corporation and even where this is not the case, the corporate device plays the principal role in the acquisition of control.

Structurally, the holding company is a convenient and flexible adaptation of any of the types of business organization which used the associ-

[4]Jones, *op. cit.*, p. 44.

[5]These companies have subsidiaries, however, for activities not related to the main product, as well as for operations in other countries. The detail for these and other companies can be found in *Moody's Industrial Manual* issued annually.

[6]For a discussion of the problems relating to the definition of a holding company, see J. C. Bonbright and G. C. Means, *The Holding Company* (New York: McGraw-Hill Book Co., Inc., 1932), pp. 7–10.

ation idea; hence, it could be a joint-stock association, a Massachusetts trust, or a corporation. From the standpoint of the law, it may be any form which the law designates as a holding company; and this may even embrace a single individual proprietorship.[7] In actual practice, the most common medium used by the holding company is the corporation, probably because of the ease with which satisfactory corporate charters can be obtained, and the insulation from responsibility and liability which they afford. The corporate form also offers more adaptability and flexibility for many purposes than do the others, even where charter privileges are circumscribed and carefully supervised. Indeed, despite the variations in the type of organization used, it is probable that the holding company would not exist apart from the corporation.

Holding companies may be classified in a number of different ways. From the standpoint of their function, they fall into two categories. The "pure" holding company is one which is set up solely for the purpose of owning the controlling interest in other companies, known as "subsidiaries." It does not engage directly in the operations of any of the controlled properties. Thus, it is strictly an ownership device. The "parent" holding company or "parent company" is one which carries on operations of its own in addition to owning or controlling other companies. For many purposes, it is also convenient to classify holding companies according to the field in which they operate. The "public utility" holding company is one which is established for the purpose of combining public utility properties under common ownership. Similarly, railroads, banks, and industrial holding companies derive their names from their respective spheres of activity. What is sometimes called the "finance company" is an enterprise which exercises control over companies in various fields of endeavor for the purposes of profiting from their operation, guiding consolidations, and perhaps stimulating their managerial efficiency.

The holding company achieves control through the ownership of a percentage of the voting stock of other companies. Because of the widespread dispersion of stock ownership in a large number of the big corporations, effective controls may be obtained by owning less than 50 per cent of the voting stock of subsidiaries. This, of itself, makes it possible to direct the affairs of subordinate enterprises through an investment which is small as compared with the total assets controlled.

Means of Effecting Control. The ease with which concentration may be achieved is enhanced by the issuance of nonvoting securities and pyramiding. Control of a single enterprise by investment in a relatively small amount of the total capital may be accomplished by the issuance of a considerable proportion of nonvoting securities. For example, the capitalization of a $500 million corporation might be composed of $250 million of bonds, $150 million of nonvoting preferred stock, and $100 mil-

[7]Public Utility Act of 1935, Public Law No. 333 (S. 2796), 74th Congress, Title I, sec. 2 (*a*), subsec. (*7B*).

lion of common stock, which alone has voting privileges. It would be necessary for the organizers to invest only $50 million to retain control of such a firm. The $400 million of bonds and preferred stock are equities which have no part in the direction of the affairs of the company.

The control of 10 such companies as the one just illustrated could be achieved by setting up a holding company which would have to make a total investment of $500 million. The funds for this could be raised by $250 million of bonds, $150 million of nonvoting stock, and $100 million of voting common stock. Ownership of 50 per cent of the common stock would involve an investment of $50 million by the promoters. They would thus have control of $5 billion of assets, with an investment on their part of only $50 million, or 1 per cent of the total. This practice is known as "pyramiding."

One further item arising from this use of the holding company that deserves mention is the pyramiding of earnings. If it is assumed, in the above illustration, that the operating companies earned 7 per cent on the investment, each company would receive an income of $35 million a year. If it is further assumed that the bonds bore interest at 5 per cent and the preferred stock dividends at 6 per cent, then interest would be $12.5 million, and preferred stock dividends would be $9 million. This would leave $13.5 million for the common stock, or 13.5 per cent. Of this, $6.75 million would go to the holding company. Thus, the holding company's total income would be $67.5 million. Again assuming the same rates of interest and dividends, $12.5 million would be paid out as bond interest and $9 million for preferred stock dividends, leaving a total of $46 million on the common stock equity in the holding company, or 46 per cent. In some instances, earnings actually amounted to over 300 per cent on the final common stock equity. This method of increasing earnings available to common stock is known as "trading on the equity."

Although the foregoing is a simplified and schematic illustration, it is not an exaggeration. The means by which holding company control is acquired are usually very complicated, but this does not limit the effectiveness of the control. Control of the extensive Standard Gas and Electric utility system, with assets of about $1.2 billion, was obtained by an investment of about $3 million, or less than three tenths of 1 per cent of the assets of the whole system.

An even more extreme illustration was afforded by the Associated Gas and Electric system.[8] The total capitalization of the Associated Gas and Electric Company amounted, in 1929, to approximately $540 million. This was made up of total debt of $310 million; preferred stock, no par, $25 million; common stock, no par, $22 million; Class A stock, no par, $165 million; Class B stock, which alone had a vote, $17.5 million. All of

[8]Federal Trade Commission, *Utility Corporations: Summary Report* (Senate Doc. No. 92, Part 72 *A*, 70th Cong., 1st sess.) (Washington, D.C.: U.S. Government Printing Office, 1935), p. 168.

the Class B stock was held by Associated Securities Corporation, an intermediate holding company whose stock was owned entirely by Associated Gas and Electric Properties, a Massachusetts trust. The beneficial interest in the last organization was owned by Mr. H. C. Hopson and Mr. J. I. Mange. The total original investment in the control of Associated Gas and Electric Company was $298,318.19. This was one twentieth of 1 per cent of the total capitalization of the Associated Gas and Electric Company. Even this does not tell the whole story, since the total property in the system amounted to over $1 billion.

Pyramiding through trading on the equity and the issuance of a variety of different kinds of securities has been most notorious in public utilities and transportation. It has not been used extensively in the industrial field, although some holding companies, before World War II, had both public utility and nonutility properties. The industrial holding company has generally aimed at 100 per cent ownership of the outstanding stock of subsidiaries, and the intermediate holding company has been of practically no consequence. This, however, has not prevented excessive issuance of stock by the holding company desiring to bring about the combination of a number of competing concerns. For example, it has been estimated that the United States Steel Corporation, when it was formed in 1901, issued the entire amount of common stock with no property back of it as well as one fifth or two fifths of the preferred stock. Security issues exceeded actual investment, based on physical valuation, by $726 million.[9]

Intercorporate stock ownership, however, is very common in the industrial field. This forms the basis for community of interest and interlocking directorates.[10] The ownership upon which these arrangements rest may be only a small percentage of the total stocks outstanding, but the influence wielded may be very significant. For example, E. I. du Pont de Nemours owned 23 per cent of the stock of General Motors. E. I. du Pont and General Motors each owned 50 per cent of the stock of the United States Rubber Company.[11] What this involved in terms of the market relations among these firms may be debatable; but the potentialities are obvious, especially when the position of du Pont and General Motors in their respective fields is recognized. Intercorporate stock ownership of this type does not come within the usual definition of the holding company, but it is of the same character as the holding company arrangement. The heart of the problem is the extent to which corporations should be allowed to own stock in other corporations and the conditions under which that ownership should be permitted.

Origin and Growth. As has already been noted, it was the legisla-

[9]Jones, *op. cit.*, pp. 207–10.

[10]See below, pp. 135–37.

[11]This arrangement was ended as the result of a decision by the Supreme Court under Section 7 of the Clayton Act. See Chapter 15, *infra.*

tion passed by the state of New Jersey that opened up the way to combination by means of intercorporate stock ownership. At the outset, the parent holding company was used more frequently, because of the feeling that it was less subject to legal attack. In the hectic merger period from 1898 to 1900, the pure holding company device was much less popular than other forms of combination. But the reorganization of the Standard Oil Company of New Jersey as a pure holding company, under an amended charter in 1899, for the purpose of continuing the Standard Oil trust, gave impetus to the use of this arrangement. In the period from 1900 to 1903, it vied with outright fusion as the principal means of effecting consolidation. During these years, the United States Steel Corporation (1901), the American Locomotive Company (1901), the Consolidated Tobacco Company (1901), the Eastman Kodak Company (1901), the International Nickel Company (1902), the E. I. du Pont de Nemours Powder Company (1903), and the National Packing Company (1903) were all organized as industrial holding companies.

The "trust-busting" program of President Theodore Roosevelt and the Northern Securities decision of 1904 put a severe damper on the formation of monopolistic combines. It was not until after the close of World War I that the merger movement again became a significant public question; and by that time, the pattern of combination had changed somewhat. New industries, such as public utilities, automobiles, aircraft manufacture, and radio, had risen to prominence. These offered attractions to combination for speculative reasons in addition to incentives to obtain economies from large-scale production.

The pure holding company, in the public utility field, proved to be an effective means for escaping some of the effects of the limitation on earnings imposed by public utility commissions. In the railroad field, the holding company was used to evade the provision of the Transportation Act of 1920, which gave the Interstate Commerce Commission control over consolidations. Bank holding companies emerged as a way of evading the legal restrictions on branch banking. The industrial holding company was used to bring together, under unified ownership, enterprises which, at least under the existing interpretation of the law, were not in competition with each other. If they were competitive, care was taken to see that the effect was such as not to fall within the legal concept of what constituted monopoly or a substantial lessening of competition.

The heyday of the holding company in American business was from the end of World War I to 1930. By 1929, the development had gone so far in the production of electricity that 16 holding company systems were responsible for generating over 80 per cent of the electricity output of private companies in the United States.[12] The United Corporation, Electric Bond and Share system, Standard Gas and Electric, Cities

[12]Federal Trade Commission, *op. cit.*, p. 38.

Service, Associated Gas and Electric, and the Insull group were some of the largest and most notorious. The activities of some of these companies resulted not only in public scandal but also in a huge loss to investors.[13] The American Telephone and Telegraph Company, a parent holding company, came to control about 90 per cent of the telephones through complete or controlling ownership of the major telephone companies throughout the country. In railroads, the Alleghany Corporation and the Penn Road Corporation were the two outstanding illustrations of the holding company device adapted purely to purposes of control and with the objective of evading the authority of the Interstate Commerce Commission. The bank holding company developed principally between 1926 and 1930. In 1929, 38 holding companies controlled 541 banks with combined resources of about $8 billion. Many of these companies also owned outright or controlled corporations engaged in a variety of other activities. The outstanding illustration of this was the Transamerica Corporation, which had 100 per cent control of a series of holding companies, which in turn owned commercial banks, foreign banks, investment corporations, iron foundries, life insurance companies, land banks, and mortgage companies.

After 1920, the pure holding company became prominent in the industrial field. Of the 200 largest nonfinancial corporations listed by the National Resources Committee,[14] 107 were industrial enterprises. Twenty of these were pure holding companies; and of the 20, only 3 were formed prior to 1910, whereas 14 were organized after 1922. Of the 3 appearing before 1910—namely, Standard Oil Company of New Jersey, United States Steel Corporation, and Eastman Kodak Company—only the last 2 remained as pure holding companies, Standard Oil assuming that status in 1927. General Motors, which had been formed as a pure holding company in 1908, became primarily an operating company in 1915 and therefore does not appear in the list of the 20 pure holding companies.

The foregoing does not tell the full story of holding company influence in industrial combination, however. Many of the remaining 87 were parent holding companies, while the Ford Motor Company alone had no subsidiaries in 1935. Indeed, of the entire 200 corporations, of which 93 were railroads and public utilities, Ford was the only one without subsidiaries.

Resurgence of the merger movement since World War II has brought the issue of intercorporate stock ownership and the holding company once more to the fore. Earlier developments were curbed by legislation in the transportation, public utility, and banking fields. Court interpretation of the Celler–Kefauver Act has probably imposed a severe

[13]N. R. Danielian, "From Insull to Injury," *Atlantic Monthly*, Vol. CLI (April, 1933), pp. 497–508. Danielian estimates that the collapse of the Insull system resulted in a loss of over $700 million to investors.

[14]National Resources Committee, *The Structure of the American Economy* (Washington, D.C.: U.S. Government Printing Office, 1939), p. 273.

check on intercorporate stockholding and the holding company where combination of enterprises is related fields is attempted. Where non-related areas of activity are involved, present legislation seems to be powerless to act. "Giant conglomerates merged, among many others, without objection from the enforcement agencies were Electric Boat and Consolidated Vultee, Remington Rand, and Sperry Gyroscope, Westinghouse and Le Tourneau, W. R. Grace's, Dewey and Almy and Davidson Chemicals, Ford and Philco, Socony-Mobil and Kordite, and Monsanto and Lion Oil."[15]

The outstanding use of the holding company recently has been in the savings and loan field, where current legislation is able to exercise only a partial check. The Federal Home Loan Bank Board reports that there were 44 known holding companies in the savings and loan field in 1959, and of these 31 own in excess of 10 per cent of the guaranty stock of a savings and loan association, but with principal business in other fields such as: insurance agencies, escrow companies, trustee companies, and other activities ranging from land development and construction companies to life insurance.[16] San Diego Imperial Corporation owns or controls a majority of stock in 15 savings and loan associations located in California, Texas, Kansas, and Colorado, as well as a number of other companies.[17]

Functions of the Holding Company. As a means of effecting consolidation, the holding company is the most adaptable device that has yet been developed. Its control of a subsidiary may be attained by exchange of the stock of the parent company for that of the company to be acquired; no investment whatsoever is required. Control over subsidiaries may be brought about even in the face of minority opposition merely by obtaining a majority of the voting stock. Furthermore, no formalities need be met, as in the case of outright fusion.

Where it is desired to retain the privileges contained in the corporate charters of the enterprises to be acquired or—as in the case of public utilities—to maintain franchise rights, the holding company device is the only feasible one by which to bring about consolidation. Expansion into foreign jurisdictions may frequently necessitate separate incorporation because of the laws of foreign countries. The establishment of branch factories by American firms in other countries is usually carried out through the means of subsidiaries. American firms have also frequently acquired enterprises in foreign countries by stock purchase.

Sometimes, the restrictions imposed upon corporations chartered in other states are such as to make incorporation in the state into which admittance is sought highly desirable, from the legal point of view. This

[15]*Administered Prices: A Compendium on Public Policy, op. cit.*, p. 109.

[16]Report of the Federal Home Loan Bank Board, *Savings and Loan Holding Companies* (Washington, D.C., 1960).

[17]See also E. S. Shaw, *Savings and Loan Market Structures and Market Performance*, Research Study prepared for the California Savings and Loan Commissioner, 1962.

seems to have been an important factor in shaping the pattern of organization in the petroleum industry. In some lines of business, separate incorporation is absolutely necessary. Thus, California forbids a foreign corporation to carry on a public utility business within its borders.

The holding company device also provides a convenient means for organizing expansion. If an enterprise decides to extend its activities into businesses that may be related to the main one but are differentiated from it, it may be advantageous, for purposes of good will or insulating risk, to set up new ventures as subsidiary corporations. This method is frequently used in the development of by-products, and it offers the advantage of complete legal separation and a decentralization of management. The American Telephone and Telegraph Company has used it as a means of separating the manufacturing, supply, and warehousing organization of its system. This is all under the Western Electric Company, 98 per cent of whose stock is owned by the American Telephone and Telegraph Company. Similarly, a subsidiary corporation, the Bell Telephone Laboratories, carries on research and owns patents for the Bell Telephone System.

Vertical integration, which often combines production processes from the extraction of the raw material through the various stages to the marketing of the finished product to the ultimate consumer, is most effectively accomplished by the holding company device. As already noted, after 1920, the merger movement in American business took on a new direction. Businesses expanded by combining various enterprises which were not competing—at least in the eyes of the law. This is exemplified in the complementary or circular type of merger. It involves the combination of businesses which produce similar types of products but which do not compete with each other. An outstanding illustration of this is General Foods Corporation, which controls production of coffee, flour, syrup, sea food, salt, and other similar products that are not com peting.

The holding company device has created some difficult problems and has produced some socially undesirable results. It has aggravated the monopoly problem[18] and has led to financial abuses and excess which have been costly.[19] These are problems which regulation in the various areas of the economic structure has had to face and will continue to face. The use of intercorporate stock ownership and the holding company have, nevertheless, been among the most decisive organizational factors shaping the pattern of American industry in the twentieth century. In

[18]See Temporary National Economic Committee, Monograph No. 13, *Relative Efficiency of Large, Medium-Sized and Small Business* (Washington, D.C.: U.S. Government Printing Office, 1941), Appendix A, by M. W. Watkins, pp. 133–39; Appendix D, by Frank Fetter, pp. 398-415.

[19]Federal Trade Commission, *op. cit.*, pp. 880–82.

spite of the evils and excesses that have accompanied their use, they have made a genuinely positive contribution to the growth of the American economy.

COMBINATION BY AGREEMENT

Agreements of various kinds among independent producers form the second major type of combination that has developed in this country. This has accompanied the growth of large-scale enterprise but is much wider in scope; and in some instances, the influence extends into branches of trade and industry where competitors are numerous and of comparatively small size. Sometimes, the purpose is to establish standards of competitive conduct that do not have a restrictive intent or effect. More often, the objective has been to bring about a limitation of competition that will result in benefits to the participating producers.

Prior to the emergence of the holding company, monopolistic agreements constituted the principal means of controlling competition. They were vulnerable at law, however, and lacked stability, especially when it was impossible to resort to binding sanctions. As a consequence, combinations under single ownership, especially after the passage of the New Jersey corporation law in 1889, became the most prominent device. In the years following World War I, there has been a marked revival of combinations based upon agreement. Today, they present problems of public policy that are of equal importance with those created by the integrated combinations.

Gentlemen's Agreements

The most informal type of combination, in so far as sanctions and organization are concerned, is the gentlemen's agreement. This is simply an understanding, usually the result of thoroughgoing discussion and close business contact on matters of common concern, especially as they relate to limitations on competition. Agreements of this kind have also covered conditions of sale, credit arrangements with buyers and division of territory. Indeed, it seems safe to say that almost every phase of competitive business has been covered at one time or another by a gentlemen's agreement.

The gentlemen's agreement is perhaps the most widespread device employed by business for the purpose of limiting competition. It was made famous in the early part of the century by the dinners which the late Judge E. H. Gary, chairman of the United States Steel Corporation, used to give. At these gatherings, over which Judge Gary presided, the leaders of the steel industry would reach accord on matters of common interest, especially control of prices; and the understandings thus arrived at formed the pattern of competitive action for the producers. Although the dinners were formally abandoned in 1911 because of public hostility to the trust movement, this did not cause the disappearance of gentlemen's agreements. Evidence of the extent of their existence cannot be readily obtained; but there is every reason to believe that they are an integral part of price leadership, sharing of the market, the basing-point system, and even nonprice competition.

Writers on combination have emphasized repeatedly that gentlemen's agreements have rarely proved successful, because they lack the requisite authority over the participating members, and because someone is constantly guilty of infractions. There is considerable truth to this point of view, for, standing alone, gentlemen's agreements are probably largely innocuous as far as public welfare is concerned. The trouble is that they do not stand alone but, instead, may be used in conjunction with other arrangements, such as community of interest and interlocking directorates. Even where competitors have no formal relations with each other, these agreements constitute an effective means of getting together and can exert considerable influence for some period of time where a few firms dominate an industry. When combined with community of interest, they probably constitute as distinct a threat to competition as more formal arrangements.

Probably the most notorious of all gentlemen's agreements took place in the electrical manufacturing industry, with General Electric and Westinghouse as the principal conspirators. They had worked out agreements involving price-fixing, identical bids, and division of markets. The conspiracy never had benefit of trial, and the facts can be pieced together only from Senate hearings. Only the subordinate officers of the corporations were punished upon pleas of guilty—the principal executives denying any complicity. Whether the latter were as innocent or ignorant as they contended may be a matter of opinion, but it is quite clear that a giant conspiracy, based only on collusion through gentlemen's agreements, existed for a good many years in the electrical manufacturing industry. If the subordinate executives were made the scapegoats, it is unfortunate for public policy that this was allowed to pass; if they were actually the guilty ones, then the whole affair is a sad commentary on the organization, at least of this segment of big business.[20]

In recent years, the courts have given recognition to what has come to be called "conscious parallelism of action." This is a pattern of behavior by a group of business firms, sufficient to convince the courts, on the basis of circumstantial evidence relating to it, that concerted action has taken place. No direct evidence of agreement is available; but very likely, gentlemen's agreements or understandings have formed the basis of the concerted action.

[20]See *Administered Prices, op. cit.*, Parts 27 and 28, 1961, for the full Senate hearings. See John G. Fuller, *The Gentlemen Conspirators* (New York: Grove Press, Inc., 1962), for a somewhat theatrical account of the conspiracy. See Chapter 15, *supra*, for further discussion of the legal aspects of the case.

Community of Interest

Community of interest is a form of combination which is the result of individuals owning stock in otherwise independent concerns, the stock ownership being used to secure unified action on matters of common interest. This is generally achieved by persons being appointed to sit on more than one board of directors. Interlocking directorates are not essential, however, to the effective operation of a community of interest, because the ultimate control lies in the hands of those who own the stock, and these owners may, in order to avoid legal restriction, merely secure the appointment of directors who will do their bidding.

Community of interest may exist among enterprises engaged in the same line of business activity; it may embrace companies who are customers of each other; or it may bring concerns with widely separated or only incidentally related interests under common direction. Probably, community of interest represents the most diffuse type of combination in use today. Its existence can be discovered from the records of stockholders and directors, but its significance and influence are difficult to evaluate. Such disclosures as have been made, however, indicate a degree of control over the major financial and nonfinancial enterprises of the nation that poses a definite threat of power without commensurate responsibility. The ultimate direction of a large proportion of the leading business concerns of this country, thanks to community-of-interest arrangements, is in the hands of a relatively limited number of people.

Combination by community of interest has attracted attention for a long time in this country. It was used by the Standard Oil trust as early as 1892 and was one of the means by which the American Tobacco Company achieved its power. It has been notorious in the railroad field and has probably been the principle means by which many of the large banking houses have exerted their influence on industry. Investigations by the National Resources Committee,[21] the Temporary National Economic Committee, and the Securities and Exchange Commission[22] all bear witness to the manifold ramifications of community of interest and the possibility of concentrated control which it poses. The interrelationships are too extensive to discuss in detail here. One or two examples will suffice to illustrate the situation.

In 1928, Aluminum Corporation of America (Alcoa) formed Alu-

[21]National Resources Committee, *op. cit.*, Part I, chap. ix; Appendix 12, pp. 298 f. For a recent compilation of interlocking directors in financial companies, see Select Committee on Small Business, *Interlocking Directors and Officials of 135 Large Financial Companies of the United States* (Preliminary Report, Part I, Union Calendar No. 496, House Report No. 1278, 85th Cong., 1st sess.) (Washington, D.C.: U.S. Government Printing Office, 1957).

[22]Temporary National Economic Committee, Monograph No. 29, *Distribution of Ownership in the 200 Largest Nonfinancial Corporations* (Washington, D.C.: U.S. Government Printing Office, 1940), chap. vii.

minium, Ltd., of Canada, and turned over all of its foreign properties to the latter. In return, Alcoa's stockholders received all of the common stock of the Canadian firm. In 1939, 11 individuals collectively held 48.9 per cent of Alcoa's shares and 48.5 per cent of Limited's. This arrangement persisted until 1950, when it was terminated by antitrust action.[23]

Interlocking directorates connecting competitors by directors serving on the board of a third corporation are common. Directors of the General Electric Corporation and the Westinghouse Electric Company, two leading manufacturers of electrical equipment, sat together on the boards of the American Telephone and Telegraph Company; New York, New Haven, and Hartford Railroad Company; and the Chase National Bank. Directors of Armour and Company and Wilson and Company, Inc., two of the "Big Four" meat packers, sat together on the boards of International Harvester Company, the Great Western Railroad Company, and the Continental Illinois National Bank and Trust Company. Directors of the Kennecott Copper Company and the Phelps Dodge Copper Products Corporation, concerns which produced 55 per cent of the American output of copper in 1937, sat together on the boards of the Continental Oil Company and J. P. Morgan and Company. Among the major oil companies, Tidewater Associated Oil Company interlocked with Standard Oil Company of California, through the Anglo-California National Bank; Gulf Oil with Continental Oil, through Pullman, Inc.; and Cities Service with Socony-Vacuum, through the Manufacturers Trust Company of New York, and with the Texas Corporation, through the Natural Gas and Pipeline Company of America.[24]

The ramifications of the connections of the United States Steel Corporation are emphasized by the fact that, in 1935, it had interlocking directorates with Pullman, Inc.; Mutual Life Insurance Company of New York; American Telephone and Telegraph Company; Guaranty Trust Company; New York Central Railroad Company: Pennsylvania Railroad Company; General Motors Corporation; the Atchison, Topeka and Santa Fe Railway Company; J. P. Morgan and Company; Drexel and Company; Equitable Life Assurance Society of the United States; Peoples Gas, Light and Coke Company; Commonwealth Edison Company; First National Bank of New York; Northern Pacific Railway Company; Chicago Great Western Railroad Company; Armour and Company of Illinois; Montgomery Ward and Company, Inc.; Delaware and Hudson Company; and Northern Trust Company. In addition, because of its position in the Morgan–First National interest group, it was also connected with the Penn Railroad Company, Marshall Field and Company, the

[23]See Chapter 14.

[24]Temporary National Economic Committee, Monograph No. 21, *Competition and Monopoly in American Industry* (Washington, D.C.: U.S. Government Printing Office, 1940), pp. 189–94.

Public Service Company of Northern Illinois, Cleveland Trust Company, Goodyear Tire and Rubber Company, and the Cleveland Cliffs Iron Company. *Life* magazine[25] described the United States Steel board of directors in 1946 as possibly the most powerful group of men in the whole industrial world. It included the president of the Pacific Gas and Electric Company, a director of the Bankers' Trust Company and of the Goodyear Rubber and Tire Company, the chairman of J. P. Morgan and Company, a vice-president of J. P. Morgan and Company, the president of International Nickel Company, the chairman of the board of Montgomery Ward, the president of the City National Bank and Trust Company of Chicago, and the president of the First National Bank of New York. *Life's* designation appears to be well taken.

The Select Committee on Small Business of the House of Representatives examined interlocking directorates, particularly with regard to 135 top financial companies in banking, insurance, and investment. It found that 134 of them had interlocks with other members of the group. Of the 1,667 leading companies in other fields, 905 had interlocking directorates with the 135. General Electric had interlocking directorates with 14 of the 135 financial companies, Pennsylvania Railroad with 30, and American Telephone and Telegraph with 50.[26]

Community of interest constitutes one of the most elusive devices for imposing restrictions on competition because of the indirect ways in which it may operate, because of the difficulties involved in preventing persons from owning stock in different companies, and because of the highly legalistic position maintained by the courts in this matter.[27] Recently, however, the courts have indicated that community of interest may be quite vulnerable under the antitrust laws if there is the probability of adverse effects on competition.

Pools

The term "pool" is used in a variety of different ways, but it generally indicates an agreement among independent producers whereby the latter delegate to a central organization control over the sale of products or property. Pools are based upon written contracts which set forth the terms of the agreement and the penalties incurred for violation. Most pooling arrangements in the industrial field are designed to control price or output, or both; but some of them are organized to provide for more orderly marketing procedures or for access to the use of property by enterprises which may, in other respects, be competitors.

[25]"Big Steel's Men," *Life* (November 11, 1946) pp. 107–15.

[26]*Final Report*, Select Committee on Small Business, House of Representatives, 85th Cong., 2d sess., Union Calendar No. 1148, House Report No. 2718 (Washington, D.C.: U.S. Government Printing Office, 1959). The details will be found on pages 4–30, together with charts for some of the banks.

[27]See *United States* v. *Aluminum Co. of America*, 148 Fed. (2d) 416, 440 (1945). But see also *United States* v. *Aluminum Co. of America*, 91 Fed. Supp. 333 (1950).

Types of Pools. There are many different types of pools; but generally, they fall into about four different categories. These are commonly known as the output or traffic pool, the market or territorial pool, the selling pool, and the patent pool. This classification is based upon functions rather than upon the characteristics oi a particular arrangement. As a consequence, a great many of the pools fall into more than one of these groupings.

The output or traffic pool is based on an agreement by which the participants allocate output or traffic, the basis of allotment depending upon relative bargaining positions. Sometimes, arrangement is made to allot the total business among these members, without any attempt to restrict total output. This has been characteristic of railway traffic pools. More frequently, however, total output is restricted for the purpose of controlling the market. The total is then divided up on some predetermined basis among the members of the pool; and penalties, such as fines for exceeding the allotment, may be imposed on those who fail to comply.

The market or territorial pool provides for the division of the market or territory among the members. Sometimes, this involves an outright agreement on the part of participants not to sell in each other's markets. This was the type of agreement entered into by the American Tobacco Company of the United States and the Imperial Tobacco Company of Britain in 1902. The arrangements that have been used in this country are frequently more complicated. In the Addyston Pipe and Steel pool, the United States was divided into three categories: reserved cities, free territory, and pay territory. The reserved cities were allotted to specific companies, and no one else was to do business there. The free territory was open to all of the members, without restrictions. Orders in the pay territory were assigned to the company which offered to pay the highest bonus to the pool. A board was set up to administer the pay territory; it fixed the price of cast-iron pipe for those regions and awarded the sale to the successful bidder; but in order to conceal the activities of the pool, the other competitors would submit fictitous bids at prices that were higher than the one which was to receive the contract.

The selling pool is a device whereby the contracting parties establish a joint sales organization which acts as sole distributor for the products covered by the agreement. Sometimes, this organization sells all the products offered to it by the members and then distributes the proceeds, minus costs, in proportion to the products contributed by the members. More frequently, however, selling pools endeavor to control prices, either by imposing limitations on output or by deliberately keeping part of the product off the market. The income or profit pool, which is a variation of the selling pool, puts the income or profits from sales into a common fund, which is then distributed according to agreement. A recent illustration of the selling pool in this country was that of Appalachian Coals,

Inc., which was organized in March, 1932. The Appalachian Coals Company was set up as the exclusive selling agency for 137 producers of bituminous coal in the Appalachian territory. Each of the producers owned stock in the company in proportion to his production. The company established standard classifications; it sold all of the coal of its principals at the best prices obtainable; and if all of that coal could not be sold, it apportioned orders upon a stated basis. The prices for coal were fixed by the officers of the company and its central office, but producers were permitted to designate subagents. They, however, had to sell on the terms and prices established by the company. This arrangement received the approval of the Supreme Court on the ground that it did not restrain competition but, rather, was a scheme designed to bring order out of chaos in the marketing of bituminous coal.[28]

The fourth important type of pool is the patent pool or patent interchange, which, as its name implies, consists of an agreement among owners of patents whereby they agree to allow the use of each other's patents in accordance with the conditions of the pool. There are several different ways by which a patent pool may be established. The patentees may retain title to the patents but agree to grant licenses to them to the other members of the pool; or they may transfer title to the patents to a trustee, who is authorized to license them to the members of the pool under conditions stipulated in the contract. Another arrangement is to establish a corporation which is owned by the members of the pool and to which the patents are assigned. This corporation is empowered to issue licenses for the patents. A fourth device is to grant power of attorney to someone authorized by the owners to issue licenses. Whatever the procedure, the purpose of the pool is to provide for the use of patents which are put into the pool by the various members who belong to it Generally speaking, the licensees pay royalties for the use of the patents; but sometimes, members are free to use all patents without paying fees. The pool may also grant licenses to nonmembers under conditions stipulated in the agreement.

In the early stages of the combination movement, the pool was the most widely used device to bring about restriction of competition. It almost invariably had a monopolistic intent. Its chief difficulty lay in the problems of reconciling the competitive interests of its members. To secure co-operation, it was necessary to impose strong sanctions. This requirement, however, was faced with severe legal barriers, because the purpose of the pool was to restrain trade or achieve monopoly. This not only was contrary to common law but also soon came into conflict with state antitrust legislation and federal antitrust laws. Today, the two principal manifestations are the sales pool, or the joint selling agency, and the patent pool. Both of these are sanctioned under the law if they do

[28]See Chapter 15, *infra.*

not restrain competition or if they are not established for the purpose of achieving monopoly. Presumably, any kind of pool would be legal if it met such conditions. The law, however, has given special sanction to certain types of selling pools; and the peculiarities of the patent laws make it possible to effect pooling arrangements without meeting court disapproval.

Present Use of Pools. One of the most prominent types of selling pool in operation at the present time is in the nonindustrial field; this is the agricultural marketing co-operative. This type of selling organization usually acts as the exclusive sales agency for the product of the farmers who are members of it. The leading illustration of this is the California Fruit Growers' Exchange, which acts as the central marketing agency for the member associations. The independent citrus fruit growers are members of associations which own title to the local packing houses. The local association holds membership in district exchanges, which, in turn, compose the membership of the California Fruit Growers' Exchange. In addition to making the sales, the Exchange carries on a nationwide advertising program; it has a traffic department to deal with transportation problems; and it includes a legal department to handle matters of taxes, insurance, legal liability, and claims. It conducts extensive marketing research and handles legislative matters of the citrus industry before the California legislature and Congress.

A second important type of selling pool in operation today is the export association, which may be organized under the Webb-Pomerene Act of 1918. This legislation made it legal for American producers to combine for purposes of export trade, provided that they did not restrain trade or substantially lessen competition within the United States, and provided also that they did not restrain the export trade of a domestic competitor. Most of the earlier associations were operating agencies, making sales abroad, allocating orders at home, assembling and shipping goods, making collections, and remitting payments to their members. In recent years, however, the associations have left most of these functions to the members, confining their activities to fixing prices or to assigning quotas, or both. Between 1918 and 1940, 120 export associations were formed; and of the 44 in existence in 1940, 30 were more than 10 years of age, and 14 were more than 20 years old. Thirty-two export associations were registered with the Federal Trade Commission in 1961.

The most important type of pool in use in industry today is the patent pool. Practically all of the large industries whose activities rely heavily on patents participate in this kind of an arrangement. By an elaborate and carefully constructed system of cross-licensing, the American Telephone and Telegraph Company has been able to maintain its prominent position in communications—both wire and radio. Leading oil companies have pooled their patents for the cracking process of manufacturing gasoline. As early as 1915, the leading automobile manufacturers pooled their patents, which each of the members might use freely without payment of any royalty. Henry Ford did not enter into the agreement but, nevertheless, allowed his patents to be used by the others. This agreement was modified in 1925 by the proviso that patents acquired during the life of the agreement were not to be included. They were placed in the pool after five years had elapsed, however. In 1935, a further modification was introduced, excluding from the pool a large number of patents utilized in the manufacture of the present-day automobile.[29]

The operation of present-day pools indicates clearly that they can be successful and stable if given adequate legal protection. Furthermore, they may contain genuine advantages that are not inimical to public welfare. When they function as a means of orderly marketing, without control of production or prices, they can bring real benefits to the producers, as well as lower costs to the consumer. Patent pools may eliminate a great deal of costly litigation and may provide for a much wider and freer use of basic processes.

Unfortunately, the abuses of pooling arrangements are very serious. The temptation seems to be too great to avoid the opportunities for restriction. Patent pools are a continuous source of complaint and have been a most successful device for enhancing monopoly. The export association is basically in conflict with competition in international trade; and the evidence warrants the conclusion that its activities, in many instances, have reacted unfavorably on domestic trade and competition.[30] Many of the agricultural marketing co-operatives are constantly pressing for legislation designed to strengthen their position by enabling them to restrict output and enhance prices. If the production enjoys a high degree of geographic concentration, such that the output of a given area is large relative to the total supply of the product, appreciable control over price may be obtained by effective organization. This appears to be the situation in walnuts and oranges.

Pooling arrangements may serve a definite public purpose; but, in order that this may be so, it is essential that steps be taken to control their restrictive potentialities. The record to date is, on the whole, unfavorable. In most instances, and especially where large enterprises are involved, pooling presents a constant threat to competition.

Trade Associations

A trade association is a voluntary organization of business enterprises engaged in a particular trade or industry and is established for

[29] Temporary National Economic Committee, Monograph No. 31, *Patents and Free Enterprise* (Washington, D.C.: U.S. Government Printing Office, 1941), pp. 115-22. For an extended discussion of patent pooling and the antitrust issues that emerge, see Chapter 21.

[30] Temporary National Economic Committee, Monograph No. 6, *Export Prices and Export Cartels* (Washington, D.C.: U.S. Government Printing Office, 1940); see also Chapter 15.

the purpose of dealing with common problems of the industry or trade. It is a form of combination in which the members maintain their separate legal independence and are usually in active competition with each other. They are free to enter or withdraw from membership at will, although eligibility for voting members requires that the candidate be engaged in business in the industry and area covered by the association. They may be local, regional, or national in scope. In 1940, there were more than 8,000 trade associations in the United States, approximately 2,000 of these being nationwide.[31] The activities of these organizations ranged all the way from those in keeping with the spirit of competition to others which were highly inconsistent with it.

Form of Organization. Trade associations may be incorporated or unincorporated. Somewhat over half of them are incorporated, this form of organization predominating in the service and retail trades; while somewhat less than half of the associations in the mining, manufacturing, and construction industries adopt this legal status. They are usually governed by a board of directors, with the actual administration in the hands of a salaried secretary (who is frequently a highly professionalized organizer) and a paid staff. Some of the most powerful and prominent associations have annual incomes of over $500,000[32] and employ executives who have gained wide experience in government or industry. In recent years, administration of trade associations by persons or firms that manage more than one organization has emerged. The activities of these management organizations are confined largely to associations in the small-income bracket. Generally speaking, the associations administered by a management organization place prime emphasis on services of an information nature.

Growth of Trade Associations. The trade association movement in the United States is a phenomenon of the post-Civil War development, although two associations at present in existence antedate 1860.[33] The movement, however, did not gain any real headway until after 1890. The principal interest in combination at this time focused on the control of the market, and other devices were more promising than trade associations. The years 1890-1915 witnessed a rapid growth of trade associations and marked the transformation of this type of organization into its present-day form and function. World War I gave a special impetus to the movement because the government, in its efforts to mobilize production, found it more convenient to deal with entire trades and industries. This not only resulted in a marked growth in numbers but also provided businessmen with valuable experience and the organizational foundation for co-operation.

[31]Temporary National Economic Committee, *Final Report of the Executive Secretary* (Washington, D.C.: U.S. Government Printing Office, 1941), p. 85.

[32]Temporary National Economic Committee, Monograph No. 18, *Trade Association Survey* (Washington, D.C.: U.S. Government Printing Office, 1941), p. 8.

[33]*Ibid.*, p. 12.

The development of the trade association movement since World War I has been characterized by marked fluctuations. As was to be expected in the years immediately following the close of the war, there was a substantial falling-off in the rate of formation; but from 1925 through 1929, a larger number of associations was organized than during any previous five-year period in the history of the movement, even including the period of World War I. The onset of depression resulted in an abrupt setback to the movement, at least in terms of formation, although the influence of the associations is evident by their impact on legislation and the basis which they formed for the administration of the National Industrial Recovery Act. The whole so-called "self-government of industry" movement, characterized by the N.I.R.A. and other legislation (both state and federal) of a similar nature, adopted the trade association as the chief means of regulating industry. The end of the N.I.R.A., as a result of a Supreme Court decision,[34] resulted in the disappearance of many associations and a temporary diminution in the importance of associations in industry.

Although the end of the N.I.R.A. and a return to the more vigorous enforcement of the antitrust laws brought about some shift in emphasis in the activities of trade associations and reopened the question of their place and function, the outbreak of World War II saw a renewal of the incentive for co-operation for purposes of increasing production. Since World War II, trade associations have been extremely active, especially in promoting legislation for the benefit of the members and in public relations. In addition, in many states, retail trade associations conduct the cost surveys, prescribe the minimum markup on cost in accordance with the state laws, and enforce compliance.

Open-Price Associations. Down to 1890, the trade association movement seems to have been directed primarily at restricting competition. After 1890, however, this form of co-operation came to place more emphasis on developing constructive activities for improving conditions of competition and performing functions for members which did not conflict with the spirit of the antitrust laws. This was given impetus by the development of open-price associations. The idea behind this development was that competition would be furthered by full knowledge of the market and market conditions by competitors. Credit for developing this concept of the functions of trade associations usually is given to Mr. A. J. Eddy, a Chicago lawyer, who, in 1911, advanced the proposal that association members should freely exchange price information with each other.[35]

In the years following 1920, open-price associations attained considerable prominence. Many of them used the exchange of price information as a means of exercising control over their members to restrict

[34] *Schechter Poultry Corp.*, v. *United States*, 295 U.S. 495 (1935).
[35] A. J. Eddy, *The New Competition* (Chicago: A. C. McClurg &. Co., 1912).

competition, especially in prices. When it can be demonstrated to the courts that price-reporting systems do result in restriction, the activities are illegal. The difficulty is that a large number of conditions have to be fulfilled if the open-price arrangement is to increase the effectiveness of competition. All too frequently, all the conditions are not met, and the association becomes a means of diminishing competition. This, however, may not be easy to prove to the courts.[36]

Functions of Trade Associations. The functions performed by trade associations for the benefit of their members are numerous and diverse. A great many of them are not in themselves inconsistent with competition, nor are they necessarily used to limit it. On the other hand, numerous restrictive practices have been employed; and many associations seem to have turned their energy primarily in this direction. Practically all of the functions which trade associations perform can be diverted into restrictive channels. Whether this happens or not depends upon the objectives and policies of a particular organization. Some practices may be strictly in the restrictive category by their very nature and have no place in a competitive picture. Typical trade association activities include:

1. *Statistics.* The collection and dissemination of statistical information relating to a particular trade is one of the most important services performed by a trade association. These statistics may cover such matters as the volume of production, inventories, unfilled orders, idle capacity, shipments, and sales. They may deal with market trends and the trend of the particular industry as related to those market trends, with employment, with future prospects, with new investments—indeed, with almost anything of a statistical nature that may be of informational value to the members.

2. *Price Reporting.* A great many associations, especially the more important ones, employ some form of price reporting. Sales prices of products and the conditions of sales are made available to members on past sales, present sales, and sometimes on future sales.

3. *Cost Accounting* A great many associations have sought to develop uniform methods of cost accounting for their members. This is partly for the purpose of making it possible to gather comparable statistical information. It also serves as a means of developing further knowledge of the cost problems of an industry.

4. *Governmental Relations.* One of the most important functions of trade associations that has grown up in recent years is that of acting as a spokesman for the industry before governmental agencies. This takes the form of presenting the case of a particular industry to the government, lobbying for special legislation, opposing legislation which is not desired by the industry, acting as spokesman on tax matters, and being a clearinghouse of information to members on matters of taxation.

5. *Public Relations.* This covers the whole field of endeavors designed to improve the standing of the industry in the eyes of the consumer. It embraces trade promotion and advertising; the popularizing of the product of the members, as compared with some substitute commodity; the stimulation of consumer demand; and the exploration of new markets. Collective market research and advertising are consequently two of the most important aspects of this activity. Some

[36]See Clair Wilcox, *Competition and Monopoly in American Industry* (Temporary National Economic Committee, Monograph No. 21) (Washington, D.C.: U.S. Government Printing Office, 1940), pp. 294–95.

trade asociations also endeavor to improve public relations by setting up machinery to settle business disputes outside of the courts. These disputes sometimes arise between members of an industry; but more frequently, they develop between the members, on the one hand, and their customers or suppliers, on the other. Trade associations also co-operate in building better public relations for business in general by supporting Better Business bureaus, which aim to warn the public against shysters and adulterated products. The public relations program of some trade associations includes educational activities designed to inform the public on facts about the industry and to present them in a favorable light. This takes the form of radio programs, distribution of literature, and research aids to educational institutions.

6. *Employer-Employee Relations.* Trade association services in this field include a variety of activities, the principal ones being the making of surveys and the giving of advice and assistance on wages, hours, working conditions, and collective bargaining; the promoting of employee welfare and safety; and the conducting of employee training programs. Since 1932, employer-employee relations have been one of the most important aspects of trade association work.

The most common type of labor relations activity relates to surveys, advice, and assistance on wages, hours, and working conditions. The second is that of promoting employee welfare and safety, with the objective of reducing industrial accidents, sickness, occupational diseases, and fatigue. A large number of associations have employee training programs. The American Bankers Association has, for years, conducted an extensive training program in hundreds of cities throughout the country. Some associations merely give advice and assistance on collective bargaining, while others conduct the bargaining arrangements with unions. This is most prominent in the apparel trades, especially in New York City.[37] Finally, some associations perform placement services, which usually involve the occasional and quite informal handling of inquiries, as well as the keeping of systematic records of applications and vacancies.

7. *Trade Practices.* This field of trade association activity is somewhat difficult to delimit, because it may be used to deal with every kind of business conduct from downright unethical practices to vigorous competition. It generally has an ethical content, however, aimed at the elimination of unfair methods of competition, on the one hand, and the establishment of standards of fair competitive conduct, on the other. The Trade Practice Conference sponsored by the Federal Trade Commission has stimulated this phase of trade-association work appreciably. The development of higher standards of business conduct by pressure from businessmen themselves is one of the leading contributions which they can make to further private enterprise.

8. *Standardization and Simplification.* Standardization refers to the establishment of uniform products; of sizes or dimensions; and, in the case of quality standards, of criteria of properties and performance as the basis for grading certification and labeling. Simplification refers to the reduction of the number or variety of product sizes, dimensions, types, models, patterns, and lines. Standardization may also include terms of contract, price lists, and differentials. One of the wastes of the competitive system, both in terms of consumer inconvenience and in terms of cost of product, arises from the multiplicity of commodities that serve essentially the same purpose and do not rely on their distinctiveness for consumer appeal. Standardization and simplification of many such goods over an entire industry depend primarily upon co-operative efforts. Trade associations have contributed notably to furthering this development. During both world wars, the government sought their aid on these matters as war economy measures. Some associations also

[37]Temporary National Economic Committee, Monograph No. 18, pp. 331–32.

follow the practice of certifying the quality of the products of their members, and this not only may protect producers against the competition of inferior goods but also may be of real benefit to the consumer.

9. *Credit Bureaus.* Many trade associations operate credit bureaus, which supply information to the members on the credit standing of customers. The pooling of credit information not only makes it possible for members to secure data on credit prospects but also reduces the cost of acquiring them. It may also assist a responsible buyer in establishing new lines of credit.

Restrictive Activities of Trade Associations

The foregoing presentation of the more important functions performed by trade associations has not dealt with the restrictive possibilities inherent in any one of them. Whether any of these activities are directed to the end of restraining competition depends upon the way they are employed by a particular association. An extensive examination of trade association practices designed to limit competition was made for the Temporary National Economic Committee by Dr. Clair Wilcox.[38] The number of instances in which endeavors to control the market were discovered and the range of trade and industry represented are startlingly great, but the effectiveness of the practices is difficult to appraise.

Price Controls. The most common means of attempting to limit competition was to exercise some control over price. At times, this involved little more than the exchange of price quotations, in the hope that price cutting would be avoided. On other occasions, it involved systematic drives to outlaw sales at or below cost, the items to be included in the latter being determined by the association. In the flour-milling industry, this was coupled with both informal and systematic exchange of price quotations. Another method, used by some household furniture associations, involved the hiring of a person to issue bulletins showing "selling values" for representative furniture items, based upon theoretical replacement costs; to attend regular sales markets for the purpose of consulting with members and inspecting their lines; and, upon request, to name selling prices for specific articles. Sometimes, prices were posted by associations; and failure to adhere to them was considered unfair and unethical. In some instances, this practice was reinforced by the imposition of monetary or other penalties upon those who failed to abide by the agreement. Some trade associations undertook to allocate markets or customers to their members. The assignment of a particular market to a member might permit others to sell in it also, but without competing for business on the basis of price. The price was determined by the producer to whom the market was assigned.

Output Controls. Trade associations also endeavored to control competition by controlling output. In some cases, this was accomplished by reduction of output based upon productive capacity or upon the volume

[38]Temporary National Economic Committee, Monograph No. 21, pp. 225–58.

of goods sold in a previous year. Reduction might also be achieved by assigning specific quotas. The producers of copper, through the Copper Institute, pledged themselves in 1930 to cut output by 16 per cent and announced in 1931 that production should be limited to 26½ per cent of capacity.[39] The National Elevator Manufacturers assigned members production quotas based upon the share of total business handled by each of them during the years 1928-33, inclusive, and adopted a rule which bound them to refuse to accept orders in excess of these shares. The California rice industry, from 1935 to 1938, added a new wrinkle by requiring each member to pay into a "miller's trust fund" 10 cents for every hundred-pound bag of rice processed within his quota and 20 cents for every bag processed beyond it. The proceeds, over and above the association expenses, were distributed among the participants, with penalties deducted from those who violated the agreement.[40]

Boycotts. Trade associations frequently undertook to enforce their programs by organizing boycotts, or by threatening to do so. This was accomplished by loyal association members applying concerted pressure, directly, by refusing to deal with noncomplying members and nonmember competitors who did not conform and, indirectly, by refusing to buy from suppliers or to sell to purchasers who dealt with the recalcitrant. Boycotts were used in a wide range of the wholesale and retail trade by jobbers of plumbing supplies; by plumbing contractors; and by manufacturers of cigars, hat frames, millinery, fireworks, power cable, and wire. Finally, it was found that local associations had been extremely active in endeavoring to restrain competition in the retail trade among automobile dealers, in the cleaning and dyeing business, and, most especially, in building construction.[41]

Appraisal. In an over-all appraisal of trade association activities, it is very difficult, if not impossible, to state in precise terms the extent to which trade associations co-operate to improve the competitive atmosphere and the degree to which they attempt to restrain competition. The line between the two types of activities is not easy to draw. In some instances, conspiracy against public interest has been obvious; in others, the opposite is just as clearly the case. In the practices of the majority of associations, there seems to have been a mixture of both. Nevertheless, of all the forms of combination among independent business concerns, the trade association appears to be the most acceptable from the public point of view. It is able to make substantial contributions to industrial development through the co-operative exploration of technical business problems and the dissemination to the public, as well as to members, of

[39] Temporary National Economic Committee, *Final Report of the Executive Secretary*, p. 91.

[40] *Ibid., p. 92.*

[41] Temporary National Economic Committee, Monograph No. 21, pp. 280–98.

much information otherwise difficult or impossible to obtain. It can assist materially in raising the ethical standards of business by education, by promoting legislation, and by exposing malpractices.

At the same time, the trade association contains many possibilities of monopoly and restriction. As in the case of the other forms of combination, if monopolistic conditions are prevalent in a particular industry, the association may be one of the means of giving more effective implementation to those conditions. Under such circumstances, public policy needs to be alert to the necessity of curbing whatever devises may be employed, but it is not likely to meet with appreciable success unless the more fundamental conditions are rectified.

CONCLUSION

The ubiquity and persistence of combinations are outstanding features of modern industrial development. The dominant forms of combination have changed, from time to time, under pressure of circumstances; and combination has manifested itself with varying degrees of intensity in different industries. In other words, these features have remained constant characteristics of business history and, at the same time, have presented a continuous problem for public policy.

Immediate factors have conditioned the dominant form of combination at a particular time; but the development of business practices and procedures, as they relate to the market, has always taken place under the influence of consultation on common interests. It is in this way that much of the institutional pattern of business conduct has emerged. When they are incorporated into the law, these procedures become part of the formally approved code of business behavior. If the practices do not receive public sanction, they may be condemned under existing law or result in new legal rules or legislation designed to eliminate the objectionable features. It is by the process of trial and error that the structure of regulation, public policy, and business behavior responds to changing conditions.

PART III

The Pricing Process and Public Policy

Chapter 7 THE SCALE OF ENTERPRISE

INTRODUCTION

The production of goods and services takes place under widely varying technical conditions. Many industries require large capital investment and can operate successfully only when large units of equipment are employed. This is the situation which obtains in hydroelectric dams, railroads, blast furnaces, steel mills, and automobile assembly plants. In other industries, much less capital investment is required, and the equipment which is used may be obtained in smaller units. Illustrations of this are to be found in agriculture, retailing, the service trades, clothing manufacture, and a large number of the manufacturing industries. The size of the enterprise in each instance will depend upon a number of different factors: technical, managerial, financial, and market. Size may also be influenced by organizational possibilities, which create the opportunity of expansion for the purpose of limiting or eliminating competition.

Much of modern industry is characterized by large-scale production as well as large-scale ownership. These two characteristics exert a fundamental influence on the structure of industry and on the way in which the forces of competition manifest themselves. In many lines of production, prices and business practices are not the result of rivalry among a large number of firms; instead, they are strongly influenced by the practices and decisions of a few. When a large amount of fixed capital plays an important part in the production process, the problem of calculating costs for particular units of output becomes very difficult; and the pricing process exhibits intricacies that simpler methods of production do not disclose. These factors have brought about significant changes in the nature of competition and in the problems of control with which public policy must deal.

Discussion of the scale of enterprise in the economy calls for an analysis of some of the significant aspects of the theory of production. This area of economic theory comprises some of the most elusive and unsettled topics of economic analysis. In this treatment, only those aspects of the theory that bear directly upon issues of public regulation will be developed, and even these will be dealt with only in so far as it seems possible to give them a content that can be applied to the public regulation of enterprise. This is not to say that further explanation is not useful; indeed, a great deal more study, both theoretical and empirical, is needed; for, while we may be able to set forth some of the economic principles which bear upon the size of plants and firms, we are as yet unable to supply much quantitative information that will tell us whether the scale of operations of firms is too large or too small, or how much bigger they may be able to grow and still be economical or socially desirable.

THE LAW OF DIMINISHING RETURNS

Statement of the Law

The production process requires the utilization of many different agents or resources. When these productive services are combined in varying proportions, the output also varies. This is the result of the operation of what is frequently called the "law of diminishing returns." This law states that if, with a fixed agent of production, successive increments of variable agents are employed, a point is reached where the increase in the output of the variable agents is less than proportional to their input. If the variables are added indefinitely, the additions to total output attributable to an additional variable unit ultimately will become zero.[1] Between these two limits is the stage which is significant in economic problems, known as the "stage of diminishing returns." This law assumes a given state of technology and relates only to the proportion of the factors used in production, not to their absolute amount.

The diagram in Figure 1 illustrates, graphically, the behavior of output as the input of one factor is increased, with the other remaining constant. As additional units of the variable factor are added, the total output rises more than proportionally to the input. For example, if the variable factor is increased from one to two units, the total output more than doubles, and the additional (or marginal output or product) increases; the average product also increases. As this process continues, a stage will be reached, sooner or later, depending on conditions of production, when the marginal product will commence to decline. This will result, at a later stage, in a decline in the average product per unit of input of the variable factor, at which time the total product will cease to increase proportionately,[2] although it will still increase. Finally, the

[1]See F. H. Knight, *Risk, Uncertainty, and Profit* (London School of Economic Reprints, No. 16, 1933), chap. iv., pp. 98–106, for a careful discussion of this; also F. M. Taylor, *Principles of Economics* (9th ed.; New York: Ronald Press Co., 1925), chap. ix. Diminishing returns may also be defined in terms of diminishing marginal productivity. The statement of the law in terms of diminishing average product seems preferable, because it is when average product begins to decline that the "stage of diminishing returns" sets in.

[2]This is also the point beyond which the "actual" increase of output resulting from additional units of the variables is less than the "proportional" increase. For an arithmetic and tabular exposition of this, see Taylor, *op. cit.*, p. 127.

marginal product will be reduced to zero—that is, there will be no additional output from an additional unit of the variable. When this point is reached, total output will commence to decline.

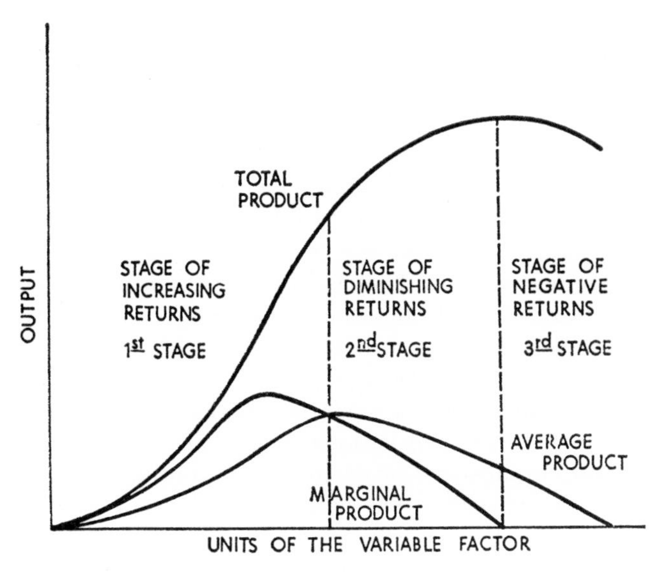

FIGURE 1

Significance of the Law

As already noted, it is the second stage of variation in returns that is the economically significant one. A producer would not continue to expand his output into the third stage, because the total output would diminish. He would not stop expanding until the end of the first stage, because he is not only increasing his total output, he is also getting more than proportional returns on the inputs of the variable. If diminishing returns did not set in at some stage of expansion, it would be possible, for example, to produce all the wheat needed in the world on a single acre of land merely by adding additional units of labor; or, to reverse the example, one man could produce all the wheat needed merely by adding additional acres of land. In other words, production is economical only within the stage of diminishing returns. This means that at any given time, there are economic limits to the scale of every enterprise, and these limits are established by diminishing returns. Even more important is the fact that without diminishing returns, there would be no problem of economic organization. "The facts of variability in the proportions of agencies in the productive organization, and of the variation of the yield relative to the different agencies in accordance with the principle of diminishing returns not merely make possible the economic organization of society through free contract, but in their absence the whole question of organization would be meaningless; there would be no such problem."[3]

The Optimum Factor Combination

The changes in output under diminishing returns are the result of varying the proportions of the productive factors which are being used. A producer, therefore, must decide what combination of factors he will employ. The combination he selects will determine where in the stage of diminishing returns his output will be. This will depend upon the relative costs of the factors which are employed. When a producer uses that combination which gives him the lowest average total cost per unit for a given output, the factors are combined in their most economical proportions for that output. That is, there is an optimum combination of factors of production. Under these circumstances, the firm obtains the maximum product from a given cost of outlay, or the minimum average unit cost for a given output.

Where the optimum combination will lie will depend upon the relative costs of the fixed and variable agents. If the fixed agent is relatively high-cost, expansion conceivably may continue until additional increments of the variables add nothing to the total product. If the variables are relatively high-cost, expansion may cease as soon as the marginal output of the variables is equal to their average output. Between these two extremes lies the most economical scale of operations. The reason for this is the unutilized or excess capacity of the fixed agents. If they are relatively expensive—that is, expensive as compared with the cost of the variables—it will pay to utilize them intensively. If the reverse is true, the variables will be used more intensively and may not even be added beyond the point where diminishing returns set in.

ECONOMIES OF SCALE

Meaning of Economies of Scale

At the outset, it is necessary to distinguish between the law of diminishing returns and the concept of economies of scale. Diminishing returns lays the foundation for the economic limits on the amount of output or the size of firms under given conditions. The law does not give an indication of the absolute economical size which a given enterprise may achieve, even under the assumption of fixed technology, because it deals only with proportions. What the most economical size of an enterprise may be depends upon the economies of scale.

Economies of scale refer to the increased efficiency or lower unit costs of production that are realized from the expansion in the size of an undertaking as a result of increasing all of the factors of production. Economies of scale therefore reflect the effects of changes in the total quanti-

[3]Knight, *op. cit.*, pp. 102–3.

ties of factors of production used by the firm on the cost per unit of output, economies of scale being realized when an increase in the size of operations yields a lower cost per unit of output. Thus, a farmer may double the amount of land he owns, increase the number of his employees, and take someone into partnership with him, thereby lowering the unit cost of his output. His larger scale of operations is more economical than the smaller one.

Reasons for Economies of Scale

There appear to be three principal reasons for the economies of scale. First, economies of scale are related to the size of the market. For example, an electric light and power plant may be serving a small community. Its generating and distribution facilities will be adapted to that market; and if it is operating most economically, it will be organized on the basis of the optimum combination. If the market expands, the firm will increase its productive capacity and will be able to lower its costs per unit of output. Again, it may operate at the optimum combination, but the increase in size will result in economies of scale. There will be a new optimum combination and a lower unit cost of output. Economies of scale may therefore arise as the market for a product expands.

Second, economies of scale may be the result of the indivisibility of some of the factors of production. Units of productive resources are not completely divisible. Some of them, like hydroelectric dams and blast furnaces, are obtainable only in relatively large units and are cheaper to obtain per unit of output capacity than technically possible smaller units. Larger outputs can therefore be obtained at a lower cost per unit of output than with the smaller plants. Indivisibilities also apply to labor and management. In the case of a hydroelectric undertaking, a very large generating establishment can be operated with nearly the same amount of labor and management as a small one. In other words, the economies of scale in this instance arise from the change in the proportion of the factors which is the result of indivisibility. Some economists contend that indivisibility in management is ultimately the most important single factor making for economies of scale. These economists also assert that without indivisibility, there could be no economies of scale. Whatever may be the merits of the controversy, it is clear that indivisibility of factors is a very important influence on economies of scale.[4]

Third, economies of scale also may arise from increased specialization in the use of factors. As a business expands, it may be able to take advantage of the specialization of labor and managerial activities in addition to being able to secure the services of more highly specialized and superior abilities. Specialization of processes and machines may also be possible with increases in size.

[4]For a discussion of this whole issue, see E. H. Chamberlin, "Proportionality, Divisibility and Economies of Scale," *Quarterly Journal of Economics*, Vol. LXII (February, 1948), pp. 229–57.

Returns to Scale

There are three stages to the economies of scale, and a firm may be in any one of them. It is also possible that an enterprise may never pass beyond the first one. These stages are the result of the operation of the forces discussed in the previous section. The first of these stages is that of increasing returns to scale. In this stage, an increase in the scale of operations—that is, an increase in the inputs or quantities of factors used—leads to an increase in output at a faster rate than the increase of inputs. The limit to increasing returns for any firm will depend upon the extent to which the influences of indivisibility and specialization create increased resistance to expansion. Indivisibilities are very important in the case of capital goods, especially in modern industry—as, for example, in railroads, the steel industry, or electric light and power. Indivisibility may also appear in connection with marketing, finance, and research activities. All of these indivisibilities encounter limitations; and although the latter may not be reached for all of them at the same time, when the resultant effect is that output ceases to increase more than proportionately to input, increasing returns arising from indivisibilities have come to an end.

Many economists are of the opinion that the most significant limitations on scale arise in connection with specialization in labor and management. Increases in labor force create problems of supervision and co-ordination, as well as the need for an increase in managerial requirements. Specialization obviously encounters limitations, and expansion leads to growing complications in co-ordination and decision making. In other words, the limitations on increasing returns arise primarily from the complexities of organization, impersonal relations, divided responsibility, and so forth. In fact, if genuine economies could be obtained without limit from such aspects of a firm's activities as finance, research, and management, particularly the latter, there seems to be no reason why a firm should encounter an end to increasing returns. "It is the economies of large-scale government rather than of large-scale technique which dictates the size of the modern business unit . . . . As in manufacture, it is the limit to the economies of large-scale government and not of large-scale technique which dictates the size of the producing unit: but unlike manufacture, agriculture runs its head into the former barrier first."[5] This is the reason why economies of the firm may exceed the economies of the plant and why multiple-plant firms may therefore be more economical than single-plant firms.[6]

[5] D. H. Robertson, *The Control of Industry* (New York: Harcourt, Brace & Co., Inc., 1923), pp. 24–25.

[6] See, however, F. A. Fetter, "The Fundamental Principle of Efficiency in Mass Production," in Temporary National Economic Committee, Monograph No. 13, *Relative Efficiency of Large, Medium-Sized and Small Business* (Washington, D.C.: U.S. Government Printing Office, 1941), Appendix D, pp. 398–415; and G. J. Stigler, *The Theory of Price* (New York: Macmillan Co., 1946), chap. 11.

Economies arising from indivisibilities may be limited, but it does not follow that further expansion promptly leads to diseconomies. When expansion has exhausted increasing returns, the firm enters the stage of constant returns—that is, output increases in the same proportion as input. This state will be the result of counteracting influences being in balance. There seems to be considerable evidence that this stage holds for a substantial range of output in many types of business and that many of our large manufacturing firms are in this stage.

The third stage, that of decreasing returns to scale, arises when the balance resulting in constant returns has been upset so that further expansion can be effected only by an increase of inputs that yield a less than proportionate increase of output. Total output, of course, may still be increasing. It is very probable that many electric light and power companies operate in this stage. They find it impossible to increase the regularity and intensity of the use of their facilities, but continue to experience growth by territorial expansion.

It should be noted that there is a difference between returns to scale and the variations in costs resulting from the change in utilization of resources at a given scale. A firm may be able to lower its costs per unit of output by a more intensive use of the facilities it possesses. Increasing output in this fashion is not the result of increasing the scale of operations, but rather that of making more economical use of the existing scale of resources in the enterprise, that is, making use of idle capacity.

LARGE-SCALE PRODUCTION

The consequences flowing from the law of diminishing returns and the influence of the forces making for economies of scale provide us with concepts that explain why there are economical limits to the size of firms at any particular time or, to put it another way, under given conditions. They also explain why firms may grow and, over a range of output, experience economies that make the larger scale more economical than the smaller one. These principles apply to all types of production and productive activity, the economical scale of operations being determined by the same forces in each case. There still remains, however, the task of applying these principles to various industries or types of industries in order to explain the differences in scale that appear among them—for example, the difference in the scale of operations typically found in agriculture from that in the manufacture of farm machinery, or in motor transport from that in rail transport. There is even the problem of deciding what we mean by large-scale production, and the usual distinction between it and economies of scale.

Meaning of Large-Scale Production

The term "large-scale production," which is frequently used to designate certain characteristics of modern industry, actually has a number of different meanings and implications. Although most of these have certain factors in common, some of them are also derived from quite different sources which require separate consideration. For example, large-scale production and giant enterprise are not necessarily synonymous terms. A holding company may own corporations engaged in many different lines of production, its own size, however, being determined merely by the amount of control which it exercises. It may exhibit none of the economies and none of the economic advantages that may derive from large size.

Large-scale production commonly refers to the contrast in size between the giant business enterprises which characterize such industries as steel, automobile manufacturing, railroad transportation, and the generation and distribution of electrical energy, on the one hand, and the multiplicity of small businesses which make up such undertakings as agriculture, the service trades, much of the building industry, and a large part of retailing, on the other hand. The term may also refer, however, to the scale of production or the size of enterprise within a particular industry. Thus, large-scale farming may be contrasted or compared with small-scale farming. Probably the most generally accepted connotation is that which comprehends both large-scale operation and large-scale organization, thereby including economies of scale of both the plant and the firm.

It is also useful to observe a distinction between mass production and large-scale production. Mass production refers to the production of highly standardized commodities in large quantities. When this is possible, the scale of production will be much larger than if each unit of output is unique—provided, of course, that there is an adequate market for the standardized products. Thus, during World War II, Liberty and Victory ships were produced on a mass basis. Ordinarily, however, the shipbuilding industry is much more individualized in terms of product; yet, it is still characterized by large-scale production. The industries which lend themselves to mass production are fewer in number than those which lend themselves to large-scale production; and from the standpoint of industrial development, mass production has followed from large-scale production as one special phase of it.[7]

In analyzing the problems connected with large-scale production, it is also frequently useful to distinguish between the plant and the firm. The plant is the basic technological unit of production. It may be conveniently regarded as the physical facilities of production located in one place and operated as a unit. The firm is the ownership organizational unit. It may operate one plant or many; it may confine its activities to one location, or it may literally spread all over the world. There is another feature which characterizes the firm: Even though it may be made

[7]M. W. Watkins, "Large Scale Production," *Encyclopedia of the Social Sciences*, Vol. IX, pp. 171–80.

up of separate legal units, the ordinary operations of the market are eliminated from among the various parts of this ownership unit. It may confine itself to a relatively limited sphere of production; or it may expand into innumerable fields, many of them having no technological connection.

When expansion of enterprise into fields of activity having little or no technological connection with each other takes place, large-scale production is succeeded by large-scale ownership. Frequently, large-scale ownership has emerged under the impetus of economies of large-scale production; but much of it is to be explained by endeavors to secure control of markets and to get insulation from the disturbing effects of competition—that is, disturbing to those seeking control. Large-scale ownership under the influence of the holding company and the privileges of intercorporate stock ownership led to large-scale control. This was a purely financial and managerial development, arising out of the existing legal status of the corporate device.

The distinction between large-scale production, as descriptive of certain industries, and large-scale production, as applied to the size of operations within particular industries, has an important bearing on public policy. Certain industries lend themselves to a scale of operations which would be characterized as large by almost any measuring rod, whereas others are typically small by similar standards. In each instance, the question may arise as to the proper public policy required to make possible the achievement of the most economical size. When public policy turns its attention to increasing productive efficiency, the scale of production is a relative matter, which must be considered in the light of each particular industry. This makes it especially difficult to impose a workable minimum or maximum size for any enterprise. However, this does not preclude the possibilities of devising practicable limitations on large-scale ownership and large-scale control. This has been done in commercial banking and in transportation. The issues arising in this connection in the field of transportation are dealt with in a later section of this book. In manufacturing, the problem is probably somewhat more complicated; some aspects of this will be examined later.

Factors Making for Large-Scale Production

The growth of large-scale production may be attributed to three main factors: market, technology, and organization. These three factors exert their influence simultaneously, although they may not be of equal significance in any particular situation. It is not necessary here to discuss the differences of opinion that have arisen over the causal relations among these forces, or to evaluate the relative importance of each in the interpretation of economic history. Historically, it was the effect of expanding markets that was first given recognition as a primary factor in the growth of large-scale production. Adam Smith first gave most explicit expression to this by demonstrating that "the division of labor is limited by the extent of the market." At the same time he explained the economic advantages of the division of labor and the specialization which accompanies it.

Reduction in the cost of production of goods by increasing the scale of output arises from the ability to specialize in processes, products, or occupations. This opportunity is present only when the market is large enough to absorb the output which is of sufficient volume to make the specialization more economical. This specialization depends upon the ability to concentrate on a limited field of endeavor and to gain proficiency by repetition of processes. If the advantages of specialization are to be obtained to any appreciable extent, the products themselves must be amenable to a considerable degree of standardization. When goods and services, however, are produced as particular units for particular individuals, or in very limited quantity, it is the extent of the market which imposes limits on the scale of production. Thus, custom-made pleasure boats are typically produced in small plants, whereas the production of automobiles illustrates the other extreme. The size of the market may be limited by consumer taste, geographic position, the transportability of the product, political considerations, population density, and standards of living.

The second factor leading to the growth of large-scale production has been technology—the development of machine techniques and the application of mechanical power to the production of goods and services. The effect of the utilization of mechanical power and machinery has been to increase enormously the productivity of human effort. Technology not only has made it possible to create goods and services otherwise unobtainable under any circumstances but also has resulted in the production of a large proportion of the commodities available today at a much lower cost than heretofore. The machine technique increases the possibilities of standardization, specialization, and coordination far beyond what would otherwise be obtainable; there is greater precision and uniformity of quality, and also a greater continuity of operation. A hydroelectric power plant, for example, can be run on a continuous basis of output for an almost indefinite period. The continuity of machine production may even carry the specialization of labor to the point where one laborer continuously performs only a single and simple operation.

The ability to realize the advantages of technology in production depends upon the market which can be obtained. Technology itself, however, is a direct factor in developing these markets. Not only is there continuous pressure for the reduction of costs so that larger markets can be reached, but also there is the constant urge to search for new markets. The possibilities of expansion and the opportunities to make new products, which industrial research is constantly uncovering, lead to intensive efforts to develop new tastes and new markets. Thus, although the ability to utilize technology depends upon the markets which are available, that technology, at the same time, is one of the most important factors leading to the development of the markets themselves.

The influence of technology on scale is illustrated in striking fashion in the field of transportation. Railroads are outstanding examples of large-scale production. Motor transport, which over a considerable range offers readily substitutable services, exhibits few of the characteristics of large-scale production. Motor transport can be supplied only by relatively small units of motive equipment, and increase in scale of operations requires extensive duplication of equipment and manpower. "Mass production" in motor transport yields little by way of economies of scale, therefore, because the technology does not lend itself to this type of activity. Strictly speaking, it is not correct to use the term "mass production" in this connection; rail transport, on the other hand, is a prime illustration of mass production.

The third factor influencing the development of large-scale production is organization. Although this is, in part attributable to the other two factors, it is also an independent force. The growth of large-scale production, under the influence of market expansion and technology, has created the opportunity for the specialization of managerial functions and has increased the scope for the exercise of entrepreneurial ingenuity. Modern industry offers one of the main outlets for the exercise of the qualities of leadership and administration and for the acquisition of power and prestige. At the same time, it encourages specialization in the various branches of industry, marketing, finance, public relations, and personnel management and in the executive aspects of nearly all the learned professions which also find a place in modern industry. Organization, however, is a distinct requirement if these branches are to be given their full scope.

The development of forms of business organization capable of integrating the various activities of large-scale enterprise has been indispensable to its growth. It is impossible to say what the structure of modern industry would have been like without the corporation; but at least, it is safe to assert that the corporate device has been one of the most potent forces that has molded modern industry and added to its efficiency. The late President Nicholas Murray Butler of Columbia University once said that the limited-liability corporation was the greatest single discovery of modern times, whether it be judged by its social, ethical, industrial, or, in the long run, political effects. In his opinion, even steam and electricity were far less important in influencing the development of modern civilization than the limited-liability corporation, and they would be reduced to comparative impotence without it.[8]

[8]Quoted in J. C. Bonbright and G. C. Means, *The Holding Company* (New York: McGraw-Hill Book Co., Inc., 1932), p. 3.

Even though this may be regarded as an extreme statement, it cannot be doubted that organization must be recognized as one of the most significant factors in the development of large-scale production and the efficiency of modern industry.

Organization is not merely a matter of form of ownership or the institutional arrangements connected therewith. It is also a question of co-ordination and effective utilization of the resources that are combined to make a producing unit or enterprise. The function of organization, therefore, is to bring together the diverse activities of the techniques of production, marketing, finance, and so forth into a co-ordinated and economical whole. Some economists refer to this as the economies of large-scale government, and they hold that this is the factor that is most significant in making for large-scale production.[9] That it is of equal significance with the other two can scarcely be denied. However, the limiting factor in industries like agriculture and motor transport appears primarily to be technology—first of all, because large-scale government or organization can effect little by way of economies; and second, because it is the technology which limits the scope of large-scale organization.

SIZE AND EFFICIENCY

Since the beginning of the present century, numerous attempts have been made to measure the success of large-scale enterprise and combinations. At first, attention was focused on the trusts or monopolistic combines. Later, it was turned to an analysis of the relative profitability of big business. A few years ago, the Federal Trade Commission endeavored to point the inquiry more directly to the question of the relation of size to efficiency in the various industries.

One of the earliest attempts to appraise the achievements of big business was made by Professor A. S. Dewing,[10] who examined 35 carefully selected consolidations that had been in existence at least 10 years prior to 1914. For a consolidation to be classified as successful, he assumed that it should yield a larger net profit than the sum of the net profits of the controlling elements that entered into the combination, that it should yield a net profit at least approximately equal to what its proponents estimated that it would yield, and that the average net earnings over a period of 10 years should show a conspicuous increase over the net earnings prior to the combination and over the net earnings obtained during its first year. Professor Dewing found that in only 5 cases did the average earnings for the 10-year period following consolidation equal or exceed the estimates made by the promoters and bankers at the time the trust was organized. Furthermore, the representative earnings of consolidation during the first year were less, by about one tenth,

[9]See Robertson, *loc. cit.*

[10]A. S. Dewing, "A Statistical Test of the Success of Consolidations," *Quarterly Journal of Economics*, Vol. XXXVI (November, 1921), pp. 84–101.

than the average earnings during the 10-year period. But the earnings of the first year after consolidation were greater than the earnings of the tenth year. In other words, after a sufficient time had elapsed for the seasoning of the consolidation, and after considerable new sums of money had been invested, the earnings gradually diminished, until they amounted to no more than they did during the first year of consolidation. Moreover, the earnings of the first year were less than the sum of the earnings of the separate plants before consolidation. Professor Dewing concluded, therefore, that the consolidations had failed to demonstrate their merits. Somewhat similar results were obtained in a study by the National Industrial Conference Board which covered mergers from 1900 to 1913.[11]

A different conclusion, however, was reached by Professor S. Livermore, who made an examination of industrial mergers from 1888 to 1905 and then followed their record through to 1937.[12] He concluded that about one half of all the mergers created at the turn of the century were successful and, furthermore, that the great majority were able to continue their position of leadership and their ability to earn profits, not by oppressive tactics toward competitors but by becoming the real leaders in their field. He also reached the further conclusion that fewer than 10 per cent of our largest companies were the result of mergers since 1905. It was his judgment that well over half of the largest industrial companies studies were the result of growth by reinvestment of their own profits and that present bigness was not necessarily the result of merger either before or since 1905.[13]

In a study designed to throw light on the question, "How profitable is big business?" the Twentieth Century Fund, Inc.,[14] found that no simple answer could be given if "profitable" meant profit on gross income. It was found that the largest corporations were the most profitable and that there was a well-marked profit trend from the smallest class through the largest among all corporations, including money-making corporations. If "profitable" meant net income on net worth or the total profit on total capitalization, then, among money-making corporations, the smallest class was the most profitable and the largest the least; and, among money-losing corporations, the smallest class was the most unprofitable and the largest class the least. In other words, largeness of size has a strong tendency to stabilize the rates of profit on capital. It tends to keep the rate of profit on profitable corporations, and the rate of loss of unprofitable corporations, within comparatively narrow limits. The

[11]National Industrial Conference Board, *Mergers in Industry* (New York, 1929).

[12]Shaw Livermore, "The Success of Industrial Mergers," *Quarterly Journal of Economics*, Vol. L (November, 1935), pp. 68–96.

[13]Essentially similar conclusions have been reached by J. F. Weston, *The Role of Mergers in the Growth of Large Firms* (Berkeley and Los Angeles: University of California Press, 1953).

[14]Twentieth Century Fund, Inc., *How Profitable Is Big Business?* (New York, 1937).

study found that larger corporations pay more liberal dividends, and it also concluded that larger corporations have sounder financial setups.

The study also pointed out that there were between 10 and 12 million different stockholders in 1932 and between 6 and 10 million individual owners of corporate bonds at the end of 1932. In addition, there are many millions of other individuals who have an indirect stage in the property of corporations because of investments in corporate securities on the part of insurance companies, banks, etc. The stabilizing effect which large corporations have on earnings of investments is a factor, the study suggested, which should be given careful consideration in view of the widespread participation of the American public in industrial investment. The smaller corporation apparently entails considerably more risk.

The Federal Trade Commission prepared an extensive study on the relative efficiency of large, medium-sized and small business for the Temporary National Economic Committee.[15] It employed six tests by which it endeavored to measure business efficiency: (1) cost of production for individual companies classified as large, medium-sized, or small; (2) cost of production for individual plants classified as large, medium-sized, or small; (3) cost of production for groups of companies classified as large, medium-sized, or small; (4) cost of production for groups of plants classified as large, medium-sized, or small; (5) rate of return on invested capital for individual companies classified as large, medium-sized, or small; and (6) rate of return on invested capital for groups of companies classified as large, medium-sized, or small. The Commission was unable to apply all of these tests to all of the companies which it studied, but it did make a total of 233 tests in its survey. The conclusion reached was that, on the whole, the largest companies made a very poor showing.

> In the 233 combined tests, large size, whether represented by a corporation, a plant, a group of corporations or a group of plants showed the lowest cost or the highest rate of return on invested capital in only 25 tests. In these combined tests, medium size made the best showing in 128 tests and small size in 80 tests. Thus, large size was most efficient as efficiency is here measured in approximately 11 per cent of the total of tests. Medium size was most efficient in approximately 55 per cent of the tests and small size was most efficient in approximately 34 per cent of the tests.[16]

These studies of the relationship of size to efficiency have achieved only inconclusive results. The general concensus of the investigators seems to be that medium-sized business is best able to meet the tests that are available for measuring that relationship and that, from the standpoint of the economies of size, the structure of industry is still competi-

[15]Temporary National Economic Committee, Monograph No. 13; see also Appendix A, pp. 133 ff., and Appendix D, pp. 398 ff.

[16]*Ibid.*, p. 14. But see John M. Blair, "The Relation between Size and Efficiency of Business," *Review of Economics and Statistics*, Vol. XXIV (1942), pp. 125–36.

tive. Investigation leaves little room for the contentions that all restraints should be removed and that monopolistic combination should be allowed to run its course to the ultimate extinction of competition.

Many questions still remain unanswered, however. The studies that have been made are subject to severe statistical limitations; and the results, at best, can be considered only tentative. What constitutes medium size is a constantly shifting measuring rod. Medium size at one time might be quite small under changed conditions of technology, or even vice versa. Furthermore, there are a great many individual differences. For example, General Motors Corporation made a good showing under the Federal Trade Commission's investigation and met the tests of social performance set up by Professor Kreps, who, in a very critical appraisal, concluded that business on the whole had failed to meet these tests.[17] Moreover, a study on large-scale organization in the food industry concluded that the enactment of various legislative measures designed to penalize and limit the growth of mass distribution has been a mistake.[18] The opinion was advanced that some form of large-scale organization is clearly needed if there is to be anything approaching maximum efficiency in the handling of food products.

Size and efficiency really present two distinct problems. For the individual enterprise, the issue is one of achieving the size which brings the most satisfactory results from the standpoint of the objectives of management. Public policy, on the other hand, is faced with the question of discovering ways and means of obtaining the advantages of the economies of size without the disadvantages of giant enterprise formed for the purpose of controlling the market, for lust for power, or for profit arising from financial manipulations.

PROBLEMS OF SIZE

Motives for Growth

The economical size of enterprises is not limited by purely technical considerations. The scale of production in many industries makes the difficulties of entry real, because of the huge amount of resources required to begin operations. The preference of consumers for many established lines of products may be difficult to overcome. Furthermore, the advantages of monopoly from the standpoint of the enterprise, the desire to restrict competition, and the power of giant corporations to blud-

[17]Temporary National Economic Committee, Monograph No. 7, *Measurement of the Social Performance of Business* (Washington, D.C.: U.S. Government Printing Office, 1940). The six tests used by Professor Kreps were (1) employment, (2) production, (3) consumer effort commanded, (4) consumer funds absorbed, (5) payrolls, and (6) dividends and interest.

[18]Temporary National Economic Committee, Monograph No. 35, *Large-Scale Organization in the Food Industries* (Washington, D.C.: U.S. Government Printing Office, 1941), p. 157.

geon competitors are strong incentives to expand beyond what would otherwise be economical limits. To these factors should be added the influence of the tariff, the restraining effects which patents may have on competition, the opportunity to adapt the corporate device to purely acquisitive ends, and the inadequacy of the law to eliminate sheer predatory behavior. So far as public policy is concerned, one of the major difficulties to date lies in the inability to secure adequate and workable standards by which it is possible to distinguish between the effects of the economies of scale of production and the other factors which provide incentives for the development of big business and combinations.

The basic issue of public policy as it relates to size and efficiency centers on the question of how size is achieved. The objective of regulation should be to prevent the utilization of devices and practices that make it possible for enterprises to grow beyond the bounds dictated by competitive ability. As long as growth is conditioned upon the economies of size, it would seem wise to allow that growth to take place and to devise ways and means of dealing with the social problems which it creates. It is apparent, however, that many of the monopolistic aspects of modern business are derived not from its economic characteristics but rather from the opportunity which business has had to acquire monopolistic power through legal arrangements which have given privileges without assessing adequate responsibilities, or through extralegal and illegal practices that have not been brought to task. Studies made so far indicate that little success can be expected from attempts to impose any absolute limit on the size of business enterprise. The alternative is to see that the methods by which growth may take place are not those which are designed to achieve monopoly power under the guise of the economies of large-scale production.

Mergers and Size

Much of the discussion bearing on the advantages of large-scale production and motivation for expansion has centered around the question of mergers, whereas the most impressive aspect of growth to present size, at least over the last forty years, has been the result of internal expansion rather than of merger. Analysis of the results of mergers may not be conclusive or even particularly relevant evidence on the effect of increasing size on efficiency, unless careful attention is given to the conditions of a merger and the purposes for effecting it. Analysis of mergers and of the motives for them generally seems to lead to adverse criticism by economists;[19] but internal expansion—vertical, horizontal, and what is sometimes called circular—does not seem to have been subject to the

[19]See, for example, J. M. Clark, *The Economics of Overhead Costs* (Chicago: University of Chicago Press, 1923), chap. vii; Stigler, *op. cit.*, chap. 11; G. W. Stocking and M. W. Watkins, *Monopoly and Free Enterprise* (New York: Twentieth Century Fund, Inc., 1951), chap. 3.

same degree of scrutiny. If evidence were conclusive that monopoly or restriction of competition was the prime motivator of mergers, the problem might be resolved by prohibiting all mergers, even though, on occasion, some social advantages might be sacrificed. If, however, the same type of integration and expansion may be obtained by internal growth, little would be gained by an outright prohibition of mergers; or, at least, the disadvantages accruing from the same type of integration or diversification through internal expansion would not be avoided. Consequently, although there may be cogent reasons for imposing definite restrictions on mergers, the basic question centering on expansion from integration would still remain unresolved.

Forms of Integration

There are really many different forms of integration, but they are rather commonly classified into three types: vertical, horizontal, and circular. The latter, being a manifestation of diversity of output, could therefore be labeled as diversified integration.

Vertical integration occurs when a firm operates at more than one stage or level of production. This is illustrated by integration of production from iron ore to finished steel products in the steel industry. Horizontal integration is the term applied to expansion across markets at the same level of production or distribution. This may involve a merger of competing firms in a given line of production; or it may manifest itself by internal expansion from an original base over a wider area, as illustrated by retail chains, mail-order houses, and branch factories. Circular or diversified integration arises when a firm diversifies its output where a common element of research, skills, or facilities may be utilized. The food manufacturing industries are examples of this, and so are transport companies that supply water, air, rail and pipe-line services. In practice, integration is seldom of any one type but instead usually involves all three, even though one of them may predominate in a particular instance.

Integration and the Process of Production

Although integration may be the result of mergers, it is, in fact, an inescapable feature of the productive process, since it is well-nigh impossible for a firm to engage in only one stage of output for a homogeneous product, even when the latter term is used with tolerable imprecision. In other words, multiple-product firms represent the various types of integration. One cannot assume these away or, for practical purposes, apply theoretical analysis which, by assumption, simplifies operating conditions beyond the point under which they can be undertaken in fact. The problem here, as in many other areas of economics, is that of developing operationally useful concepts, especially for the purpose of establishing criteria for public policy. Institutional arrangements such as the corporate device readily permit the expansion of enterprise beyond the economical limits which large-scale production may justify. Public policy should obviously seek means of preventing such expansion. How to achieve this short of purely arbitrary action is not an easy matter; and at present, to a considerable extent, economics has not been able to develop gauges that are operationally very reliable or objective. If diversity had no advantages, the answer would be simple.[20]

THE CHANGING STRUCTURE OF THE ECONOMY

The Role of Big Business

The development of large-scale production and large-scale enterprise has resulted in fundamental changes in the industrial structure. In many lines of industry, an overwhelming preponderance of output is in the hands of a few corporations. Large corporations are characteristic of the industries which market on a nationwide basis. Large-scale enterprise is so prominent in American industrial life that it is easy to get the impression that small business is no longer of significance. The corporation has come to be the almost exclusive form of organization for big business, and the ease with which it can be used to acquire control of other enterprises has made combination for that purpose one of the basic influences in the growth of giant business enterprises.

While large-scale enterprise has grown with expanding markets, it has also been a prime motivating force in that expansion. In the constant search for new outlets for products, this type of enterprise has brought an enormous increase in the variety of goods available to the consumer. Recently, product differentiation, by which the producer endeavors to attract consumer preference through some distinguishing feature of a product—whether it be name, label, or style—has undergone intensive development. As a consequence, there has been a marked increase in the influence of producers on products and on consumer preference. The cultivation of styles and tastes has become one of the most effective means of gaining markets in many products. No one can doubt, for example, that automobile manufacturers exercise considerable power in determining the styles of automobiles, even though competition and consumers' tastes impose severe limitations on them.

Today, the economy as a whole is much more integrated than it was at the beginning of the present century. The decisions of management in those industries which have nationwide markets affect a larger number of people than heretofore. When an industry operating on a national scale possesses some degree of monopoly, its actions are more

[20]See C. D. Edwards, "Conglomerate Bigness as a Source of Power," in *Business Concentration and Price Policy* (Princeton: Princeton University Press, 1955), pp. 331–52; and comment by G. W. Stocking, pp. 352–59. For a careful study of diversification in American industry, see M. Gort, *Diversification and Integration in American Industry* (Princeton: Princeton University Press, 1962).

significant to the economy than are those of the purely local monopoly; and it attracts much more attention, even though the monopoly powers, as such, may not loom large. The strategic position of some industries and firms in the economy makes them a focus of attention, especially when dislocation takes place. A shutdown of production, for example, by United States Steel or by one of the "Big Three" in automobiles, quickly becomes an issue of national importance.

Changes in Methods of Distribution

The changes in the structure of industry have also been accompanied by a fundamental shift in the methods and practices of distributing goods. Prior to the last war, the jobber and the wholesaler were the focal points of distribution between the manufacturer and the retailer. The increase in speed of transportation and communication since then has made contact between the manufacturer and the retailer much easier. The function of the jobber and the wholesaler in maintaining large inventories is no longer as useful as it once was. Nationwide advertising through the radio and press has brought the manufacturer into more immediate touch with the retailer of his product. Moreover, the stress on product differentiation has increased the necessity for manufacturers to push their own lines directly to the consumer level. As a consequence, manufacturing firms have assumed more and more the functions of distribution, with the result that the consumer may literally deal directly with the manufacturer in many lines. Many of the personal relations that formerly existed in the channels of trade have disappeared, but emphasis on brand and trade names has made the maintenance of quality of prime importance. The necessity for the manufacturer to maintain his reputation with the consumer has increased with the decline in the reliance of the buyer on the recommendations of the distributor or retailer. At the same time, these very developments have encouraged imitation and infringement, together with several forms of misrepresentation of goods and disparagement of competitors—factors which are more menacing on a national scale than could have been the case in strictly local markets.[21]

Effect on Pricing Practices

The transformation of the industrial structure has brought corresponding changes in the patterns of prices and the processes governing price formation. Pricing structures may vary all the way from thoroughly competitive situations with rapid and direct responses to market situations, to the highly formalized and slowly adaptable structures characteristic of the regulated industries. In common-carrier transportation

[21]National Industrial Conference Board, *Public Regulation of Competitive Practices in Business Enterprise* (3d ed.; New York, 1940), chap. i.

and public utilities, the law requires that all prices (rates) be publicly announced and strictly adhered to. Moreover, changes in these prices may even take years to effect because of the regulatory process. At the same time, in transportation, over one third of intercity freight, at least in interstate commerce, is hauled by nonregulated carriers, a situation that has led to serious distortions in the allocation of traffic, and a critical impasse in regulation. Over a large part of the economy, "quoted" or "announced" prices have become the customary means of informing the buyer of the price he is expected to pay. The sheer mechanics of marketing the products and services of large enterprises under modern conditions necessitates adherence by salesmen to prices as determined or sanctioned by the responsible executives. This leads to a greater systematization of policies followed by individual firms in setting the prices at which they offer their products. The complexity of the problem of arriving at the prices to be charged induces a certain amount of inertia to price changes, with the result that competition may be diverted into nonprice channels. Buyers who have become accustomed to quoted prices expect a degree of price stability that is not possible in markets where the technique of the auction prevails. Then, too, if there are relatively few sellers of a particular commodity, the knowledge that the price changes of one may be met by the other can easily lead to an element of price leadership which reduces direct price competition.

With the necessity of planning ahead for the multiplicity of products of the giant concerns in the face of many imponderables, pricing targets are bound to play a prominent part; price structures and pricing practices simply cannot respond instantaneously to the assumptions of the auction place. It may be that business firms are too tardy in adjusting to changing market situations, thereby producing distortions that react to their own disadvantage as well as to that of buyers. This seems to be the heart of the controversy over "administered" prices.[22] This does not prove that competition is less of a force than it has been. What it does emphasize is that pricing is a complex problem in a highly industrialized world, and that pricing entails the exercise of judgment and authority as well as the mere operation of impersonal forces in the market place.

Has Competition Declined?

The transformations in the industrial structure signify to many that competition has declined. It is certainly true that the question of monopoly in the last three quarters of a century has come to loom larger in the economy as a whole than it did before. The operation, on a national scale, of businesses possessing elements of monopoly power may result in a comparatively few enterprises exerting a considerable influence over important segments of the economy. It also attracts more public

[22]See *Administered Prices: A Compendium on Public Policy, op. cit.*

attention than the existence of a larger number of monopolies of purely local significance, unknown outside their own areas. This, however, does not prove that competition has declined in importance, and that there is a more widespread departure from competitive norms, or that monopoly has come to occupy a larger relative position in the economy.[23]

Attempts have been made to evaluate the comparative extent of competition and monopoly in the American economy, but no precise results have been obtained. The conclusions which Dr. Clair Wilcox reached after an extensive study of the problem seem to sum up the situation adequately:

> No sort of estimate concerning the comparative extent of competition and monopoly in American markets is justified by the available evidence. Such an estimate must wait upon the articulation of usable definitions, the development of techniques of measurement, and the collection of a body of data much larger than anything that is now at hand. Indeed, it may be doubted if such an estimate can ever be made with any assurance. Competitive industries have their monopolistic aspects, monopolized industries have their competitive aspects; the situation in both fields is constantly in a state of flux. The most that can be said today is that competition is far too common to justify the thesis that the competitive system is approaching extinction, and that monopoly is far too common to justify its treatment as an occasional exception to the general rule.[24]

The phrase "decline of competition" signifies diminution of the force of competition in the economic structure. It is clear that there are reasons for doubting the accuracy of this appraisal. It is equally clear that modern economic activity does not conform to the traditional concept of a competitive economic structure. This concept, however, was too simple and unrealistic as a description of the actual operation of the economic system, at least as we find it today. Recent theoretical analysis, in emphasizing departures from the competitive ideal, has corrected some of the misconceptions; but it seems to have given the interpretation of historical development a reverse twist. The attempt to give a more precise theoretical formulation of the operations of the economic system has led some to conclude that competition has declined, because monopoly elements may be found in every situation. Until recently, the tend-

[23]"There is a tendency to idealize the early nineteenth century and to assume that small business and the prices it charged were the result of competition. As far as I am able to see, there is little, if any, foundation for this. The village store, the village blacksmith, the village gristmill, were all monopolies. Until the advent of the automobile, they charged conventional administered prices which were not elastic. The people of the village could not go many miles to the next town. In a large measure this is still true in small towns. Such competition as there has been, curiously enough, came from large scale enterprise; mail order houses, and later the chain stores. The theory that prices were adjusted by competition under the old small scale production in small towns, as far as I can see, simply never was generally true, despite some nostalgic reminiscences which are indulged in today." (A. A. Berle, Jr., quoted in Temporary National Economic Committee, Monograph No. 21, *Competition and Monopoly in American Industry* [Washington, D.C.: U.S. Government Printing Office, 1940], p. 112).

[24]Temporary National Economic Committee, Monograph No. 21, p. 308.

ency was to put price theory into two categories—competition or monopoly. The analysis of market structures was usually based on the same dichotomy. The result was that industries and firms were classified either as monopolistic or as competitive. Because few enterprises had a complete monopoly, the industrial structure was regarded as competitive. Recent analysis, in discovering that most firms have some elements of monopoly, has gone to the other extreme and has tended to create the impression that monopoly is controlling and competition is an illusion, or, at least, so rapidly disappearing from the scene that it is impossible to retain it or revive it.

A more realistic appraisal, however, seems to justify the conclusion that competition, in practice, is more workable and more effective than envisaged by current theory.[25] Advertising, selling expenses, and product differentiation cause departures from pure competition in some respects, but they intensify it in others. Differential pricing or price discrimination has similar results; and the technological structure of modern industry makes uniform pricing, as conceived under pure competition, an impossibility, if not an absurdity. The technological structure of modern business is such that conformity to traditional concepts of the structure of competitive industry is not possible, if it ever was. This does not mean that competition is not as effective as formerly, or that it cannot be maintained as a workable system. Whether price competition has declined in absolute terms may be open to question, but there are strong grounds for believing that competition itself has broadened enormously. Price competition may have suffered a relative decline, but this is because other potent outlets for competitive forces have emerged. Public policy must recognize that behavior of modern enterprise cannot be forced into the mold of pure competition. Departures from the competitive norm must be examined carefully for their implications and significance, but such examination may frequently disclose that the effect of the departures is to bring a closer approximation to competitive standards than the elimination of them would produce. Nor, as will be shown in the following chapters, can the competitive norm be dispensed with as a guide for public policy.

[25]Clark, "Toward a Concept of Workable Competition," *loc. cit.;* also, J. M. Clark, *Competition as a Dynamic Process* (Washington, D.C.: The Brookings Institution, 1961).

Chapter 8 THE PRICING STRUCTURE

INTRODUCTION

Price theory as it relates to the economy and to public welfare deals with economic principles that bear upon the most efficient utilization of economic resources. In the broadest sense, all economic analysis is concerned with pricing problems. Price theory occupies the center of the stage, so to speak, in economic analysis because it is through prices and the price system, in some way or another, that economic resources are mobilized and utilized. This is because prices measure the basis upon which alternatives are offered and through which the rationing of scarce goods takes place. A systematic and thorough presentation of price theory would pursue it through its many and varied ramifications. In particular, it would deal with the reaction of the individual firm under varying situations and under assumptions of completely rational economic behavior, together with the implications of this for economic welfare.

Price theory as it relates to the firm mayalso undertake to analyze the forces at work in the pricing of products, on the assumption that a firm seeks to maximize its profits under the circumstances with which it is faced, or describe how it would behave if it tried to achieve this end. This same analysis may endeavor to describe and appraise the processes by which a firm undertakes to price its products where the pricing of them is one of the tasks which, by necessity, the firm must perform.

An analysis of pricing and prices as tools of regulation is somewhat more circumscribed in its purposes and potentialities than either of the foregoing. In this instance, public welfare is the focal point; but this also means that the policies which are adopted must be in keeping with the assumptions of private enterprise and with the necessary conditions of its survival. It is the function of public regulation to establish the conditions within which private management may exercise discretion in the conduct of its affairs, and it is therefore necessary for public authority to recognize the basic requirements for the survival of private enterprise. Consequently, price theory as it is applied to public regulation must endeavor to develop standards or gauges which can be utilized to establish the limits within which private management may be allowed to pursue its own interests and to establish the economic criteria for the legal framework of an acceptable private enterprise system. The following analysis attempts to develop criteria that have operational significance from the standpoint of public regulation.

CLASSIFICATION AND CHARACTERISTICS OF MARKETS

Market situations fall into a number of different categories that lie between the limits set by competition, on the one hand, and monopoly, on the other. These limits and the intermediate market patterns are economic rather than legal and are set up for purposes of analyzing particular market patterns and market behavior. For this reason, they do not necessarily establish a classification into which particular industries or firms may fit, although some may do so. More often, the market structures in which firms conduct their activities embrace more than one analytic category. As a result, it becomes impossible to describe the behavior of these firms by any one descriptive title; and, as will be shown later, it is usually not possible to speak of any industry as falling completely within any category, even though it may be primarily in one of them. These groupings or categories, then, provide an analytic framework with which the behavior of a firm may be examined to the extent that its activities fall within the particular grouping.[1]

Competition

Competition has a number of different meanings; but in whatever way it is used, it refers to the market situation in which no producer is able to control the supply of a commodity so as to be able to influence price to his own advantage. Thus, in so far as competition is effective, it always denotes complete substitutability of one seller's commodity for that of another seller, together with the inability of any one seller acting separately to influence the price of the commodity he is offering for sale so as to enhance his revenue.

Perfect Competition. Competition may be perfect, pure, or imperfect. Perfect competition is a strictly analytic concept and can never exist in fact. Nevertheless, it provides the standard or gauge for the most economical allocation of resources, because it assumes the conditions under which alternatives can be precisely evaluated and instantaneously realized. That is, perfect competition assumes that there are no obstacles of any kind to the allocation of economic resources to their most important uses. Therefore, a number of assumptions underlie the model of perfect competition.

First, it is assumed that the products which are being offered for sale are homogeneous, so that there is perfect substitutability among them. Second, buyers and sellers possess complete knowledge of the con-

[1]See J. S. Bain, *Industrial Organization* (New York: John Wiley & Sons, Inc., 1959), chap. 3 and 7.

ditions of the market at all times. Third, there must be a sufficient number of buyers and sellers, so that no one buyer or seller can exercise a significant influence on the market or by his behavior influence the market in such a way that he gains an advantage by his actions. Fourth, no kind of restraints can be imposed upon the operation of economic forces, either by law or by the actions of buyers and sellers. Fifth, there must be complete mobility of all economic resources, so that there can be complete and immediate transfer from one type of production to another and from one area of production to another. This means that resources must be both legally and economically mobile. To be legally mobile, it must be possible, as far as the law is concerned, for the resources to be free to move from one use to another and from one market to another. There must be freedom to move the physical facilities, according to the wishes of the producers, or to convert them or divert them to other uses. Similarly, the decision for investment or disinvestment must be left to the enterprisers. In other words, what is called freedom of entry, which also carries with it freedom of exist, is one of the fundamental requirements of a truly competitive structure. Economic mobility of resources requires that they be readily transferable to uses other than those in which they are presently engaged. This may be accomplished by the physical adaptation of facilities to new markets, by technological changes resulting in the production of new or different commodities and services, or by a geographic shift of plant or facilities to tap other markets.

Pure Competition. This is a less restrictive category than perfect competition, in that it does not assume that the forces of competition are able to work without impediments. For example, it recognizes that perfect knowledge of markets is not possible and that instantaneous mobility can never be achieved. It does assume, however, that buyers and sellers cannot influence the market to their advantage; that is, they must accept the market as they find it and act accordingly. Furthermore, buyers and sellers are supposed to act independently and not in collusion for the purpose of exercising control. Pure competition may be said to characterize all market situations where both buyers and sellers act independently and where each takes the market as something to which he must adapt himself. In other words, markets and prices are taken as data.

Imperfect Competition. This term does not have a universally accepted meaning. To some, it represents a condition of competition that involves more serious departures from perfect competition than does pure competition, these departures arising from rigidities in the economic system which are the result of technological conditions or institutional arrangements. The position of buyers or sellers is still the same, however, in that they must take the market and prices as data. Thus, agriculture, according to this view, may be characterized as operating under imperfect competition because of the ever-present conditions of immobility.

Some prefer to regard imperfect competition as arising from various kinds of restrictions that may be imposed by agreements, price leadership, differentiated products, and so forth. According to this view, imperfect competition means that producers, by deliberate action of some kind on their part, influence the behavior of the market in their favor. If imperfect competition is regarded in this light, it partakes of some of the characteristics of monopoly and should be viewed as a subcategory of it. If imperfect competition is used to characterize departures from competition which still leaves buyers and sellers in the position of having to take the market as datum, then it is very similar to pure competition. This is the concept that is preferred by the present writer.

Monopoly

Monopoly may conveniently be defined as that market situation in which a producer or seller has sufficient control over the supply of a commodity to enable him to exercise an influence over the behavior of the market to his advantage; that is, he can control supply so as to be able to influence price to his own advantage. There is no such thing as absolute monopoly in the sense of the world that the supplier can control the market without regard to the effect of his actions on the consumer, or without regard to the effect of his actions on the price he receives or the quantity of the commodity he can sell. In so far as a producer can act so as to influence the market in his favor, he is able to exercise monopoly power; this may be very great or very small, depending upon the circumstances.

The most complete form of monopoly arises in the case of a commodity or service for which there is no ready substitute. Possibly the leading illustrations of this in the United States today are to be found in urban water supply, electricity, natural gas, and telephone service. The buyer of these commodities or services is typically dependent upon one supplier, and there are no readily available substitutes for them. Monopoly may also be the result of collusion or agreement among sellers; and if the commodity involved does not permit ready substitutability, it will be possible for a supplier to exercise appreciable monopoly power. More frequently, monopoly power arises from control over supply for which substitutability is only somewhat limited for various reasons. In this sense, monopoly characterizes the markets of a wide variety of commodities and services.

Monopolistic Competition

This is a term which has come to be applied to markets in which the products that are offered for sale fall into the same major category but differ slightly from each other by virtue of trade-mark, brand, type of wrapping, color, style, or some other characteristic. This means that the products are quite readily and directly substitutable for one another. The differentiation gives a uniqueness to each product which makes it possible for each producer to enjoy some distinction for his product, thereby being able to exercise some control over the conditions of sale. To the extent that he is able to do so, the producer enjoys monopoly power. To the extent that the buyer finds ready substitutes, competition prevails. Monopolistic competition commonly refers, therefore, to market situations in which sellers would not be able to exercise control over the market for their product, except for the differentiation they are able to introduce. Monopolistic competition represents a departure from pure competition as a result of the uniqueness which a producer is able to give to a product that would otherwise be the same as that of his competitors.

Oligopoly

When sellers in a market are few, the market is classified as an oligopoly. Under conditions of oligopoly, no firm in an industry can afford to ignore its rivals' reactions to the policies it adopts. The importance of each seller in the market is such that any one of them, acting alone, can influence it in a significant way. In other words, each seller must take into consideration the effect of his own behavior on the market when he is deciding upon the course of action to pursue. Oligopoly assumes independence of action on the part of each of the sellers as well as homogeneity of product. If there is collusion or agreement, oligopoly becomes monopoly. Fewness of sellers does not refer to absolute numbers but rather to the situation in which a seller must recognize that his actions will affect competitors and the market. Oligopoly resembles competition in that no producer can act independently of the market; it resembles monopoly in that there is no market for the producer that is independent of his actions.

PRICING IN THE VARIOUS MARKET STRUCTURES

Pricing under Competition

Under conditions of competition, no seller is able to do anything about the prices he receives. He either takes them or leaves them; in other words, the market prices are data to him. His problem, therefore, is to adapt himself and his production policies to the market. The market prices themselves are the result of the interaction of demand and supply, each being determined by the independent decisions of all buyers and sellers. As already noted, competition is never perfect; but to the extent that competition is effective in any market, the principles that govern pricing under perfect competition are operative.

Market prices under competition are determined by the interaction of the forces of demand and supply. Demand, or the demand schedule, may be defined as the amount of a good that buyers will take off the market at all possible prices in a particular interval of time.[2] Similarly, supply, or the supply schedule, is the amount of a good that will be offered at all possible prices in a particular interval of time. In a competitive market, only one price for a good can obtain, because there is only one point at which the quantities offered and the quantities sought can meet; in other words, there is only one price that will equate exactly the amounts being offered with the amounts being sought. Given the demand and supply schedules in a competitive market, the market price will emerge where the quantity offered for sale will precisely equal the quantity that will be bought. No buyer or seller can deviate from the market price because of the complete knowledge of all traders and the complete independence of each.

Under competition, costs and prices will always equal each other because of the ability of producers to adapt their outputs to the market, because of the inducements to do so, and because of the necessity of doing so. A producer will expand his output as long as his marginal cost, which is the additional cost incurred in producing an additional unit of output, is less than the price he can obtain for the additional unit because of the extra profit he can secure. Similarly, he will contract his output when marginal cost exceeds the price that he gets for the last unit, because it is unprofitable for him to produce that unit—that is, price will be equal to marginal cost, or vice versa—and because the price is the same for all competitors, marginal cost is the same for all competitors. For the individual producer, marginal cost and average cost of output are equal when average cost is at the minimum. The reason for this is that when marginal cost is below average cost, as expansion of output takes place, rising marginal cost approaches average cost, while the latter falls. When marginal cost begins to exceed average cost, the latter will commence to rise. The most efficient level of output, therefore, is when average cost is at the minimum. No firm can continue to operate indefinitely if average cost exceeds price, or if total cost exceeds total revenue, because it would then be operating at a loss. Under perfect competition, the adjustment would take place instantaneously. Similarly, no firm can continue to operate with price exceeding average costs, because the extra profits would induce the supply of additional output until

[2] "The definition of demand singles out for consideration the relationship between possible alternative prices of the good and the quantities of it which consumers will take. The other circumstances are assumed to remain constant for purposes of defining a given state of demand. Usually we think of quantity taken as varying inversely with price. The higher the price of the good the less consumers will take, other things being equal or constant. The lower the price of the good the greater the quantity consumers will take . . . Demand refers to an entire demand schedule or demand curve" (R. H. Leftwich, *The Price System and Resource Allocation* [New York: Rinehart & Co., Inc., 1955], p. 27). A similar definition, *mutatis mutandis*, may be given for supply.

average cost and price equalized. Because marginal cost equals price and price is the same for all competitors, and because marginal cost and average cost are equal under competition, it follows that marginal cost and average cost under competition are the same for all competitors, and each firm is of the optimum size and producing its optimum output. Thus, under perfect competition, resources are allocated to their most effective use, and the price paid for those resources and the product they yield is precisely the amount necessary to secure the allocation and the product. This represents the most efficient use of economic resources. It is characterized by the fact that price equals marginal cost, which also equals minimum average cost. (See Figure 2.)

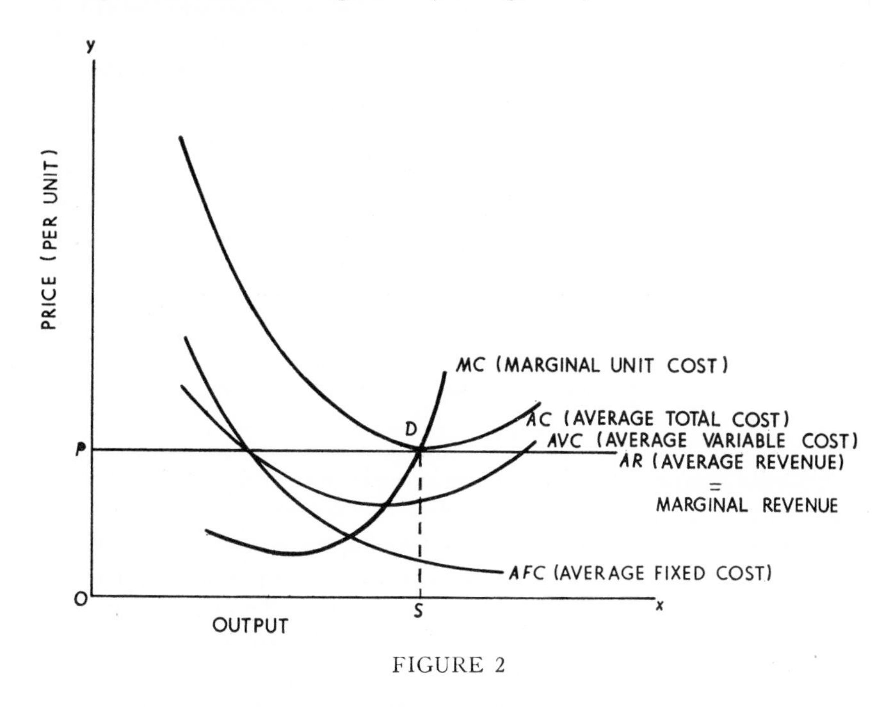

FIGURE 2

The term "cost," as used in the foregoing discussion, means all the inducements that are necessary to attract resources into a particular line of production. It thus has a different meaning from what it has in accounting and also is broader in scope, in that it includes the entrepreneurial income and earnings on proprietary capital that are necessary to maintain the enterprise. Average cost refers to the average cost of a homogeneous output; the assumption is that the firm is a single-product enterprise. The concept does not apply, therefore, to a multiple-product firm. Indeed, average cost has little, if any, meaning when applied to different products of a firm. Unfortunately, this is too rarely recognized in the administration of public policy.

Pricing under Monopoly

Monopoly pricing differs from competitive pricing in that the seller does not take prices as given. Instead, he is an active and direct participant in the price-making process. If he increases his output of a product for a given market, the effect will be to lower the price of the total which he sells in the market; and if he reduces his output, the price for the entire amount he puts on the market will rise. Therefore, when the monopolist considers the question of expanding output, he will look to the relation of his marginal cost to the additional revenue which he will receive from an additional unit of output, the additional revenue being known as the "marginal revenue." He will therefore adjust his output to that point where marginal cost equals marginal revenue. By this procedure, profits are maxamized, or losses are minimized, depending upon whether price is high enough to cover all costs.

TABLE 2

Units of Output	Marginal Unit Cost	Selling Price per Unit	Total Revenue	Marginal Revenue
100	$80	$100.00	$10,000.00	
101	81	99.90	10,089.90	$89.90
102	82	99.80	10,179.60	89.70
103	83	99.00	10,197.00	17.40

Under monopoly, price always exceeds marginal cost, because the marginal revenue curve is always below the demand or average revenue curve; that is, marginal revenue under monopoly is always less than average revenue.[3] Since price under monopoly always exceeds marginal cost, it will never be equal to minimum average cost for the plant or firm. The conditions of maximum economic efficiency that perfect competition fulfills are lacking under monopoly; or at least, they cannot all be fulfilled at the same time, as in the case under perfect competition. In other words, monopoly pricing and production under monopoly result in a less efficient allocation of economic resources than competitive pricing and production. In fact, the conditions which give rise to monopoly—be they technological, institutional, or any other kind—constitute part of the costs of any economic system because of the limitations they impose upon the effect of the forces of competition. They also constitute one of the major problems of control in a private enterprise system. Such control, in so far as it seeks to achieve economic efficiency, must limit the exercise

[3]This is because the demand curve of the monopolist is the demand curve of the industry, and therefore it slopes downward to the right, as does the demand curve for a competitive industry.

of monopoly power as much as possible at any particular time. What is possible will be conditioned by the technological circumstances of a given industry and institutional patterns and objectives within which the particular controls are imposed. (See Figure 3 and Table 2.)

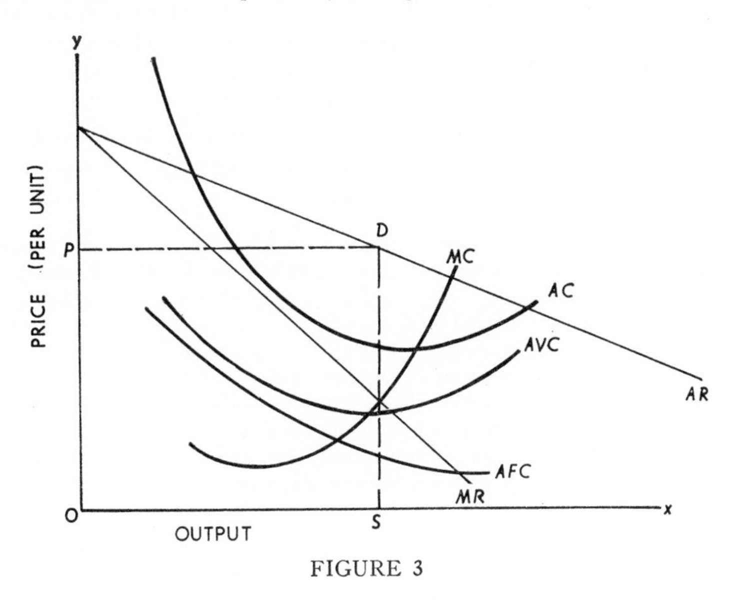

FIGURE 3

Pricing under Oligopoly

Pricing under oligopoly does not lend itself to the precise formulation that is possible with competition and monopoly. The determination of marginal revenue depends upon the unknown reactions of rivals, and the determination of marginal cost depends on the producer's assumptions regarding those unknown reactions. It is not possible, therefore, to formulate a general theory of oligopoly pricing. Professor Stigler points out that it is not even possible to enumerate all the important situations.[4] "There is no stated body of economic opinion as to the pattern that market behavior can be expected to take among oligopolists."[5] Even if one assumes the complete standardization of products among rivals, the solution to the problem of pricing in markets supplied by a few large sellers depends upon the assumption each makes regarding the reactions of others to his moves. The observer can tell what the actual particular pricing situation will be only if he knows the assumptions upon which the sellers are proceeding. Even the sellers may not know what assumptions to make or may not even be clear on the ones that are implicit in their decisions. The problem increases in complexity as

[4]G. J. Stigler, *The Theory of Price* (New York: Macmillan Co., 1946), p. 269.
[5]Alex Hunter, "The Control of Monopoly," *Lloyds Bank Review* (London: October, 1956), p. 23.

the number of rivals increases because of the greater number of uncertainties in the market situation. The analytic difficulties are complicated still further when the products are differentiated, as is normally the case. Indeed, it is improbable that buyers are totally indifferent as to the seller from whom they buy under oligopoly. Advertising, sales policies, research, and investment all make for uncertainities that contribute to results which cannot be stated in precise principles.

Professor Chamberlin has examined the problem of oligopoly pricing, first of all, on the assumption of the complete standardization of rivals' products; that is, buyers are totally indifferent as to what sellers supply the product. His conclusions are:

> 1. If sellers have regard to their total influence on price, the market price will be a monopoly one. This means that if a seller takes his total influence on price into account, he will maximize his profits, and the market price will be the same as if the total supply were offered by a single monopolist. It also means that if sellers take into account their own moves and the effects of these moves on their rivals, the result will be monopoly price. This outcome, it should be noted, is without collusion. However, it is based on the assumptions of standardization of product and fully informed and rational behavior on the part of sellers.
>
> 2. If sellers neglect their indirect influence on price, each determining his own policy as though his competitors are uninfluenced by what he does, the results vary:
>
> *a*) If each assumes his rivals' supplies to be unchanged, the equilibrium price is continually lowered as the number of sellers increases, reaching the purely competitive level only when there is an infinite number.
>
> *b*) If each assumes his rivals' prices to be unchanged, the equilibrium is the purely competitive one, even for only two sellers.
>
> 3. If sellers neglect both their direct and indirect influences, the outcome will be a purely competitive one, regardless of numbers.
>
> 4. Uncertainty regarding rivals' behavior renders the outcome indeterminate. If a seller does not know what assumptions to make, the outcome, as far as price is concerned, may lie anywhere between the limits of monopoly and competitive price.[6]

The implications of the foregoing analysis have been the basis of much debate. Some economists insist that the most likely outcome of oligopoly is monopoly pricing. They reach this conclusion by insisting that the oligopolist is likely to act quite rationally and by assuming that collusion is probable when sellers are few.[7] Others maintain that no one can predict market behavior under oligopoly and that existing theory provides few norms for evaluating the effects of oligopoly on public interest. It is quite probable, however, that pricing under oligopoly will be less flexible than under competition. What is called "nonprice" competition may be very keen. Producers may find it desirable to use prices as

[6]E. H. Chamberlin, *The Theory of Monopolistic Competition* (6th ed; Cambridge, Mass.: Harvard University Press, 1950), chap. iii.

[7]G. W. Stocking and M. W. Watkins, *Monopoly and Free Enterprise* (New York: Twentieth Century Fund, Inc., 1951), chap. 4.

targets, and compete in quality and design and so forth. In many respects this is the keenest aspect of competition under oligopoly, and may be just as effective as direct price competition. In fact, direct price competition alone can take place only with strictly standardized products that do not change from year to year. Competition in the automobile industry will have to consider quality and design as well as prices, and the fact that prices may remain relatively stable does not indicate that competition is any the less effective.

Because of the possibility of the greater knowledge of output conditions when the number of producers is small, and because of the greater opportunity for informal or secret understandings, output below the competitive level is more likely to obtain when the number of producers is limited. It is not possible, however, to predict what the outcome will be unless the conditions to which each producer gives consideration are known. Hence, it cannot be assumed that because oligopoly obtains in a particular industry, price and output will deviate from the competitive level. The facts in each case must be known before a definite conclusion can be reached. Theoretical analysis may disclose the various possibilities, but such analysis is faced with severe limitations when it endeavors to prove the conditions which obtain in a concrete case. It would seem to be reasonable to argue that public policy should aim at avoiding fewness of sellers, if possible, or, in other words, at eliminating institutional arrangements that encourage—or at least facilitate—the emergence of oligopoly.

When fewness of sellers also involves differentiated products, evaluation of pricing results is even more difficult. Differentiated products introduce an element of monopoly for each seller; and to the extent that the differentiation is really effective, the seller will be able to charge a monopoly price, because the market under such circumstances is really not an oligopoly but a monopoly instead. The fact that the products are only differentiated, however, must mean that the monopoly power is very tenuous; therefore, the oligopoly influence will predominate. Obviously, the outcome cannot be predicted, but it would not be correct to assume that the results will be socially disadvantageous.

Monopolistic Competition

If sellers are fairly large in number and the products are differentiated, then the market may be characterized as monopolistic competition. The resulting price, theoretically, will be higher than it would be if perfect competition prevailed. Selling costs, advertising, and so forth add to the cost of production; and these would not be present under perfect competition. On the other hand, markets may be broadened by such activities, and competition may become keener, with the result that the actual price, as distinct from the theoretical one, may be lower than it would be under perfect or pure competition. Neither of the latter are even possible, in fact, over a wide range of products with which the consumer is faced today. Nevertheless, the producer does have a demand curve with a downward slope to it, indicating that he does have some control over the price of his product. How effective this can be depends upon the amount of the uniqueness the producer can develop. If it is very pronounced, he becomes a monopolist, and if it is very slight, he may have practically no influence on price.

COMPETITION AND MONOPOLY IN THE ECONOMY

Markets in the real world, in contrast to the analytic classification of them, quite commonly display characteristics of some or almost all of the different kinds at the same time. As has already been pointed out, no real market exhibits or can exhibit the attributes of perfect competition. Many markets and a very considerable range of production fall within the category of pure competition, particularly if this covers imperfect competition in the way it was suggested, earlier in the chapter, that this term might be defined. The greater part of agricultural production lies in this grouping. Departures from pure competition, however, seem to be much more prevalent than adherence to it; and in terms of total volume of business in this country, there would seem to be little doubt that pure competition is less significant than the other market groupings, all of which have an element of monopoly in them. In other words, if market structures had to be classified either as competitive or monopolistic, depending upon whether monopoly power was in evidence, then the bulk of market behavior would have to be described as monopolistic. Because of the interplay of competitive and monopoly forces in our economic structure, however, the relative importance of each in the economy as a whole and the trends in the continuing role of each are the subject of much debate and considerable difference of opinion.[8]

In some industries, the element of monopoly looms so large that they are even labeled as "natural monopolies." Public utilities such as electric light and power, water supply, natural gas transmission and distribution, and telecommunication fall into this category. They may be labeled "complete monopolies" in the sense that this term can ever have any real meaning. There is practically no competition among sellers; and substitutability, even where possible, is limited to a very narrow range. Until the development of the newer means of transport, railroads supplied the overwhelming portion of the inland transport of the country. The supply of transport was predominantly from monopoly sources. Today, transport is one of the most competitive areas of economic activity. It is supplied by a group of industries with widely varying economic

[8]See, for example, E. S. Mason, *Economic Concentration and the Monopoly Problem* (Cambridge, Mass.: Harvard University Press, 1957), chap. 2; and "Symposium Review: Galbraith's 'Concept of Countervailing Power' and Lilienthal's 'Big Business,' " *Northwestern University Law Review*, Vol. 49, No. 2 (May–June, 1954), pp. 139–94.

characteristics and with a wide range of substitutability of services. Yet, at the present time, it cannot be characterized either as monopolistic or as competitive. It is a complex mixture of both that presents unique and puzzling relationships for public policy.

The classification of markets in the real world is complicated in another way. Production means the creation of goods or services which have time, form, or place utility. Thus, every commodity which has a different form is, strictly speaking, a different commodity; and even if the same good is available in different places or at different times, it is also a different commodity. This means logically that a commodity must be defined in terms of the market, and vice versa.[9] The perfect market may be described as a place where there are numerous completely informed buyers and sellers and where, therefore, the same price obtains for the same goods or services at a particular time. Anyone selling a commodity in such a market cannot sell it at a different price than any other producer. There is, however, literally an infinite variety of commodities and markets. For example, electricity generated in the daytime is a different commodity from that which is generated at night. Domestic electricity served to one house is logically in a different market from that which is served to the house next door.

One of the most critical questions relating to the development of big business in the United States is whether it is compatible with the survival of the private enterprise, competitive system. This question was explored by Dr. A. D. H. Kaplan in an extensive study entitled *Big Enterprise in a Competitive System*. Dr. Kaplan held that "the iron test of competitiveness in big business is whether it makes available increasingly numerous, varied, and significant market alternatives—or whether instead, it tends to narrow and degrade the range of choice."[10] He concluded, first of all, with regard to the structure of industries and markets in the country, that both concentration and opportunity for self-employment have persisted side by side in the American economy. Concentration was most typical where capital requirements were large, but a large part of American industry flourished in small units. Big business spreading into local markets might do more to break up the power of local monopolies than to cement its own. He also concluded that the notable feature was the wide variation in the character and number of economic opportunities and of the means to exploit them; the structure was evidently appropriate to dynamic competition.

Second, with regard to the performance of big business, he concluded that the price behavior of different commodities, as far back as price movements can be reliably traced, indicated little change in flexi-

[9]F. H. Knight, *Risk, Uncertainty, and Profit* (London School of Economics Reprints, No. 16, 1933), p. xxi.

[10]A. D. H. Kaplan, *Big Enterprise in a Competitive System* (Washington, D.C.: Brookings Institution, 1954), p. 233.

bility and inflexibility. Furthermore, if big business had not undertaken the continuous major innovations requiring large capital investment over a considerable period, the government would have had to do so, outside the market process. On the whole, big business had been kept effectively subject to a competitive system and had made an essential contribution to its scope, vitality, and effectiveness.

Some years earlier, Professor Clair Wilcox made a study of competition and monopoly in American industry for the Temporary National Economic Committee. After examining literally the whole range of productive activities in the United States, he concluded that it was not possible to make any sort of an estimate concerning the relative extent of competition and monopoly in American markets on the basis of available evidence, and he doubted that it would ever be possible to make such an estimate with assurance.[11]

WORKABLE COMPETITION

The difficulty of fitting market realities into the analytic categories provided by economic theory led Professor J. M. Clark to advance the concept of workable competition.[12] In essence, this concept was designed to provide an analytic framework with which markets could be examined as they operate in the real world and the functioning of the economic system could be more effectively evaluated. Workable or effective competition, he held, was not a matter of motives or policies of businessmen but rather one of whether the pressures of the market situation were such as to bring about the principal effects which constitute the economic reasons for the endeavor to maintain competition.

The idea of workable competition recognizes that a given industry or group of firms in an industry, each acting independently, can earn very high or low profits at any given time, and over a considerable period of time. However, no one seller, or group of sellers acting in concert, has the power to select its level of profits except within perhaps very narrow limits, by manipulating the market in some way or other. In a market where effective competition prevails, the individual seller cannot control his rivals' offerings, and those offerings set narrow limits on the discretion which he may exercise with regard to price and production. This

[11]Clair Wilcox, *Competition and Monopoly in American Industry* (Temporary National Economic Committee, Monograph No. 21) (Washington, D.C.: U.S. Government Printing Office, 1940), p. 308. See above, Chapter. 6. See also M. A. Adelman, "General Comment on the Schwartz Dissent," *Current Antitrust Problems* (Hearings before Committee on the Judiciary, House of Representatives, 84th Cong., 1st sess.) (Washington, D.C.: U.S. Government Printing Office, 1955), Part III, pp. 2668–72; for a contrary view, see T. J. Kreps, *idem*, Part II, pp. 1713–22.

[12]J. M. Clark, "Toward a Concept of Workable Competition," *American Economic Review*, Vol. XXX, No. 2, Part 1 (June, 1940), pp. 241–56. For a more extended discussion of this, see J. M. Clark, *Competition as a Dynamic Process, op. cit.* In the latter presentation Professor Clark substituted the term "effective" competition for "workable" competition.

also means that there must be genuine independence of action on the part of the firms in an industry. There can be no concerted action based on any form of collusion. By the same token, predatory tactics are excluded, because they are designed to eliminate rivals by uneconomical and even unethical practices. Price discrimination, as that term is commonly employed, is compatible with workable competition and may be a necessary part of it; this does not countenance price discrimination, however, for predatory purposes. Competitors must be permitted to meet or match each others' prices and even undercut them—provided, again, that such action is not predatory in nature. Product differentiation over a wide range of commodities is an inescapable part of any competitive economy and quite commonly increases the intensiveness of competition. Finally, relative freedom of opportunity for entry and exit is a condition of workable competition. This implies, first of all, an absence of restrictions by firms in the industry or by public authority against entry or exit. If capital requirements are very large, and if the capital equipment is severely immobile either in use or in location, entry and exit may be so restricted that the effectiveness of competition may be greatly reduced or rendered well-nigh inoperative. This is illustrated in extreme form in public utilities. To what extent this is an important factor in what are labeled the "heavy" industries is difficult to ascertain because of the presence of other imponderables, such as the corporate form of business organization, with its proclivities for growth and diversity.

Competition also manifests itself in the constant striving to produce something new and something different. This appears in the form of new products in established industries and in new industries. The pressure of innovation is such as to pose a constant threat to existing firms or industries that fail to keep pace, and it demands constant adjustment even by those that do. The innovation in transport by new agencies as well as by new techniques in the older ones is one of the most dramatic illustrations of competitive pressure induced by innovation in the world today. At the same time, innovation, because it means the introduction of new and untried products, results in monopoly power if it is successful. This monopoly power may be increased or reinforced by institutional arrangements such as patents; but even without this, the economic incentive to innovation is monopoly power, short-lived though it may be. Innovation also constitutes one of the greatest threats to monopoly and one of the most important checks on its continuance in particular situations. Professor Schumpeter held to the position that innovation is the core of effective competition.[13] Here again, departure from one of the main assumptions of perfect competition may make competition more effective in the real world than it otherwise could be.

[13]Mason, *op. cit.*, chap. 5; see also J. A. Schumpeter, *Capitalism, Socialism and Democracy* (New York: Harper & Bros., 1942), chap. vii.

What the concept of workable competition really emphasizes, therefore, is that departures from the model of perfect, or even pure, competition in the real world make competition workable in the real world. Compensating departures from some of the competitive norms, when the presence of others is excluded by technological and institutional factors, may be a necessary condition for competition to be effective at all. Thus, for example, with fluctuating demand, industry must necessarily operate short of full capacity much of the time, with the result that short-run marginal cost cannot equal average cost, at least for every product. A firm cannot afford to sell all of its products continuously on the basis of its short-run marginal costs; and most of the time, its prices are not likely to fulfill the competitive condition of being equal to marginal cost and minimum average cost. Probably, the most that can be said is that price must not be lower than short-run marginal cost. However, effective substitution of products may serve to flatten demand curves for these products so severely that managerial discretion on pricing is allowed relatively little play.

All of this seems to indicate that the real world may be more thoroughly competitive than market models, other than those of perfect or pure competition, portray. It also recognizes the interplay of competition and competitive forces throughout the entire economy. Competition is not confined to the firms in an industry; it must also comprehend interindustry rivalry. Workable competition thus arrives at a more favorable conclusion than the one to which the models of monopolistic competition, oligopoly, and monopoly seem to point. It is a multidimensional concept which recognizes that direct price rivalry is only one of the aspects of competition in the real world. The threat to competition comes not from technological conditions which, as some contend, lead to its destruction, but from arrangements, private and governmental, that attempt to mitigate or eliminate the power of competitive forces.

The idea of workable competition does not supply objective criteria or quantitative gauges by which one can judge whether particular market behavior should be deemed contrary to public policy, thereby calling for public action to limit or eliminate it. It consequently does not provide operationally usable standards for antitrust or for regulation where antitrust is inapplicable. In other words, it supplies no formula which can substitute for judgment.[14] In this respect, it adds nothing to the formal models of market behavior, for it tells us no more, from the standpoint of public policy, where competition ends and where monopoly power begins to transgress the boundaries of reasonableness, thereby requiring the limitation of it. Economics cannot offer to the law a precise

[14]See Report of the Attorney General's National Committee, *Antitrust Laws* (Washington, D.C.: U.S. Government Printing Office, 1955), p. 337.

gauge which will tell enforcement authorities when monopoly or monopoly practices have reached the point at which, in the interests of economic efficiency, they should be curbed.[15]

This does not mean that workable competition has turned out to be an empty box; on the contrary, it has exposed the fact that market realities are more complex than formal models disclose and that seemingly contradictory classifications of behavior may be found in the same firm or the same market. Thus, it is not incorrect to describe markets, or firms, as highly competitive but containing monopoly factors; nor is price discrimination (as that term is commonly used), made in good faith to meet competition, a contradiction of terms.[16] Nevertheless, it is still necessary to approach public policy from the starting point of the formal models, for they alone provide us with the conceptual apparatus, nomenclature, and criteria by which we define economic efficiency and evaluate the significance of the departures therefrom.

COMPETITIVE PRICING AS A STANDARD FOR PUBLIC POLICY

The foundation for public policy in regulation must be the competitive model and reliance on competitive standards for economical action. This is because efficient resource allocation and utilization are based on alternatives which provide the rational basis for economical decisions, regardless of the institutional arrangements within the framework of which these decisions are made. The model for monopoly or any variation of it cannot serve as the basis of an economical public policy, because it lacks the standards by which to gauge the economical allocation of resources.

One of the major problems of public policy is to establish rules for pricing within which private enterprise is permitted to make its own decisions. Where pure competition prevails, it is not necessary to set up pricing rules for producers or sellers; the market takes care of that, because there is no inducement for a seller to deviate from the market, and no harm would be done even if he attempted to do so. As has already been noted, however, pure competition does not obtain over a wide range of economic activity. Individual producers may be able to behave in such a way as to injure other producers and competition by uneconomical and/or predatory action; they may also be able to exploit the buyer be-

[15]For a detailed discussion of the need for law and economics to co-operate more effectively in formulating and applying public policy, see M. Massel, *Competition and Monopoly*, Legal and Economic Issues (Washington, D.C.: The Brookings Institution, 1962).

[16]See *ibid.*, pp. 333–36. But see also F. A. Fetter, *The Masquerade of Monopoly* (New York: Harcourt, Brace & Co., Inc., 1931), p. 313 and chap. xxvi; and V. A. Mund, *Government and Business* (New York: Harper & Bros., 1950), pp. 328–32.

cause of the inability of the latter to obtain satisfactory substitutes within a reasonable price range. Public authority intervenes for the purpose of achieving, as much as possible, the advantages of competition by reducing the disadvantages that may arise as a result of the departures from it. For this purpose, no set of rules can be devised that is uniformly applicable to the widely varying market situations that the modern industrial structure presents.

In devising rules, public authority must therefore give recognition to the different situations that are encountered. For industry in general, this involves setting minimum limits below which sellers may not be permitted to go in offering their products for sale. (Distress sales, going out of business, and similar transactions are not included in this.) The competitive standard of marginal cost equals price sets the basis for this minimum limit, although deciding what marginal cost means under particular circumstances and ascertaining precisely how much it is, present extremely difficult questions. In the field of public utilities, where monopoly is virtually complete, the problem is to limit prices, so that only fair profits are received, while efficiency is being maintained. Here again, the concepts are competitive ones, even though the application of them to situations where competition is so thoroughly lacking presents great complexities. In transport, both of the foregoing situations are encountered, with the result that extreme monopoly features are mixed with highly competitive ones in a way that requires the application of both monopoly and competitive controls at the same time. Yet, again, the starting point for a formulation of public policy, if it is to achieve an economical transport system, must be the competitive model. Utilization of the competitive norms for the formulation and application of public policy must needs be based on the nature of costs of production and the relation of these to prices and production. This is the subject of the following sections.

COSTS: MEANING AND KINDS

The relationship of costs to output and prices is one of the most important factors affecting the behavior of business and the formulation and administration of public policy. Management must constantly keep costs in mind in making its decisions, because it is the margin between costs and income which constitutes the profit which business seeks to obtain. Regulatory agencies, whether they are engaged directly or indirectly in the control of prices, have to resort to cost as a guide to many of their decisions, because the deviation of prices from costs are indications of the imperfections in the operation of competitive forces. Costs, especially under modern conditions of production, are an extremely complex phenomena, however. They vary widely under varying circumstances; they cannot be attributed specifically to each of the many products turned out by modern plants; and they cannot even be calculated precisely for a given plant or firm for a given period of operations.[17] Moreover, the costs which are significant for a particular situation may be different from those which must be taken into account in another instance.

The Nature of Cost

In the broadest sense, cost represents that which is given up in order to obtain any good or service. This is what is meant by alternative cost; and if competition were perfect, this alternative cost would always be expressed in the price of the product or service. Phrased in another way, cost, in economic theory, means the inducements which are necessary to attract economic resources into a particular use. Used in this way, cost covers the necessary or normal profits. This is a broader concept than is employed in the business world, where cost means the monetary outlays which a firm must make in order to secure the goods and services necessary to carry on operations. Thus, business costs do not include profits, although they will include such items as property taxes and interest on bonds. When decisions are being made to expand or even to continue operations, necessary profits will have to enter into the calculations; but when estimates are being made of the cost of production of firms with existing facilities, necessary profits are typically not included. One reason for this is that necessary profits for resources already committed to a particular activity are not readily ascertainable; and indeed, they may be of no significance for many policy decisions.

Costs and Rate of Output

Fixed Costs. Costs of production may be classified into a number of different categories according to the way they are related to varying rates of output or to different units or groups of commodities or services that are produced. Viewed from the standpoint of the rate of output, costs may be broken down into fixed and variable. Fixed costs are those costs which, for a given plant and given production period, are unaffected by the rate of output. A change in the scale of operations will bring about a change in the total of the fixed costs; but if this change in operations does not take place, the fixed costs will remain the same for the period. As a consequence, the average fixed cost per unit of output will vary with the number of units produced and will decrease as the output for the period increases. Interest on the funds invested in capital equipment is a fixed cost. Obsolescence of plant and equipment is largely unrelated to volume of production. Fixed assets wear out through use; but they also deteriorate as a result of the passage of time, the effects of

[17] C. R. Noyes, "Certain Problems in the Study of Costs," *American Economic Review*, Vol. XXXI, No. 3 (September, 1941), pp. 473–92.

weather, and other factors not related to rate of output. A considerable part of depreciation is, therefore, a fixed cost.[18]

Fixed costs must be calculated for a particular period of time, because in the long run, all costs are variable. Once costs are incurred and can be recovered only by the sale of the products that are derived from the services acquired by those costs and are not influenced by the rate of use of the services, they are fixed until the time arrives for the decision to renew the costs or not to renew them. It is not possible to say whether the cost of a particular type of service represents a fixed cost without examination of the particular situation. Payment for labor may be a fixed cost for a particular contract, if the contract calls for a monthly wage, for example, and must be paid for the month, regardless of the amount of time of the employee that is utilized. The investment in Hoover Dam is a fixed cost for the useful life of the dam, which may be a hundred years or more. Thus, the fixed costs of a firm will vary, depending upon the time period which is assumed, the fixed costs for a month being different from the fixed costs for a year or five years. Ascertaining what they are for a particular period also involves estimates of the prospective output of the investment in question. If equipment is estimated to be usable at full capacity for five years, the fixed cost may be calculated on that basis; but if obsolescence occurs in three years, the fixed cost per year and per unit of output will turn out to be greater than the estimate. Uncertainties such as this makes precise cost calculations impossible. Under the most favorable circumstances, average total cost per unit of output can be obtained for a given period of time only when the period has ended, because it depends upon the total output for the period. Even then, the assumption will have to be made that all the fixed costs have been included in the period under examination, and that none of them extend beyond that period.

Variable Costs. Variable costs are those which fluctuate directly with the rate of output. When the rate of output is increased, the total variable cost increases; and when that rate is decreased, the total variable cost diminishes. The variable costs for a given period of production are those which arise during that period as the result of utilizing resources. If resources are not used, there are no variable costs. A large part of the costs of labor, raw materials, selling, advertising, etc., are variable costs. Depreciation that is the result of use is also a variable. A large part of maintenance and repairs falls into the same category. For a given production period, the variable costs constitute the controllable part

[18]Fixed costs are frequently called "overhead costs," especially by economists. The use of the term in this way causes some confusion, however, because of its use by accountants to mean a different thing. Accountants use the term "overhead" to cover all expenses which are not directly attributable to output; thus, overhead costs in accounting are the indirect costs. As such, however, they include both fixed and variable expenses, because accounting classification does not typically separate the fixed from the variable expenses.

of the costs of production, for they can be discontinued with shutdowns.

All costs are variable in the long run, and the long run is the period of time during which the decision may be made whether to incur the costs. Thus, at the time when consideration is being given to future investment, this prospective investment is a variable cost to be covered by the prospective prices for the products or services which it will provide. When the commitment has been made, fixed costs have been incurred. The variable has been transformed into a fixed cost.

Although fixed and variable costs can readily be differentiated by definition, it is frequently very difficult to make an accurate distinction between them in practice. For example, the amount of depreciation which arises from use and the amount which is independent of the rate of output do not seem to be determinable except within wide limits. Quantitative relationships between fixed and variable costs in industry have been the subject of considerable study, but the results obtained so far have been somewhat inconclusive. Railroads were one of the first industries to be analyzed in quantitative terms. It is generally stated that two thirds of the costs of a railroad operating at normal capacity are fixed, and one third is variable. This means that the controllable element of costs for any railroad plant, for any particular period of time, is small relative to the total costs.

The quantitative relationship of fixed to variable costs in manufacturing industries varies widely. The proportion is considerably less, however, than it is for railroads. The United States Steel Corporation estimated that fixed costs were 25 per cent of the total in February, 1939, when the plants were operating at nearly 55 per cent of capacity. This means that fixed costs are somewhat less than 20 per cent of the total costs when operations are at 90 per cent of capacity. If this is a reasonably accurate estimate, then fixed costs at capacity operation are a relatively small part of the total.[19]

This estimate seems to be at variance with the common belief that fixed costs are a significant part of the total costs when a steel plant is operating at capacity. It also contradicts the contention, frequently advanced by management, that sizable price concessions are made to obtain large orders because of the opportunity thereby afforded to spread the fixed costs. It seems probable that, in the past, business has tended to overestimate the relative importance of fixed costs for a particular production period. The practice of using the "straight-line" method of depreciation is an illustration of this. To the extent that fixed costs are overestimated, differential pricing based on the distinction between fixed and variable costs may be overdone. The element of judgment, however, espe-

[19]Temporary National Economic Committee, Monograph No. 41, *Price Discrimination in Steel* (Washington, D.C.: U.S. Government Printing Office, 1941), pp. 31–32.

cially in allocating costs among accounting periods, looms so large in the picture that a precise separation of fixed and variable costs is not possible.

Joint and Common Costs

The problem of cost calculation is complicated by another factor; many costs are not specifically incurred for a particular product. These are known as "joint" and "common" costs. Costs are joint when the creation of one product unavoidably results in the output of another one. The familiar example is beef and hides. The raising of an animal for beef inevitably results in the production of a hide, and most of the costs incurred in rearing the animal cannot be traced to either product. The prices at which the two products sell cannot be related to their costs of production, because the joint costs are attributable to both, not to either one specifically.

Common costs are similar to joint costs in that they are incurred for the production of a number of different products, but the use of the resources to create one commodity does not unavoidably result in the production of a different one. The proportions of the different kinds of commodities turned out by a plant may be varied, frequently over a wide range. Changes in the proportions in which these are produced may result in variations in the common costs. Careful examination of these variations and experimentation with different proportions of outputs make it possible to trace a part of these common costs to a particular type of product. Practically, however, there are serious limitations to this procedure. A considerable portion of the common costs cannot be traced directly to the product. These costs are therefore nonallocable and give rise to the same problem of cost allocation as joint costs.

True joint costs, by definition, require that the joint products be forthcoming in fixed proportions and that there cannot be variations in the proportions resulting from variations in the costs. To the extent that the variability in proportions is impossible, there is no way that the joint costs can be traced to the separate products. It is frequently held that true joint costs are rare and that some variability in proportions is nearly always possible. When that is so, the marginal costs of each product are ascertainable; and therefore, within the range of variability, the total cost attributable to each can be calculated.[20] It is more probable that variability over the total range of output is not possible; and to the extent that this is so, the costs outside the range of variability are joint. A calf is always born with a hide; and at that point, the carcass and the hide are a joint product.

Whatever the actual situation may be with regard to joint costs, common costs are prevalent in almost every line of production. Vari-

[20]Stigler, *op. cit.*, pp. 306–7; see also Jacob Viner, "Cost," ***Encyclopedia of the Social Sciences***, Vol. IV, pp. 466–75.

ations in the proportions of the output may be practicable in the short run, although frequently this is not feasible. Plant facilities may be established such that variations in the proportions of the output of the various products may not affect the total costs of the facilities that are used in common. Electricity supplied before midnight is, economically, a different product from that which is supplied after midnight. The proportions of output of the two may vary, yet the same plant produces both; the capacity that is created to produce the premidnight supply inevitably results in the capacity to produce after midnight. The plant is used in common for both products, but the allocation of the plant costs between the two is not possible on the basis of traceability. Similarly, when a railroad supplies transportation in one direction, it unavoidably supplies it in the other direction. Thus, over a wide range of production, common costs that are not joint in the strictest sense are not distributable among the products in any traceable way, and the necessary average cost of each of the various products cannot be ascertained.[21]

In this connection, and adding to the complications of ascertaining actual costs, it should be borne in mind that fixed and variable costs, on the one hand, and joint and common costs, on the other, are not mutually exclusive categories. Fixed costs may be specific, or they may be joint and common. For example, the fixed costs incurred by a railroad for its passenger cars and passenger depots are specific to the passenger traffic. From the standpoint of traceability, they do not belong to the freight traffic, and they are not incurred for the business as a whole, even though losses from rendering the services may impair the financial status of the corporation. Similarly, variable costs may be specific, or joint and common.

Costs and Decision Making

Under perfect competition, costs always equal prices, marginal cost and minimum average cost being equal and the same as price. All of the costs are directly indentifiable with the products; costs and output of the individual firm are immediately adjustable to the price which the firm must accept as datum. These precise relationships between particular products and costs will not obtain, however, where competition departs from the model of perfect competition.

Fixed costs, because the amount of them is invariable for a given period of production, will be incurred whether there is any output or not. They will not, therefore, enter into the decision of management on how much to produce, because they are independent of that decision. The problem is to recover as much of the fixed cost as possible from the sale of the products. In other words, the economical thing for a firm to do is to ignore its fixed costs when deciding on its production policies. If it can

[21]See John F. Due, *Intermediate Economic Analysis* (rev. ed.; Homewood, Ill.: Richard D. Irwin, 1950), chap. xi.

recover only part of them, it will be better off than to refuse to take this course of action; if it can more than recover them, so much the better for the firm. This is why fixed costs are called "noneconomic costs."

A firm can exercise control over its variable costs, and it is on these costs that its decisions for a given production period will have to rest. If sales will only just cover the variable costs, the decision whether to produce is really a matter of indifference; but if sales will more than cover variable costs, then the economical decision will be to undertake production, because the difference between the sales price and the variable costs will contribute toward covering the fixed costs. In other words, if the firm acts economically, it will not consider average total cost in making its decisions. Average total unit costs are not, therefore, a bench mark for policy decisions, because for a given period, the variable costs are the only controllable element in them; the fixed costs are unavoidable for the period, regardless of the volume of output.[22]

Average variable costs and average total costs can be ascertained for the units of a homogeneous output. These averages, however, are not obtainable when joint and common costs are present. To the extent that these are part of the fixed costs of a firm, it is not possible to ascertain the precise fixed cost per unit of output; and to the extent that they are part of the variable costs, it is not possible to obtain the precise variable unit cost. Management decisions arising from the relation of costs to the rate of output will be unaffected by this fact, but the precise calculation of cost for each unit of output will be impossible.

The role that average cost pricing plays in the policies of firms is a matter of considerable debate[23]. This is sometimes called "full-cost pricing," the full cost per unit of output being calculated by adding to the directly ascertainable unit costs an arbitrary portion of the unallocated fixed and common costs. Thus, in the calculation of the average or full-cost basis for moving railroad freight, the total volume of freight movement for a period is divided into the total costs of freight, giving an average cost per ton-mile. The assumption is that all ton-miles of freight are homogeneous products.

There are three difficulties with this method of pricing. First of all, it contradicts the principle of marginal cost pricing, in that the price of the last unit of output may actually be below the additional cost of producing it. Even though marginal cost may be difficult to ascertain, the use of average cost pricing necessarily results in pricing being different from marginal cost except at the point of competitive equilibrium, a situation that is not likely to obtain at any particular time except under

[22]What this means is that variable costs are the only ones that ever enter into rational decision making in economics.

[23]See R. B. Heflebower, "Full Costs, Cost Changes, and Prices," in National Bureau of Economic Research, *Business Concentration and Price Policy* (Princeton: Princeton University Press, 1955), pp. 361–96.

perfect competition. In the second place, full-cost pricing requires an arbitrary allocation of the costs which cannot be traced; this allocation cannot rest on the necessary relation between the costs involved and the resulting products. Third, if average total cost is used for pricing in multiproduct firms, and if sales are not permitted at prices below full cost, variable cost pricing to utilize unused capacity is thereby prevented. If this practice is followed in public policy as a basis for establishing minimum prices below which firms cannot go, then differential pricing is practically eliminated. The result will be excess capacity and misallocation of resources. Differential pricing for railroad rates is one of the main points of controversy at the present time between rail and motor carriers.

Full-cost pricing for multiproduct firms must be arbitrary because of nontraceable, and also fixed, costs. In addition, if the practice is followed according to the logic of it, the prices of various firms in competition with each other would have to be different because their costs and product mix will not be the same. If the prices are competitive, the full-cost allocation will have to be tempered to the market, which means that the practice is not being followed to its logical conclusion. If the prices are those of a monopolist, he is not maximizing his monopoly profits, or using his resources in the most efficient way even for a monopolist.

Despite the foregoing, it is the practice of the various regulatory commissions to rely heavily on full-cost pricing. The Interstate Commerce Commission has shown some tendency to depart from the average-cost standard, although it has done so with great reluctance, and seems to resist any concessions with regard to its theory of pricing.[24]

It is not possible to calculate the precise total unit costs of output, even theoretically, in a multiproduct firm. Fixed costs should not enter into the pricing calculation. Common costs cannot be allocated except on an arbitrary basis and therefore should be considered only with the multiple products, not with the individual ones. Decision making on the basis of ascertainable and relevant unit costs can, however, use those costs only as the minimum gauge for price, below which it would not be economical to seek the sale.

If the problems of monopoly or of predatory pricing were of no concern, firms could be allowed to make their decisions without public restriction. Unfortunately, this is not the case; public authority is called upon to establish minimum price conditions, under certain circumstances, in order to deal with predatory practices and the unwarranted exercise of monopoly power. Even when the economical cost minimum is reasonably

[24]Professor Taggart reports that a Federal Trade Commission accountant stated that he did not think much of the whole idea of trying to distinguish between fixed and variable costs, and that in the accounting field in general, the attempt to designate certain overhead items as constant, is not recognized. H. F. Taggart, *Cost Justification* (Ann Arbor, Mich.: Bureau of Business Research, University of Michigan, 1959), p. 29. Evidently, there is as much need for accountants and economists, as for lawyers and economists, to get to understand each other.

ascertainable, use of it may not serve as a satisfactory check on monopoly or predatory action, because that cost minimum may be lower than a firm might need to charge except for purposes of eliminating or excluding competitors. On the other hand, effective competition also involves the privilege to undercut one's rivals; and this may lead to a price at some indeterminate amount above the minimum below which cost considerations dictate it should not go. Economics can offer no precise gauge for public policy on this point, but public administrators should recognize the fact that costs can do no more than set the limits within which they must exercise their judgment and that, in all but rare cases, average or full costs will yield the results they are trying to avoid. Government, no less than management, must give careful consideration to the problems of efficient resource utilization. Informed judgment must play a large part in arriving at the answers for public policy, because there is no simple formula by which to compute cost-price relationships that will provide a solution.

Chapter 9 PRICE POLICIES

MEANING AND FUNCTION OF PRICE POLICIES

Meaning of Price Policies

The pricing of the products or services of modern industry is rarely determined solely by the impersonal operation of the market. Instead, the seller participates directly in the process of pricing because of the general practice of quoting prices at which goods will be sold and because of the departure from pure competition in a great many market situations. When prices are arrived at partly through the action of the producer of a particular commodity, a price policy emerges. Under conditions of pure competition, the producer or seller cannot influence prices to his own advantage. He can, however, adapt his production to the current price situation. Consequently, he will have a production policy but not a price policy. The producer who is able to exercise, to his own advantage, some influence on the market of the product which he sells has the choice of fixing his price and then adjusting his supply to it or of determining the supply and letting price take its course. In other words, he will have a price policy as well as a production policy.

The marketing of most manufactured goods, as well as many other types of goods, is normally carried on through the medium of quoted prices. In arriving at the price to be quoted, the producer takes into consideration all of the many factors which affect prices, as well as the effects of his decision on his own output. He can have both a production and a price policy, but the price which he receives for his product will not be determined independently of his production policy, and vice versa. When an enterprise determines its prices in advance, the management must decide what kind of price policy it will adopt and fix its prices accordingly. This operation will entail decisions as to the price relationships of the various commodities that are to be produced and the prices to be charged to different classes of customers and in different geographic areas. It will also involve the question of frequency of price changes: "Are the prices to be quoted with the intention of maintaining them for some considerable period of time, are they to be announced for only a short period, or are they to be subject to change without notice?"

Price policies are characteristic of the present industrial structure. Only recently, however, has much attention been focused on them and their effect on the price system and production. Heretofore, price policies were regarded as an aberration from the competitive system, arising from monopoly which could be eliminated. Monopoly was viewed principally from the standpoint of the trust problem and was regarded primarily as a predatory development. As has already been pointed out, this was an overly simplified point of view. Even the breeder of a special strain of horses or dogs possesses a certain degree of monopoly and may have a price policy. Price policies have always been present, and they have covered a much larger part of the economy than is generally understood. The attention which is being given them today arises from the fact that industrial leaders and administrative agencies play a very significant role in the formation of prices. Decisions on prices are as much a part and as integral a part of business policy as decisions on products to be produced, location, and so forth.

Requisites for Price Policies

If a business enterprise is to have a price policy, it must be able to exercise some degree of control over the price of its product or service. It may be an outright monopoly; or it may possess such monopoly power that its rivals are compelled to fall in line, and it may have to consider the reaction of these rivals to its policy. The enterprise may produce patented, trade-marked, or branded articles with their own special sales appeal. Special sales appeal based upon personal connections, personal services, credit facilities, servicing of equipment, etc., may be used as a basis for market differentiation. In the case of highly standardized products where price is the deciding factor, it will be necessary to meet the price quoted by rivals if the various markets are to be tapped. Legislation may also assist the development of price policies. Resale price maintenance laws permit the manufacturers of branded or trade-marked products to determine the retail price of them. Milk marketing laws make it possible for the distributors to fix the price of milk delivered at homes and at stores. Trade associations, by encouraging uniform cost accounting and the filing of price information, also contribute to the formulation of price policies.

Although the formulation of prices is the result of many factors, one of the important variables is the judgment exercised by a business executive. The presence of the giant corporation in the industrial structure makes his decisions vital to the functioning of the economy as a whole. Price making by the producer has become an integral part of the pricing process of the present-day economic structure. Pricing cannot be a matter of purely private acquiescence to the forces of the market, because modern markets are not characterized by the techniques of the auction. Instead, the seller typically quotes the price at which his product is to be sold. For a producer or seller to be able to do this, however, there must be a uniqueness in his market situation. Whether this gives the seller much leeway for decision making with regard to the prices he sets is a different matter. If the seller sets his price according to the requirements of resale price maintenance, then he does not have a price policy. It is the manufacturer who has the price policy; the retailer has no discretion under such circumstances.

The Functions of Price Policies

Price policies perform two major functions in modern business. In the first place, they are part of the mechanics of the pricing process. Prices over a wide range of economic activity do not emerge immediately and automatically as the result of auctions or totally impersonal procedures. The seller has to state the price at which he is willing to sell, and the buyer expects him to do so. A large modern business could scarcely delegate to each member of its sales force the power to decide upon the price at which each sale should be made. The determination of what these prices are to be is a highly complex and technical task. The over-all price policy is typically determined by a conference of executives, officials, and representatives of various major departments of the company, such as sales, accounting, engineering, and manufacturing. At these conferences, the prices of a few key items are decided upon. The entire price structure is then worked out by employees, who price the large number of various items to be sold in accordance with some established formula. The United States Steel Corporation finds it necessary to set some 50,000 prices, and the International Harvester Company manufactures and stocks some 250,000 separate parts of agricultural implements that must be priced. The enormity of the task of making prices and the influence of those engaged in the sheer mechanics of it have a strong tendency to introduce price inertia. Customary procedure comes to play an important part in the process. Prices and price structures in industry are largely the result of relatively slow growth and experimentation. They do not emerge overnight; it would literally be impossible for a modern industry to start from scratch and construct a workable price structure all at once.

The second main function of price policies relates to the strategy and tactics of business. Management may prefer to protect its price structure to prevent spoiling the market. Announcements of price reductions may cause buyers to hold off in anticipation of further reductions. Management may decide that it is better to make sales appeals through other channels, such as changes in style or quality or offers of extra services, rather than through price variation. The reaction of competitors to price changes may have to be taken into consideration. The raising of prices may mean the loss of business to competitors who do not follow suit, whereas the lowering of them may result in a price war. Consideration must also be given to the effect of price changes on the volume of production. A firm may decide to maintain its prices and allow the volume of sales to take its course; or to maintain volume and adjust prices, so as to make this possible; or to effect a compromise between the two. Price policies may be used as part of the strategy to effect a stabilization of prices, or to assist in securing or maintaining monopoly. They may also be employed as one of the effective tactics for eliminating rivals or for forcing them to conform to the policies of the leaders of an industry. Promotion prices are frequently employed to get new products on the market, and "specials" are a common tactic used by stores to attract customers. Illustrations and examples of price policies as a means of furthering the goals of firms could be detailed almost indefinitely. Almost all of them can be put to illegitimate and illegal use, but the reverse is also true. Price policies form a vital and necessary part of effective competition.

Management in modern industry occupies a key role in the pricing process. Whether the policies followed further and intensify competition, or whether they restrict and limit it, depends upon the circumstances in each case; either condition can result. Quantitatively, price policies dominate the modern market; for in most instances, management exercises more or less influence on the prices at which goods are sold. The effects of this discretionary power are many and varied. Price structures and production policies are not solely the result of entrepreneurial response to the automatic and mechanical forces of the market. Management, therefore, cannot shrug off the effects of its decisions on the operation and performance of the economy, with the contention that business is merely responding to its environment. The fact that price policies exist means that business helps create that environment. Business leaders exert a significant influence on the geographic structure of industry through the influence of judgment. They play a prominent, if a not dominant, role in the growth of industrial monopoly.

Price Policies and Public Regulation

In so far as reliance is placed upon competition to establish prices, public regulation does not intervene. As has already been pointed out, however, even competition can function only under established rules of the game. In addition, price policies, in some respects, represent deviations from competition; and these deviations may be so significant as to require special attention by public authority. In any event, the existence of conditions which give rise to the emergence of price policies creates the probability of need for greater public consciousness of the processes and results of the behavior of prices than does pure competition.

Public interest in price policies arises from three considerations. First of all, price policies are important because of their relation to the over-all performance of business. The effect of price policies on the flexibility or inflexibility of prices and the relation of these to business fluctuations are matters of public concern. The bearing that price policies have on full employment and industrial productivity raises questions that are the focus of much public discussion. Public interest in these aspects or possible repercussions of price policies may not warrant direct public intervention in price making; the manner in which these reflect departures from the competitive system, however, and the way in which they indicate defects in the performance of private business may suggest measures that will vitalize competition and impose limitations on practices and procedures that impede competition.[1]

Second, price policies are important as they relate to price relationships among commodities, among customers, and among firms. It is in this connection that price discrimination is an especially important issue. Minimum prices as part of the question of discrimination and minimum prices as a weapon of economic warfare enter the picture here, too. This second aspect of price policies frequently calls for direct intervention in the pricing process, through the medium of limitations placed on the range of discrimination that may be practiced or on the minima below which particular prices may not be permitted to go.

Third, where industries such as public utilities are monopolies that must be accepted, public authority intervenes to participate in price making and price policies by establishing limitations on the over-all level of profits of the firm or industry and by sanctioning or prescribing the precise prices to be charged for the goods or services. In some industries, such as various branches of agriculture, the government may undertake to maintain minimum prices by guarantee. In the milk industry, this takes the form of precise price regulation to establish minimum prices; in some other phases of agriculture, it takes the form of support prices.

Whether competition can continue to be the workable framework for modern large-scale manufacturing rests heavily on the desire and determination of business leaders to make it work. Price policies designed to further or maintain fair competition promote the full utilization of our economic resources. Those aimed at controlling the market and limiting competition reverse the effect, and they undoubtedly aggravate the problems of the business cycle and unemployment. The extent of the influence of managerial discretion is a matter of debate, but it is clear that private business can no longer ignore the fact that price policies must give consideration to the broader questions of public policy and to their own effect on the economy as a whole. The significant role which price policies play in the operation of the economy places a heavy

[1]Se E. S. Mason, *Economic Concentration and the Monopoly Problem* (Cambridge, Mass.: Harvard University Press; 1957), Part II.

responsibility on the duties of both private management and administrative agencies.[2] In carrying out its functions, it is not in keeping with the assumptions of a private enterprise economy for public authority to limit competition. The role of regulation is to implement competition as much as possible, even in the case of public utilities. A private enterprise economy is predicated on competition, and an economical utilization of resources must use the criteria as the gauge in any type of an economy.

PRICE DISCRIMINATION

One of the most important aspects of price policies arises in connection with price discrimination. The term "price discrimination" carries the implication of arbitrary action, and it generally means unfair treatment of some buyers by a particular seller. Thus, it connotes a deviation from the competitive norm. When prices are determined solely by the forces of competition, no producer is able to exercise any control over the prices which he charges or the conditions of sale. He adapts himself to the market as he finds it. Hence, he is unable to practice price discrimination.

If a producer has sufficient control of the supply of his product to influence the market, he may be able to practice discrimination. Control over supply, however, does not always, or necessarily, give rise to discrimination. A monopolist, offering a single product for sale and marketing it under uniform conditions, may charge the same price to all customers. His is a monopoly price, but it is not usually regarded as discriminatory. On the other hand, if a firm sells different kinds of products under competitive conditions—that is, without the ability to control the market for the product—it is not usually regarded as engaging in discrimination, even though the prices of the different products are not proportionate to their cost.

The concept of price discrimination implies two things: (1) Discrimination exists when the prices which a seller charges the various buyers differ by more than the differences in the cost of the commodities or services, and (2) these price differences are possible because of the control which the seller is able to exercise over his sales. That is, discrimination arises as the result of departure from the competitive norm brought about by the exercise of monopoly power. Sometimes, the concept is defined in such broad terms as to cover all differences in prices not matched by differences in costs.[3] This presumably would include all

[2]See A. A. Friedrich and E. S. Mason, *Public Policy* (Cambridge, Mass.: Harvard University Press, 1940), chaps. ii and iii; also Mason, "Price and Production Policies of Large Scale Enterprise," *American Economic Review*, Vol. XXIX, No. 1, Part 2, Supplement (March, 1939), pp. 61–74.

[3]See M. W. Watkins, "Price Discrimination," *Encyclopedia of the Social Sciences*, Vol. XII, pp. 350–55.

prices that deviated from cost, as that term is used in connection with perfect competition. Under such circumstances, all prices that did not conform to the standard of perfect competition would be discriminatory. The most widely accepted concept, however, seems to be that of differences in prices charged by a seller that are not matched by differences in costs. Unfortunately, this concept is not as simple as it sounds.

Relation of Discrimination to Costs

A satisfactory definition of price discrimination that will adequately fit modern conditions is difficult to formulate.[4] If it is defined in terms of cost, it assumes a simplicity of costs that does not exist in fact. The complexities of costs and their calculation was pointed out in the previous chapter. Precise costs can rarely be ascertained, and the commodities and services which a firm offers for sale are rarely homogeneous. The cost concept of discrimination does not cover the case of products produced under conditions of joint cost, and does not apply to essentially different products produced by the same firm. Furthermore, there is the additional complication of deciding what are essentially the same products. For example, a motion-picture house may exhibit the same film in the afternoon and in the evening. It is the same picture, but it is not the same service. The products which are being offered are joint; how much each should share of the total cost burden is for the market to decide; cost cannot be the arbiter. Similarly, the seats in the theater differ markedly; yet, the cost of each may be the same. If price is to perform its rationing function, the market will have to decide what is to be paid for the various seats, not cost. What is more, if the same price were charged for all seats on the assumption that they all cost the same, discrimination could be said to exist, because services of differing qualities were being sold at the same price.

Average cost is not a satisfactory basis for measuring discrimination, especially where the most difficult and controversial public questions arise, because average cost in a multiproduct firm is not a meaningful concept. Marginal or incremental cost is not satisfactory as a guide, because there is no necessary relation between marginal cost and common or joint costs. If there are joint costs and the products are sold under competitive conditions, the total price will just cover the total costs. There is no discrimination in such a case, even though the prices of the products cannot be related to their respective total costs.

It does not seem to be meaningful to talk about the discrimination in prices between the carcass and the hide of an animal because the respective contributions to the joint (nonallocable) costs are market determined, and therefore vary with market conditions. There is no rational

[4]See Ralph Cassady, Jr., "Some Economic Aspects of Price Discrimination under Non-Perfect Market Conditions," *Journal of Marketing*, Vol. XI, No. 1 (July, 1946), pp. 7–20.

way of allocating the nonallocable costs. Nor is average cost in such a situation a meaningful term. These remarks are equally applicable in industry as, for example, railroads with back-haul traffic. This is also true of theater seats, where an "average" cost of production can be calculated. What the customer buys is location rather than the seat, and location cannot be averaged. Nevertheless, there does not seem to be agreement among economists on this issue, and some insist that all costs must be allocated, price differences not matched by the calculated full costs being discriminatory.[5] This seems to be the meaning given to discrimination by the regulatory agencies.

Discrimination and Monopoly

Whether price discrimination and monopoly are always interrelated is perhaps a matter of definition. Some writers prefer to treat discrimination in broader terms.[6] Monopoly, however, seems to be an ingredient of discrimination; for without the presence of any element of monopoly, a producer cannot exercise discretion in his pricing. In any event, it is the discretionary power that creates the issues in public regulation. Discrimination seems to be a definite symptom of monopoly.[7] The presence of monopoly, however, cannot be used to prove the discrimination, because monopoly is insufficient proof. As has already been pointed out, the mere presence of differential prices also does not demonstrate discrimination. It is the price differentials which are the result of the exercise of some monopoly power on the part of a producer which are discriminatory. Public authority, in dealing with the problem, therefore, not only is faced with the necessity of detecting the existence of discrimination by some rough gauge of cost but also is faced with the task of determining whether the departures from the cost standards are the result of the exercise of monopoly power on the part of the seller.

It does not follow, even then, that the public authority will decide that all such discrimination is unwarranted or unreasonable. As has been pointed out, there may be good grounds for the sanctioning of such discrimination. Contrariwise, it does not follow that the discrimination is reasonable even though the specially favored prices are made to meet competition. The fact that a producer has monopoly control in one market may make him a more potent competitor in another, but it may not be in the public interest to allow him to follow such a price policy. This would be so, for example, if a firm were selling in some area, or some products, at a loss, in order to drive a competitor out of business. Only an evaluation of the broader question of social policy, including the ef-

[5]See C. Kaysen, and D. F. Turner, *Antitrust Policy: A Legal and Economic Analysis* (Cambridge: Harvard University Press, 1959), p. 179.

[6]See Cassady, *op. cit;* also Watkins, *op. cit.*

[7]See National Bureau of Economic Research, *Business Concentration and Price Policy* (Princeton: Princeton University Press, 1955), especially pp. 435–40.

fects of the pricing practices on competition and the industrial structure, can give a clue to the appropriate conclusion.

Even though discrimination may not initially lead to the development of monopoly, it may be a potent weapon for the furthering of monopoly power which has already been acquired. It may be used as a means of warding off potential competitors, as a device for bludgeoning existing competition into subservience, or as a method of influencing the geographical growth of industry that makes the acquisition or maintenance of monopoly control easier. These factors seem to have played an important part in the development of the steel industry and in the role which the old Standard Oil trust took in the petroleum industry. The problem which public policy faces is that of eliminating unreasonable discrimination. What this means is a matter of judgment, but the issue is whether the price policy being followed by a firm constitutes an exercise of discretionary power that imposes limitations on the operation of the competitive system contrary to public interest or established public policy. Unfortunately, no precise standards can be formulated by which this can be tested. The very factors which create the difficulty, however, also seem to make it undesirable and impossible to remove all forms of discrimination, whether they be systematic or unsystematic.

Detecting Discrimination

The detection of discrimination and the gauging of its reasonableness necessitate resort to cost considerations. The presence of monopoly control in the industrial structure is difficult to ascertain independently of cost. Even if monopoly powers are known to exist—as, for example, in the case of the supply of electricity—the extent to which they are being used can be measured only in cost terms. Unfortunately, the cost of specific products or services cannot be obtained with precision. There is no logical way of allocating joint costs; and as far as cost finding is concerned, costs that cannot be directly allocated fall into the same category. Fixed costs, moreover, have to be recovered from whatever part of the business will bear them. A manufacturer may be able to obtain orders that will more than cover the costs that can be attributed to them, but at a lower price than would be necessary to cover average costs plus a reasonable profit. If the prices of all his sales were lowered to this level, he could not long continue in business. If he did not take these orders, he would be failing to make full use of his resources. Differential pricing is therefore an integral part of the structure of modern industry.[8]

Unfortunately, even precisely allocable costs do not necessarily set

[8]See Eli W. Clemens, "Price Discrimination and the Multiple-Product Firm," *Review of Economic Studies*, Vol. XIX (1), No. 48 (1950–51), pp. 1–11. Professor Clemens takes the position that multiple-product production and price discrimination are more or less universal means to the same end and differ only in degree, even when there are no joint or common costs.

the minimum below which a firm should not be permitted to sell its products. It is possible that a firm's prices may be above the specifically allocable costs and still be used as a means of eliminating competitors. If this is the purpose of the discrimination, then the pricing is not in the public interest. In other words, such discriminatory pricing is not reasonable.

The latter term carries with it an ethical connotation. The rational foundation of a private enterprise system predicates limitations on the discretionary power of enterprise. If competition is unable to afford adequate protection against the use of that discretionary power, public policy demands restriction by some form of regulation. When this is called into play, the regulatory agency has to appraise the discrimination or the exercise of monopoly powers in the light of all the considerations which bear upon the issue.

Types of Discrimination

Discrimination may manifest itself in a multitude of ways; and because of the cost problems connected with it, classification into types is, in many respects, quite artificial. If, of course, it is defined as differences in prices that are not precisely matched by differences in costs, then the classifications are more self-evident. The following groupings are the ones most commonly encountered in public regulation.

Discrimination may be classified as systematic or unsystematic. Systematic price discrimination refers to the practice of erecting price structures in which price differentials are an inherent and regular procedure of pricing policies. Unsystematic discrimination is opportunistic and does not lead to any formulated pattern of prices. Thus, when prices are arrived at by individual bargaining, discrimination may emerge; but it is not incorporated into a formal price structure.

Personal discrimination arises when a seller, by virtue of some degree of control over his market, is able to differentiate in the prices which he charges to different buyers. The price policies which he follows are dictated by the personalities of the buyers rather than by other considerations. This may be because of differences in the bargaining powers of the various buyers or because the seller wishes to give special favors, for certain reasons, to certain of his customers. Allowances under the guise of brokerage fees and special services fall into this category.

Commodity discrimination entails price differentials among the various commodities which a seller markets. He may have considerable control over the market for commodity A, for example, but none for commodity B, which he also produces. He may wish to further the sale of B by pushing it at a low price, the difference being borne by his higher price above cost for A. Special brands and brand names may be used as a basis for differential pricing; de luxe models of equipment are similarly used as a basis for commodity discrimination. Railroads commonly use it in charging different rates for different commodities.[9]

Spatial discrimination arises when a producer is able to differentiate his market on a geographic basis. A preferred position in one market may make it possible for him to penetrate others that he would not be able to reach were it not for his extra profits in the first market. The ability of some of the heavy industries to practice spatial discrimination has had considerable influence on the geographic structure of industry in this country. Spatial discrimination is also one of the most difficult problems to deal with in connection with railroad transportation.

Temporal discrimination is the result of the ability of a producer to segregate his market on the basis of time. Certain goods or services may be available at specified prices at particular times; but if they are obtained at another time, they may bear a different price. This must be distinguished, however, from mere variations in prices over a period of time. Temporal discrimination arises only when the price differentiations are part of a definite price structure. Thus, for example, an electrical utility may sell electricity in the daytime at one rate; but at night, between midnight and six o'clock in the morning, it may sell electricity for hot-water heating at an especially low rate. If the electricity is to be used for hot-water heating at any other hour of the day, it bears a higher rate.

Hard versus Soft Competition

Discrimination, at least as the term is commonly used, is an inherent and inevitable part of the structure of modern industry. The unavoidable presence of varying degrees of monopoly, oligopoly, and monopolistic competition means that departures from the competitive norm of pricing are the rule rather than the exception. Product differentiation is an integral part of the competitive structure, although at the same time, it also entails departure from the ideal of competition and makes for the continued existence of discrimination. Fixed costs give rise to more or less immobility in the utilization of resources, lay the basis for the exercise of a certain amount of discretionary power, and usually entail the continuous existence of some unused capacity. The influence of geography on markets means that they are frequently imperfectly connected with each other; and if impediments such as tariffs or other restrictions are present, the resulting variations in the effectiveness of competition can give rise to discrimination, even though a producer has not sought to acquire monopoly power. Thus, the producer of a heavy commodity, in which transportation charges loom large, may be able to obtain high

[9]This author is not impressed with the distinction between commodity and personal discrimination. The problems of discrimination, previously discussed, seem to him to make personal and commodity discrimination amount to the same thing.

profits from his product in his immediate area. Cost considerations may dictate a capacity larger than can profitably be utilized for that particular region. If contributions to the cost of this extra capacity can be obtained by reaching out into other markets that are unable to bear the full share of costs but can contribute something more than the variables incurred, it not only will pay the producer to take such business but also may mean that the average unit costs of production are lowered, so that all the buyers receive lower prices than they otherwise would. Even the monopoly price in the restricted area may be lower than it would be if the producer were unable to reach out into other markets. This consideration has played an important part in the recognition of discrimination as unavoidable in railroad transportation. Time considerations may play a similar part in the pricing policy. Differences between peak and off-peak rates in electricity are an illustration, although the question of which of the two is being discriminated against is another matter.

After 1930, fair-trade laws, unfair practices acts, and the Robinson-Patman Act were passed to limit price discrimination severely. These laws were designed to prevent sales below costs, costs in this case meaning average or fully allocated costs. The objective of the laws was to preserve the individual competitor, especially the small one. The argument was that the large firms had a competitive advantage because of discrimination. Under this point of view, all differential pricing or price discrimination is the result of monopoly and therefore should be prohibited.[10] The supporters of this position maintain that hard and soft competition are two sides of the same coin, called "monopoly."

If differential or discriminatory pricing were always a manifestation of monopoly, and if, at the same time, the monopoly was used for the purpose of driving out competitors, there would be few differences of opinion on the need for eliminating discrimination. As has already been pointed out, the matter is not that simple. Discrimination is not necessarily a question of undesirable monopoly. "The firm that does not discriminate in its pricing policy or differentiate in its product line, or invade new markets, dies in the competitive struggle."[11] If private enterprise is to be preserved, so must competition. Preservation of competition and preservation of competitors, however, are two different things. All competition is injurious to competitors that cannot survive. The essence of competition is that it drives out the inefficient and limits the rewards that the successful competitors can receive. Policy which prevents competition based on an economical utilization of resources is a denial of

[10]See Report of the Select Committee on Small Business, *Price Discrimination, the Robinson-Patman Act*, and *The Attorney General's National Committee to Study the Antitrust Laws* (House of Representatives, 84th Cong., 2nd sess., Union Calendar No. 1218) (Washington, D.C.: U.S. Government Printing Office, 1956), especially pp. 190–213.

[11]Clemens, *op. cit.*, p. 11.

the principles of competition. Admittedly, it is not easy to discern when discrimination is being used for predatory purposes and when it is not; but this is no reason for not endeavoring to do so, or for espousing a public policy based on the opposite theory.

Quantity Discounts

The problem of distinguishing between discrimination used for predatory or monopoly purposes and discrimination to meet competition is particularly difficult in the case of quantity discounts. When a lower price per unit is given for the purchase of a larger quantity of a commodity than for the purchase of a smaller quantity, when the lower price for the larger quantity is based on differences in costs, and when the purchase in varying quantity amounts is open to all buyers on equal terms, there is no price discrimination. If, however, the total per-unit cost is the same regardless of the amount of the sale, then quantity discounts cannot be justified as nondiscriminatory on a cost basis. For example, if customer A buys 2,000 units of a commodity and customer B, in order to be induced to buy 3,000 units, has to be given a lower price, and if the production of the 3,000 units lowers the average cost of the 5,000 units, it will be to the advantage of the firm to sell the 3,000 units at the lower price. The sale, however, involves discrimination against A, because if the sale had not been made to him, the lower average cost resulting from the production of the 5,000 units would not have been obtained. "The idea that the cost of serving a given buyer is less than that of serving other buyers, for no other reason than that this buyer's additional purchases spread the overhead, imputes arbitrarily to a particular buyer the savings of larger volume."[12]

Nevertheless, the increased sales resulting from the price discrimination in the foregoing illustration bring about a more economical utilization of resources. It is the market, rather than the production costs of individual sales, that is the cause of the differentiation. The market situation may be the result of competition from other producers, or the bargaining position of the buyer who may be able to command the favored price because of the threat to make his own products if he does not get it.

If one could always assume that discriminatory practices in quantity discounts were the result of competition, there would seem to be no basis for public interference with them. If they are being used as a weapon to dominate or control a market, they should be eliminated, because they are then injurious to competition. The cost test, however, except when used within a wide range, is not suitable as a basis for economical public policy; if applied strictly on an average basis, it will serve to hamper competition rather than aid it.

[12]Report of the Attorney General's National Committee, *Antitrust Laws* (Washington, D.C.: U.S. Government Printing Office, 1955), p. 334.

Functional Discounts

Functional discounts are discounts given to buyers on the basis of the functions they perform, or the activities in which they are engaged. Thus, builders may be given prices on their materials which the ordinary retail buyer would not be able to obtain. These discounts are accorded to customers on the basis of the classification into which they fall, the classification being made by the seller. The practice of functional classification grew up, in part at least, in recognition of the difference in costs of serving the buyers in the different groups. Wholesalers may perform functions for a manufacturer that retailers do not render, and these functions may warrant a price reduction for the savings to the manufacturer. The problems of discrimination that emerge here are similar to those arising under quantity discounts. Large retailers may wish to buy directly from the producer, and yet when they are not classified as wholesalers, they may be denied the price concessions given to a wholesaler who buys less and costs more to serve. There is also the problem of classification when a buyer performs the functions of both wholesaler and retailer. Obviously, there are real possibilities of discrimination which may be subject to abuse, but which may also be difficult to isolate or identify.[13]

GEOGRAPHIC PRICE POLICIES[14]

The geographical structure of prices is a result of the spatial aspect of markets, which gives rise to differences in prices in different areas because of the cost of transport and because of market imperfections which the spatial factor creates. Transporation charges loom large in the marketing of goods in this country because of the concentration of production of different commodities in certain localities—that is, because of regional specialization. The freight revenues of railroads alone in this country were $8,848 million in 1963. If competition were fully effective among the geographically separated market areas, prices for similar goods in different parts of the United States would differ only by their transportation costs. Regional discrimination and the discrimination among various commodities could still exist because of the freight-rate structure, but they would not arise as a result of the policies of the sellers of the goods; that is, the geographic structure of prices would not be influenced by the policies of sellers of commodities.

Sellers who are able to have price policies must take transportation costs into consideration if they are going to penetrate the markets of

[13]See J. F. Barron, "Mandatory Functional Discounts: An Appraisal," *The Journal of Business of the University of Chicago*, Vol. XXXV, No. 3 (July, 1962), pp. 302–16.

[14]For a good treatment of geographic price structures, see Temporary National Economic Committee, Monograph No. 1, *Price Behavior and Business Policy* (Washington, D.C.: U.S. Government Printing Office, 1940), Part II.

other geographic areas. The costs of transportation vary widely with the different commodities. Where weight is high relative to the price of a product, freight costs become a significant item in price, especially if the distance of transport involved is considerable. Where the weight is low, the transport costs may be a very small part of the total price. In either case, the spatial factor in the marketing of products must be taken into consideration, although the way in which it manifests itself in geographic price structures varies widely.

Uniform F.O.B. Prices[15]

Every firm whose products are marketed over an appreciable area has a geographic pattern of prices, the form which the pattern takes depending upon the conditions surrounding both the firm and the industry. The simplest type of geographic price structure is one in which a firm sells a given commodity at a uniform price at the point of manufacture. The buyer takes delivery and provides for his own transportation. A modification of this occurs when the seller charges a uniform price for the commodity and adds the actual transportation costs to the point of delivery. This arrangement yields the seller a net return on all sales, which is independent of the point of destination of the commodity. It is the type of price structure which characterizes any purely competitive industry. A seller who enjoys a monopoly position may also use the same method of pricing if he does not find it to his advantage to take geographical considerations into account.

Uniform Delivered Prices

At the other extreme of the uniform F.O.B. price system is the one which provides for uniform delivered prices throughout the United States. This is sometimes called "postage stamp" pricing. This may be accomplished by quoting delivered prices directly or by quoting F.O.B. prices and allowing full freight to the buyer. Many nationally advertised brands of consumer goods are sold at uniform prices throughout the country, and book publishing companies frequently follow this same practice. Uniform delivered prices are also quoted for some industrial products where freight is a minor element—as, for example, in the case of aluminum. These prices do not always mean the same margin of profit to distributors. The consumer may be charged the uniform price; but the distributor may be required, in some cases, to absorb part or all of the freight charges.

A modification of the uniform pricing system obtains when zones are established—delivered prices may be kept constant through certain specified geographic areas. Thus, music publishing companies frequently

[15]F.O.B. means free on board—that is, the seller agrees to deliver the goods without charge to a common carrier or to a means of transport provided by the buyer. In other words, it means "loaded and ready to go."

charge a uniform price for all of the area east of the Rocky Mountains and add a differential for sales made on the Pacific Coast. Practices with regard to zone systems vary widely. In some instances, the boundaries have become generally recognized throughout the industry and are observed by all competing sellers; whereas in other cases, the individual manufacturers set up their own price zones. Sometimes, zone differentials may bear no definite relationship to each other; in other instances, they have a more formal structure. One common practice is for a firm to quote uniform plant prices in all zones. The delivered price of the commodity is the uniform plant price, to which is added the shipping costs from the plant where transportation charges are the lowest to the point of delivery. The conventionalized nature of this pricing structure makes possible a high degree of price uniformity among rival producers.

Freight Equalization

In industries where competing producers are located in different geographical areas and freight is an important consideration in the price of the commodity at the point of delivery, the sellers may endeavor to overcome some of the inequalities arising from freight costs by absorbing some of the charges. This is known as "freight equalization," "freight absorption," or "market interpenetration." The practice results in varying net yields on sales to the seller at his plant, depending upon the amount of freight that is absorbed. It is obviously a form of discrimination, since the producer would not be willing to absorb a part of the freight if he could sell all of his products at the price of those which do not absorb freight. This method of meeting a rival's price arises from endeavors to expand sales on a geographic basis, without upsetting the price structure of the local market. If freight absorption can take place without extending the advantage of a lower net yield to all buyers, a firm may be able to utilize excess capacity and make higher profits than would be the case if it were forced to adopt uniform mill nets.[16]

If rivals' prices are not generally known and the policy of freight absorption is not systematic, price structures over much of the country may be highly competitive. This may still be the case even when F.O.B. prices are publicly announced, if the freight absorption does not follow a systematic pattern. Frequently, however, freight equalization takes on more conventional forms, especially where goods are highly standardized, where competitors are comparatively few in number, and where trade associations are active. Freight equalization, under these arrangements, means that the purchasers near a particular plant receive a lower price than those who are distant from it. If a plant is established in a new territory, its prices govern; and they rise as distance from the plant

[16]"Uniform mill net" would be the same net price to the producer for each unit of product, regardless of the point of delivery.

increases. The buyers in the producing centers have a price advantage over those who are located farther away, even though freight equalization may be systematized.

Basing-Point Pricing

The basing-point system is a method of pricing under which commodities are sold on a compulsory delivered price basis or its equivalent. The delivered price to the buyer is made up of the price at a given place, known as the "basing point," plus freight to the point of delivery. This arrangement differs from the more general practice of freight absorption by the limitation on the number of points at which base prices are quoted and the formalized quotation of freight rates. Prices are publicly announced F.O.B. basing point, together with the freight which applies to destination. Transportation charges are obtained from freight books prepared by leading companies or trade associations. The freight charges do not necessarily conform in every way to actual rates, but they usually follow them fairly closely. A buyer is not allowed to take delivery of the goods F.O.B. plant and transport them by any means he desires. In the steel industry, until 1949, the buyer was permitted to accept delivery at the plant and to use his own truck, but he had to pay a premium amounting to 35 per cent of the cost of the all-rail delivery for the privilege.

Single Basing Point. Under the single basing-point system, one producing center is taken as the base from which all F.O.B. prices are quoted, the delivered price of the product being this F.O.B. price plus freight from the base point to destination. Producers not located at the basing point quote the same delivered price as the firm at that place. This was the type of geographic price structure which prevailed in the steel industry from 1900 to 1926 and was known as the "Pittsburgh-plus plan." The price of steel at every locality in the United States was the base price at Pittsburgh, Pennsylvania, plus freight from Pittsburgh to the point of delivery, no matter where the actual shipment originated. All of the other producing centers were known as "nonbase" mills.

Multiple Basing Points. The multiple basing-point system is simply an extension of the single basing-point idea. A number of producing centers become basing points which quote F.O.B. prices, and the delivered price at any given destination will be the lowest combination of base price plus transportation to point of delivery. Thus, the basing point for steel sold in Los Angeles, down to the middle of 1947, was Sparrows Point, Maryland. The price of steel in Los Angeles was the base price at Sparrows Point plus the freight charges. Whether the steel was shipped from Gary, Indiana; Pittsburgh, Pennsylvania; or Birmingham, Alabama, or even produced in Los Angeles, the price was still the base price at Sparrows Point plus freight.

It should be noted that under the multiple basing-point system, the

F.O.B. prices for the product may be different at each basing point. The governing basing point for the delivered price will be the one in which the combination of base price plus freight to destination is the lowest. Of course, if all the basing-point prices happen to be the same, then the governing basing point will be the one with the lowest freight rate to destination. The fact that delivered prices are the same at any point of delivery, no matter at what production point the shipment originates, does not mean that all production or base mills or prepared to sell anywhere in the country. If they do so, they will conform to the basing-point system; but they may be unwilling to make sales to some points of delivery, because the freight absorption is too great. The prices are systemized, but it does not follow that every producer is prepared to and endeavors to sell in every market.

Although the use of the basing-point system by the steel industry has attracted the greatest amount of public attention, it has been employed in other industries. Until 1945, the Corn Products Refining Company used a single basing-point system with Chicago as the center, and competitors conformed to this arrangement. The pulp sugar, cement, and lead industries all used multiple basing points. In some other cases, basing points are used in certain parts of the country for particular products.

Is Spatial Discrimination Objectionable? An appraisal of the basing-point system necessitates, first of all, recognition of the character of the market in which it appears.[17] The product is usually highly standardized, and freight is an important element in the price at the point of delivery. Lack of product differentiation means that the price set by all sellers who offer the product at the delivery point must be the same. There is a high degree of geographical concentration of production, and a limited number of producers. The scale of production is large, and immediate markets will not utilize all of the capacity. At best, therefore, com-

[17]For recent discussion of this issue, see F. A. Fetter, "The New Plea for Basing-Point Monopoly," *Journal of Political Economy*, Vol. XLV, No. 5 (October, 1937), pp. 577–605; M. G. De Chazeau, "Public Policy and Discriminatory Prices of Steel: A Reply to Professor Fetter," *ibid.*, Vol. XLVI, No. 4 (August, 1938), pp. 537–66; Fetter, "Rejoinder to Professor De Chazeau's Reply," *loc. cit.*, pp. 567–70; J. M. Clark, "Basing-Point Methods of Price Quoting," *Canadian Journal of Economics and Political Science*, Vol. IV (November, 1938), pp. 447–89; A. Smithies, "Aspects of the Basing-Point System," *American Economic Review*, Vol. XXXII, No. 4 (December, 1942), pp. 705–26; V. A. Mund, "Monopolistic Competition Theory and Public Price Policy," *ibid.*, pp. 727–43; Clark, "Imperfect Competition Theory and Basing-Point Problems," *ibid.*, Vol. XXXIII, No. 2 (June, 1943), pp. 283–300; Carl Kaysen, "Basing Point Pricing and Public Policy," *Quarterly Journal of Economics*, Vol. LXIII, (August, 1949), pp. 289–315; Fritz Machlup, *The Basing Point System* (Philadelphia: Blakistan Co., 1949); *Law and Contemporary Problems*, Vol. XV (Durham, N.C.: Duke University, 1950); G. W. Stocking, *Basing Point Pricing and Regional Development* (Chapel Hill: University of North Carolina Press, 1954); Report of the Senate Judiciary Committee, *Administered Steel Prices* (85th Cong., 2nd sess. Report No. 1387) (Washington, D.C.: U.S. Government Printing Office, 1958), pp. 113–27.

petition is highly imperfect; and the intrusion of monopoly itself in some form seems to be inevitable. Price discrimination is unavoidable under these circumstances, and geographic price structures are merely one of its manifestations. A certain degree of formalization of the price structure is also unavoidable. The basic question, therefore, is not whether price discrimination can be eliminated but rather whether the basing-point system aggravates the problem. It is unrealistic to assume that discrimination can be eliminated or completely detected. It is unreasonable discrimination that is the problem. The circumstances under which discrimination becomes unreasonable involve a considerable element of judgment, but there seems to be no good reason why spatial discrimination should be more objectionable than other forms.

When the economical size of plants is too large for the immediate market area, geographical price discrimination may promote a more effective utilization of capacity. This is of benefit to all concerned, unless there is a definite abuse of monopoly pricing powers at the base point. On the other hand, the basing-point system may be used to prevent the rise of plants at other centers and may deprive customers located at nonbase mills of lower prices from those mills than would otherwise obtain. A considerable amount of waste may arise from the crosshauling of freight; but again, a certain amount of this is bound to occur in market interpenetration and wherever there is competition. In this connection, objection is frequently raised to what is called "phantom freight." This results from the practice of a nonbase mill setting its price by adding freight to the nonbase mill to the F.O.B. price at the base mill. It is true that the price at nonbase mills is calculated by adding an item of freight which is not actually paid, but this does not prove that the nonbase mill is getting an unjustifiable price. Indeed, that may well be the price at which it must sell in order to cover its costs. This would be so if competition were thoroughly effective. It would also have to be the price if the nonbase mill were unable to meet the demand of its own immediate market at lower prices.

The prime objection to the basing-point system seems to lie in the thoroughgoing systematization of the pricing structure, which is undoubtedly an aid to control of the market and to the restriction of competition, and in the widespread belief that the system is based upon collusion and requires collusion for its success. Whether collusion is an essential part of basing-point pricing is a matter of serious debate; but if it is, then it is probable that it is as significant in determining F.O.B. prices as it is for the delivered price system. So far, evidence has not been advanced to prove collusion in F.O.B. prices.

The practice of pricing on a quoted-price basis seems certain to lead to a degree of systematization of the pricing structure, especially in industries where competition has many imperfections; and some geographical price discrimination seems to be inevitable under such circumstances. It is the organizing of the price structure around a limited number of basing points and the strict adherence to delivered prices, however, that distinguishes the basing-point system. What the situation would be without compulsory delivered prices may not be easy to tell; but at least, it would not be basing-point pricing.

Remedies. One proposal to deal with the objectionable features of basing-point pricing is to forbid all systematic freight absorption, and this is probably what the law does at present. Some writers even advocate prohibiting all freight absorption. The prohibition of systematic freight absorption might put an end to one phase of discrimination; but it would not reach the heart of the problem, because it deals with a symptom rather than the causes; nor would it necessarily insure over-all beneficial results. Particular practices, however, might be curbed. It may be unreasonable to allow producers to make delivered prices compulsory; but it seems equally unreasonable to prohibit them,[18] although limitation on freight absorption might be imposed. This, however, would be difficult, unless a considerable amount of price regulation was instituted. A requirement that all sales yield uniform mill nets would also probably necessitate an extension of price regulation. If all firms were compelled to make sales F.O.B. mill, they would presumably have to be prevented from establishing distribution centers in other places from which sales could be made. If these centers were established, prices charged at them would have to be supervised if uniform mill nets were to be realized. In other words, an outright prohibition of freight absorption would encounter the difficult question of whether distribution centers quoting delivered prices could be set up at nonmill centers. Prohibition of the latter would be difficult to enforce and would raise several legal issues.

A more practical approach would seem to be that of dealing with clear-cut abuses in specific situations, with a view to lessening the systematic control that is possible under present basing-point arrangements. The development of the multiple basing-point system has been a move in this direction, and a further extension of it would very likely reduce the monopoly potentialities of pricing under a limited number of basing points. Other steps, such as freeing the buyer from compulsory delivered price arrangements, might also help. If the buyer were given the privilege of purchase on a delivered price basis or F.O.B. mill at his option, and if all mills were required to quote F.O.B., the possibilities of collusion, if it existed, would be severely limited. Prices at destination would not be different from F.O.B. mill prices for an appreciable period by more than actual freight from the nearest producing center. This would also eliminate freight books and other similar devices that have facilitated common action. Delivered prices as a means of maintaining a price struc-

[18]See Louis Marengo, "The Basing Point Decisions and the Steel Industry," *American Economic Review*, Vol. XLV, No. 2 (May, 1955), pp. 509–22.

ture would no longer be possible. To attack the whole problem on the basis of a simple formula, such as no freight absorption, is probably as bad as a basing-point system, which is also erected on a simple formula.[19]

RESALE PRICE MAINTENANCE

Resale price maintenance is the practice whereby a manufacturer endeavors to control the sale price of his product all the way to its ultimate purchase by the consumer. The practice can be applied successfully only to differentiated products, because if no differentiation exists, it is impossible to identify the sale price with a particular producer's product. The effect of resale price maintenance is to eliminate price competition among retailers in the sale of the particular product whose price is maintained because all sellers must maintain the same price. Resale price maintenance has covered a wide range of products, particularly in such commodities as liquors and wines, drugs, tobacco products, cosmetics, photographic equipment, electrical appliances, men's furnishings, and similar items. Where trade-ins may be important, the practice is much less effective because of the opportunities for subterfuge.

Resale price maintenance without some effective means of enforcement cannot be very successful because compliance cannot be assured and competition will bring about a breakdown. There consequently has been continuous pressure to secure legislation that will require observance on the part of retailers through legal action by the producer or even by the government. Legislative steps to make this possible have been taken in various states and at the federal level. Legality at the federal level, however, is dependent on the effectiveness of the state laws. The widespread breakdown of the latter has led to the endeavor to secure federal legislation which would legalize resale price maintenance contracts in interstate commerce without the necessity of state co-operation. This was the purpose of the Quality Stabilization Bill of 1963.[20]

In the period following World War I a widespread movement developed to curb price competition in this country. This was given added impetus by small retailers who feared the competition from the growing chain stores. One defense of resale price maintenance is that it prevents the use of "loss leaders" for the purpose of sales promotion. Another is that it prevents chain stores from taking advantage of their powerful buying position and mass marketing which, it is alleged, enables them to

[19]For example, Temporary National Economic Committee, *Final Report and Recommendations* (Washington, D.C.: U.S. Government Printing Office, 1941), p. 33.

[20]H.R. 3669. See *Quality Stabilization*, 1963, Hearings before Subcommittee on Interstate and Foreign Commerce, House of Representatives, 88th Cong., 1st sess. (Washington, D.C.: U.S. Government Printing Office, 1963); *Quality Stabilization Act*, Report of the Committee on Interstate and Foreign Commerce, House of Representatives, 88th Cong., 1st sess., Union Calendar No. 237, House Report No. 566 (Washington, D.C.: U.S. Government Printing Office, 1963). The Committee reported favorably on the legislation, but it was not acted on by Congress.

undersell smaller retailers. In other words, one of the major purposes of laws which legalize compulsory resale price maintenance is to restrict competition at the retail level. This is supposed to prevent destructive competition. Uniform markup for the retailer is provided by the manufacturer, but this does not provide real protection for the small retailer because the manufacturer will provide the margin that is to his advantage, not to the retailer, the margin presumably being that which will maximize the return of the manufacturer. This may well result in margins that are not satisfactory to the small firm.

If all retail sales were subject to price maintenance, there would be no price competition at the retail level except in rival products. This would reduce competition to the producer level only. It also furnishes opportunity to develop restraints on competition at the producer level because the ultimate sales prices are publicly announced and adhered to by compulsion. The practice leads to reduction in efficiency in distribution by limiting the competition of, and among, large retailers who may be able to pass economies resulting from mass distribution on to the consumer. It may also encourage advertising and other sales appeals because of restrictions on price competition. The effect which legalized compulsory resale price maintenance can have on retail prices has been demonstrated by the phenomenal growth of discount houses whose existence has been primarily the result of endeavors to find ways and means to evade the controls. In short, resale price maintenance without legislative support to compel adherence to it breaks down under competition. Legislative sanction for its enforcement is a contradiction of the competitive foundation upon which the antitrust laws are erected.[21]

NONPRICE COMPETITION

One of the most significant developments of business in the twentieth century has been in the field of marketing. The growth of large-scale production extending to the area of consumer goods, the standardization of products, the sale of so many products on a nationwide basis, and the increase of facilities for acquainting consumers with the availability of products have all led to an enormous intensification of sales efforts.

Price versus Nonprice Competition

The whole group of business policies designed to increase the sales of a given firm within a given price range has come to be known as "nonprice competition." To many, this term carries with it the notion of a diminution of competition as a result of a redirection of sales effort designed to avoid price competition. Although there is some truth in this point of view, it greatly oversimplifies the processes involved in the mar-

[21]For a criticism of resale maintenance laws, see Federal Trade Commission, *Report on Resale Price Maintenance* (Washington, D.C.: U.S. Government Printing Office, 1945).

keting of goods in the modern world. Price is but one of the avenues through which competition expresses itself, and price policies are only a part of a firms's sales policy. Nonprice competition, therefore, cannot be regarded as a sort of parasite on the surface of genuine and competitive effort. Such a point of view places undue emphasis on the wasteful and harmful aspects of nonprice competition and tends to create the impression that it is deliberately aimed at limiting the role of competition as a directing force in business activity.[22] It also neglects the fact that nonprice competition is an integral and inevitable part of the competitive process when products are not completely standardized or when personal effort plays any part in the disposal of goods. A great bulk of manufactured commodities are not bought and sold in markets like produce exchanges, and never have been. The personal factor, quality, and terms of sale have always played a large role. Appeals to consumers must be made on these bases as well as through price. Many elements enter into exchange transactions, and price is intimately related to the nonprice aspect of them. As a result, "price" and "nonprice competition" cannot be regarded as mutually exclusive terms but rather as integral parts of the marketing of most goods.

Quality Competition

Competition which is not expressed directly in the usual competitive cost-price relations manifests itself in a variety of ways.[23] Perhaps the most important single channel through which this competition manifests itself is in the quality of the goods sold. A producer may decide to maintain the quality of his product and vary his price, he may vary the quality and maintain the price, or he may do both. Whatever may be the basis of his decision, he cannot ignore the interrelationships of quality and price.

In the marketing of many products, price lines are established as the basis for classifying quality. Price lines appear in such diverse commodities as wearing apparel, cars, radios, refrigerators, and gasoline. Within the price lines, competition is largely on a quality and service basis. Price competition appears among the various price lines; but even here, it is limited to some extent, in that the differentials between the lines do not always correspond to differences in cost. The effect of price lining is to stratify the market somewhat; and it probably simplifies the consumer's problem, as compared with continuous pricing. Price lining also diminishes nonprice competition to a certain extent by emphasis on price appeal; but on the other hand, it tends to increase price rigidity by fostering customary prices and to complicate the consumer's problem by presenting him with a variety of choices which he cannot precisely evaluate.

[22]See A. R. Burns, *The Decline of Competition* (New York: McGraw-Hill Book Co., Inc., 1936), chap. viii.

[23]See Temporary National Economic Committee, Monograph No. 1, chap. iii and Appendix II.

Advertising

The most striking expression of sales promotion in recent years has come through the enormous growth of advertising, brands, and trade-marks. To a certain extent, advertising disseminates information on quality features and thereby assists the prospective purchaser in reaching a decision. Brands and trade-marks furnish a ready means for identifying the merchandise sold. In one respect, therefore, these sales methods are a phase of competition based upon quality. In so far as they assist in consumer education, they increase the scope and breadth of competition; and the costs involved may be more than offset by the competitive pressure which they induce.

On the other hand, advertising may emphasize the diversion of consumer purchasing from one producer to another. This may serve to increase efficiency by stimulating competition, but it has also resulted in channeling an enormous amount of effort into sheer advertising pressure. The extent to which advertising has grown may be illustrated by the expense devoted to this end by the California wine industry. This industry spent $15 million on advertising in 1946, as compared with $500,000 in 1936. A considerable amount of the advertising that is carried on is undoubtedly sheer waste; and in all too many instances, it is false and misleading. It is often designed to appeal only to prejudice or ignorance; and when it is in this category, it is not only wasteful but also may lead to positively harmful results.

Advertising may also serve materially to reduce effective competition. This is especially true in the fields of cosmetics, toiletries, and medicine. Nationally advertised brands of many such products enjoy distinct price advantages over less widely known types. Nationwide advertising of trade-marked and branded goods simplifies resale price maintenance. Reinforced by fair-trade laws, which legalize such price practices, price competition is effectively reduced in many lines; the possibilities of maintaining price differentials are enhanced; and the control of the manufacturer over his market against the inroads of competitors is substantially increased.

Thus, advertising, brands, and trade-marks may serve to increase competition in some of its dimensions and decrease it in others. In general, it seems safe to say that the over-all effect has been to stimulate competition and productive efficiency. This, however, has not been without some of the offsetting costs which competition has entailed and without restrictions on competition, which it has facilitated.

Evaluation of Nonprice Competition

Appraisal of the effects of nonprice competition must recognize, first of all, that it is an integral part of workable competition. In any industry or trade, unless there is an outright allocation of business by some authority, rivalry among competitors will assume many aspects. The competitive strategy adopted will be that which the various firms deem most suitable to the maintenance to their position. Public policy on nonprice competition, assuming continuance of a private enterprise system, will have to be directed to the maintenance of those aspects which further healthy competition and to the elimination of those aspects which undermine it. Constant vigilance by public authority can serve to limit the effectiveness of collusion in nonprice competition; the repeal of resale price maintenance laws would serve to remove another impediment. Uniform grading and standardization have many advantages, and much may be accomplished in this direction through trade associations and other industrial groups. Government standards are desirable where public health and safety are involved; and rules requiring information disclosing quality, content, etc., can also aid the consumer.

Care needs to be exercised, however, in the extension of government authority in this direction. More may be lost by compulsion than is gained in industrial efficiency, except where consumer safety and health are clearly involved. There are too many intangibles in the situation to warrant the assumption that government intervention can reduce waste and improve the consumer's lot outside of a relatively limited field. It scarcely seems to be the role of public authority to channelize taste and consumption in the interest of efficiency, especially when the possibilities of achieving the latter through this means may be very doubtful. American consumers want a large variety of goods and a wide range of choice, and they seem to be willing to pay for them. It is difficult to substantiate the position that nonprice competition has increased consumer costs. Mass production in consumer goods, which is so characteristic of the American scene, can be attributed in no small part to nonprice competition. There is considerable waste, product adulteration, costly advertising, etc., as a consequence of which prices may be higher than they would be under perfect competition or present market conditions. The question is: "Given the variety of consumer appeals, mass production, and marketing of consumer goods, how and in what ways can public authority reduce the costs which arise from some of the more obvious wastes of nonprice competition?" The answer would seem to lie in persistent efforts to improve the effectiveness of competition. Public policy can aid in accomplishing this by continuously striving to limit the effectiveness of monopolistic practices, by improving the plane of competition, and by widening consumer education.

PRICE POLICIES AND PRICE INFLEXIBILITY

Recognition of the important role played by price policies in the functioning of the economy as a whole has led to extensive study of the behavior of prices, especially in relation to cyclical fluctuations and unemployment. The depression which began in 1929 and the uneven effects which it had on prices and employment in various segments of the economy led to a search for the causes of the breakdown and the unequal distribution of its impact.

An early attack on the problem which attracted widespread attention was made by Dr. Gardiner C. Means. He used the term "administered prices" to designate prices which are set by the seller in contrast to those which are determined in a completely impersonal way in the competitive market. The latter were called "market prices," exemplified in industries like agriculture, where prices were independent of individual producers. He defined an "administered price" as one set by administrative action (management) and held constant for a period of time. But he insisted that administered prices should not be confused with monopoly, because, to him, the presence of administered prices did not mean the presence of monopoly, nor did market prices mean the absence of monopoly. He held that monopolized industries usually had administered prices, as did many vigorously competitive industries in which the number of competitors was small. Means intended to demonstrate that administered prices, as he had defined them, were inflexible prices and that the disparity between the inflexibility of administered prices and the flexibility of market prices was the basic cause of the depression. "Indeed the whole depression might be described as a general dropping of prices at the flexible end of the price scale and a dropping of production at the rigid end with intermediate effects between."[24] Means held that the growing concentration of control in industry had led to a shift from market to administrative co-ordination of economic activity, and that price inflexility was the result of industrial concentration.

This point of view has been subject to severe challenge. The concept of price flexibility itself is a very elusive one. Merely to measure price flexibility in terms of frequency, amplitude, and timing of price changes is to neglect many other factors. The impact of fluctuations of the general price level will be felt unevenly on the various prices that make up the total structure. Changes in quality are not reflected in the price index, nor is the responsiveness of price to changing conditions of cost and demand. Industries in which the elements of fixed costs and fixed capacity loom large find it difficult to adapt to rapidly changing situations. Agriculture is typically in this category—a large proportion of farming costs go on continuously; and if production is not undertaken, the services which would be derived from these costs are lost.

On the other hand, manufacturing may find it possible to postpone many of its costs, at least for the short run. Labor and material costs can be discontinued, and a plant can be shut down, so that a very consider-

[24]G. C. Means, *Industrial Prices and Their Relative Inflexibility* (Senate Document No. 13, 74th Cong., 1st sess.) (Washington, D.C.: U. S. Government Printing Office, 1935), p. 8. See Temporary National Economic Committee, Monograph No. 1, chap. ii and Appendix I.

able proportion of depreciation is postponed. In other words, manufacturing is able to adapt its costs to the downswing of the cycle more than has commonly been assumed. In addition, demand for durable goods may be postponed for some considerable time. Under the impact of falling prices and falling purchasing power, this demand shows considerable inelasticity. In other words, a severe cut in prices may not bring the increase in volume of sales necessary to compensate for the reduction. Extreme price fluctuations in certain commodities and certain industries may therefore be evidence of lack of adaptability along other lines. Professor A. C. Neal,[25] after a careful study of industrial concentration and price inflexibility, concluded that there was no reasonable presumption that the price-production behavior from 1929 to 1933 was the result of concentration and that concentration was not an adequate explanation of price behavior or of production behavior during the depression. He concluded that the amount of direct-cost changes, rather than concentration, explained the varying degrees of price declines exhibited by different industries after 1929.

The controversy has been revived since World War II, but this time it is over the relation of "administered" prices to inflation. Means now contends that inflation has been the result, at least to a very considerable extent, of action within the area of discretion in which prices are made. This he calls administrative inflation which means to him the exercise of power to increase prices significantly in excess of the increase justified by increased costs or increased productivity.[26] Means's analysis of the problem was confined to the area of industrial prices where he found that administered prices had lagged behind what he called demand inflation after World War II, but ultimately caught up and produced what he called administrative inflation in the period after 1953. The same difficulties are contained in this analysis that appeared in the earlier version. There is obviously considerable confusion of thought in Means's presentation. Administered prices can emerge only when there is some control of the market by the seller, or by some authority externals to the market itself. Administered prices, defined as inflexible prices, cover a much wider range of the pricing process that Means's study encompasses. Nor are the administered prices of indsutrial undertakings more impor-

[25]A. C. Neal, *Industrial Concentration and Price Flexibility* (Washington, D.C.: American Council on Public Affairs, 1942). See also E. S. Mason, "Price Inflexibility," *Review of Economic Statistics*, Vol. XX, No. 2 (May, 1938), pp. 53–64.

[26]See *Administered Prices*, Hearings before the Subcommittee on Antitrust and Monopoly of the Committee on the Judiciary, United States Senate, 85th to the 88th Cong., Parts 1–29 (Washington, D.C.: U.S. Government Printing Office, 1957–1963). Parts 1 and 29 present testimony of various economists on the subject. *Administered Prices, A Compendium on Public Policy*, Committee Print, 88th Cong., 1st sess. (Washington, D.C.: U.S. Government Printing Office, 1963) contains a series of papers by economists evaluating the hearings and the issues at stake. See also Gardiner C. Means, *Administrative Inflation and Public Policy* (Washington, D.C.: Anderson Kramer Associates, 1959).

tant than similar prices in other areas. Government regulation of transportation and public utility rates covers a major segment of the price structure. These rates are highly inflexible in both directions, and could at least, by this token, be given as much credit for keeping prices down as for pushing them up. Indeed, they seem to have the perverse characteristic of working in the opposite direction to the price level, thereby aggravating the distortions rather than mitigating them. The major items in Means's analysis are given the blame for aggravating inflation by carrying advances too far. Surely this, to say the least, is a contradiction of the very concept upon which the original thesis was developed.

The effect of price policies which have prevailed to date on production and employment is difficult to evaluate.[27] In the present state of our knowledge, there are reasons for believing that price rigidities have increased somewhat in the price structure as a whole. Regulated transportation charges and public utility rates, interest on an enormously larger private and public debt, and greater rigidity in the wage structure have increased the area over which price adjustments have become more difficult to make. There is also a considerable amount of monopoly in industry which resists a downward price adjustment. To the extent that ridigity in these prices represents a failure to adapt them to changing cost and demand conditions, the severity of business fluctuations is increased and the effective utilization of resources diminished. Public policy aimed at removing this impediment would be part of the general attack on business cycles and unemployment. This, however, is only a small segment of the much larger problem of economic fluctuations, and price rigidities are probably more a symptom than a cause of the difficulty. Whether price inflexibility can be blamed for wide upward surges in prices is perhaps a debatable question, but lack of flexibility in a significant segment of the economy is probably an impediment to the process of adjustment.

[27]See paper by Richard Ruggles, "The Nature of Price Flexibility and the Determinants of Relative Price Changes in the Economy," and comments, pp. 441–505, in *Business Concentration and Price Policy*, *op. cit.*

Chapter 10 THE REGULATION OF PRICES

INTRODUCTION

Price regulation in a private enterprise economy arises as a result of the inability of competition, without any public intervention with regard to specific prices, to perform adequately the task of bringing about the most economical allocation and utilization of resources. Institutional and technological conditions, without anything else, necessitate some public participation in the determination of relative prices, even under the most favorable circumstances. In a period of war, the basic assumptions of a private enterprise system are severely undermined, if not swept away; and government is forced to take over the management of the economy in order effectively to pursue the paramount goal of winning the conflict. The ensuing return to peacetime arrangements is a painful task, even though the objectives of reconstruction are thoroughly understood and agreed upon. It is too great a strain upon private enterprise and competition to bring about readjustments from the dislocations of peacetime conditions induced by the war economy. Thus, war and postwar economic problems result in much more intervention in the price-fixing process than an effective private enterprise system can permanently tolerate.

This means that there are really three separate sets of circumstances under which price regulation may be undertaken—namely, peacetime, reconstruction, and war. The principles of price regulation applying to these three situations are by no means mutually exclusive; but the circumstances surrounding each and the assumptions of the purposes underlying the price controls make for very different application in each case, especially between peacetime controls, on the one hand, and reconstruction and wartime ones, on the other.

PRINCIPLES OF PRICE CONTROL

Objectives of Price Regulation

The principles of price controls that are appropriate to any economy must be examined in the light of the underlying institutional assumptions of that economy. The problem is quite a different one if competition is severely restricted, or if there is no competition in production at all, from what it is if private enterprise and predominantly competitive conditions prevail. The following treatment, therefore, is based upon the assumptions of peacetime conditions, a private enterprise economy, and consumers' freedom of choice. When emergency situations such as war arise, the government is forced to intervene in other aspects of economic and social life with a more comprehensive participation of government in them than is compatible with democratic peacetime arrangements. The extent to which peacetime price controls may be used as a means of regulation depends upon how they fit into the program of regulation in a particular country.

The basic objective of price regulation in the United States, presumably, is to bring about the allocation and utilization of economic resources that competition would yield under existing concepts of social desirability of particular lines of action. The need for price regulation arises from the inability of public authority to establish rules apart from price controls which will make it possible for competition within those rules to achieve the desired results. Whether price controls do or can serve this purpose will depend upon circumstances; but frequently they are a device that is ill-suited to the task imposed upon them. This is particularly the case when, instead of being utilized to promote competition or to substitute for it where it is absent, they are used to restrain it on either the supply or the demand side.

The regulation of minimum prices may have one of two main objectives. The first one is to impose limitations on minimum prices where lower prices would offend public standards or result in some form of undesirable exploitation. This is one of the purposes of minimum-wage laws. In some states, the alleged purpose, at least of minimum wellhead prices for natural gas, is to prevent wasteful exploitation of this natural resource. Most minimum price controls, however, are to protect producers against some of the effects of competition, either as an aid to the industry or to make competition workable.

Maximum prices are generally imposed as a means of protecting the consumer. Here, the theory is that the seller may be able to exploit the consumer beyond what seems to be reasonable where the commodity or service is a necessity. Maximum prices may also be imposed where limitations of supply prevent adjustments to the demand other than through prices which seem to be unreasonably high. In addition, maximum prices may be utilized for the purpose of limiting the production of some commodity or service when it is desired to divert economic resources into other channels of activity.

In addition to fixing minimum or maximum prices, regulation may fix the precise price at which commodities or services may be sold. This type of price regulation usually involves the determination of the profits which the firm is permitted to receive as well as the prices of the various commodities or services which it sells. The regulatory agency, as a consequence, is engaged in determining what the total income of the firm should be as well as the relationship among the prices of the products which it sells. Although the basic purpose of this type of price regulation is to protect the buyer against exploitation because of the lack of adequate market alternatives, it also imposes upon public authority the responsibility of sanctioning prices that are adequate for the successful functioning of the firm. The purpose of such regulation, therefore, is to permit the continuation of private production where competition is unable to perform the task of establishing reasonable prices, either to the producer or to the consumer. In this situation, public regulation is supposed to act as a substitute for competition in those aspects of a firm's activities that lack the incentives or restraining pressures of competition.

The Problem of Fair Prices

Price regulation necessarily raises the question of fair prices, because regulation presupposes that the market is unable to determine the prices that are fair to both consumers and producers. What constitutes fair prices involves ethical, legal, and economic considerations. From the standpoint of economics, a fair price is one which would be established by full and free competition. The economic standard of a fair price is a competitive price, and the most precise form is that which would obtain under the model of perfect competition. It includes, therefore, normal profits for a business or "reasonable" payment for services. The problem for public regulation which fair prices presents arises, first of all, from the fact that competition does not work perfectly and substitutes have to be invoked to remedy some of the deficiencies. Ethical concepts may dictate a departure from purely competitive pricing even when the latter could be used. Minimum-wage requirements are based—in part, at least—on ideas of social justice.[1] Legal limitations may be imposed upon purely economic criteria either by statutes which may embody political and ethical considerations or by constitutional restrictions on regulation.

The fair price that is sought by public authority will present different problems, depending on whether it is a minimum price, a maximum price, or a precise one. In any event, it involves the matter of effecting ways and means of equilibrating demand and supply, because the fact that prices are being fixed means that the market processes that would operate without such price fixing are being interfered with. The interference is not that of affecting demand and supply directly by changing the rules and conditions of competition and allowing prices to work out

[1]Some economists would abolish minimum wage laws on the grounds that they produce the opposite results from those which are intended by aggravating unemployment. This does not mean that they are oblivious to the problems created by proverty or very low incomes. They would adopt various devices that would counteract the low incomes received, but would not prevent employment by the device of minimum wage laws which may lead to the unemployment of people who are not "worth" the minimum required by law. See Milton Friedman, *Capitalism and Freedom*, *op. cit.*, chap. xi.

the adjustments. Price fixing, in its various forms, prescribes the prices to which demand and supply must adjust themselves. The problem of public policy, therefore, is to determine the standards by which the appropriate prices are to be fixed.

Regulation of Minimum Prices

Minimum prices maybe established for at least three different purposes. First of all, they may be used as a means of dealing with the problem of price discrimination. This may take the form of limiting or eliminating such practices as quantity discounts, freight absorption, and so forth. In these situations, regulation does not usually take the form of setting the minimum price; but rather, it lays down the conditions of relative pricing. For example, the range and terms of quantity discounts may be prescribed; but the actual or base price on which the discounts are calculated will not be fixed by public authority. Similarly, freight absorption may be limited or permitted, under certain conditions, without determination of the base price which absorbs the freight. However, the question of the appropriate minimum does emerge, in that the basis of the differential may be questioned if predatory pricing is involved. When public authority is called upon to prevent pricing that is being used for the purpose of eliminating rivals, one of the issues that will arise is whether the differential or discriminatory prices that are being charged are warranted by the costs of the price discriminator. The difficulties involved in this question were discussed in the previous chapter in connection with price policies. It will also be dealt with again under antitrust enforcement.

Second, minimum price regulation is used in the field of transport where public authority is usually called upon to authorize all rate minima for regulated carriers. This is also true in public utility regulation. In transport, minimum price fixing was first applied to railroad rate regulation in order to deal with the problem of "ruinous" competition. Subsequently, as new agencies appeared, it was extended to them; and as interagency competition grew, it was extended to the control of competitive rates among the agencies. In the case of public utilities, the control of minimum rates is an integral part of the over-all control of rates and precise price fixing. The problems of price regulation in transportation and public utilities are discussed in detail in Part V.

Third, outside of the fields of transport and public utilities, the principal application of minimum price fixing has been in industries where the government has endeavored to put a bottom under prices for the purpose of relieving distressed conditions or as a means of establishing a predetermined status for an industry. The use of agricultural price supports based on a parity formula is an illustration of minimum price fixing for maintaining the economic status of agriculture at the relative level of a previous period that is used as a standard. The minimum price arrangements that were adopted before World War II for the bituminous coal industry were designed to afford relief to a distressed industry. The National Industrial Recovery Act embodied the minimum price device to assist in bringing about recovery from the depression of the thirties.

The fixing of minimum prices for these purposes necessitates, first of all, the determination of the required minima. This may be based on a parity concept such as is used in connection with some agricultural commodities, by average costs for an industry, by some formula device such as is used for milk price controls, or by average costs as defined in the California Unfair Practices Act. Under this legislation, a person engaged in business in California is prohibited from selling any article or product below cost. Cost of production is defined as including the cost of raw materials, labor (including salaries of executives and officers), and all overhead expenses of the producer. The law also prohibits the sale of any article or product as a "loss leader."[2] The problems connected with the administration of such a law, the totally uneconomic nature of it when applied to multiproduct firms, and the unrealistic concept of costs contained in it are too obvious to require further examination after the earlier analysis in this text on costs.

Administration of the California law entailed minimum price regulations for the individual firm, and therefore did not require minimum price fixing for an industry as a whole. Where the policy relates to minimum prices for the entire industry, it necessitates some form of production controls for the purpose of limiting supply in industries where there is more than one producer. This is the result of the fact that the minimum is imposed because supply under existing conditions will drive prices below the level which is desired. The imposition of the minimum conditions will result in unused capacity, which must be taken care of in some way. This is frequently accomplished by pooling arrangements or by cartelization. It may also be achieved by having an agency stand ready to buy whatever surplus emerges. Thus, the Lancashire cotton industry dealt with the problem by a pooling device whereby facilities were acquired and retired in sufficient amount to maintain the desired prices. The price-support policy for agricultural products in this country is made to work by the government's readiness to acquire agricultural products at the minimum prices stipulated, by its surplus crop controls, and by its soil bank payments. Whatever the device used, it is a means of restricting competition to protect a particular group of producers.

Effective minimum price fixing also raises the question of the determination of costs and the role which costs play in the pricing process. When minimum price fixing is based on a parity formula, it assumes, first of all, that the price relationship existing between the industry whose prices are being fixed and the general level of prices for a particular pe-

[2]Statutes of California, 1913, as amended in 1937, chap. 860, Sec. 3.

riod are to be maintained in future periods. Thus, it assumes that the cost relationships of the industry for the base period as compared with other industries is the "correct" one which is to be maintained for those future periods. For industries where minimum price fixing is not based on a parity formula but instead on the direct basis of costs, the problem of what and whose costs are to be used emerges. Apart from the difficulty of ascertaining the precise minimum cost basis for the products of multi-product firms, there is the question of the proper minimum to be used, because all firms will not have the same minimum. If minimum prices are to be set on the basis of the costs of the most efficient producer, they obviously can serve no real purpose, because prices will ordinarily be above those costs. If they are to be set on the basis of average cost for the industry, they meet the same objections, since they can offer no protection to the higher-cost producers. If they are set on the basis of the highest cost or most inefficient producer, no gauge is available for the amount of production that should be forthcoming; and no standard is left whereby to judge or to compel efficiency.

The basic objection to minimum price control for competitive industries is that it is based upon false assumptions with regard to the nature of costs and the role of costs in the pricing process. It assumes that the costs which are to be used for the purpose are unequivocal in nature and are readily ascertainable. The incorrectness of this viewpoint has already been discussed. In the second place, it assumes that prices are cost-determined and that the relationship is a one-way affair from cost to price. The fact is, of course, that costs and prices are interrelated; they equal each other under competitive conditions only because of the adjustments on both sides of the relationship that competition compels. Competition dictates the adjustment of costs to prices as much as it does prices to costs. The setting of minimum prices by public authority in competitive industry ignores the effect of prices on costs and ignores the compelling pressure of competition on efficiency. In other words, it dispenses with two of the most significant economic bases for decision making and replaces them by purely arbitrary action. Furthermore, it must be emphasized that such price fixing involves the determination of the prices for the individual products that each of the competitors produces, and these individual prices must be the same for all the producers, or the price relationships among the products must be established where substitutability is somewhat limited.

Maximum Prices

The prime purpose of imposing maximum limits on prices is to protect the consumer, although it may be employed as a device for limiting output. In transport and public utilities, maximum rate regulation is used to impose limitations on the power of monopoly to exploit the consumer of the commodities or services, and to limit the range of the relative prices of the monopolies. The policy here is related to the over-all price-regulation problem in these industries and is therefore a phase of the question of fair return or fair profit. These issues will be dealt with later; but it may be noted, in passing, that transport under contemporary conditions presents a peculiarly difficult problem because of the breakdown of the fair-return or fair-profit concept under the intense competition that has emerged.

Maximum price fixing in competitive industry means that the maximum prices must apply to all of the producers of the commodities that are being controlled. This destroys part of the rationing function of prices, because the prices must be fixed for the industry. They cannot be fixed for a single firm, since such a procedure would make that firm's prices lower than the market price and lower than the prices of competitors. This would force competitors to reduce their prices if they wished to continue to sell; and this, in turn, would force the high-cost producers to curtail production or go out of business. The result would be to limit supply and raise the problem of rationing, because consumers would be willing to pay higher prices than are permitted. This is the consequence of dispensing with the price mechanism as a means of deciding who shall get the product.

The same remarks apply if maximum ceilings are imposed for the purpose of restraining price advances while supply is catching up with the demand situation. Such maxima do not necessarily curtail production, because they may not be severe enough to do that; but they will necessitate some other means than price for rationing the product which is being sold at a price lower than that which would equilibrate demand and supply. In the case of rentals, for example, if controls are imposed, some means of protecting existing occupants must be found; eviction at will cannot be permitted. At the same time, those without dwellings are deprived of means of acquiring them; and in any case, they are prevented from getting what they want, even though they can afford to pay for it. In other words, maximum price fixing disequilibrates demand and supply, either by restricting output or by compelling the sale of products at a price that will leave some willing buyers unable to make purchases. This gives rise to "black" markets, "gray" markets, and under-the-counter "premiums" in the absence of some other effective rationing device. Maximum price fixing, without more, is an uneconomical and ineffective procedure for channeling the allocation and utilization of a country's economic resources.

Professor A. P. Lerner takes the position that "administered" prices have resulted in seller's inflation and administered depression.[3] As a solution he recommends the regulation of administered prices. He dis-

[3]See *Administered Prices: A Compendium on Public Policy, op. cit.*, pp. 196–212. Whether Lerner would similarly force the lowering of prices under depression is not discussed.

tinguishes this price regulation from price control. The latter he defines as an attempt by authority to establish a price below that which clears the market. Price regulation, on the other hand, does not attempt to set a price below that which clears the market. It would prohibit price advances where the effect would be to prevent clearing the market at full employment and price stability. In other words, price advances would be unlawful if resulted in less-than-full utilization of capacity Lerner recognizes some of the problems inherent in this approach, but he does not indicate whether his regulations would be for the firm or the industry, nor how his proposal would work for a firm operating at full capacity. Presumably, under such circumstances that firm would not be able to raise its prices or increase its wages. If this were so, then industrywide bargaining and wage contracts would be necessary, and capacity would have to be gauged on an industrywide basis. How cartelization could be avoided needs to be demonstrated.

The Fixing of Precise Prices

The fixing of the precise prices a firm may be permitted to charge embraces all the complexities of both minimum and maximum price fixing, because it combines them into one. It involves the additional problem of "fair" prices—that is, prices which yield to a firm the revenue which it needs to attract economic resources to its employ, so that it can supply consumers with services they desire at prices that will cover the costs of those services, but no more. To put it another way, total revenues must be such as to bring about the sort of equilibrium that would obtain under competition.

The starting point for fixing precise prices, therefore, is that of estimating the total revenue required by the firm to cover the costs of production plus the necessary fair profit. The determination of the fair profit necessitates a standard against which to measure the fairness. The gauge may be the profits being earned by similar types of industries (if there are any), or it may be the profit needed to attract the amount of capital required to produce the quantity of goods demanded at the "fair" prices. This means that some measure of the amount of capital, as well as the amount already being used, must be obtained. The standard commonly adopted in this connection is prudent investment. Having calculated the amount of profit which the firm should be allowed to earn, public authority must then ascertain the costs of doing business. This means that it must not only be able to find out what the actual costs are; it means, in addition, that it must be able to exercise control over those costs and decide whether they are reasonable—otherwise, uncontrolled costs would provide an avenue of escape for controlled profits. The complexities and ramifications of this task are too obvious to require detailed comment. When the total revenue requirements have been calculated, the burden of providing them then has to be assessed on the various commodities or services being sold.

This very general outline describes the method employed in fixing public utility rates, and it works with tolerable acceptability. The problem is simplified in this situation, however, because regulation may be applied to each firm separately. Public utility regulation is not usually complicated by any appreciable amount of competition among the firms. The difficulties which are encountered when competition is significant are thoroughly illustrated by the breakdown of this approach in the field of transport, especially since the rise of the newer agencies. This whole subject is given more extended treatment in Part V.

Industry in general is even less amenable to this type of control than is transport. In any industry where there is a number of competing firms, it would be unworkable to try to establish different individual prices for each firm. If the attempt were made to set prices for the industry as a whole, the immediate question that would arise would be what firm should be used as the standard. If the most efficient were selected, the others would earn inadequate revenues; if the least efficient were chosen, the regulation would fail of its purpose. If an average were used, the disadvantages of both of these would be encountered. In short, if precise price fixing is to be adopted for industry, it will be necessary to create monopolies by consolidation and restrict entry; or it will be necessary to resort to a program of cartelization.

THE NATIONAL INDUSTRIAL RECOVERY ACT

Purpose of the Act

The National Industrial Recovery Act (N.I.R.A.) of June 16, 1933, was passed as part of the economic program inaugurated by President Franklin D. Roosevelt to combat the disastrous depression which struck the United States with the stock market crash of October, 1929. The purpose of the legislation was to assist in bringing about recovery, in part, by increasing purchasing power or consumer demand. The theory underlying the legislation apparently was that a raising of wage rates would increase wage payments and lead to an increased demand. This would diminish the effects of what was believed to be overproduction as well as increase productivity. Income from employment could be increased by establishing maximum hours of employment and establishing legal minima for wages. Finally, "destructive" competition was to be prevented by putting a bottom under individual prices. Such price minima, it was assumed, would make it possible to pay the higher wages, by giving protection against competitors ("chiselers"), such as self-employed persons, who could not be compelled to conform to the new wage provisions. Needless to say, this sort of a program necessitated the control of production, although that was not explicitly recognized by its promulgators or by the legislation itself.

Principal Provisions

The provisions of the National Industrial Recovery Act, as they related to industry, were contained in Title I of the legislation. The purpose of the Act, as set forth in Section 1, was to remove obstructions to the free flow of interstate and foreign commerce, to provide for the general welfare by promoting the organization of industry for the purpose of co-operative action among trade groups, to induce and maintain united action of labor and management under adequate governmental sanction and supervision, to eliminate unfair competitive practices, to promote the fullest possible utilization of the existing productive capacity of industries, to avoid undue restriction of production, to increase the consumption of industrial and agricultural products by increasing purchasing power, to reduce and relieve unemployment, to improve standards of labor and otherwise to rehabilitate industry, and to conserve natural resources. To achieve the objectives, the President was empowered to delegate any of his functions and powers as he saw fit and to establish an industrial planning and research agency to assist him in carrying out the task. It was this provision that gave the authority to set up the National Recovery Administration (the N.R.A.), the organization and administration of which was assigned to General Hugh Johnson.

The Act provided that the President, upon application by one or more trade or industrial associations or groups, might approve codes of fair competition, provided that the associations did not restrict membership or were not designed to promote monopoly or oppress small enterprise. When a code was approved, it was to be the standard of fair competition for the trade or industry that it covered. The President also had the power to impose codes upon industries, as well as to license business enterprises, if that was necessary to make the codes effective. No one could engage in interstate or foreign commerce without a license if the President so ordered. All codes, licenses, and agreements executed under the Act were exempt from the provisions of the antitrust laws. Finally, the President was given the power to limit the importation of foreign goods as he saw fit, if this was necessary to carry out the purposes of the Act. In other words, the underlying idea was that of thoroughgoing cartelization of American industry.

The only specific provisions which the National Industrial Recovery Act stipulated should be contained in every code were those setting forth standards of employment. Section 7 of the Act provided that every code, agreement, and license should contain the conditions (1) that employees should have the right to organize and bargain collectively through representatives of their own choosing; (2) that no employee and no one seeking employment should be required, as a condition of employment, to join a company union or to refrain from joining or organizing a union of his own choosing; and (3) that employers should comply with the maximum hours of labor, minimum rates of pay, and other conditions of employment prescribed by the President. Where agreements could not be reached by employers and employees, the President was empowered to prescribe codes fixing the conditions of employment.

The Codes

The National Recovery Administration approved a total of 557 basic codes for industry, 189 supplementary codes, and the labor provisions of 19 codes jointly with the Agricultural Adjustment Administration. The major effect of the codes was an extensive diminution in the reliance upon private initiative and competition in the guidance of industry and a great increase in the role of government officials and specially interested groups. Code provisions varied considerably from industry to industry, but all of them contained severe restrictions on the operation of the price mechanism. Many granted the code authority the power to fix minimum selling prices, with little or no guide to determine what these should be. A very large number prohibited selling below cost, which, in effect, meant price fixing by the code authority because of denial to the producer of discretion concerning the items that were to be included in costs. The forbidding of "loss leader" selling was a common provision, the seller being required to dispose of his product at the invoice price, plus a specified markup. In some instances, prices were fixed at a stipulated minimum if the code authority decided that there was an "emergency" in the industry.

The codes also exercised control over the utilization and expansion of productive capacity. Many limited the number of hours, within a given period, that a plant could be operated; some assigned production quotas; others restricted the construction of new equipment or even the change from one type of production to another. Limitations were also imposed upon the geographical areas that producers might serve. Under these provisions, the basing-point method of pricing was legalized and systematized; and in some instances, producers in one zone were protected against competition from those in other zones. Finally, all of the codes contained elaborate provisions relating to employment that were designed to increase wages and spread work by reducing working hours.

The price-control provisions of the National Industrial Recovery Act were limited to minimum price fixing, which was administered by the insertion of minimum price prescriptions into most of the codes. These provisions prohibited sales below cost or below some prescribed minimum. The costs which were the basis of the minimum price arrangements were practically identical with those contained in the California Unfair Practices Act, which has already been discussed. Administration necessitated the establishment of an elaborate costing system. The difficulties of enforcement proved to be overwhelming, so that the National Recovery Administration literally gave up in favor of an open-price reporting system which was used in an endeavor to limit evasion of minimum price controls. The difficulty was that which has already been discussed in connection with minimum price fixing.

Failure of the National Industrial Recovery Act

The monopolistic structure erected by the National Recovery Administration, with its restrictions, the industry-by-industry approach, and the special-interest pressures of both labor and industry, engendered conflicts that soon led to a deterioration of the initial stimulus provided by the National Industrial Recovery Act. The unanimous decision of the Supreme Court in *Schechter Poultry Corporation* v. *United States* (1935),[4] declaring the Act to be unconstitutional, did not, therefore, produce the shock that otherwise might have resulted. Much of the general structure of the National Industrial Recovery Act was continued, however, by special legislation by both federal and state governments. Congress passed the National Labor Relations Act in 1935 and the Fair Labor Standards Act in 1938 to strengthen collective bargaining and to provide for minimum wages and maximum hours of employment in interstate commerce. Price control in the bituminous coal industry was embodied in the Bituminous Coal Conservation Act of 1935 and the Bituminous Coal Act of 1937, which was passed to overcome the constitutional difficulties encountered by the act of 1935. The Robinson-Patman Act was a partial response by the federal government to demands for legislation imposing cost limitations on competition in selling similar to that contained in the unfair practices acts of many states, while the Miller-Tydings Act gave sanction in interstate commerce to the resale price maintenance provisions of state fair-trade acts.

The National Industrial Recovery Act was based on the analogy of wartime economic organization. The country had mobilized to fight World War I and had achieved spectacular production results. Therefore, it was argued, the country could mobilize to combat the depression. The trouble with the analogy was that wartime organization was for a single objective and involved mobilization of a military type unsuited to peacetime conditions. Even fighting a depression does not provide a single objective in terms of the purposes of production. Mobilization for war strains the resources of a country to the utmost and necessitates the limiting of production of things not immediately needed for war. In addition, wartime economic activity is based on short-run considerations and therefore disregards long-run costs. The result may be economic exhaustion at the end or, at least, genuine economic fatigue.

[4] 295 U.S. 495. The law was declared unconstitutional on the grounds that (1) Congress lacked the authority to delegate legislative power to the President, and (2) the Act invaded the field of intrastate commerce reserved to the separate states.

Fighting depressions is the reverse of this. In a country like the United States, the wartime type of mobilization cannot be used to combat depression if a private enterprise system is to be retained. Production does not need to be restrained, it needs to be stimulated; and restraints against this need to be removed, if possible, including the lowering of barriers to foreign trade. If over-all direction of the economy is to be successful, then the comprehensive nature of the controls that are required must be understood and accepted. This is not likely to be the case. The result is that a program of the type contained in the National Industrial Recovery Act embraces too much control for a successful private enterprise system and not enough for a centrally directed economy.

Finally, the minimum price arrangements of the National Industrial Recovery Act were based on the fallacious "cost-push" theory of pricing. This, as was explained earlier, involves a misconception of the interrelationships of costs and prices. If satisfactory prices could be obtained merely by raising costs or compelling prices to abide by them, business fluctuations would present no problem, and "sick" industries simply would not emerge. Unfortunately, this does not happen to be in the nature of the economic world.

THE BITUMINOUS COAL ACT, 1937

The program which was developed before World War II to deal with the problems of the bituminous coal industry were much less ambitious than that of the National Industrial Recovery Act; but they illustrate the complexities of price controls for an industry where there are numerous producers, if the attempt is also made to maintain the continued independence of those producers. The coal industry has been beset with difficulties everywhere since the development of new sources of energy such as petroleum, natural gas, and hydroelectric power. Producers in the industry are numerous; and, new mines can be opened at relatively small expense, with the result that freedom of entry prevails. On the supply side, with an expanding market, the output of coal responds quickly. In this respect, the industry is highly competitive. Output is slow to contract, however, when demand falls. Reduction of the number of mines operated or of the output of the mines which continue operation does not respond readily to a decrease in demand. Mining towns are typically one-industry centers, and labor is specialized and highly immobile. Short-run output adjustments are very difficult to make; long-run adjustments have met with a great deal of resistance and, in addition, have been impeded by highly unstable economic conditions over the last half century, which have alternately induced periods of large outputs of coal followed by those of severely reduced requirements.

The National Industrial Recovery Act brought bituminous coal under compulsory control by a code which provided for maximum hours, minimum wages, and a delegation of power to fix minimum prices to delegated authorities. Literally no success was achieved by this attempt; and when the Act was declared unconstitutional, Congress promptly passed the Bituminous Coal Conservation Act of 1935, which was known as the Guffey-Snyder Act. It was also declared unconstitutional.[5] Congress then passed the Bituminous Coal Act of 1937, known as the Guffey-Vinson Act; and this was upheld by the Supreme Court.[6]

The Bituminous Coal Act of 1937 set up a 7-member board consisting of 2 representatives from the operators, 2 from the miners, and 3 from the public. It was empowered to establish minimum and maximum prices, the public interest in price fixing being scrutinized by a consumers' counsel. The real purpose of the law was to establish minimum prices for soft coal; and to make these effective, a 19½ per cent tax was to be imposed on the sales of the producers that failed to conform to the code.

The Act established 23 producing districts and 10 minimum price areas. The process of fixing minimum prices involved 5 steps: (1) The Commission was to determine the weighted average cost of producing coal in each of the producing districts and minimum price areas. These were to be submitted to district boards elected by the operators. (2) Each board was to propose minimum prices for each kind, quality, and size of coal produced in the district, such minimum prices to be designed to yield a return per net ton for each district equal, as nearly as could be, to the weighted average of the net costs per ton, and reflecting the relative market values of the various coals. (3) The Commission was to review the proposals, district by district. (4) The district boards were to co-ordinate their prices where coal produced in different districts competed for sale in common market areas. And (5) the resulting prices were to be submitted to the Commission for final approval.

Under its mandate, the Commission, which became the Bituminous Coal Division of the Department of the Interior in 1939, established minimum prices for every type of soft coal produced in every region of the United States and sold in every market, at every season, for every type of use. In all, some 400,000 separate minimum prices were set. This took nearly three years to complete. By that time, World War II had broken out in Europe; the demand for coal increased rapidly, prices rose, and the elaborate schedule of minimum prices was no longer needed, or of any avail.

What the results of the Bituminous Coal Act might have been can only be a matter of conjecture. The complexity of the pricing problem is indicated by the number of prices which were established. Whether an administrative agency could have kept pace with all the adjustments which changing market conditions would have required is very doubtful. There was no organized program for controlling production; and with-

[5] *Carter* v. *Carter Coal Co.*, 298 U.S. 238 (1936).
[6] *Sunshine Anthracite Coal Co.* v. *Adkins*, 310 U.S. 381 (1940).

out that, success was quite improbable. The fixing of minimum prices on the basis of average costs for all the mines would have had the effect of driving the inefficient producers to the wall. In the absence of some means for taking care of this excess capacity, which would include miners as well as mines, the difficulties of the industry would have persisted and would probably have been aggravated. In other words, a cartel policy that lacks the features of controlling production and providing for the disposition of excess capacity is only half a remedy. Monopolistic policies without control by monopoly are doomed to failure. Even though the policy had been complete, the stimulation to substitution by other fuels because of the higher coal prices would have posed a well-nigh insuperable obstacle.[7]

WARTIME PRICE REGULATION

Need for Controls

Wartime economic controls—in one respect, at least—are but a special phase of the problem of central management that in some way has to be performed in any economy. In peacetime, we rely primarily on the market mechanism operating within rules established on the assumption that competition, private interest, and private initiative can and will perform the functions of central management.[8] During a war, when it is of the magnitude of the two world wars of this century, the peacetime market mechanism cannot function adequately for this purpose. It is necessary for the government to intervene on a massive scale in directing and managing the economy. In fact, the government takes over the management of the economy to the extent that the only peacetime arrangements which are left are those which serve the wartime objectives. Of course, the government utilizes peacetime procedures as much as possible, because a total change is not feasible. Nevertheless, the massive shift in objectives and production that war compels involves the introduction of virtually an entirely new economic structure and means of control.

[7]The difficulties of regulating the prices of an industry where the traditional public utility structure is absent, and where there is a large number of producers of a product, is exemplified in the attempt of the Federal Power Commission to regulate the price of natural gas sold by producers to the natural gas pipe-line companies. The problem here is also complicated by the fact that natural gas is produced mostly in conjunction with oil, thereby raising the issue of allocation of the joint costs entailed in producing oil and natural gas. After 10 years of investigation the Commission has yet to render a decision on the matter. It now has an Examiner's report on the area price for natural gas in the Permian Basin (West Texas). For an economic analysis in natural gas regulation, see M. A. Adelman, *The Supply and Price of Natural Gas* (Oxford: Basil Blackwell, 1962); P. J. Garfield and W. J. Lovejoy, *Public Utility Economics* (Englewood Cliffs, N.J.: Prentice-Hall, Inc., 1964) chap. 15; P. W. MacAvoy, *Price Formation in Natural Gas Fields* (New Haven: Yale University Press, 1962). See also Chapter 25, *supra*. Adelman gives a careful analysis of the problem of joint cost.

[8]See M. A. Copeland, "Institutionalism and Welfare Economics," *American Economic Review*, Vol. XLVIII, No. 1 (March, 1958), pp. 1–17.

In essence, direction of the economy becomes authoritarian in nature, which explains why totalitarian states face a much easier problem in mobilizing their economies for war than do democracies.

Direct controls of various types are necessary in a war economy for a number of reasons. In the first place, production must be focused on the objective of winning the war. The insatiable demands for war material and war personnel necessitate full mobilization of the economy to meet these demands as much as possible. In the second place, a new orientation of the economy is necessary to meet the demands by focusing production on what is judged to be most essential, and to curtail the production of nonessentials. Public authority, and not the individual, will have to be the judge of what is nonessential. In the third place, the price system is inadequate to effect the massive transformation that must take place so quickly; and it is incapable of allocating resources to all the ends that must be met. Prices alone cannot be relied upon, because without other compulsions, there would be no guarantee that prices would attract resources into desired channels. This arises, in part, from the fact that both government and individuals compete for goods and services, even in war; government must get what it needs, and resources must go where it decides, even though the individual citizen does not want that to happen. In other words, the government must resort to the extensive use of compulsions, even though it may rely as much as possible on less drastic means of persuasion. The choice which the government exercises is somewhat analogous to that which the individual makes in allocating his purchasing power. He apportions the total purchasing power available to him among the various goods and services he acquires in accordance with their relative importance to him. The total which the government has available is the goods at hand and the productive capacity of the country. It has to utilize these in accordance with the estimates of combat needs. Prices may be one of the means of channeling the production, but the decisions on relative amounts to be produced will have to be made independently of the prices that may be paid for them.

Production Controls

As has already been stated, war production must be directed to the single end of prosecuting the war. Only the government is capable of judging what is necessary for this purpose and of making the decisions to achieve the objective, because it alone is able to make the estimates of what is needed, and when and where the needs must be met. It therefore must assume the task of allocating the economic resources of the country to their appropriate uses.

Manpower controls are instituted because the government must make the decision on the division of manpower between the armed forces, on the one hand, and the producers of goods and services, on the other. The price system cannot be relied upon to perform this function. The government must also undertake the task of deciding where men shall work and at what tasks. These are two very difficult kinds of decisions to make, because detailed compulsions are obviously limited in scope. The simplest means of making the decision is to utilize the mechanism of prices, but this has its limitations because of the effects of employers bidding against each other and employees using their bargaining power against the buyers of the services that must have them. Manpower controls, as a consequence, have to be a combination of compulsions, price (wage) inducements, and voluntary co-operation. This makes manpower control one of the most difficult areas of management which government faces and, at the same time, the most crucial one.

Plant and facilities controls are introduced in order to bring about as quickly as possible the transfer of existing productive capacity to wartime requirements and to undertake the construction of new plants. The conversion of old facilities and the construction of new ones will have to be in accordance with the physical estimates of war requirements, because price indices of them are not available and would take too long to manifest themselves even if markets existed to perform the task. The balance of production of various kinds of goods and services must be achieved as much as is possible by estimates of the best combinations of various outputs that can be obtained from the total resources known to be available for the purposes. Ships will have to be produced at the expense of planes, food at the expense of both, and so forth.

Control over plant facilities, particularly the construction of new plants, also involves considerations of transportation and location. Transport includes the movement of raw materials to factory, and finished goods and manpower to points of use or departure. Both impose heavy burdens on transport facilities; and endeavors have to be made to reduce these as much as possible, as with the use of other resources. There is the additional fact that the load on transport routes is more concentrated at certain points than in peacetime; and location of war plants must take this into consideration, in order to reduce it where possible. Finally, the possibility of enemy attack at certain points influences the location of war plants, at least while the conflict is in progress.

Materials controls are of three major types. The basic one is the control over the uses of materials for production. In World War II, certain types were allowed to be used only for certain purposes because of the critical nature of them in some of the manufacturing processes. Raw and synthetic rubber for new tires were prohibited for most civilian use because of military demands. Strategic metals such as copper, zinc, aluminum, nickel, and magnesium were reserved for war purposes only. Even clothing manufacturers were limited in materials they could use for civilian clothing. To prevent hoarding, and to try to prevent needed materials from lying idle, the government imposed inventory controls, endeavoring to limit the stocks of materials that firms could maintain and to facilitate the movement of idle stocks from one firm to another. Finally, in order to assist in getting the most important things done first, a system of priorities for materials, among uses as well as among plants, was developed; and producers were given allocations on the basis of these priorities.

Price Controls

Direct price controls were used as one of the many devices for managing and directing the economy in World War II. No matter how comprehensive centralized controls of a war economy may be, there is simply no escape from utilizing the price system. This is because of the rationing function which prices perform. Rationing is an extremely critical matter during a war because of the restriction of production to the essentials of war. The rationing problem is of such magnitude, however, that every means possible must be taken to reduce the administrative task to a minimum. Here, the pricing mechanism will be used as much as possible, because in so far as it works, it relieves the administrators of the burden of performing its task. In addition, prices are already acting as a means of rationing when wartime controls take over.

Price controls in World War II had two principle objectives. The first was to control the over-all level of prices, and the second was to assist in directing production into certain channels and discourage or limit it in others. The need for controlling the over-all level of prices was to restrain inflationary forces which, if uncontrolled, would rapidly lead to a breakdown of the pricing system. The intense increase of economic activity acted as a strong stimulus to the upsurge of prices. The government also suddenly stepped into the picture as purchaser of huge amounts of new goods and services. This created a problem of purchasing power for the government, which necessitated a transfer of purchasing power from private buyers to public authority. The latter was accomplished, principally, through a heavy increase in taxation and large government borrowing. Increased earnings by workers and employers added to the competition of purchase by the government. This made it necessary to develop means of sopping up the increase in purchasing power that emerged. Monetary and fiscal measures alone were inadequate for this; but it was essential that every possible step be taken by the government to limit the total that was available for spending, through its control over the monetary supply. In addition, if the monetary supply were kept under strong control, heavy war savings might be kept down, thereby reducing the threat of postwar inflation. Measures on this score were not very successful in World War II.

Direct price controls were also introduced to assist in the control of the over-all level of prices. This was to aid in limiting the payments which the government had to make for the things it bought, to limit the purchasing power available to consumers, to limit the profits of business, and to limit what consumers had to pay. Control of prices on government purchases were to be carried out by contract negotiations on a cost-plus basis, or by government purchases on the basis of prices already determined by a central agency. Wage controls were used to retard wage increases, in order to keep down production costs as well as to limit the purchasing power of the working population. Interest rates were deliberately restrained by government, in order to lower the cost of borrowing. Profits were restricted by price maxima, cost-plus contracts, and excess profits taxes.

The administrative steps taken by the government in World War II to control prices directly consisted, first of all, of the passage of the Emergency Price Control Act of January, 1942,[9] which gave legal status to the Office of Price Administration that had been set up by an executive order in the spring of 1941. The Emergency Price Control Act empowered the price administrator to put ceilings on any prices that had risen or threatened to rise and made his orders enforceable at law. The administrator's authority was limited with regard to agricultural prices, and he had no control over wages. Thus, whatever difficulties may inhere in direct price controls were aggravated by these gaps in the legislation.

The next step was for the price administrator to establish maximum prices where it was deemed necessary. This was carried out in four different ways. One method was that of establishing precise price ceilings for industries such as steel, where the products were highly standardized. This was done by adopting methods of price calculation which the industry itself had used. This necessitated careful supervision of costs, as well as acceptance of the accounting and pricing procedures previously used by the industry. A second method was to freeze prices as of a given date and prohibit sellers from charging higher prices without specific authorization. At the outset, this was relatively simple to administer; but it failed to recognize the problem of shifting price relationships. It also failed to recognize that prices may move in succession through transactions from raw materials to finished goods, and that this takes time. Hence, what seemed to be simple administration at first became extremely complicated and difficult to implement efficiently. A third method of maximum price fixing that was used where goods were not standardized was formula pricing, whereby cost factors to be used in arriving at prices were specified. The final price was supposed to be calculated according to the formula which was stipulated. Comparison of the prices proposed by the producer was made with the prices already fixed for others as a means of checking on the legitimacy of the new prices. Finally, prices were established in many instances directly by the Office of Price Administration itself. This was done by O.P.A. agents, who studied a firm's costs, after which specific ceiling prices were set.

[9]Public Law 421, chap. 26, 77th Congress, 2nd session.

Subsidies were another device used to effect maximum price controls. In the case of foodstuffs, this was done in 1943 by rolling prices back to an earlier date and subsidizing the processors for the difference. This was done to reduce the cost of living, in order to be able to offer some resistance to demands for increased wages. In other cases, subsidies were used to encourage production of additional supplies of commodities without raising prices, by subsidizing the output of producers who could not produce at the ceiling price that had been established. The government would buy the higher-cost product at the price the producers needed and then sell it to the users at the uniform ceiling price. This method was employed for only a relatively small percentage of the total supply of a commodity that was forthcoming, in order to stop the translation to the entire output of the rise necessary to bring forth the marginal output.

Rationing

The imposition of price controls severely limits the rationing function of prices. Something, therefore, must be substituted for this function. For some commodities, maximum prices were set; supply was thereby limited, and that limited supply went to buyers on a first-come, first-served basis, or whatever other means were adopted for selecting the favored purchaser. Of course, if the maximum prices were at or above the equilibrium point, no function was served in setting the maximum prices in the first place. In the case of rent controls, strict regulations against eviction were established; no other rationing device seemed suitable in this connection, but tenants could be removed for occupancy by the owner, and a considerable amount of property transfer took place to people who were unable to rent but who could find the money with which to make the purchase. The need for some form of rent control arose from the rapid shift of population to defense areas and the inability of housing supply to respond even reasonably well to the shift.

Rationing was used extensively for consumer goods, particularly those that were considered essential. In the case of things like meat, butter, clothing, and so forth, it was considered necessary to distribute the restricted supplies so that everyone could receive a specified amount, which also meant that everyone had to be limited to a specified amount. An elaborate rationing system was worked out to effect the desired distribution. The device of rationing was a very complex one, especially where the point system was used for the various kinds and cuts of meats, fats, oils, and canned goods. It has been severely criticized on the ground that it involved too many arbitrary calculations and imponderables. This criticism is valid, especially where rationing was combined with price ceilings or where rationing undertook to confine choices so severely that reasonable substitution by the buyer was prohibited. If rationing is designed to permit the distribution of a given physical amount of products, it is difficult to see why price ceilings should be imposed. A given amount of product can be sold only at a given price. If the maximum price is too low to bring forth the amount which the rationing permits, the rationing will fail; if the maximum price is above the price necessary to bring forth the desired amount, it will serve no purpose; if it is just right, then it will be by pure coincidence and unnecessary. In other words, a combination of rationing and price controls for the same commodities increases the complexities of administration and serves no purpose that they will not perform separately. In fact, the chances of their doing it effectively together are very slight.

Conclusions

The effectiveness of the administration of the war economy and wartime price controls must be evaluated in the light of conditions under which they were developed, the difficulties that were encountered, and the results that were achieved. That there were serious shortcomings, both from the theoretical and from the practical points of view, is obvious. Wage and agricultural price controls were very weak; and partly as a result of this, the control over the monetary supply was not very successful. Control over the consumer sector of the economy was also very defective. Many of these controls were carried altogether too far. For example, there was little point in imposing price controls on rattlesnake meat and Christmas cakes. Quality control was very inadequate, and product adulteration offset much that was done by the way of price control. Eliminating pocket lapels on men's coats and cuffs on men's trousers accomplished little when the cloth was cut off the suit that was already made and thrown into a barrel.

Despite the criticisms, the program must be acclaimed as a success as a whole. It may not serve as a model for another war; and many plans have been developed with the idea of eliminating the defects another time, if the occasion should arise.[10] The importance of the experience with wartime controls today is the lessons they teach for peacetime application.

Four observations on price fixing seem to emerge from the experience of the war: (1) The first thing that strikes one is the magnitude and complexity of the task, together with the enormous amount of control that must be exercised over individual action if a war is to be prosecuted successfully. This, it should be emphasized, is necessary, even under conditions where the objective is limited, well defined, and supported with patriotic fervor. (2) Even under these most favorable conditions—that is, favorable from the point of view of acceptance of the controls—the program achieved limited success and would have encountered severe resistance under peacetime conditions. (3) Direct price controls do not cure the evil they are erected against; they are only a palliative and leave unresolved the basic factors that lead to their imposition. They may retard

[10]See E. S. Shaw and L. Tarshis, "A Program for Economic Mobilizations," *American Economic Review*, Vol. XLI, No. 1 (March, 1951), pp. 30–50.

inflation for the time being; they will serve only to aggravate it in the long run because of the distortions they create and because they do not remove the pressures that bring about inflation. They do not contain in them any of the elements necessary to remove the pressures. (4) The experiences of wartime controls and their aftermath should give pause to those who wish to reinvoke price controls to control inflation. Wartime controls are for the purpose of limiting certain types of production, particularly those connected with civilian consumption. This would scarcely be the avowed objective of peacetime price controls; nor would there be any likelihood that the government would be able to impose all the other controls that have to accompany price controls. Maximum price fixing as a means of controlling peacetime inflation, standing alone, would serve, at best, to promise a subsequent period of severe inflation and, at worst, a dislocated economy immediately.

PART IV

The Antitrust Laws

Chapter 11 THE LEGAL FOUNDATIONS OF REGULATION

The preceding chapters have dealt with the institutional foundations of our economic life, the structure of industry, and the rise of the present problems of public policy. We now turn our attention to the development and application of the law to the issues which have emerged, for it is through the law that public policy finds its formal expression. This makes it necessary for us to endeavor to give our economic concepts and objectives a content sufficiently precise to enable them to be put into operation. In terms of economic policy for private business, the task is to develop rules that will set the limits within which private enterprise is left free to use its own discretion.

The control of industry embraces all the sanctions, informal and formal, which condition the behavior of businessmen. The informal sanctions consist of those forces—tradition, custom, religion, education, public opinion, the price system, etc.—which impose limits upon individual or group action without the express compulsion of law and government. The formal sanctions, on the other hand, are those which are embodied in the law of the land and are enforced by agencies constituted for that purpose. The regulation of industry refers to the formal controls which are set up to supplement, as well as to implement, the informal ones.

LAW AND ECONOMIC LIFE

The Meaning of Law

Law is that body of rules of conduct which is backed up by the coercive power of the state or the body politic. It consists of those rules which are recognized, interpreted, and applied to particular situations by the courts of the land. In the final analysis, the law, at any given time, is what the courts say it is; but to have effect, it must be supported by the power of the state to require compliance with the decrees of the courts. Thus, law constitutes those rules of behavior prescribed by the courts and enforced or supported by the agencies established for that purpose. Finally, law is coercive; obedience is required, or penalties are suffered accordingly.

Ultimately, the law is coercive and implies compulsion; but it is not a purely negative arrangement. It not only prescribes rules of conduct by saying what must not be done, but it also may set forth what may be done. The law is both prohibitive and permissive; and although it embodies rules of behavior, it does not encompass all of them. Custom plays a major role in our social behavior; and when this custom is incorporated into legislative acts or is given sanction by the courts under common-law procedure, it becomes law. Thus, law is really social policy expressed in legal rules.

Although, from a strictly legalistic point of view, the state is the supreme authority, the law is faced with definite limitations. It cannot persistently flout customary patterns of behavior because, to maintain the continuity which is characteristic of law, it must be deeply rooted in those customs. Furthermore, successful enforcement depends upon the voluntary compliance of the majority of those to whom the law applies. This is especially true of constitutional law, where custom, more than being a support, is an integral part of the law. Legislative acts may deal with temporary situations and, at times, may even do violence to established modes of conduct; but if legislation is to become an integral part of the body of law, it must rest upon widespread custom and upon generally accepted ideals. Even then, the law may be faced with limitations because of conflicting interests or objectives, since the attaining of some ideals may involve the sacrifice of others.

The Supremacy of the Law

The political institutions of the United States are characterized by the rule or supremacy of law. Government in all its actions is bound by rules, fixed and announced beforehand. Everyone is free to pursue his own personal ends and desires, within the law, presumably assured that the powers of government will not be used arbitrarily against him. The rule of law, as contrasted to the rule of men, means that those who govern are also answerable to the law. Equality before the law not only entails impartial administration but also intends that administrators must govern by law and not by personal whim.[1]

> It means in the first place, the absolute supremacy or predominance of regular law as opposed to the influence of arbitrary power and excludes the existence of arbitrariness, or prerogatives, or even of wide discretionary authority on the part of the government . . . .
>
> It means, again, equality before the law or the equal subjection of all classes to the ordinary law of the land as administered by the Law Courts . . . .[2]

Wherever the rule of law characterizes political institutions, the courts play a major role in the development of public policy. They not only interpret the Constitution and legislative acts, but also legalize cus-

[1]See *Youngstown Sheet & Tube Co.* v. *Sawyer*, 343 U.S. 579 (1952).

[2]A. V. Dicey, *Law of the Constitution* (London: Macmillan & Co., Ltd., 1920), p. 198. Quoted by permission of the publishers. See also Bernard Schwartz, *American Constitutional Law* (Cambridge, Eng.: University Press, 1955) pp. 22–26.

tom. The very nature of the judicial process, however, makes for a somewhat gradual development of the law. Legislative action may speed it up, but even this is likely to be a more or less gradual procedure. Legislation typically uses language that already has an established meaning; and it is a principle of law that a term used in a legislative act has an accepted meaning, unless it is specifically defined otherwise in statute. In any case, the meaning of legislation will be developed by the courts in the light of existing law.

Meaning of Regulation

The term "regulation of business" has three meanings. In the broadest sense, it covers all of the laws which govern the activities of business. From this point of view, all business is regulated, since it is subject to rules of conduct prescribed by the state. This, however, is no different from any other aspect of human behavior which is subject to the law. The second meaning arises from the imposition of rules of conduct by legislative action designed to limit the freedom of activity of business enterprise. These regulations arise because competition is not perfect and because economic forces, working without legislative guidance or restriction, are an independent means of achieving social objectives. Such regulations are designed to channel economic motivation by establishing conditions designed to maintain competition and to eliminate monopoly power, as far as possible. The third and narrowest meaning is used to describe the controls which have been developed to deal with industries such as transportation, public utilities, and communication. "Regulation" in this sense means the positive control of monopolistic enterprise by price fixing and other devices necessary to implement the primary objectives of limiting profits and restraining discrimination. In recent years, this meaning has been broadened somewhat to include fixing of minimum prices for the purpose of limiting competition which—in the opinion of the legislators, at least—has become destructive, with consequent socially undesirable results.

Regulation presupposes private business and economic activity independent of the government. It assumes the decentralization of responsibility for the guidance of economic life and production. It prescribes rules of conduct under which, however, enforcement agencies are allowed considerable discretion. Regulation also involves an element of deliberate direction, which, at times, creates the problem of distinguishing between regulating and managing. This is particularly true in those industries "affected with public interest," and it has also emerged in connection with many of the agricultural policies that have arisen in recent years.[3]

[3]For example, the quota arrangements established for the marketing of many agricultural products.

Interaction of Law and Business

It is almost trite to say that the influence of law on business conduct is of major significance. Yet, the position of law as a means of economic control is by no means a simple one. This is because the law—in part, at least—arises out of business practices, while, at the same time, it must also control them. One eminent writer expresses this position when he says: "The Supreme Court of the United States . . . occupies the unique position of the first authoritative faculty of political economy in the world's history . . ."[4] This has been responsible for a strongly legalistic attitude on regulation. This leads, all too frequently, to a hewing to the line of legality and to a justification of policies on the grounds that they conform to the law. Changes in the law may also lead to new activities which heretofore have been shunned, either because of doubtful legality or because the possibilities of the newer practices were not fully grasped. This was the case when, in 1889, the state of New Jersey permitted the formation of holding companies.

The expansion of regulation and the assumption by the government of a more positive role in the conduct of business may lead to a shifting of responsibility to the government, or to uncertainty as to where responsibility lies, especially if the departure from established practices is at all extreme. This has been a point of controversy in the regulation of transportation and public utilities, and has led to recrimination by both sides. Similiarly, the assumption by the government, especially since 1930, of the task of directing much of our economic activity has led to a great deal of confusion and has made business leaders wonder what their role is to be. Whatever may be the merits of the policies, the present situation calls for considerable clarification. Either business must be given more freedom of action to adapt itself, or the government must assume more and more responsibility for direction and management. This is the crucial economic question of the day, and the future of private enterprise depends on the answer to it.

While the influence of law on the conduct of business enterprise is of major significance, the reverse is at least equally true. Law, as we have seen, is largely dependent on custom; and in the end, it is custom that largely determines what the law will be. This has been the story of the common law over the centuries; it has also been true of constitutional law. Similarly, legislation may give positive recognition to existing business practices, or it may prohibit those which have come to be generally recognized as contrary to public welfare. When the courts interpret this legislation, they do it in the light of existing law and circumstances. This was illustrated in a case involving the Federal Trade

[4]John R. Commons, *Legal Foundations of Capitalism* (New York: Macmillan Co., 1924), p. 7. Quoted by permission of the publishers.

Commission, when Mr. Justice McReynolds, speaking for the majority of the Court, said:

> The words "unfair methods of competition" are not defined by the statute and their exact meaning is in dispute. It is for the courts, not the Commission ultimately to determine as a matter of law what they include. They are clearly inapplicable to practices never before regarded as opposed to good morals because characterized by deception, bad faith, fraud or oppression, or as against public policy because of their dangerous tendency unduly to hinder competition or create monopoly.[5]

The development of public policy proceeds from this continuous process of action and interaction. On the one hand, public policy, as expressed through the law, endeavors to mold business conduct so as to achieve more or less conscious objectives. On the other hand, business activity continuously creates new conditions that call for adaptations of policies in the light of altered circumstances. We endeavor to shape our destiny, while, at the same time, we are captives, within limits, of our immediate environment.

COMMON-LAW BASIS OF REGULATION

Emergence of Common-Law Control

Until comparatively recent times, the regulation of private business practices was a matter of common law. Indeed, down to the latter part of the nineteenth century, the use of statute law for this purpose was comparatively rare. Although the common law antedates the development of private business by many centuries, the development of common-law principles relating to the regulation of private business came with the breakdown of the medieval system. In medieval England, the regulation of business activity was carried on largely by the towns and the guilds. The establishment of a strong national monarchy under the Tudors in the sixteenth century led to the rapid disappearance of the power of the towns and the guilds. With their breakup, private enterprise, as we know it today, gradually emerged, although the activities were largely local in nature. Statutory regulations, upon which we rely heavily today, did not emerge until very recent times. It was the common law which bridged the gap between the breakup of the medieval system and modern methods of control. During the period of the decline of the guilds, this common law developed as a means of protecting and expanding the rights of individuals. Thus, the first manifestations of common-law regulation of business arose in connection with the freeing of labor from the restrictions imposed upon it by the guilds.

The relatively simple business conditions that obtained down

[5]*Federal Trade Commission* v. *Gratz*, 253 U.S. 421 (1920). Developments in the last 30 years, however, have given much greater scope to the decisions of commissions than this quotation implies.

through the Industrial Revolution and the acceptance of the principles of *laissez faire* in the nineteenth century resulted in very limited development of statutory regulation. As a result, the legal foundations of private enterprise evolved under common law. Gradually, there grew up a limited number of fairly well-established principles designed basically to protect private right and to prevent public injury. With the acceptance of *laissez faire*, the public injury aspect of common-law regulation declined in importance because of the belief in the beneficience of competition. When it became necessary to impose statutory controls, however, these were interpreted in the light of the common law. This was for two reasons. In the first place, the common-law doctrines were incorporated into the statutes, which were interpreted in accordance with legal precedents. In the second place, the principle had developed that statutes in derogation of the common law are strictly construed. Hence, common-law doctrines tended to survive, even where legislation provided for comprehensive regulation.

In the evolution of the common-law basis of control of private business, four basic principles or doctrines emerged. These were (1) restraint of trade, (2) conspiracy to monopolize, (3) unfair competition, and (4) the right to regulate. The first three embodied the rules of conduct for competitive enterprise. The fourth became the legal basis, in the United States, for the regulation of prices as well as other aspects of industries "affected with a public interest."

Restraint of Trade

The idea of freedom of contract did not emerge until after the breakdown of the guild system. Originally, at common law, contracts entailing an obligation to refrain from carrying on an occupation or business transaction were void and very probably illegal. Gradually, however, the idea developed that such contracts could be made at common law. Thus, in *Mitchell* v. *Reynolds* (1711),[6] court sanction was given to the sale of what we today would call "good will." The idea grew that if the major engagement was valid, the contracting parties could impose restrictions, provided that these were essential to the carrying-out of the contract. For example, one might sell a business and agree not to compete with the buyer for a period of time and in a given area. The validity of the restrictions depended upon their reasonableness, and it was for the courts to decide to what extent they were necessary in order to implement the contract. If the restraints imposed were reasonable, the contract was valid; but if they were unreasonable, it was unenforceable because of restraint of trade. Thus, restraint of trade at common law related to agreements imposing restrictions on trade which were unreasonable or unconscionable. If the commitments were essential to

[6] 1 P. Wms. 181.

private transactions, or were an incidental or ancillary result of actions that were legal and resulted in no substantial public injury, the primary transactions would be valid. If not, they would be void, because they were in restraint of trade.

At common law, then, only those restrictions on the actions of parties to an agreement which were unreasonable in regard to the geographic area embraced or the length of time covered by the agreement were held to be in restraint of trade. It was the agreements that were unreasonable that constituted restraint of trade under the law. Unreasonable acts or restraint of trade were those which would not stand the scrutiny of reason; and reason, in this sense, was the accepted standard of public policy as embodied in the common law at the time the decision on a particular case was rendered. In general, the question of whether contracts were unenforceable because the restrictive provisions contained in them were unreasonable was commonly regarded as involving considerations of the public interest. This was a broad notion, limited, in the main, to the idea that the seller's right to compete should be no more extensive than was necessary for the protection of the buyer.

In the course of the nineteenth century, restraint of trade came to take on a broader meaning, however. Agreements among rival traders to suppress or limit competition were usually viewed as incompatible with the public interest of preserving competition. Presumably, as a general rule, a party to a contract could contend that it was unenforceable on the ground that it was incompatible with public interest,[7] but such incompatibility came very close to a deliberate attempt to bring about monopoly prices. Judge Taft expressed this in the following words:

> "[Where] the sole object of both parties in making the contract is merely to restrain competition, and enhance or maintain prices, it would seem that there was nothing to justify or excuse the restraint, that it would necessarily have a tendency to monopoly and therefore would be void . . . . We do not think that at common law there is any question of reasonableness open to the courts with reference to such a contract."[8]

There was little, if any, basis for action, however, under the restraint of trade doctrine except by those who were parties to the contract, although corporations became vulnerable through challenges by public authority to the charter powers of corporate constituents of monopolistic combinations.[9]

[7]This was not so in England. "Their Lordships are not aware of any case in which a restraint, though unreasonable in the interests of the parties, has been held unenforceable because it involved some injury to the public" *Attorney General of Australia* v. *Adelaide Steamship Co.* A. C. 781 (1913). See also *Herrimen* v. *Menzies*, 115 Calif. 16 (1896); *Central Shade Roller Co.* v. *Cushman*, 143 Mass. 343 (1887).

[8]*United States* v. *Addyston Pipe and Steel Co.*, 85 Fed. Rep. 271 (1898), 282.

[9]See M. W. Watkins, *Industrial Combinations and Public Policy* (Boston: Houghton Mifflin Co., 1927), chap. xi, pp. 223–49; L. S. Lyon, M. W. Watkins, and Victor Abramson, *Government and Economic Life*, Vol. I (Washington, D.C.: Brookings Institution, 1939), pp. 252–56. For a discussion of leading cases, see Eliot Jones, *The Trust Problem in the United States* (New York: Macmillan Co., 1921), chap. xiii.

Conspiracy to Monopolize

The earliest provisions of the law in England relating to monopoly were those which forbade forestalling, regrating, and engrossing. Although these terms had different technical meanings, they all related to the one offense of cornering the market in some way or another and thus creating public injury by enhancing price. The law was aimed at preventing middlemen from cornering the market on the necessities of life, and violation of the law was a criminal offense. These common-law offenses were repealed by statute in England in 1844. They are part of the common law of this country and have been incorporated into statutes, but it is doubtful that they have ever constituted a crime in the United States. However, the common law still renders such contracts unenforceable by private suit in the courts.

The common-law doctrine against monopoly grew out of the struggle between Crown and Parliament under the Tudors and Stuarts. Under the Tudors, the Crown developed the practice of granting monopolies to private parties for special reasons. This was considered a royal prerogative, unamenable to the law, and was used as a means of rewarding royal favorites and raising money. At this time, modern taxation had not arisen; and the revenues of the Crown, for the most part, supported the government. As the pressure of finance increased, endeavors were made to circumvent the appeal to Parliament for revenues by a lavish grant of monopolies. The controversy aroused considerable popular opposition during the last years of Elizabeth's reign, and the House of Commons even proposed to introduce a bill abolishing all monopolies. Elizabeth decided to avoid an open conflict with Parliament by ending all monopolies by royal proclamation. The supremacy of the common law over royal prerogative was confirmed the next year in *Darcy* v. *Allen* (1602),[10] in which a monopoly based on the letters patent of all playing cards within the realm was declared to be invalid.

James I was unwilling to accept this position. He had no desire to acknowledge curbs on what he considered to be his royal prerogatives. The royal favorites continued to grant monopolies in scandalous fashion. Parliament responded to the challenge by reviving the ancient practice of impeachment.

Finally, in 1624, the Statute of Monopolies was passed. This legislation embodied the common-law rule by stating that all monopolies, however granted, should be absolutely void, with the exception of letters patent, which could grant the exclusive right of using, for a term of fourteen years, any new manufacture to the first and true inventor thereof. This exception became the basis for England's patent laws.[11]

[10]The case against monopolies, 11 Coke 84 *b*.
[11]See Chapter 17.

The monopoly against which this legislation was aimed was complete control of production or sale, resulting from a special legal grant of privilege. Monopoly as such, however, was never illegal at common law. The common law did not compel competition. Endeavors to suppress competition by combined action received little attention at common law until the nineteenth century. The rise of modern industry changed the situation, and the common law adapted itself accordingly. This was accomplished by an application of the ancient doctrine of conspiracy. This doctrine came to mean that a combination formed for any purpose was a criminal conspiracy if the intent of the persons combining was to injure another party. The things done by such a combination were actionable at law if they were intended to injure a third party, although the same acts might not be an offense if committed by an individual.

Thus, the common-law development of the idea of monopoly first arose from exclusive grants. This meant that monopoly referred to complete control over the production or sale of a commodity. Later, the idea, as applied to combinations, came to embody the notion of conspiracy with intent to injure. These two concepts, which were not always consistent with each other, arose to plague legislators and courts alike in the formulation and interpretation of the antitrust laws in this country.

The growth of the common law in the United States against restraint of trade and monopoly has come largely through the state courts,[12] although the federal courts have rendered decisions where the controversies have involved diversity of citizenship. In the development of the common law in this country, restraint of trade and monopoly have been used interchangeably and have been frowned upon because of the limitations imposed upon competition and the public mischief resulting therefrom. The courts have held, as illegal, agreements among competing concerns to control supply, to divide territory, to effect pooling arrangements, to form price-fixing associations, to use common marketing agencies, and to promote concerted action of competing buyers, where the purpose of these agreements was to restrain trade and promote monopoly, thereby advancing market prices to the injury of the general public. On the other hand, they have sanctioned agreements where the evidence did not show that any public mischief, such as depriving men of employment, unduly raising prices, causing monopoly, or putting an end to competition, was likely to result. At times, too, the courts have looked with more lenience upon agreements which did not involve articles of necessity.

The common law has also been used to dissolve agreements using the trustee device. In most instances, this has been done on the grounds that the acts of the corporation were *ultra vires* at common law. In *State* v. *Standard Oil Company* (1892),[13] the Supreme Court of Ohio ordered

[12]For a useful treatment of this growth, see Jones, *op. cit.*, chap. xiii.
[13]49 Ohio State 137.

the dissolution of the trust device, on the ground that it was *ultra vires* of the corporation, and also because its object was to establish a virtual monopoly in the business of petroleum. Similarly, the courts have found the combinations effected through the corporate device for the object of establishing monopoly or restraining trade illegal at common law. Pooling arrangements among competitors for the division of their earnings have also been held unlawful. In some of the cases, however, one can see a foreshadowing of the difficulties that were later to plague the Supreme Court. Thus, in *Dolph* v. *Troy Laundry Machinery Company* (1886),[14] the Court said:

> It is quite legitimate for any trader to obtain the highest price he can for any commodity in which he deals. It is equally legitimate for two rival manufacturers or traders to agree upon a scale of selling prices for their goods and a division of their profits. It is not obnoxious to good morals or to the rights of the public that two rival traders agree to consolidate their concerns, and that one shall continue business and become a partner with the other for a specified term. It may happen as the result of such an arrangement, that the public have to pay more for the commodities in which the parties deal; but the public are not obliged to buy of them. Certainly the public have no right to complain so long as the transaction falls short of a conspiracy between the parties to control prices by creating a monopoly.[15]

If this was representative of the state of the common law on monopoly and restraint of trade in this country at the time the Sherman Act was passed, there can be little wonder at the difficulties which the courts encountered in interpreting and applying that statute.

Unfair Competition

The common-law rules which established standards of competition were expressed in doctrines designed to preserve the civil rights of private parties. The common law aimed at fostering competition by the provision of a few private remedies for private wrongs. There was no positive approach to the problem by the use of measures administered by public authorities to establish a plane of competition by direct action of these authorities. The common law, relying upon competition to establish the standards of business conduct, merely sought to prevent a business from obtaining special advantages by devices designed to injure competitors.

Three major types of injury were recognized: (1) deceitful diversion of patronage, (2) misappropriation of trade secrets, and (3) malicious interference or molestation in the exercise of the right to do business.

1. *Deceitful Diversion of Patronage.* Trade-marks, which were recognized as a form of property, had long been protected against infringement. With the development of product differentiation, the protection was extended to cover the invasion of these rights by simulation, imita-

[14] 28 Fed. Rep. 553.
[15] *Ibid.*, pp. 555–56.

tion, or other means designed to take advantage of the good will which the trade-mark had given a competitor. This protection was also extended to cover trade names. These practices, known as "palming or passing off," were condemned by the law when they were used to exploit the good will of the competitor. Positive proof of fraud in the invasion of this good will was not necessary. The purpose of the law was to protect private parties in the enjoyment of the business which they had gained by legitimate competitive means.

2. *Misappropriation of Trade Secrets.* Although the common law recognized property rights and trade secrets, it did not prevent competitors from using the same or similar devices if they were legitimately developed. However, the courts of equity recognized that the unauthorized use of trade secrets acquired in bad faith was inequitable and deserving of injunctions. Secret information obtained by breach of trust or from previous employment or former employees was similarly treated. Nevertheless, the law required that a businessman should take ordinary precaution to protect his secret; and it was always necessary to prove that the defendant had obtained this information by unlawful means.

3. *Malicious Interference or Molestation in the Exercise of the Right to Do Business.* The essence of this principle was that business competition was on a different level than mere predatory action. This distinction was difficult to draw, because the common law did not take into account motive as constituting an element of civil wrong. However, it did afford protection against disparagement of products or defamation of character by a competitor. Similarly, breach of contract brought about by malicious intent or by illegal means, such as violent intimidation or some form of fraud, offered grounds for redress. Finally, practices designed deliberately to injure a competitor or interference with his right to do business were frowned upon at common law. They were regarded as injuries arising from persecution, against which the common law gave protection.

The common law, as thus developed down to the beginning of the twentieth century, was adequate for relatively simple circumstances and local trade. As an effective means of grappling with the complex conditions of modern trade and industry, it had marked deficiencies. The difficulties involved in proving malicious intent or that damages had been sustained were too great for the common law to afford adequate protection. The consumer was left out of the picture; he had to rely on the principle of *caveat emptor*. Then, too, procedure at common law was cumbersome. The injured parties had to bring suit and prove their case. Besides being expensive and slow, this afforded little protection to small enterprises against giant competitors. Moreover, adaptation to change by judicial precedents was too slow for the rapidly changing present-day conditions.[16] The growth of improved standards of fairness in business

[16]For a comprehensive discussion of the law on unfair competition, see Milton Handler, "Unfair Competition," *Iowa Law Review*, Vol. XXI, No. 2 (January, 1936), pp. 175–262.

conduct called for legislative action and positive development of the law on unfair competition. Finally, there was no federal common law. The cases which arose were settled either in the state courts or by federal ones if diversity of citizenship was involved. As the result of the Supreme Court decision in *Swift* v. *Tyson* (1842),[17] businesses were frequently operating under two interpretations of the common law, with resulting confusion.

The Right to Regulate

Another common-law concept which was to become of prime importance in the regulation of business was the right of the state to regulate. Since the Civil War, this has become the center of one of the most significant controversies in the constitutional history of the United States.

In medieval times, the guilds gave local monopoly to trades and crafts; and because of the importance of these in the local economy, they became common callings requiring close regulation. The term "common" in medieval law, indicated that employment was public, in the sense of being available to all who might want to be served. With the breakdown of the medieval economy, the control of the guilds gradually disappeared. In the succeeding development, the process by which certain occupations or callings became subject to special regulation is not clear. Lord Hale, in his treatise *De Portibus Maris*, written about 1670, distinguished between callings affected with a public interest and those which were matters of private concern only. This seems to have been based on the theory that the individual customer required protection against the seller because of the monopoly of the latter over some common necessity. These monopolies were the result of some special grant of privilege but could not escape their responsibility to the public by charging unreasonable prices. With the development of private enterprise in trade and commerce, the concept of the right to regulate became particularly applicable to means of transportation. It was not used in England, however, as a means of limiting the power of Parliament to regulate business; rather, it was a statement that monopolies obtained by special grant, especially royal patents, could not escape the authority of the common law.

When, after the Civil War, the Granger states enacted laws to control the prices and services of railroads and certain other enterprises immediately associated with transportation, the power of the legislative branch of the government to fix the prices charged by any private enterprise was challenged.[18] The courts, harking back to Lord Hale's treatise, held that it had been customary from time immemorial to regulate property "affected with a public interest." The common law, curiously enough, was, at the same time, given a reverse meaning, in that the right

[17] 16 Pet. (U.S.) 1.
[18] See *Munn* v. *Illinois*, 94 U.S. 113 (1877).

of the legislature to regulate the prices of industries not so characterized was denied. Moreover, until recently, the concept of industries affected with a public interest has been so narrowly construed that until the mid-1930's, it was almost synonymous with transportation and public utilities. Thus, the common law which was used in England to justify interference and regulation, became a bulwark against legislative action in the United States. However, the recognition that the state did have the right to regulate, under appropriate circumstances, laid the constitutional foundation for the expansion of the regulatory powers of the legislature into the much broader sphere which they encompass today.

POWERS OF THE NATIONAL GOVERNMENT

The Federal Framework

The federal form of government—consisting, as it does, of a union between political bodies which are sovereign within their own sphere of competence and a central government which has the powers deemed necessary to form a national union—requires an instrument setting forth the respective spheres of influence and containing the means to implement the division of powers. The instrument accomplishing these purposes in the United States is the federal Constitution. This document sets forth, among other things, the respective powers of the state and federal governments. Under it, the powers which the federal government enjoys are delegated and enumerated. All others, except those expressly prohibited, are reserved to the states or to the people.

The federal Constitution, however, gives Congress the authority "to make all laws which shall be necessary and proper for carrying into execution"[19] all powers vested by the Constitution in the government of the United States. This constitutional provision, known as the "doctrine of implied powers," together with the broad terms setting forth federal powers, laid the basis for expanding the scope of the national government to meet changing circumstances far beyond any possible conception which the founders of the Constitution had. Thus, although the Constitution of the United States is a written document, its meaning and scope continue to change with altering circumstances.

While the general principles dividing the powers between the state and federal governments have remained the same over our history, the application of them has wrought fundamental changes in our constitutional structure and has posed continuously the question of state versus federal authority. The enormous growth of economic activity far beyond the boundaries of the states, since the United States became a nation, has led to a great expansion of federal authority. This has brought about an increase of federal functions that has presented a continual constitu-

[19]Art. I, Sec. 8, cl. 18. See *Eli Lilly & Co.* v. *Sav-on Drugs*, 366 U.S. 276 (1960).

tional challenge. National and local economic issues have become intermingled on such a broad scale that the division of powers is not as simple a question as it was at the time the Constitution was framed. The division still exists, however, and the effective ways and means of implementing it are as pertinent considerations today as at the time when the nation was founded. The power and prestige of the national government too frequently obscure the immense importance and vital necessity of the states to our constitutional, political, and economic life.

Under the Constitution of the United States, all powers not delegated to the federal government are reserved to the states. This division between the state and federal jurisdictions is a matter of constitutional law. Within the limitations set by the federal Constitution, as its meaning is interpreted by the Supreme Court of the United States, Congress is supreme. Whether the powers thus permitted to Congress should be exercised is a political, not a legal, question. The Court decides what powers Congress possesses, but the latter decides whether it should use them. Political and legal questions are frequently badly mixed up when consititutional issues are at stake. Once the constitutional question is settled, however, the matter then becomes one of policy.

Neither state nor federal government can delegate to the other the powers which it possesses exclusively, but it is interesting to note that the courts have shown considerable willingness to sanction co-operation and that this may bring about a further diminution of strict lines of demarcation of authority. Moreover, the Supreme Court has held that the powers of Congress may be exclusive, paramount, or concurrent. If congressional powers are exclusive, the states cannot exercise any control, even though Congress would be willing to allow them to do so. If, on the other hand, congressional powers are held to be paramount, the states may exercise jurisdiction in the absence of federal action. When congressional powers are held to be concurrent, both the state and the federal governments may act at the same time in the same manner.[20] All laws of the Congress made in pursuance of the federal Constitution are the supreme law of the land.[21]

Delegated Powers

Section 8 of Article I of the Constitution of the United States, among other things, enumerates in broad terms the powers which the Congress may utilize to control, direct, and even directly participate in the conduct of the economic life of the nation. The powers relating to taxation, borrowing and spending, and money, taken together, give the national government enormously wide and varied opportunities to shape the economic activity of the nation under the general heading of

[20]For a thorough discussion, see J. E. Kallenbach, *Federal Coöperation with the States* (Ann Arbor: University of Michigan Press, 1942).

[21]Article VI, Sec. 2, Constitution of the United States.

what may be called "fiscal policy." The broad powers of taxation have been interpreted to mean that taxes may be levied for the purpose of furthering the general welfare of the United States. This concept has been given such a comprehensive interpretation by the Supreme Court that carefully worded legislation, especially when used in conjunction with other constitutional powers, makes the possibility of control by taxation virtually unlimited. Taxation may be used directly and admittedly for regulation purposes, if such purposes can be sustained under the nontaxing authority granted by the Constitution.

Congress, using its monetary powers in conjunction with the others it possesses, may coin money; regulate the issuance of bank notes; enter the banking, finance, and insurance fields; and exercise extensive control over the whole area of private finance. It may establish whatever monetary standards it wishes; and by regulating the conditions for the granting of credit, it can exert influence over the price levels, in so far as this lies within the power of any government.

The power to borrow and to spend gives Congress virtually unlimited spending opportunities, provided that the funds are properly appropriated and used for purposes of general welfare. It does not take very much legal ingenuity to devise ways and means under this heading to accomplish almost any objective which Congress may have in mind. Coupled with the powers to establish post offices and post roads, and to dispose of and make all needed rules and regulations respecting the territory or other property belonging to the United States, the federal government may enter into the public ownership of business to almost any extent it sees fit.

Utilizing these powers, the federal government owns and operates the post office, which is one of the largest businesses in the world. Through the United States Maritime Commission, the federal government is the largest shipping enterprise in this country. It also owns and operates the Panama Canal Railroad and the Alaska Railroad. It has large public utility projects, such as the Tennessee Valley Authority, Hoover Dam, and Grand Coulee. It owns and operates the federal airways, has a large investment in airports, and is the largest single investor in the highways of the country.

The basic position of the Supreme Court is that the government may engage in literally any type of business the legislature decrees and that it may operate in competition with private enterprise for the production of peacetime goods and services. It has been suggested that government competition with private enterprise may be one of the effective means of bringing about regulation.[22] Obviously, the reservation of production to private business is essentially a matter of congressional dis-

[22]See D. H. Wallace, *Market Control in the Aluminum Industry* (Cambridge, Mass.: Harvard University Press, 1937).

cretion; therefore, the policy to be followed in this country is a matter to be settled in the political, rather than in the judicial, area.

Congress may also exercise control over business activity through its powers to establish uniform laws on bankruptcy throughout the country, and to grant patents and copyrights. Bankruptcy and reorganization proceedings are means of maintaining the effectiveness of private enterprise, but they have all too often been used as a means of fleecing innocent investors. The National Bankruptcy Law, as amended by the Chandler Act of 1938, now assures conformity to reasonable standards of public accountability by corporations which have gone through reorganization under its provisions.

Congressional authority over patents and copyrights is for the purpose of promoting the progress of science and the useful arts. The rights that are conveyed to private persons constitute a monopoly privilege and, in some respects, may constitute a contradiction with the theory of competitive enterprise. On the other hand, they are an integral part of the private enterprise system and may be used effectively to further it.

Interstate Commerce

The powers which have just been discussed give Congress very wide scope for the exercise of control over economic activity, but the one which is most significant, at least from the standpoint of regulation. is that which places the control over interstate commerce in the hands of Congress. The Constitution, in Article I, Section 8, stipulates that Congress shall have the power to regulate commerce with foreign nations and among the several states. This clause gives Congress its most comprehensive direct power for the regulation of business (1) because of the broad way in which the Supreme Court has construed the provision and (2) because of the use of this provision in conjunction with others, thereby giving a wider application of the latter than otherwise might have been accorded.

The scope of congressional authority over interstate commerce is by no means self-evident or unequivocal, for there is no explanation in the Constitution of what constitutes "commerce," or "among the states." The meaning of these words and the validity of federal policies involving them has resulted in an almost continuous process of judicial interpretations.

Very early in the nation's history, the scope of federal powers was given a very broad interpretation. In *Gibbons* v. *Ogden* (1824)[23] the first case coming before the Supreme Court involving the federal powers over interstate commerce, Chief Justice Marshall said:

> Commerce undoubtedly is traffic, but it is something more; it is intercourse. . . . The subject to which the power is next applied is to commerce "among the

[23] 9 Wheat (U.S.) 1.

several states." The word "among" means intermingled with. A thing which is among others is intermingled with them. Commerce among the states cannot stop at the external boundary line of each state, but it may be introduced into the interior. . . . If, as has always been understood, the sovereignty of Congress, though limited to specified objects, is plenary as to those objects, the power over commerce with foreign nations and among the several states is vested in Congress as absolutely as it would be in a single government having in its constitution the same restrictions on the exercise of the power as are found in the Constitution of the United States. The wisdom and the discretion of Congress, their identity with the people, and the influence which their constituents possess at the election are in this, as in many other instances, as that, for example, of declaring war, the sole restraint on which they have relied to secure them from its abuse. They are the restraints on which the people must often rely solely in all representative governments.[24]

It seems clear that all of the activities controlled by Congress under the heading of interstate commerce could be completely supported by this decision. Nevertheless, it was not until near the end of World War II that Congress was able fully to assert the powers which *Gibbons* v. *Ogden* seemed to imply. In the years subsequent to *Gibbons* v. *Ogden*, the Supreme Court often found occasion to impose restrictions on the federal government. This may be explained—in part, at least—by the difficulties involved in analyzing the effects of the growth of the country on a national basis. In any event, the Court held that mining, manufacturing, farming, the generation of electricity, and insurance were not commerce. Furthermore, congressional authority was limited by a strict construction of the idea of "interstate" that required actual movement across state boundaries.

The rapid expansion of federal regulation of business came in the field of transportation with the passage of the Interstate Commerce Act of 1887. In the years since then, federal power has been extended so far in transportation as to comprehend all the agencies that directly or indirectly affect interstate commerce. Any local medium through which traffic moves in the course of interstate commerce may be subject to federal regulation. It is on this basis that federal control of grain elevators and stockyards has been upheld.[25] Similarly, railroad rates on purely local traffic may be subject to the authority of the Interstate Commerce Commission if the latter considers them sufficiently important in the rate structure to warrant their regulation.[26] Recent court decisions in other fields indicate that the legal reasoning which upheld the exercise of federal power over transportation can be applied with the same effectiveness elsewhere.

On the basis of the pattern that developed in the field of trans-

[24]*Ibid.*, pp. 189 f.

[25]*Munn* v. *Illinois*, 94 U.S. 113 (1877); *Lemke* v. *Farmer's Grain Co.* 258 U.S. 50 (1922).

[26]*Railroad Commission of Wisconsin* v. *Chicago, Burlington and Quincy Railway Co.* 257 U.S. 563 (1922).

portation, the Supreme Court has permitted the extension of authority by bringing within the powers of Congress activities that are in the stream of interstate commerce or that substantially affect interstate commerce. Finally, in *United States* v. *South-Eastern Underwriters Association* (1944),[27] the Court held that the insurance business was commerce and therefore could be regulated by the federal government whenever transactions fell into the category of interstate.[28] Thus, the circle seems to have been completed back to *Gibbons* v. *Ogden*.

If the courts decide that jurisdiction over a certain matter belongs exclusively to Congress, the states cannot act, even though the federal government would be willing for them to do so. However, there is a wide range of concurrent powers in the concept of interstate commerce, and the interstate commerce which is reserved exclusively to Congress is quite narrowly construed. As a consequence, Congress may permit the states to regulate a wide range of activities which it could appropriate unto itself if it saw fit. It is on this basis that the states have been allowed to exercise very extensive powers over motor transport, public utilities, and insurance.

Interstate Compacts

The Constitution prohibits any state from entering into any agreement or compact with any other state without the consent of Congress.[29] Put the other way around, this means that Congress has the power to sanction interstate compacts and that the states may make agreements with each other for mutual benefit or to solve common problems, if Congress is willing to give the necessary approval. Although the Constitution requires the consent of Congress for the formation of compacts, that consent does not need to be expressed; it may be only implied. Positive congressional approval is not necessary if the agreement does not increase the political power of the states involved or encroach upon or interfere with the just supremacy of the federal government.

To date, over 100 agreements among the states are on record. It is only recently that the possibilities inherent in the device seem to have become recognized. From 1936 to 1943 alone, 28 interstate compacts were formed. The most important use of the compact developed after World War I. The most noted of these compacts have related to transportation and public utilities. The New York Port Authority, the Colorado Basin Development, and the Rio Grande and the Columbia River projects are all based upon interstate compacts.[30] In 1935, a compact among the mid-

[27] 322 U.S. 533.

[28] This specifically overruled *Paul* v. *Virginia*, 8 Wall 168 (1869).

[29] Art. I, Sec. 10, cl. 3.

[30] F. A. Ogg and P. O. Ray, *Introduction to American Government* (6th ed; New York: D. Appleton-Century Co., 1952), pp. 57–58.

continent oil-producing states was entered into for the joint state control of oil conservation. In 1934, 7 northeastern states formed an interstate compact on minimum-wage regulations, although it has not yet been ratified by all the governments involved. Many other agreements covering other fields of common interest have also been entered into.

Most of the interstate compacts leave action to legislation and enforcement thereof to the individual states. The Ohio River Valley Water and Sanitation Compact, however, established a commission to administer the provisions of the agreement. Its orders are enforceable in the federal and state courts.

The negotiation of compacts offers many difficulties because, frequently, very conflicting interests are at stake. For this reason, many writers see only limited possibilities in the use of this procedure. The compact device, however, does provide a means of co-operation among the states for accomplishing ends that otherwise would be unattainable except, perhaps, through federal action. It seems to offer considerable possibilities as an intermediate arrangement between excessive centralization, on the one hand, and the hampering effect of states' rights, on the other. The present political boundaries of states all too frequently form units that are inadequate or inappropriate for the administration of economic affairs. At the same time, centralization in Washington seems to go too far in the other direction, in many cases. The recent development of a regional approach to a large number of our economic problems may have opened a new field for the use of compacts; and, vice versa, the compact may offer a workable basis for the development of regional administration. The possibilities of preserving both federal and state interests by this device are well worth exploring.

THE ROLE OF THE COURTS

General Functions

It is the function of the courts in every country where there is orderly government to interpret the laws and to settle litigation arising thereunder. The role occupied by the courts in the regulation of business in this country, however, is greater than that which is exercised by the judiciary of any other. This position is the result of two things. First, the doctrine of judicial review, which has grown up as a result of certain unique features of the Constitution of the United States, has given a leading role to the Supreme Court in the determination of public policy. Second, Congress has seen fit, especially in the Sherman Act, to give the courts the direct and immediate responsibility of interpreting very broad legislation and of developing public policy under it. The courts in this country have, therefore, four major functions in regulation: (1) the interpretation of the Constitution in terms of the framework of government, (2) the interpretation of the Constitution as it applies to the protection of personal and property rights, (3) the direct enforcement of regulatory legislation, and (4) the adjudication of disputes arising from enforcement by commissions.

The Federal Form of Government

The federal form of government makes it necessary that some authority decide on the allocation of powers between the federal and state governments in the event of disputes. This issue was settled, in *Marbury* v. *Madison* (1803),[31] by Chief Justice Marshall, who ruled that under written constitutions, "an act of the legislature repugnant to the Constitution is void." This established the supremacy of the judiciary for the interpretation of the Constitution and also the fact that the Supreme Court would be the arbiter of the division of powers between state and federal governments.

The Separation of Powers

The Constitution provides for the separation of powers of government among three departments: the legislative, the executive, and the judicial. These are co-ordinate branches, and each one must perform all the duties which come within its scope, and only such duties. Numerous legal problems have arisen in connection with this separation because, in practice, a complete separation particularly of executive and legislative powers is not feasible. Congress may make all laws "necessary and proper for carrying into operation" powers vested in it or in any office or department of the government. The Supreme Court has therefore upheld laws which delegated legislative powers to the executive branch of the government, provided that the enabling act contained a standard, that is, a limit or guide to the exercise of the power conferred. In other words, legislative power may be granted to the executive branch provided that the grant of authority is limited by prescribed standards. Where these are inadequate the delegated authority will be held to be unconstitutional. This was the basis of a unanimous decision of the Supreme Court in *Schechter Poultry Corporation* v. *United States* (1935)[32] which held the National Industrial Recovery Act to be unconstitutional because it, among other things, constituted a delegation of legislative authority to the President without providing any legislative standards to limit the exercise of the power delegated.

The position of administrative commissions whose functions are in the nature of legislative, executive and judicial has consequently given rise to considerable constitutional difficulty. The law, however, has accommodated itself by legislative action and judicial sanction, so that many regard the administrative commissions today as a fourth branch

[31] 1 Cranch 137.
[32] 295 U.S. 495.

of the government.[33] This has come about by court recognition of the legislative right to prescribe general rules, to be administered in detail by the administrative agency. At the same time, the courts retain the right to hear appeals from the decisions of these commissions.

The Regulation of Prices

With the development of regulation of business by administrative commission in the period following the Civil War, a new constitutional issue arose. The extension of regulatory powers to include price fixing met with the contention that this violated the Fifth or Fourteenth Amendments of the federal Constitution, which provided that no person should be deprived of life, liberty, or property without due process of law. The challenge to the right of the state to regulate centered around the controversy over the powers of government to fix the prices of private business. The first case coming before the Supreme Court was that of *Munn* v. *Illinois* (1877),[34] which contested the right of the state of Illinois to fix the maximum charges to be exacted by grain elevators, on the ground that this violated the Fourteenth Amendment of the federal Constitution. The Court upheld the statute, on the ground that the property was affected with a public interest and therefore could be controlled by the public for the common good. On the basis of this decision, the legislative power to regulate the prices charged by railroads and public utilities was upheld.

In 1914, the Court expanded the idea of business affected with a public interest by upholding the statute of the state of Kansas which undertook to regulate the fire insurance business. In this case, *German Alliance Insurance Company* v. *Kansas* (1914),[35] the Court held that the insurance business bears such a peculiar relation to the public interest that the right of public regulation is superinduced upon it.

The broad interpretation which the Court seemed to have given to the right to regulate suffered a severe setback, however, after World War I. In 1923, in *Wolff Packing Company* v. *Industrial Court of Kansas* (1923),[36] the Supreme Court denied the right of the Kansas Industrial Court to fix wages in the meat-packing industry. In writing his opinion, Chief Justice Taft listed three categories of business which might be said to be clothed with a public interest justifying some public regulation. These included those which were carried on under the authority of a public grant of privilege which imposed the affirmative duty of rendering a public service, such as was found in railroads, other common car-

[33]Whether it is desirable for regulatory commissions to be as independent of the executive branch of the government as they are today is a matter on which there may be a considerable difference of opinion. See M. H. Bernstein, *Regulating Business by Independent Commission* (Princeton: Princeton University Press, 1955).

[34]94 U.S. 113.

[35]233 U.S. 389.

[36]262 U.S. 522.

riers, and public utilities; certain occupations regarded as exceptional, in which the public interest had been recognized from the earliest times; and those businesses which, though not public at their inception, might be fairly said to have risen to be such and had become subject in consequence to some government regulation, and had come to hold such a peculiar relation to the public that this was superimposed upon them. The restrictive interpretation thus imposed on the right of the state to regulate was reinforced by three subsequent decisions. A New York statute, declaring that admission to a theater or other place of public amusement or entertainment was a matter of public interest, was declared unconstitutional in *Tyson* v. *Banton* (1927),[37] in which it was held that the property of ticket brokers was not affected with a public interest. Similarly, a statute of New Jersey, designed to regulate employment agencies and fix their prices, was set on one side in *Ribnik* v. *McBride* (1928).[38] Here again, it was held that the business of conducting an employment agency was not affected with a public interest. Finally, in *New State Ice Company* v. *Liebman* (1932),[39] the Supreme Court declared unconstitutional an Oklahoma statute which required a license as a prerequisite to engaging in the ice business. The Court took the position that the ice business was as essentially private in its nature as the business of the grocer, the dairyman, and the butcher, and that it bore no such relation to the public as to warrant its inclusion in the category of business charged with a public use.

The accumulation of legislative pressure, the force of dissenting opinions of the Supreme Court, and the depression which began in 1929 resulted in a thoroughgoing relaxation of the Court's restrictions on the right of the legislature to regulate. In *Nebbia* v. *New York* (1934),[40] the Supreme Court upheld a New York statute which declared that the production, distribution, and sale of milk was a business affecting the public interest and health. Under this law, the Milk Control Board established minimum prices for milk sold at wholesale and retail. In upholding the act, Mr. Justice Roberts took the position that it was entirely a matter of judgment when property was used in a manner to make it a public consequence and affect the community at large. Price control was simply one branch of the general police power; but legislation enacted under this power could not be "arbitrary, discriminatory, or demonstrably irrelevant to the policy the legislature is free to adopt." Subject to these conditions,

> . . . there can be no doubt that upon proper occasion and by appropriate measures the state may regulate a business in any of its aspects, including the prices to be charged for the product or commodities it sells, and that so far as the re-

[37]273 U.S. 418.
[38]277 U.S. 350.
[39]285 U.S. 262.
[40]291 U.S. 502.

quirement of due process is concerned, and in the absence of other constitutional restrictions, a state is free to adopt whatever economic policy may reasonably be deemed necessary to promote public welfare and to enforce that policy by legislation.[41]

This position was reaffirmed in *United States* v. *Rock Royal Cooperative, Inc.* (1939).[42] The decision in this case upheld the right of the Secretary of Agriculture, under the Agricultural Marketing Agreement Act of 1937, to fix and equalize minimum prices to be paid producers for milk sold to dealers and disposed of by the latter either in liquid form or as milk products. Said the Court:

> The people of great cities depend largely upon an adequate supply of pure, fresh milk. So essential is it for health that the consumer has been willing to forego unrestricted competition from low-cost territory to be assured of the producer's compliance with sanitary requirements, as enforced by the municipal health authorities. It belongs in the category of commodities that for many years has been subjected to the regulatory power of the state.[43]

Finally, in *Sunshine Anthracite Coal Company* v. *Adkins* (1940),[44] the Supreme Court upheld the power of the National Bituminous Coal Commission, acting under the Bituminous Coal Conservation Act of 1937, to establish minimum prices in the coal industry. This was done on the grounds that there had been increased demand for federal intervention in the coal industry and that free competition had degenerated into anarchy in the bituminous coal industry. In the words of the Court:

> It was the judgment of Congress that price fixing and the elimination of unfair competitive practices were appropriate methods for prevention of the financial ruin, low wages, poor working conditions, strikes, and disruption of the channels of trade which followed in the wake of the demoralized price structures in this industry. If the strategic character of this industry in our economy and the chaotic conditions which have prevailed in it do not justify legislation, it is difficult to imagine what would.[45]

It is quite clear, from the development of the Supreme Court's position, that legislative power over the regulation of business, by controlling prices, has been materially increased and is no longer confined to the narrow concept of a public utility. This does not mean, however, that the exercise of legislative power over regulation is not subject to review by the courts. Time alone will tell how the Supreme Court will react to the developments of the future. It seems unlikely that the ground gained will be lost by judicial action. Nevertheless, it is well to remember that future legislation will be subject to court scrutiny, and that it is for the judiciary to determine what constitutes the proper occasion and appro-

[41] *Ibid.*, p. 537.
[42] 307 U.S. 533.
[43] *Ibid.*, p. 570.
[44] 310 U.S. 381.
[45] *Ibid.*, p. *395*.

priate measures by which the state may regulate a business in any of its aspects.[46]

Reasonable Prices

When the Supreme Court has granted to the state the right to regulate prices, a new and even more complex issue may arise. This focuses on the question of what constitutes reasonable rates or prices. Private business continuously contends that prices fixed by legislative action must be reasonable to the producer; otherwise, there is violation of the constitutional protection of private property. This issue was first raised in the case of *Munn* v. *Illinois* (1877);[47] but in that instance, the Court declared that price fixing was a matter of legislative discretion, once the right to regulate had been established, and that the courts would offer no protection. Doubts as to the validity of this position, however, were expressed by the Court in *Stone* v. *Farmer's Loan and Trust* (1886),[48] when is said: "This power to regulate is not a power to destroy, and limitation is not the equivalent of confiscation. Under pretense of regulating fares and rates, the state cannot require a railroad corporation to carry persons or property without reward."[49] The hint contained in this opinion was erected into law in *Chicago, Milwaukee and St. Paul Railway Company* v. *Minnesota* (1890).[50] In its decision, the Court said: "The question of reasonableness of a rate of charge for transportation by a railroad company involving, as it does, the element of reasonableness, both as regards the company and as regards the public, is eminently a question for judicial investigation requiring due process of law for its determination."[51]

In *Smyth* v. *Ames* (1898),[52] the Court gave effect to this position by prescribing the so-called "rule of rate making." It held that rates are reasonable when they give a fair return on the fair value of the property being used for the convenience of the public. The opinion also listed the items to be given consideration in determining reasonable rates.

Since *Smyth* v. *Ames*, the controversy on public utility rate regulation has centered on two issues. The first of these relates to what constitutes fair return and fair value, especially the latter. It is not necessary here to go into the difficulties and complexities of this problem. Suffice it to say there is anything but agreement among economists, lawyers, and public authorities as to the proper answer.

The second aspect of the controversy raises the question of who shall determine what is a fair return on a fair value. Down to 1930, the

[46]See *Olsen* v. *Nebraska*, 313 U.S. 236 (1941).
[47]94 U.S. 113.
[48]116 U.S. 307.
[49]*Ibid.*, p. 331.
[50]134 U.S. 418.
[51]*Ibid.*, p. 458.
[52]169 U.S. 466.

Supreme Court held to the position that the Court itself was the final arbiter on this matter and that the commissions must follow its instructions. In 1933, however, in the case of *Los Angeles Gas and Electric Corporation* v. *Railroad Commission of California* (1933),[53] the Supreme Court indicated that it was willing to leave the determination of the procedures to be employed in the fixing of reasonable rates to the administrative commissions. In that decision, the Court said:

> We have emphasized the distinctive function of the Court. We do not sit as a board of revision, but to enforce constitutional right. . . . The legislative discretion implied in the rate-making powers necessarily extends to the entire legislative process embracing the method used in reaching the true legislative determination, as well as that determination, itself. We are not concerned with either so long as constitutional limitations are not transgressed.[54]

There has been much discussion of the implications of the Court's reasoning in this case, and the issue was again raised in *Federal Power Commission* v. *Natural Gas Pipeline Company* (1942).[55] In upholding an order of the Federal Power Commission, the Court said:

> The Constitution does not bind rate-making bodies to the service of any single formula, or combination of formulas. Agencies to whom this legislative power has been delegated are free, within the ambit of their statutory authority, to make the pragmatic adjustments which may be called for by particular circumstances. Once a fair hearing has been given, proper findings made, and other statutory requirements satisfied, the courts cannot intervene in the absence of a clear showing that the limits of due process have been overstepped. If the Commission's order, as applied to the facts before it, and viewed in its entirety, produces no arbitrary result, our inquiry is at an end.[56]

This position was reaffirmed in *Federal Power Commission* v. *Hope Natural Gas Company* (1944).[57]

The implication of these decisions seems to be that the Court has thrown the responsibility for public utility price making directly into the laps of the regulatory commissions; but it should be noted that the Court reserves the right to interfere if there is a clear showing of the violation of due process and presence of confiscation. Whether this means that henceforth the courts will confine themselves entirely to procedural matters, leaving all matters of fact to the commissions, remains to be seen. Under the pressure of violent price changes, the whole issue might be reopened; and the courts might find occasion once more to inquire extensively into the facts and pass judgment upon the methods used to fix fair prices.

[53]289 U.S. 287. See also *Simpson* v. *Shepard*, 230 U.S. 352 (1913).

[54]*Ibid.*, p. 304.

[55]315 U.S. 575. See also M. G. Glaeser, "The Supreme Court Redeems Itself," *Journal of Land and Public Utility Economics*, Vol. XVIII, No. 2 (May, 1942), pp. 146–54.

[56]*Ibid.*, p. 566. See also *Interstate Commerce Commission* v. *Union Pacific Railway Co.*, 222 U.S. 541 (1912).

[57]320 U.S. 591.

The clear conclusion to be drawn from the controversy over reasonable rates is that price fixing is an extremely complex problem, involving difficult economic and constitutional issures. The Sunshine Coal Company case established the fact that the government could fix both minimum and maximum prices for coal. In *Yakus* v. *United States* (1944),[58] the constitutionality of the Price Control Act of World War II was upheld, Mr. Justice Stone stating that there was no requirement under the statute that the petitioners sell at a loss. They could withdraw from the business at their pleasure, a privilege which is denied to public utilities. Just what the application of such a principle would mean for price fixing in such industries as steel and automobile manufacturing is an open question. To date, no method appears to have been devised to deal satisfactorily with the problem. Maximum price fixing that will result in an effective policy for competitive industry has many serious economic complications, and we have yet to explore the constitutional difficulties which may beset any such attempt.

Frequently, there is impatience in this country at the checks which the courts place on the legislatures, and the feeling prevails that the supremacy which Parliament enjoys in England is a more desirable procedure. Apart from the fact that our federal form of government is much more complicated than that of England, a far larger role by the courts and a much greater emphasis and reliance on growth of accepted procedures, before they are recognized as law, obtain there than has been understood in this country. The supremacy of Parliament, in the technical sense, has too frequently obscured the strong hand which custom imposes upon the exercise of that technical supremacy. The more obvious role of the courts in the United States tends to exaggerate the actual part played by them as compared with that in England. The position which our courts occupy shifts the arena of discussion and controversy somewhat by placing less immediate responsibility upon the legislature. To say that this is ultimately a retarding force on public policy, however, is very debatable. Under pressure of circumstances and zeal for change, it is too easy to assume that the legislature need not respect the law but that, on the contrary, it is the sole creator of the law. This attitude seems to ignore the fact that stable government has developed within the law and that, if one check does not work, another one will. If there were no judicial checks on legislatures in the United States, others would most certainly have grown up.[59]

[58]321 U.S. 414.

[59]For an excellent discussion of this whole problem and its complexities, see B. Schwartz, *op. cit.*

Chapter 12 ANTITRUST LEGISLATION

INTRODUCTION

Meaning of "Antitrust"

The term "antitrust legislation," as it has come to be used in the United States, refers to all of the various legislative attempts to grapple with the practices of private enterprise designed to restrict or destroy competition, and to improve the position of the individual producer by deliberately limiting competition or creating monopoly, and also with those practices which may have the effect of achieving these results. The underlying objectives of the legislation are to foster conditions whereby healthy and free competition may be maintained and to eliminate activities that are inimical to it.

"Trust" is a generic term derived from the early use of the trustee device to create a monopoly, and it is still used in popular language to refer to all of the various schemes that are employed in attempts to evade governmental restrictions on the discretionary powers of private enterprise. The laws which embody these restrictions have consequently come to be known as "antitrust" laws.[1] They prescribe, by prohibiting certain types of conduct, the general forms of competitive behavior for all enterprise, except where exemptions are provided by special legislation. Even such exemptions are limited to a strict interpretation of the statutes; and businesses acting beyond the exemptions granted are liable to prosecution under the antitrust laws, even though, at the same time, they are subject to special regulation. Thus, the basic assumption of control of private enterprise in the United States is that competitive standards must be adhered to, unless and to the extent that specific permission is given to depart therefrom.

[1]Antitrust laws as defined in the Clayton Act include the Sherman and Clayton Acts. Section 5 of the Federal Trade Commission Act has been applied and interpreted so broadly as to include mere incipient Sherman Act violations. ". . . the general practitioner who advises a client on compliance with the antitrust laws would do well to bracket together the Sherman and Federal Trade Commission Acts, and to view their collectively broad commands as a flaming sword which turns every way to guard the competitive tree of life of our economy." J. G. Van Cise, *Understanding the Antitrust Laws* (New York: Practising Law Institute, 1963) pp. 34–35. The Select Committee on Small Business of the House of Representatives includes these Acts and a large number of other statutes or parts thereof as antitrust statutes. *Congress and the Monopoly Problem, Fifty Years of Antitrust Development*, 1900–1956, House Doc. No. 240, 85th Cong., 1st sess. (Washington, D.C., 1957).

The Need for Legislation

For all practical purposes, the move for legislative control of business enterprise in the United States came after the Civil War. The growth of large-scale industry, the rise of the railroad problem, the predatory practices of young and aggressive industrial leaders with their "public be damned" attitude, and widespread financial abuses led to vigorous public demand for governmental action. On top of this, the difficulties of reconstruction after the Civil War, the long depression of 1871-79, and a price level that declined steadily until 1896 afforded the setting for legislative action which created the framework for present-day public control of business in the United States.

The common law was totally inadequate for the problems which emerged during this period. Although it provided the bases upon which the foundations of regulation were erected, it was too simple in structure and lacked adequate means of application to meet the new situation which had arisen. As has already been pointed out, restraint of trade and unfair competition at common law did not provide the basis for positive action by the state. Only conspiracy to monopolize was positively illegal. In addition, the common law as a means of regulating business was confined to the states. Regulation by the federal government of practices that might be dealt with at the state level through the common law could be carried out only through the medium of federal statutes.

Early State Legislation

The first attempts to regulate business were made by the various states. The Granger laws of the midwestern states signalized the advent of regulation in the special field of railroad transportation. At the same time, many of the states introduced legislation to deal with monopoly in the industrial field. They enacted laws against monopolies, restriction of competition, pooling, price control, limitation of output, division of territory, and price discrimination.[2] The most thoroughgoing measures to deal with the latter issues were adopted by Texas and Missouri, especially the former. In most cases, however, state action was weak and enforcement only halfhearted. Even Texas and Missouri found their scope limited because of the predominantly interstate nature of the activities of those enterprises which were the worst offenders. The Supreme Court had made it quite clear that the states could not exercise control over interstate commerce, even though the federal government had not acted.[3] It was not difficult for legal ingenuity, in the absence of federal action, to escape the effects of state legislation. Furthermore, the laxity of many states and their charter-mongering proclivities made any concerted program at the

[2]H. R. Seager and C. A. Gulick, Jr., *Trust and Corporation Problems* (New York: Harper & Bros., 1929), chap. xvii.

[3]This was explicitly stated in *Wabash Railway Co.* v. *Illinois*, 118 U.S. 557 (1886).

state level impossible. This situation, together with the restrictions of the Standard Oil trust, the sugar trust, and various kinds of monopoly agreements in whiskey, meat products, steel rails, structural steel, linseed oil, etc., necessitated federal action. The result was the Sherman Antitrust Act of 1890.

THE SHERMAN ANTITRUST ACT, 1890

Public sentiment against trusts and industrial monopolies crystallized in the United States in the 1880's and brought forth the first declaration against them in 1888. In that year, all the parties in the presidential campaign declared against monopolies; and the platforms of the four leading parties contained specific planks relating to monopoly, combinations, and trusts. Several bills were introduced into both houses of Congress in 1888 and 1889, the most important one being presented by Senator Sherman on December 4, 1889, entitled "A bill to declare unlawful, trusts and combinations in restraint of trade and production." Although this bill was never enacted into law, the leading role played by Senator Sherman in formulating the general scope and in securing the passage of the first federal antitrust law resulted in that legislation being known by his name.

As the result of the extensive debate on the nature of the legislation to be passed, a number of proposals were made; and all of these were referred to the Senate Judiciary Committee. From that Committee finally emerged a substitute which, after extensive discussion, was enacted into law by both houses of Congress and approved by President Harrison on July 2, 1890. It was entitled "An Act to protect trade and commerce against unlawful restraint and monopoly." This has since been known as the Sherman Antitrust Act.[4]

Provisions of the Act

1. The first two sections of the law set forth the practices which are prohibited under it. Section 1 declares "every contract, combination in the form of trust or otherwise, or conspiracy in restraint of trade or commerce among the several states or with foreign nations" to be illegal. Section 2 provides that "every person who shall monopolize or attempt to monopolize, or combine or conspire with any other person or persons to monopolize, any part of the trade or commerce among the several states or with foreign nations shall be deemed guilty of a misdemeanor." Section 3 extends the geographic scope of the Act by declaring illegal "every contract, combination in form of trust or otherwise, or conspiracy, in restraint of trade or commerce in any Territory of the United States or of the District of Columbia, or in restraint of trade or commerce between any such Territory and another, or between any such Territory or Terri-

[4] 26 Stat. 209, chap. 647; 15 U.S.C.A. 1.

tories and any State or States or the District of Columbia, or with foreign nations, or between the District of Columbia and any state or states or foreign nations."

2. The Act also provides that every person, for each violation, "shall be deemed guilty of a misdemeanor and on conviction thereof shall be punished by fine not exceeding $50,000, or by imprisonment not exceeding one year, or by both said punishments in the discretion of the court."[5] The definition of the word "person," as used in the law, is set forth in Section 8, which states that "the word 'person' or 'persons' wherever used in this Act, shall be deemed to include corporations and associations existing under or authorized by the laws of either the United States, the laws of any of the territories, the laws of any state, or the laws of any foreign country."

3. It is the duty of the federal district attorneys, acting under the supervision of the Attorney General of the United States, to prosecute violations of the law; and the federal courts are given jurisdiction over the proceedings. The government is empowered to proceed against offenders by criminal action, by action to seize and condemn the property of offenders moving in interstate or foreign commerce, or by instituting suit in equity to prevent and restrain violation. Any person injured in his business or property by violators of the law may bring suit in the federal courts and recover threefold damages and the cost of the suit, including a reasonable attorney's fee.[6]

4. For enforcement, interpretation, and application, the Sherman Act relies solely upon the courts. They alone have jurisdiction; no administrative machinery was provided for securing compliance with the law. This was not surprising at the time the legislation was passed, because the development of regulation by commission in this country was in its infancy. Despite the change that has taken place in this respect, Congress has not yet deemed it fit to place the Sherman Act under a federal commission. The duty of detecting violations of the law and of bringing the offenders to trial has devolved primarily upon the Antitrust Division of the Department of Justice, which endeavors to secure compliance, either by suit in criminal proceedings or in equity or by settlement out of court before trial and arrived at by negotiation, the agreement receiving the approval of a court. This is known as a "consent decree."

Objectives of the Act

The underlying idea of the Sherman law was the elimination of various forms of restraints and monopoly that were designed to avoid

[5]The provision in the original law was $5,000; but this was increased to the above figure in 1955, by Public Law 135, 84th Congress, 1st session, chap. 281.

[6]The provision regarding recovery of threefold damages by private suit (Section 7) was repealed in 1955 and was superseded by Section 4 of the Clayton Act which contains a similar provision except it applies to all the antitrust laws as defined in the Clayton Act (Public Law, 137, 84th Cong., 1955), whereas Section 7 of the Sherman Act applied to the Sherman Act only.

competition or make it impossible. To achieve this objective, the common-law doctrines of restraint of trade and monopoly were incorporated in the Sherman Act. Debate in the Senate indicated that the intent of Congress was to give statutory recognition to the common-law meaning of these terms. Congress felt that the economic evils with which it was trying to grapple could be dealt with on a basis of precedent, because everyone knew the nature of the evils. The law was framed in the broadest possible terms by deliberate intent, with the objective of bringing within its ambit all action designed to thwart the forces of competition. The underlying assumption was that competition was the "natural order" of private business and that monopoly would emerge only as the result of some sort of deliberate intent and action to eliminate or forestall competition or competitors.

The Sherman Act, therefore, has been the target of frequent criticism, on the grounds that it was erected on the blind faith of beneficence of competition and that it proclaimed statutory adherence to unvarnished *laissez faire.* It is clear that the legislators abhorred monopoly and sought to lay firm statutory foundations for competition. To contend, however, that the validity of the legislation stood or fell with *laissez faire,* in the nineteeth-century sense, is unwarranted. As long as private enterprise is relied upon as the prime means of implementing industry, competition will have to be its mainspring. Even regulated monopoly relies heavily upon it and uses competitive standards as its principal guide. By giving statutory recognition to the common-law rules, and by providing for governmental responsibility in their enforcement, the Sherman Act followed the American tradition of proceeding to the solution of new problems by a gradual process. The outstanding industrial evils of the time centered around predatory monopoly. The solution of them demanded immediate attention. It was hardly to be expected that Congress could foresee the developments that were to unfold so rapidly or could diagnose the nature of the problems that would emerge as the Sherman Act became effective. There is no reason to believe that any legislator felt that this would be the last or final development in the regulation of industry in the United States; that it was the first necessary step is obvious. Moreover, there seems to be few, if any, grounds, even today, for eliminating or curtailing the broad general provisions of that law. Supplementation and better administration are in order, but not elimination.

It has frequently been urged that England has found no need for antitrust laws and that she has not been plagued by the antitrust problem. The Balfour Committee on Industry[7] gave support to this point of view by stating that England was fortunate in not being hampered by such antitrust legislation as prevailed in the United States. This ap-

[7] *Final Report of the Committee on Industry and Trade* (London: His Majesty's Stationery Office, 1929), p. 191.

pears to assume that the Sherman Act has fostered, rather than hindered, the growth of industrial monopoly; but evidence on this score is lacking, to say the least. Moreover, it is instructive to note that Great Britain initiated a positive antimonopoly policy in 1948 with the passage of the Monopolies and Restrictive Practices Act.[8]

To support the Sherman Act is not to argue that it alone is adequate; but to argue for its repeal is to contend, in effect, that the whole common-law foundation of our regulatory structure should be swept away. To do this and, at the same time, to retain private enterprise would launch us on uncharted seas without any recognizable points of reference. As one writer forcefully puts it:

> The Sherman Act is thus in accord with the Great American tradition. . . . In any venture into regulation, every party has a right to insist that it be accorded an equivalent for the protection of the open market which he is called upon to surrender. In a world where the unknown crowds upon us, public policy can have no enduring ultimate. For its guidance, we may discover a more reasonable scheme of values than we now know; but until that time, the objectives of the common right and the Sherman Act must continue to direct. However the pattern of industrial government is modified, the ideal they embody will remain the reference for economic justice.[9]

The Miller-Tydings Amendment

The first and only direct and substantive amendment to the Sherman Act came in 1937 with the passage of the Miller-Tydings Resale Price Maintenance Act,[10] which legalized resale price maintenance in interstate commerce. The basic objective of resale price maintenance is to secure, through control of the resale price of products, whatever advantages may inhere in trade-marked or differentiated goods. Thus, it is simply a practice designed to impose limitations upon certain aspects of competition. Until the passage of the Miller-Tydings Act, resale price maintenance by contract or coercion constituted a violation of the Sherman law; but a manufacturer or wholesaler was not guilty of restraint of trade if he endeavored to control the resale prices of his product by persuasion.

In the period following World War I, a widespread movement to curb price competition developed in the United States. This was given added impetus by small retailers, who feared the growth of the chain store. Although there was need for devising means to prevent predatory practices and the disparagement of good will of trade-mark products, the pressure for resale price maintenance was, at bottom, part of the

[8] 11 and 12 George VI, chap. 66 (1948).

[9] W. H. Hamilton, "Common Right, Due Process and Antitrust," *Law and Contemporary Problems* (Durham, N.C.: Duke University Press, 1940), Vol. VII, No. 1, pp. 24–41.

[10] Public Law 314, 75th Congress, 1st session, H.R. 7472, August 17, 1937, Title VIII, chap. 690. Statutes legalizing resale price maintenance are known as "fair-trade laws."

general atmosphere of the period after the war. During these years, there emerged, for various reasons, strong resistance to adjustments to conditions of the market by price competition. The depression of 1929, and the collapse of prices that ensued, gave rise to a general movement and concerted effort to bolster the price structure. On of the manifestations of this was the widespread adoption of legislation legalizing resale price maintenance.

The state of California took the lead in this direction by passing, in 1931,[11] a law which became the model for the other states. This law legalized price maintenance contracts of a commodity "which bears, or the label or content of which bears, the trademark, brand, or name of the producer or owner of such commodity, and which is in fair and open competition with commodities of the same general class produced by others." An amendment, added in 1933, provided that "willfully and knowingly advertising, offering for sale or selling any commodity at less than the price stipulated in any contract entered into pursuant to the provisions of Section 1 of this Act, whether the person so advertising, offering for sale or selling is or is not a party to such contract, is unfair competition and is actionable at the suit of any person damaged thereby." This was the "nonsigner" clause of resale price maintenance legislation. Another section of the law prohibited price agreements among competitors on any level. In the following years, forty-five other states passed similar legislation.

In 1937, Congress amended Section 1 of the Sherman Act by passing the Miller-Tydings Resale Price Maintenance Act. This legalized resale price maintenance contracts in interstate commerce, when such contracts were lawful as applied to intrastate transactions, and declared that such arrangements were not an unfair method of competition. This law was jammed through Congress as a rider to a revenue bill for the District of Columbia and was opposed both by the President and by the Federal Trade Commission. It constituted a definite reversal of the established antitrust policy but was fully in keeping with the spirit of the times. It was a logical addition to the legislation of the period, which was restrictive in spirit and inimical to free and competitive market conditions. This piece of legislation was challenged in *Schwegmann Bros.* v. *Calvert Distillers Corporation* (1951).[12] The Supreme Court held that the law applied only to those who had signed interstate contracts. This literally eliminated fair-trade contracts in interstate commerce. However, Congress took steps to remedy this situation by amending the Federal Trade Commission Act in 1952[13] so as, once again, to legalize resale price maintenance in interstate commerce.

[11]Fair Trade Act, Statutes of 1931, Chap. 278.
[12]341 U.S. 384.
[13]Public Law 542 (the McGuire Act), 82nd Congress, 2nd session, 1952.

THE CLAYTON ANTITRUST ACT, 1914

Purpose of the Clayton Act

Although the Sherman law lays down the broad foundation for statutory control of private enterprise and is basic to the maintenance of conditions of competition, taken alone, it is quite inadequate as a preventive for the development of practices inimical to competitive and capitalistic organizations. Administration of the law soon disclosed three fundamental difficulties which clearly necessitated supplemental legislation. In the first place, there was the inadequacy of an enforcement procedure that relied solely on the courts and that necessarily placed emphasis upon punitive, rather than preventive, measures. Secondly, there was the difficulty of securing a reasonable consistency in policy regarding restraint of trade and monopoly, because of the inability of this approach to develop policy through purely judicial channels, and also because of the variations in enthusiasm for the objectives of the Sherman Act by different administrations in Washington. Thirdly, the successful prosecution of some practices and devices led to the resort to others which proved less vulnerable under existing laws and to the emergence of new ones previously unknown.

The disclosure of abuses by the investigations of the Industrial Commission in 1901 and the destruction wrought upon competitive enterprise by some of the monopolistic combines before they could be brought to successful trial, together with the rapid growth of corporate giants, gave rise to widespread insistence on further action. As the result of these demands, the trust problem became one of the main issues of the presidential campaign of 1912. All of the major parties proposed remedies in their platforms. Woodrow Wilson took the stand that private monopoly was indefensible. He proposed to introduce legislation that would eliminate interlocking directorates, prohibit—item by item—practices of monopoly which experience had disclosed, set up an interstate trade commission, impose penalties on individuals responsible for breaches of the law, and make it possible for private suits for redress to be filed. All of these were embodied on his message to Congress in January, 1914, together with requests for consideration of the question of individuals owning stock in several companies which should have been expected to be independent of each other but which were, in effect, brought under common control. This message resulted in two acts of Congress: the Clayton Act, designed to prohibit certain practices which had escaped the Sherman Law; and the Federal Trade Commission Act, which set up administrative machinery for the first time to deal with antitrust problems.

There was general agreement in Congress on the necessity for further legislation, and there was substantial agreement on the basic nature of the legislation to be enacted; but there was much disagreement on detail. This was to be expected in the light of the complex nature of the problem with which Congress was trying to deal and also because of the lack of experience. Congress was still groping its way; and up until that time, there had not been adequate means of discovering the precise nature of the problem and of developing distinctions between those things which were harmful to public interest and competition and those which were not. There had been no administrative development in antitrust such as that which had characterized the Interstate Commerce Commission in transportation. Control by legislative enactment and judicial enforcement suffered from the fundamental defect that the formulation of policy could not be a continuous process; and a clear-cut distinction between the good and bad results of similar policies could not be drawn. As a consequence, much congressional debate centered around definitions and practices; and the legislation that emerged was indefinite, conglomerate, and diffuse.

Nevertheless, the legislation of 1914 introduced a new concept of the trust problem. It acknowledged that the simple and generalized prohibitions of the Sherman Act were inadequate, that preventive measures were required, and that the readily discernible abuses would have to be eliminated. It also recognized the necessity of establishing machinery for the purpose of developing continuity in the control of industrial enterprise. Unfortunately, this promising beginning was stifled almost in its infancy by the outbreak of World War I and the events which followed in the next thirty years.

Provisions of the Clayton Act

The Clayton Act,[14] known as "An Act to supplement existing laws against unlawful restraint and monopoly, and for other purposes," was avowedly a supplement to the Sherman law. It was designed to forestall monopoly by nipping it at the beginning. Although its purpose was to overcome some of the shortcomings of the Sherman Act, it should be noted that the courts have stressed that the Clayton Act stands independent of the Sherman Act. The new law contained four main provisions relating to monopoly and restraint of trade.

1. Section 2 prohibited discrimination in price between different purchasers of commodities, which commodities were sold for use, consumption, or resale, "where the effect of such discrimination may be to substantially lessen competition or tend to create a monopoly in any line of commerce." This prohibition was qualified by the provisos that "nothing herein contained shall prevent discrimination in price between purchasers of commodities on account of differences in the grade, quality or quantity of the commodity sold, or that makes only due allowance for differences in the cost of selling or transportation, or discrimination in

[14] 38 Stat. 730, chap. 323; 15 U.S.C.A. 12.

price in the same or different communities made in good faith to meet competition," and that "nothing herein contained shall prevent persons engaged in selling goods, wares or merchandise in commerce from selecting their own customers in bona fide transactions and not in restraint of trade."

It is clear that this section of the law was aimed at eliminating price discrimination as a means of achieving monopoly or restraint of trade. It was easier to state the purpose, however, than to devise the effective means of carrying it out. If the Clayton Act had been administered with a thoroughgoing understanding of the issues involved and a clear-cut picture of the objectives to be achieved, the law might have been sufficient to deal with price discrimination. But what constitutes price discrimination is subject to a great deal of difference of opinion. Furthermore, even the objectives involved in the elimination of the practice were, and still are, anything but clearly defined or understood, as will be seen shortly in the discussion of the Robinson-Patman Act.

2. Section 3 of the Clayton law prohibited the use of tying contracts and exclusive-dealer arrangements, where the effect of these "may be to substantially lessen competition or tend to create a monopoly in any line of commerce." The practices against which this section was directed were tying contracts and exclusive-dealer arrangements, which had frequently been used for the purpose of suppressing competition or achieving monopoly. A tying contract is one in which a seller or lessor agrees to sell or lease a commodity only on the condition that other commodities used in conjunction with the first are purchased or leased from the same party. An exclusive-dealer arrangement is one in which the seller obligates the distributor to refrain from selling like products of any competitor of the seller. This also includes what are known as "full-requirements" contracts.

Both of these arrangements may be quite legitimate and productive of no harmful results. Modern production may necessitate the use of certain commodities in conjunction with others and may, as a means of protecting the manufacturer, justify the imposition of restrictions or conditions upon sale. As a consequence, tying contracts may even enhance competition. Similarly, exclusive-dealer arrangements may lead to economies of production or marketing, when they bring about a concentration of distribution that results in greater marketing efficiency. On the other hand, both devices may be used effectively to restrain competition or maintain monopoly. The purpose of the law was not to outlaw these business practices but only to prevent their use when the result would be substantially to lessen competition or to tend to create a monopoly in any line of commerce. It is the difficulty of drawing the line between the desirable and undesirable aspects that has rendered the enforcement of the law halting and uncertain.

3. Section 7 of the Clayton Act forbade any corporation from ac-

quiring the stock of any other corporation engaged in commerce, where the effect of such acquisition might be substantially to lessen competition between any such corporations, or where it might result in the restraint of commerce or might tend to create a monopoly in any line of commerce. The prohibition did not apply to stock acquired solely for investment purposes or to the formation of subsidiaries for carrying out immediately lawful business. The purpose of the section was to provide means for preventing the establishment of monopoly or the lessening of competition by the device of intercorporate stockholding.

The wording of this section seems to have been particularly inept, at least in the light of court decisions down to 1957. It was still possible to acquire the stock of an enterprise and use the control thereby gained to merge the assets and dissolve the former owner. A further difficulty which stood in the way of effective legislative proscription of intercorporate stock ownership for purposes of control was to ascertain how much stock had to be owned in order that any effective control could be exercised. That the whole problem of intercorporate stock ownership was a real one was all too evident, but the means of dealing with it effectively remained obscure for at least forty-three years.

4. Section 8 of the Clayton Act prohibited, among other things, any person from being at the same time a director in any two or more corporations, any one of which had a capital, surplus, and undivided profits aggregating more than $1 million, where the corporations were or heretofore had been competitors to the extent that the elimination of competition by agreement between them would constitute a violation of the antitrust laws. This was designed to end the use of interlocking directorates as a means of evading the antitrust laws. Even more than Section 7, this part of the Act has proved to be particularly ineffective. It did not deal with the possibility of electing dummy directors through common ownership of stock in competing corporations; and it did not prevent the use, by competitors, of the same officers who were not stockholders.

Section 8 has been criticized on the ground that it may be positively harmful by preventing men of outstanding executive capacity from using their talents in more than one enterprise. This does not seem to be a very pointed criticism, however, because the law does not prevent such arrangements if the firms are not competing; and it is difficult to see why businesses that are genuinely competitors should want to have common officers. It is even more difficult to understand how such common officers can serve competitors conscientiously except, perhaps, in a strictly technical capacity. The evils envisaged in Section 8 are especially difficult to deal with by legislative action. The element of judgment must loom large in each case. The remedy would seem to lie in the administrative development of a coherent and consistent policy, but it appears that the furtherance of this approach must await congressional action.

5. The Clayton Act made directors, officers, or agents guilty if they

were in any way responsible for corporate violation of the penal provisions of the antitrust laws. Punishment was fixed at a maximum of $5,000 fine or one year of imprisonment, or both. Individuals injured by violation of the law were entitled to sue for threefold damages and costs of the suit. Relief by injunction could also be obtained by suit in the courts to prevent threatened loss or damage. The Department of Justice was given jurisdiction over all violations of the Act and could bring suit against any offender. The Federal Trade Commission was also made responsible for enforcing Sections 2, 3, 7, and 8 and, consequently, had co-ordinate authority with the Department of Justice. This dual and bifurcated control indicates clearly that Congress had not reached the point where it was willing to embark upon a definitely integrated antitrust policy. Unfortunately, this situation still obtains.

THE ROBINSON-PATMAN ACT, 1936

In June, 1936, Congress passed the Robinson-Patman Antidiscrimination Act.[15] This legislation was enacted for the purposes of amending Section 2 of the Clayton Act, by completely rewriting it to add some additional provisions against price discrimination and to clarify the status of the transactions of co-operative and nonprofit institutions under the antidiscrimination provisions. The enforcement of Section 2 of the original Clayton Act by the Federal Trade Commission had not only proved a disappointment but also had become the center of much controversy. The reversals which the Commission met at the hands of the courts, particularly in regard to quantity discounts, the emergence of new and subtler marketing and price policies, and the lack of objective standards of price discrimination all pointed to further legislation if any real progress was to be made in dealing with price discrimination. In addition to this, the impact of the depression, coupled with the demise of the National Industrial Recovery Act, created widespread demand for restrictions against competitive price cutting. There was also the desire, in many quarters, to limit the advantages which large distributors might obtain from quantity buying, which, in the belief of many, threatened the existence of small-scale, independent retailers. The spirit of the times was to keep everybody in business and put a bottom under prices. Consequently, there was a demand for the extension of price regulation, especially as it applied to minimum prices. At the same time, the idea of using average or fully allocated costs as the standard for measuring price discrimination was also taking hold. The result was legislation which exhibited poor draftsmanship and conflicting objectives.

1. The new law prohibited discrimination in price by any person engaged in commerce between different purchasers of commodities of like grade and quality, where the effects of such discrimination might be

[15] 49 Stat. 1526, chap. 592; 15 U.S.C.A. 13.

substantially to lessen competition or to tend to create a monopoly in any line of commerce. Price differentials to different purchasers, however, were permitted if they made only due allowances for differences in the cost of manufacture, sale, or delivery resulting from different methods or quantities "in which such commodities are to such purchasers sold or delivered." The Federal Trade Commission was empowered, after due investigation and hearing, to fix and establish quantity limits on particular commodities, or classes of commodities, if it found that available purchasers of greater quantities were so few as to render differentials, on account thereof, unjustly discriminatory or promotive of monopoly in any line of commerce. In other words, quantity discounts could be limited, even though justified by cost reduction, if the Federal Trade Commission concluded that differentials based on such costs would give an undue advantage to large-scale marketing. The law permitted price changes from time to time in response to changing conditions affecting the market—such as, but not limited to, actual or immediate deterioration of perishable goods—or sales made in good faith in discontinuance of business in the goods concerned. It also permitted sellers to select their own customers in bona fide transactions which were not in restraint of trade.

Just how much leeway to adapt price policies to changing market conditions is afforded a producer is difficult to ascertain. When a bill of particulars charging price discrimination has been drawn up, the burden of proof that such discrimination has not taken place is on the shoulders of the seller charged with violation. He may, in rebuttal, however, argue that his lower price was made in good faith to meet an equally low price of a competitor. Whether the defense set up on these grounds by a particular seller is adequate is, presumably, a matter for the Commission and the courts to decide. This has given rise to a long-drawn-out controversy, on which the outcome is as yet by no means settled.

2. The law also endeavored to grapple with brokerage, advertising, and other service allowances that might be used as a cloak for price discrimination. The Act prohibited any person engaged in commerce to pay or grant or to receive or accept anything of value as a commission, brokerage, or other compensation, or any allowance or discount in lieu thereof, except for services rendered in connection with the sale or purchases of goods, and declared it unlawful for any person engaged in commerce to pay or contract for the payment of anything of value to or for the benefit of a customer of such person, unless such payment or consideration was available on proportionally equal terms to all other customers competing in the distribution of such products or commodities. Provisions regarding brokerage fees and other compensations were applicable equally to buyers and sellers, and it was unlawful for any person engaged in commerce knowingly to induce or receive a discrimination in price, which is prohibited by the legislation.

3. Section 3 of the Act forbids any person to be a party to or assist

in sales which discriminate against competitors of the purchaser by the granting of any discount, rebate allowance, or advertising service charge that is greater than that which is available to the competitors. It forbids sale in one locality at lower prices than those exacted by the same seller in another locality, where the purpose is to destroy competition. Finally, it prohibits sales at unreasonably low prices for the purpose of destroying competition or eliminating a competitor. All of these offenses are punishable by a maximum fine of $5,000 or a year's imprisonment, or both.

In some respects, the Robinson-Patman Act marks a definite advance in dealing with the problem of price discrimination, in that it moves in the direction of establishing standards of discrimination. The problem which the legislation endeavors to grapple with is a real one and has been the source of much difficulty to administrative agencies. Discrimination as a predatory or protective device needs to be eliminated, but all price differentials are not in this category. The attempt to measure discrimination by cost standards is extremely difficult, not only because of problems of cost allocation but also because the costs to be used in measuring the advisability of certain sales vary widely with the different transactions. Furthermore, the restrictions that may be imposed upon large-scale producers against passing on to their customers savings which result from volume orders is a definite limitation upon competitive pricing. The preservation of small-scale enterprise at the expense of the consumer is a forthright curtailment of price competition and imposes a barrier to the efficient utilization of resources. Whether the resulting social cost will be offset by advantages obtained from the elimination of certain abuses may be difficult to ascertain and must await evidence gained from enforcement. Until it can be shown, however, that the evils of discrimination cannot be limited without sacrifice of the advantages of large-scale production, it would seem to be wise to rely on more administrative discretion than now seems possible and to modify the law so as to make it less restrictive against legitimate competition.

THE CELLER-KEFAUVER ACT, 1950

Section 7 of the Clayton Act was rendered completely innocuous by a series of decisions by the Supreme Court. The resulting inability of this section to accomplish any of the objectives that had led to its passage finally resulted in the Celler-Kefauver Act of 1950,[16] which was an amendment to the Clayton Act. The amendment prohibited any corporation engaged in commerce from acquiring, directly or indirectly, the whole or any part of the stock or share capital, or the whole or any part of the assets of another corporation, where, in any line of commerce or in any

[16]Public Law 899, 81st Congress, 2nd session, 1950. That the original Section 7 was not as innocuous as had been inferred from earlier court decisions was evidenced by the decision in *United States* v. *E. I. du Pont de Nemours et al.*, 353 U.S. 586 (1957). This decision was rendered, however, after the passage of the Celler-Kefauver amendment.

section of the country, the effect of such acquisition might be substantially to lessen competition or to tend to create a monopoly. The prohibition also extended to the use of such stock by the voting or granting of proxies or otherwise.

One purpose of this legislation was to plug the loopholes of the original Section 7. It also had a wider objective, in that it was intended to apply to the lessening of competition in any line of commerce in any section of the country as well as between the corporation acquiring the stock and the one whose stock was acquired.[17] In addition, it was intended that mergers that would probably lessen competition would be checked in their incipiency.

THE FEDERAL TRADE COMMISSION ACT, 1914

Reasons for the Legislation

The Federal Trade Commission Act of 1914 was the second part of President Wilson's program to provide for more effective control of business practices. The idea of regulation by an administrative commission had been growing in this country since the introduction of that device to deal with railroad companies by the Granger laws of the 1870's. As early as 1893, Judge Harlan had pointed out the need for the establishment of a permanent federal administrative agency to deal with antitrust problems. In 1902, the Industrial Commission recommended that a permanent bureau be set up for the purpose of registering all corporations doing an interstate business and of making investigations that would furnish Congress with information for future legislation. In 1903, legislation was passed creating a Bureau of Corporations, under the Secretary of Commerce and Labor, to secure publicity in the affairs of corporations.

During the ensuing ten years, there was widespread agitation for the formation of some kind of an administrative agency. These demands arose primarily from two sources. On the one hand, businessmen and others, exasperated at the uncertainties of the law, wanted a more precise statement of what was legal; and they advocated an administrative tribunal which could give advance opinions as to what business might or might not do. On the other hand, there were those who thought that the courts had appropriated too much authority to themselves in interpreting the Sherman Act. They felt that this took too much power out of the hands of Congress, and they wanted an administrative commission to develop policy. On all sides, there was recognition of the need for an

[17]*Current Antitrust Problems* (Hearings before Committee on the Judiciary, House of Representatives, 84th Cong., 1st sess.) (Washington, D.C.: U.S. Government Printing Office, 1955), Serial No. 3, Part I, pp. 26 f. Exemptions from the application of Section 7 are set forth in Section 11 of the Clayton Act. To date, these have been narrowly construed by the Supreme Court. See *United States* v. *Philadelphia National Bank,* 374 U.S. 321 (1963).

administrative body that could combine all the varied talents necessary to deal with the myriad problems which the regulation of competitive enterprise presented.

Although President Wilson favored the protection of small business and regarded monopoly as intolerable, he recognized that much of the difficulty arose from the inadequacies of the law and existing enforcement procedures. In his message to Congress, he said: "The Government and businessmen are ready to meet each other half way in a common effort to square business methods with both public opinion and the law." It was clear that he envisaged an administrative agency not only as a means of enforcing the law but also as a device whereby the problems of competitive business could be settled outside the restrictive procedures of the judicial process. Except for unanimity of opinion on the need for an administrative commission, there was well-nigh universal disagreement on the function and powers which should be given to that body. As a consequence, the agency which was established enjoyed neither the power nor the prestige of the Interstate Commerce Commission, which served as the prototype. This was to be expected in light of the uncertainties, except as to the most general objectives, and the lack of experience in administrative regulation of competitive enterprise.

Provisions of the Act

The legislation creating the Federal Trade Commission was signed by President Wilson on September 26, 1914.[18]

1. The law provided for a commission of 5 members, appointed for 7 years by the President, with the advice and consent of the Senate. The terms of the first appointees were fixed so as to obviate the retirement of all members at one time. Not more than 3 of the 5 commissioners could be from the same political party. To keep them independent of political interference, the law provided that they might be removed from their position by the President only for inefficiency, neglect of duty, or malfeasance in office.

2. The newly constituted Commission was instructed to take over the Bureau of Corporations, its records, and its personnel, and to continue the investigations that the Bureau had commenced. The Act provided the Commission with extensive investigatory powers, to be used for the purpose of securing publicity in business practices and aiding in the enforcement of the antitrust laws. The tribunal was given the authority to investigate the organization, business, conduct, practices, and management of any corporation engaged in commerce, except banks and common carriers, and to require, by general or special orders, annual or special reports, or answers in writing to specific questions from corporations subject to its control. Upon the direction of the President or either house of Congress, it was required to investigate any alleged violations of the

[18] 38 Stat. 717, chap. 311; 15 U.S.C.A. 41.

antitrust laws by any corporation. The Act directed the Commission to examine corporate practices or arrangements not in conformity with the antitrust laws, if requested to do so by the Attorney General, and to recommend readjustments which would secure such conformity. It was given the task of acting as master in chancery to ascertain and report an appropriate form of degree in any suit in equity brought under the direction of the Attorney General, as provided in the antitrust laws, if it was instructed to do so by a federal court. The legislation provided the Commission with the power to investigate trade conditions in and with foreign countries which might affect the foreign trade of the United States, and to report the results of its findings to Congress, with whatever recommendations it considered advisable. It was given permission to make public such portions of any information gathered by it, except trade secrets and names of customers, as it deemed expedient in the public interest; to prepare annual and special reports to Congress; and to submit therewith recommendations for additional legislation.

3. In addition to the enforcement duties connected with Sections 2, 3, 7, and 8 of the Clayton Act, which it shared co-ordinately with the Attorney General, the Commission was given the sole responsibility for enforcing Section 5 of the Trade Commission Act, in which unfair methods of competition in commerce were declared unlawful. Much congressional debate centered around the wording of this section of the law, some congressmen contending that it was necessary to enumerate illegal practices item by item. Others felt that the term "unfair competition" had a definite meaning at common law and that such wording would confer adequate powers upon the Commission. The phrase "unfair methods of competition," which was finally adopted, was intended to give wider scope to the Commission than it would have had if the phrase "unfair competition" had been used. Then, too, the use of unfair methods of competition now constituted a violation of the law which the Commission was required to prevent as a matter of federal responsibility.

4. Another source of contention centered on the question of judicial review of the orders of the Commission. Some wished to prevent the courts from having the power to review the discretion and judgment exercised or the facts passed upon by the Trade Commission. As the law emerged, it vested the power of review in the courts if either party to the controversy requested judicial evaluation, with the proviso that the findings of fact of the Commission were to be conclusive, if supported by evidence. Unfortunately, the Act provided no penalties for disobedience of the Commission's orders, but made it necessary for that body to appeal to the courts for enforcement of its orders if they were not obeyed.[19] This

[19]This procedure continued to apply to Commission enforcement of the Clayton Act, including the Robinson-Patman Act, until the amendment to Section 11 of the Clayton Act in 1959 (73 Statutes 243–246) in 1959. As the result of this amendment, Clayton Act enforcement was brought into conformity with that which was provided in the Wheeler-Lea of 1938 for violations of Section 5 of the Federal Trade Commission Act.

saddled upon the Commission the necessity of taking the initiative and considerably weakened its authority to prohibit unfair methods of competition.

The standard of fairness that Congress had in mind when it enacted the legislation was at once ethical and economic. The law was accordingly designed to deal with the plane of competition, as well as practices which would limit the free play of competitive forces. The Commission interpreted this to mean that it had a duty to consumers as well as to competitors. The difficulties encountered in proving in each instance that the methods of competition complained against always injured competitors of alleged offenders, and the Commission's concern for consumer welfare, together with the weakness inherent in the existing procedure of enforcing the Commission's orders, finally led to the Wheeler-Lea Act of 1938.[20]

THE WHEELER-LEA ACT, 1938

By this legislation, Section 5 of the Federal Trade Commission Act was changed to read: "Unfair methods of competition in commerce and unfair or deceptive acts or practices in commerce are hereby declared unlawful." This was designed to widen the Commission's powers in dealing with the plane of competition and also to make it possible for the Federal Trade Commission to require the discontinuance of practices which it considered injurious to the consumer, even though competition was unaffected. The Commission was also given the power to prevent the dissemination of false advertising of foods, drugs, cosmetics, or curative or corrective devices. Enforcement provisions of the Federal Trade Commission Act were strengthened by making it an offense, subject to a penalty of $5,000 for each violation, to disobey a cease and desist order after it became final. This penalty was increased in 1950 by making each day's failure to obey the law a separate offense. Any order which was not contested by either party became final at the expiration of sixty days from its issuance.[21] The Commission was also authorized to institute injunction proceedings in any district court to prevent violation of the provisions relating to false advertising, until the Commission had time to dispose of the case. Finally, the Wheeler-Lea Act made it a criminal offense to violate the section regarding false advertising "if the use of the commodity advertised may be injurious to health because of results from such use under the conditions prescribed in the advertisement thereof, or under such conditions as are customary or usual, or if such violation is with intent to defraud or mislead." The enforcement of this provision was placed in the hands of the Attorney General, who was required to institute proceedings upon certification by the Commission.

[20]52 Statutes 111, chap. 49; 15 U.S.C.A. 41.

[21]None of this applied to the sections of the Clayton Act which were under the Federal Trade Commission. (But see footnote 18, *supra*.)

THE McGUIRE ACT, 1952[22]

This law was passed to remedy the deficiencies that had been exposed in the Miller-Tydings amendment to the Sherman Act. This time, the legislation amended Section 5 of the Federal Trade Commission Act by declaring that interstate contracts fixing resale prices were not to be held in violation of Section 5 of the Federal Trade Commission Act or any of the antitrust laws "when contracts or agreements of that description are lawful as applied to intrastate transactions under any statute, law or public policy now or hereafter in effect in any State, Territory, or the District of Columbia in which such resale is to be made, or to which the commodity is to be transported for such resale." The law confined the exemption to products that were in free and open competition with commodities of the same general class produced by others, but it made the resale price arrangements binding on those sellers who were not parties to the contracts. At the same time, it prohibited agreements among competitors. Under the Act, enforcement of the agreements was left to private suit. The Federal Trade Commission has no responsibility on this score.[23]

OTHER LEGISLATION

A number of other laws designed to eliminate unfair methods of competition and to protect both competitors and consumers are also administered by the Federal Trade Commission.[24] The Wool Products Labeling Act, 1939,[25] declares that trading in wool products in this country that are misbranded constitutes an unfair method of competition. Mandatory labeling of wool products is required and the labels are required to disclose by percentages the constituent fibers contained in them. Similar provisions are included in the Fur Products Labeling Act, 1940[26] which requires that the true English name, as set forth in the official name guide promulgated by the Commission in 1952, of the animal from which the fur came be on the label, advertising and invoicing of the fur products offered for sale. Sellers must also state if the furs were new or used, dyed or bleached, and if they are composed of paws, bellies, or waste furs. The country of origin of imported furs must also be stated. The Textile Products Identification Act, 1958,[27] applies to textile fiber

[22]Public Law 542, 82nd Congress, 2nd session, 1952.

[23]See Federal Trade Commission, *News Summary*, No. 9 (February 25, 1955).

[24]A complete text of all antitrust laws administered by the Department of Justice, the Federal Trade Commission and other agencies having any jurisdiction is presented in *The Antitrust Laws*, Staff Report to the Antitrust Subcommittee (Subcommittee No. 5) of the Committee on the Judiciary, House of Representatives, 85th Cong., 2nd. sess., H.Res. 107 (Washington, D.C.: Government Printing Office, 1959).

[25]54 Stat. 1129.

[26]65 Stat. 175 (1951).

[27]72 Stat. 1717.

products, other than wool, and requires labeling similar to that for wool products. The Flammable Fabrics Act, 1953[28] forbids the marketing of apparel or fabrics which are considered dangerously inflammable. The Federal Trade Commission is authorized to issue rules and regulations to conduct tests and to make investigations and inspections to obtain compliance with the law. The flammability tests are devised by the Bureau of Standards.

DEPARTURES FROM ANTITRUST

Nature of the Departures

The traditional and fundamental policy of the United States toward private business has been that of maintaining competition and eliminating monopoly wherever and whenever possible. In the years since the Sherman Act was passed, however, significant deviations have developed. Two major types of legislative enactments have given effect to this.

1. One type of legislation is that which has permitted arrangements that are designed to reduce competition among the members of a particular type of economic activity on the theory that free competition among them is harmful to the group and also to the country. The theory is that some sort of co-operation among the members with regard to prices and/or output is necessary for their general interest. Here, the members of the group, within the limits set forth by the permissive or exempting legislation, are allowed to act as a group in controlling their activities. The principal manifestations are export associations, agricultural organizations, and labor.

2. The second type of legislation assigns the regulation of a particular industry or group of industries to a public agency which regulates the prices, conditions of service, and so forth, of the firms. The principal examples are transportation, public utilities, and insurance. The transport and public utility industries form a special category for which, it is assumed, regulatory controls must be established, not to limit competition but rather to correct the evils of inescapable monopoly. Whether the assumptions underlying this approach are wholly valid is a matter which will be given extended treatment later in this text. The present status of insurance is the result of historical factors which are explained below.

Export Associations

One of the most significant exemptions to the antitrust laws is that afforded to associations of American firms for export trade under the Webb-Pomerene Act of 1918. In the years of the twentieth century preceding World War I, the growth of American foreign trade, as compared with that of Great Britain and Germany, did not present a very favorable

[28] 67 Stat. 111.

picture. The expansion of American industry into foreign markets, together with nationalistic foreign trade policies as manifested by Germany, led to the feeling that American exporters were hampered by laws against combinations and cartels which placed them in an unfavorable competitive position with many foreign exporters. With the outbreak of World War I, the United States was placed in the position of the world's greatest exporter. The desire to maintain this position after the war and recognition of the fact that reconstruction would result in severe competitive rivalry and great uncertainty led to the demand that American exporters be able to combine with each other for the purpose of meeting their foreign rivals. The growing spirit of economic nationalism lent strong support to this point of view.

In 1916, the Federal Trade Commission presented a two-volume report on *Cooperation in American Export Trade* to Congress. This document stressed the importance of our foreign commerce and the need for understanding the conditions which American exporters would have to meet it in competing for the trade of the world. It called attention to the unsettling effects of the war and to the difficulty of foreseeing the economic and business conditions that would result after the peace. It also emphasized the fact that in foreign countries, combinations or cartels among producers and dealers were well established and that American exporters would have to face the competition of these groups. Furthermore, the report stated that in many countries, American exporters were selling to buying combinations or cartels. As a result, the Commission strongly recommended legislation that would allow American exporters to form combinations for foreign trade purposes. Even President Woodrow Wilson supported this position. Congress responded by passing the Webb-Pomerene Act.[29]

This legislation afforded exemption from the Sherman Act to associations entered into for the sole purpose of engaging in export trade, and actually engaged solely in such export trade, and to agreements made, or acts committed, in the course of export trade by such associations. Whatever arrangements were made, however, were not to be in restraint of trade within the United States and not in restraint of export trade of any domestic competitor. The prohibition in the Federal Trade Commission Act against unfair methods of competition also extended to unfair methods of competition used in export trade against American competitors engaged in export trade. This provision applied, however, only to American competitors; and it seems clear that Americans could employ methods of competition against foreign competitors which would have been unfair had they been used in the United States.

The law required every association to file with the Federal Trade Commission a verified written statement setting forth the location of its

[29]40 Stat. 516, chap. 50 (1918); 15 U.S.C.A. 61.

offices or places of business, and the names and addresses of all its officers and of all its stockholders. An association was also required to furnish the Commission with such information as the latter might require on organization, business, conduct, practices, management, etc. Whenever the Federal Trade Commission had reason to believe that an association or agreement under the Act was in restraint of trade within the United States, or in restraint of the export trade of any American competitor, it could conduct an investigation into the alleged violations of the law. The Commission could make recommendations to the association for readjustment of its business, if the Commission found that the law had been violated. If the association failed to comply, the Commission was instructed to refer its findings and recommendations to the Attorney General of the United States for such action as the latter deemed proper.

The Webb-Pomerene Act constitutes a direct contradiction of the basic antitrust policy of this country. Although it specifically applies only to export trade, the implications for domestic policy are such as to call for careful examination of the possible effects on the latter. This examination will be undertaken in the chapter on International Cartels,[30] where the interaction of policies in the foreign and domestic fields will be discussed.

Agricultural Marketing and Production Controls

A second major field of economic activity which has been granted substantial exemption from the operation of the antitrust laws, and from the philosophy upon which they are erected, is agriculture. The rapid growth of industrialization in the United States prior to World War I resulted in a basic shift in the structure of the economy and forced a readjustment in agriculture to a position of less relative importance than it had heretofore enjoyed. This change was not only suddenly halted by the outburst of World War I but also—temporarily, at least—was completely reversed. The tremendous demand for American agricultural products led to a disastrous expansion of productive capacity. Furthermore, the rapid development of mechanization and the substitution of motor for animal power only served to enhance the changes that were in evidence when the war broke out.

As a consequence, agriculture was faced with readjustments of major proportions after the price collapse of 1920. This situation precipitated a crisis in agriculture which led to a multitude of attempts to improve and stabilize agricultural prices, as well as to restrict competition in marketing and to reduce production. The success of co-operative marketing in California in certain agricultural specialities led to a good deal of legislation designed to extend this device. The attack on the California Associated Raisin Company in 1920, under the Sherman law, on the

[30]See Chapter 19, *infra*.

grounds that this organization was operating in restraint of trade, and the resulting consent decree, gave rise to the demand that agricultural co-operatives be given greater protection against the operation of the antitrust laws.

These various influences resulted in the passage of the Capper-Volstead Act in 1922.[31] This law provided that persons engaged in the production of agricultural products could act together in associations, corporations, or otherwise, for the purposes of collectively processing, preparing for market, handling, and marketing, in interstate and foreign commerce, such products of persons so engaged. The associations so formed could have marketing agencies in common, and such associations and their members could make the necessary contracts and agreements to effect their purposes. To reap the benefits of the Act, it was necessary that no member of the association be allowed more than one vote, that the association not pay dividends in excess of 8 per cent per annum, and that it should not deal in the products of nonmembers to an amount greater in value than such as were handled by it for members. If the Secretary of Agriculture had reason to believe that any association monopolized or restrained trade to such an extent that the price of any agricultural product was unduly enhanced, he was required to draw up a complaint. In the event that the association failed to obey the order to cease and desist from monopolization, the Secretary was instructed to request the appropriate district court to enforce his orders. The Secretary was also to notify the Attorney General of the filing of the complaint.

The principle that the formation of a joint agency by farmers, solely for the economical conduct of their own business, was not a violation of the antitrust laws was clearly enunciated in the Clayton Act. It was not necessary to pass legislation merely to permit co-operative marketing designed to bring about more efficient marketing of agricultural products. What the Capper-Volstead Act did was to signalize the beginning of the development of a federal program of pricing and production control in agriculture. That was in contradiction to our basic policy of competitive pricing.

Under the euphemistic term "stabilization," subsequent legislation expanded the restrictive possibilities of the Capper-Volstead Act and aided and abetted them by a variety of arrangements designed to limit production, enhance prices, and raise farm incomes by subsidies. Thus, the Co-operative Marketing Act of 1926[32] authorized agricultural co-operatives to exercise powers in handling statistical and other information that had been denied to open-price associations. The Agricultural Marketing Act of 1926[33] set up the Federal Farm Board, which became a special propaganda and service agency to agricultural co-operatives. The poli-

[31] 42 Stat. 388; 7 U.S.C.A. 291.
[32] 44 Stat. 802; 7 U.S.C.A. 451.
[33] 46 Stat. 11; 7 U.S.C.A. 601.

cies embodied in this legislation were extended after 1933. In 1937, the Agricultural Marketing Agreement Act[34] added further amendments to the law and re-enacted provisions set up in 1935, which explicitly authorized the Secretary of Agriculture to compel a minority of handlers of any line of produce to abide by a plan of distribution drawn up by and approved by the majority, or even (with the expressed approval of the President) without the approval of a majority of the handlers, if two thirds of the producers (three fourths in the case of California citrus) agreed to the arrangement. Furthermore, it was provided that, once a majority of occupiers decided that community regulation of grazing or farming operations would promote their mutual advantage, and once they drew up a code of fair range practice or a soil-use program, the minority must conform to the group plan, which was also to be policed by the group, not by the courts.[35]

Legislation in the years since World War II has been characterized by a continuous succession of laws designed to limit agricultural output and raise farm prices and incomes. That no solution to the "farm problem" has as yet been even remotely achieved is all to obvious. How the problem will be resolved is not at all apparent at the present time, but it is quite clear that the policies being pursued with regard to agriculture are in direct contradiction to the basic assumptions which underlie our professed attitude toward industry. It must be recognized that it was and will be necessary to take steps to bring about some fundamental readjustments in agriculture. However, a program which, by various devices, enables a large segment of our economic life to depart from the pattern of competition and private enterprise with governmental blessing and aid induces demands for similar privileges in other segments. Apart from the expensive nature of a policy that cannot bring the adjustments which the situation calls for, it is difficult to imagine that success can attend a vigorous and comprehensive attempt to control monopoly power over prices or to eliminate bigness, as such, when so large a group is excluded. A further contradiction is injected if one endeavors to reconcile this with a "Good Neighbor" policy and amicable international economic relations.

Labor

In many respects, the problems of labor occupy a unique position with regard to the antitrust laws. On the other hand, labor-management arrangements involving union agreements covering collective bargaining,

[34]50 Stat. 246; 7 U.S.C.A. 601.

[35]During the same period, a number of other laws were passed by Congress providing for price supports, commodity loans, crop insurance, soil conservation payments, surplus disposal, and export subsidies (L. S. Lyon, M. W. Watkins, and Victor Abramson, *Government and Economic Life*, Vol. II, [Washington, D.C.: Brookings Institution, 1940], chap. xxiii).

hiring and firing, closed shop, and so forth, have resulted in restrictions on competitive processes that are a far cry from the original philosophy of the Sherman Act. The limitations that may be imposed upon the freedom of action of the individual would not be tolerated for one moment under the law if engaged in even by small business. On the other hand, the position of the individual workman is such that union activity and collective bargaining over a wide range of employment are recognized as necessary substitutes for the lack of an effectively competitive market process.

Limitations imposed by the Sherman Act on the activities of organized labor led Congress to enact Sections 6 and 20 of the Clayton Act, granting what were believed to be extensive exemptions of the activities of organized labor from the antitrust laws. Court interpretation of these sections gave them a rather limited sphere of application. The passage of the Norris-LaGuardia Act in 1932[36] was intended to restore the broad purpose which Congress thought it had formulated in the Clayton Act. The final significant step in "emancipating" labor from the restrictions of the antitrust laws came with the National Labor Relations Act of 1935.[37] This gave positive recognition by federal law to the right of collective bargaining and required management to bargain with a union duly certified by the National Labor Relations Board.

The National Labor Relations (or Wagner) Act was modified by the Taft-Hartley Act[38] whereby there was added to the former list of unfair practices by employers a corresponding list of unfair practices by unions. This law forbade the closed shop, but it permitted the union shop in which workers, not members of a union, could be employed provided that they joined the union after they had been hired. The employers could present their views to employees concerning the desirability of unionization and they could petition the NLRB for an election. The Act also contained provisions designed to protect union members against misconduct by their leaders.

Nevertheless, as the result of public policy, organized labor has come to enjoy very extensive monopoly privileges. This is inescapable under the present concept of collective bargaining. There seems to be a rather widespread feeling, however, that the monopoly power of organized labor has gone too far. Whatever may be the facts and the judgment on them, it seems to be clear that labor presents sufficiently differentiated problems to warrant special treatment under antitrust. This does not mean that it should be totally exempt, nor does it mean that public policy toward labor should be contradictory to the philosophy of the antitrust laws. What it does mean is that the problems presented by organized labor should be dealt with by a comprehensive labor-manage-

[36] 47 Stat. 70 (1932).
[37] 49 Stat. L. 449 (1935). This is commonly known as the Wagner Act.
[38] 61 Stat. 136 (1947).

ment code which is separate from the antitrust laws but not in conflict with or contradictory to them.

Transportation and Public Utilities

Transportation and public utilities have long fallen into the category of industries affected with a public interest. As a result, they have been subject to more control by the state than most other economic enterprises. With the coming of the railroad, telephone, electricity, and so forth, technical developments imposed such severe limitations on competition among firms that competition became a thoroughly inadequate device for bringing about an economical allocation of resources and protecting the consumer. Regulation by public authority was developed as one of the means of remedying this deficiency. This regulation was designed to achieve what competition and the antitrust laws could not have achieved. This has, on occasion given rise to conflicts of jurisdiction,[39] as well as controversies over the effectiveness of the regulatory agencies in carrying out the duties assigned to them. These are matters that can be dealt with only after careful examination of the industries and the policies which have been adopted to control them. This is done in a later section of this book. The point to be made here is that the antitrust laws are not applicable over a wide range to these industries because of the technical structure of the latter and because of the authority which must be accorded to the regulatory agencies if these agencies are to be effective.

Insurance

The insurance business was not subject to federal laws until the decision of the Supreme Court in the Southeastern Underwriters case. Previously, insurance had been subject only to state laws. No federal legislation had been developed to deal with the special problems of that business. Congress was not prepared to enact comprehensive legislation and has not yet seen fit to do so. To fill the gap, however, it passed, in 1945, the Walter-McCarran Act,[40] which exempts the business of insurance from the federal antitrust laws if it is regulated by the state, but which states that such laws "shall be applicable to the business of insurance to the extent that such business is not regulated by state law."

Limitations on Exemptions

A word of caution should be injected on the scope of exemptions from the antitrust laws such as apply to transportation, public utilities, and other activities which are supposed to be accompanied by controls that are not of themselves contrary to the antitrust laws. These exemp-

[39] *Judicial Doctrine of Primary Jurisdiction as Applied in Antitrust Suits* (Staff Report, Committee on the Judiciary, House of Representatives, 84th Cong., 2nd sess. [Washington, D.C.: U.S. Government Printing Office, 1957]).

[40] 59 Stat. 33 (1945).

tions should be distinguished from policies such as agricultural price supports that run counter to competition and the free market. The Supreme Court has been very strict in construing these exemptions by requiring that they be explicit and exclusive. Thus it has held that milk-marketing arrangements and co-operatives[41] may be subject to the antitrust laws; that national banks are not exempt from the Sherman and Clayton Acts;[42] that resale price maintenance must move along the route strictly marked out by the resale price maintenance laws;[43] and that the Federal Power Commission does not have control over mergers of natural gas companies achieved by stock acquisition.[44] In *Pan-American World Airways* v. *United States* (1963),[45] the majority of the Supreme Court, on an issue of alleged violation of Sections 1, 2, and 3 of the Sherman Act, held that the narrow questions presented by the complaint had been entrusted to the Civil Aeronautics Board and that the lower court should have dismissed the complaint which had been filed by the Aeronautics Board. However, the majority stated that "While the Board is empowered to deal with numerous aspects of what are normally thought of as antitrust problems, those entrusted to it encompass only a fraction of the total . . . We, therefore, refuse to hold that there are no antitrust violations left to the Department of Justice to enforce."[46] In a vigorous dissent, Mr. Justice Brennan, joined by Chief Justice Warren, took the position that even this interpretation was too broad in its grant of authority to the Civil Aeronautics Board. ". . . although this Court has not until today passed on the question whether the Aeronautics Act repealed by implication any part of the antitrust laws, the lower federal courts have uniformly held that it did not.—this Act [Sherman] embodies perhaps the most basic economic policy of our society, basic and continuing: abhorrence of monopoly."[47]

Until the passage of the Reed-Bulwinkle Act in 1948, railroad rate-making through rate bureaus was held to be illegal, even though the rates, after having been drawn up by the bureaus, were submitted to the Interstate Commerce Commission for its consent.[48] The authority of the Interstate Commerce Commission over railroads, and other common

[41] *United States* v. *Borden Co.* 308 U.S. 188. (1939); *Maryland and Virginia Milk Producers Association, Inc.* v. *United States* 362 U.S. 458 (1960).

[42] *United States* v. *Philadelphia National Bank* 374 U.S. 321 (1963); *United States* v. *First National Bank and Trust Co. of Lexington*, 376 U.S. 655 (1964).

[43] *United States* v. *Bausch and Lomb Optical Co.*, 321 U.S. 707 (1944); *United States* v. *Univis Lens Co.*, 316 U.S. 241 (1942); *United States* v. *McKesson and Robbins, Inc.* 351 U.S. 305 (1956).

[44] *California* v. *Federal Power Commission*, 369 U.S. 482 (1962).

[45] 371 U.S. 296.

[46] *Ibid.*, p. 305.

[47] *Ibid.*, pp. 323, 324. See also *U.S.* v. *Radio Corp. of America*, 358 U.S. 334 (1959) for application of Sherman Act to enterprises under control of the Federal Communications Commission.

[48] *State of Georgia* v. *Pennsylvania Railroad Co.*, 324 U.S. 439 (1945).

carriers, excepting air, would appear to be exclusive, but this may be open to challenge because the Commission is given the responsibility of enforcing the amended Section 7 of the Clayton Act as it applies to carriers under its jurisdiction. The Commission, however, may have to justify its avoidance of the tests of illegality that have been laid down, on the grounds of overriding considerations in transport policy and the Interstate Commerce Act. In a vigorous dissenting opinion to Commission approval of the Seaboard Air Line-Atlantic Coast Line railroad merger,[49] Commissioner Webb stated, "What the statement says, in effect, is that the meaning of Section 7 of the Clayton Act in merger proceedings is not to be found in the opinions of the judiciary, but is to be determined exclusively by transportation expertise. This is a bold grab for power in which the courts are not likely to acquiesce."[50]

STATE ANTITRUST

Since the passage of the Sherman Act, antitrust has become almost completely a matter of federal concern. Most of the states legalize resale price maintenance by fair-trade laws; and many impose limitations on competition by unfair practices acts which prohibit selling below cost—a term which, in California, is defined as average cost for the industry. These state laws are clearly in conflict with the theory of antitrust. Some states, however, do have antimonopoly laws. Enforcement, unfortunately, is either nonexistent or at a very low ebb. This ought not to be so, for there is much to be done that can be really effective only at the state level. Here is an area where the advocates of states' rights can demonstrate their readiness to deal with problems at the local level.

Ironically, the states have proved to be the jurisdictions where the most extensive restrictions on competition have originated and have been maintained. California, an allegedly progressive state, has the original fair-trade law (1931), an unfair practices act, state control of milk prices, state enforcement of resale prices in liquor, and state-sanctioned price fixing in some trades such as barber shops,[51] together with the most complete control anywhere of public utilities and motor transport. Local activities and small business scarcely seem to be a bulwark against monopolistic practices at least as far as their own activities are concerned.

[49]*Seaboard Air Line Railroad Company-Merger-Atlantic Coast Line Railroad Company*, Interstate Commerce Commission, 320 I.C.C. 122 (1963).

[50]*Ibid.*, p. 227.

[51]See Wm. F. Brown and Ralph Cassady, Jr., "Guild Pricing in the Service Trades," *Quarterly Journal of Economics*, Vol. LXI (February, 1947), pp. 311–38.

Chapter 13 AGENCIES FOR ENFORCING THE ANTITRUST LAWS

The responsibility for the enforcement of the antitrust laws of the United States is placed primarily in the hands of three agencies: the courts, the Attorney General of the United States, and the Federal Trade Commission. Each of these agencies enjoys a unique status and plays a distinct and separate role in the nation's antitrust policy. Because of this division of authority, there has been a lack of a unified and co-ordinated approach which has frequently led to contradictory results. Congress has decided to maintain the separate means of enforcement, however; and the agencies have therefore had to develop their own concepts of policy within their respective spheres of competence and responsibility.

THE ROLE OF THE COURTS

In the final analysis, all laws are interpreted and enforced by the courts. It is for them to decide what the law means and what authority the other agencies enjoy under the law, and to be the last resort in the event of dispute over the application of the laws. In this sense, the courts enforce all the laws of the land. In so doing, however, they merely sit in judgment to resolve the issues between the disputants. The initiative for court action must be taken by some party. This may be done by private suit, by suit brought by some agency of the government with authority for that purpose, or by appeal against the order of some government agency which has the power to issue orders and enforce them in the absence of appeal to the courts. Thus, the courts are the ultimate legal authority on all matters relating to antitrust and the regulation of industry.

Specific Functions in Antitrust

As was pointed out in the previous chapter, enforcement of the Sherman Act is entirely through the medium of the federal courts. Sections 2, 3, 7, and 8 of the Clayton Act may be enforced in the same manner. This procedure imposes upon the courts the responsibility of deciding the meaning and application of these laws, assessing penalties, awarding damages in private suits, and devising appropriate remedies to prevent future violations. Of themselves, these are not unique functions for courts to perform; indeed, they are the essence of court responsibilities. However, "in the antitrust field the courts have been accorded, by common consent, an authority they have in no other branch of enacted law."[1] It is the part which the courts play in the formation of public policy that gives them their unique role in antitrust and in regulation in the United States.

The Courts and Public Policy

The interpretation and application of the Sherman and Clayton Acts and the devising of remedies to prevent firms from violating them in the future involve broad and fundamental problems of economic policy. Restraint of trade, monopolizing, price discrimination, and activities the effect of which may be substantially to lessen competition, are not concepts that can be given a precise content; at least, they have not been given one in the legislation. Application of these concepts to modern business situations necessitates an evaluation in terms of public policy and public interest.

The courts are also assessed with the responsibility of devising remedies to prevent future violations. Here again, considerations of public interest and public policy weigh heavily. The dissolution of a huge industrial enterprise or divestment of ownership of stock or assets entails problems of organization and impact upon markets that require a thoroughgoing evaluation of public as well as private effects. With these responsibilities imposed upon them, the courts cannot escape the role of molding economic policy in antitrust. This may too frequently lead to bad law; but if so, Congress must supply the remedy by assigning initial enforcement to some other agency.

THE DEPARTMENT OF JUSTICE

The Antitrust Division

The initiative for judicial enforcement of the antitrust laws is vested in the Attorney General of the United States. In 1903, the Antitrust Division of the Department of Justice was established under an assistant attorney general in charge of antitrust.

The function of the Antitrust Division is primarily that of a prosecutor of those who violate those antitrust laws which the Attorney General is charged with enforcing. To carry out its work, it employs a staff of attorneys, economists, and special investigators. It also receives assistance from the Federal Bureau of Investigation. The appropriations for the Division to carry out its functions were $5.9 million in 1962 and $6.24 million in 1963—not very impressive sums considering the importance and volume of the work to be done, although the amount in 1963 was nearly twice that which was available in 1953.

[1] *United States* v. *United Shoe Machinery Corp.*, 110 Fed. Supp. 295, 348 (1953).

Investigative Procedures

Investigations by the Antitrust Division, and the cases that originate therefrom, stem from complaints of private citizens or government agencies and from surveys made by the Division's own staff of economists. The identity of complainants is, on request, preserved as confidential, and no formal method is necessary to inform the Division of an alleged violation. If it is decided to make an investigation, four types of inquiries may be made—the preliminary inquiry, an F.B.I. investigation, a grand jury investigation, and investigation under the Antitrust Civil Process Act.[2]

Preliminary Inquiry. If a complaint is considered to be of sufficient importance to warrant attention, the Assistant Attorney General authorizes a preliminary inquiry. This may be made by the personnel of the Division or by the Federal Bureau of Investigation. The decision whether to proceed further will depend upon the outcome of the investigation.

F.B.I. Investigation. If a broader investigation is warranted, the Division usually requests the F.B.I. to make a full-scale investigation. This agency engages in an exclusively fact-finding examination.

Grand Jury Investigations. If the potential defendant refuses to give the F.B.I. the information it requests, the Division may present the matter to a federal grand jury. Grand jury investigations usually are instituted by the issuance of *subpoenas duces tecum* which require the production of designated documents. Persons called before the grand jury to appear and testify in an antitrust investigation are granted immunity from criminal prosecution "for or on account of any transaction, matter, or thing concerning which he may testify or produce evidence documentary or otherwise." The grand jury may be used only when criminal proceedings are contemplated.

The Civil Investigative Demand. Under the Antitrust Civil Process Act the Assistant Attorney General may issue a Civil Investigative Demand to any corporation, association partnership, or other legal entity not a natural person, calling for the production of any documentary material relating to any suspected antitrust violation. The C.I.D. may be enforced by compulsory court procedure and is subject to the same limitations as a grand jury *subpoena duces tecum.* The custodian to whom the documents are to be made available is always either a staff attorney or an F.B.I. agent. A C.I.D. can be used only to secure documentary evidence, not to compel testimony.

In 1961 the Antitrust Division established a new section to represent the public interest in preserving a free and competitive economy when issues of competition are involved in proceedings before executive, administrative, and regulatory agencies. It is this section that has intervened in railroad merger applications before the Interstate Commerce

[2]Public Law 87–664, statute 7C548 (1962). 10 U.S.C. 9342(E).

Commission, and the merger application of American Airlines and Eastern Airlines before the Civil Aeronautics Board.[3]

Criminal versus Civil Actions

The Sherman Act gives the Attorney General the choice of civil action, criminal action, or both. By commencing criminal prosecution, he is not barred from filing a companion civil case against the same defendants. This is done when, in addition to criminal penalties, injunctive relief to prohibit certain types of future conduct is also sought.

In general, the Antitrust Division proceeds criminally against (1) price fixing; (2) other violations of the Sherman Act, where there is proof of a specific intent to restrain trade or to monopolize; (3) a less easily defined category of cases, involving proof of use of predatory practices (boycotts, for example) to accomplish the objective of the combination or conspiracy; (4) defendants previously found guilty of similar antitrust violations; (5) a defendant who knows that practices similar to those charged had been outlawed, in a prior civil or criminal suit against other persons.[4]

Before a criminal trial begins, the defendant may issue a plea of *nolo contendere*, in which he states that he does not wish to contest the charge. Although the defendant does not admit guilt the "no contest" plea is an implied admission of guilt and equivalent to a guilty plea for the purpose only of a criminal case under the antitrust laws. If the court accepts the plea, the defendant is subject to the imposition of the same punishment under either a guilty or a *nolo contendere* plea, but the *nolo contendere* plea cannot be used as an admission of guilt in litigation with other parties, such, for example, as a private antitrust damage suit.

Consent Decrees

Civil action under the antitrust laws may be concluded before the completion of trial or, in certain cases, even before the filing of a civil complaint, by an agreement between the defendants and the government, known as a "consent decree." The defendants explicitly deny admission of guilt but agree to accept provisions arrived at by negotiation. The agreement, when approved by a court, embodies the essential force of a litigated judgment. From 1935 to 1954, 72 per cent of civil actions brought by the Antitrust Division were terminated by consent decrees.[5]

The device has been used by the government to save the expense of protracted trials as well as to secure the advantage of informal negotiations where issues of fact might offer difficulties of proof in a court trial. The defendants may derive advantage because the Clayton Act permits

[3]*Annual Report of the Attorney General of the United States* (June 30, 1962), p. 100.

[4]Report of the Attorney General's National Committee, *Antitrust Laws* (Washington, D.C.: U.S. Government Printing Office, 1955), p. 350.

[5]*Ibid.*, p. 360.

treble-damage plaintiffs to introduce final judgments or decrees, rendered in government antitrust actions against the same defendants, as prima-facie evidence of all issues determined in the prior adjudication, thereby simplifying the task of the plaintiff. If the action is terminated by a consent judgment or decree before any testimony has been taken the defendants are exempt from the statutory provision of the Clayton Act.

The Clearance Program

The Attorney General is not permitted to give legal advice to private parties. Since the amendment of Section 7 of the Clayton Act, however, a "clearance" program has been set up, under which counsel for corporations may discuss with the Antitrust Division the legality of proposed mergers. If the counsel requests clearance and the Division believes that violation of the law is likely, it will inform him that it will not undertake to withhold proceedings should the merger be consummated. If no violation is apparent, counsel receives a letter stating that no action is presently contemplated. Merger clearance is not obtainable unless both parties to the merger have already agreed to proceed with it. Careful evaluation of all the relevant data is undertaken by the Antitrust Division before it gives its answer.[6]

Private parties may also submit certain matters to the Antitrust Division for "release" or "clearance" letters. These "release" letters permit and advance review of business plans for proposed operations so as to ascertain whether they involve risk of criminal prosecution if adopted. Release and clearance commitments are given only in formal written communications, and constitute a waiver of the government's right to proceed in a criminal case. They do not preclude civil action, however.[7]

THE INDEPENDENT REGULATORY COMMISSION

Development of the Regulatory Commission

The independent regulatory commission is literally an "invention" of the United States and one of this country's unique contributions to the regulation of private industry. It has now been in existence for over 70 years as an agency of the federal government. The Interstate Commerce Commission was the first of these federal agencies. It was established in 1887, with limited powers to regulate railroad rates and services. During the present century, its scope and authority have been extended so that, today, it stands as the most comprehensive and powerful commission in the country.

[6]J. G. Van Cise, *Understanding the Antitrust Laws* (New York: Practising Law Institute, 1955), pp. 136ff.

[7]For a summary of the procedures of the Antitrust Division, see L. Loevinger, "The Department of Justice and the Antitrust Laws" in J. G. Van Cise, *Understanding the Antitrust Laws* (New York: Practising Law Institute, 1963) pp. 191–210.

The idea of the independent regulatory commission has been extended to other spheres of federal control in the last 45 years. Those of immediate interest to the subject of this presentation are the Federal Trade Commission, which was set up in 1914; the Federal Power Commission, in 1930; the Federal Communications Commission, in 1934; and the Civil Aeronautics Board, in 1938. This type of commission now occupies a well-established position in our framework of government and has gained a wealth of experience in the many and varied aspects of the regulation of business.

Nature of the Regulatory Commission

The theory underlying the functions and organization of the independent regulatory commission is that it is an expert body composed of individuals appointed for the purpose of providing a continuity of business regulation that neither the courts nor the legislature can supply. The courts are unable to do it, because they can act only on the basis of litigation and only on the issues brought before them. They cannot act on their own initiative. Legislatures, by their very nature, are unable to act in an administrative capacity and are unable to supply the day-to-day and individualized regulations that modern business conditions require.

The regulatory commission is supposed to be a nonpolitical agency administering the law, within the framework of the Constitution, according to the intent of Congress, as expressed in the governing statutes. It is for this reason that it is considered essential that such a commission enjoy independent status. Accordingly, commissioners are appointed by the President and approved by the Senate for a fixed term of office. They are removable during their terms only for substantially the same reasons as judges.[8] They may not engage in any other business, vocation, or employment while they are in office.

The regulatory commission is regarded as an arm of the legislative and judiciary branches of the government, and is free from control of the executive. In other words, it occupies a dual position, which has been characterized as quasi-legislative and quasi-judicial.[9] This means that it acts in a legislative capacity when it fills out legislation by promulgating rules. Congress may prescribe broad standards to carry out its purposes, such as requiring that rates be just and reasonable, or by prohibiting unfair methods of competition. Congress, however, can seldom lay down detailed rules to carry out these standards, because this would be too rigid for effective regulation. The commission takes over this task.

[8]See *Humphrey's Executor* v. *United States*, 295 U.S. 602 (1935).

[9]For an extended discussion of these functions, see dissenting opinion of Mr. Justice Jackson in *Federal Trade Commission* v. *The Ruberoid Co.*, 343 U.S. 470 (1952). See Chapter 20 for an appraisal of the independent commission in antitrust enforcement and Chapter 24 on transportation.

When it interprets the law and requires compliance with the rules it has established, it then acts in a judicial capacity. In this capacity, it is predominantly a fact-finding body, by which activity it provides the basis upon which detailed regulations may be issued and public policy developed. Most of the statutes under which the commissions operate specify that commission findings as to the facts shall be conclusive, if supported by adequate evidence.

In enforcing the laws assigned to them, commissions in effect may also discharge executive functions in that they endeavor to ascertain violations of the laws and then undertake to bring the alleged violators before them for trial. Thus, a commission may be said to occupy the position of both prosecutor and judge, although the commissioners themselves never act as trial lawyers. This task is left to the attorneys of the staff or to independent counsel. Commission procedures may vary in the cases that are presented for adjudication. All complaints coming before the Federal Trade Commission under the antitrust laws are prosecuted by the attorneys of its staff. There are no adversary proceedings. The Interstate Commerce Commission, on the other hand, entertains adversary proceedings under which the contestants supply their own counsel. Thus, commissions are not always in the position of both prosecutor and judge.

The quasi-judicial, quasi-legislative functions of commissions commonly put them in the position of assuming the tasks of legislator, prosecutor, and judge, all at the same time. Within their statutory power, they promulgate rules and regulations, take the necessary steps to enforce them, and sit in judgment upon those who fail to comply. In performing these tasks, however, they are primarily engaged in prescribing and defining the future privileges and duties of persons subject to regulation. In large measure, this involves making and applying policies to carry out the objectives and standards of the governing statutes. In the strict sense of the word, commissions do not act as prosecutors. They may hail alleged violators before them, but they do not seek or impose penalties. Instead, they issue orders designed to prevent future violations or to secure compliance with announced rules of conduct. Commissions with broad regulatory powers such as those possessed by the Interstate Commerce Commission also exercise authority over such matters as the rates to be charged by the enterprises under their control, service standards, certificates of entry, issuance of securities, and accounting procedures. The statutes usually contain penalties for failure to obey orders, unless relief from them is obtained by prescribed procedures, but the imposition of the penalty rests in the hands of the courts.

In their formal proceedings, commissions function in much the same way as courts. The commissioners sit as judges on the presentations of the commission's attorneys and/or those of the interested private parties. Evidence is read into the record by the usual procedure of direct examination and cross-examination, just as in a court trial, except that the rules of evidence are not as strict. As a consequence, matters may be introduced into the record for the information of the commission that would be ruled out in a court case. A commission may also request testimony on matters not called for in the proceedings when they started, on the grounds that such information is pertinent to the question at hand. A commission may take its own initiative in this regard, just as it may do in instituting a case. A court cannot take such initiative under either circumstance. When the trial is concluded, the commission may issue an opinion and order which may be embodied in a written document very similar to a court decision. The orders are usually self-enforcing, in the sense that they are binding upon respondents unless set to one side by court order arising from an appeal.

In addition to performing their functions as regulatory agencies, commissions may also act as fact-finding bodies for the purpose of securing information that may be used as a basis for the formulation of public policy toward business and for recommendations to Congress for legislative action. The investigations may be made by the staff under commission direction, or they may be made by the members of the commission holding hearings like a congressional committee. Investigations are usually confined to the field over which the commission has regulatory authority, but the Federal Trade Commission has been asked to undertake investigations in areas quite outside of those covered by its enforcement responsibilities.

Courts versus Commissions in Regulation

When, as in the case of the Sherman Act, the courts alone are given the power of enforcement, the regulatory commission plays no part. When, however, a commission is assigned the responsibility for initial enforcement, as in the Interstate Commerce Act, the courts still have a function to perform. The courts are really the sole judges of the law, and only court decisions act as legal precedents. The courts alone can try criminal cases, assess penalties, and award damages. Finally, only the courts can compel observance of a commission order if a respondent refuses to comply.

On the other hand, the commission is the expert body on policy, the authority on matters of fact, and the agency through which the regulatory program is carried out. Over the years, the courts have come to recognize this status of the commission and have gradually placed limitations upon their restriction of commission authority. They now confine their review of commission deliberations to three main considerations:[10]

[10]Commission on the Organization of the Executive Branch of the Government, *Task Force Report on Regulatory Commissions* (Washington, D.C.: U.S. Government Printing Office, 1949), p. 15.

1. The courts will review the proceedings of the commission to assure that they have been conducted in accordance with procedures required by the statute and by due process of law. This insures that interested parties have a fair opportunity to present their evidence and arguments.

2. The courts may also review the activities and orders of commissions to make sure that they do not exceed the powers conferred by the legislation. This serves to keep the commissions within the statutory bounds prescribed by Congress.

3. Where action of a commission depends upon a factual record, the courts can review a decision or order to determine whether it was supported by substantial evidence in the record. Where substantial evidence does exist, the action of the commission will be sustained, even though the court might itself have come to a different conclusion.

Thus, judicial review of commission decisions is a safeguard against arbitrary or capricious actions, or actions which do not conform to statutory standards or authority, or actions which are not in accordance with fair procedure or substantial evidence. Finally, court review of commission decisions is in keeping with our legal procedure, whereby, upon appeal, a higher court is able to review the decisions of a lower one.

THE FEDERAL TRADE COMMISSION

The basic conception behind the establishment of the Federal Trade Commission and the legislation underlying it was twofold: (1) a reinforcement of the laws against monopoly and restraint of trade; and (2) a continuous administrative supervision of general business policies, with the objective of preserving and promoting healthy and thoroughgoing competition. To this end, the Clayton Act proscribed specific practices which had escaped the general prohibitions of the Sherman law. The more evasive methods which, in devious and subtle ways, injured competition or destroyed its effectiveness were left for the Federal Trade Commission to discover, under the powers to prohibit unfair methods of competition set forth in Section 5 of the Federal Trade Commission Act. It was believed that only an administrative tribunal could provide the continuity of policy and enforcement necessary for the satisfactory development of a detailed code of conduct. The idea was that rules of the game evolved under continuous supervision would maintain a competitive atmosphere that would insure the existence of competition, which, in turn, would adequately and effectively protect public interest. Thus, it was the intent of the legislation to establish an agency which would develop a coherent public policy in the field of competitive business.

The Federal Trade Commission was consequently given two broad functions: (1) the combatting of interference with competition by enforcing the specific provisions of the Clayton Act and Section 5 of the Federal Trade Commission Act and (2) the investigation of business activity. The second function had two aspects. As an additional agency to aid in the enforcement of the antitrust laws, the Commission had the power to investigate the manner in which court decrees under the antitrust laws were being complied with; and at the request of the Attorney General, it was compelled to do so. The courts were authorized to refer civil suits to the Commission for recommendations on the appropriate decree. The Commission was also required, upon the direction of the President or either house of Congress, to institute investigations into alleged violations of the antitrust acts by any corporation. Upon application by the Attorney General, it was to investigate the activities of any corporation alleged to be in violation of the antitrust act and to make recommendations, in order that the corporation in question could bring itself into conformity with the law. Finally, the Commission was empowered to make investigations into the conduct and structure of business, in order to provide publicity and to secure information upon which the further development of public policy could be predicated.

The difficulties which the Commission encountered in discharging its responsibility to promote the kind of competition that would, among other things, give adequate protection to the consumer, led to an expansion of the legislation so that the protection of the consumer alone became sufficient grounds for administrative action. As a consequence, in the period subsequent to the Wheeler-Lea Act of 1938, Commission attention came increasingly to be focussed on practices that deceived, or were alleged to deceive, the consumer. These practices were held to be inimical to healthy competition, but it was necessary to prove only injury to consumer. Protection of the consumer has thus become an additional objective of the Federal Trade Commission Act, as amended, and enforcement of this aspect of the law has come to occupy a large portion of the Commission's time and budget. In the fiscal year 1963 about $4 million of its total budget of $11½ million was spent to halt the cheating of consumers, principally by false advertising.[11]

Administrative Organization

The administration of the Commission is centered in the hands of the chairman who is appointed by the President from one of the five members of the Commission. The detailed administrative task of guiding the activities of the staff is in the hands of the executive director, who is the chief operating official. He exercises direct supervision over the administrative offices and the operating bureaus. The offices of the General Counsel, Hearing Examiners, Secretary and Special Legal Assistants report directly to the chairman. The secretary of the Commission is the legal custodian of all the records and he signs the official documents. In addition he is the liaison officer with Congress and with other government agencies.

The internal organization of the Commission has been changed a number of times since 1914, the most recent shifts coming as the result

[11] *Annual Report of the Federal Trade Commission*, 1963 (Washington, D.C.: U.S. Government Printing Office) p. 11.

of activities of the Hoover Commission and the endeavors of President Eisenhower to revitalize the agency. The result is an organizational structure quite different from that which previously obtained, and one that is designed to focus responsibility for the discharge of functions.[12] (See Figure 4.) The description of organization which follows is taken from the *Annual Report* of 1962.

Office of the General Counsel

The general counsel is the chief law officer of the Commission and the principal legal adviser to it and to the staff. He and his staff represent the Commission in all cases advancing beyond the agency or otherwise arising in the courts. All litigation arising in the U.S. courts of appeal,

FIGURE 4

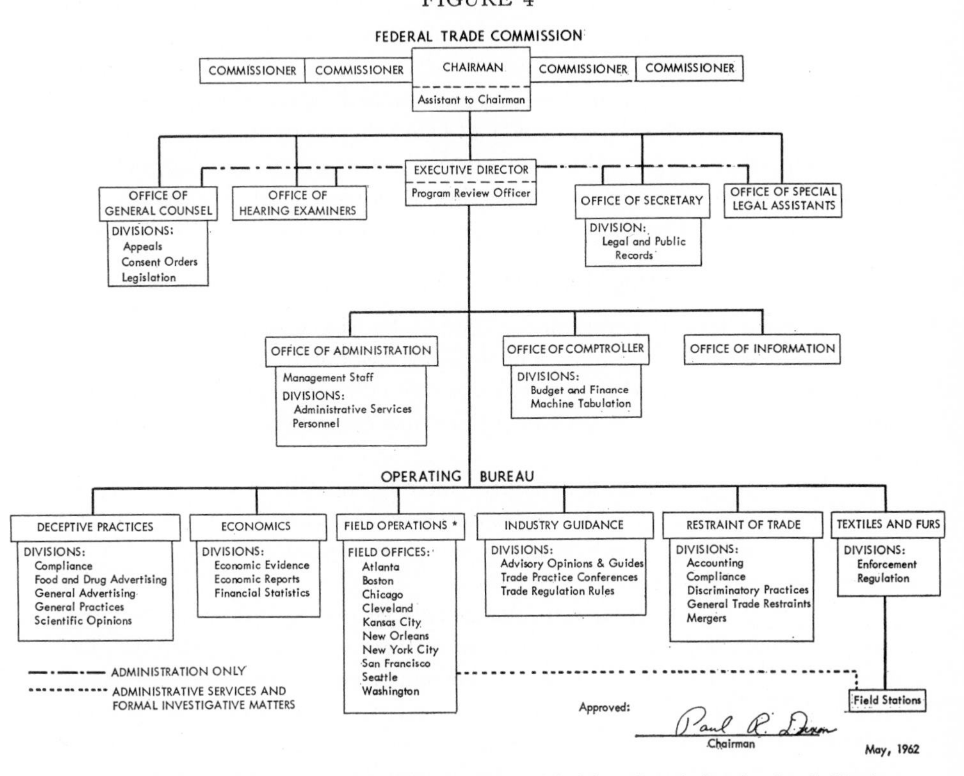

*To these should be added a field office in Arlington, Virginia and one in Los Angeles, California.

Reproduced from the *Annual Report* of the Federal Trade Commission (1962), p. 21.

[12]See *Current Antitrust Problems* (Hearings before Committee on the Judiciary, House of Representatives, 84th Cong., 1st sess.) (Washington, D.C.: U.S. Government Printing Office, 1955), Part III, Serial No. 3, pp. 2368 f.; Federal Trade Commission. *Annual Reports* (Washington, D.C.: U.S. Government Printing Office, 1956).

or the Court of Customs and Patents Appeals, is handled by the Office of the General Counsel. Commission cases that reach the Supreme Court, however, are handled by the Department of Justice, which represents the Commission in that court. The cases are prepared for presentation with the collaboration of the Office of General Counsel. Civil suits involving the assessment of penalties or firms charged with violating case and desist orders are prosecuted by the Department of Justice.

The Office of General Counsel passes upon all trade practice rules and "guides" prior to their appeal and issuance by the Commission. The Office also has charge of the review, analyses, and preparation of the reports of the Commission on new legislation. In addition, the General Counsel represents the Commission in hearings before congressional committees.

It should be noted that the general counsel is the legal officer who acts for the Commission to secure compliance with its program and in cases which go before the courts. He does not participate in the legal proceedings which lead to the issuance of orders by the Commission. These matters are the responsibility of other departments of the Commission. Thus, there is an endeavor to make a clear-cut distinction between those who present the evidence to the Commission for its decision and those who are responsible for enforcement when the order has been issued.

Office of Hearing Examiners

When a formal complaint is issued by the Commission, it is assigned to a hearing examiner who has the responsibility of taking testimony in support of and in opposition to the allegations of the complaint. During the year 1962, a staff of 22 hearing examiners served the Commission.

The Administrative Procedure Act outlines the powers and duties of all hearing examiners in the federal service, including the Federal Trade Commission. Their appointment and tenure are under the authority of the Civil Service Commission.

Hearing examiners are in charge of cases from the time the Commission issues its complaint until the initial decision is rendered. They hold pretrial conferences; conduct hearings; rule upon offers of proof, admissibility of evidence, and all procedural and other interlocutory motions; and make and file an initial decision in each proceeding. In the performance of their duties as adjudication officers, hearing examiners are exempt from direction, supervision, or control of the Commission except for administrative purposes.[13]

When a hearing examiner has completed the taking of testimony

[13]For a discussion of the problems of the role of the hearing examiner, see *Major Administrative Process Problems*, Hearings, Subcommittee on Interstate and Foreign Commerce, House of Representatives, 86th Cong., 1st sess. (Washington, D.C.: Government Printing Office, 1959) pp. 542–66.

in any case, he allows the attorneys for both parties to file proposed findings of fact and draft of order. Thereafter he prepares and files an initial decision which, under the Administrative Procedure Act and the Commission's rules, becomes the decision of the Commission if no petition for review is granted or if the Commission itself does not put the case on its own docket for review. In any event, the decision of the hearing examiner becomes a part of the formal record and is taken into consideration by the federal courts in any review of the case. The Commission may adopt, in whole or in part, the decision of the hearing examiner or may set it aside completely, in which case the Commission either rewrites the decision or remands it to the hearing examiner for the taking of further testimony.

Operating Bureaus

To assist it in discharging the duties imposed upon it by various laws, the Commission has six operating bureaus. The law enforcement activities are carried on primarily through the Bureau of Restraint of Trade, the Bureau of Deceptive Practices, and the Bureau of Textiles and Furs. The Bureau of Field Operations is responsible for field investigational work; the Bureau of Industry Guidance deals with voluntary compliance through co-operation with industry; and the Bureau of Economics undertakes economic investigations.

Bureau of Restraint of Trade. This bureau makes all preliminary investigations of restraints of trade under Section 5 of the Federal Trade Commission Act and alleged violations of Sections 2, 3, 7, and 8 of the Clayton Act. It conducts the trial work connected with these sections of the law. In addition it, upon request of the Department of Justice, investigates and reports on compliance with decrees obtained by the Department of Justice under the Sherman Act. The Division of Mergers analyzes acquisitions and mergers within the jurisdiction of the Commission and takes action against those that appear to be unlawful. The Division of General Restraints has the responsibility for all matters relating to restraint of trade within the scope of Section 5 of the Trade Commission Act. Finally, the Division of Accounting prepares accounting analyses and policies of respondents in connection with: (1) alleged discrimination under the amended Section 2 of the Clayton Act; (2) cost data submitted by respondents in justification of price discrimination under the Robinson-Patman Act; (3) alleged price-fixing cases under Section 5 of the Trade Commission Act; and (4) alleged sales below cost in violation of Section 5 of the Trade Commission Act.

Bureau of Deceptive Practices. This bureau is responsible for investigation and trial of all cases involving acts or practices alleged to be deceptive under Sections 5 and 12 of the Trade Commission Act and for maintaining compliance with cease and desist orders entered in such cases. The actions under Section 12 are directed at preventing false advertising of foods, drugs, cosmetics, and therapeutic devices, while those under Section 5 cover all types of goods and services sold in commerce, and all possible forms of deception including false advertising, misbranding, oral misrepresentation, and deceptive sales schemes. Investigation and trial work is carried on by the Divisions of Food and Drug Advertising, General Advertising, and General Practices. Obtaining and maintaining compliance with cease and desist orders on deceptive practices is the responsibility of the Division of Compliance. The Division of Scientific Opinion furnishes the other divisions with information and advice on matters involving medical and scientific questions.

Bureau of Textiles and Furs. This bureau is responsible for administering and enforcing the Wool Products Labeling Act, the Fur Products Labeling Act, the Flammable Fabrics Act, and the Textile Fiber Products Identification Act. The Division of Regulation counsels the textile and fur industries on the legislation and regulations, and also conducts routine inspections of manufacturers. The Division of Enforcement prosecutes major violations and also maintains a screening laboratory for testing fabrics and furs. The Division of Compliance polices the cease and desist orders.

Bureau of Field Operations. This bureau conducts the field investigations of the Commission through offices located in the major cities of the country.

Bureau of Economics. The function of this bureau is to given economic and statistical assistance to the Commission in its investigation and trial work, to make economic studies in response to requests of the President, of the Congress, or of the Commission, and to carry on a continuing program of quarterly financial statistics. The Division of Economic Evidence has primary responsibility for providing economic assistance to the legal bureaus and divisions in connection with the investigation and trial of cases. It is responsible for identifying, recording, and developing information regarding acquisitions and mergers. In addition, it reviews surveys made under Section 6 of the Trade Commission Act by the legal bureaus and assists in processing such surveys. The Division of Economic Reports undertakes to prepare the studies requested by the President, the Congress, or the Commission. A complete list of those that have been made since 1915 will be found at the end of each Annual Report. The Division of Financial Statistics has been responsible since 1947 for summarizing for each calendar quarter, uniform, confidential, financial statements collected from a probability sample of all enterprises classified as manufacturers, except newspapers, which are required to file U.S. Corporation Income Tax Form 1120. These quarterly summaries are published under the title of "Quarterly Financial Report for Manufacturing Corporations."

Bureau of Industry Guidance. This bureau administers the program of the Commission developed for the purpose of obtaining voluntary compliance with the laws administered by the Commission. On June 1, 1962, the bureau was given two new functions: (1) the administration of the new Trade Regulation Rule Procedure, and (2) the preparation of advisory opinions which are binding on the Commission.

The newly established Trade Regulation Rule procedure is administered by the Division of Trade Regulation Rules. Rules promulgated under this procedure express the experience and judgment of the Commission, based on facts of which it has knowledge, derived from studies, reports, investigations, hearings, and other proceedings concerning the substantive requirements of the statutes it administers. Industry members may apply for rules and may participate in the proceedings for establishing them. When a rule is related to an issue in an adjudicative proceeding thereafter instituted, the Commission may reply upon such a rule, provided that the respondent has been given a fair hearing on the legality and propriety of applying the rule to the particular case.

The Division of Advisory Opinions and Guides performs two functions: it prepares advisory opinions for the Commission which represents its official views, and it prepares and recommends the adoption of Guides to aid businessmen to comply voluntarily with the law. Prior to June 1, 1962, advisory opinions were given only at the staff level, and were not binding on the Commission. Now, however, whenever practicable, the Commission will render an advisory opinion, subject only to the right to reconsider its advice should such reconsideration be in the public interest. The "Guides" issued by the Division are a restatement in laymen's language of the law as previously decided by the Commission and the courts.

The Division of Trade Practice Conferences. The Division of Trade Practice Conferences administers the trade practice conference program. As a means of encouraging and maintaining free and fair competition in business by industrial co-operation, and of assisting in eliminating the burden arising from overcrowded dockets, the Federal Trade Commission instituted the trade practice conference procedure. The purpose of this is to develop fair-trade practice rules by conferences with particular industries, on the theory that if the majority of the competitors know clearly what the rules are, they will willingly conform to them. The Commission's approach to the problem is based upon the assumption that a large number of violations of the law arise either from ignorance or from misunderstanding. To the extent that these difficulties are eliminated and clarified by conference, the Commission is then left only with the task of proceeding against deliberate recalcitrants. Additional ideas behind the development of the trade practice conference are that problems of specific industries will be brought out and that rules designed to meet new situations and heretofore unrecognized difficulties will be constructed in such a way as to further healthy competition. In other words, the trade practice conference procedure is designed to develop a sort of "law merchant," on the generally valid assumption that the rules of competition must grow out of the workshop of competitive business. In 1962, 166 industries were operating under trade practice rules.

Adjudicative Procedures

The formal proceedings of the Commission commence with the investigation of alleged violations of the law. These investigations may stem from complaints of consumers, businessmen, governmental agencies, or the Commission's own motion. Any individual or business organization may lodge either a formal or an informal complaint with the Commission. Such a complainant is not regarded as a party to any proceedings, and the Commission does not disclose his identity. If formal action is decided upon, the case is that of the Commission. There are no adversary proceedings.

If the Commission decides that a complaint should be issued, the respondent is given the opportunity to negotiate an agreement containing a consent order prior to the opening of formal proceedings. Under current Commission procedure, the respondent is served with a copy of the complaint the Commission intends to issue and a proposed form of order, prior to any formal filing of complaint or any public announcement of alleged violation of the law. If the respondent indicates a desire to settle, an appropriate agreement is then entered into with the Commission.

When a formal complaint is issued by the Commission, it is assigned to a hearing examiner who has charge of the proceedings until an initial decision is rendered. The hearing examiner holds pretrial conferences; conducts the hearings (trial); and renders an initial decision. After the trial is concluded, the hearing examiner is required to render an initial decision. This must include a statement of (1) findings and conclusions, with the reasons or basis therefor, upon all the material issues of fact, law, or discretion presented in the record; and (2) an appropriate order based upon a consideration of the whole record and supported by reliable probative and substantial evidence. In the absence of further action, the initial decision becomes the decision of the Commission thirty days after it is filed.

Any party to a proceeding may appeal an initial decision to the Commission. In acting upon an appeal from or review of an initial decision, the Commission may consider any part of the record necessary to resolve the issues of the appeal and may exercise all of the powers it could have exercised if it had made the initial decision. In rendering its decision, the Commission is required to adopt, modify, or set aside the findings, conclusions, and order contained in the initial decision, and must include in the decision a statement of the reasons and bases for its action. It is unfortunate that, over the years, the Commission has not seen fit to write opinions in all cases in a manner similar to that which is employed by the other regulatory commissions. Only in this way can it explore and develop a field of law in the area of its competence and make the record publicly available.

Commission orders become final sixty days after service on respondents unless the order is appealed. This may take the form of a request for a rehearing or an appeal to the courts for review in a United States Court of Appeals. Violation of an order of the Commission after it becomes final subjects the violator to civil penalties up to $5,000 for each day the violation continues. Assessment of the penalties is obtained by appeal to the courts.

Chapter 14 MERGERS AND CONSOLIDATIONS UNDER THE SHERMAN ACT

INTRODUCTION

The Sherman Act is the only antitrust law that relies solely on the judiciary for its interpretation and enforcement. If the Attorney General believes that the law is being disobeyed, he cannot issue orders; but he is empowered to instigate judicial proceedings against alleged offenders. It is for the courts to decide the question of guilt or innocence of the defendants and to prescribe the appropriate penalties or remedies. The law at the present time consists of generalized statutory prohibitions applied to specific cases presented to the courts for adjudication.

This procedure undoubtedly has its advantages in an experimental period, for it allows more flexible exploration for discovering the issues involved and for furnishing the basis of further legislation which can more precisely formulate public policy. Sole reliance on the courts for enforcement, however, renders well-nigh impossible the development of a satisfactory legal code of business conduct. Matters of economic policy can scarcely be settled by the ordinary processes of litigation and judicial decision. Yet, this is what is bound to happen if enforcement is left to the judiciary. Emphasis turns to legality of practices rather than to the wisdom of them, although the courts have not failed to express their judgment on the latter. For this, they are not entirely to blame, since Congress has failed to take steps to declare its own position. This enforcement procedure has, however, placed upon the courts a burden which they are ill-equipped to carry. Prosecution involves the collection of all the available evidence needed to prove the alleged guilt, and concentration in the proceedings is on the securing of a conviction. The trial itself becomes a battle of lawyers; and from the evidence submitted by them, the court must reach its decision. Judicial enforcement of the antitrust laws, as a consequence, is a matter of strict legal procedure, in marked contrast to administrative regulation.

Despite the accumulation of decisions under the Sherman Act, it is difficult to arrive at a classification of what is legal and what is not. Little more can be done in the present state of affairs than to recite the significant cases that have been decided and to attempt to give the reasons for the verdicts. This is in keeping with common-law procedure and, given sufficient time and stability of conditions, a reasonably precise set of rules may emerge, although developments at the present time do not seem to offer much ground for optimism. Modern business problems are comparatively young, exceedingly complex, and changing rapidly. As a consequence, a clear-cut pattern of the substance of the antitrust laws, as developed in court interpretation, is literally impossible to draw, although certain practices, once acceptable, seem to have been outlawed. "The laws have been unpredictable because the corporate executive has been able to rely neither upon precision in the congressional legislation nor upon precedent in the judicial legislation."[1] The Attorney General's National Committee went so far as to say that the application of Sections 1 and 2 of the Sherman Act to cases involving mergers revealed no consistent pattern, and so it refrained from a detailed analysis of the cases involving this problem.[2]

Because of the all-inclusive scope of the Sherman Act, its enforcement and interpretation are confronted with an almost infinite variety of possible situations. The Act itself does not give any indication of the meaning of monopoly or restraint of trade, but it does intend that the prohibitions shall apply to individual as well as group action; and in either case monopoly and restraint of trade, if unreasonable in the eyes of the court and if monopoly is accompanied by monopolization, are illegal. Proof of violation of the law has, generally speaking, however, been much more difficult to establish where only single enterprises have been involved. There is no satisfactory legal test of what constitutes a monopoly, since expansion to an influential position in the market may be the result of strictly economic forces and completely honorable. Furthermore, large combinations have usually been shrewd enough in more recent years to avoid practices that may reasonably be interpreted as disclosing intent to monopolize or to restrain trade. Finally, the courts have shown a distinct tendency to look with disfavor upon certain practices if they result from group action, apparently because they regard the competitive market as one in which individual concerns must act independently of their competitors. The same practices may be sanctioned, however, if indulged in by a single enterprise. For purposes of analysis, therefore, it is convenient to classify the cases arising under the Sherman Act on the basis of the distinction between allegations of violation of the law by firms acting alone and allegations of violation from concerted behavior.

INITIAL ENFORCEMENT

The first case to come before the Supreme Court under the Sherman Act was *United States* v. *E. C. Knight* (1895).[3] The government

[1]J. G. Van Cise, *The Federal Antitrust Laws* (Washington, D.C.: American Enterprise Association, 1962) p. 59.

[2]*Report of the Attorney General's National Committee, Antitrust Laws* (Washington, D.C.: U.S. Government Printing Office, 1955), p. 115.

[3]156 U.S. 1.

challenged the lawfulness of a combination effected by exchange of stock of companies in the sugar refining industry. In 1892, the American Sugar Refining Company, the successor of the sugar refining trust, acquired, through the exchange of stock, the E. C. Knight Company and three other independent refineries located in Philadelphia. The American Sugar Refining Company produced about 65 per cent of all the sugar refined in the United States; and the four independents, approximately 33 per cent. Thus, the new combination controlled 98 per cent of the output of all refined sugar in this country. The government requested dissolution of the combination, the return of the stock exchanged to previous owners, and an injunction to prevent the further performance of agreements entered into.

The issue at stake, in the opinion of the Court, was whether monopoly in manufacture could be directly suppressed under an act of Congress. In answering this question, the Court concluded that the power to control the manufacture of a commodity involved, in a certain sense, the control of its disposition. But the latter was a secondary and not the primary result. It affected commerce only incidentally and indirectly, because commerce succeeds to manufacture and is not a part of it. The law was intended to deal with combinations, contracts, and conspiracies to monopolize trade and commerce among the several states or with foreign nations, whereas the contracts and acts of the defendants related exclusively to the acquisition of the Philadelphia refineries and the business of sugar refining in Pennsylvania. These contracts bore no direct relation to commerce between the states or with foreign nations. There was nothing in the proof, in the opinion of the Court, to indicate any intention to put a restraint upon trade or commerce. Consequently, the Court refused to order the dissolution of the combination and dismissed the suit.

In refusing to recognize that the sugar combination came within the Sherman law, the Supreme Court set a precedent which would have rendered the law impotent in merger and consolidation cases had it been rigidly adhered to. However, subsequent extension of the idea of interstate commerce and recognition of the fact that manufacture may affect commerce and therefore come within the control of the federal government have overcome the severe limitations which the Knight case appeared to impose upon federal control.[4] These developments have also answered the objections to the verdict rendered by Mr. Justice Harlan in his dissenting opinion.

[4]The difficulties encountered in interpreting the terms "commerce" and "interstate" as applied to professional sports are exemplified in *Federal Baseball Club of Baltimore* v. *National League of Professional Baseball Clubs*, 259 U.S. 200 (1922); *Toolson* v. *New York Yankees*, 346 U.S. 356 (1953); U.S. v. *International Boxing Club*, 346 U.S. 236 (1955); *Radovich* v. *National Football League*, 352 U.S. 445 (1957); *International Boxing Club* v. *U.S.*, 358 U.S. 242 (1959); and the dissenting opinions in these cases.

Many explanations, such as inadequate pleading, have been advanced for the Court's decision in this case. Whatever may have been the reason, it seems clear that the early attempts to enforce the Sherman Act were of an exploratory nature. The law remained to be defined, and only by trial and error could this be accomplished. The case also exposed some of the problems connected with legal enforcement of the antitrust law, and experience was necessary to indicate what constituted legal proof of violation. Finally, it should be noted that the government at the time was not particularly enthusiastic about using the law to restrain large consolidations. A more vigorous attempt at enforcement later on proved to be more successful.

THE PERIOD OF "TRUST BUSTING"

The immediate effect of the Knight case was the creation of the impression that the Sherman law was virtually powerless to deal with industrial mergers. In addition, demonstration by the Court, through its decisions on cases involving agreements among competitors, that the Sherman Act possessed teeth to prevent restriction of competition among independent enterprises,[5] together with a period of prosperity and stock market speculation, resulted in a veritable orgy of giant combinations. This movement was brought to a rather abrupt conclusion by the collapse of the stock market boom and by a more vigorous prosecution of industrial monopoly by the federal government. In addition, the Supreme Court soon came to recognize that a successful federal antitrust policy was impossible if state corporation laws gave immunity from the federal statutes and if the meaning of commerce was as severely restricted as in the Knight case.

Although the broad scope of the Sherman Act with regard to interstate commerce had been settled by the beginning of the twentieth century in cases involving agreements among competitors, the form of organization which might be used to escape the force of the law had not been settled. This was achieved, however, in *Northern Securities Company* v. *United States* (1904).[6] The Northern Securities Company was a holding corporation organized in the state of New Jersey in 1901 for the purpose of combining the Great Northern and the Northern Pacific railways. A previous attempt to combine these two had been thwarted by the decision of the Supreme Court in *Pearsall* v. *Great Northern Railway Company* (1896),[7] on the grounds that the arrangement violated the statutes of Minnesota. In 1901 the two roads acquired joint control of the Chicago, Burlington, and Quincy Railway. This line was also of supreme importance to E. H. Harriman, who controlled the Union Pacific;

[5]Discussion of the Sherman Act as applied to agreements is deferred to Chapter 16, *infra*.

[6]193 U.S. 197.

[7]161 U.S. 646.

in the hands of his northern rivals, it constituted a threat to his ambitions for a railroad empire. As a consequence, he set out to acquire the controlling stock interest of the Northern Pacific. The resulting financial scramble left considerable doubt as to who controlled the Northern Pacific. A compromise was agreed upon to resolve this situation. The Northern Securities Company was formed; and to it was transferred, by stock exchange, approximately 90 per cent of all the stock of the Northern Pacific Company and 76 per cent of the stock of the Great Northern Company. Thus, the two northern roads were merged through the medium of a holding company.

In appraising the decision of the Supreme Court in the Northern Securities case, it should be remembered that the Great Northern and Northern Pacific jointly controlled the Chicago, Burlington, and Quincy, and that Mr. Harriman controlled the Union Pacific and the Southern Pacific. Although the Northern Securities Company controlled only the Northern Pacific and the Great Northern directly, controlling interests in the combine completely dominated the transcontinental lines of central and northern United States. This undoubtedly impressed the Supreme Court that a monopoly in transportation had been created, despite the fact that the holding company itself combined only the Northern Pacific and the Great Northern railways.

The government brought suit against the Northern Securities Company, under the Sherman Act, and asked for dissolution of the combine. The Supreme Court upheld the government's request. In so doing, it held that the Sherman Act did not refer merely to manufacture or production of articles or commodities within the limits of several states, but embraced every contract, combination, or conspiracy, in whatever form or of whatever nature, and whoever might be party to it, if such arrangement directly or necessarily operated in restraint of trade or commerce among the several states or with foreign nations. Moreover, the Act encompassed all direct restraints imposed by any combination, conspiracy, or monopoly. The Court overruled the contention that application of the Sherman Act would constitute an unwarranted interference by the federal government with the right of states to create corporations, by stating that a state cannot, by any means it chooses, project its authority into other states so as to prevent Congress from exerting the power it possesses under the Constitution over interstate and international commerce. No device is beyond the reach of the supreme law of the land if such a device directly restrains commerce among the states or with foreign nations in violation of the acts of Congress.

The decision was of supreme importance, in that it corrected much of the damage done by the Knight case and also made it clear that the holding company was not immune to attack. On the other hand, the case clearly set forth many of the difficulties involved in enforcing the Sherman law. The Court voted 5 to 4 in favor of the dissolution; and among the dissenters was Mr. Justice Holmes, who contended that ownership in stock of railroads was not commerce at all and that there was no combination in restraint of trade until something was done with the intent to exclude strangers to the combination from competing with it. He urged that a holding company did not fall within the definition of contract, combination, or conspiracy and therefore was not covered by the statute.

Whatever may be the legal merits of Mr. Holmes's arguments, the events leading up to the combination indicated beyond doubt that it was part of a movement toward a railroad monopoly. For this, there was clearly no public sentiment or statutory authority at the time. On the other hand, the case established no criteria whereby one might judge whether a combination constituted a monopoly or was in restraint of trade. What it did was to declare that the holding company was not a means whereby the Sherman Act could be evaded and that states could not, by granting corporate charters, project their authority into interstate commerce in defiance of federal laws.

The Northern Securities decision in the words of one author "represented the first major milestone in the evolution of antitrust after the enactment of the Sherman law and that in reaching that milestone antitrust had finally become institutionalized, had gained general recognition as an important American public policy."[8] The decision was followed by a determined effort to enforce the law by central direction and implementation. In 1903, the year in which the lower court decision was rendered, Congress made available special funds for antitrust enforcement. It also passed the Expediting Act to make possible the direct and speedy appeal of antitrust cases from the courts of first instance to the Supreme Court of the United States.

The effectiveness of the Sherman Act as a means of bringing to task giant industrial combinations that had deliberately engaged in practices of restraint of trade and resulted in monopoly, literally without conscience, in the abuse of the power which their position afforded them, was demonstrated in two momentous decisions rendered by the Supreme Court in 1911. The first of these was the decision against the Standard Oil Company of New Jersey in *Standard Oil Company of New Jersey, et al.* v. *United States* (1911).[9] The growth of the Standard Oil monopoly met its first rebuff in 1892, when the Supreme Court of Ohio declared the trust agreement of 1882 to be illegal. Not satisfied with the methods used by the company to comply with the decree, the Attorney General of Ohio initiated contempt proceedings in 1897. The trustees of the original combine then took new steps to maintain their control of the petroleum industry. In 1899, they secured an amendment to the charter of Standard

[8]Hans Thorelli, *The Federal Antitrust Policy* (Baltimore: The Johns Hopkins Press, 1955) p. 560. This is the most authoritative account available on the origination and development of antitrust policy down to 1904.

[9]221 U.S. 1.

Oil of New Jersey, so that the latter could hold stock in other companies. The New Jersey company, by an exchange of stock, then acquired the stock of those companies previously controlled by the trustees. It was against this combination that the government instituted suit for dissolution.

The Supreme Court, in a unanimous decision, upheld the contentions of the Department of Justice and ordered a dissolution of the trust. The company itself was particularly vulnerable to attack. In 1904, it controlled almost 90 per cent of all the refined oil produced in the United States. In addition, it controlled all of the important pipe lines by which the crude product was transported to the refinery. It had acquired its position by the most flagrant practices and by almost every conceivable predatory device. It had deliberately set out to obtain monopoly and to exclude all possible competition. In achieving this end, it not only secured dominance in the refining and pipe-line capacity of the country but also resorted to espionage and bribery, secret railroad rates, and rebates. It bludgeoned the railroads into giving special rates, resorted to price cutting whenever necessary to choke independents, and prevented the successful operation of competing refineries by charging exorbitant rates for the transportation of crude oil over its own lines. This record left no doubt in the mind of the Court that the company had deliberately and grossly violated the Sherman Act and that a drastic remedy was necessary to eliminate undue restraint on, or monopolization of, trade or commerce. The dissolution decree was formulated as a remedy to correct the existing situation, not as a penalty for past acts.

Although this verdict added much-needed life to the antitrust laws, it did little to clarify the meaning of monopoly or restraint of trade, especially as these terms apply to the activities of a single firm. The Court noted the absence of prohibition of monopoly as such, as distinguished from monopolization, in the Sherman Act. The verdict turned, therefore, on the evidence of intent and purpose to maintain dominance over the oil industry, although the position occupied by Standard Oil was regarded as prima-facie presumption of intent and purpose.

One of the most important aspects of the decision was the adoption by the Court of the so-called "rule of reason." The Court found Standard Oil guilty of violating the Sherman Act, not because it restrained trade but because this restraint was unreasonable. The adoption of this point of view, which had been advocated by the minority in earlier cases involving agreements, did not effect the decision, since the company was guilty of violating the law under any standard, once it was conceded that interstate commerce was involved. The enunciation of the rule, however, did introduce a broader interpretation of the Sherman Act, in that it indicated that the Court intended to weigh questions of public policy when industrial mergers were under judicial consideration. This position brought forth a vigorous protest from Mr. Justice Harlan, who argued for a more rigorous interpretation of monopoly and restraint of trade.

He felt that the introduction of the rule of reason constituted judicial legislation.

The second landmark decision rendered in 1911 was in *United States* v. *American Tobacco Company* (1911).[10] This trust had its beginning in 1890, when the American Tobacco Company was formed in New Jersey to control five manufacturers of cigarettes who produced 95 per cent of the domestic production. The company then began an aggressive campaign to monopolize the tobacco industry. The Continental Tobacco Company was formed, in 1898, to secure control of the plug-tobacco business. In 1901, the American Cigar Company was set up for the purpose of acquiring control over cigar manufacturing. The Consolidated Tobacco Company was organized in the same year as a holding company to own the stocks of the American Tobacco Company and the Continental Tobacco Company. An agreement was reached, in 1902, with the Imperial Tobacco Company of Great Britain, whereby the tobacco markets of the world were divided between the British and American companies. In 1904, probably in order to safeguard against possible effects of the Northern Securities decision, a new American Tobacco Company was formed to take over the assets of the combine. It was against this company that the government instituted suit for violation of the antitrust laws. The company placed heavy reliance on the ruling in the Knight case, contending that this precedent excluded the tobacco company from the operation of the antitrust laws. The Supreme Court refused to be impressed by the argument. Instead, it based its decision on the ground that the intended purpose of the combine was to monopolize the tobacco industry and to stamp out competition, as evidenced by the following facts:

1. The original combination was impelled by a previously existing fierce trade war, inspired by one or more parties to the combination.
2. The combination used its powers to further its monopoly by trade conflicts designed to injure others by driving them out of business or forcing them into the combination.
3. The company was continuously conscious of wrongdoing, as evidenced by frequent changes in the structure of the combine to conceal its intent, but at the same time, to retain control in the hands of a small group.
4. Control over all the elements essential to the successful manufacture of tobacco products was secured in such a way as to present perpetual barriers to the entry of others into the tobacco trade.
5. There was a persistent expenditure of millions of dollars for the purpose of buying up plants in order to close them down.
6. The company used the constantly recurring practice of executing contracts with persons binding them not to compete with it, generally for long periods of time.

In addition to these facts, the record also showed that at the time of the suit, the American Tobacco Company manufactured 86.1 per cent of the output of cigarettes in this country, 91.4 per cent of little cigars, 96.5

[10] 221 U.S. 106.

per cent of snuff, 84.9 per cent of plug tobacco, 76.2 per cent of smoking tobacco, 79.7 per cent of fine-cut tobacco, and 14.4 per cent of cigars. In the light of these facts, the Court, after affirming the rule of reason as set forth in the Standard Oil case, ordered the dissolution of the American Tobacco Company and instructed the lower court to effect a decree in accordance with the findings.

Emphasis by the Court on the abuse of power by Standard Oil and American Tobacco and the holding that this constituted an unreasonable restraint of trade afforded no clue as to how the law would apply where abuse was absent, nor how much power was necessary to constitute a violation of the law. The answer to this question was not to be forthcoming for over thirty years. A foreshadowing of subsequent developments was contained in *United States* v. *Union Pacific Railroad Company* (1912).[11]

The Union Pacific had obtained 46 per cent of the stock of the Southern Pacific Company. The Justice Department sought the dissolution of the combination. The Court held that any combination which placed railroads engaged in interstate commerce in such a relation as to create a single dominating control in one corporation, thereby eliminating competition between them, violated the Sherman Act without reference to the strength or weakness of whatever competition remained.

> "It is urged that this competitive traffic was infinitesimal when compared with the gross amount of the business transacted by both roads, and so small as only to amount to that incidental restraint of trade which ought not to be held within the law; but we think the testimony amply shows that while these roads did a great deal of business for which they did not compete and that the competitive business was a comparatively small part of the sum total of all traffic, state and interstate, carried over them, nevertheless such competing traffic was large in volume, amounting to many millions of dollars. Before the transfer of stocks this traffic was the subject of active competition between these systems, but by reason of the power arising from such transfer, it has since been placed under a common control. It was by no means a negligible part, but a large and valuable part, of interstate commerce which was thus directly affected."[12]

The Court therefore ordered the dissolution of the combination. It seems clear that the test of substantiality had emerged at the same time as the abuse theory.

Dissolution Problems

The dissolution decrees in the Northern Securities, Standard Oil, and American Tobacco Company cases have been widely criticized, on the ground that they did not effectively dissolve the combinations. Although the legal connections between the corporate constituents of the

[11] 226 U.S. 61.

[12] *Ibid.*, pp. 88–89. This passage was quoted with approval by the Supreme Court in *United States* v. *First National Bank and Trust Co. of Lexington*, 376 U.S. 665 (1964), 670–671.

combines were severed, the distribution of stock ownership in the resulting corporations was such as to leave in control, in each instance, the same individuals who had controlled the original combines. In other words, a community of interest continued to exist in each case. Although the latter is a much more unstable type of control than outright consolidation, it may nevertheless be an effective device for securing monopoly power or for achieving restraint of trade for a considerable period of time. The courts, in their emphasis on the corporate fiction, do not seem to have recognized that a community of interest of stockholders may be as effective as any other device for exercising monopoly power or restraint of trade.[13] Perhaps it is because the law is inadequate on this point; but whatever the reason may be, concerted action can neither be implied nor assumed merely because of the existence of community of interest. Moreover, dissolution proceedings are a remedy designed to establish as much as possible the competitive conditions envisaged by the Sherman Act. In addition, the Court has emphasized that one of the fundamental purposes of the Act is to protect, not to destroy, property rights. This presents a difficult problem of reconciling property rights and public interest. It requires a comprehensive understanding of the organizational structure of the industry in question as well as of industry in general. This entails a fact-finding task and economic analysis that a court is not well equipped to perform. The problem, as we shall see, continues to plague the application of the law to the giant enterprise which is also the dominant firm.

In the years following the Standard Oil and American Tobacco decisions, the Department of Justice was successful in prosecuting a number of cases involving railroad companies including the Union Pacific-Southern Pacific case and, in 1916, secured a consent decree against the National Cash Register Company, whereby the latter agreed to discontinue the use of a large number of predatory practices by which it had secured dominance in the manufacture and sale of cash registers. At the same time, the government failed in its prosecution of the United Shoe Machinery Company[14] because of the company's successful defense, based on the contention that it was merely making lawful use of its patent rights.

RECESSION OF ANTITRUST

The outbreak of World War I may be said to mark the end of the "trust-busting" era. This may be attributed to a number of factors. In the first place, big business had learned a lesson; and the grosser forms of abuse which had been employed by the earlier trusts were discontinued

[13]At a later date Judge Knox recognized this fact and acted accordingly in *United States* v. *Aluminum Co. of American*, 91 Fed. Supp. 333 (1950).

[14]*United States* v. *Winslow*, 227 U.S. 202 (1913); *United States* v. *United Shoe Machinery Co.*, 247 U.S. 32 (1918).

because of their vulnerability before the law. Not only had the more obvious cases been prosecuted by the Department of Justice, but astute legal counsel of the corporations had discovered more effective ways of presenting their defense. Moreover, corporate expansion took on the newer form of extension into complementary and noncompeting lines.

Judicial tolerance of mere size and the existence of unexerted power when unaccompanied by unlawful conduct in the exercise of that power was clearly set forth in two of the most important merger cases coming before the Court between World War I and World War II. The first of these was *United States* v. *United States Steel Corporation* (1920).[15] The United States Steel Corporation was formed in 1901, as a holding company in New Jersey, with a total capitalization of $1,402,846,817, of which it has been estimated over $600 million consisted of watered securities. Accumulated evidence pointed overwhelmingly to the fact that the corporation had achieved a dominant position in the industry; that its purpose was to achieve a monopoly position; that it engaged in various practices designed to fix and maintain prices; and that it pursued methods of conduct which, had they been in use at the time of the suit, would have brought condemnation.

The Supreme Court, in a 4-to-3 decision, decided that the corporation was not guilty of violating the Sherman Act. Two justices did not participate in the decision; and it is quite possible that, had they done so, the verdict would have gone the other way. Suit against the company was originally begun in 1911, and the government received an unfavorable verdict at the hands of the District Court in 1915.[16] Appeal was carried to the Supreme Court in 1917, but the outbreak of the European war led the attorneys of the government to request postponement of the case on the ground that, if dissolution were ordered, the result might interfere with the government's war effort. It is probable that the long delay in prosecuting the case had some effect on the outcome.

In reaching its decision, the majority of the Court emphasized that the corporation did not possess a monopoly, since it did not have greater power than all its competitors combined. The Court recognized that United States Steel was greater in size and productive power than any of its competitors—nearly equal, in fact, to all of them combined—but held that its power over prices was not at any time commensurate with its power to produce. (This pronouncement was in spite of the fact that the Pittsburgh-plus system of steel pricing still prevailed.) Furthermore, failure to achieve monopoly had caused the corporation to resort to co-operation with competitors through pools, associations, trade meetings, social dinners, and price agreements. These, however, were transient in their purpose and effect; and, convinced of their futility, the company had

[15]251 U.S. 417.
[16]223 Fed. 55.

abandoned them nine months before the suit was instituted. The company had resorted to neither an inclusive nor an exclusive monopoly. The Court held that the existence of mere size or unexerted power was not an offense. Finally, the Court was unable to see that public interest would be served by bringing about a dissolution but, on the contrary, felt that such a requirement would entail a risk of injury to the public interest, including material disturbance of, and material detriment to, the foreign trade of the United States. The application of the law, it said, required that public interest be of paramount regard. Despite the narrow margin by which the case was lost,[17] the government dismissed its appeal from a number of other adverse decisions of the lower courts.

That the Court's decision in the steel case was not merely transitory but, on the contrary, represented its considered judgment on antitrust as applied to single firms seemed to be borne out by the decision in favor of the defendant in *United States* v. *International Harvester Company* (1927).[18] In this instance, the Court refused to dissolve the International Harvester Company into three independent enterprises, as requested by the Attorney General, on essentially the same grounds on which it decided the steel case. The law, stated the Court, does not make the mere size of a corportion or the existence of unexerted power on its part an offense, when unaccompanied by unlawful conduct in the exercise of power. Thus, the Court apparently condoned what have frequently been referred to as "good" trusts, in contrast to the "bad" ones which ran afoul of the law. Be that as it may, it should be recognized that the Court lacked objective criteria by which it could judge whether an enterprise had too much power over prices for the public good. Economic criteria useful for establishing rules of law on this score are still sadly lacking.

Although the decisions in the steel and harvester cases appeared to impose severe limitations on the application of the Sherman Act to mergers and consolidations, generalizations on the reasons given for the verdicts are virtually impossible to make. This is emphasized by the decisions rendered in the anthracite coal cases of *United States* v. *Reading Company* (1920)[19] and *United States* v. *Lehigh Valley Railroad Company* (1920).[20] In both instances, the holding company device was used to effect, directly or indirectly, the integration of competing railroads, competing coal companies, and railroad and coal companies. As a result of the combinations, however, the Reading Company controlled only about 33⅓ per cent of the annual production of anthracite coal, and the Lehigh Company did not control more than 20 per cent. The companies

[17]The verdict was 4 to 3, with two justices, McReynolds and Brandeis, not participating.

[18]274 U.S. 693.

[19]253 U.S. 26.

[20]254 U.S. 255.

had continuously altered their organizations to escape the antitrust laws, but the Hepburn Act of 1906 was designed to eliminate the combination of railroad companies and coal mining. On strictly technical grounds, these combinations would seem to have escaped the Hepburn Act and, in the light of the reasoning in the steel case, presumably had a strong defense against the Sherman Act. The Court, however, ordered the dissolution of both combinations. The reasoning appears to mirror the dissenting opinion of the steel case rather than the majority opinion, and clearly followed the path of the earlier Union Pacific-Southern Pacific decision.[21]

Two factors may possibly have accounted for the verdicts. In the first place, Congress had declared its intent to separate production from transportation of coal by the Hepburn Act; and the Court has been careful to carry out the intent of Congress when it is clear and constitutional. In the second place, it has been easier for the Justice Department to secure favorable verdicts in antitrust cases involving the railroads. The reason for this is probably that railroad companies have always been regarded as a natural monopoly. Hence, any combination to which they are a party and which joins together competing lines involves the extension of an already existing monopoly. Consequently, it is much easier to make out a convincing case, without the necessity of quantitative demonstration of monopoly, and to show that the combination results in restraining trade and competition. At any rate, the hand of the law has fallen more severely upon railroad than upon industrial mergers; and factors that have weighed heavily in the former cases seem not to have been decisive in the latter. The application of the Sherman Act to railroads appears to have laid the foundation for a broader approach to mergers and combinations than did the cases involving industrial firms, just as the interpretation of the scope of interstate commerce gained its initial breadth from cases pertaining to transportation.

REVIVAL OF ANTITRUST

The depression of the thirties brought about a virtual suspension of the operation of the antitrust laws. This resulted not only from a court attitude that made dissolution of mergers extremely difficult but also from lack of vigor in prosecution—a deficiency that was aggravated by the National Industrial Recovery Act and other legislation encouraging business co-operation and limitations on price competition. Just before the outbreak of World War II, however, there developed a renewed interest in the problems of monopoly and competition. Under the aggressive leadership of Mr. Thurman Arnold, the Department of Justice set out

[21]See also *United States* v. *Southern Pacific Co.*, 215 U.S. 214 (1922) which was decided on the same principle as the Union Pacific-Southern Pacific case. The reasoning in this decision was also quoted with approval by the Supreme Court in *United States* v. *First National Bank of Lexington*, 376 U.S. 665 (1964).

to put new life into the enforcement of the antitrust laws. Despite the outbreak of World War II and our entry into it, the vigor of the movement was not dimmed by the momentous events of the period. This revival of antitrust marks the beginning of what has been called the new Sherman Act. Power over markets, whether exercised or not, became subject to challenge, and even demonstration of the existence of monopoly power no longer seems to be necessary to bring combinations to task under the Sherman Act.

The initial decision that marked this change in the application of the law was rendered in *United States* v. *Aluminum Company of America* (1945).[22] This is one of the most important decisions ever handed down in a merger case under the Sherman Act. Technically, this was not a Supreme Court decision. The government had appealed the case from the District Court of the United States for the Southern District of New York to the Supreme Court. The latter was unable to get a quorum to hear the case and, as a consequence, certified it to the Circuit Court of Appeals, Second Circuit. The decision handed down by this Circuit Court of Appeals, therefore, has the effect of a Supreme Court ruling.[23]

The Department of Justice sought dissolution of the Aluminum Company of America, on the grounds that this company had a monopoly in the manufacture and sale of "virgin" aluminum ingot, and that it and Aluminium, Ltd., had entered into a conspiracy in restraint of interstate and foreign commerce. The opinion of the Court was divided into four sections.

First of all, it considered the question of whether the aluminum company known as Alcoa possessed a monopoly of "virgin" ingot. The distinction between "virgin" and "secondary" ingot is that the latter is made from aluminum scrap. From 1902 to 1928, Alcoa made "virgin" ingot in Canada through a wholly owned subsidiary. In 1912, this, together with that which Alcoa made in the United States, amounted to nearly 91 per cent of the total amount of "virgin" ingot available for sale in the United States. In 1913, it was about 72 per cent; in 1921, about 68 per cent; and in 1922, about 72 per cent. In all other years, it was always over 80 per cent; and for the five years from 1934 to 1938, inclusive, it averaged over 90 per cent. The Court considered the question of whether "secondary" ingot should be included in computing Alcoa's control of the aluminum market and decided that it should not. Not only did the Court find that Alcoa had controlled the supply of "secondary" ingot in the past but also that failure to monopolize the "secondary" ingot would not

[22]148 Fed. (2d) 416. See also *United States* v. *Pullman Co.*, 50 Fed. Supp. 123 (1943), which required the Pullman Company to divorce manufacturing from transportation. The Pullman Company decided to remain in the manufacturing field by disposing of its transportation properties to the railroads.

[23]Later, in *American Tobacco Co.* v. *United States*, 328 U.S. 781 (1946), the Supreme Court specifically endorsed key portions of Judge Learned Hand's decision.

eliminate the monopoly over "virgin" aluminum ingot, which was the relevant market for the case at bar.

The fact, however, that Alcoa had acquired a monopoly did not alone prove to the Court that it had "monopolized" the ingot market. Monopoly may have been thrust upon Alcoa; that is, monopoly may have been acquired by the company without intention to put an end to existing competition or to prevent competition from arising where none had existed. The Court did not feel, however that Alcoa was the beneficiary of a passive monopoly. It felt that, in expanding, Alcoa had effectively anticipated and forestalled all competition and had succeeded in holding the field alone. The Court was convinced, from the evidence, that Alcoa's monopoly stemmed from a deliberate policy pointed to that end. Alcoa had, therefore, monopolized the ingot market; and because it had a monopoly of that market, it was not necessary for the government to prove "specific" intent. Had Alcoa not acquired a monopoly, the government would have been compelled to prove specific intent; and on the record that was presented, it is doubtful that this would have been possible. What Judge Hand did, therefore, was to emphasize market power by holding that when this amounted to monopoly in the eyes of the law, the defense must prove that monopoly was thrust upon it; if it could not do this, it would be guilty of monopolization, and therefore in violation of the law.

The government alleged that Alcoa's profits on "virgin" ingot were extortionate by virtue of tariff protection and that they amounted to over 10 per cent. While the Court did not feel that 10 per cent was an unreasonable profit, it held that the issue was irrelevant, because a monopoly is not excused merely on the grounds that it makes only fair profits. Fair profits, said the Court, were no evidence that a fair profit could not have been made at lower prices. The Court held that Congress did not condone good trusts and condemn bad ones. It forbade all of them. This clearly laid the International Harvester ghost to rest.

> Moreover, in so doing it [Congress] was not necessarily actuated by economic motives alone. It is possible because of its indirect social or moral effect to prefer a system of small producers, each dependent for his success upon his own skill and character, to one in which the great mass of those engaged must accept the direction of a few. These considerations which we have suggested only as possible purposes of the act, we think the decision [of the lower court] proved to have been in fact its purposes. . . .[24]
>
> Throughout the history of these statutes, it has been constantly assumed that one of their purposes was to perpetuate and preserve for its own sake and in spite of possible costs, an organization of industry in small units which can effectively compete with each other.[25]

The Court stated that all contracts to fix prices are unconditionally prohibited and that monopoly, which involves the power to fix prices, when accompanied by monopolization, must therefore also be prohibited.

[24] 148 Fed. (2d) 416, 427.
[25] *Ibid.*, p. 429.

The second matter which the Court considered was Alcoa's alleged unlawful practices. Alcoa was found guilty of only one of them—namely, the "price squeeze." This was a practice by which, it was alleged, the defendant intended to put the manufacturers of aluminum sheet, who were its competitors, out of business by selling ingot to these manufacturers at such a high price that they could not produce sheet and sell it at a profit at the price at which Alcoa itself sold sheet. Because of the difficulties involved in allocating costs, the Court found it hard to determine whether Alcoa had been holding ingot at a higher than fair price. It did feel, however, that the price of ingot had been changed in 1933 because the company feared some action by the Department of Justice. After considering all the facts before it, the Court held that it was an unlawful practice for Alcoa to set the price of sheet so low and hold the price of ingot so high that the price of the latter was above a fair price, as shown by the record. This was only a consequence of Alcoa's monopoly of ingot, and the Court did not use it as part of the reasoning by which it concluded that Alcoa's monopolization was a violation of the Sherman Act. The Court did feel, however, that it was an unlawful exercise of Alcoa's power after it had been put on notice by the sheet rollers' complaint; and therefore, after 1932, the practice constituted a wrong. This is a somewhat curious ruling, since it would seem to imply that sale of a commodity above a fair price is unlawful, even though monopoly has not been proved.

The third aspect of the case which was considered by the Court was that of Aluminium, Ltd., known as "Limited."[26] This was a company which had been incorporated in Canada on May 31, 1928, to take over all of those properties of Alcoa which were outside the United States, with the exception of a Dutch company which owned bauxite deposits in Dutch Guiana and a Canadian power transmission company. In exchange for all the properties conveyed, Limited issued all its common shares to Alcoa's common shareholders, in the proportion of 1 of the former for every 3 of the latter. At first, there were some officers common to both companies; but by the middle of 1931, this practice was discontinued. In 1939, 11 individuals collectively still held 48.9 per cent of Alcoa's shares and 48.5 per cent of Limited's. The companies had a number of transactions with each other, and the Justice Department tried to prove that they did not deal at arm's length. The Court, however, felt that the evidence was insufficient to prove any violation of the law.

In 1931, Alliance, a Swiss corporation, was formed as an international cartel to establish quotas of production and to control prices. The Court was of the opinion that the agreement affected imports into the United States and, as a consequence, influenced prices. It concluded that

[26]Judge Learned Hand referred to the Canadian company as *Aluminum*, Ltd. (p. 421). The correct name of *Aluminium*, Ltd., was given in the District Court case, 44 Fed. Supp. 97 (1941), and again by Judge Knox in 91 Fed. Supp. 333 (1950), for which see n. 28.

Aluminium, Ltd. violated the laws of the United States, even though it was a foreign corporation, because it did business in the United States, and that it made agreements outside of this country which affected prices and production in domestic trade. There was the question, however, whether the Aluminum Company of America had any part in these proceedings. The Court recognized that there was a community of interest between the two companies, although the group owning stock common to each composed less than a majority. However, it was large enough, for practical purposes, to control each company. The Court held that the existence of the same large minority interest in the two corporations was not enough, in itself, to identify the two. It said: "Alcoa would not be bound unless those who held the majority of its shares had been authorized by the group as a whole to enter into the alliance, and considering the fact that, as we shall show, it was an illegal arrangement, such an authority ought convincingly to appear. It does not appear at all." The Court therefore concluded that Alcoa was not a party to the practices of Alliance.

This situation presents the difficulties arising from community of interest that have been noted in earlier cases. Whatever may be the legal niceties, it is hard to believe that there was no common action between the interested parties in Aluminium, Ltd. and Aluminum Company of America in the activities of Alliance. This situation clearly demonstrates the need for some means, other than lawyers' battles in the courtroom, of solving many of the fundamental problems of monopoly and monopolistic practices and the means by which they are carried out.

The fourth part of the case dealt with the remedy. The Department of Justice requested a dissolution of Alcoa but also requested a stay of execution of the plan until after the war. The Department also asked for a termination of all shareholding in common between Alcoa and Limited, and for an injunction against the unlawful practices. The Court recognized that the war had made fundamental changes in the aluminum industry. It refused to take notice of this fact, however, as far as the correctness of the findings was concerned; but it did take notice of certain facts relevant to the remedy to be adopted. It stated that dissolution is not a penalty but a remedy, and that the need for such a remedy was for the District Court in the first instance to decide.

There was another persuasive reason why the Court was not willing to prescribe dissolution of any kind. The Surplus Property Act of 1944 provided the method by which surplus properties of the government were to be disposed of. The designated disposal agency was required to give careful consideration to all factors necessary to promote free and competitive enterprise. The Court felt that this would require some plan or design for the industry as a whole and that such a plan would necessitate the assignment of a place to Alcoa. Whatever the results might be, it was felt that no decision with regard to the treatment of Alcoa should be made until a plan for the whole aluminum industry was announced.[27]

After finding Alcoa guilty of monopolizing the ingot market, the Court remanded the case to the District Court. At the same time, it issued an injunction against any resumption of the "price squeeze" and enjoined Limited from entering into any cartel or agreement like that of 1931.

The remedy that was finally adopted for this case came as the result of an appeal to the courts, upon completion of the disposal program by the War Assets Administration. Alcoa petitioned the Court to declare that it no longer had a monopoly of the ingot market. The government filed a petition alleging that competitive conditions had not been re-established and accordingly requested that Alcoa be divested of such of its properties as would accomplish this purpose. Judge Knox[28] denied both petitions but did grant some relief to the government. He concluded that effective competitive conditions had not been restored in the aluminum industry, but that Alcoa was clearly the dominant firm in a field of three competitors, the other two of which were Reynolds Metals and Kaiser Aluminum. At the same time, he felt that vertical divestiture of Alcoa so as to create another fully integrated competitor would be a highly speculative venture and might well be detrimental to the national welfare. Accordingly, he decreed a modification of Alcoa's patent-licensing arrangements so as to eliminate the restrictive effect of these on effective competition in the aluminum industry; and he ordered the shareholders of Alcoa to dispose of their stock interest in either Aluminium, Ltd. or Alcoa. This termination of the community of interest was ordered because Limited, the largest producer of aluminum in the world, would then, in Judge Knox's opinion, become an effective competitor in the domestic market of the United States.[29]

During a period of over a quarter of a century, the motion-picture industry had been involved in a series of Sherman Act cases in which the defendants were single firms, closely affiliated enterprises, and independent concerns. The main issue in all these cases has centered around the relationship that developed among the producers of motion pictures, the distributors of the pictures, and the exhibitors (owners of the theaters in which the pictures are shown), especially with regard to the practices

[27]See Report of the Surplus Property Board to the Congress, *Aluminum Plants and Facilities* (Washington, D.C.: U.S. Government Printing Office, September 21, 1945), for a discussion of proposals for disposal of government-owned aluminum plants and the restoration of competition in the industry.

[28]*United States* v. *Aluminum Co. of America*, 91 Fed. Supp. 333 (1950).

[29]For an appraisal, see Walter Adams, "The Aluminum Case: Legal Victory—Economic Defeat," *American Economic Review*, Vol. XLI, No. 5 (December, 1951), pp. 915–22.

followed in distribution and exhibition.[30] This long period of attack by the Justice Department culminated in a suit against the 5 major motion-picture companies which, in the words of one author, represented "the most important experiment in vertical disintegration under the Sherman Act."[31] In this case, *United States* v. *Paramount Pictures, Inc.* (1948)[32] the 5 major defendants produced films and, through subsidiaries or affiliates, distributed and exhibited them. The charge was that the vertical combination of producing, distributing, and exhibiting motion pictures by each of the 5 major defendants violated Sections 1 and 2 of the Sherman Act. The Court examined the charges under two main headings. The first of these was restraint of trade, and the second was competitive bidding.

The charge of restraint of trade was dealt with under six headings:

1. *Price Fixing.* No film is sold to an exhibitor in the distribution of motion pictures. The right to exhibit under copyright is licensed. Here, it was found that two price-fixing conspiracies existed—a horizontal one between all the defendants, and a vertical one between each distributor defendant and its licensees. The Court held that even patentees cannot regiment an entire industry by licenses containing price-fixing agreements. Nor was the situation any different in the case of vertical conspiracy, because the licenses were but part of a general plan to suppress competition.

2. *Clearances and Runs.* Clearances and periods of time were designed to protect a particular run or exhibition of a film against a subsequent run. The evidence showed that many clearances had no relation to the competitive factors which alone could justify them. The Court concluded that the defendants either participated in evolving a uniform system of clearances or acquiesced in it and so furthered its existence.

3. *Pooling Agreements: Joint Ownership.* The District Court found the exhibitor defendants had agreements with each other and their affiliates by which theaters of two or more of them, normally competitive, were operated as a unit, or managed by a joint committee or by one of the exhibitors, the profits being shared according to prearranged percentages. The District Court found that both the pooling arrangements and the joint ownership violated the law. The Supreme Court concluded, however, that in some instances, the joint ownership involved no more than innocent investments by those who were not actual or potential operators.

4. *Formula Deals, Master Agreements, and Franchises.* A formula deal is a licensing agreement with a circuit of theaters in which the license fee of a given feature is measured for the theaters covered by the agreement by a specified percentage of the feature's national gross. The circuit was allowed to allocate playing time and film rentals among the theaters as it saw fit. The District Court held that the formula deals and master agreements constituted a restraint of trade, because they eliminated the possibility of bidding for films theater by theater, and because the pooling of purchasing power was a misuse of monopoly power.

[30]See *Paramount Famous Lasky Corporation* v. *United States*, 282 U.S. 30 (1930); *United States* v. *First National Pictures, Inc.* 282 U.S. 44 (1930); *Interstate Circuit Co. Inc.* v. *United States*, 306 U.S. 208 (1939); *United States* v. *Crescent Amusement Co.*, 323 U.S. 173 (1944); *Schine Chain Theatres, Inc.* v. *United States*, 334 U.S. 110 (1948); *United States* v. *L. C. Griffith*, 334 U.S. 100 (1948).

[31]Simon N. Whitney, "Vertical Disintegration in the Motion Picture Industry," *American Economic Review*, Vol. XLV, No. 2 (May, 1955) pp. 491–98).

[32]334 U.S. 131.

5. *Block Booking.* This is the practice of licensing one feature or group of features on condition that the exhibitor will also take another feature or features released by the distributors during a given period. This prevented competitors from bidding for single features on their individual merits. The Supreme Court held that it was illegal to refuse to license one or more copyrights unless another copyright was accepted.

6. *Discrimination.* The District Court found that the defendants had discriminated against small independent exhibitors and in favor of large affiliated and unaffiliated circuits through various kinds of contract provisions.

The second main problem was that of competitive bidding. The District Court concluded that the only way competition could be introduced was to require that films be licensed on a competitive bidding basis. The Supreme Court recognized the force of the District Court's recommendation but concluded that competitive bidding would involve the judiciary so deeply in the daily operations of this nationwide business and promised to offer such dubious benefits that it should not be undertaken. "Yet delegation of the management of the system to the discretion of those who had the genius to conceive the present conspiracy and to execute it with the subtlety which this record reveals, could be done only with the greatest reluctance."[33] The District Court had decreed competitive bidding as the means of dealing with the violations of the Sherman Act, because it felt that divestiture was too harsh a remedy. The Supreme Court disagreed. It set aside the findings on divestiture, so that a new start on this phase of the cases could be made on remand.

Between 1948 and 1954, the integrated companies were split by 5 consent decrees into 2 parts each, creating 5 disaffiliated theater circuits—which, in turn, were allowed a period of time to sell a quarter to a half of their theaters.[34] Whether the results of all this ligitation will be to provide a workable solution to the marketing problems of the motion-picture industry remains to be seen. After a careful study of the motion-picture industry, Professor Michael Conant concluded that the Paramount decrees destroyed the nationwide combination that had controlled the motion-picture industry. The decrees of divestiture and divorcement effectively put an end to the organized control of the industry. The decrees were deficient, however, in that they failed to dissipate circuit-buying power completely because the Court failed to break up the circuits into sufficiently small units.[35] Professor Simon Whitney evaluates the results in the following words: "In brief, attempts by a single company to monopolize the motion picture industry have been defeated by competition, with relatively minor aid from the antitrust laws; and the

[33]*Ibid.*, pp. 163 and 164.

[34]Consent decree, United States District Court, Southern District of New York, 1948–49, Commerce Clearing House, Trade Reports, ¶62,377. See also *ibid.*, ¶57,254 (1952).

[35]Michael Conant, *Antitrust in the Motion Picture Industry* (Berkeley and Los Angeles: University of California Press, 1960), pp. 218–20.

effects of the 1948 divorcement decree against the dominant group have been mixed: a rigid pattern of control has been abolished and independent theatres have won the right to show features sooner; but this plunge into a free market has given them a new appreciation of the advantages of integration; and the benefits to the public have been uncertain and, at best, moderate."[36] Once again, however, the atmosphere of the courtroom does not seem to be the most conducive milieu for arriving at economical patterns in an intricate industrial structure.

That the tests of the Sherman Act, when applied to single combinations or consolidations, are anything but precise or unequivocal was demonstrated clearly in *United States* v. *Columbia Steel Corporation* (1948).[37] In this case, the government filed suit under the Sherman Act to enjoin the United States Steel Corporation, through its Pacific Coast subsidiary, Columbia Steel, from acquiring the assets of Consolidated Steel Corporation, which was the largest independent steel fabricator on the Pacific Coast. The government claimed that if the sale were consummated, competition in the sale of rolled steel products would be restrained and that the contract indicated an effort on the part of United States Steel to attempt to monopolize the market in fabricated steel products.

Prior to the contract for the acquisition of Consolidated, United States Steel had bought the steel plant at Geneva, Utah, from the United States government, for the sale of which to United States Steel the War Assets Administrator had received the approval of the Attorney General. This acquisition increased the ingot capacity of United States Steel to 32.7 per cent for the nation as a whole, 39 per cent for the Pacific Coast and Mountain states, and 51 per cent for the Pacific Coast area. With this acquisition, United States Steel then looked to the problem of acquiring fabricating structural steel plants as outlets for its ingot production. Before contracting to buy Consolidated, it even considered building plants for making structural steel products in Los Angeles and San Francisco.

The majority of the Court concluded that acquisition of Consolidated by United States Steel would not constitute an unreasonable restraint of trade, because the competition between Consolidated and the subsidiaries of United States Steel in the relevant market was not substantial. The Supreme Court agreed with the lower court that the purchase agreement was entered into for sound business reasons and with no intent to monopolize the production and sale of fabricated steel products. The Court stated that, in evaluating possible violation of the Sherman Act, it looked (1) to the percentage of business controlled, (2) the strength of the remaining competition, (3) whether the action sprang from business requirements, (4) the probable development of the industry, (5) consumer

[36]Simon N. Whitney, *Antitrust Policies* (New York: The Twentieth Century Fund, 1958), Vol. II, p. 195.

[37]334 U.S. 495.

demands, and (6) other characteristics of the market. The Court declined to set any percentage figures to measure reasonableness; but it made it clear that there was no direction of public policy as yet that forbade, per se, an expansion to meet the new markets of a community, whether that market was nationwide or countrywide.

Failure to prove unreasonable restraint or monopolizing placed a heavy burden on the government to prove specific intent. On this count, the Court felt that the unobjected acceptance of the bid for the Geneva plant negated the contention of specific intent.

Mr. Justice Douglas, speaking for the four dissenting justices, said:

> "This acquisition gives it [United States Steel] unquestioned domination [on the Pacific Coast] and protects it against growth of the independents in that developing region. That alone is sufficient to condemn the purchase. Its serious impact on competition and the economy is emphasized when it is recalled that United States Steel has one-third of the rolled steel capacity of the entire country. The least I can say is that a company that has that tremendous leverage on our economy is big enough."[38]

Judge Knox summarized the verdict by saying: "The conclusion is inescapable from the Columbia Steel decision, that the possession of monopoly power is something other than the status in a market of a dominant firm. The dominant firm may have neither the power to exclude competitors, nor the power to fix prices."[39]

Judged by the reasoning of the majority and the verdict in this case, the tests of the Sherman Act certainly remained severe. Suit under Section 7 of the Clayton Act as it was worded at that time was not possible because Columbia Steel had acquired the assets of Consolidated directly, thereby leaving the corporate structure of the latter intact.

The perennial questions of the meaning of monopoly in the eyes of the law and the relevant market for deciding whether it exists came to the fore again in *United States* v. *E. I. du Pont de Nemours and Company* (1956).[40] The issue was given a new twist, however, in that what constituted the relevant market required consideration of substitute products, a matter that had heretofore been avoided. The charge was monopolization of cellophane; the defense, that cellophane was merely a part of the relevant market for packaging materials. The government asserted that cellophane and other wrapping materials were neither substantially fungible (readily substitutable) nor like-priced. Hence, it argued that the market for other wrappings was distinct from the market for cellophane and that the competition afforded cellophane by other wrappings was not strong enough to be considered in determining whether Du Pont had monopoly powers.

The Court stated that previous cases determined that a party has

[38]*Ibid.*, pp. 539–40.
[39]*United States* v. *Aluminum Co. of America*, 91 Fed. Supp. 333 (1950), 346.
[40]351 U.S. 377.

monopoly power if it has, over any part of the trade or commerce among the several states, a power of controlling prices or unreasonably restricting competition. "Whatever the market may be, we hold that the control of price or competition establishes the existence of monopoly power under section 2. Section 2 requires the application of a reasonable approach in determining the existence of monopoly power just as surely as did section 1. This of course does not mean that there can be a reasonable monopoly."[41] The Court recognized that, strictly speaking, all differentiated products give rise to monopoly but that "where there are market alternatives that buyers may readily use for their purposes, illegal monopoly does not exist merely because the product said to be monopolized differs from others."[42]

The relevant market for this case, the Court held, was other flexible wrapping materials. To determine whether these other materials were reasonably substitutable for cellophane, it was necessary to consider the cross-elasticity of demand. The conclusion drawn from the record was that cellophane's interchangeability with the other materials sufficed to make it a part of the flexible packaging material market. The record showed that Du Pont produced 75 per cent of the cellophane in this country but only 17.9 per cent of the flexible wrapping materials.

On the basis of the record, the majority of the Court held that Du Pont did not monopolize cellophane within the meaning of the law. The issues of attempt and conspiracy to monopolize were not involved, because the government specifically excluded them in its appeal. The question which the Court was called upon to answer was strictly one of fact, and the answer to be derived from the facts clearly involved the exercise of judgment.

The emphasis on the relevant market concept and the utilization of cross-elasticity will draw commendation from economists, but it has not simplified their problem. However, they may be able to work in rather broad categories of product and market classification, since it is unlikely that the courts will accept very fine distinctions; nor should they.[43]

The influence of the Alcoa decision, which seemed to have lost considerable of its sting in the litigation involving Columbia Steel, came to the fore again in *United States* v. *United Shoe Machinery Corporation* (1953).[44] This was a federal and not a Supreme Court decision; but it is

[41]*Ibid.*, p. 393.

[42]*Ibid.*, p. 394.

[43]The type of analysis used by Stocking and Mueller to prove that Du Pont had a monopoly within the meaning of the law over cellophane will not go unchallenged by economists, especially when the authors question that effectiveness of interchangeability on the ground that the evidence does not indicate that Du Pont at any time carried quality competition so far as to equalize average cost and selling price (G. W. Stocking and W. F. Mueller, "The Cellophane Case and the New Competition," *American Economic Review*, Vol. XLV, No. 1 [March, 1955]), pp. 39–63.

[44]110 Fed. Supp. 295.

important for three reasons: (1) the government finally secured a verdict under Sections 1 and 2 of the Sherman Act against United Shoe, (2) the case summarized clearly lower court views of the new interpretation of the Sherman Act, and (3) the old problem of remedy reared its head again.

Over the years since 1911, a number of antitrust suits have been brought against United Shoe and its officers. These had never succeeded in getting at the major problem of United's position under the Sherman Act because of the company's success in defending its position by virtue of its patent rights over shoe machinery used in various stages or processes of shoe manufacture.

The Court, in this case, found that United was the largest source of supply of shoe machinery for some 1,460 shoe manufacturers, in that it was supplying over 75 per cent, and probably 85 per cent, of the current demand in the American shoe machinery market. The aggregation of patents which United held impeded potential competition to some extent and furnished a trading advantage. United followed the practice of never selling but only leasing its machines; and these leases, the Court felt, created barriers to entry by competitors. The Court also found that United followed a discriminatory pricing policy of sharp and relatively durable differentials which gave a higher rate of return where competition was of minor significance and a lower one where the reverse was the case.

Judge Wyzanski held that the facts showed that (1) the defendant exercised such overwhelming strength in the shoe market that it controlled the market; (2) the strength excluded and limited some actual competition; and (3) the strength was not attributable solely to the defendant's ability, economies of scale, research, natural advantages, and adaptation to inevitable economic laws. He noted that where market control exists, a defendant may escape statutory liability if it bears the burden of proving that it owes its monopoly solely to superior skill. This, he held, United was unable to do. United's position did not rest on predatory practices; but it could not properly be described as resulting from inevitable consequences of ability, natural forces, or law. Moreover, the defendant intended to engage in the leasing practices and pricing policies which maintained its market power.

The government wanted to break United into three separate manufacturing companies. Judge Wyzanski held that the petition for dissolution should reflect greater attention to practical realities than was shown in the government's presentation. He rejected the remedy of dissolution. Instead, he ordered a considerable modification of the company's leasing practices and ordered the company to divest itself of the business of manufacturing and distributing supplies such as nails, tacks, and eyelets, which United had monopolized. Whether the decree afforded a remedy that will establish effective competition in the shoe machinery industry in this country remains to be seen. The verdict, on appeal, was sustained by the Supreme Court in a *per curiam* decision.[45]

Another case arising under the Sherman Act may be discussed here. It did not add anything significant to the substance of interpretation, but it did emphasize the difficulties which may arise in connection with the court application of it to complicated factual situations. This was *United States* v. *New York Great Atlantic and Pacific Tea Company* (1949),[46] also a federal court case. The Department of Justice brought criminal suit against A. & P., several of its subsidiaries, and certain of its officers. Judge Minton upheld the conspiracy conviction of the lower court, whereupon A. & P. paid the fine of $175,000 without carrying an appeal to the Supreme Court.

In reviewing the record Judge Minton held that there was substantial evidence to show conspiracy. He based his conclusion on the fact that A. & P. was organized so as to have a centralized buying policy, which also gave it control over such things as advertising allowances and label and bag allowances. He held that A. & P. used its power to get lower prices than its competitors and that it used the threat of withholding its patronage if it did not get better prices. It even threatened to manufacture its own products if it did not receive the prices it wanted. Furthermore, it used the Atlantic Commission Company (ACCO), a wholly owned subsidiary, to act as a buying agent for A. & P. and as a buying and selling agent for the rest of the trade.[47] This, Judge Minton held, enabled A. & P. to get better produce and to use the profits to further retail competition with other sellers. By owning manufacturing and processing plants, A. & P. was able to "subsidize" its retail competition. Finally, the Court found that in highly competitive areas, A. & P. lowered its prices over those it charged in other areas, even to the point of selling below cost of operation.

After settlement of the criminal suit, the government instituted proceeding in equity which sought to break up the A. & P. chain. The suit was based on reasoning similar to that employed by Judge Minton. One may agree with Judge Minton that A. & P. was a hard competitor and broke the law, but the offenses seem to fall primarily under the Robinson-Patman Act. If, however, the economic reasoning relating to the buying practices and advantages, and the relationships between the manufacturing and selling activities of A. & P. were to be the basis for dissolution, no vertically or horizontally integrated enterprise could withstand the impact of the Sherman law. It is immaterial, from the standpoint of effec-

[45]347 U.S. 521 (1954). For a complete analysis of the entire case, see Carl Kaysen, *United States* v. *United Shoe Machinery Corporation* (Harvard Economic Studies) (Cambridge, Mass.: Harvard University Press, 1956).

[46]173 Fed. (2d) 79.

[47]See *Great Atlantic & Pacific Tea Co.* v. *Federal Trade Commission*, 106 Fed. (2d) 667 (1939); certiorari denied, 308 U.S. 625 (1940).

tive competition, at what price a manufacturing concern turns over its product to its subsidiary seller. The question of predatory activities and "fighting" branches is another matter. These questions, again, are matters of fact, which courts are not particularly adept in appraising.

The civil suit was settled by consent decree[48] in which A. & P. agreed to dissolve the Atlantic Commission Company. A. & P. was enjoined from purchasing any food on behalf of or for the account of the outside trade, or from selling any food to competitors except that processed in its own plants. It was also forbidden to sell at less than regular billing prices to any of its units in order to circumvent state minimum mark-up laws or to defeat local competition. Whether the decree will substantially alter A. & P.'s competitive position remains to be seen but it does not appear to have done so as yet, even though the decree subjects the company to certain limitations that do not apply to its competitors.

The latest step in the development of the Sherman Act as applied to consolidations is the decision of the Supreme Court in *United States* v. *First National Bank and Trust Co. of Lexington* (1964).[49] The First National Bank and Trust Co. of Lexington, Kentucky, and the Security Trust Co. of Lexington, had consolidated to form the First Security National Bank and Trust Co. It was charged by the Justice Department that the consolidation constituted a combination in restraint of trade in violation of Section 1 of the Sherman Act, and an attempt to monopolize trade and commerce in violation of Section 2. Reports requested by the Comptroller of Currency pursuant to the Bank Merger Act of 1960 from the Attorney General, the Federal Deposit Insurance Corp., and the Board of Governors of the Federal Reserve System, all concluded that the consolidation would adversely affect competition among commercial banks in Lafayette County. Nevertheless, the Comptroller of the Currency approved the consolidation and the District Court upheld him. Upon appeal the Supreme Court reversed the decision of the District Court.

The Supreme Court ruled that commercial banking was the relevant market for determining the Section 1 issue in the case, and that the consolidation should be judged in light of its effect on competition in Lafayette County, the relevant geographic market. The Court found that the bank established by the consolidation was larger than all the remaining banks combined, having 52.7 per cent of the banking assets, 51.95 per cent of the deposits, and 54.2 per cent of the loans. The combined trust assets of the two banks amounted to 94.82 per cent, trust department earnings, 92.2 per cent, and the number of trust accounts, 79.62 per cent. The Court held that significant competition would be eliminated by the consolida-

[48]Consent decree, January 19, 1954 (Commerce Clearing House, *Trade Reports*, ¶67, 658). See M. A. Adelman, "The A & P Case," *Quarterly Journal of Economics*, Vol. LXIII (1949), pp. 238–57.

[49]376 U.S. 665.

tion, and that this constituted unreasonable restraint of trade even though there was no "predatory" purpose. The Court than went on to cite the railroad cases, already discussed earlier in this chapter, as precedents for its decision. It also stated that the tests for violation set set forth in Columbia Steel were met in this instance. It did not rule on the questions posed under Section 2 of the Sherman Act, violation having been established under Section 1.

Justices Brennan and White concurred in the findings, but felt that the decision should have rested solely on the factors relied on in Columbia Steel. Mr. Justice Harlan, joined by Mr. Justice Stewart, dissented from the verdict and the reasoning. The dissent contended that the railroad cases were of questionable relevance and that the Columbia Steel tests should have been held to favor the consolidation. The only criterion in Columbia Steel which favored the government was "bigness." "In sum, the Court's analysis of this case ends where it begins; the conclusion that the consolidation violates the Sherman Act collapses into the agreed premise that First Security is 'big.' "[50] Finally, Justice Harlan felt that this, if anything, was a Clayton Act case masquerading in the garb of the Sherman Act.

On the surface, this case seems to be a direct contradiction of Columbia Steel. If it may be taken to indicate the position of the Court in future cases, then the tests for Section 1 of the Sherman Act may have come to be essentially those of Section 7 of the Clayton Act. The fact that seven of the Justices felt that the tests of Columbia Steel were applicable may indicate that these tests will have a much sharper cutting edge than the majority applied in that case.

RÉSUMÉ OF MERGERS UNDER THE SHERMAN ACT

The Pattern of the Decisions

It was pointed out at the beginning of this chapter that cases under the Sherman Act seem to reveal no consistent pattern of application of the law. Nevertheless, at some risk one may venture to make some generalizations because the issues today are not on all fours with those of 70 years ago. A recital of the leading cases clearly indicates that the Sherman Act at the present time has a much broader scope than it had when it was first applied. Immunity from the law on the ground that a firm's activities do not involve interstate commerce is extremely difficult to establish. The crude and arrogant tactics of the earlier trusts have been eliminated, because they could not stand the scrutiny of the law. Monopolization is now illegal if monopoly has been achieved, unless the accused can prove that the monopoly was thrust upon it. The difficulties of establishing specific intent have therefore been largely overcome.

Down to the Alcoa case in 1944 it appeared that mere size was not

[50] *Ibid.*, p. 679.

an offense, nor was the existence of unexerted power by a single enterprise. Abuse of power by clearly illegal practices and intent to monopolize by industrial firms were the requisites of successful prosecution. This led to the distinction between good and bad trusts, and the latter have apparently disappeared. On the other hand, another line of reasoning had been enunciated in the railroad cases, which appears to have emerged from oblivion in the Lexington Bank case. In the railroad cases the substantial volume of business controlled became the test, although the quantitative measure of this was not discussed. In the Alcoa case the initial test became monopoly in the relevant product market. Here the product market was given a narrow interpretation, although the measure of monopoly seemed to be left vaguely high, but the need for proving specific intent was eliminated. The Du Pont cellophane case turned on a relatively broad interpretation of the relevant market, with the resulting conclusion that monopoly was not established to the satisfaction of the Court. The Columbia Steel case enumerated a number of tests for violation, but curiously, to the economist at least, the Court found these inapplicable in this instance. Mr. Justice Douglas, however, in his dissent, did put his finger on bigness and concentration which have become the focal point of mergers under the Clayton Act. In the Lexington Bank case the Court also emphasized concentration, and found that possession of something over 50 per cent of the market was too much. Since this was a merger case that could have been handled under Section 7 of the Clayton Act, it gives no indication of the tests that might be applied to those that can be prosecuted only under the Sherman Act. Nor did the Court pass judgment on how this might have fared under Section 2 of the Sherman Act. Whether reliance of the Court on the precedents of the earlier railroad cases has any significance for possible prosecution under Section 2 of situations not involving mergers, only the future can tell.

The passage of the Celler-Kefauver amendment to Section 7 of the Clayton Act has resulted in a basic change in the law on mergers such that meeting the tests of the Sherman Act is no longer necessary. However, this legislation does not meet the entire problem because many existing combinations of giant proportions are apparently not subject to it, nor is the growth of a giant combination by internal expansion. When such an enterprise may come under attack under the Sherman Act is not discernible under decisions to date, nor have economists yet devised tests that meet with sufficient general acceptability to be legally applicable. The position in the market to which a single enterprise might be permitted to grow without violating the law, at least under the tests supplied by the Alcoa case, cannot be discerned at this time. Nor would the test of intent as suggested by Professor Kahn or that of market performance by Professor E. S. Mason seem to offer very useful criteria.[51]

[51]See Edwin Mansfield (ed.), *Monopoly Power and Economic Performance* (New York: W. W. Norton & Co. Inc., 1964), pp. 144–71. See also *Antitrust Laws, op. cit.*, chap. vii, "Economic Indicia of Competition and Monopoly," pp. 315–42.

This problem, if there be one, of growth, corporate size, and market dominance, will have to be met through other approaches that focus on the structure and privileges of the corporation and the scope of powers which this form of business organization possesses. In other words, methods of achieving the position are the ones that now call for comprehensive examination.

THE RULE OF REASON

Antitrust legislation must, of necessity, over a considerable range, leave appreciable discretion in the interpretation and application of it to the appropriate governmental agencies. This led, at the very outset of judicial proceedings under the Sherman Act, to controversy over what came to be known as the "rule of reason."

At common law, restraint of trade was a concept developed by court precedents over the centuries. Its meaning had changed with the growth of modern business and was less restrictive than in earlier times. The rapid emergence of new conditions by the end of the nineteenth century made the task of the courts much more difficult, however, because of the variety of new situations with which they had to deal. Moreover, the courts had always construed the common-law concept in the light of what circumstances seemed to require. They were, in fact, applying generally accepted standards of business practice that conformed to prevailing economic philosophy.

The Sherman Act did nothing to clarify the situation. In fact, apart from making restraint of trade a positive offense—and therefore illegal, presumably—it merely applied common law to interstate commerce. Thus, what constituted restraint of trade or monopoly was still for the courts to decide in the light of circumstances. There was no definition in the legislation.

The issue was first joined in the Trans-Missouri Freight Association case, in which the majority of the Court took the position that a contract might be in restraint of trade and still be valid at common law. Even so, it was nevertheless a contract in restraint of trade and, as such, was forbidden under the Sherman Act. The majority was unwilling to concede that only contracts in unreasonable restraint of trade violated the Sherman law. The minority, on the other hand, argued that the words "restraint of trade" embraced only contracts which unreasonably restrained trade and that, consequently, reasonable contracts—although they, in some measure, imposed restraint—were not within the meaning of the law.

The minority opinion became the majority position in the Standard Oil case; and although the issue did not affect the decision, nevertheless, the Court took occasion to state that the Standard Oil Company had violated the Sherman law, not because its acts were in restraint of trade, but because they were in unreasonable restraint of trade. This position undoubtedly influenced the decisions in the United States Steel and the

International Harvester cases. The Court's concern for the foreign trade of the United States and its failure to detect monopolizing in either case, led to the belief that the Court was usurping legislative powers. What effect on the outcome of litigation the "rule of reason" has had since the Alcoa case is an open question. Of course, the Court has been forced to exercise its judgment, both under the Sherman Act and the Clayton Act, just as the Federal Trade Commission has been required to do under the Trade Commission Act. But exercise of judgment does not seem to cover the scope of the controversy over the rule of reason. The latter involved the injection of broader judgments on the desirable public policy in the mind of the judiciary that a strict interpretation of the law did not call for. It is still necessary for the Court to use reason in deciding whether monopoly exists within the meaning of the law, just as economists must, but approaching the problem in this manner eliminates much of the issue of desirability or undesirability, and makes the administrative problem more amenable to economic considerations centering on competition and the circumstances that may impose limitations on it. The existence of power itself is open to examination regardless of how it may be used.

Although the acceptance of the rule of reason by the Supreme Court in cases involving outright consolidations seemed to broaden judicial discretion and to introduce considerations of public policy of a legislative nature, at least in industrial cases, the Court did not retreat significantly from its strict construction of the law relating to restraint of trade as applied to price-fixing and similar arrangements. The issue of the rule of reason that was first exposed in cases involving agreements became a center of controversy primarily in connection with the application of the Sherman Act to single enterprises acting alone. Despite the Alcoa case, the problem of the good giant enjoying a marked degree of concentration still remains.

THE REMEDY FOR VIOLATION

The problem of remedy for violation of the Sherman Act presents a particularly difficult issue when it involves dissolution or divestiture. The remedies that have been applied to date have raised serious questions as to their effectiveness. The courts are conscious of the need for protecting property rights, but they do not seem to have taken the position that protection of these must be at the expense of establishing conditions that will prevent continued violation. The difficulty in drawing up decrees for remedies seems to have arisen primarily from the economic facts and conditions of the industry or firms in question. This again becomes a matter of economics and economic policy rather than law; and again, the restrictions of the courtroom and the capacities of judges do not seem to provide the best available means for resolving the difficulties. There seems to be a definite need for further development of machinery for administering the antitrust laws. This will be discussed later.

Chapter 15 MERGERS UNDER THE CLAYTON ACT

INTRODUCTION

The Sherman Act as applied to consolidations and mergers was supplemented by Section 7 of the Clayton Act of 1914. This section provided, among other things: "That no corporation engaged in commerce shall acquire, directly or indirectly, the whole or any part of the stock or other share capital of another corporation engaged also in commerce where the effect of such acquisition may be to substantially lessen competition between the corporation whose stock is so acquired and the corporation making the acquisition or to restrain such commerce in any section or community or tend to create a monopoly of any line of commerce." Presumably, Congress intended to stop in its incipiency undue concentration of economic power through intercorporate stock ownership by competing corporations where the effect would be substantially to lessen competition between them. Such a combination might be achieved by partial or by the complete ownership of the stock of one firm by another. Combination by acquisition of assets was apparently deliberately omitted from the law. The fact that Section 7 was included in the Clayton Act warrants the assumption that the tests of illegality under it were to be different from and less stringent than those of the Sherman Act. Unfortunately, these tests were not spelled out, the law leaving them for the courts and the administrative agencies to delineate and detail.[1]

The enforcement of the legislation as provided in Section 11 of the Clayton Act was vested in the Interstate Commerce Commission where applicable to common carriers, in the Federal Reserve Board where applicable to banks, and in the Federal Trade Commission where applicable to all other character of commerce. Section 15 assigned jurisdiction over violations also to the district courts of the United States and provided that "it shall be the duty of the several district attorneys of the United States, in their respective districts, under the direction of the Attorney-General, to institute proceedings in equity to prevent and restrain such violations." The problem of delineating the spheres of

[1]See David D. Martin, *Mergers and the Clayton Act* (Berkeley and Los Angeles: University of California Press, 1959). A complete history of Section 7 of the Clayton Act and its administration down to 1958 is presented in this treatise.

authority of the Justice Department and the various administrative agencies has given rise to considerable controversy under the Clayton Act as now amended.

ENFORCEMENT OF THE ORIGINAL SECTION 7

The Federal Trade Commission

For some twelve years after the passage of the Clayton Act the Federal Trade Commission acted without benefit of definitive court adjudication. The first order of the Commission was issued in 1921 against the Aluminum Company of America, which had acquired a majority of the capital stock of the Aluminum Rolling Mills Company. The Commission ordered the Aluminum company to divest itself of the stock, and this order was upheld in the courts.[2] The effectiveness of this decision, however, was destroyed by a subsequent ruling of the Circuit Court of Appeals, which permitted the Aluminum company to buy, at a sheriff's sale, the physical properties of the Aluminum Rolling Mills Company.[3] The Commission continued its investigations of alleged violations, but it apparently developed no consistent, workable criteria for distinguishing between those acquisitions that were and those which were not in the public interest. Reversal of its major decisions by the Supreme Court and a narrow interpretation by the latter of the standard of illegality ended any possibility of successful enforcement of the law by the Trade Commission.

The first of the important cases arising from Commission action to be decided by the Supreme Court was *Federal Trade Commission* v. *Western Meat Co.* (1926).[4] It was in three cases, decided in a consolidated proceedings, that the real possibilities of evasion of the law were fully established. The Western Meat Company had acquired all of the stock of the Nevada Packing Company, a competitor, but none of its plant or other property. The Supreme Court held that the Commission's order requiring a divestment of this stock was within the Commission's authority, and that the Commission also had the power to prevent the Western Meat Company from using the control of the stock to dissolve the packing company and to acquire its assets. The Thatcher and Swift companies, however, had acquired controlling interest in competitors; and they used this to obtain the properties and dissolve the subsidiaries before the Commission instituted proceedings. The Court held that these companies were within their rights and that the Commission had no

[2]*Aluminum Co. of America* v. *Federal Trade Commission*, 284 Fed. Rep. 401 (1922); certiorari denied, 261 U.S. 616 (1923).

[3]*Aluminum Co. of America* v. *Federal Trade Commission*, 299 Fed. Rep. 361 (1924).

[4]*Federal Trade Commission* v. *Western Meat Co.; Thatcher Manufacturing Co.* v. *Federal Trade Commission;* and *Swift and Co.* v. *Federal Trade Commission*, 272 U.S. 554 (1926).

jurisdiction, even though the acquisition of the competitor's property and business was brought about through stock which had been purchased unlawfully.

The jurisdiction of the Commission was subject to still further limitations by the decision of the Court in *Arrow-Hart and Hegeman Company* v. *Federal Trade Commission* (1934).[5] In this instance, a holding company was formed to acquire the stock of two competing corporations. The Federal Trade Commission instituted proceedings, whereupon the holding company was dissolved and the assets of the competitors were merged into the new company of Arrow-Hart and Hegeman Electric Company. The Commission ordered the dissolution of this new company. The Court held that the jurisdiction of the Commission was ousted by the merger, and that the Commission had no power to bring in the new corporation as a respondent and require it to divest itself of one or the other of the operating plants. Mr. Justice Stone filed a vigorous dissent, declaring that this case contradicted the holding in the Western Meat Company case and that the decision left the Commission powerless to act, no matter how flagrant the violation of the Clayton law.

Prior to the Arrow-Hart and Hegeman decision, the powers of the Federal Trade Commission had been limited in another direction. In *International Shoe Company* v. *Federal Trade Commission* (1930),[6] the Supreme Court set aside an order of the Federal Trade Commission which had required the International Shoe Company to divest itself of stock ownership of the McElwain Company. The latter had been in severe financial difficulties, and its recovery was a matter of doubt. The Court found, first of all, that there was no substantial competition between the two companies in respect of 95 per cent of their business, because they manufactured different grades of shoes and sold in different markets. It also concluded that the McElwain Company might have disappeared altogether because of its financial difficulties. Consequently, it overruled the Commission's order. Mr. Justice Stone filed a dissenting opinion, with which Justices Holmes and Brandeis concurred. The interpretation of the phrase "substantially lessen competition" was so narrow as to limit it practically to firms between which only pure competition obtained. Introduction of the "failing business" concept opened up another avenue of conjecture by which evasion might be achieved.

For various reasons the Federal Trade Commission failed to accomplish anything under Section 7 of the Clayton Act down to its amendment in 1950. It failed to give specific content to the general language of the standard of illegality of the section, and it failed in its attempts to prevent general evasion of the law.

[5]291 U.S. 587.

[6]280 U.S. 291. But see *United States* v. *Diebold, Inc.*, 369 U.S. 654 (1962).

The Department of Justice

Enforcement of Section 7 by the Interstate Commerce Commission added little, if anything, to the Commission's program of consolidation of railroads as part of the over-all transportation policy, and the Federal Reserve Board was unsuccessful in its attempt to compel Transamerica Corporation to divest itself of a controlling interest in banks in the five western states of California, Washington, Oregon, Nevada, and Arizona.[7]

Original Section 7

As the result of the decisions of the Supreme Court on Federal Trade Commission attempts to enforce Section 7 of the Clayton Act, it was generally assumed that the law was virtually useless. That this section did possess real teeth, however, was demonstrated by the decision of the Supreme Court in *United States* v. *E. I. du Pont de Nemours et al.*, (1957)[8] commonly known as the Du Pont-General Motors case. The original suit was filed by the Department of Justice in the District Court for Northern Illinois, before the passage of the Celler-Kefauver amendment, and was carried on an appeal to the Supreme Court. In this case, Du Pont was charged with violating Sections 1 and 2 of the Sherman Act and the original Section 7 of the Clayton Act. The government charged that the business conduct of the defendants had three objectives: (1) obtaining control of management and policies of Du Pont, General Motors, and United States Rubber, (2) creation and exploitation of protected markets for certain products of Du Pont and United States Rubber, and (3) reservation of certain exclusive fields of production to the Du Pont company. Violation of the Clayton Act was claimed, because the ownership by Du Pont of 23 per cent of General Motors stock, and the joint ownership of United States Rubber by General Motors and Du Pont resulted in arrangements among the corporations that substantially lessened competition. The District Court dismissed the case for lack of evidence, on the ground that the government had failed to demonstrate that any of the business relationships had not been the result of sound and honest business practices.

The government appealed the case, and the Court dealt only with the issue under Section 7 of the Clayton Act. The Court held that this section was designed to arrest in its incipiency a substantial lessening of competition arising from the acquisition by one corporation of the whole or any part of the stock of a competing corporation, as well as to arrest in their incipiency restraints or monopolies, in a relevant market, which

[7]*Board of Governors of the Federal Reserve System* v. *Transamerica Corporation*, 184 Fed. (2d) 311 (1950); *Transamerica Corporation* v. *Board of Governors of the Federal Reserve System*, 206 Fed. (2d) 163 (1953).

[8]353 U.S. 586.

as a reasonable probability might result from the ownership. The Court held that the statute applied to horizontal as well as to vertical acquisitions although this matter had not previously been adjudicated, and then went on to say:

> "We hold that any acquisition by one corporation of all or any part of the stock of another corporation, competitor or not, is within the reach of the section whenever the reasonable likelihood appears that the acquisition will result in a restraint of commerce or in the creation of a monopoly in any line of commerce."[9]

The Court held that automotive finishes and fabrics were sufficiently distinct from all other finishes and fabrics to make them a "line of commerce" within the meaning of the Clayton Act. Furthermore, "incipiency" did not denote the time when the stock was acquired, but any time when the acquisition threatened to ripen into a prohibited effect. It was not requisite to the proof of a violation of Section 7 to show that restraint or monopoly was intended. The test of violation was whether, at the time of suit, there was a reasonable probability that the acquisition was likely to result in the condemned restraints. The judgment of the lower court was reversed and the cause remanded to it for the necessary equitable relief.

What the results of this decision will be remains to be seen, but the dissenting remarks of Mr. Justice Burton are worth noting:

> All that is required, if this case is to be our guide, is that some court in some future year be persuaded that a "reasonable probability" then exists that an advantage over competitors in a narrowly construed market may be obtained as a result of stock interest . . . . Every corporation which has acquired a stock interest in another corporation after the enactment of the Clayton Act in 1914, and which has had business dealings with that corporation is exposed, retroactively, to the bite of the newly discovered teeth of section 7.[10]

No cases have since been adjudicated that deal with the effect of stock ownership accumulated over the years since 1914, but the statement of the majority of the Court that the test of the violation is whether, at the time of the suit, there is a reasonable probability that the acquisition is likely to result in the condemned restraints would seem to present the possibility of a wide range of action by an aggressive Department of Justice or Federal Trade Commission. Furthermore, the restriction of the "line of commerce" to automotive finishes and fabrics and not to the total market for finishes and fabrics indicated a much narrower market to which the test of substantially lessening competition was to be applied than was theretofore supposed.

[9]*Ibid.*, p. 592. In a footnote, the Court states that the Celler-Kefauver amendment is inapplicable to acquisitions prior to 1950 (p. 588). However, the Celler-Kefauver Act amended, but did not repeal, the original Section 7. Its provisions still remain in force.

[10]*Ibid.*, p. 611.

ENFORCEMENT UNDER THE CELLER-KEFAUVER AMENDMENT

Enforcement of the provisions of Section 7 of the Clayton Act as amended by the Celler-Kefauver Act inaugurated a new era in antitrust as related to concentration and mergers in business. The scope of the law, when applied to the various kinds of amalgamations or mergers that might take place, the impact of the law on the bearing of such mergers on restraint of trade, monopoly and substantiality of competition, all called for interpretation because the legislation left much of this to be spelled out by the various agencies charged with administering it. In addition, the jurisdictional authority of the numerous federal agencies that were involved, required court clarification. The principal matters upon which the Supreme Court has been called upon to pass judgment to date may be grouped into five categories: (1) jurisdictional authority over mergers that come under Section 7; (2) the meaning of merger under the law; (3) line of commerce or the relevant product market; (4) section of the country or the appropriate geographic market; and (5) the substantiality of competition.

Jurisdictional Authority

As has already been noted, the Clayton Act, as amended, assigns the responsibility of enforcement to a number of administrative federal agencies where their authority is applicable, and concurrently to the Department of Justice. This has given rise first of all to the question of where primary jurisdiction resides, that is, where authority for initial action resides, and second, to the question of the exclusive jurisdiction of the particular agency involved.

The question of jurisdictional authority has been dealt with in a number of recent cases. In *Maryland and Virginia Milk Producers Association Inc.* v. *United States*(1960),[11] the Association had purchased the assets of Embassy Dairy in Washington, D.C. It contended that the purchase was pursuant to the authority given by the Secretary of Agriculture. The Court held that there was no such statutory authority to approve such a transaction, and that Section 7 was therefore applicable. The case of *California* v. *Federal Power Commission* (1962)[12] arose out of the purchase of the stock of Pacific Northwest Pipeline Corp. by El Paso Natural Gas Co. which then applied to the Federal Power Commission for authority to acquire the assets pursuant to Section 7 of the Natural Gas Act. Prior to this action, the federal government commenced proceedings against the companies under Section 7 of the Clayton Act. The companies filed a motion to dismiss the antitrust suit, but this was

[11]362 U.S. 458. This case also involved charges of violating the Sherman Act.
[12]369 U.S. 482.

denied by the Court. The Federal Power Commission proceeded with its hearings, however, and authorized the merger. The Supreme Court noted that immunity from the antitrust laws is not lightly to be implied, and then pointed out that the Natural Gas Act does not give relief to the companies in the case of mergers and that the Power Commission did not have the authority to adjudicate antitrust issues; it was not included in the list of agencies enumerated in Section 11 of the Clayton Act. Furthermore, Section 7 of the Natural Gas Act gave the Power Commission jurisdiction over the acquisition only of assets of natural gas companies, not over stock acquisitions. Finally, the Court said that where primary jurisdiction is in the agency, courts withhold action until the agency has acted, but that primary jurisdiction did not rest with the Power Commission in this instance.

The same problem was dealt with at greater length in *United States* v. *Philadelphia National Bank* (1963).[13] This case arose out of a proposed merger of the Philadelphia National Bank and the Girard Corn Exchange Bank, both with head offices in the Philadelphia metropolitan area. The Comptroller of the Currency approved the merger, although the reports of the Federal Reserve Board, the Federal Deposit Insurance Corporation, and the Attorney General advised him that the proposed merger would have substantial anticompetitive effects in the Philadelphia metropolitan area. The Supreme Court held that the merger violated Section 7 of the Clayton Act.

In passing judgment on the matter of jurisdiction, the Court observed that Section 7 reached acquisitions of corporate stock by any corporation engaged in commerce, but reached acquisitions of corporate assets only by a corporation "subject to the jurisdiction of the Federal Trade Commission." The Trade Commission had no jurisdiction over banks and, therefore, if the proposed merger was deemed to be an assets acquisition, it was not within Section 7. The Court held, however, that Congress intended to bring the entire range of amalgamations within the scope of the law. "Thus, the stock-acquisition and assets-acquisition provisions, *read together*, reach mergers which fit neither category perfectly, but lie somewhere between the two ends of the spectrum . . . . So construed, the specific exception for acquiring corporations not subject to the FTC's jurisdiction, excludes from the coverage of Section 7 only assets acquisitions by such corporations when not accomplished by merger."[14] The Court then ruled that the Banking Act of 1960 gave no express immunity from the antitrust laws.

ENFORCEMENT BY THE DEPARTMENT OF JUSTICE

To date only a limited numer of cases has come before the Supreme Court for adjudicating on the meaning of amended Section 7 of the Clay-

[13]374 U.S. 321.
[14]*Ibid.*, p. 342.

ton Act as applied to the vertical and horizontal aspects of mergers, the "line of commerce," and any "section of the country." The first of these was *Brown Shoe Co. Inc.*, v. *United States* (1962).[15]

After dispensing with a jurisdictional matter the Court listed eight of the factors relevant to a judgment as to the validity of a given merger, specifically discussed by Congress in redrafting Section 7: (1) Congress intended to "plug the loophole" and to include the acquisition of assets no less than the acquisition of stock; (2) Section 7 applied not only to mergers between actual competitors, but also to vertical and conglomerate mergers whose actual effect may be to lessen competition in any line of commerce in any section of the country; (3) a keystone in the erection of a barrier to the rising tide of concentration was the provision for arresting mergers at a time when the trend to a lessening of competition in a line of commerce was still in its incipiency; (4) Congress rejected as inappropriate the application to Section 7 cases the standards for judging the legality of business combinations adopted by the courts in cases arising under the Sherman Act; (5) while Congress sought to create an effective tool for preventing all mergers having demonstrable anticompetitive effects, it did not intend to impede a merger between two companies which would enable the combination to compete more effectively with larger corporations dominating the relevant market, nor to prevent a merger between a corporation that is financially healthy and a "failing" one; the purpose is to protect *competition*, not *competitors;* (6) Congress neither adopted nor rejected specifically any particular tests for measuring the relevant market, nor did it adopt a definition of the word "substantially"; (7) Congress provided no definite quantitative or qualitative tests, but it indicated plainly that a merger was to be functionally viewed, in the context of a particular industry; (8) Congress used the words "*may be* substantially to lessen competition" to indicate that its concern was with probabilities, not certainties. The Court then proceeded to deal separately with both the vertical and the horizontal aspects of the merger, examining each of these in terms of the product market, the geographic market, and the probable effect of the merger.

The Vertical Aspects of the Merger. The Supreme Court stated that the primary vice of a vertical merger or other arrangement tying a customer to a supplier is that the foreclosing of the competitors of either party from a segment of the market otherwise open to them may act as a "clog on competition." The area of effective competition, therefore, must be determined by a reference to a product market (line of commerce) and to a geographic market (section of the country). The outer boundaries of a production market are determined by reasonable interchangeability of use between the product itself and the substitute for it. Within this broad market well-defined submarkets may exist which con-

[15]370 U.S. 294.

stitute well-defined submarkets for antitrust purposes, and each economically significant submarket must be examined to see whether there is a reasonable probability that the merger will substantially lessen competition. The Supreme Court upheld the District Court's finding that the relevant lines of commerce were men's, women's, and children's shoes. It refused to sanction a further breakdown, as requested by the appellant, on the ground that the boundaries of the relevant market had to be drawn with sufficient breadth to include the competing products of each of the merging companies, and to recognize competition, where, in fact, competition existed.

The relevant geographic market was held to be the entire nation. The relationships of product value, bulk, weight, and consumer demand, enable manufacturers to distribute shoes on a nationwide basis as Brown and Kinney did.

Appraisal of the probable effects of the merger led the Court to observe that it is necessary to examine the nature and purpose of the arrangement. The test of illegality is virtually identical to that of Section 3 of the Clayton Act where tying contracts, unless employed by a small company attempting to break into a market, can rarely be harmonized with the strictures of the antitrust laws. Congress intended to preserve the "failing company" doctrine and to permit the merger of small companies if the purpose was to enable them to compete with larger corporations dominating the market. But the merger under consideration involved neither small companies nor failing companies. In 1955, Brown was the fourth largest manufacturer in the shoe industry, and Kinney the largest independent chain of family shoe stores in the nation. The Court stated that the trend toward concentration had to be considered because a prognosis of the probable future merger was required. There was a tendency for acquiring manufacturers to become increasingly important sources of supply for their acquired outlets. Remaining vigor of competition could not immunize a merger if a trend in that industry was toward oligopoly; Congress was desirous of preventing the formation of further oligopolies with their attendant adverse effects upon local control of industry and upon small business.

The Horizontal Aspects of the Merger. The horizontal aspects of the merger required consideration of: the relative size and number of parties to the transaction; whether it allocates shares of the market among parties; whether it fixes prices at which the parties will sell the product; or whether it absorbs or insulates competitors.

The Court found the product market to be the same as for the vertical aspects of the merger, namely, men's, women's, and children's shoes. Brown and Kinney had sold their shoes in competition with one another through the enumerated outlets characteristic of the industry.

Consideration of the geographic market at the retail level required examination of submarkets. The Court agreed with the District Court's finding that shoe stores in the outskirts of cities compete with stores in central downtown areas, and that the most intense competition in retail sales will be confined to stores within the particular communities in a single "standard metropolitan area" and their immediate environs. The relevant geographic market in this case consisted of those cities with a population exceeding 10,000 people, and the environs in which both Brown and Kinney retailed shoes through their own outlets.

The probable effect of the merger was ascertained by the District Court by a detailed analysis of competition in shoe retailing in St. Louis, and by hearing witnesses from 40 other cities in which the parties to the merger operated. The Supreme Court felt that this was a fair sampling of the evidence. After noting that the combined market share of Brown and Kinney sales in the separate cities ranged from 5 per cent to 49 per cent in the three different kinds of shoes, the Court went on to state: (1) that the market share which companies control is one of the most important factors to be considered when determining the probable effects of the combination on effective competition in a relevant market; (2) in this fragmented industry, even if the combination controls but a small share of a particular market, the fact that this share is held by a large national chain can adversely affect competition; (3) this merger creates a large national chain which is integrated with a manufacturing operation, but the expansion is not rendered unlawful by the mere fact that small independent stores may be adversely affected because it is competition, but not competitors which the Act protects. Other factors also had to be considered, such as: (1) the history of the tendency toward concentration in the industry. By this merger, the largest single group of retail stores still independent of one of the large manufacturers was absorbed into an already substantial aggregation of retail outlets with the result that Brown moved into second place in terms of retail stores directly owned, with about 7.2 per cent of the nation's shoe stores and 2.3 per cent of the nation's total retail outlets; (2) Congress gave a mandate that tendencies toward concentration in industry were to be curbed in their incipiency; (3) "At the same time appellant has presented no mitigating factors, such as business failure or the inadequate resources of one of the parties that may have prevented it from maintaining its competitive position, nor a demonstrated need for combination to enable small companies to enter into a more meaningful competition with those dominating the relevant market."[16] The Supreme Court affirmed the District Court's order divestiture.

Emphasis on the tests of illegality set forth in the Brown Shoe case was added in *United States* v. *Philadelphia National Bank* (1963),[17] the jurisdictional aspects of which were dealt with earlier. Only the evaluation of the Court on the lawfulness of the merger will be discussed here.

[16] *Ibid.*, p. 346.
[17] 374 U.S. 321.

After holding that the relevant market was commercial banking which was sufficiently inclusive to be meaningful in terms of trade realities, the Court turned to discuss the relevant geographic market. It stated that the "areas of effective competition in the known line of commerce must be charted by careful selection of the market area in which the seller operates and to which the purchaser can practically turn for supplies."[18] It held that the four-county area was the appropriate one because that was where the vast bulk of the appellees' business originated. Although large customers might find it practical to do a large part of their business outside the area, "some fair intermediate delineation which avoids the indefensible extremes of drawing the market either so expansively as to make the effect of the merger upon competition seem insignificant, because only the very largest bank customers are taken into account in defining the market, or so narrowly as to place appellees in different markets, because only the smallest customers are considered."[19]

Determination of the question of whether the effect of the merger may be to substantially lessen competition led the Court to emphasize intense congressional concern with the trend toward concentration. This warranted dispensing with elaborate proof of market structure, market behavior, or probable anticompetitive effects, and required that a merger be enjoined in the absence of evidence clearly showing that it was not likely to have such anticompetitive effects. The Court found that the merger would control 30 per cent of the commercial banking business in the four-county area which presented a threat of undue concentration. In addition, the result would be to give the two largest banks in the area control of over 59 per cent of the commercial banking, an increase of 33 per cent over the present control of 44 per cent in the hands of the two largest. A purpose of amended Section 7 was to arrest the trend toward concentration, the *tendency* to monopoly, before consumers' alternatives disappeared through merger. The alternative to the merger route is the opening of new branches, and "one premise of an antimerger statute such as Section 7 is that corporate growth by internal expansion is socially preferable to growth by acquisition."[20] To this the Court added "Congress determined to preserve our traditionally competitive economy. It therefore proscribed anticompetitive mergers, the benign and the malignant alike, fully aware, we must assume, that some price might have to be paid."[21] The Supreme Court accordingly reversed the findings of the District Court and ordered it to enjoin the merger.

In 1959, Aluminum Company of America acquired the stock and

[18] *Ibid.*, p. 359, and citing *Tampa Elec. Co.* v. *Nashville Coal Co.*, 365 U.S. 320 (1961), 327.

[19] *Ibid.*, p. 361.

[20] *Ibid.*, p. 370.

[21] *Ibid.*, p. 371.

assets of the Rome Cable Corporation, and the government claimed that this violated Section 7 of the Clayton Act. The matter came before the Supreme Court in *United States* v. *Alcoa* (1964)[22] on appeal from the District Court, which had dismissed the complaint. The Supreme Court reversed the District Court by holding that the merger violated the law.

The initial and most significant issue concerned the identification of the "line of commerce." Rome produced both copper conductor and aluminum conductor for electrical utilities. Prior to the merger it produced 0.3 per cent of total industry production of bare aluminum conductor, 4.7 per cent of insulated aluminum conductor, and 1.3 per cent of the broader aluminum conductor line. Alcoa produced no copper conductor, but did produce 32.5 per cent of the bare aluminum conductor, 11.6 per cent of the insulated aluminum conductor, and 27.8 per cent of aluminum conductor. The District Court found that bare aluminum conductor was a separate line of commerce, but that the broader aluminum conductor was not because insulated aluminum conductor was not an appropriate line of commerce separate and distinct from its copper counterpart. The Supreme Court recognized that the competition between insulated aluminum conductor and its copper counterpart was enough to justify grouping aluminum and copper conductors together in a single-product market (which would have made them the same thing), but that their degree of competitiveness did not preclude their division into separate submarkets. The price spread between insulated aluminum and copper conductors was so great that the prices did not respond to each other. The Supreme Court held that "where insulated aluminum conductor pricewise stands so distinctly apart, to ignore price in determining the relevant line of commerce is to ignore the single, most important practical factor in the business."[23] In other words, there was the possibility of substitution even though it was not very great.

Having established aluminum conductor as the appropriate line of commerce (product market) within the meaning of Section 7, the Court then proceeded to examine the effect of the merger on competition and on concentration. In 1958, Alcoa was the leading productor of aluminum conductor with 27.8 per cent of the total output of the market, and only nine concerns (including Rome with 1.3 per cent) accounted for 95.7 per cent of the output. Alcoa ranked third in the production of insulated aluminum conductor with 11.6 per cent, and Rome eighth with 4.7 per cent. Nine companies controlled 88.2 per cent of the total output. This, according to the Court, showed highly concentrated markets. The acquisition of Rome added only 1.3 per cent to Alcoa's control of the aluminum conductor market, "but in this setting it seems to us reasonably likely to produce a substantial lessening of competition within the mean-

[22]377 U.S. 271.
[23]*Ibid.*, p. 276.

ing of Section 7."[24] The Court held that the record showed that Rome was an aggressive competitor, and that it was the prototype of the small independent that Congress aimed to preserve. The case was remanded to the District Court to carry out divestiture proceedings.

Mr. Justice Stewart, joined by Justices Harlan and Goldberg, wrote a vigorous dissent which contended that the government had failed to show substantial percentages of market shares in competitive markets, and that aluminum conductor was not a line of commerce. The combination, the dissent held, was essentially that of an aluminum and a copper manufacturing company and that this did not violate the law. Rome's production of bare aluminum cable was only 0.3 per cent of the market.

This is an utterly confusing case. What the verdict would have been if Rome Cable had produced no aluminum conductor cannot be guessed. The indicia set forth for ascertaining the line of commerce will leave both economists and lawyers thoroughly mystified.[25] The conclusion seems to be warranted, however, that mergers are illegal under Section 7 if there is substitutability of products, even though that substitutability be decidedly remote. The division of the produce market into submarkets apparently is to be made to fit each case, leading to the suspicion that the division is for the purpose of rationalizing the verdict rather than establishing the basis for it.

The status of joint ventures under the Clayton Act was the issue at bar in *United States* v. *Penn-Olin Chemical Co.* (1964).[26] Pennsalt Chemicals Corporation and Olin Mathieson Chemicals Company jointly formed Penn-Olin Chemical Company to produce and sell sodium chlorate in the southeastern United States. Each owned 50 per cent of the stock, and a plant was built at Calvert City, Kentucky. The previous sales arrangement for sodium chlorate, produced only by Pennsalt, by which Olin marketed the sodium chlorate in the southeast, was superseded by the joint venture. The District Court held that the joint venture did not violate the law because the reasonable probability that both companies would build plants in the southeast was lacking. At the time of the suit neither company had a plant in the southeast area.

The Supreme Court took the position that "If the parent companies are in competition, or might compete absent the joint venture, it may be assumed that neither will compete with the progeny in its line of commerce."[27] Basically, the same considerations apply to joint ventures as to mergers. Furthermore, in reply to the lack of proof that both companies would build in the area, the Court said, "There still remained for consideration the fact that Penn-Olin eliminated the potential compe-

[24]*Ibid.*, p. 280.
[25]A summary can scarcely do justice to the "*wortspielerei*" of the opinion.
[26]378 U.S. 158. Violation of Section 1 of the Sherman Act was also alleged.
[27]*Ibid.*, p. 169.

tition of the corporation that might have remained at the edge of the market continually threatening to enter."[28] The joint venture ended that threat. The Court felt that the District Court had given inadequate attention to the probability of a substantial lessening of competition by the joint venture. It then set forth the following criteria for the trial court to take into account: ". . . . the number and power of the competitors in the relevant market; the background of their growth; the power of the joint ventures; the relationship of their lines of commerce; the competition existing between them and the power of each in dealing with the competitors of the other; the setting in which the joint venture was created; the reasons and necessities for its existence; the joint venture's line of commerce and the relationship thereof to that of its parents; the adaptability of its line of commerce to non-competitive practices; the potential power of the joint venture in the relevant market; an appraisal of what the competition in the relevant market would have been if one of the joint venturers had entered it alone instead of through Penn-Olin; the effect in the event of this occurrence, of the other joint venturer's potential competition; and such other factors as might indicate potential risk to competition in the relevant market. In weighing these factors the court should remember that the mandate of the Congress is in terms of probability of a lessening of substantial competition, not in terms of present restraint."[29] The case was then remanded to the lower court.

Mr. Justice Douglas dissented from the majority ruling on the ground that all agreements to divide markets are a per se violation of Section 1 of the Sherman Act. This, he held, was such an arrangement and the Court should have ended it. Mr. Justice Harlan would have sustained the dismissal verdict of the lower court. The fate of this joint venture appears to be sealed, but the prolonging of litigation in this fashion would seem to call for either a clarification of the respective roles of the trial courts and the Supreme Court or a more definitive statement of the tests of the law that can be understood by both. Perhaps both remedies are in order at the present time.

That the question of what constitutes the line of commerce or the relevant product market is as unclear as it was immediately following the Brown Shoe case is evident from the opinion of the Supreme Court in *United States* v. *Continental Can Co.* (1964).[30] In 1956, Continental Can Co., the second largest producer of metal containers in the United States, acquired all of the assets and goodwill of Hazel-Atlas Glass Co., the third largest producer of glass containers in the country. The District Court established three product markets—metal containers, glass containers, and metal and glass beer containers. The issue was whether the

[28]*Ibid.*, p. 173.
[29]*Ibid.*, p. 177.
[30]378 U.S. 441.

admitted competition between metal and glass containers for uses other than packaging beer was of the type and quality which should serve as the basis for defining the relevant market. In *Times-Picayune* the Court had held that for every product substitutes exist, but a relevant market cannot encompass that infinite range. In the Du Pont cellophane case it said it was improper to require that products be fungible to be considered in the relevant market. "In defining the product market between these terminal extremes, we must recognize meaningful competition where it is found to exist."[31] The Supreme Court held that metal and glass containers competed over a broad range and that "Interchangeability of use and cross-elasticity of demand are not to be used to obscure competition but 'to recognize competition where, in fact, competition exists,' . . . . Thus, though the interchangeability of use may not be so complete, and the cross-elasticity of demand so immediate as in the case of most intraindustry mergers, there is over the long run the kind of customer response to innovation and other competitive stimuli that brings the competition between these two industries within § 7's competitive-preserving proscriptions."[32] The purpose of delineating a line of commerce is to provide an adequate basis for measuring the effects of a given acquisition, and therefore the contours must, as nearly as possible, conform to competitive reality. Where the area of effective competition cuts across industry lines, so must the relevant line of commerce. "Where a merger is of such size as to be inherently suspect, elaborate proof of market structure, market behavior, and probable anticompetitive effects may be dispensed with in view of § 7's design to prevent undue concentration."[33] Finally, the Court closed the opinion by saying "And even though certain lines are today regarded as safely within the domain of one or other of these industries, the pattern may be altered, as it has in the past. From the point of view not only of the static competitive situation, but also the dynamic long-run potential, we think that the Government has discharged its burden of proving prima facie anticompetitive effect."[34] The verdict of the District Court was reversed, and the case was remanded for further consideration.

Mr. Justice Goldberg concurred in the judgment, but stated that as he read the opinion, the Court did not purport finally to decide the determinative line of commerce. Mr. Justice Harlan wrote a vigorous dissent in which he was joined by Mr. Justice Stewart. He contended that "the Court is, in effect, laying down a '*per se*' rule that mergers between two large companies in related industries are presumptively unlawful under §7 . . . . I have no idea where §7 goes from here, nor will businessmen or the antitrust bar."[35]

[31] *Ibid.*, p. 449.
[32] *Ibid.*, pp. 453, 455.
[33] *Ibid.*, p. 458.
[34] *Ibid.*, p. 466.
[35] *Ibid.*, pp. 476, 477.

Summary of Enforcement by Department of Justice

Whatever may have been the intent of Congress when it passed the original Section 7 of the Clayton Act, the results were negligible until the decision of the Supreme Court in the Du Pont-General Motors case. In this instance, the Court indicated clearly, however, that the legislation possessed formidable provisions and that it could be used effectively against intercorporate stock ownership where there was reasonable likelihood that such ownership would result in a restraint of commerce or in the creation of monopoly in any line of commerce. Moreover, the line of commerce (relevant product market) was given a narrow construction, thereby foreshadowing a strict interpretation of limitations on mergers under the Celler-Kefauver amendment. No subsequent cases have been decided under the original section, but the possibility of other suits remains if the Department of Justice should see fit to take action.

The application of the law to banks and natural gas companies is indicative of the wide range of application which the Supreme Court may sanction. This may be broadened to cover companies under the jurisdiction of the other regulatory commissions, perhaps including even the Interstate Commerce Commission. The Court has thus indicated that it intends to give the widest possible scope to what it believes is a congressional determination to limit the growth of concentration by merger and the consequent probability of lessening competition.

Although the Court has not declared mergers to be illegal per se, it appears to have come very close to that position. The exceptions seem to be those where the combination of very small firms would, in the opinion of the Court, enhance competition, or where one of the parties was a failing business. The Court's position is that mergers represent a trend toward concentration, and that it was the congressional intent to put an end to this. The "line of commerce" has been interpreted broadly or narrowly to suit the needs of each particular case; the same remarks apply to "any section of the country." Vertical as well as horizontal mergers have fallen within the prohibitions of the law, although the application to vertical combinations so far has been confined to those involving manufacturing with retail outlets. Joint ventures also seem to entail a genuine risk of illegality if the parties thereto engage in an undertaking in which each of them might engage separately. The scope of this prohibition remains to be seen, but it possesses a vast potentiality.

Interpretation of the new Section 7 thus presents a difficult hurdle for mergers to overcome, and thereby imposes real limitations on concentration by this means. The impact of this on the development of the industrial structure is not easy to foresee. The merger movement at the beginning of the century clearly aided in a rapid development of concentration, but subsequent growth of big business came mostly through other channels. Whether this resulted in further concentration is a matter of serious debate, but certainly it was followed by the era of big business. The present law contains nothing to prevent the further growth of giant enterprises by reinvestment of profits or by appeal to the security markets. Furthermore, these giant enterprises can expand into almost any activity they wish to undertake. Whether they can, by merger, acquire firms that engage in totally unrelated activities remains to be tested, for this will depend upon how broadly the Court interprets the phrase "line of commerce" in its determination to end the trend of concentration by merger. It is clear, however, that if there is a trend toward concentration, and if the conglomerate enterprise poses a threat to competition, then opportunities under existing legislation are ample to accomplish both.[36]

Enforcement by the Federal Trade Commission

The passage of the Celler-Kefauver amendment to Section 7 of the Clayton Act has resulted in a renewed attack on various kinds of mergers by the Federal Trade Commission. Activity of the Commission in this area has gained considerable momentum since 1959. Thus, in the fiscal year 1961, the Commission recorded 1,032 acquisitions, while 55 formal investigations were initiated; in 1962 recorded acquisitions amounted to 1,633, and 26 formal investigations were initiated. In 1962 the Division of Mergers had a backlog of 73 formal investigations and 24 complaint matters in various stages of trial. The program of enforcement for 1963 placed emphasis on completing these cases. Two new complaints were added and only 15 of the total of 26 cases remained in trial status at the end of the year. The other 11 went to the Commission, which issued five orders of divestiture, dismissed two cases, and retained four under advisement.[37]

None of the Commission's orders have as yet been adjudicated by the Supreme Court, nor did the Commission have the benefit of Court interpretation of amended Section 7 until the Brown Shoe case (1962). As a consequence, the Commission has been struggling with its own interpretation of the law as applied to the various mergers against which it has proceeded. In 1953 it issued a complaint against Pillsbury Mills.[38] This company, the second largest flour miller in the United States, acquired the assets of Ballard and Ballard Company and Duff's Baking Mix. The record showed that Pillsbury and Ballard were leaders in the southeastern part of the United States in the sale of family flour, bakery flour, and

[36]For a summary of the enforcement of the Celler-Kefauver Act, see *Administered Prices: A Compendium on Public Policy,* Subcommittee on Antitrust and Monopoly, Committee on the Judiciary, United States Senate, 88th Cong., 1st sess. (Washington, D.C.: Government Printing Office, 1963), pp. 166–75, by A. E. Kahn.

[37]*Annual Report of the Federal Trade Commission,* June, 1963 (Washington, D.C.: Government Printing Office), p. 17.

[38]50 FTC 555 (1953). For an evaluation of the meaning of the amended section, see Federal Trade Commission, *Report on Corporate Mergers and Acquisitions* (Washington, D.C.: U.S. Government Printing Office, 1955), chap. vi.

mixes. The Commission discussed the meaning of the new legislation and the requirements of proof under it. It concluded that the tests were not so severe as those of the Sherman Act. The Clayton Act, as amended, was to arrest potential violations of the Sherman Act in their incipiency. The Commission stated that the law gave no blanket prohibition but instead required a case-by-case examination of all the relevant factors. It held that a prima-facie case had been established against Pillsbury, but that the evidence was as yet inadequate to prove that the situation in the southeast had been converted from a competitive to an noncompetitive situation. At the same time, the pattern in the urban markets exhibited a trend that might be threatening. The case was remanded to the hearing examiner, who had previously dismissed the complaint, for further consideration. After rehearing by the Examiner in the light of the factors which the Commission said had to be given consideration, the Commission issued an order to divestiture. This case is now on appeal in the courts, still awaiting settlement after over 11 years of litigation.

The only case decided so far by the Trade Commission that has been terminated by final court action was that involving the merger of Crown Zellerbach Corp. and St. Helens Pulp and Paper Co.[39] Crown Zellerbach Corporation, the nation's second largest producer of paper and paper products, acquired by exchange practically all of the common stock of St. Helens Pulp and Paper Company of Oregon on February 17, 1953. In September, 1955, St. Helens was fully merged into Crown Zellerbach. In deciding the case, the Commission held that the coarse paper line—including wrapping, bag and sack papers, and converting papers, which both companies manufactured—was within the meaning of "any line of commerce" as set forth in the Du Pont–General Motors case, because these papers were in a relatively allied line in respect to markets and end use. The Commission found that 85 per cent of St. Helens' domestic sales were in the 11 western states, that sales in the Pacific Coast states comprised 88.7 per cent of this and 75.4 per cent of its sales in the United States. At the same time, Crown Zellerbach sold 80 to 85 per cent of its products which were comparable to those produced by St. Helens, in the 11 western states. The Commission also held that the relevant market was a substantial one, in which Crown Zellerbach produced 51.5 per cent and St. Helens, 11 per cent. This, in the opinion of the Commission, constituted a predominant share of the market, considering its relative isolation. Finally, the Commission declared that there was little likelihood that the competition represented by St. Helens would be effectively replaced in the foreseeable future by other paper mills. Crown Zellerbach was consequently ordered to divest itself of all the St. Helens' assets which had been acquired. Action by the Federal Trade Commission ob-

[39] 51 FTC 1105 (1955). See also Luria Brothers, Docket 6156 (1954) now wending its way through the courts.

viously relied on the Supreme Court decision in the Du Pont–General Motors case.

The case was appealed to the courts, and the Circuit Court of Appeals[40] upheld the Commission, but the Court went even further than the Commission in dealing with the relevant line of commerce and the section of the country by adding manufactured bags to those included in the coarse paper line by the Commission, and by stating that the three Pacific Coast states were the proper section of the country.

Just what this decision portends, however, remains to be seen. The tests of illegality employed by the Commission would appear to square well with the decisions on Section 7 rendered so far by the Supreme Court. However, the case-by-case examination may, for various reasons, be subject to serious pitfalls. For example, in the Erie Sand and Gravel case,[41] the company was ordered to divest itself of the assets it had acquired by the purchase of the Sandusky division of the Kelly Island Co. The Commission held that the acquisition tended to lessen competition substantially and to give Erie a monopoly in the sale of lake sand along the southern shore of Lake Erie from Buffalo, N.Y. to Sandusky, Ohio. The Commission also distinguished between "lake sand" and "pit or bank sand." The case was carried to the courts, where the Court of Appeals[42] rejected the distinction between lake and pit sand, although it recognized that the high cost of transportation prevents lake sand from competing with pit sand very far inland. In arguing the case, the Commission's attorneys substituted eight discontinuous areas around the port cities for the continuous strip along the southern shore of Lake Erie. This led the Court to remand the case to the Commission for further consideration.

Recently, the Commission has embarked on a program of investigating firms on an industrywide basis. The milk industry was the first to come under examination. The complaint against *Foremost Dairies* (Docket 6495) resulted in an order of divestiture in 1962.[43] In 1963 *National Dairy Products Corp.* (Docket 6651) entered into a consent settlement- The cases against *Beatrice Foods Co.* (Docket 6653) and *Borden Co.* (Docket 6652) have yet to be decided. The program in the cement industry involves complaints against *Permanente Cement Co.* (Docket 7939), *Diamond Alkali Co.* (Docket 8572), and the *Lone Star Cement Co.* (Docket 8585), all of which await final disposition. In addition, the complaint against American Marietta Co. which had acquired some 46 companies engaged in the manufacture and sale of concrete pipe, cement, lime, and

[40]*Crown Zellerbach Corp.* v. *Federal Trade Commission*, 296 Fed. (2d) 800 (1961), certiorari denied 370 U.S. 937 (1962).

[41]FTC Docket 6670 (1956).

[42]*Erie Sand and Gravel Co.* v. *Federal Trade Commission*, 291 Fed. (2d) 279 (1961).

[43]Foremost Dairies has recently disposed of its properties in both the northeastern and southeastern regions of the United States (*Los Angeles Times*, September 8, 1964).

other products, became the case against *Martin-Marietta Co.* (Docket 8280) as the result of the merger of American Marietta and the Martin Co. of Baltimore. This was settled by a consent decree with an order of divestiture.

The complaint against *Consolidated Foods, Inc.* (Docket 7000) arose out of the acquisition by Consolidated Foods, a large diversified processor and seller of food products, of Gentry, Inc., a company engaged in the production of dehydrated onion and garlic. The issue at stake is the competitive effect of the practice of "reciprocity" or "reciprocal buying," whereby Consolidated, it is alleged, is now afforded the opportunity to use coercion, expressed or implied, to induce suppliers to purchase all or some of their dehydrated onion and garlic requirements from the Gentry Division of Consolidated. The case is now on appeal to the courts.

It is obvious that the Trade Commission has embarked upon an aggressive and sweeping attack on mergers in industries under its jurisdiction. It is unfortunate that in the fourteen years since the Celler-Kefauver Act was passed, none of the Commission's decisions have had the benefit of adjudication by the Supreme Court. Some basis of optimism for success may be gained from the results of the Crown Zellerbach case. With the guide lines afforded by the Supreme Court in the cases prosecuted by the Justice Department, the Commission should be able to shape its orders to conform to the tests of illegality that have been supplied.[44]

INTERLOCKING DIRECTORATES

Section 8 of the Clayton Act has not been very effective,[45] and the Supreme Court has not yet elected authoritatively to construe its provisions. There appears to be no legal barrier to interlocks among potential competitors, and apparently none against sellers and market outlets. However, in *United States* v. *Sears Roebuck & Co.* (1953),[46] a federal court interpreted the law in a way that indicates it may have more scope than was theretofore assumed. Sidney J. Weinberg was a director of Sears, Roebuck and Company and of B. F. Goodrich. The Court stated that the basic question was whether Sears and Goodrich are "competitors so that elimination of competition by agreement between them would constitute a violation of any of the provisions of the anti-trust laws." The

[44]Private suit has also been used with success as a basis of action under Section 7. The Benrus Watch Co. acquired 24 per cent of the voting stock of Hamilton Watch Co., and Hamilton brought suit for an injunction to restrain Benrus from voting the stock and from acquiring additional shares. The suit also sought an order requiring divestment of the stock. The District Court granted a temporary injection which was affirmed by the Court of Appeals after which Benrus disposed of the stock. *Hamilton Watch Co.* v. *Benrus Watch Co.;* 114 Fed. Supp. 307 (1953); 206 Fed. (2d) 738 (1953). See also *American Crystal Sugar Co.* v. *Cuban-American Sugar Co.* 152 Fed. Supp. 387 (1957); affirmed 259 Fed. (2d) 324 (1958).

[45]See Federal Trade Commission, *Report on Interlocking Directorates* (Washington, D.C.: U.S. Government Printing Office, 1951).

[46]111 Fed. Supp. 614.

Court also noted that this was the first construction of this section since the Clayton Act was passed in 1914.

The Court held that the intention of the law was to nip incipient violations in the bud and that the legislation was essentially preventive. It held that Section 8 omits the Section 7 test and substitutes its own substantiality standard by the $1-million-dollar capital, surplus, and undivided profits requirement for any one corporation. An agreement between Sears and Goodrich to fix prices on the seven products specified would eliminate competition. In fact, an agreement to this effect would be a per se violation of the law. Therefore, this interlocking directorship violated Section 8.

The possibilities of evasion by other means are such that this decision may not be very effective. Furthermore, this decision has not had the benefit of Supreme Court adjudication; and the vague tests used by the lower court might well fall short of winning final approval.

The Commission in its report on interlocking directorates pointed out their possible anticompetitive effects, and recommended amendments to the law to Congress. No action was taken. Perhaps the rigorous application of the amended Section 7 of the Clayton Act and the attack on "reciprocity" or "reciprocal buying" will lead to a reawakening of the need to examine the effects of interlocking directorates on competition. In any case, a comprehensive antitrust policy in keeping with the new program of enforcement calls for careful reconsideration of the problem of interlocking directorates by all the public agencies concerned.

Chapter 16 AGREEMENTS RESTRICTING COMPETITION

INTRODUCTION

Attempts to control the market by various forms of agreements among independent enterprises have continuously come before the courts. The way of the transgressor may be hard; but it is also characterized by so many ingenious, disingenious, and variegated devices that the way of law enforcement is even harder. The task of the analyst is frequently almost insuperable. Each case under consideration presents new issues, new devices, and new pleadings; and each case is decided on its merits. As a consequence, classification of offenses under the law, on the basis of principles enunciated, is extremely difficult. The following treatment groups the cases, in general, according to the methods used to restrict competition. Withing each group, the chronological approach has been adopted, in order to bring out, as far as possible, the development of the law and the shifting nature of the issues.

One generalization on the application of the law to agreements, as contrasted with mergers, may be made. The courts have interpreted the law more strictly in the case of the former than the latter, presumably because the issues are clearer when independents agree among themselves to restrict their freedom of action. Even this generalization must be qualified by the latitude granted to the holders of patent rights, which is reserved for separate treatment. The facts, nevertheless, are still subject to a reasonable interpretation; but the scope of application of the rule of reason is much narrower as a general rule.

AGREEMENTS AMONG INDEPENDENTS

The status of price fixing by agreement under the Sherman Act first came before the Supreme Court in the Traffic Association cases. The first of these was *United States* v. *Trans-Missouri Freight Association* (1897).[1] In 1889, a number of railroad companies operating south and west of the Missouri River formed the Trans-Missouri Freight Association for the purpose of establishing and maintaining reasonable rates, rules, and regulations. The Association continued to operate after the passage of the Sherman Act, and the government brought suit to have

[1]166 U.S. 290.

it dissolved. The railroads advanced the defense that the Sherman Act did not apply to them because of the passage of the Act to Regulate Commerce in 1887, and that, in any case, the agreement was reasonable and therefore legal under the law. The Court denied both contentions and stated that the Act included every contract, combination, in the form of trust or otherwise, or conspiracy in restraint of trade or commerce among the several states or with foreign nations.

The defendants argued that the law was aimed only at those contracts which were in unreasonable restraint of trade. In discussing this contention, the majority of the Court stated that a contract may be in restraint of trade and still be valid at common law; but, although valid, it is still a contract in restraint of trade and, consequently, illegal under the Sherman Act. The Court insisted that Congress intended to outlaw all contracts in restraint of trade and that to rule otherwise would be judicial legislation. Finally, the majority stated that the direct, immediate, and necessary effect of the agreement was to put a restraint upon trade and commerce within the meaning of the Sherman law. This was held to be illegal.

Four Justices rendered a vigorous dissenting opinion, in which they contended that the words "restraint of trade" embraced only contracts which unreasonably restrained trade. Reasonable contracts, therefore, they contended, although they in some measure restrained trade, were not within the meaning of the Sherman Act.

The same issue came before the Court again in *United States* v. *Joint Traffic Association* (1898).[2] This association was formed, as the result of an agreement of a number of railroads operating east of Chicago, to establish and maintain reasonable rates, fares, rules, and regulations. The defendants not only maintained that they did not restrain trade at all but also argued for a reconsideration of the Trans-Missouri case. They urged that the effect of the decision in the latter was to render illegal most business contracts or combinations, however indispensable and necessary they might be.

The majority of the Court disagreed with this contention. It stated that the statute applied only to those contracts whose direct and immediate effect was a restraint upon interstate commerce. The Act was not intended to deal with agreements whose effect on interstate commerce was indirect or incidental only. The law had to be given a reasonable construction; and nothing that the Court had ever said justified the conclusion that an agreement entered into for the purpose of promoting the legitimate business of an individual or corporation, with no purpose thereby to affect or restrain interstate commerce, and which did not directly restrain such commerce, was illegal. The majority felt that the effect of the agreement was to prevent lower rates which would re-

[2]171 U.S. 505. See also *Hopkins* v. *United States*, 171 U.S. 578 (1898).

sult from the interplay of free competitive forces; therefore, it was illegal and void.

The division of opinion among the Justices of the Supreme Court in these cases over what came to be known as the "rule of reason" really centered on questions of public policy and the role the Court was to play in passing upon them. Competition among railroads of the type required by this interpretation of the Sherman Act was unworkable, but Congress had not yet seen fit to put railroads in a separate category. Given the assumption that one of the purposes of antitrust is to maintain competition among independent firms, the majority was undoubtedly right in its reasoning. Subsequent decisions were to confirm the position taken in these cases and to place such price-fixing agreements in the category of per se violations of the law.

The restrictive decision in the E. C. Knight case which distinguished between commerce and manufacturing was largely overcome in *Addyston Pipe and Steel Company* v. *United States* (1899).[3] This case settled the question as to whether an agreement to restrict competition among sellers, even though they were manufacturing concerns, was a restraint on interstate commerce. In addition, the Court also held that the restraints that went beyond the ancillary restrictions sanctioned by common law were illegal under the Sherman Act.

The association, of which Addyston Pipe and Steel was a member, was formed by 6 cast-iron pipe companies, 2 each in Alabama and Tennessee and 1 each in Ohio and Kentucky, for the purpose of ending competitive bidding among them in 36 states. In 1895, they agreed that prices were to be fixed by the association for each contract; and except in reserved cities, the bidder was to be determined by competitive bidding of the members, the one agreeing to give the highest bonus for division among the others getting the contract. The reserved cities were allotted by agreement, and the other members were excluded therefrom. It was contended by the members of the association that the contract was only a reasonable restraint upon ruinous competition among themselves and that it was formed solely for the purpose of protecting them in securing prices that were fair and reasonable to themselves and to the public. It was also argued that the agreement was not one which amounted to regulation of interstate commerce.

The Supreme Court disagreed with this defense and ordered the association dissolved. In reaching its conclusion, the Court agreed that the pool did not possess a complete monopoly. The pool was tempered by the fear of competition, and it affected only part of the price. However, in order to vitiate a contract or combination, it was not essential that its result should be a complete monopoly. It was sufficient if it really tended to create a monopoly and to deprive the public of the ad-

[3]175 U.S. 211. See also *Swift & Co.* v. *United States*, 196 U.S. 375 (1905); and *Eastern States Retail Lumber Dealers Assn.* v. *United States*, 234 U.S. 600 (1914).

vantages which flow from free competition. The association maintained that the prices at which cast-iron pipe was sold in pay territory were reasonable. The Court did not think that, at common law, there was any question of reasonableness open to the Court with reference to such a contract. In addition, the Court did not think that the price being charged for cast-iron pipe was a reasonable one. The association also argued that the ruling of the Supreme Court in the Knight case removed it from the operation of the Sherman law. In answering this, the Court pointed out that the prime purpose of the contract was the sale and delivery of pipe, and that a sale for delivery beyond a state boundary made the transaction a part of interstate commerce. The direct and immediate result of the combination was necessarily a restraint upon interstate commerce.

Adoption of the "rule of reason" by the Supreme Court in the Standard Oil case posed the question of its possible application to price-fixing agreements. The Supreme Court answered this decisively in the negative in *United States* v. *Trenton Potteries Company et al.* (1927).[4] This is the leading case decided by the Supreme Court on direct price fixing by agreement. It not only summarized the status of the law to that date; it is also the law today. Trenton Potteries was a member of the Sanitary Potters Association, which was a trade organization whose members produced 82 per cent of the vitreous pottery fixtures in the United States. The members of the Association combined to fix prices and to limit sales in interstate commerce to jobbers. It was the contention of the Association that the essence of the law was injury to the public. Not every restraint of competition and not every restraint of trade worked injury to the public; only an undue and unreasonable restraint of trade had such an effect and was deemed to be unlawful. The trial court refused to charge the jury with this contention.

The Supreme Court was unwilling to accept the view that agreement to fix or maintain prices was reasonable restraint and therefore permitted by the statute, merely because the prices themselves were reasonable. Although the Court held that reasonableness was not a concept of definite and unchanging content, it was nevertheless the assumption of the Sherman law and the judicial decisions interpreting it that the public interest was best protected from the evils of monopoly and price control by the maintenance of competition. The Court then stated:

> The aim and result of every price-fixing agreement, if effective, is the elimination of one form of competition. The power to fix prices, whether reasonably exercised or not, involves power to control the market and to fix arbitrary and unreasonable prices. The reasonable price fixed today may, due to economic and business changes, become the unreasonable price of tomorrow. Once established it may be maintained unchanged because of the absence of competition secured by the agreement for a price reasonable when fixed. Agreements which create such potential

[4] 273 U.S. 392.

power may well be held to be in themselves unreasonable or unlawful restraint, without the necessity of minute inquiry, whether a particular price is reasonable or unreasonable as fixed, and without placing on the government in enforcing the Sherman law the burden of ascertaining from day to day whether it has become unreasonable through the mere variation of economic conditions. Moreover, in the absence of express legislation requiring it, we should hesitate to adopt a construction making the difference between legal and illegal conduct in the field of business relations depend upon so uncertain a test as whether prices are reasonable—a determination which can be satisfactorily made only after a complete survey of our economic organization and a choice between rival philosophies.[5]

Then, after an extensive review of the rulings of prior cases decided by the Supreme Court, the verdict of the trial court, which found the defendants guilty of violating the Sherman antitrust law, was upheld. Whatever the status of price-fixing power of single combinations may be, it is clear that its mere existence as the result of agreement violates the Sherman Act.

Despite what seemed to be a decisive ruling on the status of agreements among independent producers, an element of serious doubt was introduced by the Supreme Court verdict in *Appalachian Coals, Inc., et al.* v. *United States* (1933).[6]

Appalachian Coals was an exclusive selling agency formed by 137 producers of bituminous coal in the Appalachian territory. The defendants produced 74.4 per cent of the coal of this area. The government contended that the plan violated the Sherman Act, because it eliminated competition among the defendants themselves and gave the selling agency power substantially to affect and control the price of bituminous coal in many interstate markets. The defendants insisted that the primary purpose of the formation of the selling agency was to increase the sale, and thus the production, of Appalachian coal through better methods of distribution, intensive advertising, and research, and that it was designed to achieve economies in marketing and to eliminate destructive trade practices.

The Court took the position that, in applying the Sherman Act, realities must dominate judgment, and the mere fact that the parties to an agreement eliminated competition among themselves was not enough to condemn the arrangement. The Court ruled that, in applying the statute, attention must be given to intent and effect; and this could not be determined by arbitrary assumption. It found that conditions in the coal industry were severely depressed and chaotic. The defendants contended that the purpose of the plan was to bring about a better and more orderly marketing of coal from the region, so that through more orderly marketing, the producers would be able to compete more effectively for a fair share of the available coal business. No attempt, how-

[5] *Ibid.*, pp. 397–98.

[6] 288 U.S. 344; see also *Standard Oil (Indiana)* v. *United States*, 283 U.S. 163 (1931).

ever, was to be made to limit production. The producer was to be able to produce, and the selling agent to sell, as much coal as possible. The Court agreed that the defendants' intentions were good; but this, of itself, would not have saved the plan. However, knowledge of actual intent, the Court found, was an aid in the interpretation of fact and the prediction of consequences. It was held that the agency had no intent or power to fix prices, that abundant competitive opportunities still existed in all the markets where the defendants' coal was sold, and that nothing was shown to warrant the conclusion that the defendants' plan would have an injurious effect upon competition in these markets. Finally, the Court ruled that, when a suit was brought under the Sherman Act, there had to be a definite factual showing of illegality; and this the government failed to make. The Court decided that Appalachian Coals did not violate the Sherman law; but because the effects of the plan could not be discovered at that time, it instructed the District Court to retain jurisdiction, with power to institute further proceedings if future developments justified them.

Two factors seem to have influenced this decision. First of all, the United States was at the bottom of the Great Depression. Everywhere, steps were being taken to restrict competition and to restrain price cutting. The Supreme Court was responding—in part, at least—to this development. In the second place, the rule of reason seems to have played its part, for the Court felt that the agreement did not constitute an unreasonable restraint of trade.

The controlling effect of the Trenton Potteries decision was emphasized a few years later, however, in *United States* v. *Socony-Vacuum Oil Company* (1940)[7] which held that price-fixing agreements were illegal per se. The government charged that 12 major oil companies and 5 individuals combined and conspired arbitrarily to fix the tank-car prices of gasoline in the midwestern area, exacted contracts that made the price to the jobber dependent upon the average spot-market price, and intensely raised the general level of retail prices prevailing in the midwestern area. The Court took cognizance of the acute conditions which prevailed in the petroleum industry and the wholesale market in the early 1930's. It noted that the government, through Secretary of the Interior Ickes, had set up a code of fair competition to be administered by him. The Court found, however, that the respondents had not obtained immunity from prosecution under the antitrust laws by securing authorization under the National Industrial Recovery Act for the agreement. It was brought out that the agreement had not received the approval of the petroleum administrator. Moreover, the arrangements continued after the National Industrial Recovery Act had been declared unconstitutional in 1935. Besides trying to prove that they had con-

[7]310 U.S. 150.

formed to the spirit of the National Industrial Recovery Act, the defendants also relied upon the ruling in the Appalachian Coals case.

The Supreme Court held that the fact that the buying program might have been consistent with the general objectives and ends sought to be obtained under the National Industrial Recovery Act was irrelevant, since price-fixing combinations which lack congressional sanction are illegal, per se. It also ruled that Appalachian Coals was not controlling, since in that instance, there was no attempt to fix prices, and the arrangement would not contribute to that end. Instead, the Court relied heavily on the Trenton Potteries case and stated that agreements which create potential power for such price maintenance, exhibited by its actual exertion for that purpose, are in themselves unlawful restraints within the meaning of the Sherman Act. It held that the elimination of so-called "competitive evils" is no legal justification for price-fixing arrangements. "Congress has not left with us the determination of whether or not the particular price-fixing means are wise or unwise, healthy or destructive. It has not permitted the age-old cry of ruinous competition and competitive evils to be a defense in price-fixing conspiracies"[8] And further: "Under the Sherman Act a combination formed for the purpose and with the effect of raising, depressing, fixing, pegging or stabilizing the price of a commodity in interstate or foreign commerce is illegal *per se*."[9] The Court admitted that price-fixing agreements might be useful to members of a group, even though the power possessed or exerted fell far short of domination and control; but it asserted that proof that a combination was formed for the purpose of fixing prices or that it contributed to that result was proof of the completion of a price-fixing conspiracy. It would thus seem that no price-fixing agreement, no matter what degree of control is exercised, can stand the test of the Sherman law.

Price fixing, even when evidence of formal agreement is lacking, has also been condemned with the inference of unanimity of action cannot be escaped. This was the situation in *Interstate Circuit Company, Inc.*, v. *United States* (1939).[10] The manager of two major exhibitors of motion pictures, located chiefly in Texas and controlling most of the first-run theaters in that area, wrote identical letters to 8 major distributors of motion pictures. This letter stated that Interstate Circuit would not agree to purchase films to be exhibited in its "A" theaters at a price of 40 cents or more for night admission, unless the distributors agreed that this "A" product would never be exhibited at any time or in any theater at a smaller admission price than 25 cents for adults in the evening. It also required that these "A" pictures should never be exhibited in conjunction with another feature picture, under the so-called "policy of

[8]*Ibid.*, p. 221.
[9]*Ibid.*, p. 223.
[10]306 U.S. 208. See also *United States* v. *Masonite Corp.* 316 U.S. 265 (1942) 275.

double features." Conferences were then held with representatives of each of the distributors; and a uniform contract was entered into, in line with the letter. Although there was no direct proof of agreement among the 8 distributors, the Court felt that the unanimity of action must have been the result of understanding, and rejected, as beyond the range of probability, the idea that it was the result of mere chance. It was acceptance of this type of proof of agreement that later led to the idea of conscious parallelism of action.[11]

The line of reasoning in the Interstate case was given more explicit recognition in *American Tobacco Co.* v. *United States* (1946).[12] Here the identity of behavior of the defendants pointed to a common plan of action and knowledge of that plan by them. This was a criminal case against the American Tobacco Company, Liggett and Myers Tobacco Company, R. J. Reynolds Tobacco Company, and American Suppliers, Inc., a subsidiary of American, and certain officials of the respective companies. The defendants were convicted by jury in a district court trial. The appeal to the Supreme Court was on the convictions under Section 2 of the Sherman Act.

Mr. Justice Burton, speaking for the Court, stated that the crime of monopolizing under the Sherman Act was "to combine or conspire to acquire or maintain the power to exclude competitors from any part of the trade or commerce among the states or with foreign nations provided that [the parties] also have 'such a power' that they are able, as a group, to exclude actual or potential competition from the field and provided that they have the intent and purpose to use that power."[13] No formal agreement is necessary to constitute an unlawful conspiracy. Neither proof of exertion of the power to exclude nor proof of actual exclusion of existing or potential competitors is essential to sustain a charge of monopolization.

This reasoning was in keeping with the Trenton Potteries case. The difference came in the proof of violation. The conspiracy was established not through the presentation of a formal written agreement but through evidence of widespread effective conduct on the part of the tobacco firms in relation to their existing or potential competition. In other words, the evidence was entirely circumstantial. Statistics showed that the "Big Three" enjoyed the title by virtue of their commanding position in most of the tobacco industry. The record showed that the "Big Three" spent over $40 million a year for advertising, and the Court noted that such tremendous advertising was a warning that these com-

[11]The Court may have been influenced by the fact that the motion-picture industry seemed to be in almost continuous difficulty with the law. See *Paramount Famous Lasky Corp.* v. *United States*, 282 U.S. 30 (1930); *United States* v. *First National Pictures, Inc.*, 282 U.S. 44 (1930); *United States* v. *Crescent Amusement Co.*, 323 U.S. 173 (1944).

[12]328 U.S. 781.

[13]*Ibid.*, p. 809.

panies possessed and knew how to use a powerful offensive and defensive weapon against new competition. The government also presented evidence of common action, such as refusal on the part of one of the companies to purchase tobacco at auction markets unless the others were present, adherence of their buyers to common price ceilings, and in simultaneous price changes.

The basis for determining guilt in this case was what has come be be labeled as "conscious parallelism of action." The jury arrived at the verdict of criminal conspiracy from evidence that presumably convinced it that the uniform behavior of the defendants was not mere coincidence but, on the contrary, was part of a planned course of action. If the defendants had agreed to what they did, they would clearly have violated the law. If they had acted completely independently of one another, they would not have done so.

The same issue has arisen on other occasions, but it gained its greatest prominence in the basing-point controversy. Here, the Supreme Court said: "It is enough to warrant a finding of 'combination' within the meaning of the Sherman Act, if there is evidence that persons with knowledge that concerted action was contemplated and invited, give adherence to and then participate in a scheme."[14] Persons familiar with price and market theory will recognize that mere parallelism of action in price and market behavior is not of itself evidence of collusion or agreement, and therefore alone does not provide a sound legal basis for proceeding against alleged violators. The Court has recently given recognition to this.

> To be sure, business behavior is admissible circumstantial evidence from which fact the finder may infer agreement. . . . But this Court has never held that proof of parallel business behavior conclusively establishes agreement or phrased differently, that such behavior itself constitutes a Sherman Act offense. Circumstantial evidence of consciously parallel behavior may have made heavy inroads into the traditional judicial attitude toward conspiracy; but "conscious parallelism" has not yet read conspiracy out of the Sherman Act entirely.[15]

However, it should be noted that conscious parallelism might carry more weight under the Clayton Act or before the Federal Trade Commission.

Violation of the Sherman Act may even result from agreement among the members of a single corporate family. Thus, in *Schine Chain Theatres, Inc. et al.* v. *United States* (1948),[16] the conspiracy charged was between the Schine defendants themselves, and between them and the distributors. The Court held that "the concerted action of the parent company, its subsidiaries, and the named officers and directors in that endeavor was a conspiracy which was not immunized by reason of the

[14]*Federal Trade Commission* v. *Cement Institute*, 333 U.S. 683 (1948) 716.

[15]*Theater Enterprises, Inc.* v. *Paramount Film Distributing Corp. et al.*, 346 U.S. 537 (1954) 541.

[16]334 U.S. 110, 116.

fact that the members were closely affiliated rather than independent." To this, the Court added, in *United States* v. *L. C. Griffith et al.* (1948),[17] that "monopoly power whether lawfully or unlawfully acquired, may itself constitute an evil and stand condemned under section 2 even though it remains unexercised." So also, a conspiracy to monopolize violates Section 2, even though monopoly power was never acquired.

> "The substance of the Supreme Court decision is that concerted action between a parent and a subsidiary or between subsidiaries, which has for its purpose or effect coercion or unreasonable restraint on the trade of strangers to those acting in concert, is prohibited by Section 1. . . . Where such concerted action restrains no trade and is designed to restrain no trade other than that of the parent and its subsidiaries, Section 1 is not violated."[18]

Probably the most widespread and incredible price-fixing conspiracy in the history of antitrust enforcement was that in which the Department of Justice charged 29 manufacturers of electrical equipment, including General Electric and Westinghouse, and 45 of their executives, with criminally conspiring to fix prices and allocate markets in violation of the Sherman Act. The defendants, which did not include the top executives of the corporations, sought to plead *nolo contendere*, but attorneys for the government opposed this, and the judge rejected the pleas. The defendants then changed their pleas to guilty, and penalties were assessed without trial.[19] The offenses to which the defendants pleaded guilty were: price fixing, price rigging, allocation of business, and division of markets. Sentences imposed by the Court included both fines and imprisonment, the total fines amounting to nearly $2 million, and seven of the executives were sentenced to jail. In addition, the pleas of guilty exposed the convicted firms to suits from buyers for treble damages. A large number of these are still being processed in the courts.

Guilt of the top executives in the conspiracy has never been established legally. If they were not guilty, then the shortcomings of organization and top management are alarmingly great in these giant enterprises. Whatever the situation may be, the case and the verdicts indicate clearly that responsible executives cannot flout the law without accepting the consequences of doing so, regardless of the orders of their superiors.

[17]334 U.S. 100, 107. See also *Kiefer-Stewart Co.* v. *Joseph E. Seagram & Sons, Inc.*, 340 U.S. 211 (1951).

[18]The Attorney-General's National Committee, *Antitrust Laws* (Washington, D.C.: U.S. Government Printing Office, 1955), p. 34. See also *United States* v. *Timkin Roller Bearing Co.*, 83 Fed. Supp. 284 (1949), affirmed 341 U.S. 593 (1951).

[19]For a scathing description of the whole conspiracy and the proceedings involved therein, see John G. Fuller, *The Gentlemen Conspirators* (New York: Grove Press Inc. 1962). See also *Collusion Among Electrical Equipment Manufacturers*, Wall Street Journal (January 10, 12, 1962); *Administered Prices*, Hearings, Subcommittee on Antitrust and Monopoly, Committee of the Judiciary, United States Senate, 87th Cong., 1st sess., S.Res. 52, Parts 27 and 28 (Washington, D.C.: U.S. Government Printing Office, 1961).

TRADE ASSOCIATION ACTIVITIES

The use of trade associations to effect control of the market was a rather common device in the early days of the development of the trust movement. Its generally adverse reception at the hands of the courts, however, led to a change in organization and procedure immediately prior to World War I. This came about in the form of what were known as "open-price associations," in which the trade association was set up for the purpose of collecting and disseminating extensive information on a particular trade to the competitors who were organized in the association. It was believed that such a procedure would promote the good of the trade, advance business ethics, and insure healthy and free competition.

Government policy during the first World War, by its emphasis on co-operation for increased production, lent support to the movement. The period of prosperity following the war, together with the live-and-let-live policy that ensued therefrom and the development of the idea of self-government of industry, served further to promote the trade association movement. However, the difficulty that emerged was that of distinguishing between the activities of the so-called "open-price associations" which led to the furtherance of healthy competition and those which were designed to restrict it. The issues involved have come before the courts in a number of significant cases, and the opinions which the Supreme Court has rendered indicate the complexity of the issues involved and the difficulty of establishing bench marks which satisfactorily delineate restrictive practices from those which further the bases of competitive enterprise.

Proceedings against trade associations that have employed "open-price" policies have been initiated principally by the Department of Justice. The first of the cases involving these issues to appear before the Supreme Court was that of *American Column and Lumber* v. *United States* (1921).[20] The American Hardwood Manufacturers Association was a unincorporated association formed in December, 1918, out of a combination of two previous similar associations. From one of the latter, the Hardwood Association took over an activity known as "the open-competition plan." The government alleged that the plan constituted a combination and conspiracy in violation of the Sherman Antitrust Act.

According to the records of the Association, the open-competition plan was a central clearinghouse for information on prices, trade statistics, and practices. This resulted in a certain uniformity of trade practices, although there was no agreement among the members to follow the practices of each other. But it was recognized that members do

[20]257 U.S. 377.

naturally follow their most intelligent competitors, if they know what these competitors have actually been doing. Each member of the Association was required to make 6 reports to the secretary. These consisted of a daily report of all sales actually made, with the name and address of the purchaser and the commodity which he bought; a daily shipping report, with exact copies of all invoices and other information; a monthly production report, showing the production (during the previous month) of the member reporting; a monthly stock report by each member, showing the stock on hand on the first day of the month—sold, unsold, greens, dry, etc.; price lists filed at the beginning of each month, showing prices F.O.B. shipping point; and inspection reports, made by the Association and established for the purpose of checking on grades of the various members, the stocks of the members being checked by a chief inspector of the Association periodically. All of the reports were subject to complete audit, and any member who failed to report for 12 days in 6 months was to be dropped from the membership. The voluminous disclosures made to the Association were then communicated to the members, periodically, in a condensed and interpreted form.

The majority of the Court found that the whole arrangement lacked only a definite agreement as to production and prices to make it the familiar type of competition-suppressing organization. However, the Association possessed sufficient coercive power to make this unnecessary. Moreover, at meetings held throughout the year in every part of the territory covered, every effort was made to induce the members to cooperate in restricting production. The record disclosed a persistent drive to encourage members to unite in pressing for higher and higher prices, and this seemed to be not only the prime purpose of the plan but also its achievement. The Court found that the whole plan constituted conduct "of men united in an agreement, expressed or implied, to act together and pursue a common purpose under a common guide that, if it did not stand confessed a combination to restrict production and increase prices in interstate commerce, and as therefore a direct restraint upon that commerce, as we have seen that it is, that conclusion must inevitably have been inferred from the facts which were proved."[21] This, the Court held, was an old form of combination in restraint of trade and, therefore, in violation of the Sherman law. The whole scheme seemed to be a definite arrangement to restrict competition by a device which would escape the condemnation of the Sherman law.

The differences of opinion on the validity of such schemes which can easily arise, however, are well illustrated by the fact that Mr. Justice Holmes and Mr. Justice Brandeis wrote strong dissenting opinions, contending that the ideal of commerce is "an intelligent interchange made with full knowledge of the facts as a basis for a forecast of the future

[21] *Ibid.*, p. 410.

on both sides."[22] They could find no evidence of coercion or purpose to curtail production, or any intent to enhance prices. Justice Brandeis felt that the members merely intended to rationalize competition; and if they failed by this method, they might be induced to turn to outright consolidation. With all due respect to the minority opinions, it would seem that, if any arrangement other than an outright agreement to restrict production and enhance prices violated the Sherman law, this one did.

The differences of opinion seem to have arisen from the endeavor of the minority to apply to literally the assumptions of perfect competition.[23] These assumptions are made in the construction of an analytic model for the purpose of ascertaining the most economical allocation of resources. It does not follow that competition in fact will possess all the attributes of the model, or that it is even necessary for competitors to exchange information. In fact, unrestricted opportunity to do so is one of the easiest ways to arrive at collusion.

In *Maple Flooring Manufacturers Association* v. *United States* (1925),[24] the Supreme Court rendered a verdict favorable to the activities of this trade association, on the ground that the activities, as conducted, did not have the necessary tendency to cause direct and undue restraint of competition, as condemned by the Sherman law.

Chief Justice Taft, Mr. Justice Hanford, and Mr. Justice McReynolds dissented from the majority opinion, because they felt that the case fell within the rule of the American Column and Lumber Company and the American Linseed Oil Company cases, since the evidence disclosed carefully developed plans to eliminate normal competition in interstate commerce.

The majority of the Court pointed out that there was no allegation in the indictment of any agreement among the members of the Association either to affect production, to fix prices, or to insure price maintenance. The activity of the Association showed that members were left free to sell their product at any price they chose and to conduct their business as they pleased. Furthermore, there was no direct proof that the Association had affected prices to consumers adversely. On the contrary, there was evidence that the prices were fair and reasonable. The Court examined the business of the Association at great length and found that in no instance was there evidence of any necessary tendency to restrain competition. The majority opinion concluded by saying:

> We decide only that trade associations or combinations of persons or corporations, which openly and fairly gather and disseminate information as to the cost of their product, the volume of production, the actual price which the product has

[22] *Ibid.*, p. 412.

[23] See also *United States* v. *American Linseed Oil Co.*, 262 U.S. 371 (1923), in which an arrangement very similar to that of the Hardwood case was held to be illegal.

[24] 268 U.S. 563.

brought in past transactions, stocks of merchandise on hand, approximate cost of transportation from the principal point of shipment to the points of consumption, as did these defendants, and who, as they did, meet and discuss such information and statistics without, however, reaching or attempting to reach any agreement or any concerted action with respect to prices or production or restraining competition, do not thereby engage in unlawful restraint of commerce.[25]

The majority also insisted that "each case arising under the Sherman Act must be determined upon the particular facts disclosed by the record, and that the opinions in those cases must be read in the light of their facts and of a clear recognition of the essential differences in the facts of those cases and in the facts of any new case to which the rule of earlier decisions is to be applied.[26]

It is clear that the facts were slightly different from those presented in earlier cases. This was, in part, the result of a change in activities of the Maple Flooring Association, as the consequence of earlier decisions involving trade associations. However, that change does not seem to have been sufficient to warrant the conclusion that there was any material difference in the situations. It seems more reasonable to assert that, had the case been decided four years earlier, the verdict would have been in accordance with the earlier decisions. Once again, the dissenting opinions seem to have become the majority—such are the vicissitudes of the law.

On the same day that it disposed of the Maple Flooring case, the Supreme Court handed down the decision in *Cement Manufacturers Protective Association* v. *United States* (1925).[27] The facts in this instance are sufficiently similar to the previous case to warrant the omission of a recitation of them. The Court held that the purposes of controlling the production and price of cement could not be inferred from the activities of the organization, and that they were not, in themselves, unlawful restraints of commerce prohibited by the Sherman law.

One point to which the Court referred in the Maple Flooring case was discussed at greater length in the Cement case. That related to the effect of competition on price uniformity. Many distinguished economists testified that in the case of a standardized product, sold wholesale to fully informed professional buyers, as with the dealers in cement, uniformity of price will inevitably result from active, free, and unrestrained competition. The government alleged that price uniformity was evidence of agreement. No proof of agreement was established, and the Court evidently relied on the theory of the operation of the perfect market to reject any inference of agreement. That a theoretically perfect market would result in price uniformity seems to be beyond dispute, but the facts disclosed in the case seemed to indicate that price uniformity must

[25] *Ibid.*, p. 586.
[26] *Ibid.*, p. 579.
[27] 268 U.S. 588.

have resulted from the activities of the association or by the rarest coincidence.

A further modification of the rulings on the legitimate activities of open-price associations came in *Sugar Institute* v. *United States* (1936).[28] The members of this Institute refined practically all of the imported raw sugar processed in the United States and, after 1927, supplied from 70–80 per cent of all the sugar consumed in this country. During the first World War, the government fixed prices and forbade all forms of concessions and rebates. After government control was removed, and probably as early as 1921, some of the refiners developed the practice of giving secret concessions. This practice spread widely, and the Court felt that one of the reasons for it was lack of statistical information on the sugar industry. The evidence left no doubt that the industry was in a demoralized state, which called for remedial measures. A basic agreement was drawn up, under a code of ethics adopted in 1928, by which all discriminations between customers were to be abolished and sugar was to be sold only upon open prices in terms publicly announced. This was in accordance with established conditions in the trade, but the distinctive feature was a requirement of adherence without deviation to the prices and terms which were publicly announced. The lower court held that the range and effect of this restriction constituted an unreasonable restraint of trade.

A number of other practices designed to support the basic agreements were condemned by the lower court. The Sugar Institute required that the activities of broker, warehouseman, and merchant, or other user of sugar, should be separated. Prior to the formation of the Institute, these functions frequently had been combined; and the lower court concluded that such a combination of functions led to a definite possibility of lower prices to ultimate consumers. The lower court also found that the Institute introduced a policy of delivered prices in place of the old F.O.B. arrangement; that the members concertedly policed these delivered prices and investigated alleged departures therefrom; and that, furthermore, the prices were patently unreasonable. The evidence satisfied the Court that the defendants acted concertedly with respect to the elimination and reduction of consignment points, reconsignment points, and ports of entry. The record showed that all long-term contracts—that is, those permitting the buyer to take delivery more than thirty days after date—were prohibited and that the Institute condemned, as unbusinesslike and uneconomical, all concessions made to purchasers on the basis of quantity of sugar bought. This was done despite economies of operation that might be achieved as the result of large-volume orders. Finally, statistical information relating to production and deliveries of individual refiners, etc.—information which would have been valuable in the various trade areas where competitive setups differed widely—was withheld

[28]297 U.S. 553.

from purchasers. The lower court concluded that this gave the members of the Institute an unfair advantage over purchasers.

The Supreme Court agreed with most of the conclusions of the lower court. It pointed out that previous decisions did not prevent the adoption of reasonable means to protect interstate commerce from destructive or injurious practices and to promote competition upon a sound basis. Co-operative effort, however, could not justify unreasonable restraint merely because of laudable purpose. The Court recognized that the refiners occupied a dominant position in the industry and that—because of their standardized product—price, rather than brand, was generally the vital consideration in their competition. It took the position that because sugar is a standardized commodity, there was a strong tendency to price uniformity; and this tendency made it all the more important that opportunity for fair competition should be afforded, not impaired. "The unreasonable restraint which defendants imposed lay not in advance announcements, but in the steps taken to secure adherence without deviation to prices and terms thus announced. It was that concerted undertaking which cut off opportunities for variation in the course of competition, however fair and appropriate they might be."[29] The Court recognized, however, that the custom of the trade involved advance price announcement and that it was not apparent that arrangements merely to circulate or relay the announcement threatened competitive opportunity. From this, it drew the conclusions that if the requirement that there must be adherence to prices and terms openly announced in advance was abrogated, and if the restraints which followed that requirement were removed, the just interests of competition would be safeguarded, and the trade would still be left with whatever advantage might be incidental to its established practice. The Court also held that statistical information, which might be received in relation to the affairs of the refiners, which might be rightly treated as having a confidential character, and in which distributors and purchasers had no proper interest, did not need to be disseminated by the Institute.

Although the Court did not order the dissolution of the Sugar Institute, it did outlaw a great many restrictive practices. The decision, however, was evidently quite effective, because the Institute was dissolved soon after. This case and current interpretation of the Sherman Act as it relates to agreements indicate that trade associations are very vulnerable to the antitrust laws. On the other hand, trade associations seem to be susceptible to the temptation to use this form of organization as a means of achieving secret understandings for price stabilization and price leadership. The comparative ease with which their activities may pass from the lawful to the unlawful makes the potential abuses difficult to control at the present time.

[29] *Ibid.*, p. 601.

The Federal Trade Commission has proceeded against the restrictive activities of trade associations under Section 5 of the Trade Commission Act as unfair methods of competition. In this it has had considerable success. Early in its administration, its action against a trade association was sustained by the Supreme Court in *Federal Trade Commission* v. *Pacific States Paper Trade Association* (1927).[30] This involved a simple agreement to abide by uniform prices on paper and paper products in intrastate commerce. The same price lists, however, were used by salesmen making interstate sales, although there was no evidence of a definite price agreement with respect to this trade. The Commission inferred that the use of the price lists lessened competition, and it issued a cease and desist order. The Supreme Court sustained the order, holding that the weight to be given the facts and circumstances admitted, as well as the inferences reasonably to be drawn from them, was for the Commission to decide, and that the latter was fully warranted in its conclusion. No reference was made to the Commission's power to deal with restraint of trade as comprehended by the Sherman Act.

This was specifically passed upon, however, in *Fashion Originators' Guild of America, Inc.* v. *Federal Trade Commission* (1941).[31] The Guild consisted of garment manufacturers who claimed to be creators of original and distinctive designs of women's clothes. After these designs entered channels of trade, other manufacturers systematically copied them. The Guild members claimed that this piracy was unethical, even though the designs were neither copyrighted nor patented. To combat the copying, the members of the Guild combined to destroy all competition from the sale of these copied garments by systematic boycott of retailers who sold them. The Supreme Court held that, if the purpose and practice of the combination of garment manufacturers and their affiliates ran counter to the public policy declared in the Sherman and Clayton Acts, the Federal Trade Commission had the power to suppress the combination as an unfair method of competition. The Commission has so ruled, and the Court sustained the cease and desist order.

Although the Commission has had considerable success in dealing with price-fixing arrangements by trade associations, it suffered a reversal at the hands of the courts in *Tag Manufacturing Institute et al.* v. *Federal Trade Commission* (1949).[32] The members of the Institute manufactured and distributed approximately 95 per cent of the tag products purchased and used in the United States, with 55 per cent of the industry shared by the four largest manufacturers The issuance of price lists by tag manufacturers had become established as a general practice

[30] 273 U.S. 52.

[31] 312 U.S. 457. See also *Millinery Creators's Guild* v. *FTC*, 312 U.S. 469 (1940). For an attack on price discrimination through trade association activity, see the discussion on basing-point pricing in Chapter 17, *infra.*

[32] 174 Fed. (2d) 452. The Commission did not appeal.

in the industry prior to the formation of the Institute. After the National Industrial Recovery Act was invalidated, the members of the industry adopted an agreement to report prices, terms, and conditions of each sale of or contract to sell tag products to the secretary of the Institute. All such information was available to public agencies, but failure to make reports was punishable by fine. The Commission issued a cease and desist order, on the ground that the manufacturers had fixed and maintained prices with a dangerous tendency to hinder price competition. The Court held that the agreement merely facilitated the assembling of price data and that the Commission had not advanced evidence to prove a price-fixing agreement. The Court also could find nothing secret about any of the arrangements. This decision followed the precedent of the Maple Flooring case.

The Commission has also used the consent decree in settling important price-fixing controversies. As the result of its investigation into coffee prices in which it reported that the coffee price spiral of 1953-54 could not be explained in terms of the competitive laws of supply and demand,[33] it issued a complaint against the New York Coffee and Sugar Exchange, Inc.[34] The examiner held that the contract used by the exchange had the effect of limiting trading in coffee futures to less than 10 per cent of United States coffee imports. The examiner, in the initial decision, ordered the exchange to permit trading in all types of coffee which are in general use in the United States. This would include Arabica coffees from all of the exporting countries, which coffees constitute about 90 per cent of the world's supply. The Exchange contract, which had been used since 1948, first specified Santos as the only Brazilian point of origin of coffee for futures trading in the United States. Even after the contract was modified in 1953 to include three other ports, the coffee shipped from them was deliverable only at fixed penalties under the values for Santos coffee. The consent decree embodied the recommendations of the examiner.

In a consent order against the West Coast Tuna Industry,[35] the Commission ordered the producers, supplying well over half the nation's pack, to stop fixing prices for the tuna fish they produced, as well as to cease in attempts to suppress competition in the industry. The Commission had charged that associations of tuna boat owners had negotiated with the canners to fix the prices paid for raw tuna. The three unions

[33]Federal Trade Commission, *Economic Report of the Investigation on Coffee Prices* (Washington, D.C.: U.S. Government Printing Office, 1954).

[34]FTC Docket 6235. The consent order was issued on April 3, 1955.

[35]"California Fish Canners Association and 137 others," FTC Docket 6623 (1957). See also "Puget Sound Salmon Canners, Inc., et al.," Docket 6376 (1956), settled by consent decree. But see "Women's Sportswear," FTC Docket 6325 (*News Summary*, February 4, 1958). The Commission has also issued a complaint against 15 tire and tube manufacturers and 2 trade associations charging them with a conspiracy to fix prices. Docket 7505.

involved were charged with entering into working agreements with the boat owners on the basis of illegally fixed prices, while the canners were alleged to have conspired among themselves to maintain fixed prices and suppress competition. Finally, some of the parties were charged with conspiring to prevent competition with the Japanese tuna industry. As is now the practice in all the consent agreements obtained by the Commission, this agreement did not constitute admissions by the respondent parties that they had violated the law.

RESALE PRICE MAINTENANCE

The endeavor of producers to control the price of their products after they had left their hands, by the device of resale price maintenance, emerged after the Civil War with the growth of business on a national scale and the development of nationwide advertising. The passage of the Sherman Act brought the various devices for price maintenance under the scrutiny of the federal government and raised the issue of the extent to which private rights, in fixing resale prices, were limited by the prohibition against restraint of trade. Early cases, such as *Bobbs-Merrill* v. *Straus* (1908).[36] and *Bauer & Cie* v. *O'Donnell* (1913),[37] held that mere notice to sellers setting the resale price by copyright or patent owners did not establish an enforceable contract. Therefore, the sellers could dispose of the product at any price they wished.

The leading decision on resale price maintenance under the Sherman Act before it was amended by the Miller-Tydings Act was *Dr. Miles Medical Company* v. *John D. Park and Sons* (1911).[38] In order to control prices all the way down to the consumer on its product of unpatented (but proprietary) medicines, the company used a sales contract by which wholesalers were treated as consignees without title until the goods were sold. The contract fixed the price at which the products were to be sold to retailers. Not only did the Miles company select the retailers, but it also required them to sign contracts fixing the resale price. John D. Park & Sons secured a supply of the medicines without signing the contract and proceeded to sell them below the prices fixed. The Miles company brought suit to prevent this practice. The Supreme Court, in upholding the lower court's decision against the Miles company, held that the restrictions were invalid both at common law and under the Sherman Act, on the ground that the retailers were not agents but purchasers, and that the Miles company, having sold its product, had no right to control subsequent resale prices. Thus, resale price fixing by contract, when title to the commodity had passed, was declared illegal under the Sherman law.

[36]210 U.S. 339.

[37]229 U.S. 1.

[38]220 U.S. 373. See also *Straus* v. *Victor Talking Machine Co.*, 243 U.S. 490 (1917). The role of patents in price fixing is discussed in the chapter on patents, *infra*.

What appeared to be a serious limitation on the seemingly stringent rulings against resale price maintenance emerged in *United States* v. *Colgate Company* (1919).[39] In this instance, the company did not resort to signed contracts to maintain resale prices but, on the contrary, merely used various forms of persuasion. It informed the dealers, by various means, of the prices it wished them to charge and urged them to adhere to such prices. It stated that no sales would be made to price cutters and requested information on such offenders. It placed price cutters on suspended lists and refused to renew arrangements with them until they gave assurance that they would conform. The Court upheld the company, on the grounds that there was no agreement and that any private business had the privilege of selecting the customers with whom it wished to deal and of refusing to sell whenever it so desired. Although the decision turned, in part, on the technicalities of the indictment, it nevertheless posed the difficult problem of distinguishing between those forms of business pressure which were legal and those which were not. However, where agreement is inferred from actions, the Dr. Miles ruling still held.[40]

Early in its history, the Federal Trade Commission undertook to curb the practice of resale price maintenance but, in so doing, confined its activities largely to co-operative efforts between manufacturers and their distributors, presumably because of the uncertainty of the status of resale price maintenance in the courts. The leading case to which the Commission was a party involved the Beech-Nut Packing Company.[41] The Commission found that the Beech-Nut company had worked out an elaborate system of regulations and means of checking its customers. All who dealt in its products were informed that they were expected to maintain the established prices and that no sales would be made to anyone who deviated therefrom. The company kept an extensive record of price cutters; and although it did not require its customers to sign any contracts of resale price maintenance, it was nevertheless successful in securing their co-operation in reporting price cutters. The Commission ruled that this was an unfair method of competition within the meaning of Section 5 of the the Trade Commission Act.

A cease and desist order was issued against the Beech-Nut company; and this was finally sustained by the Supreme Court, although the latter required that the order of the Commission be made more specific in some respects. In reaching its decision, the Court held that a trader was not guilty of violating the Sherman Act if he simply refused to sell to others, but that he could not, by contracts or combinat'ons, express or implied, unduly hinder or obstruct the free and natural flow of commerce. In the opinion of the majority of the Court, the Beech-Nut

[39] 250 U.S. 300.

[40] *United States* v. *A. Schrader's Son, Inc.*, 252 U.S. 85 (1920).

[41] *Federal Trade Commission* v. *Beech-Nut Packing Co.*, 257 U.S. 441 (1922).

system went far beyond the simple refusal to sell goods to persons who would not market at stated prices. This seemed to be in keeping with the ruling in the Colgate case.

The difficulties involved in the application of the law, however, are emphasized by the fact that Mr. Justice Holmes dissented from the verdict, on the grounds that he could see no dangerous tendency unduly to hinder competition or to create monopoly and that he did not understand to whom the conduct of the respondents was unfair. Mr. Justice McReynolds wrote a dissenting opinion with similar import.

The legalizing of resale price maintenance by a majority of the states and the Miller-Tydings Act of 1937 suspended the Commission's prosecution of resale price maintenance, but it nevertheless continued its attack on the problem. After a careful investigation of the whole subject, it submitted a lengthy report to Congress in 1945,[42] in which it vigorously opposed the practice and the Miller-Tydings amendment. This report stated, in part:

> The purpose of this amendment, as this report shows, is not to legalize contracts whose object is to prevent predatory price cutting for an ulterior purpose. The anti-trust laws do not condemn such contracts. The Miller-Tydings amendment legalizes contracts whose object is to require all dealers to sell at not less than the resale price stipulated by contract without reference to their individual selling cost or selling policies. The Commission believes that the consumer is not only entitled to competition between rival products but to competition between dealers handling the same branded product.[43]

The requirement that there be competition from similar commodities, if exemption under the Miller-Tydings Act was to be obtained, was the basis of the ruling in *Eastman Kodak Co.* v. *Federal Trade Commission* (1946).[44] The cease and desist order of the Commission required Eastman Kodak to abandon its arrangements with its dealer customers, was upheld by a District Court. The Commission had held that Eastman had a resale price maintenance policy designed to control the prices at which dealers might sell. The Court held that the purpose of the Miller-Tydings Act was to validate resale price agreements when the products involved were in competition with similar commodities produced by others. The Court agreed with the Commission that Eastman's products were not sold in free and open competition with commodities of the same general class.

The limitations imposed by the Supreme Court on the practice

[42]Federal Trade Commission, *Report on Resale Price Maintenance* (Washington, D.C.: U.S. Government Printing Office, 1945).

[43]*Ibid.*, p. lxiv. For an analysis of this report, see E. T. Grether, "The Federal Trade Commission versus Resale Price Maintenance," *Journal of Marketing*, Vol. XII, No. 1 (July, 1947), pp. 1–13.

[44]158 Fed. (2d) 592. The Supreme Court denied certiorari, 330 U.S. 828 (1947). See Walter Adams, "Resale Price Maintenance: Fact and Fancy," *Yale Law Journal*, Vol. LXIV, No. 7 (June, 1955), pp. 967–90.

of resale price maintenance were severely circumscribed by the Miller-Tydings Act. This legislation, however, did not give complete immunity from those decisions, as was brought out in *United States* v. *Bausch & Lomb Optical Company* (1944).[45] Bausch & Lomb sold lenses to Soft-Lite Lens Company. The latter was the sole distributor of pink-tinted lenses, sold under the trade name of "Soft-Lite," on which there were no patents or secret processes. The agreement with Bausch & Lomb provided that the latter would not sell pink-tinted glass to lens manufacturers or pink-tinted lenses to the optical trade. Soft-Lite sold only to wholesalers who were willing to co-operate with its policy, and the wholesalers were allowed to sell only to retailers who held licenses from Soft-Lite.

The Court found that the case did not come under the Colgate decision, as argued by counsel for Soft-Lite, because an agreement between the seller and the purchaser to maintain resale prices had been made. The Court also found that there was a conspiracy with wholesalers to restrain commerce. The company contended that its fair-trade contracts were legal under the Miller-Tydings Act, but the District Court had ruled that these contracts "came into existence as a patch upon an illegal system of distribution" and as an integral part of that system. With this, the Supreme Court agreed. It did grant, however, that Soft-Lite had the privilege of selecting its customers and that it could execute new resale price maintenance contracts which moved strictly along the route marked by the Miller-Tydings Act.[46]

In many respects, the status of resale price maintenance at the present time is quite uncertain. The federal constitutionality of the McGuire Act seems to be established;[47] but a number of the state laws have been invalidated by state courts,[48] and a number of legal aspects of "fair-trade" protection and statutory interpretation remain unsettled.[49]

Aggressive action which went beyond a simple refusal to sell constituted the basis upon which the Supreme Court held in *United States* v. *Parke Davis & Co.* (1960)[50] that the defendant had violated Sections 1 and 3 of the Sherman Act. The thorough review by the Court of the leading cases on resale price maintenance where fair-trade laws do not apply warrants a full presentation of this case.

The Department of Justice charged that Parke Davis combined and conspired in violation of the Sherman Act with retail and wholesale druggists in Washington, D.C. and Richmond, Virginia, to maintain

[45]321 U.S. 707.

[46]See also *United States* v. *Univis Lens Co.*, 316 U.S. 241 (1942). This situation also holds under the McGuire Act (*United States* v. *McKesson & Robbins, Inc.*, 351 U.S. 305 [1956]).

[47]*Eli Lilly & Co.* v. *Schwegmann Bros. Grand Super Market*, 205 Fed. (2d) 788 (1953); certiorari denied. 346 U.S. 856 (1953).

[48]See *Journal of Marketing*, Vol. XX. No. 1 (July, 1955), pp. 77–78.

[49]See Report of the Attorney General's National Committee, *Antitrust Laws* (Washington, D.C.: U.S. Government Printing Office, 1955). pp. 152–53.

[50]362 U.S. 29. Also *United States* v. *Parke Davis Co.*, 365 U.S. 125 (1961).

the prices of Parke Davis pharmaceutical products. There is no fair-trade law in Washington, D.C. or in Virginia.

Sometime before 1956, Parke Davis announced a retail price maintenance policy in its wholesalers' and retailers' catalogues, and listed suggested minimum resale and retail prices. The catalogue stated that it was the company's policy to deal only with drug wholesalers who observed the schedule and who sold only to drug retailers authorized by law to fill prescriptions. Parke Davis also sold directly to retailers, giving them volume discounts which the wholesalers could not grant. In 1956, drug retailers in Washington and Richmond advertised and sold several Parke Davis vitamin products at prices substantially below the suggested minimum, and in some instances even below the prices listed in the wholesalers' Net Price Selling Schedule. To secure compliance of the retailers, "representatives of Parke Davis visited the wholesalers and told them that not only would Parke Davis refuse to sell to wholesalers who did not adhere to the policy announced in their catalogue, but also that it would refuse to sell to wholesalers who sold Parke Davis products to retailers who did not observe the suggested minimum retail prices. Each wholesaler was interviewed individually, but each was informed that his competitors were also being apprised of this. The wholesalers without exception indicated a willingness to go along."[51] Representatives also called on the retailers, and told each that if he did not observe the suggested minimum retail prices, Parke Davis would refuse to deal with him directly or through wholesalers. Each retailer was told that his competitors were similarly being informed. Some retailers refused to co-operate, with the result that Parke Davis and also the wholesalers refused to sell any of Parke Davis products to them. The program did not succeed and, in September, Parke Davis stopped trying to promote the retailers' adherence to the suggested prices, but this was done only after the Department of Justice had begun an investigation of possible violation of the antitrust laws. When the case came before the District Court, the latter held for Parke Davis on the ground that "the actions of [Parke Davis] were properly unilateral and sanctioned by law under the doctrine laid down in the case of *United States* v. *Colgate*."[52]

The Supreme Court recognized that the Colgate case had created some confusion, but held that subsequent decisions had eliminated this. "Thus, whatever uncertainty previously existed as to the scope of the *Colgate* doctrine, *Bausch & Lomb*, and *Beach-Nut* plainly fashioned its dimensions as meaning no more than that a simple refusal to sell to customers who will not resell at prices suggested by the seller is permissible under the Sherman Act. In other words, an unlawful combination is not just such as arises from a price maintenance *agreement*, express or

[51]*Ibid.*, *p. 33.*
[52]*Ibid.*, p. 36.

implied; such a combination is also organized if the producer secures adherence to his suggested prices by means which go beyond his mere declination to sell to a customer who will not observe his announced policy. . . . Both cases teach that judicial inquiry is not to stop with a search of the record for evidence of purely contractual arrangements."[53] The Court held that the Parke Davis arrangements plainly exceeded the limitations of the Colgate doctrine in that Parke Davis "created a combination with the retailers and wholesalers to maintain retail prices and violated the Sherman Act. . . . . It was only by bringing about substantial unanimity among the competitors that Parke Davis was able to gain adherence to its policy."[54] The Court also was convinced that Parke Davis discontinued its efforts because of the investigation and possible litigation.

Mr. Justice Harlan wrote a vigorous dissent in which he was joined by Justices Frankfurter and Whittaker. Justice Harlan took the position that the Colgate doctrine, as originally understood, would have required the affirmance of the judgment of the District Court. He could not find that the Beech-Nut or Bausch & Lomb cases introduced a narrowing concept. He argued that we are left wholly in the dark as to what the purported new standard is for establishing a "contract, combination—or conspiracy,"[55] and that "the lower court had found no coercion but only unilateral action."

> "To be sure, the Government has explicitly stated that it does not ask us to overrule Colgate, and the Court professed not to do so. But contrary to the long understanding of bench and bar, the Court treats Colgate as turning not on the absence of the concerted action explicitly required of Sections 1 and 3 of the Sherman Act, but upon the Court's notion of 'countervailing' policies. I can regard the Court's profession as no more than a bow to the fact that *Colgate*, decided more than 40 years ago, has become part of the economic regime of the country upon which the commercial community and the lawyers who advise it have justifiably relied.
>
> "If the principle for which *Colgate* stands is to be reversed, it is, as the Government's position plainly indicates, something that should be left to the Congress. It is surely the emptiest of formalisms to profess respect for Colgate and eviscerate it in application."[56]

Economists and lawyers may surely be excused if they find it difficult to understand the status of resale price maintenance at the present time.[57] It appears, however, that suggestion backed up by a simple refusal to deal, narrowly interpreted, is about as far as the seller can go.

[53]*Ibid.*, pp. 43–44.
[54]*Ibid.*, pp. 45–46.
[55]*Ibid.*, p. 53.
[56]*Ibid.*, p. 57.
[57]The Federal Trade Commission issued a cease and desist order against *Brown Shoe Co. Inc.*, Docket 7607 (1963), based on the Colgate ruling. This may be sustained under the Parke Davis ruling.

Recently, some of the major oil companies have endeavored to maintain the retail prices of their gasoline through the use of "consignment" agreement, under which the oil company retains "title" to the gasoline until it is sold, and fixes the selling price for it. The legality of this arrangement under the Sherman Act was the issue in *Simpson* v. *Union Oil Co. of California* (1964).[58] This case arose out of a suit for damages under Section 4 of the Clayton Act for violation of Sections 1 and 2 of the Sherman Act. Union Oil had a "consignment" agreement with lessees of its retail outlets under which the company set the prices at which the retailer sold the gasoline. The "consignment" was for one year and terminable at the end of any year by either party, as was the lease. Title to the gasoline remained in Union Oil until it was sold by the dealer, the latter being compensated by a minimum commission. Simpson sold below the authorized price allegedly to meet a competitive price, and Union Oil refused to renew the agreement. Simpson brought suit for damages. The Court reiterated its previous rulings that a supplier may not use coercion on its retail outlets to achieve resale price maintenance; Union Oil tried to do just that. The Court noted that resale price maintenance of gasoline through the "consignment" device was increasing. "By reason of the lease and 'consignment' agreement, dealers are coercively laced into an arrangement under which their supplier is able to impose non-competitive prices on thousands of persons whose prices otherwise must be competitive—when the device is used to cover a vast gasoline distribution system, fixing prices through many retail outlets, the antitrust laws prevent calling the 'consignment' an agency. . . . resale price maintenance through the present, coercive type of 'consignment' agreement is illegal under the antitrust laws." All other issues in the case were remanded to the District Court for trial.[59]

Mr. Justice Stewart wrote a strong dissenting opinion on the ground that legitimate consignment arrangements came with the rule of *United States* v. *General Electric* (272 U.S. 476)[60] and that resale price maintenance was legal under the circumstances. He argued that the case should be remanded for trial on the merits of whether this was a bona fide lease-and-consignment arrangement. Regardless of legal technicalities, the situation set forth in this case clearly seems to be an endeavor to engage in retail price maintenance; the problem that will now come before the courts will be that of identifying, legally, consignment arrangements that are genuinely bona fide.

The Federal Trade Commission had already issued two cease and desist orders under Section 5 of the Federal Trade Commission Act, one against *The Atlantic Refining Co.* (Docket 7471) and the other against

[58]377 U.S. 13.

[59]*Ibid.*, pp. 21, 24. This case did not settle the validity of resale price maintenance under the McGuire Act. This was to be dealt with, on remand, by the lower court.

[60]Discussed in Chapter 18 on patents, *infra.*

Sun Oil Co. (Docket 6934), both in 1963. The facts seem to be essentially the same as in the Union Oil case, and the Commission held that the consignment arrangements were a fiction and a subterfuge and did not constitute genuine consignment under the law of agency. These cases are now in the courts for adjudication.

TYING CONTRACTS AND EXCLUSIVE-DEALER ARRANGEMENTS

One of the purposes of the Clayton Act was to curb restrictions on competition by such devices as tying contracts, exclusive-dealer arrangements, and full-requirements contracts, the latter two meaning essentially the same thing. A tying contract is one in which the seller of a product makes the sale on condition that the buyer purchase other products or services from him. This may also involve what is known as "full-line forcing," where a distributor of one item may have to accept other products in the seller's line. Exclusive-dealer arrangements that come under the law are those by which a seller compels the distributor to deal in his products only and to exclude all rivals' merchandise. These contracts may also require a distributor or buyer to fill all his needs from a seller for a specified time. These devices were specifically prohibited by Section 3 of the Clayton Act "where the effect . . . may be to substantially lessen competition or tend to create a monopoly in any line of commerce." The scope of the application of the provisions therefore became a matter ultimately to be settled by the courts.

This section of the law was aimed particularly at restricting competition or maintaining or enhancing monopoly through products protected by patents and which had escaped the law by Supreme Court interpretation.[61] The section was worded, however, to cover unpatented as well as patented commodities. Although most of the cases have arisen out of attempts to extend control through patent rights and copyrights, some of the landmark decisions have involved neither of these.[62] Furthermore, recent decisions have also brought these arrangements under the Sherman Act.

Tying Contracts

The increase in the scope of the antitrust laws as a result of the Clayton Act was emphasized in the litigation involving the United Shoe Machinery Company. In a civil suit under the Sherman Act *United States* v. *United Shoe Machinery Company* [1918],[63] the government requested dissolution of the company. The request was based on two con-

[61]*Henry* v. *A. B. Dick Co.*, 224 U.S. 1 (1912). This case was overruled in *Motion Picture Patents Co.* v. *Universal Film Manufacturing Co.*, 243 U.S. 502 (1917).

[62]Issues relating primarily to the patent rights themselves are dealt with in the chapter on patents, *infra.*

[63]247 U.S. 32. See also *United States* v. *Winslow*, 227 U.S. 202 (1912), a criminal suit against the president of United Shoe Machinery Company, which the government also lost.

tentions: first, that the shoe company was a combination of competing concerns, engaged in the manufacture of shoe machinery and combined for the purpose of forming a monopoly; and second, that by an elaborate system of leases and tying contracts, the company sought to further and maintain that monopoly On the first count, the Court held that the combination did not violate the Sherman law, since the original members of the combine did not compete with each other, and since subsequent acquisitions consisted of noncompetitive firms or were made to resolve patent difficulties. The Supreme Court agreed with the lower court that competition had not been removed in any real sense. On the second count, the Court held that the leases and tying clauses were justifiable exercises of the patent rights possessed by the combine. The Court referred to previous rulings that patent rights were limited to the privileges granted by the patent laws and that such rights could not be used as a guise to violate the Sherman law, but it held that the company had stayed within the legitimate limits of these rights. This suit had been started in 1911.

The failure to secure a conviction and the passage of the Clayton Act led the Department of Justice to file a new suit alleging that the company's leases violated that law. This time, the prosecution was successful. The company had modified its leases in the meantime; but the Court held that while there was no specific agreement that lessees would not use the machinery of a competitor, the practical effect of the restrictive provisions was necessarily to lessen competition and to tend to create a monopoly. Consequently, the company was enjoined to abandon the restrictive practices.[64]

The illegality of tying arrangements that would suppress competition and result in monopoly was emphasized in *International Business Machines Corporation* v. *United States* (1936),[65] the government brought suit for violation of Section 3 of the Clayton Act, on the ground that this manufacturer of business machines leased them upon the condition that the lessee use only those tabulating cards manufactured by the International Business Machines Corporation. The company contended that this lease arrangement was lawful because of its patent on the cards and on the machines in which the cards were used. The Court found that other cards were suitable for use in these machines. It did not deny the company the right to proclaim the virtues of its own cards or to warn against the danger of using, in its machines, the cards which did not conform to the necessary specifications, or even to make leases conditional upon the use of the cards which conformed to those specifications.

[64] *United Shoe Machinery Corp.* v. *United States*, 258 U.S. 451 (1922). For an earlier case on the issue of tying contracts, see *Henry* v. *A. B. Dick Co.*, 224 U.S. 1 (1912). The latter was overruled in *Motion Picture Patents Co.* v. *Universal Film Manufacturing Co.*, 243 U.S. 502 (1917).

[65] 298 U.S. 131. See *International Salt Co.* v. *United States*, 332 U.S. 392 (1947).

Such a procedure would have protected good will without creating monopoly or resorting to suppression of competition. The Court held, however, that the Clayton Act gave no exception to its prohibition of monopolistic tying clauses and that the arrangement, in this instance, resulted in the elimination of business competition and the creation of monopoly. Furthermore, the Court held that the company's good will could be achieved by methods which did not tend to create monopoly and were not otherwise unlawful.

Subsequently, the Supreme Court was to make tying agreements based on patents practically a per se violation of the Sherman and Clayton Acts. In *International Salt Company* v. *United States* (1947),[66] the Court pointed out that patents confer no right to restrain the use of, or trade in, unpatented salt. International Salt licensed the use of its patented vending machines on condition that the lessees purchased all unpatented salt and salt tablets used in the machines. The Court ruled that under the Sherman and Clayton Acts, it was unreasonable, per se, to foreclose competitors from any substantial market, and that the law did not have to wait arrival at the goal of monopoly before condemning the direction of the movement. Rules for the use of leased machinery could not be disguised restraints of free competition, even though they set reasonable standards which all suppliers must meet.

International Salt had protested against the decree of the lower court, which directed it to lease its machines on nondiscriminatory terms, on the ground that International Salt had not been charged with discrimination and also that the decree might hamper its competitive position by preventing it from discriminating in good faith to meet competition. The Court held that International Salt had wedged itself into the salt market by methods forbidden by law and that, therefore, the decree was warranted. A court, it stated, was not obligated to prohibit only those practices which had been previously employed.

The distinction between the tests of illegality of tying agreements under the Sherman Act and the Clayton Act was the focal point of *Times-Picayune Publishing Company* v. *United States* (1953).[67] The government instituted suit against the New Orleans publishing company, charging it with violating the Sherman Act by employing tying arrangements (really full-requirements arrangements) in connection with its sale of advertising. The *Times-Picayune* was the only morning newspaper in New Orleans. In 1933, it bought out the *States*, one of the two evening newspapers, the other being the *Item*. Since 1950, general and classified advertisers had not been able to buy space in either the *Times-Picayune* or the *States* alone, but had to insert identical copy in both or neither. The Court felt that advertisers viewed the city's newspaper

[66]332 U.S. 392.
[67]345 U.S. 595.

readers, morning or evening, as fungible customer potential. The common core of unlawful tying arrangements is the forced purchase of a second distinct commodity with the desired purchase of a dominant "tying" product; but in this case, the Court held that the products were identical and the market the same. The Court could see nothing in the factual record which disclosed that demonstrably deleterious effects could be inferred. Lacking proof of monopoly, it was necessary for the government to demonstrate specific intent.[68] This it was unable to do.

After discussing preceding cases dealing with tying arrangements the Court said: "From the 'tying' cases a perceptible pattern of illegality emerges: when the seller enjoys a monopolistic position in the market for the 'tying' product, *or* if a substantial volume of commerce in the 'tied' product is restrained, a tying arrangement violates the narrower standards expressed in §3 of the Clayton Act because from either factor the requisite potential lessening of competition is inferred. And because for even a lawful monopolist it is 'unreasonable, *per se*, to foreclose competitors from any substantial market,' a tying arrangement is banned by §1 of the Sherman Act whenever *both* conditions are met. In either case the arrangement transgresses §5 of the Federal Trade Commission Act, since minimally that section registers violations of the Clayton and Sherman Acts. . . . In this case, the rule of *International Salt* can apply only if both ingredients are met."[69]

That this strict differentiation, or at least application, of the tests of illegality still obtains may be doubted in light of the decision in *Northern Pacific Railway Co.* v. *United States* (1957).[70] The Northern Pacific disposed of land in which a large number of its sales contracts and most of its lease agreements contained "preferential routing" clauses which compelled the grantee or lessee to ship over its lines all commodities produced or manufactured on the land, provided that its rates were equal to those of competing carriers. Alternative means of transportation, including those of two other major railroad systems, existed for a large portion of the shipments. The government charged that the "preferential routing" agreements violated Section 1 of the Sherman Act. The Court held that the railway company possessed substantial economic power by virtue of extensive land holdings and that a "not insubstantial" amount of interstate commerce was affected by the preferential routing agreements. The District Court granted a summary judgment in favor of the government and the Supreme Court affirmed it.

The Court held that certain agreements such as price fixing, di-

[68]But it is not necessary to show that success rewards the attempt to monopolize. See *Lorain Journal Co.* v. *United States*, 342 U.S. 143 (1951). It is interesting to note that the *Times-Picayune* subsequently acquired the *Item*, with the acquiesence of the Department of Justice.

[69]*Ibid.*, pp. 608–9. In *Brown Shoe Co.* v. *United States* 370 U.S. 294 (1962) the Court discussed tests of illegality under Section 3 of the Clayton Act, pp. 329–31.

[70]356 U.S. 1.

vision of markets, group boycotts, and tying arrangements are per se unreasonable, and that this avoids the necessity of an incredibly complicated and prolonged economic investigation into the entire history of the industry, as well as related industries, in order to determine whether a particular restraint has been unreasonable. Tying agreements violate the law "whenever a party has sufficient economic power with respect to the tying product to appreciably restrain free competition in the market for the tied product and a 'not insubstantial' amount of interstate commerce is affected."[71] The purpose of the railroad was to fence out competitors and stifle competition. The fact that the tying product was not patented was of no consequence. The Court reconciled its verdict with *Times-Picayune* by stating that the latter case made clear "that the vice of tying arrangements lies in the use of economic power in one market to restrict competition on the merits in another, regardless of the source from which the power is derived, and whether the power takes the form of monopoly or not."[72]

Mr. Justice Harlan, together with Justices Frankfurter and Whittaker, dissented on the ground that *Times-Picayune* "has made it clear beyond dispute that *both* proof of dominance in the market for the tying product *and* a showing that an appreciable volume of business in the tied product is restrained, are essential conditions to judicial condemnation of a tying clause as a *per se* violation of the Sherman Act."[73] These requirements, the dissent held, were not met in this case.

The Federal Trade Commission has not been particularly successful in its attack on tying agreements. This arises, in part at least, from the fact that the Commission has not attacked the problem in a realistic and concrete fashion designed to eliminate practices patently harmful to the public and clearly restrictive of competition. The first reversal at the hands of the courts came in *Federal Trade Commission* v. *Gratz* (1920).[74] The Commission took action under Section 5 of the Trade Commission Act by charging Gratz with employing unfair methods of competition. The Gratz company sold steel ties for cotton bagging, on the condition that buyers also take a proportionate amount of bagging. The Court reversed the cease and desist order of the Commission, on the ground that such a tying contract did not constitute an unfair method of competition. The fact that the Commission had filed to allege, in specific terms, injury to the public or to competitors may have affected the decision.

The most important case involving tying contracts arose out of twenty-seven orders issued by the Commission against gasoline companies which had adopted the practice of leasing tanks and pumps to

[71]*Ibid.*, p. 6. See also *United States* v. *Lowe's Incorporated*, 371 U.S. 38 (1962).
[72]*Ibid.*, p. 11.
[73]*Ibid.*, pp. 13–14.
[74]253 U.S. 421.

dealers, on condition that the latter confine the use of the equipment to the storage and sale of gasoline purchased from the gasoline companies. There was no charge of monopolistic control, because the dealer could also lease the equipment of any competitor company. Small independent refiners objected, however, because they felt that they would have to supply tanks and pumps in order to obtain market outlets for their gasoline. The Commission's cease and desist order was appealed to the courts and finally passed upon by the Supreme Court in *Federal Trade Commission* v. *Sinclair Refining Company* (1923).[75] The Court held that, since the contract between the oil companies and the dealers did not limit the lessees' right to use or deal in the goods of a competitor of the lessor, but left him free to follow his own judgment, there was no violation of the Clayton Act. The Court also held that there was no unfair competition, because there was no evidence of bad faith, fraud, or oppression. It further stated that the Federal Trade Commission was limited by the statute and had no general authority to compel competitors to a common level or to interfere with ordinary business methods. Accordingly, it sustained the opinion of the Circuit Court, which held that there was no violation of the antitrust laws. The Commission, however, is able to eliminate tying contracts where the arrangements are essentially the same as those which the courts condemned in the International Business Machines case,[76] and it has issued several cease and desist orders to that effect.[77]

Exclusive-Dealing Arrangements

The application of Section 3 of the Clayton Act to exclusive-dealer agreements was passed upon by the Supreme Court in *Standard Fashion Company* v. *Magrane-Houston Company* (1922).[78] The Standard Fashion Company had entered into a contract with Magrane-Houston Company by which it agreed to sell the Magrane company patterns at a discount of 50 per cent from retail prices and to allow that company the privilege of returning discarded patterns. The Magrane company, in turn, agreed to purchase only the Standard patterns and to sell them at the agreed price, which appeared on the label. The Magrane company discontinued the exclusive sale of Standard patterns and placed on sale patterns of a rival company, whereupon Standard Fashion brought suit for violation of contract. It claimed that the contract was one of agency; but the

[75]261 U.S. 463. See also *Pick* v. *General Motors*, 80 Fed. (2d) 641 (1935), affirmed, *per curiam*, 291 U.S. 3 (1936); and *U.S.* v. *J. I. Case Co.*, 101 Fed. Supp. 856 (1961).

[76]298 U.S. 131 (1936).

[77]*American Flange and Manufacturing Co.*, 27 FTC 1286 (1938); *Signode Steel Strapping Co.*, 33 FTC 1049 (1941); *Signode Steel Strapping Co.* v. *Federal Trade Commission*, 132 Fed. (2d) 48 (1941). For recent case involving a sales commission arrangement, see *The Goodyear Tire and Rubber Co.* v. *Federal Trade Commission* and *Atlantic Refining Co.* v. *Federal Trade Commission*, 331 Fed. (2d) 394 (1964) in which the Court of Appeals upheld the Commission's cease and desist order.

[78]258 U.S. 346.

Court held that it was a sale, since the Magrane company had full title to the pattern.

The question was: "Did this contract violate the Clayton Act because it might substantially lessen competition or to tend to create a monopoly?" The lower court answered this question in the affirmative, since it found that of 52,000 so-called "pattern" companies, Standard Fashion controlled two fifths of such companies. It was held that the restricting of each merchant to the patterns of one pattern manufacturer amounted to giving that single pattern manufacturer a monopoly of the business in each community, and this was in violation of the Clayton Act. The Supreme Court upheld the lower court's findings. The test for violation in this case was the amount of control over the market which Standard Fashion enjoyed as the result of its contracts.

The market test of a substantial share of commerce was the basis of the Court's decision, in *Standard Oil of California and Standard Stations, Inc.* v. *United States* (1949)[79] that the full-requirements contracts of Standard Oil supported the inference that competition probably had been or would be substantially lessened. This was a suit seeking to enjoin the defendants from enforcing or entering into exclusive-supply contracts with any independent dealer in petroleum products and automobile accessories. Standard of California had exclusive-supply contracts which bound the dealers to purchase from Standard all of their supply of one or more products; but all dealers were not required to purchase from Standard all of the petroleum products and accessories which they sold. The Court found that the full-requirements contracts affected an annual gross business of $58 million, comprising 6.7 per cent of the total area. This, it was felt, went far toward supporting the inference that competition had been or probably would be substantially lessened. The Court distinguished between tying contracts and full-requirements contracts. Tying contracts, it stated, served hardly any purpose beyond the suppression of competition. Full-requirements contracts, on the other hand, might have advantages to buyers, sellers, and the consuming public. In the instant case, the Court noted that Standard was a major competitor when the system under challenge was adopted and that it was possible that the company's position would have deteriorated but for the adoption of that system. All the other major suppliers used full-requirements contracts, and the relative share of business that fell to each remained the same during the period of their use. The theory of the antitrust laws is, said the Court, that the long-run advantage of the community depends upon the removal of restraints upon competition. Proof that competition has been foreclosed in a substantial share of the line of commerce affected establishes violation of Section 3 of the Clayton Act.[80]

[79]337 U.S. 293.

[80]See also *United States* v. *Richfield Oil Corp.*, 99 Fed. Supp. 280 (1951); sustained *per curiam*, 343 U.S. 922 (1952).

The importance of evaluating the reasonableness of an exclusive-dealing contract was emphasized in *Tampa-Electric Co.* v. *Nashville Coal Co.*, (1961),[81] which arose from a private suit under Section 3 of the Clayton Act. Tampa Electric had entered into a contract with the Nashville Coal Co. whereby it contracted for its total requirements of fuel for a period of 20 years. Just before delivery of the coal was to start, the Nashville company sought to break the contract on the ground that it violated the antitrust laws. Tampa Electric sued for enforcement. The lower courts held for Nashville Coal, holding that the effect of the contract would be "to substantially lessen competition." The Supreme Court, with Justices Black and Douglas dissenting, reversed the lower courts by ruling that the contract did not violate Section 3 of the Clayton Act.

The Court stated that in practical application an exclusive-dealing arrangement does not violate the law unless the Court believes that performance of the contract will foreclose competition in a substantial share of the line of commerce affected. This required (1) consideration of the line of commerce, (2) selection of the market area in which the seller operates, and (3) whether the competition foreclosed constitutes a substantial share of the relevant market. "To determine substantiality in a given case, it is necessary to weigh the probable effect of the contract on the relevant area of effective competition, taking into account the relative strength of the parties, the proportionate volume of commerce involved in relation to the total volume of commerce in the relevant market area, and the probable immediate and future effects which pre-emption of that share of the market might have on effective competition therein. It follows that a new showing that the contract itself involves a substantial number of dollars is ordinarily of little consequence."[82] The Court then added: "It may well be that in the context of antitrust legislation protracted requirements contracts are suspect, but they have not been declared illegal *per se*—we seem to have only that type of contract which 'may well be of economic advantage to buyers as well as to sellers.' "[83]

The Federal Trade Commission has had considerable success over the years in proceeding against exclusive-dealing arrangements under both Section 3 of the Clayton Act and Section 5 of the Trade Commission Act. Its initial success came with *Butterick Company et al.* v. *Federal Trade Commission* (1925).[84] The Butterick Company, which controlled the Standard Fashion Company and several other pattern-making concerns, had contracts similar to those which had been declared illegal in *Standard Fashion Company* v. *Magrane-Houston Company* (1922).[85]

[81]365 U.S. 320.
[82]*Ibid.*, p. 329.
[83]*Ibid.*, pp. 333–34.
[84]4 Fed. (2d) 910 (1925).
[85]258 U.S. 346 (1922).

The dominant position of the Butterick Company in the manufacture of dress patterns led the Court to uphold the Commission's cease and desist order, issued under Section 3 of the Clayton Act.

A similar situation led the Court to sustain the Federal Trade Commission in *Q. R. S. Music Company* v. *Federal Trade Commission* (1926).[86] The Q. R. S. company controlled over 50 per cent of the business in music rolls for player pianos, and the Court held that this dominant position made exclusive-dealer arrangements a means whereby free competition was threatened. The importance of the dominant position of a producer in affecting the position of the courts was emphasized in the earlier case of *B. S. Pearsall Butter Company* v. *Federal Trade Commission* (1923).[87] Here, the Commission was reversed, on the ground that the respondent manufactured only a small fraction of the total supply of oleomargarine and, therefore, its contract did not substantially lessen competition.

Since 1938, the Commission has renewed its attack on practices under Section 3 of the Clayton Act but, seemingly, has been more circumspect in its action. Many of the complaints have been against automobile manufacturers; and in *Federal Trade Commission* v. *Carter Carburetor Corporation* (1940),[88] the Commission's cease and desist order was upheld. In this instance, the Carter company, holding a predominant position in the sale of carburetors, announced to all of its dealers and customers that, if they handled a competitor's product, they would no longer receive preferential discounts. The Commission held that this practice had a tendency substantially to lessen competition or to create a monopoly, and the Court agreed with the Commission's findings.

This was also the position of the Commission in the matter of the Automatic Canteen Company (1950).[89] The Commission found that the rapid business growth of Automatic Canteen had been primarily the result of its exclusive-dealing contracts with the distributors of its automatic vending machines, combined with the favorable buying contracts for confectionery which it had obtained. The exclusive-dealing contracts required that the distributors purchase exclusively from Automatic Canteen all of the confectionery products sold in the machines and that they not buy or deal in the confections of any other seller or competitor of Automatic Canteen. The Commission held that because of the sub-

[86] 12 Fed. (2d) 730 (1926). See also *Federal Trade Commission* v. *Eastman Kodak Co.*, 274 U.S. 619 (1927).

[87] 292 Fed. Rep. 720.

[88] 112 Fed. (2d) 722.

[89] 46 FTC 861. This case was before the Supreme Court in 346 U.S. 51 (1953), but only on the matter of price discrimination. The issue of exclusive dealing did not go to the Supreme Court.

stantial volume of business involved, the exclusive-dealing contracts violated the law.[90]

In *Federal Trade Commission* v. *Motion Picture Advertising Service Company* (1953),[91] the Supreme Court sustained a cease and desist order of the Commission under Section 5. The respondent produced advertising motion pictures and had exclusive contracts with 40 per cent of the theaters which exhibited such films in the areas in which it operated. It and three other companies had exclusive contracts with 75 per cent of such theaters in the United States. The Federal Trade Commission held that the evidence showed that the contracts unreasonably restrained competition and tended to monopoly. It issued an order prohibiting the respondent from entering into a contract that granted exclusive privileges for more than one year. Mr. Justice Frankfurter wrote a dissenting opinion, in which he criticized the Commission severely for its failure to relate "its analysis of this industry to the standards of illegality in section 5 with sufficient clarity to enable this Court to review the order."[92] This echoes a recurring criticism of the Commission's administration of antitrust that it would do well to heed if it wishes to continue to be an important arm of the government in this field.

The Commission is continuing its enforcement policy along the lines laid out in the two preceding cases, and the Supreme Court decision in the Tampa Electric case would seem to augur well for its success. In 1960, two consent orders of some significance were issued. The first of these settled a complaint which charged the Rayco Manufacturing Co. with entering into exclusive-dealing contracts and illegal price-fixing agreements with independent dealers in violation of Section 3 of the Clayton Act and Section 5 of the Trade Commission Act. The Commission alleged that Rayco's competitors were foreclosed from making sales to the dealers and that competition among dealers was suppressed. The order forbade Rayco from engaging in practices that led to these results.[93] In the same year a consent order forbade Procter & Gamble from entering into unlimited exclusive contracts with manufacturers of automatic washing and dishwashing machines to pack samples of P&G detergents or bleaches in the appliances.[94]

A complaint against Brown Shoe Co., Inc.[95] resulted in an order

[90]See also *Dictograph Products, Inc.*, v. FTC 217 Fed. (2d) 821 (1954), certiorari denied 349 U.S. 940 (1955). and *Harley-Davidson Motor Co.*, 50 FTC 1047 (1954). See also *Maico Co., Inc.*, 51 FTC 1197 (1955); and *Insto-Gas Corp.*, FTC Docket 5851 (1954).

[91]344 U.S. 392.

[92]*Ibid.*, p. 399. See discussion of this problem in *Antitrust Laws*, *op. cit.*, pp. 137–49.

[93]Federal Trade Commission, *Annual Report* (1960), p. 48.

[94]*Ibid.*, p. 49.

[95]Order 7606 (1963) reported in Federal Trade Commission, *News Summary* (March 13, 1963). This order has been appealed by Brown Shoe to the courts. See also Orders 8558–8559 (1964), *Central Linen Service Co. Inc. et al.*, in which the Com-

(*Continued on next page.*)

which forbade it from precluding independent franchised dealers from buying competing shoes, at the same time requiring them to adhere to its suggested resale prices. The Commission held a restrictive provision in Brown's franchise agreements—equally applicable to signer and nonsigner franchise holders alike—was an unlawful restraint of trade because it foreclosed competitors from selling to the independent holders of franchises. This provision required franchised retailers (766 stores as of October, 1961) to concentrate on Brown's shoes and prohibited the purchase of "conflicting" lines.[96] This plan effectively foreclosed Brown's competitors from selling to a significant number of retail shoe stores and therefore constituted an unfair-trade practice. Brown's resale price policies went beyond the mere unilateral declaration of policy coupled with a refusal to sell as sanctioned by the Colgate ruling.

Mention should also be made here to the use of the agency device in connection with exclusive dealing. In confining the application of the law to arrangements which limit competition, the courts have held that Section 3 does not apply to agency contracts. This was established in *Federal Trade Commission* v. *Curtis Publishing Company* (1923).[97] The Curtis company refused to allow the wholesale distributors of its publications to handle those of any other company. The Commission issued a cease and desist order, but the Supreme Court held that the contract was one of agency and not one of conditional sale. The law, said the Court, applied only to outright sales or leases and, therefore, could not apply to agency contracts.

SUMMARY

When the Sherman Act alone is applicable, price-fixing agreements among independent firms are illegal per se. Exemptions claimed under other legislation are narrowly construed by the Supreme Court. The development of the law has followed the construction originally given by the Court in the Traffic Association cases. The rule of reason seems to have had no application here. Even the corporate cloak where subsidiaries are involved may not afford protection if action among the members of a corporate family has for its purpose or effect the coercion or unreasonable restraint on the trade of strangers.

Activities of trade associations fall into a less unequivocal category,

mission ordered that exclusive-supply contracts with customers be limited to one year, except that contracts for special articles—not usable by another customer—might be for not more than two years. Federal Trade Commission, *News Summary* (April 8, 1964).

[96]But note that exclusive franchises are granted by manufacturers to automobile dealers and these are legal. However, under the Automobile Dealer Franchise Act of 1956 provides that dealers can collect damages if they can prove that a manufacturer, in terminating a franchise, has not acted in good faith, but has used coercion, intimidation, or threats.

[97]260 U.S. 568. This issue has presented difficulties in connection with patents. See *United States* v. *General Electric Co.*, 272 U.S. 476 (1926) which is discussed in the chapter on patents, *infra*.

but their scope is severely circumscribed. The rule of reason has played its part, but the rule in this situation seems to be more in the category of judgment on whether the arrangements or practices involve the presumption of restriction or competition.

The status of resale price maintenance arrangements is somewhat more ambiguous because of Court rulings and also because of the effect of resale price maintenance laws. The latter will remain somewhat precarious in their status and effects, unless Congress passes the controversial quality stabilization legislation. The scope of the ruling in the Colgate case, which has been used as the precedent for upholding no more than simple refusal to sell as a basis for suggested resale prices, is quite uncertain as the result of the Parke Davis decision. In any case, resale price maintenance rests on a very narrow base at the present time. Subterfuge by "consignment" arrangements also seems to be circumscribed drastically, if not eliminated. Agency contracts are also a hazardous means for enforcing price maintenance, and the General Electric precedent may well be relegated to the scrap heap before long.

Tying contracts and exclusive-dealer arrangements (including full-requirements' contracts) are illegal where the effect in the judgment of the courts is substantially to lessen competition. This means that they are not illegal per se. However, the Courts have sanctioned permissible tying contracts in such a restrictive way as to render them illegal per se in the opinion of some judges. Thus, the rule of reason plays its part in this connection also, but thus applied it really means that the adjudicating agencies are forced to exercise judgment in the absence of precise legislative standards. This seems to be a rule that is much narrower in scope than that which emerged in the original Standard Oil of New Jersey decision.

Chapter 17 ENFORCEMENT BY THE FEDERAL TRADE COMMISSION

INTRODUCTION

The enforcement activities of the Federal Trade Commission, as one of the agencies established to deal with antitrust problems, have embraced both the relevant sections of the Clayton Act and Section 5 of the Federal Trade Commission Act. The former, as has already been pointed out, enumerated specific practices which were prohibited because of their tendency to lessen competition. The Trade Commission Act gave the Commission power to prevent unfair methods of competition. The principal design of this legislation was to eliminate behavior which lessened competition, but it also sought to raise the plane of competition. It therefore had a significant ethical content. The prime intent of both laws was to achieve a more thoroughly competitive structure. In practice, the administration of the provisions relating to unfair methods of competition has leaned heavily in the direction of consumer protection, with little regard to the effect of decrees on competition as such. Under the Wheeler-Lea amendment, the Commission can proceed against practices which it considers injurious to the consumer, even though competition is unaffected. In dealing with alleged violations of the Clayton Act, particularly Section 2, the Commission frequently charges violations of Section 5 of the Trade Commission Act at the same time. This is done on the theory that practices which violate the Clayton Act are threats to competition and other competitors and are, therefore, unfair methods.[1]

The administration of the two laws by the Commission has tended to merge them, so that, at times, it is difficult to know upon what grounds it is actually proceeding. It frequently brings a complaint under both at the same time and has even extended the idea of unfair methods of competition so as to comprehend practices which also have come under the prohibitions of the Sherman Act. Congress probably did not contemplate that the law would evolve in this fashion when it passed the Clayton and Trade Commission Acts, but developments have pointed to the gradual unification of the idea of limitations on competition. In this respect, the Federal Trade Commission has moved in the direction of becoming the only antitrust enforcement agency to deal with practices that fall under

[1]Enforcement of Sections 3, 7, and 8 of the Clayton Act by the Commission were discussed in previous chapters.

all of the laws. This aspect of the Commission's activities has, by and large, been overshadowed by its concern for consumer protection.

PRICE DISCRIMINATION

The Clayton Act, Original Section 2

The provisions of the Clayton Act regarding price discrimination have been administered primarily by the Federal Trade Commission. The original Section 2 apparently was aimed at the use of discretionary power in furthering monopolistic control or subduing competitors. It thus prohibited specific practices which the Sherman Act could not get at before the damage was done.

Many economists, bound by overly simplified concepts of competitive price making, have heaped considerable ridicule on this legislation, without realizing, apparently, the difficulties of defining discrimination in concrete terms, and without recognizing that, short of perfect competition, differences in price may emerge from the effects of many diverse factors. The problem is to differentiate between the variations which arise from market conditions and those which are the result of arbitrary action, which, in turn, may perpetuate situations that make such action possible. That the Federal Trade Commission faced real difficulties in administering the law is apparent. It seems to have been bound at the outset by a too-rigid concept of the competitive market. In addition, it met early reversals at the hands of the courts which virtually ended its attempts to enforce the law.

In two early cases the Justice Department was successful in its action against violators of the Act. In *Porto Rican American Tobacco Co. v. American Tobacco Co.* (1929),[2] the defendant, the American Tobacco Company, was forbidden to engage in price discrimination in cigarettes because of its obvious intent to drive its competitor, the Porto Rican American Tobacco Company, out of business in Porto Rico. The Circuit Court of Appeals found that American Tobacco had discriminated in favor of its Porto Rico sales customer as compared to its American customers, and had also given its sole customer in Porto Rico a guarantee of a profit of $20,000 a year on his entire business. It was established that, in addition to this, the American Tobacco Company lost $10,147 per month on the same business. As a result of the price war the Porto Rican company, which had previously made from $200,000 to $250,000 profit per year, was suffering a loss of from $150,000 to $180,000 per year. The Court held that the tactics employed by American Tobacco violated the Clayton Act.

The Supreme Court, in another case, decided that price discrimination violated the Clayton Act if the effect was substantially to lessen

[2]30 Fed. (2d) 234; certiorari denied, 279 U.S. 858 (1929).

competition between *buyers* of the same products. This was the basis of the ruling in *George Van Camp and Sons* v. *American Can Company* (1929).[3] George Van Camp and Sons and the Van Camp Packing Company were both engaged in the business of packing and selling food products in tin cans. The American Can Company manufactured the cans used by these two firms. It sold the cans to the Van Camp Packing Company at a discount of 20 per cent below the announced standard prices at which it sold the same cans to George Van Camp and Sons. It also charged the George Van Camp and Sons a fixed rental for the sealing machines but furnished them to the Van Camp Packing Company without charge. The issue at bar was whether price discrimination was forbidden by the Clayton Act when the effect of such discrimination was to lessen competition among the buyers of the American Can Company's products. The Court held that the law applied just as much under such circumstances as it did when the discrimination lessened competition in the line of commerce in which the seller was engaged. It consequently ordered the American Can Company to cease its discriminatory practices.

The Federal Trade Commission's attack on various kinds of quantity discounts met with severe rebuffs by the courts. In *Mennen Company* v. *Federal Trade Commission* (1923),[4] the Commission met its first reversal at the hands of the courts. The Mennen Company, manufacturer of various toilet articles, had adopted a plan for allowing trade discounts in marketing groups, whereby it classified its customers into wholesalers and retailers, allowing different rates of discounts for the same quantity and quality of product to purchasers according to the way they were classified by the Mennen Company. The Commission contended that this constituted an unfair method of competition in violation of Section 5 of the Federal Trade Commission Act, and constituted price discrimination in violation of Section 2 of the Clayton Act. In listing its customers, the Mennen Company classified as retailers a class of mutual or co-operative corporations which purchased large quantities of the Mennen products. These mutual or co-operative corporations consisted solely of the retailers in the same line of trade, the stock of the corporation being held exclusively by the retailers. The Circuit Court of Appeals held, first of all, that the Mennen Company had not engaged in anything heretofore regarded as opposed to good morals and, therefore, did not violate the Trade Commission Act. It also found that the co-operative concerns were buying for themselves to sell to ultimate consumers; and the Mennen Company, therefore, was within its rights in classifying them as retailers. The Court also held that the primary intention of the Clayton Act was to eliminate local price discrimination and to prohibit only those practices which lessened competition between the offender

[3]278 U.S. 245.
[4]288 Fed. Rep. 774 (1923); certiorari denied, 262 U.S. 759 (1923).

and his competitors. It found no indication that the Mennen Company intended to create or maintain a monopoly. Therefore, the cease and desist order of the Federal Trade Commission was not sustained. The Supreme Court denied certiorari.

One of the issues posed in this case was that of what is known as functional discounts. A common practice in distribution is for manufacturers to classify buyers into wholesalers and retailers. The former are given special discounts not available to the latter, on the ground that the wholesalers relieve the manufacturers of many distributive functions. The retailers do not qualify for these discounts even though they may buy in larger quantities than many of the wholesalers and may relieve the manufacturer of many of the distribution functions. The problem is complicated by the fact that some buyers engage in both wholesale and retail activities in the same product.

The Commission met a second reversal in its proceedings against the National Biscuit Company (1924).[5] The National Biscuit Company offered discounts on its products on the basis of quantity purchased. It treated chain stores as a unit but, at the same time, refused to recognize as units independents who banded together for the purpose of joint buying. Although the Circuit Court of Appeals found that the manager of a branch store of a chain might possess such discretion as to make it possible for him to buy as an individual unit, he was, nevertheless, in such a case, acting as an employee or agent of the owner of the chain system and therefore could not be regarded as a different purchaser. Indebtedness was incurred by the company, the payment was made by it, and the goods were delivered to it. The Court further held that, even through the cost of selling through the chain was the same as the cost of selling to the owner of but one store, this did not sustain the charge of price discrimination, because there was no provision in the Clayton Act, or elsewhere, that stated the price to two different purchasers must be the same merely because it cost the seller as much to sell to one as it did to the other. The Court also ruled that the practice of granting discounts was not an unfair method of competition under the statute, unless it was prejudicial to the public, and that the policy of the National Biscuit Company in refusing to sell to co-operative or pooling buyers was fair in every respect as to all of its competitive customers. The Supreme Court denied certiorari.

The severe limitations which these decisions imposed upon the Federal Trade Commission's endeavors to deal with price discrimination were somewhat alleviated in the American Can case,[6] to which the Commission was not a party. Mr. Justice Sutherland, in delivering the opinion of the Supreme Court, rejected the position which the lower courts had

[5] *National Biscuit Co.* v. *Federal Trade Commission; Loose-Wiles Biscuit Co.* v. *Same*, 299 Fed. 733 (1924); certiorari denied, 266 U.S. 613 (1925).

[6] 278 U.S. 245 (1929).

taken in the Mennen and National Biscuit cases by declaring that Section 2 of the Clayton Act applied to practices which lessened competition among purchasers, as well as those which lessened competition among competing sellers. Possibly, the difference lay in the fact that the Antitrust Division had stressed the effect on competition, while the Federal Trade Commission attacked quantity discounts and cost differences.

The Commission interpreted the American Can decision as opening the way for a new assault on price discrimination; and in 1933 it issued a complaint against the Goodyear Tire and Rubber Company.[7] In 1926, this company had entered into a contract with Sears, Roebuck and Company, whereby Goodyear agreed to supply all of the tire requirements of Sears, Roebuck on a basis of cost plus 6 per cent. The tires were similar in every respect, except as to trade-mark and tread pattern, to those which Goodyear had distributed under its own name through some 25,000 retailers. The Commission found that the net average price discrimination over a period of seven years, in favor of Sears, was between 12 and 22 per cent. This estimate made an allowance for differences in cost arising from differences in quantities sold and in selling expenses. Goodyear argued that only the additional costs arising from the additional volume sold should be included in the cost computations and that the contract gave Goodyear advantages of a minimum volume of business, thereby insuring stability by avoiding the fluctuation of profit inevitable in Goodyear's other business and by passing risks of price declines in raw materials and credit losses on to Sears. The Commission's basic position was that the Clayton Act limited price differentials to differences in cost.

Goodyear appealed to the courts, and the Circuit Court of Appeals reversed the Commission's order.[8] In the meantime, as a result of the passage of the Robinson-Patman Act in 1936, Goodyear had discontinued the contract. On this ground, the Circuit Court held that the case had become moot. However, the Commission carried the matter to the Supreme Court,[9] which held that the Circuit Court was in error and remanded the case to the latter for determination on its merits. The Circuit Court then ordered that the Commission's order be vacated.[10] Subsequently, the Supreme Court denied certiorari.[11]

Again, had the Commission centered its attack on the effects on competition, instead of on cost differences, it might have secured different results. The issue, however, of the effects of the contract on competition is not an easy one to resolve. Goodyear found the contract profitable,

[7]22 FTC 232.

[8]*Goodyear Tire and Rubber Co.* v. *Federal Trade Commission*, 92 Fed. (2d) 677 (1937).

[9]*Federal Trade Commission* v. *Goodyear Tire and Rubber Co.*, 304 U.S. 257 (1938).

[10]*Goodyear Tire and Rubber Co.* v. *Federal Trade Commission*, 101 Fed. (2d) 620 (1939).

[11]308 U.S. 557 (1939).

and competition with other tire manufacturers was not lessened. The tires which Goodyear sold to Sears were marketed under the Sears name. The resulting competition was no harder on dealers in Goodyear tires than it was on those handling Firestone or Goodrich tires. If consumers wished to buy Sears tires, they were the beneficiaries. The Commission's position seemed to reflect a greater concern for protecting competitors than for protecting competition. Furthermore, the Commission evidently used a physical comparison approach, since it did not recognize distinctions which arise because of brand names.[12]

The Clayton Act, Amended Section 2 (Robinson-Patman Act)

It is evident that the Commission lacked any significant power to deal with price discrimination under the original Section 2 of the Clayton Act. The Robinson-Patman Act was designed to give the Commission sweeping powers over the whole field of price discrimination. The main factors responsible for the passage of the legislation set the stage for the way in which the Commission has endeavored to administer it. In the first place, the Commission, in its exhaustive study of the chain store problem, emphasized its powerlessness to deal with discriminatory practices, even where public interest demanded it. In the second place, numerous complaints by small-scale independent merchants, who felt they were threatened by chain store competition, created widespread demand for legislation which would protect the small businessman. There was not only the belief that large buyers were able to obtain unfair advantages but also that this large buying power, even when based upon economies, threatened small-scale enterprise, which needed to be preserved in the interests of society. Finally, there was the impression, on every hand, that competition had become too severe and that limitations had to be imposed upon it if private enterprise was to survive. "Soft competition" was considered to be preferable to "hard competition," the former offering protection to the competitors, with injury to the competitor rather than to competition in general being the main issue.

The Commission's hand in administering the law was also strengthened by placing upon the respondent the burden of proof of rebutting the charge that discrimination existed if price differentials were greater than warranted by due allowance for differences in cost. The respondent, however, could urge in defense that the lower prices were made in good

[12]For an analysis of this problem as applied to the Robinson-Patman Act, see Ralph Cassady, Jr. and E. T. Grether, "The Proper Interpretation of 'Like Grade and Quality' within the Meaning of Section 2(*a*) of the Robinson-Patman Act," *Southern California Law Review*, Vol. 30, No. 3 (1957), pp. 241–79. Interestingly enough, in the Cement Institute case (1948), the cement manufacturers argued that identity of product led to the need for identical prices in competitive markets. The Federal Trade Commission undertook, by chemical analysis, to prove that the products were not "identical." The cellophane and Du Pont (General Motors) cases also emphasize the difficulties of competing products and "relevant markets."

faith to meet the equally low price of a competitor or the services or facilities furnished by a competitor.

The Commission's approach to the administration of the Robinson-Patman Act was foreshadowed in the Goodyear case, in which the company's use of additional costs as a defense for its price policy was rejected. Administrative faith in the efficacy of modern cost accounting was evidenced by the statement that a sound method of allocating joint costs may be based upon an analysis of the service or function for which the cost is incurred.[13] This attitude is reminiscent of the administration of the codes under the National Industrial Recovery Act and is suggestive of the Unfair Practices Act of California,[14] in which selling below cost is forbidden and provision is made for the allocation of all costs to any article sold. The same position was manifest by the Interstate Commerce Commission in its class-rate decision,[15] indicating faith of commissions in the possibilities of cost allocation that is certainly not in accordance with the findings of economic theory or in keeping with flexible market conditions. The prevailing predilection of commissions for the use of "average costs" practically precludes a cost defense in discrimination cases.

The Federal Trade Commission promptly proceeded to deal with various quantity discount schemes, under the new Section 2(*a*), which it had tried to cope with unsuccessfully under the previous legislation. In the Pittsburgh Plate Glass Company case,[16] the manufacturers and distributors of window glass were ordered to cease classifying buyers into two groups—namely, quantity buyers, who purchased directly from the manufacturers, and carlot buyers, who purchased only indirectly through quantity buyers at a substantial mark-up. The practice of allowing cumulative discounts on total purchases for a specified period of time, rather than upon the size of individual orders, was the basis of a cease and desist order in the matter of the H.C. Brill Company.[17] The Commission felt that this policy was not justified by differences in cost, since it ignored the fact that the large buyers frequently placed numerous small orders, and the average size of these orders was often less than the average size of those of buyers whose aggregate annual purchases were less in volume. The decision was aimed at the concessions frequently obtained by large wholesalers and chain retailers. In a similar vein, the Commission, in its case against Standard Brands, Inc.,[18] struck at volume discounts given to purchasers irrespective of the quantities delivered to the separate plants or units of a purchaser. Standard Brands based its sales dis-

[13]Federal Trade Commission, *Annual Report* (Washington, D.C.: U.S. Government Printing Office, 1941), p. 26.

[14]Statutes of California, Chap. 860 (1937). This amended the law of 1913 (Deering's General Laws, Act No. 8781, secs. 3–7).

[15]Class-rate Investigation, 262 I.C.C. 447 (1945).

[16]25 FTC 1228 (1937).

[17]26 FTC 666 (1938).

[18]29 FTC 121 (1939).

count on yeast on the aggregate monthly requirements of the individual buyer, regardless of the source of purchase. The arrangement which had been the bone of contention in the Goodyear case was disposed of in the matter of the United States Rubber Company.[19] The Commission ordered the company to discontinue the price concessions made to large buyers of tires that were to be marketed as private brands where these were of like grade and quality with those sold under the regular trade name.

The first indication of the sweeping powers possessed by the Commission over quantity discounts under the Robinson-Patman Act was given in *Federal Trade Commission* v. *Morton Salt Company* (1948).[20] The Commission had held that Morton Salt had discriminated in price among different purchasers of table salt of like grades and qualities by the use of a pricing system which required the purchasers to pay delivered prices, the latter differing according to quantities purchased. The Commission found that only five companies ever bought sufficient quantities of salt from the Morton company to qualify for the lowest price. In addition, it found that special allowances were granted to certain favored customers who competed with other customers to whom these allowances were denied. The Commission issued a cease and desist order which forbade different prices to competing wholesalers, different prices to competing retailers, or lower prices to any retailer than those charged to a wholesaler whose customers competed with such retailer.

The Supreme Court held that, theoretically, the discounts were equally available to all but that, functionally, they were not. The law, it said, was especially concerned with protecting small businesses which were unable to buy in quantities; and the company had failed to prove that the full amount of the discounts was based upon actual savings in cost. The Court also held that the burden of showing justification rested on the one who was shown to have discriminated in prices. Finally, the Court stated that it was necessary, under the law, to show only that there was a reasonable *possibility* that the discriminations might harm competition.

In a dissenting opinion, Mr. Justice Jackson argued that the law required that the record show a reasonable *probability* of harm. He interpreted the majority opinion to mean that no quantity discount would be valid if the Commission chose to say that it was not.

This was evidently the way in which the Commission chose to interpret the verdict. In a cease and desist order against the Minneapolis-Honeywell Regulator Company, it ordered the company to discontinue the discriminatory pricing of automatic burners. In *Minneapolis-Honeywell Regulator Company* v. *Federal Trade Commission* (1951),[21] the Seventh Circuit Court of Appeals noted that the pricing system used

[19] 28 FTC 1489 (1939).

[20] 334 U.S. 37.

[21] 191 Fed. (2d) 786. The Supreme Court dismissed a writ of certiorari on jurisdictional grounds, 344 U.S. 206 (1952).

by the company was a standard quantity discount system and that the discounts were allowed to customers according to trade channels in which the customers were engaged. The Court held that Minneapolis-Honeywell did not need to justify the discounts on the basis of cost differences unless the pricing system did or might tend to injure competition. (The trial examiner for the Commission had found no such injury, and on-dissenting commissioner agreed.) The Court found no injury to come petitors or customers and, therefore, the order was reversed. "We construe the Act to require substantial, not trivial or sporadic, interference with competition to establish violation of its mandate."[22]

The Commission utilized the quantity limit proviso of the Robinson-Patman Act in the "Quantity Limit Rule on Replacement Tires."[23] In this proceeding, it found that available purchasers of rubber tires and tubes in quantities of annual dollar volume greater than $600,000 were so few as to render differentials on the greater quantities unjustly discriminatory against purchasers of smaller quantities. In order to eliminate the existing discrimination, the Commission ruled that the carload quantity of 20,000 pounds was the amount to be used for the maximum price differential. The basis for this order was that only 63 out of 48,198 purchasers bought over $600,000 of tires and tubes annually, and that the Robinson-Patman Act permitted the limitation of discounts where sellers were so few. The 20,000-pound limit was imposed because it was the carload quantity for rate making for tires and was used as a basis for carload discounts. This limitation was necessary, said the Commission, if the discount was to be available to the larger proportion of total buyers.

In a vigorous dissent, Commissioner Mason disagreed totally with the basis of the reasoning. He insisted that the evidence was so fragmentary and inconclusive as to be incapable of supporting a finding.

The order of the Commission has been subject to considerable litigation; but in *Federal Trade Commission* v. *B. F. Goodrich* (1957),[24] the United States Court of Appeals for the District of Columbia reversed the Commission, on the grounds that the dollar-volume standard did not justify the poundage limitation that the Commission wrote into the rule. The Court also held that the Commission did not furnish the necessary findings of fact. This case and the Minneapolis-Honeywell case seem to indicate that the Federal Trade Commission will have to justify its rulings more effectively than it has done to date.

The sweeping nature of the Commission's orders against price discrimination that has already been noted came up for consideration in *Federal Trade Commission* v. *Ruberoid Company* (1952).[25] The Com-

[22]*Ibid.*, p. 790.

[23]File No. 203–1 (1951).

[24]242 Fed. (2d) 31 (1957). This affirmed the decision of the District Court, which had reversed the Commission's decision, 134 Fed. Supp. 39 (1955).

[25]343 U.S. 470.

mission ordered the company to cease and desist from discriminating in price by "selling products of like grade and quality to any purchaser at prices lower than those granted to other purchasers who in fact compete with the favored purchaser in the resale or distribution of such products."[26] Thus, the Commission prohibited all price differentials among competing purchasers, on the ground that very small differences in price were material factors in competition among Ruberoid's customers. The Court felt that there was ample evidence that Ruberoid's classification of customers did not follow real functional differences and stated that it would not interfere except where the remedy selected had no reasonable relation to the unlawful practices found to exist. The law, said the Court, entitled Ruberoid to grant price differences if it could offer a cost defense or good faith; but it was not necessary for the Commission to make these exceptions in issuing an order, because they are necessarily implicit in every order under the Act. Mr. Justice Black concurred in the opinion, except that he held that the Commission order should explicitly state the exceptions. Mr. Justice Jackson wrote a lengthy dissent on the lack of specificity in the order. If the Commission could not establish a set of guiding yardsticks, he said, "there should be no judicial approval for an order to cease and desist from we don't know what."[27] In commenting upon this case the Attorney General's National Committee stated: "As administered, blanket cease and desist orders produce a system of mounting penalties for Robinson-Patman violations, the first violation provoking an order to cease and desist while subsequent transgressions result in Court injunctions, followed by penalties for contempt, without at any stage supplying legal guidance beyond what the perplexing text of the Act reveals."[28]

The meaning of price discrimination under the law has recently been set forth explicitly by the Supreme Court in *Federal Trade Commission* v. *Anheuser-Busch Inc.* (1960).[29] This case arose out of a complaint issued by the Federal Trade Commission in 1955 in which it was alleged that Anheuser-Busch had discriminated in price between different purchasers of its beer of like grade and quality by selling it to some of its customers at higher prices than to others, and that there was a reasonable probability that this would substantially lessen competition in the respondent's line of commerce The issue, therefore, was that of a pricing pattern that had adverse effects only upon sellers' competition, commonly termed primary-line competition, and not upon buyers' competition, commonly called secondary-line competition. The Court of Appeals held that the threshold statutory element of price discrimination had not been established.

[26]46 FTC 379, 387.
[27]343 U.S. 470.
[28]*Antitrust Laws, op. cit.*, p. 168.
[29]363 U.S. 536.

The Supreme Court first of all emphasized that Section 2(*a*) is violated where there is price discrimination which deals the requisite injury to primary-line competition even though secondary-line and tertiary-line competition are unaffected, and that even the original Section 2 of the Clayton Act was for the purpose of curbing the use by financially powerful corporations of localized price-cutting tactics which gravely impaired the position of other competitive sellers. The respondent urged that price discrimination is not synonymous with a price difference, and that Section 2(*a*) penalizes sellers only if an anticompetitive effect stems from a *discriminatory* pricing pattern, not if it results merely from a low price. Unless there is proof that high prices in one area have subsidized low prices in another, the price differential does not fall within the compass of the section.

The issue in the case was solely that of whether there had been price discrimination. The Court held that the term was synonymous with price differentiation because "it is only by equating price discrimination with price differentiation that §2(*a*) can be administered as Congress intended."[30] This interpretation of the law did not lead to a flat prohibition of price differentials, because price differences constitute but one element of a Section 2(*a*) violation. The Supreme Court reversed the Court of Appeals but this did not preclude further action by Anheuser-Busch, because it was still possible for it to advance the defenses available for price discrimination under Sections 2(*a*) or 2(*b*).

The nature of the cost defense for price discrimination under Section 2(*a*) was the issue at bar in *United States* v. *Borden Co.* (1962)[31] in which the District Court held that the cost showing by the Borden Company, and the Bowman Dairy Company, was an adequate one. The Supreme Court reversed the District Court on the ground that the cost classifications used by the companies did not satisfy the burden of showing that their respective discriminatory pricing plans reflected only a due allowance for cost differences.

The pricing arrangements of the dairy companies gave most of their customers—the independently owned stores—percentage discounts off list price which increased with the volume of purchases to a specified maximum, while granting to a few customers—the grocery store chains—a flat discount without reference to volume, and substantially greater than the maximum discount available under the volume plan offered to the independent stores. Borden's cost justification was built on comparisons of its average cost per $100 of sales to the chains in relation to the average cost of sales to each of the four groups of independents. Various methods of cost allocation were utilized, depending on the cost involved. Bowman's cost justification was based on differences in volume and methods of delivery. It relied heavily on a study of the cost per

[30]*Ibid., p. 550.*
[31]370 U.S. 460.

minute of its routemen's time. It determined that substantial portions of this time were devoted to three operations, none of which were ever performed for the 163 stores operated by its two major chain customers. It was on the basis of the costs of these services that the price discrimination was justified.

The Supreme Court recognized the elusiveness of cost data, but held that the classifications did not support the cost defense. It found that the classifications made by the dairy companies were not sufficiently homogeneous. "In sum, the record here shows that price discriminations have been permitted on the basis of cost differences between broad customer groupings, apparently based on the nature of ownership, but in any event not shown to be so homogeneous as to permit the joining together of these purchasers for cost allocation purposes. If this is the only justification for appellees' pricing schemes, they are illegal."[32] Just what would be legal is difficult to ascertain from this decision. Nor did it help to state that "We do not believe that an appropriate decree would require the trial court continuously to 'pass judgment on the pricing practices of these defendants.' "[33]

Section 2(*b*) of the amended Clayton Act places the burden of rebutting the prima-facie case of price discrimination upon the person charged with a violation, but permits the defense that the lower price to any purchaser was made in good faith to meet an equally low price of a competitor. The defense in *Standard Oil Company* (Indiana) v. *Federal Trade Commission*[34] was that the price discrimination in question was made in good faith to meet competition. Standard Oil of Indiana sold its Red Crown gasoline at two different wholesale prices. It sold to its "jobber" customers at tank-car prices, which were 1½ cents per gallon less than the tank wagon prices to service station customers. Each of the so-called "jobber" customers was free to sell at retail or wholesale. Two of these customers who sold at both wholesale and retail reduced their resale prices of gasoline below prevailing rates. The Commission held that the reduced resale prices resulted in injuring, preventing, and destroying competition. Standard's defense was that the lower price to the jobber was made in order to retain the jobber as a customer and in good faith to meet an equally low price offered by one or more competitors. There was no cost defense for the differentials.

Mr. Justice Burton, speaking for the majority of the Court, held that under the Robinson-Patman Act, the "good faith defense" is an absolute defense for price discrimination and that the effects of discrimination, under such circumstances, on competition are irrelevant. "It is enough to say that Congress did not seek by the Robinson-Patman

[32]*Ibid.*, p. 471. See also *In the matter of Champion Spark Plug Co.*, 50 FTC 30 (1953).

[33]*Ibid.*, p. 471.

[34]340 U.S. 231.

Act either to abolish competition or so radically to curtail it that a seller would have no substantial right of self-defense against a price raid by a competitor."[35] The order of the Commission was set aside.

Mr. Justice Reed dissented from the majority opinion, on the ground that the majority decision made "good faith" an absolute defense. Instead, he held that injury to competition should also be considered. The Commission has since endeavored to attack the good faith defense of Standard, with sharp division in its own ranks;[36] and Congress has debated the matter. So far, however, there has been no change in the law. Whether there should be depends upon one's viewpoint on "hard" versus "soft" competition and on protection of competitors versus protection of competition.

This case also indicates the complexity of the issues which can arise in connection with functional discounts. Two of the jobber customers sold at both wholesale and retail, and received the tank-car prices. A group of retailers proposed to establish their own bulk plant facilities and to purchase in tank-car quantities. Standard refused to grant the requested discounts. These dealers could not turn to other suppliers because of their leasing arrangements.[37]

Availability of the good faith defense of Section 2(*b*) to a seller who discriminates in favor of a customer to enable the latter to meet the price of his (the customer's) competitor was the issue in *Federal Trade Commission* v. *Sun Oil Co.* (1963).[38] The Sun Oil Company is a major integrated refiner that customarily distributes its products through retail service station operators who lease their stations from it. In 1955, Gilbert McLean was the operator of a Sunoco station in Jacksonville, Florida, in a sales territory composed of eight Sun stations, one of which was only about 11 blocks away from McLean's. McLean was an independent contractor and bore the direct and immediate risk of profitability of the station.

In June, 1955, the Super Test Oil Company, which operated about 65 retail service stations, opened its only service station in Jacksonville, across the street from McLean. Super Test began by selling its regular gasoline at 2 cents a gallon below McLean, and this seemed to be a normal difference. Super Test later cut its price, and McLean told Sun Oil that he would have to post a price of 25.9 cents a gallon in order to meet competition. Sun gave McLean a discount of 1.7 cents a gallon, and McLean dropped his retail price from 28.9 cents to 25.9 cents, thereby reducing

[35]*Ibid.*, p. 249.

[36]49 FTC 923 (1953). Good faith as a complete defense was finally established in *Federal Trade Commission* v. *Standard Oil Co.*, 355 U.S. 396 (1958). See also *A Study of the Antitrust Laws*, Part 3 (Hearings, Committee on the Judiciary, U.S. Senate) (Washington, D.C.: U.S. Government Printing Office, 1955).

[37]See also *Purolator Products Inc.*, FTC Docket 7850. Federal Trade Commission, *News Summary* (May 13, 1964).

[38]371 U.S. 505.

his gross margin from 4.8 cents a gallon to 3.5 cents. This meant that McLean absorbed 1.3 cents and Sun 1.7 cents of the price reduction. Sun did not give a corresponding reduction to any of its other dealers, although some of these complained about the favored treatment accorded to McLean.

The Federal Trade Commission charged Sun Oil with entering into a price-fixing agreement with McLean, and found that there had been actual competitive injury to the nonfavored Sun dealers. The Commission rejected the good faith defense on the ground that Sun was not meeting its own competition because the allowance was made to McLean to meet his competitor's. The Court of Appeals reversed the Trade Commission's findings, first on the ground that Super Test was an integrated supplier-retailer, and second that the price competition of Super Test was as much a threat to the continued existence of McLean as a customer as a direct competing lower offer to McLean would have been.

The Supreme Court found that the record indicated that Super Test was engaged solely in retail operations, and was not the beneficiary of any enabling price cut from its own supplier. It held that 2(*b*) contemplates that the lower price which may be met by one who would discriminate must be the lower price of his own competitor; the language of the section contains no implication that it comprehends a two-stage price reduction effected by two separate economic units at different levels of distribution. The general purpose of the Robinson-Patman Act is to protect the small independent businessman. The record showed that Sun's other dealers in the area were hurt by the discrimination in favor of McLean, and Sun took no steps to protect them. "It is the very operators of the other Sun stations which compete with McLean who are the direct objects of protection under the Robinson-Patman Act."[39] The fact that McLean was a small dealer did not make the good faith defense applicable, since Congress sought generally to obviate price discrimination practices threatening independent merchants and businessmen, presumably from whatever source. "To allow a supplier to intervene and grant discriminatory price concessions designed to enable its customer to meet the lower price of a retail competitor who is unaided by his supplier would discourage rather than promote competition. . . . To permit a competitor's supplier to bring his often superior economic power to bear narrowly and discriminately to deprive the otherwise resourceful retailer of the very fruits of his efficiency and convert the normal competitive struggle between retailers into an unequal contest between one retailer and the combination of another retailer and his supplier is hardly an element of reasonable and fair competition. . . . So long as a wholesaler can meet challenges to his pricing structure by wholly local and individualized responses, it has no incentive to alter its overall pricing

[39]*Ibid.*, p. 519.

policy."[40] In reply to Sun's contention that it would have to grant concessions over an unwarrantedly wide geographic area, perhaps even nationwide, the Court replied that in cases in which the economic facts so indicate, carefully drawn submarkets may be the proper measure of competitive impact among purchasers.

The Federal Trade Commission has held that the good faith defense is not available to a seller who discriminates in price to obtain new customers; it is limited in its scope to those situations in which a seller acts in self-defense against competitive price attacks. In Sunshine Biscuits, Inc.,[41] it found that the respondent had granted discounts of 5 per cent plus 2 per cent on potato chips to four customers in Cleveland, Ohio, and discounts of 5 per cent to fifteen customers in the same area. The purchasers who received discounts competed with other purchasers of the respondent in the sale of the same potato chips. Sunshine Biscuits claimed that it had granted the discounts in good faith to prevent the loss of customers to its competitors in some instances, and in others to obtain new customers. The Commission held that the discounts might injure the competitive ability of those who did not receive the discounts, and that the respondent was not acting defensively, as required by law, when it granted the discounts to obtain new customers. The case was appealed to the courts. In *Sunshine Biscuits, Inc.* v. *Federal Trade Commission* (1962)[42] the Court of Appeals held that the Commission had misinterpreted the statute and that as a matter of law the defense of meeting in good faith the equally low price of a competitor is available to the seller, whether the purchaser to whom the lower price is granted is a new customer or an old customer. The Commission did not seek Supreme Court review, but stated publicly that failure to do this did not reflect a change of position by the Commission on the question. It held that another federal court had sustained the Commission in a similar situation[43] and that now there was a split of court authority on the question.[44] Thus this issue still remains to be settled.

The Robinson-Patman Act, directed primarily against sellers who discriminate in favor of large buyers, also has a provision (Section 2[*f*]) of the amended Clayton Act under which proceedings may be instituted against buyers who knowingly induce or receive discriminatory prices. The construction of this section of the Act came before the Supreme Court for the first time in *Automatic Canteen Company* v. *Federal Trade Commission* (1953).[45] The company was a large buyer of confectionery products which were sold through automatic vending machines. It received price concessions on its purchases; and the Commission claimed that the

[40] *Ibid.*, pp. 522–23.

[41] FTC Docket 7708 (order issued in 1961).

[42] 306 Fed. (2d) 48.

[43] *Standard Motor Products Inc.*, v. FTC 265 Fed. (2d) 674 (1959).

[44] Federal Trade Commission, *News Summary* (November 30, 1962).

[45] 346 U.S. 61. See also "Automotive Parts and Supplies," FTC Docket 6889 (Federal Trade Commission, *News Summary*, February 4, 1958).

company knew that the prices the company induced were below list prices and that these prices were induced without inquiry of the seller, or assurance from the seller, as to cost differentials which might justify the price differentials.[46] The issue before the Court was the burden of proof under Section 2(*f*).

Mr. Justice Frankfurter, writing the opinion for the majority of the Court, said that the Commission had made no finding as to the company's knowledge of actual cost savings of particular sellers, and found only as to knowledge that the company knew what the list prices to other buyers were. He held that the Commission's interpretation of the term "knowingly to induce or receive" was such as to comprehend any buyer who engaged in bargaining over price and to place the buyer at his peril whenever he engaged in price bargaining. He concluded "that a buyer is not liable if the lower prices he induces are within one of the seller's defenses such as the cost justification or not known by him to be within one of those defenses."[47] He stated that, too often, no one can ascertain whether a price is cost-justified and that the burden of justifying a differential rests on the one who has at his peculiar command the cost and other record data by which to justify such discriminations."[48] Furthermore, he said that the Commission should "not shelter behind uncritical generalities or such looseness of expression as to make it essentially impossible for us to determine what really lay behind the conclusions which we are to review."[49] He therefore held against the Commission.

Mr. Justice Douglas dissented, on the ground that the burden of proof lay on the buyer who knew that he received discriminatory prices. This difference of opinion serves to emphasize Mr. Justice Frankfurter's understatement that "precision of expression is not an outstanding characteristic of the Robinson-Patman Act."[50]

The Attorney General's National Committee[51] approved the "rule of convenience" promulgated by this case as a future guide even though the precise application to concrete cases could not be foretold. Others[52] have felt that the burden placed on the Commission was a forbidding one. In any case, enforcement against buyers under the present circumstances will continue to be a difficult task, since "the court's interpretation firmly established *knowing* receipt of an illegal concession as the essential element of the buyer's offense."[53]

[46]46 FTC 861.
[47]346 U.S. 61, 75.
[48]*Ibid.*, p. 79.
[49]*Ibid.*, p. 81.
[50]*Ibid.*, p. 65.
[51]*Antitrust Laws, op. cit.*, p. 197.
[52]See Corwin Edwards, *The Price Discrimination Law* (Washington, D.C.: The Brookings Institution, 1959), p. 511.
[53]*Antitrust Laws, op. cit.*, p. 194. But see N. W. P. and Bryant M. Smith, Sr., FTC Docket 8039 (Federal Trade Commission, *News Summary*, January 8, 1964). This was a cease and desist order in which the Commission held that jobbers of automotive parts knowingly induced and received discriminatory prices through an agent they are partners in, and own and control, namely, National Parts Warehouse.

Section 3. Robinson-Patman Act

Section 3 of the Robinson-Patman Act makes it a crime for any person to be a party to the practices forbidden in Section 2 of the amended Clayton Act. The constitutionality of this provision was passed on by the Supreme Court in *United States* v. *National Dairy Products Corp.* (1963).[54] The company and Raymond J. Wise, a vice-president, were charged with violating Section 3 by making sales below cost for the purpose of destroying competition. In five of its markets, National Dairy's pricing practice was alleged to have resulted in severe financial losses to small dairies, and in two others the effect was claimed to have been to eliminate competition and drive small dairies from the market. The District Court dismissed the Section 3 charges on the ground that the section was unconstitutionally vague and indefinite.

The Supreme Court held that "sales made below cost without legitimate commercial objective and with specific intent to destroy competition would clearly fall within the prohibitions of §3."[55] It felt that if Section 3 gave National Dairy and Wise sufficient warning that selling below cost for the purpose of destroying competition is unlawful, the statute is constitutional as applied to them. The Court found that they were adequately forewarned, and remanded the case to the lower court for trial. Mr. Justice Black, joined by Justices Stewart and Goldberg, dissented and stated that the judgment of the District Court should have been upheld. Justice Black quoted with approval a statement from the Attorney General's National Committee: "Doubts besetting Section 3's constitutionality seem well-founded; no gloss imparted by history or adjudication has settled the vague contours of this harsh criminal law."[56]

Basing-Point Pricing

Over the years, since the end of World War I, the Federal Trade Commission has conducted an almost continuous assault on the basing-point method of quoting delivered prices. It has contended that this procedure destroys free competition, that it is a method of systematic price discrimination involving practices that deprive customers of the advantage of location, and that it tends toward monopoly. Under the original Section 2 of the Clayton Act, the Commission, in 1924, ordered the United States Steel Corporation to cease and desist from quoting prices under what was known as the "Pittsburgh-plus" system.[57] Under this arrangement, the price of rolled steel products consisted of the price F.O.B. Pittsburgh plus railroad freight, either hypothetical or real, to the point of delivery. All buyers were required to purchase at delivered prices; and the delivered price at any given destination was the same, re-

[54] 372 U.S. 29.
[55] *Ibid.*, p. 37.
[56] *Antitrust Laws*, *op. cit.*, p. 201.
[57] 8 FTC 1.

gardless of the origination point of the steel. This, the Commission contended, was discrimination in violation of Section 2 of the Clayton Act and also an unfair method of competition. The United States Steel Corporation accepted the order, "insofar as it is practicable to do so," and thereafter adopted a multiple basing-point system, by which it established a number of basing points from which prices to different parts of the country were quoted.

For approximately the next twenty years, however, the Commission was powerless to do anything about this method of pricing. Continued complaints by buyers, together with the passage of the Robinson-Patman Act, led to a new assault on the basing-point practice. The Commission also found additional strength by employing Section 5 of the Trade Commission Act, under which it contended that such pricing constituted an unfair method of competition.

The first significant regulatory breach in the basing-point method of pricing came in *Corn Products Refining Company* v. *Federal Trade Commission* (1945).[58] In this case, the Supreme Court sustained an order of the Commission against the Corn Products Refining Company. The latter used a basing-point system in pricing sales of glucose, by which it sold only at delivered prices. These were computed by adding to a base price at Chicago the published freight tariff from Chicago to the several points of delivery. The company also made deliveries from its factory in Kansas City, but used the Chicago base price. In other words, it was using a single basing-point method of pricing. The Commission found that this method of quoting prices gave an advantage to candy manufacturers in Chicago and resulted in discrimination in price among purchasers of glucose located elsewhere, and that this discrimination resulted in substantial harm to competition among the purchasers. The company argued that there was no discrimination under its basing-point system between buyers at the same points of delivery and that Section 2(*a*) of the Clayton Act was directed only at price discrimination between buyers at the same delivery point. The Court did not agree with this contention but held, on the contrary, that the discriminations involved in the petitioner's pricing system were within the prohibition of the Act. Furthermore, it ruled that the statute was designed to reach discriminations in their incipiency, before the harm to competition was effected, and that the Commission's inference that there was a reasonable probability that the effect of the discrimination was substantially to lessen competition had been sustained. It also held that it was for the Commission, and not for the courts, to determine what weight was to be attributed to the facts proved or stipulated and the inferences to be drawn therefrom.[59]

[58]324 U.S. 726.

[59]The Commission, in addition, charged Corn Products with other violations of Section 2(*a*), such as special discounts to favored purchasers, and with violating Section 2(*e*) by favoring Curtiss Candy company with advertising services not proportionately available to others. The Court upheld the Commission's order on these counts also.

The Supreme Court also condemned, in a companion case, the practice of emulating a competing seller's pricing system when it resulted in systematic discrimination. The case of *Federal Trade Commission* v. *A. E. Staley Manufacturing Company* (1945),[60] decided on the same day, was similar to that involving the Corn Products Refining Company, except that the Staley company justified its practices on the grounds that they were made in good faith and that a producer had the right to meet the low price of a competitor. The Court upheld the Commission's findings that the Staley company had slavishly followed the pricing policy of the Corn Products company by using the Chicago base price and had not sustained the "good faith" defense. The Court found that the Staley company had never endeavored to set up a nondiscriminatory pricing system, but then added: "It does not follow that respondents may never absorb freight when their factory price plus actual freight is higher than their competitor's price, or that sellers, by so doing, may not maintain a uniform delivered price at all points of delivery, for in that event there is no discrimination in price." These cases established the fact that a single basing-point system violated the law if a producer had factories at various places, but it left entirely unsettled the question of the legality of multiple basing points and uniform delivered prices. However, the reasoning of the Court certainly foreshadowed its decision in the Cement Institute case.

In *Federal Trade Commission* v. *Cement Institute et al.* (1948)[61] the Supreme Court upheld the Commission in its proceedings against the Cement Institute and the manufacturers of Portland cement who were members of it. The litigation arose out of a lengthy investigation by the Federal Trade Commission of the pricing practices employed by the manufacturers of Portland cement and the activities of the Cement Institute. The latter was a trade association whose membership comprised practically every manufacturer of Portland cement in the United States. The target of attack by the Commission was the multiple basing-point system of pricing to which the cement industry adhered. The Commission held that this pricing structure in the cement industry was the result of combination and conspiracy to restrain competition; that it and all the practices connected therewith constituted unfair methods of competition, in violation of the Federal Trade Commission Act; and that it resulted in price discrimination, in violation of the Clayton Act, as amended by the Robinson-Patman Act.

As a result of its findings, the Commission ordered the respondents "to cease and desist from entering into, continuing, cooperating in or carrying out any planned common course of action, understanding, agreement, combination, or conspiracy between and among any two or more of said respondents, or between any one or more of said respondents

[60] 324 U.S. 746.
[61] 333 U.S. 683.

and others not parties hereto, to do or perform any of the following things":

> 1. Quoting or selling cement at prices calculated or determined pursuant to, or in accordance with, the multiple-basing point, delivered price system; or quoting or selling cement pursuant to or in accordance with any other plan or system which results in identical price quotations or prices for cement at points of quotation or sale or to particular purchasers by respondents using such plan or system, or which prevents purchasers from finding any advantage in price in dealing with one or more of the respondents against any of the other respondents.
> 2. [Prohibits specific practices designed to support any method of pricing outlawed above.]
> 3. Discriminating in price between or among their respective customers by systematically charging and accepting mill net prices which differ by the amounts necessary to produce delivered costs to purchasers identical with delivered costs available to such purchasers through purchases from other respondents.
> 4. Using any means substantially similar to those specifically set out in this order with the purpose or effect of accomplishing any of the things prohibited by this order.[62]

The respondents appealed the order to the courts; and when the case came before the Supreme Court, the latter upheld the order of the Commission in its entirety. In so doing, the Supreme Court agreed with the Commission that the respondents collectively maintained a multiple basing-point, delivered price system for the purpose of suppressing competition in cement sales. The Court also agreed that the respondents had employed the multiple basing-point system as a practice rather than as a good faith effort to meet individual competitive situations. This applied to situations involving both phantom freight and freight absorption. The multiple basing-point system of pricing was clearly outlawed if it was based upon collusion of any type among the sellers. In addition, the Court held that the Commission had the jurisdiction to conclude that conduct resulting in a combination to restrain trade which constituted a violation of the Sherman Act might also be an unfair method of competition.

The verdict in the Cement case had apparently rested on the existence of an agreement among the companies using the basing-point system of pricing. In *Triangle Conduit and Cable Co. Inc.* v. *Federal Trade Commission* (1948)[63] however, where the facts were substantially the same, the Circuit Court of Appeals took the position that no direct proof of agreement or conspiracy was necessary. This could be shown by circumstantial evidence. Triangle Conduit contended that the individual use of the basing-point method, with the knowledge that other sellers used it, did not constitute an unfair method of competition. The argument was that individual freight absorption was not illegal, per se, and that the Commission's order was a denial of the right to meet competition.

[62]*Cement Institute et al.*, 37 FTC 87 (1943), pp. 259–61.
[63]168 Fed. (2d) 175.

The Court of Appeals was unwilling to say that the individual use of the basing-point method, as used in this instance, was not an unfair method of competition. The Commission's cease and desist order was therefore allowed to stand. The case was carried to the Supreme Court, which divided 4 to 4 on the appeal.[64] This sustained the ruling of the lower court. There was no written opinion.

The confusion as to the legality of freight absorption and spatial price differentiation was well exemplified by Mr. Walter Wooden, associate general counsel of the Federal Trade Commission, when, in testifying before a congressional committee, he said, "The only absolutely safe method is to have a non-discriminatory price. If an f.o.b. mill price is that, and as I understand it, it would be, it is safe."[65]

In short, these decisions seemed, practically, to have ruled spatial competition out of the picture. Congress endeavored to grapple with the problem by passing legislation designed to legalize basing-point pricing that was not based on conspiracy. The trouble was that the legislation was no clearer than the confusion it tried to correct. President Truman vetoed the bill, on the ground that it would create more confusion than already existed and would lead to endless litigation.

In 1953 the Federal Trade Commission attacked the zone-delivered pricing system of National Lead Company under Section 5 of the Trade Commission Act as an unfair method of competition. It changed its previous position on the discriminatory character of delivered pricing by holding that the price that is relevant in determining the legality of discrimination is not net realization at the mill, but the price charged at the point of delivery.[66] The complaint was based upon an alleged concert of action on zone-delivered pricing to which National Lead was a party. In *Federal Trade Commission* v. *National Lead Co.* (1957)[67] the Supreme Court held that the Commission order in effect prohibited a concert of action among the respondents in utilizing a zone-delivered pricing system, by directing each respondent individually to cease and desist from adopting the same or a similar system of pricing for the purpose or with the effect of "matching" the prices of competitors.

According to the Commission, under the National Recovery Administration, there had been an agreement among the respondents to use flat delivered prices in designated zones and uniform differentials applicable as between such zones. The zone boundaries were highly artificial. Uniform discounts, terms of sale, etc., were also adopted. The

[64] *Clayton Mark and Co.* v. *Federal Trade Commission*, 336 U.S. 956 (1949).

[65] See D. F. Pegrum, "The Present Status of Geographic Pricing," *Journal of Marketing*, Vol. XV, No. 4 (April, 1951), pp. 425–35.

[66] *National Lead Co.* 40 FTC 840 (1953). This accords with the Supreme Court's definition of price discrimination in *Federal Trade Commission* v. *Anheuser-Busch, Inc.*, 363 U.S. 536 (1960).

[67] 352 U.S. 419. See also *Chain Institute* v. *Federal Trade Commission*, 246 Fed. (2d) 231 (1957), certiorari denied, 355 U.S. 895 (1957).

arrangements were continued after the demise of the N.R.A. The Commission ordered the abandonment of a "planned common course of action" to sell at prices determined pursuant to a zone-delivered price system. National Lead argued that the order and remedy were too sweeping.

The Court noted, first, that the order was temporary and solely for the purpose of creating a breathing spell in which an independent pricing system might grow up. Second, the order was aimed at a delivered-zone pricing system. Third, zone-delivered pricing, per se, was not banned. The Court held that the order did not prohibit the practice of absorption of actual freight, as such, in order to foster competition. "It is our conclusion that the order was not intended to and does not prohibit or interfere with independent delivered zone pricing *per se*. Nor does it prohibit the practice of the absorption of actual freight as such in order to foster competition."[68]

The earlier controversy over basing-point systems seems to have disappeared even without new legislation. Compulsory delivered pricing and with it "phantom freight" are gone.[69] Freight absorption based on a systematic pricing system also seems to be out, but the Commission is proceeding against unsystematic territorial price variations under the Robinson-Patman Act.[70] The Commission is now conducting an investigation into the pricing structure of the cement industry to ascertain compliance with the orders given in the Cement Institute case,[71] but no report has yet been prepared.

The Commission is also engaged in proceedings against two trade associations and fifteen tire and tube manufacturers under a charge of conspiracy to fix prices. The principal charge is that the manufacturers have adopted and maintained a single-zone delivered pricing system for tires and tubes. The Big Four (Goodyear, Firestone, United States Rubber, and Goodrich) quote identical, or substantially matched, prices to all customers of a class throughout the country, regardless of location and differences in freight costs. Those quoted by General Tire and Rubber and the "minors" are lower by agreed-upon differentials.[72] Economists have long recognized that identical prices may be as discriminatory as nonidentical ones. If the final outcome of this complaint establishes this fact at law, it will constitute a step forward in dealing with the problem of discrimination. If it turns out to be merely another case of conspiracy, no clarification is likely to merge.

[68]*Ibid.*, p. 431.

[69]But see S. M. Loescher, "Inert Antitrust Administration: Formula Pricing and the Cement Industry," *Yale Law Journal*, Vol. LXV (1955), pp. 1–22; and Marvin J. Barloon, "Institutional Foundations of Pricing Policy in the Steel Industry," *Business History Review*, Vol. XXVIII, No. 3 (September, 1954), pp. 214–35.

[70]See Corwin D. Edwards, *op. cit.*, chaps. 11–13.

[71]Federal Trade Commission, *Annual Report* (1961), p. 59.

[72]Docket 7505 (Federal Trade Commission, *Annual Report*, 1959), pp. 42–43.

Brokerage Allowances and Services

The interpretation of the section of the Robinson-Patman Act [Section 2(*c*) of the amended Clayton Act] on brokerage has resulted in its becoming a highly restrictive provision. In the complaint against the Biddle Purchasing Company, the respondent was ordered to cease and desist splitting brokerage payments with purchasers. The Biddle company sold market information to a large number of distributors and, at the same time, placed orders for many of its clients. The goods, however, were delivered and billed directly to the buyer. The seller paid the Biddle company a brokerage fee, which the latter then passed on to the purchaser. The company appealed to the courts for relief; but the Commission was upheld, despite the fact that the company had long been conducting its business openly on this basis.[73]

The cease and desist order against the Great Atlantic and Pacific Tea Company required the company to refrain from accepting brokerage allowances from its field agents. The latter executed purchasing orders for the company and also rendered certain services to the seller. Although some modifications in the arrangement were made as a result of the passage of the Robinson-Patman Act, the Commission insisted that the agents were still acting on behalf of both buyer and seller, and that the Congress intended that compensation to an agent must be a bona fide brokerage fee. The Commission's position was sustained in the lower courts, and review was denied by the Supreme Court.[74] It appears that the Commission's position on this matter is the same when applied to independent retailers acting in groups as it is when applied to chain stores.[75]

In *Webb-Crawford* v. *Federal Trade Commission* (1940), a court of appeals declared that all payments of "brokerage" to anyone connected with the buyer were illegal, whether granted in return for genuine services or not.[76] Thus, the payment of middlemen's commissions to any but pure "brokers" was apparently illegal, per se, even though valuable distributive services was performed, and even though no adverse competitive effect resulted. The fact that the concessions reflected actual savings in the seller's distribution costs did not lessen the illegality.

The interpretation of the section of the Robinson-Patman Act relating to allowances and services has not been so completely restrictive at that which involves brokerage. Thus, in the Corn Products Refining

[73]*Biddle Purchasing Co.* v. *Federal Trade Commission*, 92 Fed. (2d) 687 (1938); certiorari denied, 305 U.S. 634 (1938).

[74]*Great Atlantic and Pacific Tea Co.* v. *Federal Trade Commission*, 106 Fed. (2d) 667 (1939); certiorari denied, 308 U.S. 625 (1940); petition for rehearing denied, 309 U.S. 694 (1940).

[75]*Oliver Bros.* v. *Federal Trade Commission*, 102 Fed. (2d) 763 (1939).

[76]109 Fed. (2d) 268. See also *Southgate Brokerage Co.* v. *Federal Trade Commission*, 150 Fed. (2d) 607 (1945).

case,[77] the Commission, among other things, contended that the Corn Products company had entered into an arrangement with the Curtiss Candy Company whereby, from 1936 to 1939, it spent over $750,000 in advertising Curtiss candy as being rich in dextrose. The Curtiss company made a similar advertisement. During the same period, the purchase of dextrose and glucose by the Curtiss company from the Corn Products company increased rapidly, but the latter did not furnish proportionally equal advertising services to its other customers. The Supreme Court upheld the Commission's contention that the Corn Products company thus furnished a service connected with the sale, or offering for sale, of a commodity upon terms not accorded to other purchasers. The statute, said the Court, was aimed at discrimination made in favor of one purchaser and denied to another or other purchasers of a commodity.

The Commission expects the seller to offer bona fide alternative means to all qualified customers, whereby all buyers are able to participate in some form. The Commission has approved the practice of the large soap manufacturers of granting advertising allowances to their customers.[78] Those allowances were given for services actually rendered. The Commission found that these allowances were not substantially in excess of the cost of these services to the distributors or their value to the manufacturers.

The issue of "proportionally equal terms" came before the Supreme Court in *Federal Trade Commission* v. *Simplicity Pattern Co.* (1960).[79] Unfortunately, the opinion did nothing to clarify the meaning or interpretation of this phrase.[80] This case presented for the first time the availability of certain defenses to a prima-facie violation of Section 2(*e*) which forbade discrimination without furnishing services to all purchasers on proportionally equal terms. The Federal Trade Commission found that the Simplicity Pattern Company, one of the nation's largest manufacturers of dress patterns, discriminated in favor of its larger customers by furnishing to them services and facilities not accorded to smaller customers on proportionally equal terms. The customers of Simplicity fell roughly into two categories. One, composed largely of department and variety stores, comprised only about 18 per cent of the total number of customers, but accounted for 70 per cent of the total

[77]See *Corn Products Refining Co.* v. *Federal Trade Commission*, 324 U.S. 726 (1945), above, pp. 427–28.

[78]*Lever Bros. Co.*, *Procter and Gamble Co.*, *Colgate-Palmolive-Peet Co.*, FTC Dockets 5585, 5586, 6687 (1953). See also report of the Attorney General's National Committee, *Antitrust Laws* (Washington, D.C.: U.S. Government Printing Office, 1955)., pp. 187–93.

[79]360 U.S. 55.

[80]In a footnote the Court stated: "The parties did not explore, before the Commission, the possibility that this tailoring of services and facilities to meet the different needs of two classes of customers in fact constituted 'proportionally equal terms.' " *Ibid.*, p. 61.

sales volume. The remaining 82 per cent of the customers were small stores whose primary business was the sale of yard-goods fabrics. The retail prices of Simplicity patterns were uniform, and so was the price to the two groups of buyers. Simplicity furnished the patterns to the large stores on a consignment basis, thus affording them an investment-free inventory. The small stores had to pay cash. The large stores were furnished with cabinets and catalogues free of charge, while the small stores were charged for them. Finally, Simplicity paid all transportation charges in connection with the business with the large stores. Simplicity contended that there was no real competition in patterns between the variety (large) stores and the fabric (small) stores, and further that the discriminations were not unlawful if it could be shown that the differential treatment only reflected differences in costs.

The Supreme Court held that competition among the two groups of buyers did exist, and that the absence of proof of competitive injury was not a defense under 2(*e*). The Court held that the proscriptions of 2(*c*, *d*, and *e*) are absolute, and that none of them requires as proof of prima-facie violation a showing of injurious or destructive effect on competition. ". . . . false brokerage allowances and the paying for or furnishing of nonproportional services or facilities are banned outright . . . . neither 'cost-justification' nor an absence of competitive injury may constitute 'justification' of a prima facie §2 violation."[81] The decision of the Federal Trade Commission was upheld.

In *Federal Trade Commission* v. *Henry Broch & Co.* (1960),[82] the Supreme Court dealt with Section 2(*c*) of the Clayton Act which makes it unlawful for any person to make an allowance in lieu of brokerage to the other party of the transaction. Broch was a broker for a number of sellers of food products. He agreed to act for Canada Foods, Ltd. for a 5 per cent commission. Other brokers worked for Canada Foods, but Broch received a higher commission because he stocked merchandise in advance of sales. Canada Foods established a price of $1.30 a gallon for its 1954 pack of apple concentrate in 50-gallon drums. J. M. Smucker offered $1.25 a gallon for a 500-gallon purchase, through another broker named Phipps. Canada Foods refused to meet this by stating that the only way it could give the lower price was through a reduction in brokerage, and informed Broch to this effect. Broch agreed to lower his brokerage from 5 per cent to 3 per cent with the result that a contract was entered into with Smucker at $1.25 a gallon. The reduction in brokerage amounted to 50 per cent of the total price reduction granted by Canada Foods to Smucker. The Federal Trade Commission charged a violation of Section 2(*c*).

The Supreme Court stated that the Robinson-Patman Act was enacted to prohibit all devices by which large buyers gained discrimina-

[81]*Ibid.*, pp. 69–71.
[82]363 U.S. 166.

tory preferences over smaller ones by virtue of greater purchasing power. The majority of the Court held that "Congress enacted the Robinson-Patman Act to prevent sellers and sellers' brokers from yielding to the economic pressures of a large buying organization by granting unfair preferences in connection with the sale of goods. . . . An 'independent' broker is not likely to be independent of the buyer's coercive bargaining power. . . . A price reduction based upon alleged savings in brokerage expenses is an 'allowance in lieu of brokerage' when given only to favored customers."[83] Mr. Justice Whittaker, joined by Justices Frankfurter, Harlan, and Stewart, wrote a strongly dissenting opinion against upholding the cease and desist order of the Commission. He noted that the respondent was an independent broker and that the buyer knew nothing of the agreement to reduce the commission. He held that Congress did not intend that Section 2(*c*) would affect negotiated charges for legitimate brokerage services. "Until today, it seems always to have been generally understood that a truly independent broker, such as respondent, was free to negotiate the rate or amount of his commissions with his principle without fear of violating §2(*c*). . . . But the Court now holds that an independent broker who has once agreed with the seller on a general rate of commission may not renegotiate that rate with his principal in order to effect a sale that would otherwise be lost to him."[84] It is thus impossible to reconcile Section 2(*c*) with Sections 2(*a*) or 2(*b*), and it eliminates a defense under these by the independent broker. The majority and dissenting opinions both in this case and in the Simplicity Pattern Company might lead the Commission to give more careful thought to the costs that are relevant to decision making in situations involving differential pricing and the relation of these to discrimination in the economic sense.

Summary of Price Discrimination

The Robinson-Patman Act has now been on the statute books for nearly 30 years. The results of enforcement are somewhat difficult to appraise because interpretation of the law has cut across desirable and undesirable practices in indiscriminate fashion. The Federal Trade Commission has been in almost continuous internal controversy over the meaning and application of the law, and the decisions of the Supreme Court have been marked by a similar division. Neither the courts nor the Commission have made any substantial contribution to an understanding or elucidation of the economic issues of the cases coming before them. Sections 2(*c*), (*d*), (*e*) on advertising allowances, brokerage allowances, and proportionally equal terms have been construed as to make their prohibitions absolute even though many transactions in these categories may be economically desirable and defensible; at least they seem to

[83] *Ibid.*, pp. 174–76.

[84] *Ibid.*, pp. 183–84. But see *Hruby Distribution Co.*, FTC Docket 8068 (Federal Trade Commission, *News Summary*, January 11, 1963).

encompass practices for which the defense under 2(*a*) and (*b*) should be available.

Price discrimination presents an extremely complex issue which is not simplified by court definition, which equates it with price differentiation. Economists have long recognized that price discrimination may be used as a weapon to destroy competition, to enhance monopoly, or retain it. However, cost is an elusive and blunt weapon, particularly when used alone to deal with the problem under modern conditions of multiple-product firms and widespread geographic markets. Neither the Federal Trade Commission nor the courts have done much to clarify the issues or give the law tolerably ascertainable content. Whether by intent or accident, the results of decisions to date have been more in the direction of protecting competitors than in protecting competition. Interpretation of the good faith defense has had similarly unsatisfactory results. It has limited price discrimination to that of meeting competitors only, thereby preventing a firm from pricing its products below those of a rival, even though it might be economical to do so, and it is possible that it may even prevent the use of a good faith defense to secure new customers, as contrasted with that of retaining old ones.[85]

The Robinson-Patman Act has been subject to severe criticism both on the grounds of the provisions in the law and of their interpretation. Proposals for rectification have even gone as far as recommendation for repeal of it. However, existing legislation without the Robinson-Patman Act is inadequate to deal with the problems presented by the price policies that are an inescapable part of modern business. Repeal of the present law is an unlikely prospect, particularly in view of the difficulties of writing an acceptable substitute. Modification by amendment would have advantages, but agreement on such modifications, especially as to wording would be difficult to obtain. What seems to be most necessary is a more statesmanlike interpretation by the Federal Trade Commission, which should interpret the legislation more in keeping with the spirit and intent of the antitrust laws. The Commission has concentrated its attention too much on narrow types of injury to competition, and has participated too much in what has come perilously close to price regulation to develop a broad program of public policy.[86] The most urgent need to correct the shortcomings of the Robinson-Patman Act is a reorientation on the part of the Federal Trade Commission to a position as major policy-developing agency for antitrust enforcement.

[85]This is a particularly acute issue in transportation, as is pointed out in Part V of this book, *infra.*

[86]For a careful analysis of the Robinson-Patman Act, see Corwin D. Edwards, *The Price Discrimination Law* (Washington, D.C.: The Brookings Institution, 1959). A thorough analysis of cost justification is presented in H. F. Taggart, *Cost Justification* (Ann Arbor: University of Michigan, 1959). Appraisal and recommendations will also be found in *Antitrust Laws, op. cit.*, ch. iv, and in C. Kaysen and D. F. Turner, *Antitrust Policy: An Economic and Legal Analysis* (Cambridge: Harvard University Press, 1959).

UNFAIR METHODS OF COMPETITION

In enforcing Section 5 of the Federal Trade Commission Act, the Commission has manifested a dual approach. First of all, as has already been pointed out, it recognized that the Act was designed to supplement the antitrust laws. As a consequence, the Commission has attacked, as unfair competition, practices which could have been prosecuted under them. In the second place, it has applied the law with a view to maintaining or establishing standards of conduct which it considers essential to the maintenance of fair and healthy competition. To this end, it has proscribed practices which it considers harmful to competitors, contrary to public interest, and inimical to the welfare of the consumer. In this respect, the standards which the Commission has applied are ethical in nature and are designed to protect both the competitor and the consumer. Congress may not have foreseen, in the first instance, that this would come to occupy the major part of the Commission's activities, but subsequent legislation—such as the Wheeler-Lea amendment and the Wool Products Labeling Act (1939), the Furs Products Labeling Act (1951), the Flammable Fabrics Act (1953), and the Textile Fiber Products Identification Act (1958)—has given sanction to the importance which the Commission has attached to both of these. In fiscal 1963, approximately four elevenths of the appropriation for the Trade Commission were spent to halt the cheating of consumers, principally by false advertising.[87]

Interpreting the Law

The statute did not define "unfair methods of competition" but, instead, left the meaning of this phrase to be developed out of experience. The question of location of final jurisdiction on what constitutes unfair methods of competition arose in *Federal Trade Commission* v. *Gratz* (1920).[88] The Supreme Court stated that the words "unfair methods of competition" were not defined by the statute and did not have any exact meaning, and that it was for the courts, not the Commission, ultimately to determine, as a matter of law, what they included. The Court also held that the law was clearly inapplicable to practices not theretofore regarded as opposed to good morals because they were characterized by deception, bad faith, fraud, or oppression, and not theretofore regarded as against public policy because of their dangerous tendency unduly to hinder competition or to create monopoly.

This severe limitation on the powers of the Commission to expand the concepts of unfair methods was modified considerably by the decision in *Federal Trade Commission* v. *Winsted Hosiery Company* (1922).[89]

[87]Federal Trade Commission, *Annual Report* (1963), pp. 11 and 31.
[88]253 U.S. 421.
[89]258 U.S. 483.

The Commission issued a cease and desist order against the Winsted company, on the ground that its labeling and advertising created the impression with the public that its product was all wool, whereas, as a matter of fact, it was composed largely of cotton. The company contended that it was merely adopting a common practice of the trade and that no one, either competitor or consumer, was deceived. The Court upheld the Commission's ruling, on the ground that the practices were inherently unfair and "the fact that misrepresentation and misdescription have become so common in the knit underwear trade that most dealers no longer accept labels at their face value, does not prevent their use being an unfair method of competition."[90]

Under the original wording of Section 5, the Commission was directed to proceed against unfair methods of competition if such a proceeding would be in the interest of the public. Presumably, this provision limited jurisdiction to unfair methods which constituted injury to the public and did not cover controversies which merely involved the private rights of competitors. This was the ruling of the Supreme Court in *Federal Trade Commission* v. *Klesner* (1929).[91] This case involved a dispute over good will and the use of the name "The Shade Shop." The Court held that the issue was one between private parties and therefore could be settled by private suit in a court of law. Although this ruling limited the Commission's jurisdiction, it also authorized the Commission to refuse to act if, in its judgment, public interest was not involved.

The original wording of Section 5 was interpreted to mean that it was necessary to prove injury to competitors if action was to be taken against alleged violators. This was the interpretation of the Supreme Court in the original case of *Federal Trade Commission* v. *Raladam Company* (1931).[92] The Raladam Company manufactured and sold a fat-reducing preparation, which, it claimed, was safe and effective. The Commission held that this claim was misleading and deceptive, and that the cure competed with the advice of professional physicians and other means and remedies for reducing weight. It therefore issued a cease and desist order, on the grounds that Raladam's practices constituted unfair methods of competition. The Supreme Court assumed that the methods were unfair and that the Commission's proceedings were in the interest of the public. However, the Court held that unfair trade methods are not, per se, unfair methods of competition, and that the Commission had failed to prove that the practices of the Raladam Company had effected any substantial injury upon competitors. The Supreme Court therefore affirmed the lower court's reversal of the Federal Trade Commission's cease and desist order.

The Commission commenced an entirely new action against Rala-

[90] *Ibid.*, p. 494.
[91] 280 U.S. 19.
[92] 283 U.S. 643.

dam in 1935, and this case finally reached the Supreme Court in *Federal Trade Commission* v. *Raladam* (1942).[93] This time, the Commission's findings were upheld. The Commission had taken great care to demonstrate the competitive effect of Raladam's practices; and the Supreme Court ruled that when the Commission found, as it did in this instance, that misleading and deceptive statements were made with reference to quality of merchandise in active competition with other merchandise, it was authorized to infer that trade would be diverted from competitors who did not engage in such unfair methods and that this constituted substantial injury to competitors. The ruling in the Winsted Hosiery case was cited as a precedent.

Meanwhile, the Court had softened its restrictions considerably by its ruling in *Federal Trade Commission* v. *R. F. Keppel & Bros., Inc.* (1934).[94] Here, the Court upheld a cease and desist order against a candy company which used the lottery device in the sale of penny candies. The Commission contended that this device had resulted in the substantial diversion of patronage from other manufacturers of candy. In a unanimous decision, the Supreme Court ruled that the Commission's jurisdiction was not confined to practices which had previously been passed upon by the Court, and that Congress did not intend to limit the forbidden method to fixed and unyielding categories. The Court further held that it was for the courts to determine what practices of methods of competition are deemed to be unfair, but that the opinion of the Federal Trade Commission carried weight on this issue, and that new or different practices must be considered as they arose in the light of the circumstances in which they were employed.

The Wheeler-Lea amendment strengthened the Commission's position and broadened the scope of its powers by adding unfair or deceptive acts or practices in commerce[95] to the prohibition of unfair methods of competition. By this legislation, Congress accorded its support to the Commission's concern with consumer protection and thus, either by intention or inadvertence, contributed further to the diversion of the Commission's attention from the major problems of monopoly and competition.

INDUSTRY GUIDANCE

Trade Practice Conferences. In its endeavor to secure compliance with the law, raise the plane of competition, and protect the consumer,

[93] 316 U.S. 149.

[94] 291 U.S. 304. See also *Topps Chewing Gum, Inc.* FTC Docket 8463 (1964) re: Baseball Picture Cards.

[95] In *Federal Trade Commission* v. *Bunte Bros.* 312 U.S. 349 (1941), the Supreme Court held that the Commission did not have an express grant of authority over transactions that merely affected interstate commerce. Its authority was limited to practices *in* interstate commerce, and the granting of additional powers over transactions affecting interstate commerce was not necessary to implement the Trade Commission Act.

the Trade Commission has used a number of different devices. The longest established of these is the trade practice conference which has been in operation for more than 40 years.

The trade practice conference began as an informal procedure in 1919, when the Commission was faced with a large number of similar complaints alleging unfair practices in the creamery industry. It was felt that many of these could be eliminated en masse by a conference procedure. This led to the establishment of a Division of Trade Practice Conference in 1926. Business participants in the conferences at the time were desirous of incorporating restrictions such as those which later characterized the National Recovery Administration code. The Commission seems to have been somewhat sympathetic with this point of view, but criticism in 1930 by the Department of Justice caused the Commission to reconsider all of its trade conference rules. As a result, business lost its enthusiasm for the trade practice conference; and the latter was completely eclipsed during the period in which the National Industrial Recovery Act was on the statute books. The end of this legislation, as the result of the Schechter decision, together with the subsequent passage of the Robinson-Patman and Wheeler-Lea Acts, brought about a revival of the trade practice conference.

Trade practice conferences usually originate from a request by members of an industry that such a conference be held, but they may also be initiated by the Commission if it feels that such a conference may be helpful. In either case, participation is purely voluntary. When a conference has been decided upon, the Commission gives public notice of the time and place of the gathering. The Division holds preliminary meetings and discussions with interested parties to work out the problems to be dealt with. A general industry conference is then held at some convenient place; and at that time, problems of the industry are explored, and proposals and suggestions developed for their solution. After a draft of suggested rules has been prepared, public notice is given of a public hearing to be held in connection with these proposals. The Division then recommends final rules to the Commission for its approval. Copies of the rules are supplied to all members of the industry. Each one is afforded the opportunity of signing a contract agreeing to comply with the rules, but this acceptance has no binding force at law.

The rules adopted by the trade practice conference are divided into two classifications.[96] Group I consists of mandatory requirements which proscribe practices that violate any of the laws administered by the Commission. Proceedings, undertaken in the usual manner, are instituted

[96]Temporary National Economic Committee, Monograph No. 34, *Control of Unfair Competitive Practices through Trade Practice Conference Procedure of the Federal Trade Commission* (Washington, D.C.: U.S. Government Printing Office, 1941); also Federal Trade Commission, *Trade Practice Conferences* (Washington, D.C.: U.S. Government Printing Office, 1933).

against anyone who is charged with engaging in these practices, whether he has agreed to the arrangements adopted by the conference or not. The regulations promulgated under Group I add nothing to the prevention of willful violation of the law except, perhaps, as they encourage co-operation in disclosing the offenders to the Commission. If carefully drawn so as to specify, in detail and concrete fashion, practices in specific lines of trade which are illegal, the rules may be of considerable assistance in clarifying the law for those who earnestly wish to conform, thereby simplifying the Commission's task of enforcing the law.

Group II comprises those practices which do not, in the opinion of the Commission, violate the law but which, nevertheless, are not conducive to sound business and healthy competition. The prime purpose of rules in Group II seems to be to eliminate irrational methods and unnecessary wastes in competition, on the one hand, and to develop higher standards of ethics and more economical competition, on the other. In other words, the purpose is to set forth more uniform rules of competitive conduct, which all are expected to observe.

The trade practice conference has been subject both to caustic criticism and to uncritical praise. The idea itself seems to warrant wholehearted support and can be an effective means of disclosing the complexities of competitive industry and of enforcing, by co-operation, the rules necessary to make competition genuinely workable. To date, however, this whole approach has lacked adequate implementation. A mere recitation of the law does not help to clarify it, nor do statements couched in glittering generalities, such as the following: "The practice of selling goods below the seller's cost with the intent, and with the effect, of injuring a competitor, and where the effect may be to substantially lessen competition or tend to create a monopoly or unreasonably restrain trade, is an unfair trade practice; all elements recognized by good accounting practice as proper elements of such cost shall be included in determining costs under this rule."[97] Moreover, so far, little has been done to grapple with the problems of major industries which form the heart of endeavors to make private enterprise and competition work satisfactorily. Little in the nature of a real contribution to this issue can come from holding conferences on paper bags, wax paper, and china recess accessories.[98] Still further, no additional means of law enforcement have been provided by the trade practice conference.

Industry Guidance Program. Prior to 1962 there was no way by which a businessman could obtain a binding opinion from the Commission on whether his proposed course of action would violate the law. On June 1, 1962, the Bureau of Industry Guidance was given two new functions:

[97]Temporary National Economic Committee, Monograph No. 34, *op. cit.*, "Trade Practice Rules for the Rubber Tire Industry," p. 49.

[98]*Ibid.*, p. 7. See Federal Trade Commission, *Annual Report* (1956), pp. 63–64, for a list of the trade practice rules promulgated for 1956.

(1) the administration of the Trade Regulation Rule procedure; (2) the preparation of advisory opinions which are binding upon the Commission when rendered by it. Trade Regulation Rules are intended to advise all members of an industry on what the Commission considers to be lawful. In the event of litigation it is necessary only to present proof that the alleged violator had engaged in the banned practice.[99] The first trade regulation rule promulgated dealt with misrepresenting the size of sleeping bags.[100]

The Commission has also undertaken to issue Industry Guides whose purpose is to clarify legal requirements as applied to a particular problem within an industry or common to many industries. In January, 1964, it issued a revised "Guides against Deceptive Pricing." This was intended to serve as a practical aid to the honest businessman who seeks to conform his conduct to the requirements of fair and legitimate merchandising through truthful advertising. Commissioner MacIntyre stated that he was in accordance with the professed aim of the Guides, but felt that they raised more problems than they resolved. "A considerable number of cases will have to be brought and considered by the courts and the Commission before either our staff or the business community can be expected to operate with any confidence under the new standard." The Commission has always expressed enthusiasm for its industry guidance activities, but just what has been accomplished is a matter of conjecture. Whether the new approach will constitute an improvement remains to be seen, but issues of any real consequence will have to be settled by formal procedures.

INVESTIGATIONS

Section 6 of the Federal Trade Commission Act gave the Commission broad general authority to investigate business activity and to make public such information as it deemed in the public interest. The Commission was to take over the records and activities of the Bureau of Corporations. The purpose of the legislation was to maintain a continuity of information on business activities, in the belief that such a policy would provide for effective publicity of business practices. This would discourage the use of those that would not stand the scrutiny of public opinion and, at the same time, would supply information upon which a more satisfactory public policy could be developed.

In the course of its inquiries, the Commission has had occasion to touch upon almost every phase of industrial life and has published reports under some 150 different titles, comprising several hundred volumes. Investigations by the Commission have been undertaken on its own initiative, in compliance with congressional resolutions, and upon request

[99]Federal Trade Commission, *Annual Report* (1962), p. 38.

[100]Federal Trade Commission, *News Summary* (October 23, 1963). Others have dealt with the size of tablecloths, and misrepresentation of dry-cell batteries as "leak-proof."

of the President, the Attorney General, and other agencies. They have covered the basic economic conditions in a wide range of industries, such as cement, chain stores, coal, electric and gas utilities, meat packing, grain trade, newsprint, and textiles. They have also embraced economic and statistical analyses of such subjects as national wealth and income, taxation and tax-exempt income, social and economic consequences of grain-futures trading, resale price maintenance, comparative incomes of farmers and manufacturers, stock dividends, and basing-point systems. In addition, very extensive investigations were undertaken at the request of various governmental agencies in both World War I and World War II. Many of the studies provided the factual information upon which legislation was subsequently adopted by Congress. Thus, for example, the Webb-Pomerene Act was the result of a report on co-operation in American export trade. The Packers and Stockyards Act was passed in response to inquiry into the meat-packing industry. The public utility inquiry led to the Public Utility Holding Company Act, and the chain store investigation resulted in the Robinson-Patman legislation.[101]

Despite its extensive accomplishments, the investigatory work has fallen far short of the original goal, both as to objectives and results. This may be attributed, in the first place, to the attitude of Congress and the courts. The Bureau of Economics has always operated under severe budget restrictions because of lack of adequate congressional support for general fact-finding activities. Moreover, in 1934, Congress provided that no new investigations were to be initiated by the Commission in compliance with a legislative resolution, unless the latter was the result of a concurrent resolution of the two houses of Congress. This further restricted the Commission's activities, since most general investigations have originated from instructions of one of the houses of Congress or the President. In short, the Commission has not received the necessary congressional support to make it work effectively.

The Commission also suffered curtailment of its investigatory powers at the hands of the courts. The first important rebuff came from the lower courts in *Federal Trade Commission* v. *Claire Furnace Company* (1923).[102] This case arose out of an attempt on the part of the Commission to inaugurate a regular and periodic publication of data on supplies, cost of production, investment, and profit in a number of industries, including the iron and steel industry. The Claire Furnace Company, among others, refused the information and sought an injunction in the courts to restrain the Commission. The lower court granted the injunction; but when the matter was finally carried to the Supreme Court in 1927, the latter reversed the ruling on purely technical grounds.[103] The long delay in handling this case seriously impeded the activities of the Commission.

[101]For a list of these investigations, see Federal Trade Commission, *Annual Report* (1962), pp. 137–61.

[102]285 Fed. Rep. 936 (1923).

[103]*Federal Trade Commission* v. *Claire Furnace Co.*, 274 U.S. 160 (1927).

A more direct blow came in the decision of the Supreme Court in *Federal Trade Commission* v. *American Tobacco Company* (1924).[104] The Commission had undertaken to investigate the tobacco industry in pursuance of a Senate resolution. The Court set aside the Senate resolution, on the ground that it was not based on any alleged violation of the antitrust acts, as required by the Federal Trade Commission Act, and also held that it was contrary to the first principles of justice to allow a search through all the respondent's records, relevant or irrelevant, in the hope that something would turn up. "Anyone who respects the spirit as well as the letter of the Fourth Amendment would be loath to believe that Congress intended to authorize one of its subordinate agencies to sweep all our traditions into the fire, and to direct fishing expeditions into private papers on the possibility that they may disclose evidence of crime."[105] The lower courts gave some relief from these restrictions,[106] but the major change came in *United States* v. *Morton Salt Company* (1950).[107] This was a controversy which arose over the power of the Commission to require corporations to file reports showing how they had complied with a decree enforcing a cease and desist order. The Commission ordered the Morton Salt Company and International Salt Company to file additional and highly particularized reports to show continuing compliance with the decree. The respondents challenged the Commission's jurisdiction to require further reports, on the grounds that since the Commission had made no charge of violation of the decree or the statute, it was engaged in a mere "fishing expedition." The Court took the position that an administrative agency had "a power of inquisition, if one chooses to call it that, which is not derived from the judicial function. It is more analogous to the Grand Jury, which does not depend on a case or controversy for power to get evidence but can investigate merely on suspicion that the law is being violated, or even just because it wants assurance that it is not."[108] Then the Court added: "A governmental investigation into corporate matters may be of such a sweeping nature and so unrelated to the matter properly under inquiry as to exceed the investigatory power. . . . . But it is sufficient if the inquiry is within the authority of the agency, the demand is not too indefinite and the information sought is reasonably relevant."[109] The Court accordingly upheld the Commission's order. Thus, it appears that, while what is "reasonably relevant" is a matter for judicial determination, the Commission is no longer subject to the severe legal restictions that previously

[104]264 U.S. 298 (1924).
[105]*Ibid.*, p. 306.
[106]See *Federal Trade Commission* v. *National Biscuit Co.*, 18 Fed. Supp. 667 (1937) (S.D.N.Y.); and *Federal Trade Commission* v. *Smith*, 34 Fed. (2d) 323 (1929).
[107]338 U.S. 632.
[108]*Ibid.*, p. 642.
[109]*Ibid.*, p. 652.

circumscribed it. "Corporations can claim no equality with individuals in enjoyment of the right to privacy."[110]

Recently, in *St. Regis Paper Co.* v. *United States* (1961),[111] the Court gave the Commission almost unlimited powers to secure valid information. The Commission had ordered St. Regis Paper to submit various reports. St. Regis refused to submit its file copies of certain reports made previously to the Census Bureau on the ground that these were confidential. The Court ruled "[that the Census Act] does not require petitioner to keep a copy of its reports, nor does it grant copies of the report not in the hands of the Census Bureau of an immunity from legal process."[112] Furthermore, through requests for special reports the Commission could require the identical information filed with the Census Bureau. Mr. Justice Black, joined by Justices Whittaker and Stewart, dissented strongly from the ruling that the Census reports were not secret.

The effectiveness of the Commission's investigations has been limited by improper orientation of inquiry. The Commission has placed too much emphasis on furthering competition and limiting monopoly. This is not to say that these are not desirable goals but rather that the studies should be directed to discovering the problems of industry and the reasons for the lack of effective competition. The results could then be used to lay constructive foundations for public policy which would recognize that not all industrial activity can conform to the standards of perfect competition. Crusading investigations based upon the assumption that departures from the competitive norm are solely the result of practices contrary to public interest are not likely to be productive of results conducive to a realistic solution of problems. The conclusions of the findings are too preordained. To be really useful, the investigations should be made primarily for the purpose of discovering information essential to the development of policy in the public interest.

A final difficulty is that too much of the Commission's energies has been spent on general inquiries, which are but incidentally related to its main function. For example, the time-consuming examination of the public utility holding company should have been assigned to the Federal Power Commission, not only because it was the agency familiar with the field but also because that body should ultimately develop public policy on that problem.

DECEPTIVE PRACTICES

Over the years, the Commission has issued cease and desist orders against a large number of methods and practices which it considers unfair; and it now lists thirty-one principal types of these, many of which

[110] *Ibid.*, p. 652.
[111] 368 U.S. 208.
[112] *Ibid.*, p. 218.

have numerous subdivisions.[113] These unfair methods include such practices as various forms of false or misleading advertising, numerous kinds of misrepresentation, harassing tactics, trade espionage, disparagement, bogus independents, boycotts, price conspiracies, lotteries, passing-off, and sharp practices with customers or competitors.

In proceeding against deceptive practices, the Commission, at first, had to prove that honest competitors had suffered. The first important case involving only unfair methods of competition to reach the Supreme Court was that of *Federal Trade Commission* v. *Winsted Hosiery Company* (1922).[114] This company labeled its products as marino, natural wool, and natural worsted, when, in fact, they were composed largely of cotton. The Commission found that a substantial section of the consuming public was deceived by these labels and that, even though the practice was of long standing, competitors of these goods who used honest labels were injured because trade was diverted from them. The Court agreed with this finding, on the ground that honest competitors suffered and the public was misled by the labels.

As a result of this decision, the Commission continued a vigorous campaign against misbranding, but it encountered some difficulties in the courts. It met reversal at the hands of the lower courts on a cease and desist order against the Berkey and Gay Furniture Company (1930),[115] in which case, the Commission had ordered the company to cease labeling, as "mahogany," furniture which had only a veneer of that wood. For some reason, this case was not carried to the Supreme Court, despite a ruling of the latter tribunal in *Indiana Quartered Oak Company* v. *Federal Trade Commission* (1928),[116] which had sustained the Commission's order. In Berkey and Gay, the Commission had objected to the use of the label "Philippine mahogany" to describe furniture made from wood from the Philippines which merely resembled mahogany. The Commission held that such designation was unfair to the importers of genuine mahogany, as well as to the general public, and issued a cease and desist order. Differences of opinion within the Commission caused it to reverse its position later on this matter.[117] It decided that a wood which was not mahogany and which did not have the qualities of mahogany might be called "mahogany" if the sellers merely indicated the geographic origin of the wood so named.

The confused and unsatisfactory legal and administrative status of misbranding was brought to an end by the Supreme Court in *Federal*

[113]Federal Trade Commission, *Annual Report* (Washington, D.C.: U.S. Government Printing Office, 1959), pp. 85–90.

[114]258 U.S. 483.

[115]*Berkey and Gay Furniture Co.* v. *Federal Trade Commission*, 42 Fed. (2d) 427.

[116]26 Fed. (2d) 340 (1928); certiorari denied, 278 U.S. 623 (1928).

[117]*Gillespie Furniture Co.*, 15 FTC 439 (1931).

Trade Commission v. *Algoma Lumber Company* (1934).[118] This decision upheld a cease and desist order issued against western lumber manufacturers. In 1931, the Commission ordered thirty-nine manufacturers to cease advertising their products under such names as "California white pine" and "Western white pine." The Commission found that Western white pine was inferior in quality to genuine white pine and that, as a result of confusion of ultimate buyers, many purchasers were being supplied with an inferior product without their knowledge. Fourteen of the firms involved carried their case to the Circuit Court of Appeals,[119] which rendered a verdict in their favor. The Commission appealed to the Supreme Court for review. Respondents defended their position by arguing that dealers were aware of the difference; but the Court refused to be impressed, because it believed that the ultimate consumers were misled. It held that the consumer was prejudiced if, upon giving an order for one thing, he was supplied with something else. The fact that lower prices were charged for Western white pine was not important, because the practices indulged in created an atmosphere in which misrepresentation and confusion could flourish. The Supreme Court also reprimanded the lower court for disregarding the Commission's findings of fact.

In its endeavor to protect the consuming public against sales promotion policies designed to attract trade by misrepresentations of value or fictitious trade status, the Commission has also received the support of the Supreme Court. The practice of business purporting to be manufacturers selling directly to the public and therefore being able to eliminate the costs of the middleman has been held by the Commission to be deceptive. The Supreme Court sustained a cease and desist order which dealt with the issue in *Federal Trade Commission* v. *Royal Milling Company* (1933).[120] In the opinion, the Court said that consumers or purchasers have the right to purchase the article of a particular manufacturer if they wish, and that this right cannot be satisfied by imposing upon them an exactly similar article or one exactly as good but having a different origin. The Royal Milling Company had never, in fact, been a miller, since it did not grind grain but merely mixed and processed flour.

[118]291 U.S. 67. For an earlier case involving an analogous situation, see *Jas. S. Kirk & Co.*, v. *Federal Trade Commission*, 59 Fed. (2d) 179 (1932); certiorari denied. 287 U.S. 663 (1932). In this case, the company was selling Castile soap which was not made entirely of olive oil. The Commission recognized that the name "Castile" no longer implied that soap came from a certain region in Spain, but it maintained that the name carried an implication of quality. The federal court reversed the Commission's order. This case illustrated the difficulties of setting standards for misbranding, but the Algoma ruling widened the discretion of the Commission. See also *Top Form Mills Inc.*, FTC Docket 8454 (1963); *Windsor Pen Corp.*, FTC Docket 8521 (1964).

[119]64 Fed. (2d) 618 (1933).

[120]288 U.S. 212.

Similarly, the practice of eliciting sales by giving the purchaser the impression that he is in a select class and is getting an article at a special price when, in fact, this is not the case, has been prohibited by the Commission. Its endeavors in this direction finally received court support in *Federal Trade Commission* v. *Standard Education Society* (1937).[121] The Commission found that not only did this company advertise, as contributors and reviewers, many persons who had never been either, but also that it claimed that the price of $69.50 for the publication of the company and its loose-leaf extension service was a reduced price, the regular price being $150 and, sometimes as high as $200. Actually, $69.50 was the regular standard price. The Court took the position that, even though the falsity of a statement might be obvious to those who were trained and experienced, this did not take away its power to deceive others who were less experienced. Nor was any citizen given the duty of suspecting the honesty of those with whom he transacted business.

The Commission has issued a large number of cease and desist orders against the use of lotteries as a means of promoting sales. This practice, which is confined chiefly to the confectionery trade and has been prohibited by statute in many states, is an ethical rather than an economic issue. The suppression of lotteries is therefore primarily a matter of protecting the consuming public. The leading court decision which sustained the Commission was handed down in *Federal Trade Commission* v. *R. F. Keppel & Bros., Inc.* (1934).[122] The Keppel company manufactured chocolate creams for retail distribution at one cent each. A few of the packages contained a penny, and each retailer had a display placard advertising this and explaining that the purchaser of a piece of candy containing the penny had his purchase price returned and thus received the candy free of charge. The Supreme Court agreed that this device exploited consumers, especially children, who were unable to protect themselves, and that it was a means whereby the return received from the expenditure of money depended upon chance. Such practices, the Court remarked, had long been deemed contrary to public policy, both by common law and by criminal statutes, and were regarded by a large share of the industry as unscrupulous.

The record of these cases and the amount of time and energy spent by the Commission on consumer protection indicate that it regards this as one of its most important functions. The gradual, although limited, support which it came to receive from the courts, together with the passage of the Wheeler-Lea Act (1938), which gave the Commission jurisdiction over false and misleading advertising in foods, drugs, devices, or cosmetics, greatly expanded the functions of the Commission in this

[121] 302 U.S. 112. See also *General Motors Corp.* v. *Federal Trade Commission*, 114 Fed. (2d) 33 (1940); certiorari denied, 312 U.S. 682 (1941).

[122] 291 U.S. 304. See also *Dandy Products, Inc.*, FTC Docket 8467 (1963); *Great Western Distributing Co.*, FTC Docket 8525 (1964).

direction. To this must be added the responsibilities under the Wool Products Labeling Act, the Fur Products Labeling Act, and the Flammable Fabrics Act, already mentioned. "From a numerical standpoint, deceptive practices account for the largest percentage of the Commission's work."[123] This is probably to the severe disadvantage of the other functions of the Commission. Unfortunate, too, is the amount of repetition of effort that is involved. The Commission can assess no penalties; and an offender, therefore, can carry on unfair practices until ordered to cease and desist, without fear of punishment, even though he knows that what he is doing violates the law.

Consumer protection against dangerous or deceptive practices is clearly necessary today, when mass advertising and impersonal sales relations are so prevalent. Whether the Commission's accomplishments have been commensurate with its efforts may be an open question. Whatever it may have achieved in its campaigns against cigarette advertising, Carter's Little Liver Pills, and correspondence courses in theology seems to be insignificant compared with the major tasks with which the Commission is saddled. Time-consuming hearings on the misbranding of pillows[124] scarcely seem to fit into the latter category. Similar remarks apply to the controversy over the advertising of the Book-of-the-Month Club that used the word "free" when a designated book was offered to new members. The vigorous dissent of Commissioner Mason[125] indicated that the Commission was severely divided and confused, as it was in the cases before the Wheeler-Lea Act. The Commission cannot escape its responsibilities under the laws it has to administer. It is difficult to see, however, how five commissioners can establish and administer consumer standards in the minute detail that the majority of the dockets indicate and, at the same time, devote the necessary attention and energy to administering the laws and developing policies for a vigorous and aggressive private enterprise system. A clear indication by the Commission that it had decided to devote its energies and limited funds to the really important matters would signalize a most welcome change.[126]

APPRAISAL OF THE FEDERAL TRADE COMMISSION

In the fifty years of its existence to date, the Federal Trade Commission has engaged in a wide variety of activities. Despite this, however, it has not fulfilled the purpose for which it was originally created.

[123]Federal Trade Commission, *Annual Report* (1956), p. 37.

[124]FTC Dockets 6132, 6133, 6134, 6135, 6136, 6137, 6161, 6188, 6189, 6208 (1955) ("Feather Pillows").

[125]FTC Docket 5572 (1952). In 1963 the Commission held a public hearing to obtain the reaction of businessmen and the public regarding the use of the word "free." Federal Trade Commission, *Annual Report* (1963), p. 8.

[126]No great contribution to public regulation is likely to arise from a complaint charging The Quaker Oats Co. with misrepresenting that the briquets it manufactures from corncobs are "charcoal." Federal Trade Commission, *Annual Report* (1961), p. 41.

It has not been very effective as an agency for enforcing competition, and it has afforded scant aid in bringing about a solution to the problem of monopoly. In fact, it has made little or no contribution toward formulating broad policies of industrial control.

On the other hand, it has achieved considerable success in furthering consumer protection; and it has advanced and broadened the common-law concepts of unfair methods of competition. This has been accomplished, however, in a rather unsystematic way; and broad principles of unfair competition have not been enunciated. Failure to do this is the result—in part, at least—of overemphasis on the protection of the consumer. Safeguarding the interests of the consumer is undeniably an important function of regulation; indeed, one of the fundamental tenets of competitive economics is that thoroughgoing competition is the best protection the consumer can receive. Regulatory agencies may, however, focus much of their attention on the consumer without relying on competitive forces and without endeavoring to further them. This is the situation in public utility regulation. In the industrial field, on the other hand, principal emphasis needs to be placed on the maintenance of competition and the preservation of the competitive structure, unless we are prepared to abandon the private enterprise economy. Anything short of thoroughgoing monopolization of various segments of the industrial structure must rely primarily on competition for effective utilization of economic resources because of the complexities of regulation and price control where competition exercises any major influence.

All this is not to say that the Commission has ignored its mandate with regard to competition, for its activities have been characterized by two lines of action: (1) the endeavor to eliminate practices which have threatened to stifle competition or restrain trade and (2) the prohibition of tactics which have had the effect of preying upon and deceiving the consumer. It is the undue emphasis on the second which is the point of criticism. The Commission has developed very largely into an agency for consumer protection; and its activities in this direction have assumed prime importance, both in the volume of work and in the orientation of its policy.

This diversion from the purpose originally contemplated in the legislation may be attributed to a number of reasons. In the first place, the Commission has lacked a clear-cut congressional mandate. At the outset, there was considerable difference of opinion on the functions which a trade commission should perform and divergence of ideas on the authority which it should possess. As a result, the legislation which it was to administer was badly drafted, and there was also an unwillingness to give the Commission the authority essential to a successful and full-fledged administrative agency. Perhaps this was to be expected in the beginning because of the necessity of experimentation and exploration; but the persistent refusal of Congress to clarify the laws or to amend them when court decisions disclosed the deficiencies proved to be a continual source of weakness. When judicial rebuff is followed by congressional silence, this must be attributed either to acquiescence or to inability to formulate definitive policies. Part of the responsibility for this must be placed on the shoulders of the Commission because of its failure to formulate and develop its own conception of an antimonopoly policy; but enactment of legislation which was contrary to the expressed antitrust policy of this country, as well as contrary to the theory upon which the Federal Trade Commission was operating, can scarcely be regarded as conducive to administrative initiative. This was the situation created by the National Industrial Recovery, Miller-Tydings, and McGuire Acts.

The Robinson-Patman and Wheeler-Lea amendments strengthened the Commission's hand somewhat belatedly, but the latter added consumer protection to its function and has therefore tended further to divert the Commission's efforts from emphasis on monopoly and competitive problems. The Wool Products Labeling and similar acts moved in the same direction. In addition, the division of administration of the antitrust legislation created by the Clayton Act has been matched at the other end of the scale by conflict between the Wheeler-Lea amendment and the Pure Food and Drug legislation. Finally, the failure of both the courts and the Antitrust Division to make use of the Commission, as contemplated in the Trade Commission Act, has prevented the Commission from becoming an integrated part of the enforcement machinery.

Another obstacle faced by the Commission has been that of prolonged conflict with the courts. Our courts have exhibited an almost traditional hostility to commissions in the early years of their existence. This has arisen, in part, from the clash of administrative and judicial authority; in part, from the necessity of clarifying the law; and in some measure, from the inexperience and ambitions of the commissions. The Federal Trade Commission has had a particularly trying time because of the difficulty of establishing standards in its field of regulation and because of the failure of Congress to indicate its support of the Commission by remedying the deficiencies at law as they appeared. In recent years, the courts have exhibited a tendency to be more sympathetic with the Commission's rulings, partly because of the legislative broadening of the Commission's powers and partly because of a better understanding on the part of the Commission of the limits to which it may go in administering the law. Fortunately, as the result of the Wheeler-Lea amendment, the burden of proof is now on the respondent when violation of the Federal Trade Commission Act is charged and a cease and desist order has been issued; and furthermore, penalties are imposed for failure to comply with the Commission's orders.

To these difficulties must be added the particular ineptitude of the Commission in interpreting and applying the laws under its jurisdiction. Apart from the Robinson-Patman Act, the Antitrust Division has had much more success with the Clayton Act than has the Federal Trade Commission. This seems to be because the Justice Department has shown considerably greater insight, as well as greater capacity for presentation of its cases before the courts. In enforcing the Robinson-Patman Act, the Commission has exhibited a crusading zeal that has shown more concern for protecting competitors than for protecting competition. As a result, it has come very close to an interpretation of that law which establishes per se violations. Examples of this are seen in the Cement, Morton Salt, Rubber Tire, and Standard Oil (Indiana) cases. Perhaps the statute is to blame for this situation; but the Commission does not appear to have tried to reconcile this legislation with the other antitrust laws, nor does it seem to have endeavored to give it a reasonable interpretation. Recently, the Commission seems to have retreated from its extreme position—partly, perhaps, because of court criticism. Whether this signalizes a real change remains to be seen. Finally, the Commission has not, through carefully worded and reasoned opinions, endeavored to develop its own body of case law, which is essential to the building of a coherent program of public policy.[127]

The Commission has suffered considerably because of its personnel. It has had many able and sincere commissioners, but the severe cross-currents of politics during the chaotic period of its existence have not been conducive to the selection of men who were willing to pursue the prosaic and laborious tasks of developing an administrative agency of first-rate caliber. Furthermore, there has been a lack of that continuity and permanence of tenure essential to the development of high-grade administrators. Finally, the Commission has never had on its staff the experts in the many fields which its legal mandate calls for. Part of the explanation for this surely must lie in a budget which has always been inadequate for competent discharge of the multifarious functions assigned to it. The total appropriation by Congress for the Commission for the fiscal year 1955 was $4,129,000[128] and total employees, 587, although the budget for the fiscal 1963 was increased to $11,456,007 with a staff of 1,178 persons.

Today, the Commission stands at the crossroads. It is clear that there is need for consumer protection, but there is also need for an administrative body to carry out the purposes for which the Federal Trade Commission was originally established—namely, to deal with competitive and monopoly problems. The question is: "Which of these functions is the Federal Trade Commission to perform?" The task of fulfilling both of them is too great for one agency. The time has now arrived to remold the laws and clarify the status and duties of the Commission.

[127]For a scathing criticism of the Commission, see Lowell Mason, *The Language of Dissent* (New York: The Long House, Inc., 1961). Mr. Mason was a former Commissioner.

[128]Federal Trade Commission, *Annual Report* (1955), p. 71.

If its functions are to be primarily those of protecting the consumer, then a new commission needs to be established for the purpose of dealing with the antitrust laws and competition. On the other hand, if the Federal Trade Commission is to be the agency for carrying out the latter functions, then legislation should be passed to strengthen it to that end. The task of affording specific and direct protection to the consumer should be transferred to another agency of government established for that purpose.

Chapter 18 PATENTS AND THE ANTITRUST LAWS

THE PATENT SYSTEM

Nature and Purpose of Patents

A patent is a grant by the government to an inventor which gives to the latter exclusive control of his discovery or invention for a stipulated period of time. During the period covered by the grant, no one else may make the patented item or use it to produce goods or services, except by permission of the owner and under the conditions laid down by him. Nor can anyone imitate the invention during the life of the grant. The basis of the grant is the originality of the idea, and the recipient is entitled to exclude others from using the substance of the idea. This is in contrast to copyrights, which secure the exclusive right to copy but give protection only to the distinctive way in which an idea is expressed. The idea itself is not protected and does not need to be original. Even if it is unique, no proprietary interest in it can be obtained. The type of protection which copyrights afford and the contrast of this with patent privileges deserve consideration when proposals for patent reform are being evaluated.

Patents are the creation of statute law, and the patent arrangements of this country are conditioned by the statutes and their administration at any particular time. The fact that patents are a creation of Congress has given rise to the question whether the owner of a patent has a property right therein or whether, on the other hand, it only constitutes a privilege granted by the government. Both points of view have been expressed by justices of the Supreme Court. While the latter treats the patent as an item of property, it nevertheless emphasizes the fact that the rewards to the patentee are secondary to considerations of public welfare. If a patent were regarded as property in the usual sense, the owner would possess greater rights respecting his ability to disregard public welfare than is now the case. In any event, patents can be abolished by congressional action, and Congress may establish such conditions for patent grants as it deems in the interests of public welfare.

The purpose of the patent grant is to stimulate invention and encourage progress in the development of the useful arts, by giving the owner protection whereby he may reap such gains as may accrue to him from his discovery. Stimulation to the application of research and invention for the production of goods to be sold in the market place necessitates a prospect of reward for those who spend time, effort, and money on such activities. If there were no patents, anyone would be free to copy all new developments, without having to entail the risk or expense of pioneering. This would not stop industrial progress, because competition would constantly exert pressure to outdo one's rival, but it might possibly act as a serious impediment to extensive private research. In any case, it would serve to deprive the inventor of the rewards of his discovery or, at least, seriously curtail them, at the same time giving others the opportunity to reap returns on developments to which they made nothing by way of original contribution.

Patents and Private Enterprise

The necessity for patents in a private enterprise economy arises from the inability of an inventor or owner, in the absence of a patent, to prevent others from using the invention. If such appropriation were to be permitted, those who did this could reap the benefits of the efforts, ingenuity, and investment of the inventor, without making any corresponding contribution to the development, and without in any way reimbursing the inventor, who might thus be deprived of an adequate market in which to recoup his outlays. Without protection against immediate appropriation of his creation, the innovator could not secure a return for the unique thing he has created except, perhaps, as he might have a head start on competitors for a short period, or in his productive superiority by the use of that which would be, in effect, common property. Modern technology and research is, on the whole, very expensive; and a great deal of time and money must be spent on it if continued advance is to be maintained. This investment in the furtherance of technology needs protection against appropriation by others as much as does the protection of investment in manufacturing plant and equipment or in land.

Patents are a device of a private enterprise economy. There is no place for them in a socialist system. The latter recognizes no differentiable rights in the means of production or in the ideas connected therewith. In a private enterprise economy, on the other hand, private property in the means of production is one of the cornerstones of the competitive system. The question is frequently asked, however, whether patents are a necessary or useful part of the capitalist order.[1] The answer to this has already been indicated and clearly seems to be in the affirmative as long as private property is used as a means of furthering the competitive

[1]For an extensive discussion of economic thinking on patents, see Fritz Machlup, *An Economic Review of the Patent System*, Study of the Subcommittee on Patents, Trademarks, and Copyrights, Committee on the Judiciary, United States Senate, 85th Cong., 2d sess. S.Res. 236 (Washington, D.C.: United States Government Printing Office, 1958), especially Part IV.

organization of production. If it does not do this, then the rationale of a private enterprise system fails in any case.

A good deal of emphasis is frequently placed on the monopoly aspects of patent grants. It is true that the owner of a patent is protected in his ownership of a unique product for which there is—in theory, at least—no precise substitute. Because this unique product cannot be used or reproduced without the consent of the owner, the latter enjoys a monopoly position and can charge monopoly prices, if it is commercially valuable. As a consequence, it is often held that the granting of patents, copyrights, and trade-marks is in conflict with the policies embodied in our antitrust laws. This point of view, however, does not seem to place patents quite in their proper perspective. The antitrust laws necessarily assume private property. Furthermore, these laws do not forbid monopoly, as that term is used in economics; they only forbid monopolizing and that amount of monopoly which is considered to be unreasonable in the light of circumstances. Monopoly, in the economic sense, is a common characteristic of uniqueness in a private enterprise system; and the concept of private property recognizes that fact. It is not in the special privileges of the grants, per se, that the conflict arises but rather in the particular laws which may make it possible to acquire monopoly positions beyond those contemplated by the grant of privilege. In other words, patent rights may be used knowingly or otherwise to bring about violation of the antitrust laws, just as may other practices that have already been discussed.

Patent Laws and the Patent System

It is necessary, in dealing with patent problems under antitrust, to distinguish between patent laws and the patent system. The patent system is part of the institutional arrangement of private property and, as has already been noted, is an integral part of a capitalistic economy. The system may manifest itself in different ways in different countries, but its common characteristic is a grant of exclusive privilege over a new invention. What the grant of exclusive privilege covers and the terms upon which it is made depend on the patent laws. The latter constitute the legal framework within which the patent system operates. The laws differ in their content from one country to another.

Although the patent system remains a permanent feature of private enterprise, the laws may undergo more or less continuous change by legislative action and by court interpretation. In this respect, the role of the courts has played a greater part over the last one hundred years in the United States than elsewhere. This—in part, at least—is because of the antitrust laws in this country and the way in which they are administered.

Patent Problems in the United States

The phenomenal role played by rapidly changing technology in modern industrial life has presented a profound challenge to the concept of patents and patentable rights. The original idea of patentability was based on the assumption that inventions were rare and clearly distinguishable from each other. The mechanization of industry has changed that. Invention in industry has become the order of the day. Thus, 91,091 patents were applied for in 1963 and 48,970 were issued by the United States Patent Office.[2] A large percentage of these were trivial and in the category of useless, but many were basic and of such importance that the owners enjoy strategic control in basic devices and processes. Furthermore, the patenting of improvements and adaptations frequently develops into a race to guard against would-be competitors to such an extent that much time and effort is devoted to warding off competition, rather than meeting it directly. Product differentiation, achieved in many lines of merchandising by trade names and brands, is furthered in the field of industry, on occasion, by patent rights acquired more for the purpose of limiting competition than for increasing or improving production.

The fact that patents are an integral part of a system of private enterprise does not mean that property rights in patents, as they exist today, are not open to serious challenge. On the contrary, both the patent laws and their administration, in many instances, present such contradictions with the competitive economy, which they are supposed to further, that a thoroughgoing and fundamental revision of the whole system seems to be in order.

Patents may present very subtle conflicts between private rights and public interest because of the abuses that may result from the endeavors of owners of patents to use the indirect powers of the patent grant to amplify the monopoly position which the grant bestows. The result is that patent problems have become one of the focal points of the present-day issue of monopoly. Patents are one of the instruments by which giant combinations have been able to achieve or fortify their monopoly powers. The relative importance of patents, as compared with other devices, in assisting in the growth of industrial empires is difficult to appraise because, as has previously been pointed out, the combination movement is a complex one. It is evident, however, that the potentialities of the patent laws have frequently been exploited to the full extent of legal and business ingenuity, and have been significant factors in the achievement of industrial concentration in many lines.

Perhaps of even greater significance has been the opportunity that patents have afforded industrial monopoly to reap the benefits of financial power. The complexities of the patent laws, inadequacy of administration, corporate utilization of vast resources to acquire literally every conceivable patent necessary to exclude competition, threatened lawsuits, and protracted litigation have all served too frequently to per-

[2]U.S. Department of Commerce, *Statistical Abstract of the United States* (Washington, D.C.: U.S. Government Printing Office, 1964). Applicants from foreign countries received 5,501 patents.

vert the basic objective of the patent laws. These shortcomings have served to enhance or create the very kind of monopoly the antitrust laws were designed to inhibit or destroy. Furthermore, the rights which the law has come to bestow upon patentees are, to a considerable extent, in direct opposition to the fundamental tenets of private enterprise and public policy as expressed in the antitrust legislation. The challenge of the patent problem today, therefore, is to bring the private rights of patentees into conformity with the requirements of a workable system of private enterprise. As long as the latter is considered a desirable social arrangement, private property rights must be adapted to that end. Patents are no exception to this rule.

DEVELOPMENT OF THE PATENT LAWS

Origin of the Patent System

The origin of the American patent system is to be found in developments that took place in England prior to the American Revolution. The practice of granting and selling many valuable privileges had been exercised by the Crown ever since the Norman Conquest. After 1485, under the Tudor monarchs, exclusive rights in trading were granted on an ever-increasing scale. The Crown bestowed these monopolies by issuing what were known as "letters patent." This device was extended by Elizabeth I to inventions and new industries, and marked the introduction of the patent system, as a system, into England.[3]

The right of the Crown to grant monopoly privileges became one of the focal points of the struggle between Crown and Parliament under Elizabeth I. The House of Commons protested that the monopolies had become a grievous burden. Finally, in 1601, the Queen promised that existing patents would be repealed and no more issued. Her successor, James I, however, disregarded the promise and made extensive use of monopolies for the purpose of obtaining revenue. Finally, in 1624, the Statute of Monopolies[4] was passed. This legislation declared that all grants of monopoly in the future were to be illegal and that they had been so in the past. An exception to this sweeping prohibition permitted the granting of letters patent which gave the exclusive right to use, for a term of fourteen years, "any new manufacture to the first and true inventor thereof." The theory behind this exception was that public benefit would result from these monopoly grants because of the stimulus they were expected to give to the development of manufacturing. The present patent laws of England and the United States are the result of the special exception to the general prohibition against monopoly contained in the statute of 1624.

[3] W. S. Holdsworth, *A History of English Law* (Boston: Little, Brown & Co., 1924), Vol. IV, p. 345.

[4] 21 James I, chap. 3 (1624); see also Holdsworth, *op. cit.*, pp. 352–56.

Patents were issued in the American colonies on grounds similar to those for which the grants were made in England. They were used to encourage the development of new inventions and the introduction of new industries. They rested upon special acts of the legislatures and, like the patents in England, did not conform to any clearly defined standards and were not for strictly prescribed purposes. There were, however, definite limits to the privileges granted. Thus, in 1641, the General Court of Massachusetts decreed that there "should be no monopolies but of such inventions as are profitable to the country and that for a short time only." The first patent on this continent was issued by the Massachusetts General Court, in 1641, to Samuel Winslow, for a novel method of making salt. The first patent on machinery was granted by the same body to Joseph Jenks, in 1646, for a mill for making scythes. Each colony, of course, issued patents independently of the others.

The Articles of Confederation of 1781 continued the arrangements whereby the issuance of patents was left with the separate states, but this procedure led to confusion and uncertainty. The advantages of uniformity led to the adoption of the provision in the Constitution of the United States which gave Congress the power "to promote the progress of science and useful arts, by securing for limited times to authors and inventors the exclusive right to their respective writings and discoveries."[5]

Patent Laws in the United States

On the basis of this provision, Congress enacted the first patent law of the United States in 1790.[6] This act made it possible for anyone to obtain a patent if he could meet the conditions set forth in the legislation. This was a unique development that marked a complete departure from previous arrangements. It was this feature of general applicability of the patent law that inaugurated the modern system of granting patents. The basic test which the applicant had to meet was that he had invented or discovered a useful art, manufacture, engine, machine, or device, or any improvement therein, which had not been used or known before.

Authority for granting patents was placed in the hands of a committee composed of the Secretary of State, the Secretary of War, and the Attorney General. This was an unsatisfactory method of administration; and it was changed by the statute of 1793, which provided for the issuance of patents by registration only. The validity of the patents so obtained was to be decided by the courts, which, it was assumed, would develop the necessary standards by judicial precedent. The statute also omitted any reference to usefulness or importance as a condition of issuance.

[5]Art. I, Sec. 8, cl. 8.

[6]For a historical summary of the patent laws, see U.S. Department of Commerce, Patent Office, *The Story of the American Patent System,* 1790–1940 (Washington, D.C.: U.S. Government Printing Office, 1940).

The last fundamental change in the American patent laws was made in the act of 1836. Numerous amendments have been added since then, most especially to widen the scope of patentable items; and the meaning of the law has grown under the constant scrutiny of the judiciary. But the legislation of 1836 established the basic legal and administrative framework of the present patent system in this country.

Conditions of the Patent Grant

The patent laws of the United States give an inventor the exclusive right to his invention for a period of seventeen years. At the end of that time, the subject matter of the invention becomes public property and may be used by anyone. To obtain a patent, the applicant must show that there has been an invention, that the invention is useful, that it is not vicious or against public policy, and that it is new or has not been in use heretofore. The applicant must also demonstrate that his invention will actually work. Patentable items include mechanical devices, chemical processes, ornamental designs, and botanical plants.

The application for a patent is made to the Commissioner of Patents. It consists of six parts: (1) the petition that the patent be granted; (2) the power of attorney, which provides for the legal appointment of a person to represent the applicant before the Patent Office; (3) the specifications; (4) the claims upon which the request for the patent rest; (5) the official drawings; (6) the oath, which states the applicant's belief that he is the original first inventor of the thing for which he solicits a patent. The purpose of the specifications and drawings is, first of all, to provide adequate information by which the Patent Office can reach a decision as to issuance. The second purpose is to make certain the disclosure of full information on the invention, so that the public may be able to use it after the period of the grant has expired.

Patents may be granted only to individuals; but the law allows the recipient of the grant to rent, license, sell, or assign it. Extensive research by corporations in modern times has led to the practice whereby employees, by contract, assign to the employer all inventions made and patent rights obtained during their employment. This is a development that was not contemplated in the original patent law, and it has created problems of control and concentration of patents that necessitate consideration for fundamental revision of the laws. Although the data available do not offer any conclusive evidence of concentration, the ability of large corporations to control technically superior processes by the astute use of patents serves as a means of enhancing their strategic position in industry.

Once a patent has been issued, it cannot be canceled, except upon showing of fraud. However, the government does not underwrite the patents which it grants; competing claims are settled at law. This is usually accomplished by private action, and many persons may be drawn into a case. For example, a patent may be licensed to others by a defendant; and the licensees may also be charged with infringement, even though they are unaware that this may have taken place.

Because patents are grants of privilege by governments, they are limited to the territory over which the granting government has jurisdiction. An American who wishes to protect his invention in another country must secure a patent in that country. Foreigners must do likewise in the United States. If Americans wish to license others to use their patents in foreign countries, they must first secure those patents in those countries. The same remarks apply to foreigners who wish to license Americans to use their patents in this country.

Protection of the Patent

Patent pendency is one of the important issues in the present administration of the patent laws. After a patent has been applied for, and during the time which elapses before the grant is made, absolute secrecy cloaks the invention. The patent itself does not begin to run until it has been issued. As a consequence, the right, in effect, may be enjoyed for much longer than 17 years. The Fritts patent in motion pictures, for example, afforded protection to the inventor for a total period of 53 years.[7] The large number of applications imposes a heavy task on the Patent Office. The number of patents pending in 1938, for example, was 116,041.[8] This accumulation of applications and the long pendency of many are, in part, the result of an overburdened Patent Office and, in part, the outgrowth of rules that make for delay. A further factor is the advantage that may be obtained from deliberate procrastination and resort to every possible technical means for lengthening the period of application.

Another problem centers around the multiplicity of patents which are issued. The patent laws, presumably, were designed to protect distinctive inventions. The latter, however, have been multiplied to the point that, for example, a single stainless steel wristband for a watch is covered by four patents. The distinctiveness of invention is lost in such a maze. Furthermore, the social merits of such patents may be seriously questioned. They serve largely to increase the costs of patent applications and certainly afford little public benefit. Patents on ornamental designs only add to the confusion. Design protection may be desirable, but patenting does not seem to be the appropriate means.

The legal technicalities involved in securing and maintaining patent rights frequently give rise to protracted and costly lawsuits. If two or

[7] L .S. Lyon, M. W. Watkins, and Victor Abramson, *Government and Economic Life* (Washington, D.C.: Brookings Institution, 1939), Vol. I, p. 133.

[8] *Ibid.*, p. 132. In 1963 the total was 209,131. Commissioner of Patents, *Annual Report*, Fiscal Year 1963 (Washington, D.C.: U.S. Government Printing Office, 1963) p. 11.

more applications are pending to the Patent Office at the same time, interference proceedings may be instituted. These may have to run the gauntlet of an examiner, the examiner-in-chief, the Commissioner of Patents, and the Court of Customs and Patents Appeals or the Circuit Court of Appeals for the District of Columbia. Finally, appeal may be had to the Supreme Court of the United States.

Suits for infringement of patent rights may also result in lengthy and costly litigation. This is aggravated by the present chaotic legal situation resulting from lack of unified jurisdiction. The district courts have original jurisdiction in infringement suits. Appeal from these courts is to the Circuit Court of Appeals for the district. The circuit courts are not bound by each other's decisions, except in a suit between the same parties. As a result, a litigated patent is not secure until it has been sustained by the Court of Appeals in every circuit, or by the Supreme Court of the United States. When the Circuit Courts of Appeals differ as to the validity of a particular patent, or when a novel or important point of law is involved, the Supreme Court may grant certiorari. The possibilities of intimidating or ruining would-be competitors by interference proceedings or infringement suits are all too obvious.[9]

PATENTS AND THE ANTITRUST LAWS

The owner of a patent is given exclusive control of his invention by statute. At the same time, the antitrust laws are designed to prohibit monopolies and contracts or agreements in restraint of trade in interstate commerce. Since the patent laws do not specifically exclude patents from the antitrust legislation, and, conversely, since the antitrust legislation does not mention patents as outside of its scope, patent holders have been held subject to the antitrust laws if they endeavor to extend their monopoly beyond that which is contained in the grant. The amount of control allowed under the patent monopoly that is consistent with the antitrust laws is left for judicial determination.

The courts, in dealing with issues that have arisen, have had to pass judgment upon a wide variety of practices. At the outset, the issues seemed to be rather simple; but with the growth in the use of patents for the purpose of limiting competition, and the development of new means to evade the antitrust laws, the legal problem has become exceedingly technical and complex. In one of its earliest decisions dealing with the conflict between the antitrust laws and patent monopolies, the Supreme Court declared that the object of the patent laws of the United States was monopoly and that the rule, with very few exceptions, was that any conditions that were not by their very nature illegal would be upheld by the Court. The fact that the conditions in the contract

[9]See for example, *Hartford-Empire Co.* v. *United States*, 323 U.S. 386 (1945).

between patentee and licensee maintained monopoly did not render them illegal.[10]

Gradually, however, the Court came to hold that owners of patents could not use the right obtained for the purpose of making agreements or forming combinations, on the basis of the patent right, which would have been illegal had no patent been involved. In other words, the exclusive right to enjoy the benefits of invention conflicts with the antitrust laws when the patentee attempts to use his legal monopoly to evade the antitrust laws and thus act contrary to public policy. If the Court feels that the patent privileges are being used to evade the will of Congress, it will impose limitations on the use of those privileges. Just how far the patentee may extend his monopoly before it comes into conflict with public policy and the antitrust laws is still, however, very much an unsettled question.

Patent Pools and Cross-Licensing

A patent pool is an arrangement whereby the owners of patents co-operate in the use of them by employing various practices. They may transfer title to the patents to a single owner, who then licenses the use of them to each of the parties to the agreement; or the co-operating owners may cross-license each other, or even use some other method of reciprocity by which the participants are enabled to use each other's patents under specified conditions. Although pooling agreements, in general, are illegal under the Sherman Act, where patents are involved, they may be completely within the law. In fact, this may be the only way in which a particular product can be produced if two or more firms own separate patents, all of which are necessary to the completion of the product. Thus, patent pools may be used as a means of facilitating the use of patents by the manufacturers who are members of the pool, but they may also be employed as a means of bringing about combinations in restraint of trade. The line between the legitimate and illegitimate use of these pools is not easy to draw. In general, however, over the years, the Supreme Court has come to scrutinize more carefully the purpose for which the pool is formed, and to declare it in violation of the antitrust laws if the objective seems to be that of effecting a combination in restraint of trade.

Early in the administration of the Sherman Act, the Supreme Court recognized the conflict between the patent and antitrust laws where the monopoly arises from the combination and not from the exercise of rights conferred by the letters patent. This was the basis of the decision in *Standard Sanitary Manufacturing Company* v. *United States* (1912),[11]

[10]*Bement* v. *National Harrow Co.*, 186 U.S. 70 (1902).
[11]226 U.S. 20.

frequently referred to as the "bathtub" case. The Standard Sanitary Manufacturing Company controlled about one half of the production of enameled ware in the United States in 1912. This company owned the Arrott patent, which was a process for the application of enamel to ironware. Other manufacturers were using inferior processes and had patents which were regarded as infringing upon the Arrott patent. To deal with this situation, an association was formed in which all patents were assigned to the secretary, who issued licenses to the manufacturers and jobbers of enameled ware; 83 per cent of the manufacturers and about 90 per cent of the jobbers were brought into the network of license agreements. A committee of manufacturers, chosen by the association, determined the selling prices of both manufacturers and jobbers; territorial pools, royalty rebates, and penalties to prevent violation of the license contract were provided for. The secretary of the association licensed the various manufacturers to use the patent, if they agreed to adhere to selling prices fixed by the association. In addition, the jobbers were brought into the association by resale price agreements.

The government charged the Standard company with violation of the Sherman Act. The company pleaded that the combination was immune from the law, because it was based upon patents. The secretary claimed he had not devised the plans to suppress competition but to eliminate second-rate enamel ware.

The Supreme Court held that the arrangement was a subterfuge for direct price fixing. It ruled that the agreements transcended what was necessary to protect the use of the patent and accomplished a restraint of trade condemned by the Sherman law. The rights conferred by patents, said the Court, were very definite and extensive; but they did not give a universal license against positive prohibition such as contained in the Sherman law. The Court therefore held that the agreement violated the Sherman Act. This case made it clear, as a Circuit Court said in a later case, that "if the end is monopoly, and the means the restraint of trade, the inquiry is directed to the character of the restraint. If that is undue and unreasonable and was directly intended and the monopolistic result came as a direct and not a merely incidental consequence, the combination through which it is brought about is illegal."[12]

The complications that can arise in the application of this doctrine, however, were illustrated in *Standard Oil Company* (*Indiana*) v. *United States* (1931).[13] The Standard Oil Company of Indiana, the Texas Company, the Standard Oil Company of New Jersey, and the Gasoline Products Company had entered into an agreement for the pooling and cross-licensing of patents for the manufacture of cracked gasoline. The

[12] *United States* v. *Motion Picture Patents Co.*, 225 Fed. Rep. 800, 811 (1915); appeal dismissed, 247 U.S. 524 (1918). See also *Ethyl Gasoline Corp.* v. *United States*, 309 U.S. 436 (1940); *Hartford-Empire Co.* v. *United States*, 323 U.S. 386 (1945).

[13] 283 U.S. 163.

government contended that the purpose was to effect a monopoly and therefore violated the Sherman Act. The Supreme Court stated that any agreement whatsoever between competitors may be illegal if it is a part of a larger plan to control interstate markets. It held also that an agreement for cross-licensing and division of royalties violated the Sherman Act only when it was used to effect a monopoly or to fix prices, or otherwise to impose an unreasonable restraint on interstate commerce. In the opinion of the Court, no such monopoly or restriction of competition had been proved. It found that, in 1924 and 1925, after cross-licensing arrangements went into effect, the 4 primary defendants owned or licensed, in the aggregate, only 55 per cent of the total cracking capacity and that the remainder was distributed among 21 independently owned cracking processes. The Court held that this was evidence that there was no concentration of control in the production of cracked gasoline. Furthermore, the output of cracked gasoline was only about 26 per cent of the total gasolines produced. Because ordinary or straight-run gasoline was indistinguishable from cracked gasoline and the two were either mixed or sold interchangeably, the Court concluded that the defendants could not effectively control the supply or fix the price of cracked gasoline by virtue of their patent control over the cracking processes. The Court also held that the evidence showed active competition among the defendants themselves, and with others. As a result, these agreements providing for patent pooling and the division of royalties did not violate the Sherman law. "An agreement for cross-licensing and division of royalties violates the [Sherman] Act only when used to effect a monopoly, or to fix prices, or to impose otherwise an unreasonable restraint upon interstate commerce."[14]

This appears to be the tenor of the decision of the Supreme Court in *United States* v. *National Lead Co.* (1947),[15] although there is also the additional implication that cross-licensing may violate the Sherman Act if two competing producers control the market between them.[16] This case involved international cartel arrangements, but one aspect of it related to patent pooling in the domestic market. The lower court found that, apart from the international aspects of the agreements that were in question, National Lead and Du Pont controlled 100 per cent of the commerce in titanium products in the United States. They agreed to exchange all future patents, patent applications, and know-how. Although these exchanges were not on an exclusive basis, the Court stated that it was clear that the capacity to dominate the market and exclude outsiders was vastly increased by the combination. Another inevitable consequence was that of the proliferation of patents which, under the

[14]*Ibid.*, p. 175.
[15]332 U.S. 319.
[16]Commerce Clearing House, *Anti-Trust Law Symposium* (New York, 1952), p. 163.

arrangements, were forged into instruments of domination of an entire industry. The Supreme Court agreed entirely with the lower court, and quoted its statements on these matters extensively and apparently with approval.

Because this was a suit in equity, the issue before the Court was the appropriate remedy to prevent future violations of the law. Despite the fact that the defendants were found guilty, the Court refused to order royalty-free licensing or to issue a permanent injunction prohibiting the patentees and licensees from enforcing the patents. Instead, it held that licenses should be issued on the basis of reasonable royalties.[17] Mr. Justice Douglas dissented on this point. As the law now stands, whenever it can be proved that patent pools and cross-licensing are used for the purpose of evading the antitrust law, they are illegal devices. The owner of a patent "may grant licenses to make, use, or vend, restricted in point of space or time, or with any other restriction upon the exercise of the granted privilege, save only that by attaching a condition to his license he may not enlarge his monopoly and thus acquire some other which the statute and the patent together did not give."[18] That the issues involved, however, are far from settled is quite clear when one examines the question of price-fixing privileges when cross-licensing is used. Patent pools and cross-licensing under the existing interpretation of the law still seem to offer considerable scope, beyond that contemplated in the single patent grant, for exerting control over the market.

Combinations

What is sometimes called a "patent trust" is a consolidation of companies owning patents over processes that have to be combined to make a finished product. The combination may be such that it would be contrary to the Sherman law were it not for the fact that it brings under single ownership the patented processes which are complementary and not competing. It is the patents which are involved that make the combination legal. This is illustrated by the United Shoe Machinery Company, whose long history of litigation brings out one of the basic conflicts of the Sherman Act and the patent laws.[19] The principal machines connected with the manufacture of shoes are the lasting machines, welt-sewing machines, outsole stitching machines, heeling machines, and the metallic fastening machines. By 1899, each of these machines was in the hands of a separate manufacturer. In that year, the United Shoe Machinery Company was incorporated, and it acquired the various concerns which owned the machines and the patents upon which they

[17]*Hartford-Empire Co.* v. *United States*, 323 U.S. 386 (1954) and 324 U.S. 570 (1945).

[18]*Ethyl Gasoline Corp.* v. *United States*, 309 U.S. 436, 456 (1940).

[19]For an early history of this trust, see Eliot Jones, *The Trust Problem in the United States* (New York: Macmillan Co., 1921), chap. viii.

were based. As a result of the original combination and some subsequent acquisitions, the United Shoe Machinery Company came to be the only American concern possessing a full line of the so-called "bottoming room machines."

The first case against the United Shoe Machinery Company was a criminal proceeding under the Sherman Act in *United States* v. *Winslow*.[20] United Shoe Machinery Company was charged with forming a combination in restraint of trade and with forming a conspiracy. The Supreme Court opinion, written by Mr. Justice Holmes, held that the business of the several companies that had been combined, as it existed prior to the combination, was assumed to be legal. The machines were patented, making them a monopoly in any event; and the success of the various companies was because they had the best patents. Since the companies did not compete with each other, the Court could not see why the collective business was any worse than its component parts. Moreover, the Court could see no greater objection to one corporation manufacturing 70 per cent of three noncompeting groups of patented machines, collectively used for making a single product, than to the three corporations making the same proportion of one group each.

Contemporaneously with the criminal proceedings, the government instituted a suit in equity. This was heard by the Supreme Court in *United States* v. *United Shoe Machinery Company*.[21] The government charged that the combination was in violation of the Sherman law and also that the tying agreement under which the lessees of the machinery were forbidden from using machines of any other company, either for the process for which United machines had been leased or in connection with any of the other processes or stages incident to the manufacture of shoes, also was contrary to that act. On the first count, the Supreme Court held that the companies that united to form the United Shoe Machinery Company were complementary and not competitive. It was recognized that the constituent companies were patent monopolies, but these patent monopolies did not compete with each other. The Court held that the leases and tying clauses were a legitimate exercise of a patentee's right.

Passage of the Clayton Act in 1914, with its prohibition against tying contracts, resulted in further litigation. On this occasion, the Court decided that the tying agreements violated the Clayton law. This decision, however, did not have any vital effect on the dominant position held by United in the manufacture of shoe machinery;[22] and the company continued to occupy the dominant position in the shoe machinery market in the United States, supplying over 75 per cent, and probably 85 per cent, as late as 1953.

Under the revitalized attack on antitrust following World War II,

[20] 227 U.S. 202 (1913).
[21] 247 U.S. 32 (1918).
[22] 258 U.S. 451 (1922).

the government again instituted suit against United Shoe.[23] This time, the government was successful in its prosecution. Judge Wyzanski recognized what Mr. Justice Holmes earlier had failed to grasp—namely, that the combination of a number of complementary patents under single ownership does give a degree of market control which separate ownership of them cannot achieve, and second, that concentrated management of those patents may be utilized to further and maintain the monopoly beyond the scope comprehended by the individual patent grants. The Court found that United had followed the practice of never selling, but only leasing, its machines and that the leases in the context of the existing shoe machinery market had created barriers to entry by competitors. The Court also concluded that United intended to engage in the leasing and pricing policies which maintained its market power. Therefore, in light of the Alcoa decision, it had violated the law. It would thus appear that if a firm has achieved a monopoly position by acquisition of patents, it violates the Sherman Act, even though, apart from this, it has not engaged in any illegal practices. This is a far cry from the earlier decisions.

A somewhat different situation arose in *Hartford-Empire Company* v. *United States* (1945),[24] because in this case, there was no doubt about the illegal practices of the defendant in acquisition of monopoly. Here, the Supreme Court found one of the most widespread combinations in American industry guilty of violating the Sherman Act and Section 3 of the Clayton law. The original complaint named as defendants 12 corporations and 101 individuals associated with them as observants or directors. However, the charge against 3 of the corporations and 40 individuals was dismissed. In an extensive review of the complicated facts involved in achieving a monopoly in the glassmaking industry, the Court found the defendants guilty of conspiring and combining to monopolize and restrain trade by acquisition of patents, exclusion of competitors, exclusive-dealer arrangements and tying contracts, cross-licensing, collusion, and pools. They also used a trade association to assign quotas and exchange statistical data. As a result, thoroughgoing control of the glassmaking industry had been obtained. There was no doubt as to the guilt of the combination; and the Court restated its position in the Standard Sanitary case, in which it said that rights conferred by patents were very definite and extensive, but they did not give, any more than any other rights, a universal license against positive prohibition.

There was never any doubt about the guilt of Hartford-Empire under the Sherman and Clayton Acts; but because this was a suit in equity, the question before the Supreme Court was that of remedy, not punishment. The government had requested dissolution of Hartford,

[23] *United States* v. *United Shoe Machinery Corp.*, 110 Fed. Supp. 295 (1953). See Chapter 14 for a discussion of the details of this case.

[24] 323 U.S. 386; clarified in 324 U.S. 570 (1945).

the keystone of the combination. The Court decided, however, that adequate remedy could be obtained that would preclude the resumption of unlawful practices without dissolution. The decree set forth elaborate conditions for the future use of patents and also prohibited intercorporate stock ownership among the guilty companies. The Court, however, refused to require royalty-free licenses, holding that a patent is property protected against appropriation both by individuals and by government. "A patent owner is not in the position of a quasi-trustee for the public or under any obligation to see that the public acquires the free right to use the invention. He is under no obligation to use it or to grant its use to others."[25] Mr. Justice Rutledge wrote a strong dissent, on the ground that the remedies were totally inadequate and did not meet the needs of the situation.

This case presents, once again, the age-old problem of dissolution of a combine whose tentacles spread to every corner of the industry under the use of every conceivable device. Admittedly, the problem is one of remedy, not of punishment; but the line is not easy to draw. In the Alcoa and United Shoe cases, the courts were unable to see how dissolution would restore effective competition. In this case, that question was not raised. It seems clear, however, that adequate dissolution can be affected only by a competent administrative tribunal which is able to give careful consideration to the pattern of industry and the requisites of effective competition. Furthermore, there is strong argument in favor of dissolution if it can restore effective competition, even though less drastic remedies might be effective, in those cases where giant combines have come to dominate an industry. As to patents, it would seem that the patent laws should be changed to deprive owners of patent protection when they have used the rights deliberately to violate the antitrust laws. Present remedies scarcely fit the violations that have occurred.

Acquisition of patents of foreign firms for the purpose of excluding importation into the United States of rival products was the subject of litigation in *United States* v. *Singer Manufacturing Co.* (1964).[26] The Singer company was charged with violating Sections 1 and 2 of the Sherman Act on the ground that it conspired with two of its competitors, Vigorelli, an Italian corporation, and Gegauf, a Swiss corporation, on the matter of importation, sale, and distribution of zigzag sewing machines in order to exclude Japanese manufacturers from the market in the United States. The appeal to the Supreme Court was only under Section 1 of the Sherman Act. Each of the three companies had acquired patents on multiple-cam mechanisms for household sewing machines. Uncertainty over the status of the patents of these companies in the various countries of the world posed the threat of infringement suits,

[25] *Ibid.*, p. 432.
[26] 374 U.S. 174.

and Singer was in danger of losing its patent rights in the United States. Singer, therefore, entered into negotiations with both Vigorelli and Gegauf, without, however, disclosing all the facts to Gegauf. Gegauf was particularly concerned over the inroads that Japanese machines were making in the United States market. Singer was also concerned with the Japanese competition. It therefore undertook a series of arrangements with Vigorelli and Gegauf for the purpose of ridding all three of infringements by the Japanese machines. This was to be accomplished by the assignment to Singer of the patent rights of all three in the United States. The Court held that "by entwining itself with Gegauf and Vigorelli in such a program, Singer went far beyond its claimed purpose of merely protecting its own 401 machine—it was protecting Gegaug and Vigorelli, the sole licensees under the patent at the time under the same umbrella . . . the conspiracy arises implicitly from the course of dealing of the parties here resulting in Singer's obligation to enforce the patent to the benefit of all three parties."[27] The controlling purpose was to destroy the Japanese sale of infringing machines in the United States. This went beyond the limited monopoly which a patent grants, and therefore violated the Sherman Act.

Restrictive Licensing and Patent Infringement

Owners of patents frequently seek to impose restrictions upon the use of the patented article that is sold or leased. Sometimes, this is for the purpose of extending the monopoly conferred by the patent right into the control of products that are not in any way covered by the patent. Sometimes, restrictions on the use of the patented article may be imposed in order to be able to exploit more completely the patent grant itself.[28] The restrictions are usually achieved either by notice or by tying clauses in the contract.

The majority of cases involving restrictive licensing of this sort are the result of private suit. Frequently, however, the defense is based on the contention that the licensor is guilty of violating the antitrust laws. The courts may accept this as a defense, even though an antitrust suit is not the matter before them. Furthermore, the earlier position of the courts was one of the factors bringing about the passage of the Clayton Act, which forbade tying clauses. In the early litigation on this matter, the position taken by the lower courts was that a patentee could sell his patented device on his own terms, including a restriction upon the use and conditions under which the patented article could be used. A transgression of the restriction constituted an infringement of the patent right, and one who assisted in such infringement was a contributory infringer. Thus, tying clauses were enforceable by infringement remedy.

[27] *Ibid.*, 194.

[28] See *Mercoid Corp.* v. *Mid-Continent Investment Co.*, 320 U.S. 661 (1944); dissenting opinion of Mr. Justice Jackson, p. 678.

This doctrine of contributory infringement was upheld by the Supreme Court in *Henry* v. *A. B. Dick Company* (1912).[29] The Dick company made mimeographing machines and sold them under the license restriction that the machine might be used only with the stencil paper, ink, and other supplies made by the Dick company. Henry, a dealer in ink, sold ink to a purchaser of one of the Dick machines. The Dick company sued Henry for infringement. The Supreme Court upheld the provisions in the license which the Dick company had attached to the mimeographing machine, on the ground that the owner of a patent might impose license restrictions which gave the licensee the right to use the machine only for specified purposes, under specified conditions, and at specified prices, because a patent monopoly gave a separate right to manufacture, sale, and use.

In 1914, the Clayton Act was passed. This led to reversal of the Dick doctrine in *Motion Picture Patents Company* v. *Universal Film Manufacturing Company* (1917).[30] The Motion Picture Patents Company sold motion-picture projecting machines, with the stipulation that these machines should be used solely with film leased from a manufacturer licensed by the Motion Picture Patents Company. The suit claimed infringement by a distributor and a motion-picture exhibitor who had furnished and used films that were not made by the plaintiffs. The Court held that the owner of a patent could not extend the scope of a patent monopoly by restricting the use of it to materials necessary for its operation but not part of the patented invention. "The scope of every patent is limited to the invention described in the claims contained in it, read in the light of the specification."[31] The inventor can claim nothing beyond this. The latter point was clarified by the Supreme Court later in *Carbice Corporation* v. *American Patent Development Corporation* (1931).[32] The Supreme Court held that a patent may not be broadened to include unpatented material or machines, even though the material was included in the claim of the patent.

The limitations which transgression of the antitrust laws may impose on suits for contributory infringement was illustrated in *Morton Salt Company* v. *Suppiger Company* (1942).[33] The defendant contended that the plaintiff should be estopped from maintaining an infringement suit, because even though the patents themselves were valid, the owners had attempted to use their patents to eliminate competition in products not directly within their scope. The Court held that the patent owner had violated the antitrust laws and therefore could not sue for contributory

[29] 224 U.S. 1.

[30] 243 U.S. 502; see also *United Shoe Machinery Corp.* v. *United States*, 258 U.S. 451 (1922); *International Business Machines Corp.* v. *United States*, 298 U.S. 131 (1936).

[31] *Ibid.*, p. 510.

[32] 283 U.S. 27; also *Leitch Manufacturing Co.* v. *Barber Co.*, 302 U.S. 458 (1938).

[33] 314 U.S. 488; also *American Lecithin Co.* v. *Warfield Co.*, 105 Fed. (2d) 207 (1939); certiorari denied, 308 U.S. 522 (1939).

infringement. The Court stated that public policy forbids the use of a patent to secure an exclusive right or limited monopoly not granted by the Patent Office. Where such use occurs, equity may rightly withhold its assistance from such use by declining to entertain a suit for infringement. It appears also, from this decision, that the imposition of any extra-patent restraint on competition will preclude relief, without inquiry into the amount or substantiality of the commerce outside the grant.

The doctrines developed in the foregoing cases were further extended in *Mercoid Corporation* v. *Mid-Continent Investment Company* (1944).[34] The Mid-Continent Investment Company owned a patent on a domestic heating system that it licensed to the Minneapolis-Honeywell Company. The latter manufactured a combustion stoker switch, which because of its shape and design, could be used only in conjunction with the Mid-Continent patent. The Mercoid Corporation manufactured a similar stoker switch, which could also be used only in conjunction with the Mid-Continent patent. The lower court held that the Mercoid Corporation was guilty of contributory infringement, because there was no other use for the stoker device except in conjunction with the Mid-Continent patient. The Supreme Court held that the owner of a patent may not use it to secure a limited monopoly of an unpatented device employed in practicing the invention, even though the unpatented device is itself an integral part of the patented combination. Furthermore, misuse of the patent to protect an unpatented element from competition may be used as a defense by contributory infringers. If the patent is used or misused so as to result in restraint of trade in unpatented materials, the patent owner will be denied the aid of the court in enforcing his rights. The position taken in this case, however, resulted in strong differences of opinion among the members of the Supreme Court because of the possible implication that under the Mercoid ruling, a patent misuse would in every case be a per se antitrust violation. Whether contributory infringement suits constitute misuse seems to be a debatable question.[35]

A limitation on the application of the ideas of misuse and patent validity doctrine was set forth in *Automatic Radio Manufacturing Company* v. *Hazeltine Research, Inc.* (1950).[36] In this case, Hazeltine Research, Inc., sought to recover royalties on patents it had leased to Automatic. The royalties were based on a percentage of the selling price of complete radio broadcasting receivers which were manufactured and sold by Automatic. The latter contended that this arrangement constituted a misuse of patents by Hazeltine, because the royalties were derived from prices covering both patented and unpatented items. The

[34]320 U.S. 661; and *Mercoid Corp.* v. *Minneapolis-Honeywell Regulator Co.*, 320 U.S. 680 (1944).

[35]Report of the Attorney General's National Committee, *Antitrust Laws* (Washington, D.C.: U.S. Government Printing Office, 1955), pp. 250 f.

[36]339 U.S. 827.

Court held that there were no "tie-in" requirements but that only a method of calculating the royalty was involved.[37] This did not constitute a misuse. At the same time, however, Automatic challenged the validity of the patents. To this, the Court replied: "The general rule is that the licensee under a patent license agreement may not challenge the validity of the licensed patent in a suit for royalties due under a contract."[38] However, when the agreement also contains price-fixing provisions, the validity of the patent may be challenged in a suit for royalties.[39] The confused and unsatisfactory state of the law on these matters is indicated by the continuous and sharp division of the Court on them.[40]

The Federal Trade Commission has ruled that practices based on patents obtained by misconduct before the Patent Office constitute a violation of Section 5 of the Trade Commission Act. In a decision involving Chas. Pfizer & Co., Inc. and a number of other respondents, the Commission held that unclean hands and bad faith played a major role in the issuance of a patent on the antibiotic drug tetracycline.[41] The Commission found that some of the respondents had conspired to prevent relevant information bearing on the patentability of tetracycline from coming to the attention of the Patent Office. The Commission ruled that it could prevent enforcement of a patent obtained by unclean hands, and that it could arrest the continuance of an absolute monopoly (i.e., a patent from being enforced) under Section 5. It therefore issued a cease and desist order against the price-fixing arrangements that had been entered into by the respondents.

In a misuse case, the Commission ruled that the Lapeyre family in Louisiana (Laitrum Corp. and Laitrum International Inc.) had abused their patent-based monopoly in shrimp processing machinery.[42] Abuse was alleged on the grounds of (1) charging northwest shrimp-canner lessees of this indispensable machinery more than double that which Gulf canners were charged, and (2) selling the machinery to foreign canners while refusing to sell to domestic canners. The Commission held that the actual intent of the respondents was to preserve their own interests as canners of shrimp by the Grand Caillon Packing Co., which they owned. The Commission decided that these practices constituted unfair methods of competition under Section 5, and issued a cease and desist order. The economic reasoning left considerable to be desired, and its interpretation of the law relating to patents certainly seems to be novel. Under the Commission's interpretation, a misuse occurs if the lessor discriminates in price among the lessees even if the patent is valid.

[37]But see *United States* v. *United States Gypsum Co.*, 333 U.S. 364 (1948).
[38]*Ibid.*, p. 836.
[39]*MacGregor* v. *Westinghouse*, 329 U.S. 402 (1946).
[40]See *United States Gypsum Co.* v. *National Gypsum Co.*, 352 U.S. 457 (1957).
[41]Order 7211 (1963) (Federal Trade Commission, *News Summary*, August 6, 1963).
[42]Order 7887 (Federal Trade Commission, *News Summary*, June 12, 1964). See also *A. C. Neilsen Co.*, Consent Order C-13 (*News Summary*, November 2, 1963).

Price-Fixing Arrangements

The issues of price fixing under patent grants should be distinguished from resale price maintenance. A patentee may, under appropriate circumstances, fix the prices at which a licensee may sell the products; but the patent owner cannot establish, by notice or any other arrangement, the sale price of the product if the ownership of it has passed from him. An attempt to dictate prices by an elaborate licensing contract and license notice came before the Court in *Straus* v. *Victor Talking Machine Company* (1917).[43] In the endeavor to retain control of prices, the company granted a license to use machines, even to the ultimate consumer, only upon the payment of a fixed royalty. R. H. Macy and Company acquired some of the machines, without agreement to maintain prices, and proceeded to sell them below the royalty. The Victor company brought suit, on the ground that patent rights had been infringed. The Supreme Court found the whole plan to be illegal under the Miles company ruling,[44] declaring that the scheme was the same as previous ones which had been held illegal, except that it was "adroitly modified on the one hand to take advantage if possible of distinctions suggested by these decisions, and on the other to evade certain supposed effects of them."

This position was maintained even after the passage of the Miller-Tydings Act in *United States* v. *Univis Lens Company* (1942).[45] Univis Lens Company held a majority of the stock of the Univis Corporation. The corporation owned patents and trade-marks on eyeglass lenses. The corporation licensed the lens company to manufacture lens blanks and to sell them to licensees designated by the corporation. The corporation issued three classes of licenses: to wholesalers, to finishing retailers, and to prescription retailers. The lens company sold only the blanks which were covered by patent, the wholesalers and the finishing retailers completing the process of grinding the lens. The license contract called for price fixing right through to the ultimate consumer. The Supreme Court held that the patent monopoly ended with the sale of the blanks and that the stipulation for the maintenance of prices derived no support from the patent. The Court also held that the Miller-Tydings Act did not apply, since the lens company manufactured the blanks and not the finished lens to which the resale price applied, and that the licensees, therefore, were not engaged in the resale of the same commodity that they bought.

One of the earliest and leading cases upholding the right of a patent owner to fix prices was that of *Bement* v. *National Harrow Com-*

[43]243 U.S. 490.
[44]*Dr. Miles Medical Co.* v. *John D. Park & Sons*, 220 U.S. 373 (1911).
[45]316 U.S. 341.

pany (1902).[46] The National Harrow Company was a combination of 6 manufacturers of harrows formed for the purpose of holding patents and licensing the respective manufacturers under it. Eighty-five patents were acquired by assignment from the several manufacturers. The National Harrow Company, through this pooling arrangement, acquired most of the business of manufacturing and distributing spring-tooth harrows in the United States. Bement and Sons was one of the 6 manufacturers to assign patents to the combination. By agreement, each manufacturer was required to pay a royalty of $1.00 for each harrow sold and to sell the harrows at the price stipulated by the agreement. The National Harrow Company accused Bement and Sons of violating the conditions of the agreement. Bement argued that the contracts violated the Sherman Act. The Court, however, held otherwise. In holding the agreements to be legal, it took the position that, as a general rule, there should be absolute freedom in the use or sale of patent rights under the patent laws of the United States, because the very object of the patent laws was monopoly. The fact that the conditions in the contract kept up the monopoly and fixed prices did not render them illegal. It should be noted, however, that the decision was based upon the legality of the specific contracts presented to the Court. The existence of a combination to control the sale and the price of the harrows was not established, and so the Court did not find it necessary to pass upon the legality of such a combination when based on patents.

In *United States* v. *General Electric Company* (1926).[47] two issues regarding price-fixing privileges under patents came before the Supreme Court. The first was the right of a patentee to fix the price of the products manufactured by the licensee under the patent, and the second was the validity of price fixing under agency contracts for the same product. General Electric had acquired the patent right in this country on tungsten filament lamps. It licensed Westinghouse to manufacture these lamps, on condition that Westinghouse sold the lamps only at the prices fixed by General Electric. At the same time, in order to secure control over the sale price of the lamps which it manufactured itself, General Electric worked out a selling program through a series of agency contracts between itself and distributors. Under this program, General Electric retained title to the lamps until they were sold to the ultimate consumer.

On the first issue, the government charged that the contracts violated the Sherman Act. The Court upheld the right of General Electric to limit the selling prices of the licensee, saying that this was legal "provided the conditions of sale are normally and reasonably adapted to secure pecuniary reward for the patentee's monopoly. . . . When the

[46]186 U.S. 70.
[47]272 U.S. 476.

patentee licenses another to make and vend, and retains the right to continue to make and vend on his own account, the price at which his licensee will sell will necessarily affect the price at which he can sell his own patented goods."[48] Under such circumstances, the Court found such price fixing to be entirely reasonable.

On the second question, the government contended that the agency arrangements were a subterfuge. The Court held that a true agency had been established, and that the purpose and effect of the marketing plan was to secure for the patentee only the reward for his invention to which he was entitled.

However, when the agency device is used as a cloak to establish a price-fixing combination of competitors, it violates the Sherman Act. This was the basis of the decision in the *United States* v. *Masonite Corporation* (1942).[49] In this instance, the Masonite Corporation, the owner of certain patents for making hardboard, entered into agency agreements with a number of competitors of similar products for the sale of Masonite hardboard. The terms of the contract were definitely such that they violated the antitrust laws if a true agency could not be established at law. The Supreme Court stated that a patentee may employ the del credere agency device to distribute his product but

> when he utilizes the sales organization of another business—a business with which he has no intimate relationship—quite different problems are posed since such a regimentation of a marketing system is peculiarly susceptible to the restraints of trade which the Sherman Act condemns. And when it is clear, as it is in this case, that the marketing systems utilized by means of the *del credere* agency agreements are those of competitors of the patentee, and that the purpose is to fix prices at which the competitors may market the product, the device is, without more, an enlargement of the limited patent privilege.[50]

Furthermore, relief was not available under the Miller-Tydings Act, because it did not legalize resale price agreements among competitors.

Price fixing under the guise of licenses designed to preserve patent rights, even though no agreements or contracts for price maintenance existed, was declared to be a violation of the Sherman Act in *Ethyl Gasoline Corporation* v. *United States* (1940).[51] Ethyl Gasoline Corporation manufactured and sold a patented fluid compound containing tetraethyl lead to oil refiners, solely for use in the production of improved motor fuel. It entered into license agreements with most of the large oil refiners, which prohibited them from selling the manufactured product to any except other licensed refiners, to jobbers licensed by the Ethyl corporation, and to retail dealers and consumers. Jobbers gener-

[48]*Ibid.*, p. 490.

[49]316 U.S. 265. See also *United States* v. *United States Gypsum Co.*, 333 U.S. 364 (1948).

[50]*Ibid.*, p. 279.

[51]309 U.S. 436.

ally were required to apply for licenses to the refiners, and extensive restrictions were thus imposed upon the jobbers.

The Supreme Court found that the licensed refiners refined 88 per cent of all the gasoline sold in the United States and that the gasoline processed by them, under the license agreements, was 70 per cent of all the gasoline sold in this country and 85 per cent of all gasoline processed to obtain a high-octane rating. These licensing agreements served to exclude all unlicensed jobbers from the market. In addition, the licenses placed restraints on the sale prices of the refiners by establishing prescribed differentials between regular and ethyl gasoline. The Court stated that the company had acquired the power to exclude, at will, from participation in the nationwide market for lead-treated motor fuel, all of the 12,000 motor fuel jobbers of the country by refusing to license any of the 1,000 unlicensed jobbers and by being allowed to cancel the licenses of any of the 11,000 licensed jobbers. The practice of investigating the business ethics of jobbers applying for licenses made it possible for the company to exercise sufficient control over prices and marketing policies of jobbers to be persuasive in eliminating price cutting in the jobbers' trade.

The Court held that the practices of the company did not constitute the exercise of the right to refuse to sell, or to refuse to permit the licensee to sell, the patented product to price cutters, in accordance with the Colgate rule, but that, on the contrary, they constituted a combination capable of use, and actually used, as a means of controlling jobbers' prices and suppressing competition among them.

To be exempt from the antitrust laws, price-fixing agreements now must be based on valid patents. Until 1942, patent monopolies were frequently maintained by license arrangements, even though the validity of the patent might be in question. This was accomplished either under the doctrine of estoppel, by which a licensee was prevented from challenging the validity of the patent because he was a licensee, or by specific agreement, in which the licensee agreed not to challenge the validity of the patent. The first of the issues came before the Supreme Court in *Sola Electric Company* v. *Jefferson Electric Company* (1942).[52] The Jefferson company licensed the Sola company to manufacture and sell patented transformers throughout the United States on payment of the stipulated royalty on each transformer. The contract provided that the license was granted on condition that the prices and conditions of sale throughout the licensed territory should not be more favorable to Sola's customers than those prescribed from time to time by Jefferson for its own sales. The Sola company also manufactured another type of transformer, which the Jefferson company claimed to be covered by certain broader claims in its patent. The Circuit Court of Appeals ruled that

[52] 317 U.S. 173.

the Sola company, having accepted a license under the Jefferson patent, was estopped from denying its validity. The Supreme Court held that where, owing to the invalidity of a patent, a price-fixing stipulation in a license to manufacture the patented article and sell it in interstate commerce was in conflict with the Sherman law, the licensee was not estopped to set up the invalidity against the licensor in a suit by the latter.

The second question, concerning the effectiveness of contracts prohibiting challenge of patent validity was dealt with in *Edward Katzinger Company* v. *Chicago Metallic Manufacturing Company* (1947).[53] In this instance, the license contract contained price-fixing provisions and also a provision that the licensee would not challenge the validity of the patent. A controversy arose over the scope of the patent. The Supreme Court held that the contract did not prevent the licensee from challenging the validity of the patent because the contract contained price-fixing provisions. The fact that Katzinger did not enforce these provisions did not matter. Furthermore, because the agreement to fix prices and pay royalties was an integrated consideration for the license grant, the royalty provisions were also not enforceable.[54]

One of the two major issues in the General Electric case was the right of the patent owner to fix the prices at which the licensee could sell the products manufactured under the patent. That case, however, did not deal with price fixing where cross-licenses are involved. This was the issue in *United States* v. *Line Material Company et al.* (1948).[55] In this instance, there was a cross-licensing arrangement between Line Material Company and Southern States Equipment Company, by which the two companies licensed each other to use the complementary patents held by each company. Each patentee agreed that it would fix the price on the product made by the licensee and that each could license other producers to use the patents, provided that the licenses required that the prices fixed by Line Material be maintained. The Supreme Court agreed that the licensees knew of the price-fixing provisions in the licenses of others, that the licenses were the result of arm's-length bargaining in each instance, and that all licensees were forced to accept the terms or cease manufacture. The Court divided three ways on the interpretation of the General Electric precedent. A minority wanted to overrule it. A majority adhered to the precedent but could not agree on its interpretation.

The decision in the Line Material case held that the arrangement

[53]329 U.S. 394; rehearing denied, 330 U.S. 853 (1947).

[54]See *MacGregor* v. *Westinghouse Electric and Manufacturing Co.*, 329 U.S. 402 (1947). Four Justices dissented from this and the Katzinger decision in a vigorous dissent written by Mr. Justice Frankfurter.

[55]333 U.S. 287. See also *United States* v. *United States Gypsum Co.*, 333 U.S. 364 (1948), decided on the same day. The decision in this case was made on the Masonite precedent; also *United States* v. *New Wrinkle, Inc.*, 342 U.S. 371 (1952).

violated the Sherman Act. No case, said the opinion, has construed the patent and antimonopoly statutes to permit separate owners of separate patents, by cross-licenses or other arrangements, to fix the prices to be charged by them and their licensees for their respective products. Therefore, the General Electric rule did not apply. A concurring minority wanted to abolish the Bement and General Electric precedents. A dissenting minority wished to reaffirm those cases. Furthermore, this group contended that the instant case was on all fours with those precedents and that they should be upheld because Congress has not seen fit over the years, after much debate, to enact any statutory amendments. The uncertainty of the situation certainly calls for congressional action. It is unfortunate that the issue should be decided in the forum of the Court rather than in the forum of Congress.[56]

Summary

The foregoing discussion of patents and the antitrust laws brings out the fact that there are limits to the rights conferred by patents and that the patent monopoly cannot be used to effect control not comprehended by the patent grant. Recent judicial action, in particular, has gone a long way toward reconciling patent rights with the theory of the antitrust laws. A staff report to the Subcommittee of the Judiciary of the House of Representatives concludes:

> Analysis of the leading judicial decisions in the patent-antitrust area discloses no discernible threat to the integrity of the American patent system and no basic incompatibility or irreconcilable conflict between the patent laws and the antitrust laws . . . for the courts have been alert to recognize and condemn the use of patents in monopolization and in combinations to restrain trade. The present statutory scheme and judicial climate afford ample means for preserving rights of patent owners in the legitimate exploitation of their property, while at the same time correcting patent abuse and safeguarding competitive opportunity.[57]

With this encomium, it is difficult to agree.

The scope of the patents monopoly and the rights of ownership are still so extensive that monopoly can be achieved or preserved through patent ownership within the limits imposed by the antitrust laws. Ownership of a patent on a key invention can place a patentee in a position of dominance in a particular field of manufacture. Cross-licensing and pooling may extend this control in such a way as to make it extremely difficult, if not impossible, to bring it under the antitrust laws. Enterprises whose activities relay heavily on patented processes or devices may devote

[56]Uncertainty concerning the status of the General Electric ruling on agency contracts has been enhanced still further by the decision of the Supreme Court in *Simpson* v. *Union Oil Co.*, 377 U.S. 13 (1964) discussed in Chapter 16, *supra*.

[57]*Anti-Trust Problems in the Exploitation of Patents* (Subcommittee of the Judiciary, House of Representatives, 84th Cong., 2d sess.) (Washington, D.C.: U.S. Government Printing Office, 1957), p. 25.

large sums to research to maintain their technical superiority and, also, to ward off competition.[58] The practices of "fencing in" and "blocking out" are frequently used in this connection. Fencing in is accomplished by accumulating all possible patents which may impinge upon those that are of especial importance to a business. Recourse may also be had to the practice of buying up patents, in order to suppress them if they offer a threat to investment that it is desired to preserve.[59] A patentee may also take out patents on alternative items, in order to protect his basic idea. This is known as "blocking out." As the law now stands, it is not necessary for an owner to use his patent or to license others to use it, even though nonuse may result in suppressing competition because of the strategic position which the patent occupies.[60] Furthermore, the severe division of opinion on the present Supreme Court on what the law is, as well as differences of opinion on what it ought to be, calls for congressional assumption of the responsibility for clarifying existing law as well as determining what policy ought to be.

PROPOSALS FOR REFORM

The patent laws of the United States are the most generous of any country in the world: patents are easier to acquire than elsewhere, the grants are less circumscribed, the costs of obtaining and maintaining patents are less, and there are no compulsory working or licensing requirements. These privileges, as we have seen, are not without their shortcomings. In recent years, many suggestions for reforming the patent laws have been advanced, with a view to eliminating the abuses and to the end of adapting the patent system to its social objectives.[61] These proposals fall into two main categories—procedural and substantive. The procedural reforms relate to such matters as shortening the total period of protection from the date of filing, simplifying the interference procedure, establishing a single court of patent appeals, and providing technical advisers for the court. The substantive reforms include suggestions for limiting the classes of patentable inventions, restricting the privileges of assignment, making compulsory the licensing of patents, and allowing the granting of unrestricted licenses only.

[58]See Federal Communications Commission, *Report on the Investigation of the Telephone Industry in the United States* (House Document 340, 76th Cong., 1st sess). (Washington, D.C.: U.S. Government Printing Office, 1940), especially chap. viii, for an evaluation of the role of patents in the growth of the Bell Telephone System. See also Chapter 18, "International Combinations."

[59]*Special Equipment Co.* v. *Coe*, 324 U.S. 370 (1945).

[60]*Hartford-Empire Co.* v. *United States*, 323 U.S. 386, 433 (1945). For an extensive recitation of patent problems, see *Patents* (Hearings before the Committee on Patents, U.S. Senate, 77th Cong., 2d sess.) (Washington, D.C.: U.S. Government Printing Office, 1942).

[61]In dealing with proposals for reform it is necessary once more to distinguish between the patent system and the patent laws. Reform relates to the laws, while at the same time retaining the system.

The Temporary National Economic Committee

This Committee conducted extensive hearings on patents and, in its final report, submitted a number of recommendations for changes in the patent laws.[62] The following is a summary of these:

1. *Licensing Patents.* Any future patent should be available for use by anyone who may desire to use it and who is willing to pay a fair price for the privilege. Machinery should be set up to determine the fairness of the royalty.

2. *Unrestricted Licenses.* The owner of any patent should be required to grant only unrestricted licenses, and he should not be permitted to impose restrictions upon the buyer with regard to the sales of articles that might be produced by the use of the patented device.

3. *Recording of Transfers and Agreements.* All transfers and agreements should be registered in writing, and a copy should be filed with the Federal Trade Commission within thirty days of its execution.

4. *Limitation on Suits for Infringement.* No action based upon a charge of patent infringement should be permitted against any licensee under a patent, unless the plaintiff had previously secured a judgment against the grantor of the license.

5. *Forfeiture of Patent for Violation.* Any person violating the provisions of items 1 or 2 should forfeit his license, and the patent should become part of the public domain.

6. *Single Court of Patent Appeals.* There should be a single Court of Patent Appeals for the United States and its territories to replace the present eleven different and independent jurisdictions.

7. *Limitations on Period of Patent Monopoly.* The life of a patent should be so limited that it will expire not more than twenty years from the date of the filing of the application.

The Committee noted that the patent privilege had been shamefully abused and that it had been used as a device to control whole industries, to suppress competition, to restrict output, to enhance prices, to suppress inventions, and to discourage inventiveness. It also warned that "if the pattern of control which has been achieved through patent monopoly continues in spite of the changes we suggest, and it is entirely possible that it will, a complete reexamination of our patent laws should be made with a view to determining whether, under present-day conditions, they are calculated to achieve their avowed purpose."[63]

The National Planning Patent Commission

An executive order issued by President Franklin D. Roosevelt on December 12, 1941, established the National Planning Patent Commission, under the chairmanship of Dr. Charles F. Kettering of General Motors Corporation. The function of this Commission was to study the American patent system and its operation.

[62]Temporary National Economic Committee, "Investigation of Concentration of Economic Power," *Final Report of the Temporary National Economic Committee* (Senate Document No. 35, 77th Congress, 1st session) (Washington, D.C.: U.S. Government Printing Office, 1941), pp. 36–37.

[63]*Ibid.*, p. 36.

In its first report,[64] the Commission expressed its faith in the patent system of the United States by stating that this system was the foundation of American enterprise and that it had demonstrated its value over a period coextensive with the life of the government of this country. Its principal recommendations were:

1. Public interest should be protected by requiring that all patent agreements be recorded with the United States Patent Office; that, in a suit for infringement, a patent owner should be limited to reasonable compensation without prohibiting the use of the invention when a court finds that the manufacture of the invention is necessary to the national defense or required by the public health or safety; and that issued patents should be canceled if later information shows they should not have been issued.
2. A patent owner should be given the opportunity to declare publicly his willingness to grant licenses under reasonable terms.
3. Congress should declare a national standard whereby patentability of an invention should be determined by the objective test as to its advancement of the arts and sciences.
4. A patent term should not endure more than twenty years after the application is filed.
5. The Court of Customs and Patent Appeals should be designated as the sole reviewing body if a license is denied by the Patent Office.

It is evident that the Commission viewed the problems and difficulties relating to patents with much less alarm than did the Temporary National Economic Committee. The enactment into law of many of the proposals of the two foregoing reports would undoubtedly make for considerable improvement in the patent situation in this country. The recommendations of the National Planning Patent Commission, however, appear to be too inadequate, by themselves, to make a real impression on the fundamental difficulties.

Supplementing the proposals of the National Planning Commission by the recommendations regarding procedural reform of the Temporary National Economic Committee would be an important step in simplifying the patent procedure. There is definite need for improving the standard of patentability by reducing the scope of patent coverage and by confining patents to inventions that represent really significant additions to technology. Procedures involving defense of patent rights and infringement suits need to be simplified and modified, so they cannot be so readily used as a means of intimidation and bludgeoning; and a single court should replace the present divided and frequently contradictory jurisdictions.

Price-Fixing Restrictions

It also seems desirable to remove the price-fixing privileges which the courts have permitted the owners of patent grants to exercise through their licenses. Despite the lengthy argument of the minority in the Line

[64]House of Representatives, Document No. 239, 78th Congress, 1st session (Washington, D.C.: U.S. Government Printing Office, 1943).

Materials case, there does not appear to be any convincing economic argument to support the position that such price fixing is necessary to reap the benefits of the patent grant. This can be done through the royalties charged. The price-fixing privileges are simply a resale price maintenance device carried on under the guise of a monopoly grant. As such, they are no more justified than any other form of price maintenance; whatever the reason may be, price fixing by license provisions is not covered by the fair-trade laws. Finally, other restrictive provisions —such as relate to output, territories served, and so forth—should be eliminated, because they seem to serve no useful public purpose.

Remedies

Where patent arrangements are found to violate the antitrust laws, the courts prescribe remedies to prevent the continuance of these violations in the future. This may be done by decrees which require compulsory licensing of the patents in question, as was done in the Hartford-Empire case. In this instance, the licenses were to be available to all who wished them at standard royalties, without discrimination or restriction. The company was also prohibited from further prosecution of infringement suits that were pending at the time the original suit was filed against Hartford.[65] This sort of remedy now seems to be well established. As yet, the Supreme Court has not seen fit to require royalty-free licensing, but it did prescribe compulsory licensing at reasonable rates in the National Lead case. It may be noted that the Department of Justice has secured royalty-free licensing in a number of consent decrees.

In the United Shoe Machinery case, the Court went further than it had previously done by requiring United to offer for sale the same type of machine it chose to lease, to eliminate discriminatory provisions and full-capacity clauses from its leases, and to grant licenses under its patents at reasonable royalties. In addition, United was divested of its business of manufacturing certain types of supplies for the shoe machinery market. Most of these provisions, however, were in lieu of dissolution as a remedy for the antitrust violations by the combination.

The remedies that have been prescribed on patent offenses alone, however, seem to leave the offenders with the fruits of their illegal acts, even though they cannot continue to reap all of them in the future. This comes perilously close to permitting companies to play the game of "heads I win and tails you lose," which can be very profitable if none of the winnings have to be given up when it is terminated. What is needed is legislation which will impose penalties under the patent laws when conviction is obtained under the antitrust laws.

[65]See also *United States* v. *United States Gypsum Co.*, 340 U.S. 76 (1950); *Besser Manufacturing Co.* v. *United States*, 343 U.S. 444 (1952). In *Mercoid Corp.* v. *Minneapolis-Honeywell Regulator Co.*, 320 U.S. 680 (1944), Mercoid was awarded treble damages for the patentee's violations of the antitrust laws.

Compulsory Licensing

In the opinion of many students, the compulsory licensing of patents offers the most satisfactory available remedy for the restrictive abuses of the patent system. Compulsory licensing might mean that a patentee would be required to grant licenses to all who applied for them at a reasonable price and on nondiscriminatory terms. It might also mean that the granting of licenses would be compulsory if public welfare demanded it or if the patentee had abused his monopoly rights. This is the basis for compulsory licensing in most European countries.[66] Recommendation 1 of the Temporary National Economic Committee was for compulsory licensing with administrative machinery for the determination of fair royalties.

A system of compulsory licensing, whether it were made manditory for all patentees, or whether it were compulsory only when an administrative tribunal decreed it in the public interest, would necessitate the establishment of administrative machinery to determine the conditions of licensing and the fees to be paid by the licensees. Some students believe that this is not a particularly compelling objection. They feel that the mere existence of compulsory licensing provisions would ordinarily be sufficient to secure voluntary agreements without restrictions. This may be too sanguine a view, however, since the root of the patent problem lies in patents which are of such importance as to make fighting for them worthwhile. Moreover, the difficulties of establishing fair prices in this country for industries like public utilities indicate that formidable obstacles would have to be overcome. Compulsory licensing as a remedy for antitrust violation may be very useful, but it is most likely that employment of it as a condition of a patent grant would do considerably more harm than good. More fundamental restrictions, designed to narrow the limits of the original grant, would appear to offer a more promising approach than a device that first establishes a monopoly and then endeavors to regulate it.

Proposals for reform of the patent laws must recognize the fact that present arrangements are of long standing. No fundamental change has been made in the patent laws since 1836. While it is not legitimate to argue, as some do, that this demonstrates that the laws are fundamentally sound,[67] it nevertheless does offer some ground for somewhat gradual reform.[68] Present patent procedures and practices are deeply embedded in our economic structure. A drastic revision of existing laws could create a considerable disturbance of property rights, work serious injustice, and

[66]See Richard Reik, "Compulsory Licensing of Patents," *American Economic Review*, Vol. XXXVI, No. 5 (December, 1946), pp. 813–32.

[67]See O. R. Barnett, *Patent Property and the Anti-Monopoly Laws* (Indianapolis: Bobbs-Merrill Co., 1943), p. 399.

[68]See Fritz Machlup, *op. cit.*, p. 80.

give rise to a great deal of legal uncertainty. Immediate and obvious abuses should be dealt with at once; and steps should be taken to prevent their perpetuation by legislative enactments designed to eliminate, from new patent applications and grants, the more clearly definable opportunities for evading the intent of the system. At the present time, there exists a sufficient understanding—and, probably, concensus of opinion—on the more significant requirements of revision in the patent laws to provide Congress with the necessary basis of immediate action.[69]

On the broader issues, business must assume a major responsibility. If executives insist on exploiting the monopolistic and predatory possibilities of patent rights to their limit, there will be little chance of saving the system. The latter cannot do much more than reflect the atmosphere of business morality that surrounds it. On the other hand, a genuine recognition on the part of business that the patent system is one of the valuable devices for stimulating private initiative will aid greatly in simplifying the problem of reform. Business can shirk its responsibility only at the peril of losing one of its most valuable privileges.

[69]For more detailed discussion of proposals for patent reform, see Corwin Edwards, *Maintaining Competition* (New York: McGraw-Hill Book Co., Inc., 1949) pp. 236–48. C. Kaysen and D. Turner, *op. cit.*, pp. 171–79; G. W. Stocking and M. W. Watkins, *Monopoly and Free Enterprise* (New York: The Twentieth Century Fund, 1951), pp. 486–590. The international aspects of the patent problem are dealt with in Edith F. Penrose, *The Economics of the International Patent System* (Baltimore: The Johns Hopkins Press, 1951).

Chapter 19 INTERNATIONAL COMBINATIONS

INTRODUCTION

The problems of public policy relating to the regulation of private business are not confined to activities on the domestic scene. Much of modern industry transcends national boundaries, just as it does state lines; and some type of business, such as shipping, are primarily international in scope. Government policy on economic activity extending beyond national geographic limits or on that which emanates from other countries is largely a matter of foreign economic policy and international economics. However, the line between domestic and foreign policy is very difficult to draw at times. The interactions between the two are such that decisions on many domestic issues may condition the type of action that has to be taken on foreign policy if the program at home is to be carried through. Similarly, decisions on foreign economic policy may limit the choice of action within a country. "Antitrust is but one of several interrelated governmental policies touching on the foreign trade and national security programs of the United States."[1]

This interplay of forces is clearly manifest in the current issues raised by the activities of combinations in foreign trade. American business participates in foreign trade in a number of different ways. It makes sales to foreign buyers who purchase the goods in the United States and export them to their own country. It also sells abroad through representatives located in foreign countries. Purchases of foreign goods are also made by both means. Another method is to establish or acquire subsidiaries in other countries in order to set up branches of American firms. The penetration of foreign markets through branch factories or stores which may be separately incorporated in the foreign country has been a characteristically American means of expanding export trade. General Motors, Ford, Chrysler, General Electric, Woolworth, Standard Oil (New Jersey), Standard Oil (California), and Texaco are familiar establishments in many parts of the world. The holding company, or intercorporate stock ownership, is the common form of organization for this type of expansion.

[1]Report of the Attorney General's National Committee, *Antitrust Laws* (Washington, D.C.: U.S. Government Printing Office, 1955), pp. 65–66.

The control of competition and monopoly in international trade raises essentially the same questions as it does in domestic markets, except, however, that nations, to date, have not shown any great concern for the competitive practices which their nationals have used against those of other countries. The theory of conduct to which the nations of the world have generally subscribed, so far, is that the international scene is a "no man's land," over which no one exercises any jurisdiction. Protection against undesirable or unwarranted practices by foreign competitors may be afforded by legislation that excludes the foreigner from the domestic market by imposing limitations on his entry to it or by threats of retaliation of one sort or another if the grievances are not removed. Competition in markets in third countries, however, may readily degenerate into little short of piracy, especially if those countries do not have industries of their own which are affected by the rivalry.

It is consequently not surprising that business enterprises get together to work out arrangements to govern their relationship with each other in the field of international trade. As has already been pointed out in connection with the combination movement in the United States, co-operation among business firms on matters of common concern is one of the most significant factors shaping the pattern of the industrial structure. In the absence of an expressed public policy, the agreements or understandings that emerge may have little regard for public interest and may frequently be highly detrimental to it. This, however, is not a very good reason for condemning co-operation; rather, it emphasizes the necessity for recognizing the conditions underlying the co-operation and for initiating public action to curb the abuses arising therefrom.

The many diverse factors which have influenced the course of the combination movement in its various manifestations in the different countries of the world have also been at work on the international scene. No separate explanation of the causes of this development seems to be necessary. The problems of control and the impact of international combinations on domestic policy, however, raise additional issues. Some countries, such as Germany, have openly recognized and even encouraged combination at home and abroad.[2] Others, like the United States, have followed a policy aimed at preventing or eliminating arrangements at home that were designed to restrain competition or to create a monopoly. This has also been applied, in the United States, to combinations in international trade which have the effect of limiting competition in the domestic market.

[2]This has now been changed by Germany's new cartel law of July 4, 1957, which is their version of antitrust. For recent developments in foreign countries see Michael Conant, "British Antitrust in Action," *Michigan Law Review*, Vol. 59, No. 6 (April, 1961), pp. 855–902; Corwin Edwards, *Foreign Antitrust Laws in the 1960's* (Washington, D.C.: the Brookings Institution, 1962) Reprint No. 56; *Economic Policies and Practices* (Paper No. 4, Private Trade Barriers and the Atlantic Community, Joint Economic Committee, 88th Cong., 2d sess. (Washington, D.C.: U.S. Government Printing Office, 1964).

Even if the world were committed to free trade and competition, the structure of much of modern industry would give rise to problems of restrictive agreements and monopolistic practices. This has been amply demonstrated by the continuous problem of enforcement of the antitrust laws in the United States. The spread of business activity on a major scale, far beyond national boundaries, has created the need for regulatory machinery that comprehends that fact and for arrangements among governments that have sufficient elements of common purpose to make control beyond national boundaries workable. Combination of business on an international scale can now neither be ignored nor be eliminated. The recent rise to prominence of the issues presented by combination has focused attention on the restrictive aspects of this development and the use to which these have been put by aggressive nationalism. It needs to be emphasized, however, that the problems are not confined solely to economic nationalism; nor are all combinations necessarily restrictive in nature. The development is wider in scope and more profound than this.

This chapter is confined to the relation of the antitrust laws to the activities of American and foreign business enterprises in other countries as they affect the foreign trade of the United States as well as its internal commerce, and also to arrangements between foreign firms when these arrangements affect American foreign commerce and/or the American domestic market, provided, of course, that there is some way of apprehending these foreign firms. At the present time, there is no effective international machinery for dealing with the questions that arise. Divergence of the laws of the various countries, together with the sovereign position asserted by nations, means that this country must by various devices deal with the issues through its own agencies and in accordance with its own laws. This presents problems of conflict of jurisdiction, problems of co-ordination among the agencies of government, and reconciliation of concepts of national welfare applicable to a free-trade area for the domestic market with world market situations that exhibit no such barrier-free opportunities.

COMBINATIONS AND INTERNATIONAL CARTELS

The widespread growth of restrictive and monopolistic practices in the years which followed World War I has brought the word "cartel" into front-page headlines. Like the term "trust" in American usage, it has come to have an almost wholly sinister content and is frequently used as an epithet that immediately condemns any arrangement to which it is applied. Combinations for restricting trade in the United States have assumed many different forms; yet, the name "cartel" has not been used to designate any of them. On the other hand, similar arrangements in Germany have usually been so described. Commodity agreements among governments are aimed at some kind of trade restriction;

yet, the term "cartel" is not usually applied to them or to the numerous shipping conferences that have been formed on many ocean routes of the world. There thus appears to be no clear-cut delineation or application of the use of the term.

The Nature of Cartels

A great deal has been written on the cartel concept and on what constitutes the essence of the cartel device. Unfortunately, there has not been very widespread agreement on the matter. Some writers define cartels as agreements between firms in the same branch of trade which limit the freedom of these firms with respect to the production and marketing of their products. Others prefer to define them as combinations of otherwise independent business concerns for the purpose of regulating their relations in the marketing of competitive goods. Some would designate the marketing arrangements set up under the Agriculture Adjustment Administration as cartels, and many would include the giant chemical combine of I. G. Farbenindustrie. One author, at least, feels that the ramifications of the cartel concept are so great as to make it necessary to define cartels as "business arrangements which have the purpose or effect of reducing or regulating competition."[3]

The essence of the idea of the cartel, however, seems to be that of arrangements involving otherwise nominally independent business enterprises which have the purpose or effect of restricting competition among those enterprises in some way or another so as to effect control over the market. This would include pools, community of interest, interlocking directorates, price agreements, etc.; but it would exclude commodity agreements, outright combines, and arrangements designed to improve the ethics of competition. Thus, plans for regulating, but not restricting, competition would not be termed cartels. International cartels are business arrangements among otherwise nominally independent enterprises entered into for the purpose of restricting, or at least controlling, competition in international trade.

Reasons for the Rise of Cartels

The rise of the issue of cartels and international combinations in American economic policy dates from the end of World War I. This country's dependency upon the German chemical and dye industry was the result, to a considerable extent, of cartel policies and the ramifications of arrangements among manufacturers of explosives that focused attention on cartel activities. The foundations for cartels and international combinations were well established before 1914, however. One of the first of the modern cartels was the Neckar Salt Association, which was formed

[3]C. D. Edwards (ed.), *A Cartel Policy for the United Nations* (New York: Columbia University Press, 1945), essay by Fritz Machlup, p. 5.

in Germany in 1828. In 1867, this Association took on an international aspect by making an agreement with the Eastern French Salt Work, Syndicate. Dr. Liefmann, in 1897, was able to enumerate 40 international cartels concluded by German producers with English, Austrians Belgian, or French firms.[4] By the outbreak of World War I, 114 such cartels were known to exist;[5] and by this time, some American participation had emerged. The most important branches of industry in which cartels played a part, according to Liefmann, were those relating to chemical products, shipping (in which there were no less than 80 agreements), metals, stone, and earth industries, especially glass and electrical products. The outbreak of World War I put an end to the development of international cartels for nearly 10 years. In the period between World War I and World War II, however, they took on a new significance that made them a matter of public interest by the time of our entry into World War II.

Estimates of the amount of world trade subject to some degree of cartel control in recent years have varied from 32 per cent to 50 per cent. Stocking and Watkins[6] tentatively concluded that 87 per cent, by value, of mineral products sold in the United States in 1939, 60 per cent of agricultural products, and 42 per cent of manufactured products were cartelized. In 1939, there were 179 known cartels, and American companies were apparently members in 109 of these.[7] Whatever the precise facts may be, it is evident that cartels played a major role in international trade in the period between the two wars.

Prior to World War I, international cartels and combinations were considered primarily from an economic point of view. They developed largely out of arrangements among individual enterprises, with little direct participation or interference by national governments; and attention was focused almost entirely on their effect on competition and prices. In general, more interest was manifested in the growth of giant business enterprises and their individual penetration of other countries. The growth of industrial giants in the United States and the establishment by them of branch factories in many different countries of the world gave rise to considerable attention abroad, because of the threat of competition to domestic producers that this penetration posed. After World War I, international cartels and combinations became a political problem, first of all, because of the much greater concern of government with the specific direction and control of industry and, second, because of the direct use of economic policy as a means of reviving or establishing national power.

[4]Robert Liefmann, *Cartels, Trusts and Concerns* (New York: S. P. Dutton & Co., 1932), p. 148.

[5]Alfred Plummer, *International Combines in Modern Industry* (London: Sir Isaac Pitman & Sons, Ltd., 1938), p. 3.

[6]G. W. Stocking and M. W. Watkins, *Cartels in Action* (New York: Twentieth Century Fund, Inc., 1946), p. 5.

[7]Edwards, *op. cit.*, p. 10. This did not include shipping conferences.

The control of industry for national purposes, after World War I, was the result of a number of factors. The reconstruction of peacetime economic life, especially in the war-devastated countries of Europe, required action on a national scale and could scarcely be left to industry alone. Furthermore, the mobilization of industry for war purposes and the success which attended that mobilization created a pattern which it was all too easy to continue. The loss of foreign markets, especially to strong American competitors, and the desire of European countries to regain their place in international trade acted as powerful incentives to cartelization as a means of regaining international markets. Further emphasis was given to this by the resurgence of national feeling and the economic nationalism that accompanied it. The extreme national consciousness which was a heritage of World War I led most of the countries of the world to pursue policies of self-sufficiency and to seek foreign markets through cartels in international trade. Currency disturbances and the rationalization of industry by conscious government action led to the widespread extension of control over trade, and the use of cartels was one of the convenient means of exercising that control. There was also severe loss of faith in the competitive system and a growth of the belief that competition in international trade, especially among one's own nationals, would give advantages to the producers of other countries. Many of the extractive industries had suffered from wartime expansion, which created demands for the goods that they produced considerably beyond those existing in peacetime. This called for public programs designed to correct the difficulties. Unfortunately, the policies adopted were almost uniformly of a restrictive nature, designed to raise prices rather than reallocate resources.

A final fillip to the whole development was given by the economic collapse of 1929. The depression, with its paralyzing effect on economic activity, led to a virtual world-wide development of government economic planning, with the resultant agreements among producers to control prices and output in almost every line of industry. Domestic cartelization became characteristic of the postwar world. This ended whatever possibilities may have remained for reducing restrictions on competition in international trade. Thus, the development of the cartel problem after World War I was one phase of the world-wide movement toward economic nationalism. It would have been difficult for one to thrive without the other.

Organizational Structure of Cartels

The organizational structure of cartels follows pretty much the same pattern as that of the various forms of combinations that have been described in connection with the combination movement in the United States. They may be grouped conveniently under the three headings of agreements, associations, and combines.

1. *Agreements.* Agreements, imposing restrictions of one kind or

another on the foreign trade activities of the co-operating parties, probably constitute the most common type of cartel arrangement. These may take the form of simple understandings in the nature of gentlemen's agreements, which are strictly informal in nature, or they may be reduced to a written document. In all probability, informal devices are not very effective or very numerous on the international scene, unless other conditions, similar to those necessary to make them effective in the domestic field, are present. They are difficult to detect, although their existence may be suspected when there are interlocking directorates or a community of interest. Thus, community of interest arising from the ownership of 48.9 per cent of the shares of Aluminum Corporation of America and 48.5 per cent of the shares of Aluminium, Ltd. of Canada, by the same 11 individuals, makes it difficult to believe that concerted action in international trade did not exist between the two. Even though this could not be legally demonstrated, the existence of some officers common to both companies, prior to 1931, serves to strengthen the belief.

The most important type of agreement today is that which relates to patents. It has been estimated that nine tenths of the cartels involving firms of other countries and American firms have taken the form of patent-licensing agreements.[8] Since the end of World War I, this device has probably become the most important basis for effecting cartels in industry. The most comprehensive agreements govern the licensing of patents issued, as well as patents to be issued, together with allocation of territories or industries, the right to use secret processes, and unpatented industrial experience or know-how. Such arrangements, involving extensive interchange of knowledge between the contracting parties, frequently lead to agreements whereby members cannot pass on any information to outsiders or license patents to them without the consent of the other members. Competition among the contracting parties may also be eliminated in the unpatented as well as the patented areas of their activities.

Where a network of interrelated patent and process agreements has been developed, it may be necessary for a company to accept agreements to which it was not even a party. Thus, in the extraordinarily complicated cartel structure erected by I. G. Farben, the latter constantly played off one American partner against another by using its commitments to one as a pretext for limiting its concessions to others. When Hercules Powder Company requested a license from I. G. Farben to use certain processes, the latter found it necessary to consult with Du Pont to see whether this could be done and under what conditions. To further its position in the American chemical market, I. G. Farben entered into an arrangement with Standard Oil of New Jersey in 1930,

[8] E. S. Mason, *Controlling World Trade* (New York: McGraw-Hill Book Co., 1946), p. 49.

whereby I. G. Farben's primacy in chemicals was recognized in return for Standard's primacy in petroleum. As a result, Standard obtained a dominating position in patents required for petroleum refining, while I. G. Farben reinforced its hold on the manufacture of new chemical products derived from petroleum or natural gas. Arrangements such as these, multiplied many times where patents and industrial processes are involved, constitute a story of business diplomacy reminiscent of the rivalry carried on among nations.

2. *Associations.* A great many of the international cartels are organized into associations, the function of which is to administer the agreements which are the bases of the arrangement. These organizations are analogous to the trade associations. Prior to 1920, this type of cartel organization was considered as typifying the cartel. The members of these international cartel associations are the producing companies in the various nations. Sometimes, they have permanent executive officers, with headquarters in some country selected because of its convenience or tolerance of cartel activities. Thus, the international lamp cartel chose Geneva as its domicile, while the international steel cartel, with its executive and business agencies, was located in Luxemburg. The audit service of this organization was carried on by a Swiss firm located in Basel. Many of these associations, on the other hand, have had no permanent headquarters but have carried on their activities by periodic meetings of representatives of the various members, who elect the officers from among themselves and carry on their business at these meetings.

Cartels of this type are usually formed for the purpose of fixing prices; limiting and apportioning output, sales, or exports; allocating market territories; and redistributing profits in accordance with an agreed formula. They may even sell to a jointly maintained sales agency. Very frequently, means—such as deposits or similar arrangements—are employed to provide for penalties for failure of a member to adhere to the agreement.

3. *Combines.* The third form of organization used by the international cartel is the combine. Since the end of World War I, this has come to assume an almost dominant role in cartel organization. This type of cartel uses the corporate form of organization to achieve its objective. Sometimes, it is a corporation in which the members of the cartel own stock or have membership. On occasion, it may consist of jointly owned subsidiaries; while in other instances, a concern may have subsidiaries in other countries linked with competitors by intercorporate stockholding and interlocking directorates. Thus, in the case of the aluminum cartel, Alliance was set up as a Swiss corporation that issued shares to those participating in the agreement. Aluminum of America was not a party to this; but, as has been pointed out, there was a community of interest with Aluminium, Ltd. of Canada, which was a party to the alliance. In the chemical industry, the Du Pont company shared, with a subsidiary of I.

G. Farbenindustrie, ownership of the Bayer-Semesan Company, through which both corporations carried on all their business in the United States pertaining to seed disinfection. Canadian Industries, Ltd. of Canada, is the jointly owned subsidiary of Du Pont and Imperial Chemical Industry; and in Brazil and Argentina, the same two companies organized subsidiaries in each under the name of Duperial.

Probably the leading cartel of this kind is in the field of petroleum production, transportation, refining, and marketing. According to a study made by the staff of the Federal Trade Commission,[9] control over the international oil industry is largely in the hands of 7 companies: Anglo-Iranian Oil Company, Ltd., Royal Dutch-Shell, Standard Oil Company (New Jersey), Standard Oil Company (California), Gulf Oil Company, Socony-Vacuum Oil Company, and the Texas Company. These 7 companies, 5 of which are American, controlled 31.5 per cent of crude oil production in the United States, 80.5 per cent in other Western Hemisphere countries, 99 per cent in the Near and Middle East, and 79.8 per cent in other Eastern Hemisphere countries, or 54.6 per cent of world production, excluding Russia and the satellite countries. The 5 American companies, through stockholding, all participate in the ownership of oil companies in the Middle East; in the case of the Arabian American Oil Company (Aramco), Standard of California, Standard of New Jersey, and the Texas Company, each owns 30 per cent of the stock, while Socony-Vacuum owns 10 per cent.

The report also asserts that the same 7 companies controlled, in 1950, 44 per cent of the crude-oil-refining capacity in the United States, 75.6 per cent in other Western Hemisphere countries, 79 per cent in the Eastern Hemisphere, and 56 per cent of world capacity (excluding U.S.S.R. and the satellites). The percentage for capacity of cracking plants is almost the same. A report of the Secretariat for the Economic Commission for Europe states that both the United States price for crude oil and the world-wide structure of prices are equally divorced from normal competitive forces.[10] In 1953, the Department of Justice filed an

[9] *The International Petroleum Cartel* (Staff Report to the Federal Trade Commission, submitted to the Select Committee on Small Business, U.S. Senate Committee Reprint No. 6, 82nd Cong., 2d sess.) (Washington, D.C.: U.S. Government Printing Office, 1952). The Commission has expressly stated that it neither approved nor disapproved of the statements made in the study; nor did the Commission authorize the publication of the document, because of the international implications and complications. The decision to publish was left to other agencies of the government. See Federal Trade Commission Release, January 17, 1953. See also *Petroleum, the Antitrust Laws and Government Policy* (Report of the Subcommittee on Antitrust and Monopoly, Committee on the Judiciary, Senate Report No. 1147, 85th Cong., 1st sess.) (Washington, D.C.: U.S. Government Printing Office, 1957).

[10] See *Current Antitrust Problems* (Hearings before Committee on the Judiciary, House of Representatives, 84th Cong., 1st sess.) (Washington, D.C.: U.S. Government Printing Office, 1955), Serial No. 3, Part I, pp. 269–78; Part II, pp. 765–1521, 1563–1651.

antitrust suit against the 5 American companies,[11] although much of the documentary evidence is classified and not available for public scrutiny. Whatever may be the facts regarding agreements and control of world trade in oil, it is evident that international trade in petroleum has been guided by cartel arrangements since the early 1920's. Moreover, this cartel has probably had the greatest scope of any that has yet come into existence. It is safe to say that it has had a marked impact on the structure and operation of the petroleum industry in this country, but the extent to which events have been influenced by activities of the government cannot be ascertained. Nor is it possible, at present, to discover the extent to which the private companies may be able to defend themselves against antitrust on the ground that they have entered into the arrangements with the consent and active participation of certain departments of government.

Although this particular case was settled by a consent decree,[12] the extent to which the executive branch of the government may be able to shield the activities of private enterprise on the international scene against antitrust raises some difficult questions of co-ordination with programs for national security and promoting foreign trade. Antitrust proceedings that include activities abroad by American or foreign firms may affect a variety of government programs, as well as relations with other countries.[13]

International Combinations

One of the most significant and complicated developments of international business organizations in recent years has been the growth of giant corporations operating on an international scale. This is really the counterpart of the American trust or outright consolidation. It may be headed by a pure holding company or by a parent operating company with subsidiaries in other countries. The widespread ramifications of the Ford empire are based upon the latter device. This is also true of General Motors, Woolworth, and many other American firms. At one time, the

[11] *Ibid.* pp. 830–1521. See in re *Investigation of World Arrangements*, 107 Fed. Supp. 628 (1953). This involved argument over *subpoena duces tecum*, which was ultimately denied, and the case was adjourned until further notice.

[12] Commerce Clearing House, Trade Cases (1960), ¶ 69, 849 and ¶ 69, 851.

[13] The Attorney General's Report discusses at some length the views of various divisions of the Executive branch of the government on the need for advance discussion with affected agencies concerning projected antitrust proceedings seriously involving any of the government's foreign programs. *Antitrust Laws, op. cit.*, pp. 92–98. Controversy over shipping rates in the North Atlantic Shipping Conference is an illustration of the conflict between national interests and "cartellization." See Wytze Gorter, *United States Shipping Policy* (New York: Harper & Bros., 1956), also *Discriminatory Ocean Freight Rates and the Balance of Payments*, Hearings before the Joint Economic Committee, Congress of the United States, 88th Cong., 1st sess. (Washington, D.C.: U.S. Government Printing Office, 1963–64); Parts I to V.

Ford Motor Car Company of England, a subsidiary of the American company, owned a subsidiary in Germany, 40 per cent of whose stock was sold to I. G. Farbenindustrie.[14] In 1934, Ford disposed of all of the stock of the subsidiary to I. G. Farben. The giant soap trust of Unilever, Ltd., which controlled over 600 companies before the war, consists of two separate holding companies, one English and one Dutch, which are contolled by two private companies, one English and one Dutch, each of which owns 50 per cent of the stock of the two Unilever companies. Prior to World War II, the largest and most famous of international combinations was I. G. Farbenindustrie, the giant German chemical and dye trust. It had subsidiaries in a large number of countries of the world and was also the active participant or instigator of numerous cartel agreements. It was completely reorganized by the allied governments at the conclusion of the war.

During the period since the end of World War II, American investment abroad has grown rapidly. Over the last few years, new direct investments of American companies in western Europe have been running at a little over $1 billion each year, and their total book value has now passed the $9 billion mark. In 1960, a survey by the Department of Commerce showed that exports from a sampling of United States companies to their European subsidiaries amounted to more than $500 million, while imports into the United States amounted to less than $100 million. Nevertheless, sales from United States controlled plants may have tended to retard in a small degree the growth of exports from the United States. In 1962, United States companies with direct investments abroad sold almost three times more of electrical machinery, rubber products, paper, and chemicals from their foreign plants than they exported that year. However, most of these sales could not have been made from this country, and this accounted for the establishment of the plants in Europe. The substantial share of some markets in other countries has led to complaints that there is an increasing degree of United States domination over European industries.[15] The same development has led to even stronger complaints from Canada.

The list of giant corporations operating on an international scale grew rapidly in the years between World War I and World War II, and covered such fields as rayon, chemicals, automobiles, electrical equipment, sewing machines, motion pictures, cable communications, and telephones. Many of the corporations could not be regarded as international trusts, but the development has created a situation very similar

[14]Plummer, *op. cit.*, p. 53.

[15]The foregoing account is taken from *Report on Western Europe* (The Chase Manhattan Bank, New York, November, 1963). This report concludes that the total balance of payments impact of American corporate activity in Europe is relatively small, and is not responsible for the balance of payments deficit.

to the trust issue in this country. The modern corporation now poses a problem that transcends national boundaries.

WEBB-POMERENE ASSOCIATIONS

Permissible Activities

Export associations may be set up under the Webb-Pomerene Act, which authorizes co-operation among business rivals in export trade of the United States. Since 1920, the number of such associations in existence has varied somewhat but has approximated fifty from year to year. Thirty-two such associations were registered with the Federal Trade Commission in 1961. They have the power to fix prices and output for export trade; and they may engage in price discrimination in the foreign market, provided that they do not influence the domestic market thereby or do not prejudice independent American exporters. Available evidence indicates that they have been able to make widespread use of international price discrimination. The first pronouncement of policy on foreign activities of export associations was set forth in the Commission's "Silver Letter" of 1924. In this, the Commission stated: "There is nothing in the act which prevents an association formed under it from entering into any cooperative relationship with a foreign corporation for the sole purpose of operation in a foreign market. The only test of legality in such an arrangement would be the effect upon domestic conditions within the United States."[16] Under this interpretation of the law, the Steel Export Association of America, a Webb-Pomerene Association, was able to collaborate with the International Steel Cartel on price and quota agreements. In 1938, representatives of the export association took part in policy-making decisions of the cartel and its affiliated syndicates. The Association agreed to recognize the domestic market of other cartel members and, in return, received recognition of certain areas as American spheres of influence. American exporters were given export quotas, and the Association assumed responsibility for keeping American exports within those assigned quotas. If the Association was unable to maintain this control, it obligated itself to pay penalties, even though the excess of exports was the result of the failure of independents to co-operate in the program.

In July, 1955, however, the Commission alerted export trade associations that price-fixing arrangements with foreign competitors could not be considered exempted by the Webb-Pomerene Export Trade Law from antitrust consideration under the Sherman Act.[17] The Commission gave as its reasons for changing its position the legislative history of the

[16]Federal Trade Commission, *News Summary*, No. 31 (July 15, 1955).
[17]*Ibid.*

act and court decisions in the United States Alkali Export Association and Minnesota Mining and Manufacturing cases.[18]

Commission Activities

Under the Webb-Pomerene Act, the Federal Trade Commission may make investigations to see whether export associations have violated the law. If the Commission concludes that this has happened, it may make recommendations to the association for the readjustment of its activities to end the violations. In accordance with these provisions, the Commission recommended[19] that the Pacific Coast Forest Industries and Export Trade Association discontinue the use of contracts which required all members to sell their products through the Association, because the Commission considered that these contracts restrained the trade of other domestic competitors. Similarly, it recommended that the Export Screw Association[20] discontinue activities aimed at buying out foreign competitors in order to restrict imports into the domestic market and to exclude foreign manufacturers.

The role of the Commission in Webb-Pomerene supervision has been very limited, and no antitrust suits have resulted from its findings. It now proposes to take a more active part in securing compliance with the law. "For the first time in Webb-Pomerene history the Office of Export Trade is ascertaining the activities of each export association to spotlight possible antitrust violations and joining with the Department of Justice and the Department of State to formulate a common course of antitrust action."[21]

The first court decision treating the liability of Webb-Pomerene Associations under the antitrust laws, was *United States Alkali Export Association, Inc.* v. *United States* (1945).[22] It was brought by the Department of Justice without previous examination by the Federal Trade Commission. The Supreme Court upheld the District Court, which had ruled that agreements through the Association by major American producers of alkali products with foreign associations and companies dividing world alkali markets, assigning international quotas, and fixing prices in certain territories violated the Sherman Act. The Webb-Pomerene Act did not sanction cartel agreements, because they were not agreements in the course of export trade. The Court held that imposing upon the domestic market restraint which banned all imports of a given commodity violated the law, and so did the use of an export association

[18]See below for discussion.

[19]40 FTC (1945). See Report of the Attorney General's National Committee, *Antitrust Laws*, p. 111.

[20]43 FTC 980 (1947); see also *Carbon Black Import, Inc.*, 46 FTC 1425 (1949).

[21]Federal Trade Commission, *Annual Report* (Washington, D.C.: U.S. Government Printing Office, 1956), p. 56.

[22]325 U.S. 196.

to stabilize domestic prices by removing products of its members from the domestic market. The fact that the Commission had not examined the activities of the Association made no difference.

There are two possible areas of conflict between the Webb-Pomerene Act and the Common Market based on the Treaty of Rome (1958). The first of these depends on the interpretation of Article 85 by the Common Market Cartel Commission. It is possible that a Webb-Pomerene Association that is exempt from United States antitrust laws might be engaging in practices in the Common Market which violate Article 85. The second area of conflict may emerge from interpretation of the antitrust provisions of the Treaty of Rome such as to make them applicable only to agreements or practices which affect trade within the Common Market. American antitrust laws apply to export cartels and extraterritorial agreements. American firms are forbidden from participating in such cartel arrangements, even if they are Webb-Pomerene Associations if such arrangements in any way affect United States commerce.[23]

Appraisal of the Webb-Pomerene Act

It is difficult to see wherein this legislation merits anything but condemnation. The demand for it on the part of some businesses is understandable. It also might be defended on the grounds that it had a use in protecting American interests in markets which were too often cartelized and that this country was determined to pursue an aggressive policy in foreign trade. This presupposes, of course, that the United States intended "to fight fire with fire." If this was to be done, the mere permitting of combinations was inadequate. To be effective, they needed to be backed up by government action. Furthermore, domestic antimonopoly policy needed to be changed. An antimonopoly policy at home and the reverse abroad were bound, at least in certain respects, to be self-defeating and in outright conflict with each other.[24]

The United States has been unwilling at any time to proclaim that, as a matter of national policy, it intends to enter into an economic struggle with the other nations of the world. Nor would such a pronouncement have been consistent with its stand at the Versailles Conference. When the First World War ended, this nation was in a position to exer-

[23]*Economic Policies and Practices*, Paper No. 4, Private Trade Barriers and the Atlantic Community Joint Economic Committee, 88th Cong., 2d sess. (Washington, D.C.: U.S. Government Printing Office, 1964). The laws of Great Britain do not impose such severe restrictions on corporations in that country. See Michael Conant, *op. cit.*, pp. 874–75.

[24]Leslie T. Fournier, "The Purposes and Results of the Webb-Pomerene Law," *American Economic Review*, Vol. XXII, No. 1 (March, 1932), pp. 18–33; Eliot Jones, *The Trust Problem in the United States* (New York: Macmillan Co., 1921), chap. xvi. For a different point of view, see Wendell Berge, *Cartels: Challenge to a Free World* (Washington, D.C.: Public Affairs Press, 1944), chap. xii.

cise effective leadership in world affairs and to lend strong persuasion to end economic conflict that aided in bringing on the war. The Webb-Pomerene Act was interpreted by many foreigners as a deliberate effort to capture markets abroad.[25] In any case, it was a clear indication that the United States was being swept into the vortex of postwar economic nationalism. It is consequently difficult to understand the support given to it by President Woodrow Wilson. It may be true that American exporters were subjected to certain handicaps; but many of these arose from inexperience in foreign trade, from preoccupation with domestic issues, and from lack of development, because of this, of a highly specialized foreign trade service. In the light of this country's interest in world peace, the handicaps to peaceful trade presented by foreign combinations should have been met by government action designed to bring about the elimination by foreign governments of those policies which were adopted for economic aggression. Whether such an approach could have succeeded may be an open question; but the moral position of the United States was weakened by this legislation and by the tariff policy, both of which resulted in foreign hostility and retaliation.

The defense that is advanced for the Webb-Pomerene Act is deplorable, in view of the fact that we are presumably endeavoring to break down world barriers. More important from the standpoint of antitrust, the legislation also constitutes a threat to the antimonopoly policy on the home front. It is true that associations are not excluded from the operations of the Sherman Act within the United States; but surely, it is naïve to believe that this can have much real meaning. Not only does common action in associations for foreign trade present convenient means for getting together on domestic policy, but also the very fact that these associations are to control foreign trade makes influence on domestic prices a simple matter. Surely, we have had enough experience with trade associations to be fully aware of the difficulties of distinguishing between legitimate and illegitimate activities. When producers are encouraged to pursue monopolistic practices in foreign trade, it will take more ingenuity than we have shown thus far to prevent them from effecting highly favorable results to themselves on the domestic scene. This was recognized by Judge Wyzanski in the Minnesota Mining case, when he said: "Now it may very well be that every successful export company does inevitably affect adversely the foreign commerce of those not in the joint enterprise and does bring the members of the enterprise so closely together as to affect adversely the members' competition in domestic commerce. Thus every export company may be a restraint. But if there are only those inevitable consequences an export association is not a re-

[25]D. B. Copland and J. G. Norris, "Some Reciprocal Effects of Our Anti-Trust Laws with Special Reference to Australia," *Annals of the American Academy of Political and Social Sciences,* Vol. CXLVII, No. 236 (January, 1930), pp. 117–24.

straint."[26] Furthermore, even though an association comprises almost an entire industry, it may lawfully fix export prices. It seems clear that legislation which sanctions this contradicts both our domestic and our foreign economic policies.[27]

FOREIGN COMMERCE AND THE ANTITRUST LAWS

Trade or Commerce with Foreign Nations

Antitrust is one of several interrelated governmental policies bearing on the foreign economic policy of the United States. As a result, evaluation of the administration of antitrust policy as applied to the foreign commerce activities of the American firms or foreign firms doing business in this country must take into consideration the impact of that administration on both domestic and foreign policies. The Sherman and Clayton Acts specifically include trade or commerce with foreign nations in their provisions. Therefore, such commerce is subject to their prohibitions, and no department of government can grant exemption thereto without congressional sanction. The territorial scope of the jurisdiction of antitrust legislation consequently presents some difficult questions of both law and economics.

Antitrust legislation is not applicable to foreign corporations if they do not do business in this country, even though their actions affect our commerce. Nor, apparently, is it applicable to the activities of an American enterprise within a foreign country in the absence of the firm's being a party to some concerted action in direct and substantial restraint of commerce of the United States.[28] Because of differences in the laws of different countries, it is possible that enterprises in other countries might execute arrangements in their country of allegiance comparable to our Webb-Pomerene Associations, thereby restricting their trade with this country. Presumably, if they transacted business in the United States, they would be violating the Sherman Act, for ". . . it is settled law . . . that any state may impose liabilities, even upon persons not within its allegiance, for conduct outside its borders that has consequences within its borders which the state reprehends."[29] The courts find it necessary, therefore, to pay attention to the international complications that are likely to arise and to treat them with considerable circumspection, in order that the defendant may not get caught in the laws of conflicting jurisdictions.[30]

[26] *United States* v. *Minnesota Mining and Manufacturing Co.*, 92 Fed. Supp. 947 (1950) 965.

[27] But see Report of the Attorney General's National Committee, *Antitrust Laws*, pp. 113–14. The majority of this Committee favored retention of the law, but the minority supported the above evaluation.

[28] See *ibid.*, pp. 67–70; also *American Banana Co.* v. *United Fruit Co.*, 213 U.S. 347 (1909).

[29] *United States* v. *Aluminum Co. of America*, 148 Fed. (2d) 416 (1945) 443.

[30] *United States* v. *General Electric Co. et al.*, 82 Fed. Supp. 753 (1949) 878.

Some Leading Cases

The detailed study made for the Twentieth Century Fund, Inc., by Professors Stocking and Watkins,[31] covering eight case histories in sugar, rubber, nitrogen, iron and steel, aluminum, electric lamps, and chemicals, showed that American enterprises participated in all of them and, in many instances, played a leading role. Concern over national defense in this country resulted in extensive government investigations and aggressive action by the Antitrust Division. Practices disclosed by the investigations indicated that American participation in internal cartels in some products and industries resulted in cartel domination of domestic and world markets in those fields.

In the case of *United States* v. *Aluminum Company of America* (1945),[32] the courts were called upon to deal with the problem of violation of the Sherman Act by a foreign corporation. Over a period of many years, participation of the Aluminum Company of America in international cartels had taken two lines of action. Alcoa was able to obtain a monopoly of the domestic market prior to World War I, and it participated actively in the organization of international cartels. As a result of antitrust proceedings, Alcoa signed a consent decree in 1912 that canceled cartel agreements entered into in 1908. Moreover, Alcoa did not enter the new cartel agreement of 1912; but its wholly owned Canadian subsidiary, the Northern Aluminum Company, was a member. The restrictions in the 1912 agreement applied solely to the sales of aluminum outside the United States.

After World War I, Alcoa resumed its endeavors to secure control of the domestic market. At the same time, Alcoa expanded its activities abroad, especially in Europe, and after 1923 entered into express agreements with major European aluminum interests regarding exports to the American markets. In 1928, Alcoa formed a new company in Canada to represent it in all international arrangements and transactions. This new company was called Aluminium, Ltd. At first, Alcoa and Limited had interlocking directorates; but after 1931, Alcoa relied upon a community of interest. In 1931, a Swiss corporation, Alliance, was set up, the stock being owned by the members of the cartel, one share for each hundred tons of their several annual capacities, as set forth in what was known as the "Foundation Agreements," signed on July 3, 1931. Aluminium, Ltd. held stock in Alliance.

Alcoa, as noted earlier,[33] was found guilty of violating the antitrust laws in its domestic activities but was adjudged not to be a member of the

[31]Stocking and Watkins, *op. cit.* See also Stocking and Watkins, *Cartels or Competition?* (New York: Twentieth Century Fund, Inc., 1948).

[32]148 Fed. (2d) 416. See also *United States* v. *General Dyestuff Corp.*, 57 Fed. Supp. 642 (1944).

[33]Chapter 14.

cartel. The Court held that Limited had participated in the cartel but that this did not involve Alcoa because the two companies were—formally, at any rate—completely separate. The Court did not think that there was sufficient evidence to conclude that Alcoa was a party to the alliance. Limited, however, by its participation, had violated the Sherman Act. The Court issued an injunction forbidding Limited from entering into any cartel or agreement like that of 1931. The Court was able to do this because of Limited's business in the United States. In 1950, Judge Knox even ordered the termination of the community of interest in Alcoa and Limited because of the possible effect on competition in aluminum production in the United States.[34]

Violation of the Sherman Act as it relates to foreign commerce was one of the issues in *United States* v. *National Lead Company, et al.* (1946).[35] National Lead and Titan Company, Inc., were charged with participating in an international cartel that dated back to 1920. The lower court found that National Lead, through its wholly owned subsidiary, Titan Company, Inc., owned substantial stock interests in competing enterprises in other countries. This and a series of agreements entered into between 1920 and 1944 led the court to conclude that competition among the producers of titanium was nonexistent. No titanium pigments entered the United States except with the consent of National Lead. Furthermore, the court found that the suppression of world commerce was not limited to articles produced by patented processes but extended to all products within the "licensed field." The cornerstone of the system was the private regulation of international trade brought about by illegal international agreements.

> No citation of authority is any longer necessary to support the proposition that a combination of competitors, which by agreement divides the world into exclusive trade areas, and suppresses all competition among the members of the combination, offends the Sherman Act . . . . Indeed the major premise of the Sherman Act is that the suppression of competition in international trade is in and of itself a public injury; or at any rate, that such suppression is a greater price than we want to pay for the benefits it sometimes secures.[36]

The complexities that may arise in applying the Sherman Act to the foreign commerce of the United States are exemplified in a lower court case, *United States* v. *Minnesota Mining and Manufacturing Company* (1950),[37] decided by Judge Wyzanski. The record showed that the four defendants in this case organized the Export Company, a Webb-Pomerene Association, in 1929. This company sought to sell abrasives, made in the United States, to foreign buyers when they could be sold as

[34]*Ibid.*

[35]332 U.S. 419. This decision upheld completely the lower court ruling and opinion on this issue.

[36]*United States* v. *National Lead Co. et al.*, 63 Fed. Supp. 513 (1945) 523–24.

[37]92 Fed. Supp. 947.

profitably as abrasives made by its foreign subsidiaries, which operated under the name of Durex. In 1929, also, the defendants entered into the main patent agreement under which each member licensed its foreign licenses to Durex. The latter agreed, in turn, not to import into the United States any product in which patented inventions were used. The record showed that Durex sales in England and Canada increased rapidly after World War II, while Export Company's business declined in those countries.

The nub of the question, said the court, was whether the evidence in the case proved that the defendants could not profitably have exported from the United States a substantial volume of coated abrasives to the area supplied by their jointly owned factories abroad. They obviously made larger profits through the subsidiaries than if they had sold from this country.

The court found that the four American manufacturers controlling four fifths of the export trade in the industry agreed to do their business in particular areas through jointly owned factories. This constituted a conspiracy, and the court also felt that the arrangement precluded other American competitors from these foreign markets. The fact that what was done may have been "in the interest of American enterprise" was no defense. Financial advantage, said the court, is a legitimate consideration for an individual nonmonopolistic enterprise. It is irrelevant where the action is taken by a combination and the effect, while it may redound to the advantage of American finance, restricts American commerce. "Nothing in the statute [Webb-Pomerene] nor in its legislative history, nor in the penumbra of its policy justifies or has any bearing upon the right of defendants to join in establishing and financing factories in foreign lands. Export capital is not export trade."[38] Judge Wyzanski also remarked that if the establishment of individual plants by firms restricted American commerce, that would not be a conspiracy. It should be noted, however, that the courts have ruled that conspiracy can exist between a firm and its subsidiaries; in addition, the Timken case, to be discussed in a moment, casts doubt on Judge Wyzanski's dictum. In any case, joint ownership of factories in other countries rests on very precarious legal grounds at the present time, as far as the Sherman Act is concerned.

This was emphasized by the decision of the Supreme Court in *Timken Company* v. *United States* (1951)[39] and the dissenting opinion of Mr. Justice Jackson. As early as 1909, Timken Roller Bearing and British Timken's predecessor had made comprehensive agreements for a territorial division of world markets for antifriction bearings. In 1928, Dewar,

[38]*Ibid.*, p. 963. On a similar basis, a lower court in *United States* v. *Imperial Chemical Industries et al.*, 100 Fed. Supp. 504 (1951), found that joint ownership of Duperial in Argentina and Brazil by Du Pont and Imperial Chemical Industries violated the Sherman Act. The history of the activities of these two companies constitutes an amazing story of high diplomacy in the industrial field.

[39]341 U.S. 593.

an English businessman, and Timken co-operated in purchasing all the stock of British Timken. Some of the stock was later sold to the public; and at the time of the suit, Timken owned 30 per cent and Dewar 24 per cent. In 1928, Dewar and Timken organized French Timken and together owned all of its stock. The three companies allocated trade territories, fixed prices on products, co-operated to protect each other's markets, and participated in arrangements for imports to and exports from the United States. The Supreme Court held that the fact that there was common ownership of control of the contracting corporations did not liberate them from the impact of the antitrust laws. Nor did it find any support in reason or authority for the proposition that agreements between legally separated persons and companies to suppress competition among themselves and others could be justified by labeling the project a "joint venture." The Court took the position that the provisions in the Sherman Act against restraints of foreign trade are based on the assumption that export and import trade in commodities are both possible and desirable.

The real meaning and import of the Timken case remains to be seen. To this writer, this case and preceding cases seem to identify foreign commerce with the physical movement of goods and commodities, and also seem to make the Sherman Act more restrictive of operations in foreign commerce than in domestic. Mr. Justice Jackson did not feel that it should be regarded as an unreasonable restraint of trade for an American industrial concern to organize foreign subsidiaries, each limited to serving a particular market area. If branches, instead of corporations, had been used, there could have been no conspiracy, and the law would not have been violated, he argued. Perhaps the fact that the subsidiaries were not 100 per cent owned influenced the Court. Whatever may be the explanation, the meaning of foreign commerce under the law appears to be unduly restrictive and, if maintained, may well impose uneconomic limitations on American investments in foreign countries.[40]

Consent Decrees

The Department of Justice has settled, by consent decree, a large number of alleged violations of the Sherman Act by cartel arrangements. These consent decrees do not establish any proof of violation or points of law; but they do indicate that American firms, in various ways, have participated extensively in cartel arrangements over the years. Nor can there be any doubt that most of these have been to the detriment of the foreign and domestic commerce of the United States.[41]

[40]For a more extended discussion of this problem, see *Antitrust Laws, op. cit.*, pp. 88–91. For a possible conflict that may arise in connection with the Common Market in Europe, see *Economic Policies and Practices, op. cit.*, p. 18.

[41]See *United States* v. *Alba Pharmaceutical Co.*, consent decree, Commerce Clearing House, *Trade Cases*, ¶ 5, 2650 (1941); *United States* v. *Standard Oil Co. of New Jersey, ibid.*, ¶ 5, 2927 (1942); *United States* v. *Bendix Aviation Corp., ibid.*, ¶ 5, 7444 (1946);

(*Continued on next page.*)

PROBLEMS OF NATIONAL POLICY

Importance of American Participation

American firms have participated extensively in cartel and international combinations, especially since the close of World War I. The cases which have come before the courts have arisen from charges by the Department of Justice that the agreements to which American companies have been a party have restricted competition in both the domestic and the foreign markets, in violation of the antitrust laws. These allegations have been sustained in court in a large number of cases. Moreover, the record, as disclosed in these legal proceedings, as well as in the investigations conducted by the United States Senate, emphasizes the fact that effective participation by American business in international trade restrictions is dependent upon restriction in this country of the market for the products involved. One of the principal requisites of successful cartelization in international trade has been membership by American firms which were in a position, or whose arrangements with the cartel would put them in a position, to exercise sufficient control over production in this country to remove the threat of disruption of market restraints by competition from other American firms.

Thus, the focal point of the cartel problem is on the domestic scene. Cartels can achieve little success in international trade if they are unable to secure the co-operation of powerful producers in the industrialized countries. The promise to respect each other's domestic markets is of little value if competition is already vigorous in those markets. The pledge to restrict competition in foreign countries can be of advantage only if interlopers can be curbed. The competitive power of American firms is such that they stand as a constant threat to cartels if they are not included. If they are included, they immediately endeavor to restrain, directly or indirectly, the foreign commerce of the United States. When they are also parties to agreements that restrict foreign competition in the American market, they not only violate the antitrust laws but also, for the sake of private gain, decide what foreign goods shall be available to American buyers. It goes without saying that American firms should not be permitted, by themselves, to make agreements with foreign producers to limit foreign competition in the markets in this country. Unfortunately, the record in the cartel cases indicates, all to clearly, that this has been done.

Agreements among independent firms in the United States to re-

United States v. *Precipitation Corp.*, *ibid.*, ¶ 5, 7458 (1946); *United States v. Diamond Match Co.*, *ibid.*, ¶ 5, 7456 (1946). See also C. D. Edwards, *Economic and Political Aspects of International Cartels* (U.S. Senate, Committee on Military Affairs, Monograph No. 1) (Washington, D.C.: U.S. Government Printing Office, 1944). The consent decree involving the American participants in the International Oil Cartel was noted earlier in this chapter (footnote 14).

strain trade have met with systematic disapproval by the courts. Vigorous prosecution of agreements with foreign firms that restrain either the import or the export trade of this country, on the same basis that the Sherman Act has been applied to domestic restrictions, would serve as a healthy deterrent to such arrangements. It would also impose a serious handicap to international cartels. The Department of Justice is to be commended for its aggressive action and the substantial progress it has achieved in the last few years. Moreover, foreign firms may be prohibited from participating in cartel agreements that affect the American market if they operate in the United States and wish to continue to do so. This was the situation which made it possible for the Court to enjoin Aluminium, Ltd. of Canada, from entering into cartel agreements that would restrict production in aluminum so as to have an effect upon imports into this country. Recent court decisions indicate clearly that the antitrust laws possess ample power to deal with American firms or foreign firms which wish to do business in this country, if they enter into arrangements to restrict imports and exports. This will not catch enterprises that deal with American businesses outside this country, where the American firms are not party to any agreement. This appears to be a minor part of our foreign commerce, however.

Patents

In recent years, patents have come to play a major role in the formation of industrial cartels. The right of a patentee to exercise exclusive control in the country in which a patent is granted over the invention or technical process which is patented has given to industry a means of restricting competition by agreement that frequently makes cartelization a simple process. Standard Oil (New Jersey) and I. G. Farben made agreements designed to buttress Standard's position in the oil industry and I. G. Farben's in chemicals by cross-licensing, which eliminated competition from each other in the respective fields. Patent-licensing agreements have commonly been reinforced by arrangements and understandings whereby secret processes and so-called "know-how" have been made available to cartel members. Although the courts in this country have held that the rights conferred by patents cannot be used to extend the monopoly beyond that contained in the grant, the powers thus conferred are so extensive as practically to assure monopoly, especially when they are the means of obtaining exclusive use of the patents of powerful and aggressive foreign enterprises. Moreover, secret agreements are facilitated, because the strategic points of control can be maintained within the law under present patent legislation. It should be noted, however, that when patent agreements are clearly an instrument for effectuating a conspiracy to divide markets, they will be held to violate the law.[42]

[42] *United States* v. *Imperial Chemical Industries, Ltd.*, 100 Fed. Supp. 504 (1951

Technical knowledge and processes are not the sole possession of any one country. It is highly desirable to encourage their interchange; and the patent laws are designed—in part, at least—to make foreign inventions available in this country. It is argued that lack of adequate protection would encourage secrecy and discourage interchange. There is some truth in this contention; but present arrangements may lead to the very results which we desire to avoid, and, what is more, the price is too great. The argument for "adequate protection" is too frequently advanced as a guise for protection far beyond that afforded to domestic firms. There seems to be no need for a more "liberal" interpretation of the laws than that which applies to American patentees. Patent agreements frequently have aimed at keeping important products from the American market; and when they have been available, it has been at the price of monopoly control.

One may also doubt that secrecy constitutes a serious threat. In the highhanded game of economic nationalism, as played by the totalitarian states, basic inventions are hardly likely to be made accessible to nationals of other countries. Moreover, the tremendous amount of technical and scientific knowledge available to American industry makes serious lag improbable. The thoroughgoing curbing of the monopoly powers inherent in present patent rights would force industry to rely on its competitive ability to protect its position, and there seems to be little doubt that this would overcome any handicap secrecy might impose. As has already been pointed out, reform in this direction is needed to deal with domestic monopoly. Revision of the patent laws of the United States, so as to make them more compatible with competitive enterprise, would go a long way toward diminishing the potency of cartels. Unfortunately, to date, "the foreign commerce cases have typically involved such an integration of patent rights with an overall unlawful purpose and the use of unlawful means that the courts have had little occasion to adjudicate the legality of patent practices as separable conduct."[43]

The Corporate Device

Of equal, if not greater, importance as a means of organizing cartels is the corporate device. Under present-day legal conditions, it is possible to adapt the corporation to meet almost any obstacle that may arise. Community of interest, interlocking directorates, foreign subsidiaries interlocked with domestic corporations and vice versa, joint ownership with foreign corporations of subsidiaries in third countries, and even twin holding companies related only by the fact that the same group con-

[43]Report of the Attorney General's National Committee, *Antitrust Laws*, p. 86. The case of *United States* v. *Singer Manufacturing Co.*, 374 U.S. 174 (1963) discussed in Chapter 18, *supra*, concerned "only the United States trade and commerce arising from the importation into the United States of a particular type of household sewing machine" (176). There were no international complications or conflicts with laws of other countries.

trols the stock of each, as in the case of the Lever trust, all serve to aid in the formation of either giant international combines or cartels. Cartels are frequently headed up by a corporation receiving a charter from Lichtenstein or Switzerland or some other unimportant industrial state, the members of the cartel each owning stock in the corporation. Sometimes, as in the case of Alcoa, the connections are indirectly established by a community of interest with a foreign company that is a party to the cartel. International combines, as distinct from cartels, are simply the counterpart on the foreign scene of outright consolidation in this country.

Remedies for the corporate phase of international combines and cartels are parallel to, and part of, the domestic problem of corporate control. The rights and privileges conveyed by corporate charters, like those of patents, are all out of proportion to the responsibilities imposed. Perhaps the greatest single source of power arises from the right of one corporation to own the stock of another, although community of interest is a close second and is more elusive. Legislation capable of solving corporate difficulties in this country would probably deal effectively with international combines and cartels as far as American firms and the domestic markets of the United States are concerned. However, the ownership of foreign subsidiaries presents a somewhat more difficult problem that needs careful study. The joint control of Duperial by Imperial Chemical Industries and Du Pont is a case in point. It may not be easy for this country to pass judgment upon the desirability or undesirability of such ownership; yet, it may be embarrassing if one policy is followed at home and another abroad. Recent decisions, such as in the Minnesota Mining and Timken cases, leave the legal status of the single international combine in doubt; but Imperial Chemical Industries indicates that joint ownership may be a per se violation of the law.[44]

Unilateral versus International Action

The complex problems that have arisen as the result of the growth of business to an international scale emphasize the difficulties of unilateral action. The fact that modern industry transcends national boundaries in many cases points to the desirability of international action for dealing with the issues that have emerged. Progress in this direction is bound to be slow, especially in view of the present state of world affairs.

There are those, however, who feel that strong action on the basis of international agreement should be undertaken now. A minority of the Attorney General's National Committee believes that the "government [should] support, negotiate and sign, and the Congress, by appropriate procedures ratify an international treaty or convention against restraints of trade and monopolistic practices."[45] Professor Corwin Edwards

[44]See also *United States* v. *Minnesota Mining and Manufacturing Co.*, 92 Fed. Supp. 947 (1950) 963.

[45]*Antitrust Laws, op. cit.*, pp. 98–108.

takes the position that American policy has been isolationist in this respect, and that it is necessary for this country to alter its present position of nonsupport if we do not wish to leave the leadership toward harmonizing cartel policies in the hands of the European countries.[46] The report to the Joint Economic Committee states "the fact that national and regional laws exempt export cartels and extraterritorial agreements from their competency demonstrates the recognition and necessity of international agreement, if these types of cartel agreements are to be prevented. The passage of the Trade Expansion Act of 1962 indicated to an economically unifying Europe that the United States is ready and willing to move toward a closer trading relationship with the nations of the Atlantic community through the reduction of tariffs and the elimination of quotas and other nontariff barriers of trade. Once this step has been taken, the need for international agreement regulating restrictive business practices will be more apparent than ever before."[47]

While cartels, patents, and the irresponsible use of the corporate device are definite impediments to the freeing of the world markets and are constant challenges to the successful administration of the antitrust laws at home, they do not seem to constitute the most pressing problems. Professor E. Mason expresses this in the following words:

> He [Mason] would venture as his opinion . . . that the injury inflicted by tariffs on domestic competition and American foreign trade has been several times greater than the effect of cartels; the current agricultural policy is likely to be much more damaging to exports than the total of American cartel practices; the intergovernmental commodity agreements will reduce the volume of postwar world trade more drastically than international cartels; and that the problem of dealing with state trading monopolies will far overshadow the difficulty of dealing with cartels.[48]

Prospects of decisive results through international treaty arrangements do not appear to be very bright at the present time. However, as long as the United States pursues an antitrust program at home, it is necessary to pursue it on all fronts. An antitrust policy in this country cannot meet with success if American business is allowed to enter into cartels and other restrictive arrangements in international trade. At the present time, American industry has the greatest competitive capacity in the world. The contention of foreign competitors that they have to combine to meet American competition cannot very well be met by American insistence on participation in cartels. If international trade is to be freed from restrictions, this country must refuse to allow its nationals to restrict. If antitrust is to be successful at home, it must also be anticartel.[49]

[46]*Foreign Antitrust Laws in the 1960's*, *op. cit.*, p. 69.

[47]*Economic Policies and Practices*, *op. cit.*, pp. 21–22.

[48]Mason, *op. cit.*, p. 28. Reprinted by permission of the publishers.

[49]See Stocking and Watkins, *Cartels or Competition?* chap. 12, "Report of the Committee on Cartels and Monopoly of the Twentieth Century Fund."

Chapter 20 CAN THE ANTITRUST LAWS SUCCEED?

INTRODUCTION

The continuance of a private enterprise system in the United States depends upon our ability to maintain an industrial structure that is primarily competitive in nature. If we are to be successful in doing this, the basic ideas which underlie the antitrust laws will have to form the foundation of public policy. The question is frequently raised, however, whether the antitrust laws can succeed. If the answer to this is given in the affirmative, the next question is: "What is necessary to assure their success?" The first query raises a doubt as to the possibility of success and suggests the inference of failure—or, at least, very severe shortcomings—to date. The answer to the second question depends, in part, upon the kind of a world in which we are going to have to live for some years to come. If the world were to be engulfed by a war which used all of the weapons now available for international conflict, any discussion of what the organization of society might be like afterwards would be utterly futile at this time. For purposes of present discussion, therefore, this possibility must be eliminated by assumption.

There remains, of course, the question whether the "cold war," with its heavy demands upon resources for armament purposes, places such a severe strain upon the economy as to render the continuance of a vigorous private enterprise system impossible. This raises the fundamental issue of the survival of the democratic way of life in the modern world. Unless one assumes that freedom and democracy are solely, or primarily, matters of economics, it will take more than armament pressures to devitalize private enterprise. A free society cannot exist under a state monopoly of the processes of production,[1] and it seems reasonable to assume that the people of the United States are more interested in freedom than in anything else.

Lack of Support for Antitrust

In the years since World War I, and most especially since 1930, serious doubts have risen in many quarters as to the possibility of successful application of the antitrust laws. Some regard a competitive private enterprise system as a thing of the past because of the effects of technol-

[1]This matter was discussed at some length in Chapter 1.

ogy, and take the position that any attempt to retain or revitalize the regulatory framework of competition is simply harking back to a dead era. Then there are those who aver their faith in private enterprise but who insist that experience with the Sherman Act demonstrates the impossibility of halting the growth of giant combinations and of compelling competition in many industries. They view the growth of big business as a natural one that should be allowed to follow its preordained course. In between these extremes are those who support the general idea of preventing monopoly and of enforcing competition but who find all kinds of compelling reasons why they themselves should be treated as exceptions if an attempt is made to apply the policy to them.

Where lack of support for the antitrust laws arises from the belief that private enterprise is finished, the discussion is shifted to new ground, because antitrust can have no meaning except in a private enterprise economy. It has no application where the state has a monopoly of the production processes; in fact, it has no application to publicly owned enterprises even in a private enterprise economy. Those who oppose the antitrust laws on the ground that big business is solely the result of natural growth which, if impeded or limited, will lead to a reduction of economic efficiency, fail to recognize two things. First of all, the growth of big business is not a purely natural growth process. It is institutionally conditioned. The legal privileges given to business and the modern corporation are by no means inconsequential in their influence on the size of the enterprise and the number who are able to compete. Second economic efficiency is important, but it is not the only factor to be considered. If economic efficiency results in organizational patterns that constitute a threat to other significant aspects of the social and political structure, it may be necessary to make a choice. If this has to be done, it does not follow that efficiency always will be selected, because it is the means to an end, not an end in itself. Furthermore, the proponents of the natural growth argument are taking the position that environment is the decisive factor, when, in point of fact, their own actions are based on quite the contrary assumptions. The regulation of private enterprise assumes that environment may be shaped, at least within limits, to attain desired goals.

Where lack of support for the antitrust laws rests on special interests, it indicates either a failure to grasp the nature of the basic issues involved in the regulation of private enterprise or individual selfishness. Generally speaking, those who oppose the antitrust laws on the ground that their particular kind of endeavor is of such a nature as to require exemption are equally insistent that this is not applicable to all other types of activity. They believe in competition and in rules that compel conformity to its precepts; but they find reasons why they should be put in a distinct category, either as a matter of emergency treatment or because of special circumstances surrounding the type of productive activity in which they are engaged. Motor transport, ocean shipping, milk supply, numerous areas of agriculture, and labor are illustrations of this. It is not necessary, in rebuttal, to argue that all private enterprise, under all circumstances, should be subject to precisely the same rules of conduct; nor do we, as a matter of public policy, put them all in the same category. The exceptions to antitrust, however, should be based upon economic characteristics of the industries which are sheltered or partially sheltered from it; otherwise, political pressures and special interests enter the picture. Unless industries fall into the very narrow category of public utilities, competition must be the prevailing rule if private enterprise is to perform the functions which establish the rationale of its existence. Where the exception is granted to these enterprises, the alternative is strict regulation or public ownership, not freedom to operate contrary to antitrust, without controls designed to replace the competition which has been eliminated or was not feasible in the first place.

Limitations of Antitrust

The structure of modern industry is such that no prohibition against monopoly can be of universal application. Industries such as public utilities and transportation that require special types of control are placed under commissions whose responsibility is to regulate them in the public interest. Separate treatment for some of our natural resources may be necessary in the interests of conservation. The importance of coal in the economy and the disruptions it has suffered have led to attempts in many countries to deal with the problems that have arisen. Petroleum has also been a matter of considerable public concern because of fears of depletion of resources through wasteful exploitation arising from rivalry among some of the oil-producing states in this country and because of outmoded property rights in mineral resources. Emergency controls and programs may also be called for in some major industries as a result of serious dislocations arising from war. Agriculture is a case in point. The expansion of American agricultural production under the impact of World Wars I and II created maladjustments, the correction of which, it was felt, could scarcely be left to the uncurbed forces of supply and demand.

The danger of the special treatment approach is that it can easily be diverted or distorted into special privilege. Yet, few would deny that precisely the same program for all industry, without any exceptions, is not feasible. Separate regulations, designed to deal with specific problems that are not amenable in any satisfactory way to the general or exclusive application of the antitrust laws, seem to be the most practicable remedy.[2]

[2]When the regulation is imposed because of the unavoidability of monopoly, there is the alternative of government ownership and management. Whether this is desirable or not depends upon one's evaluation of a number of other issues. These questions will be discussed in Part V.

If this regulation is to fit into the structure of a private enterprise economy, however, it should be focused on making competition work to the fullest extent and on eliminating the advantages of monopoly by every endeavor on the part of public authority to approximate the competitive norm. Where the controls are of an emergency nature, they should be set up with the clear-cut purpose of remedying the difficulties in such a way that competitive conditions are restored and once more put into operation.[3]

Apart from special exemptions specifically accorded, the antitrust laws should be universally applicable, as a constant warning that the exceptions are made for specific purposes and only on condition that other regulations are imposed in their place and enforced by public authority in the public interest against the abuse of monopoly. All special legislation should be viewed in this light and should be consciously integrated with the general policy of control.

Requisites for Successful Enforcement

The successful application of the antitrust laws will have to be based upon careful consideration of four key factors: (1) the political atmosphere, (2) the adequacy of the laws to meet the various situations to which they are to be applied, (3) the technological conditions of industry, and (4) the effectiveness of the administrative procedure.

Probably the greatest single impediment to the success of the operation of the antitrust laws over the last thirty years has been the generally inhospitable political atmosphere. This may be attributed—in part, at least—to the pressures of war and the dislocations that it has generated. In part, the lack of enthusiasm may be traced to bewilderment arising from rapid technological change and to a rather widespread belief in the technological inevitability of monopoly over a large area of industry. Possibly the most important factors, however, have been a lack of positive expression of faith in the virtues of a private enterprise economy and a lack of positive action to implement that faith. Either we have taken such an economy for granted, or else we have had serious doubts about its efficacy. To these impediments must be added the unremitting pressure of special group interests which, mistakenly or otherwise, have constantly advanced their cause on the grounds of social justice or the interests of the economy as a whole. This has found expression in the welter of legislation enacted in the late twenties and thirties that not only nullified the effectiveness of the antitrust laws in large segments of the

[3]The most unfortunate aspect of our agricultural policies has been that they have not been aimed at permanently removing the surplus capacity which called forth the program in the first instance. Instead, they have perpetuated and even aggravated the initial source of the difficulty. Now, they are giving rise to some serious international questions, especially with countries like Canada and Australia, and with the Common Market group.

economy but also even took positive steps to diminish the impact of competition by price controls, subsidies, etc. It is not surprising that enforcement of the antitrust laws, where they remained applicable, was pursued with little vigor or that Congress was unwilling to take any significant steps to strengthen them in content or enforcement. Proposals for the strengthening of the laws relating to competition and monopoly must assume a reawakened interest in the virtues of competition and a determination to establish the conditions under which it can operate effectively.

Whether the antitrust laws can succeed really turns on two questions: (1) Is it possible for private enterprise and competition to survive under modern conditions of technology and organization? (2) Is the antitrust approach to the control of private enterprise, assuming its continuance to be possible, the appropriate one? The answer to the first question turns on institutional considerations rather than economic ones. As was pointed out in earlier chapters, the evidence that concentration has increased and that competition has declined in the present century is lacking. If private enterprise and competition disappear, it will not be because of inexorable economic principles or laws but because of other factors. The point to be made here is that whether private enterprise and competition can and do survive will depend upon political and social considerations and influences. If private enterprise is to remain, however, it must be in a competitive environment. In other words, whatever the future may hold with regard to private versus some other form of ownership organization, competition is a *sine qua non* for a successful private enterprise economy. If it can be assumed that we want private enterprise and competition, then it is essential that public policy be focused on that objective. This brings up the question whether antitrust is the appropriate means of achieving it.

THE NEED FOR ANTITRUST

The Problem of Federal Regulation

The policy which the Sherman Act was intended to embody was that competition should be maintained and that monopoly engendered by the desire to enhance profits by strategic control over supply should be proscribed. Subsequent antitrust legislation has been intended to supplement this basic policy, even though legislation such as the Robinson-Patman Act—at least in the way in which it has been applied—has included clauses which seem to contradict the basic philosophy. It seems safe to say, however, that such contradictions as may arise out of lack of precision of expression in the legislation, or court and administrative failure to maintain consistency in the applications of the law, are not evidences of intent to weaken antitrust. These remarks, of course, are not applicable to many of the exemptions and special privileges that have been granted. How these fit into antitrust is a matter of consistency in over-all economic policy rather than the underlying objectives of the antitrust laws themselves.

The Sherman Act was a continuation of the tradition of public hostility to monopoly resulting from special privilege or deliberately acquired by predatory action, and of public support of free and fair competition. This had been embodied in the common-law doctrines of restraint of trade, conspiracy to monopolize, and unfair competition. With the development of railroad transportation in the nineteenth century and the rapid spread of interstate industrial and commercial activities after the Civil War the federal government could no longer ignore its responsibility for establishing rules of conduct for private competitive business at the federal level. This was because there were no applicable federal rules in the absence of federal legislation, and the states found themselves powerless to act on matters strictly concerned with interstate commerce as the result of Supreme Court decisions. The application of standards of conduct for private competitive business by the states was incapable, therefore, of grappling with the rapidly growing problems of large business, and especially the business corporation, even if the states had been unanimously enthusiastic about enforcing effective controls.

It was but natural that Congress should resort to the common-law rules applicable to private competitive business as the basis for federal policy. This was strictly in the common-law tradition, as has already been pointed out. It was only at common law that impairments of competition, such as restraint of trade and monopoly, had found any legal limitations. Congress apparently felt that it was giving recognition to the common-law rules, at the federal level, except that it was making them more positive, both in the prohibitions contained in the statute and in the means of enforcement. In both of these, the major change was with regard to restraint of trade, which was not an offense at common law that called for positive public action. Whether Congress envisaged more with regard to the limitations on monopoly than was contained in the common law may be a matter of debate, especially since it was assumed that monopoly was only the result of deliberate attempt and could not exist if competition were maintained. Whether the Sherman Act would have been passed had federal action under common law been possible cannot be answered. In the absence of such a basis of action, some sort of legislation to fill the gap was unavoidable. From the vantage point of over seventy years of experience, it is difficult to see what else could have been done. In other words, the federal antitrust laws were a necessary part of a private enterprise economy in a country with a federal form of government such as that which is found in the United States.

The Success of Antitrust

Viewed in its historical setting, antitrust must be regarded as a success. Private enterprise and competition can operate only within established rules of conduct, and those rules must be such as to promote competition and restrain the deliberate development of monopoly. It was on this presupposition that Congress had to act; and on this basis, the Sherman law was passed. The United States has developed the largest, the most complex, and—by quantitative standards—the most efficient industrial structure in the world. Perhaps it would have been even more impressive with different federal legislation, but it would hardly be reasonable to contend that it would have been better without any. In addition, given the assumption of a private enterprise economy and the desire to maintain it, generalized proscriptions with regard to competitive conduct are necessary because of the fundamental assumption of common law that a person may do anything that he is not specifically prohibited from doing. Limitations on his freedom of action, therefore, must be developed out of experience as the particular objectionable practices emerge.

If the law and its enforcement have failed to keep pace with these, the difficulties should be traced to shortcomings in developing policies on the foundations of antitrust, unless one assumes that the problems which have emerged are incapable of being resolved under private ownership. Ignoring this assumption for the moment, it may be pointed out that what constitutes the shortcomings of the antitrust laws is by no means a matter of agreement.[4] There seems to be rather general agreement that there are shortcomings, but ideas regarding these range from the one extreme that argues that the laws are far too restrictive in nature, to the other, that they are practically useless. In between these points of view lies the vast majority of opinion that sees in antitrust as it has developed to date the foundations of a continuing program adaptable to the changing requirement for rules of conduct for an industrial society, the outlines of which can never be discerned far in advance.

One final point may be made with regard to the success of antitrust. The vigorous policy of enforcement pursued in the years immediately preceding World War I served to bring to an abrupt halt the more brazen and ruthless behavior of the "trusts." The Northern Securities case may not have eliminated the holding company as a device for organizing combinations with considerable monopoly power; but had such a decision not been rendered, the holding company would have provided a

[4]See, for example, the sharp differences of opinion exhibited in Report of the Attorney General's National Committee, *Antitrust Laws* (Washington, D.C.: U.S. Government Printing Office, 1955). See also D. M. Keezer (ed.), "The Antitrust Laws: A Symposium," *American Economic Review*, Vol. XXXIX, No. 3 (June, 1949), pp. 689–724; G. W. Stocking and M. W. Watkins, *Monopoly and Free Enterprise* (New York: Twentieth Century Fund, Inc., 1951), chap. 16; *Current Antitrust Problems* (Hearings before Committee on the Judiciary, House of Representatives, 84th Cong., 1st sess.) (Washington, D.C.: U.S. Government Printing Office, 1955), Serial No. 3, Part I, especially pp. 203–412; C. Kaysen and D. F. Turner *Antitrust Policy: An Economic and Legal Analysis* (Cambridge: Harvard University Press, 1959); M. S. Massel, *Competition and Monopoly, Legal and Economic Issues* (Washington, D.C.: The Brookings Institution, 1962).

means for effectuating monopoly, the sole limitation on which would have been the lack of ingenuity of lawyers and promoters in exploiting the uncurbed opportunities available to them. The Standard Oil case ended ruthless and bare-faced bludgeoning of rivals. Perhaps subsequent practices were more subtle; but, at least, a large number of convenient and effective methods were removed. Similarly, deliberate control of the market by price-fixing agreements was outlawed very shortly after the Sherman Act was passed; and in the period following World War I, this was extended to much more subtle arrangements, which even gave rise to the protest that "conscious parallelism of action" became a violation of the law.[5] Resale price maintenance by contract was declared to be illegal and came to be recognized as a legitimate business practice later on, not as a result of interpretation of antitrust but as a consequence of a legislated exception to the laws by Congress. Renewed vigor of enforcement in recent years has narrowed the concept of monopoly which may escape the condemnation of the laws; and corporate integration is faced with more hurdles today than it was suspected, heretofore, that the law provided.

THE SHORTCOMINGS OF ANTITRUST

Even though antitrust may be appraised as having been a success—at least, in the sense of the word that it has supplied the legal framework for the development of a vigorous system of private enterprise—there are, nevertheless, shortcomings at the present time that call for serious public attention. Some of the deficiencies are external to the antitrust laws themselves, and many observers would probably regard these as the most formidable obstacles to a successful policy at the present time.[6]

In some respects, the most stubborn of these external factors is the inconsistent approach to public policy for private business that is manifest in the mass of federal legislation that grants various kinds of special exemptions, without careful consideration of the bases for the special treatment or the impact of it on the general policy of maintaining competition. There is no gainsaying the fact that atomistic competition is not possible throughout the entire economy. The economic advantages of large-scale production impose limitations in many industries which preclude it. In transportation, as will be pointed out in Part V, competition, for a long time, was able to play only a limited role. In public utilities, it is still very severely circumscribed by technology, which compels

[5]In the order against *Chas. Pfizer and Co. et al.* (7211) of the Federal Trade Commission, Commissioner Anderson protested "For the first time, to my knowledge, it appears that we are prohibiting consciously parallel behavior, even though such behavior does not stem from agreement, tacit or express, but is merely the independent decision of one firm to follow the price leadership of another." *News Summary*, Federal Trade Commission (August 16, 1963).

[6]See W. Adams and H. M. Gray, *Monopoly in America* (New York: Macmillan Co., 1955).

recognition of the fact that these enterprises are public utilities because they are monopolies and not vice versa. Where technological conditions lead to monopoly in the production of goods and services which are essential to the consuming public and for which there are no very ready substitutes, the antitrust laws are inapplicable. But no one has ever tried to apply them to conditions of local monopoly of this character, nor has it been necessary to pass legislation exempting them from antitrust. Exempting legislation has been passed primarily to permit the limitation of competition in industries where technology precludes monopoly and where competition comes as close to being atomistic as can be obtained. This has been done in the name of preventing competition from being ruinous or of protecting small business from the predatory onslaughts of powerful competitors. This is exemplified in fair-trade legislation, present regulatory policies with regard to motor transport, and agricultural legislation not only permitting but even compelling market agreements to restrict price competition.[7] What this means is that public policy is denying the validity of the competitive process precisely where the economic structure of industries is most favorable to competition. A private enterprise system is not likely to exhibit unusual vigor if public policy insists on curbing competition by legislative compulsion.

Perhaps the most difficult part of the whole problem of developing a unified and coherent antitrust policy lies in securing a consistent approach at the legislative and executive levels of the federal government. Solutions to the contradictions and conflicts that arise from this source are not easy to find. Congress and the executive branch of the government must assume the final responsibility for formulating public policy toward business and for expressing that public policy in legislation. It is the duty of the courts and the administrative agencies to interpret and apply the law. Apart from constitutional limitations which the courts may place on the legislative authority of Congress, the latter can correct contradictions, inconsistencies, or shortcoming if it sees fit to do so. The courts and the administrative agencies cannot do this. They may struggle to apply the laws that conflict with each other, and they may try to weave the statutes into patterns that are as consistent as the legislation may permit; but they are supposed to carry out the will of Congress, as expressed

[7]The problem of the relation of labor to the antitrust laws is by-passed in this discussion. If labor is to be excused from the operation of the antitrust laws because of the technical difficulties of applying these laws where collective bargaining is recognized as a legitimate means of arriving at wage contracts, and as not being inconsistent with a competitive system, then a new corpus of law should be developed which reconciles collective bargaining and a competitively oriented economy. Monopolizing and conspiracy to monopolize are not the exclusive tactics of private business. A restoration of freedom of choice to the workingman to join or not to join a union would go far toward reducing the present monopoly position of some of the unions. The compulsions that are permitted under existing legislation are no less tyrannical because they are imposed for the "good" of the laborer. Nor is the competitive process as a means of efficiently allocating resources aided by these compulsions.

in the laws passed by it. No matter how unwise they may think the legislation is in terms of public interest or how much some of the legislation contradicts the fundamental tenets of the Sherman Act, they can but apply the law as they read it, if it is within the power of Congress to enact it. Administrative agencies may be able to advise Congress within the ambit of their authority, but the courts cannot even do this. Nor can these agencies, by co-operative action among themselves, bring about a unified approach to interpretation and application, in the absence of congressional mandate.

A solution to this difficulty may not be easy to find, but it would appear that the leadership should come from the executive branch of the government. Public regulation of business by the antitrust laws occupies such an important position in government in this country today that a spokesman for antitrust in the federal cabinet is called for. The Attorney General is not the one for this. The policy problems go far beyond the legal arm of the executive branch of the government. The problem here is somewhat parallel to that which is faced in the field of transportation, which is discussed in Part V.

Another shortcoming in antitrust administration and policy arises from the failure of the states to shoulder their responsibilities with regard to public policy for competitive business. Some of the states have been active and aggressive in regulating transportation and public utilities. None of them has undertaken an effective program for the control of competitive business, and a majority of them has enacted legislation which contradicts the national policy as expressed in the antitrust laws. The federal government cannot be expected to deal with the problem at all levels of business activity. Protests against the encroachment of the federal government on state powers, if the states deliberately fail to shoulder their responsibilities of regulation, are likely to fall on deaf ears. Federal agencies are unlikely to permit, willingly, escape from their controls if the states fail to show some interest and initiative.

SUBSTANTIVE ISSUES

Legislative Revisions

In the previous chapters which dealt with their interpretation and enforcement of various sections of the antitrust laws, specific recommendations for legislative action were advanced where it was felt that substantive changes were necessary to clarify or strengthen the laws. Some of these recommendations called for the repeal of legislation such as the Miller-Tydings Act, the McGuire Act, and the Webb-Pomerene Act; others called for revision of the Robinson-Patman Act so as to clarify congressional intent and to remove contradictions between it and the Sherman law. Revision of the patent laws was proposed, in order to eliminate some of the restrictive potentialities of patents that are not necessary to an effective patent system and to resolve some of the differences of opinion that have arisen within the Supreme Court. Congressional clarification of the application of the Sherman Act to American firms operating directly through subsidiaries in other countries, and the policies which these firms may be permitted to follow with regard to home office and branch or subsidiary activities, was also recommended. In this same connection, consideration should be given to the application of the doctrine of conspiracy under the Sherman Act to parent corporations and subsidiaries. At the present time, practices may be followed by a firm operating through branches or divisions that would be condemned as conspiracies if undertaken by subsidiaries, even though the latter were 100 per cent owned. Some people advocate removing the application of the conspiracy doctrine to subsidiaries. This author would recommend an attempt to do just the reverse—namely, to endeavor to secure legal means to provide the same restrictions to activities of branches and divisions that are now applicable to subsidiaries.

Frequently, it is not easy to distinguish between requirements for change in antitrust that are the result of substantive shortcomings in the law and those that arise from procedural inadequacies. Where difficulties arise from court interpretation and enforcement, these may be—in part, at least—the result of the procedure of direct enforcement through the courts. Where the deficiencies are revealed through commission decisions, they may also be procedural in nature. For example, the Robinson-Patman Act may require substantive changes through legislative action, but the greatest difficulties seem to have arisen through the faulty enforcement procedures of the Federal Trade Commission. To the extent that this is so, the remedy is first to reform the Commission and then to change the law after new attempts at enforcement have disclosed where the real difficulties lie. Before dealing with procedural issues, however, some aspects of the corporate problem as it relates to antitrust should be examined.

The Business Corporation and Antitrust

For the most part, the corporate form of business organization presents no special problems, either in size or control, because the number of persons interested in particular businesses may be just as few as those connected with partnerships and other such types, and the relationship between ownership and management is almost as close in one case as it is in the other. The crux of the issue which the modern corporation presents lies with large-scale enterprise and large financial institutions, which present problems of concentration of power and control over wealth that call for special public attention. Most of these giants are corporations; but it should be noted, in passing, that large private banking houses which are not incorporated at all have exercised great power in the financial field and that the Massachusetts trust, although less widely used, presented the same difficulties as corporations in holding company development in the public utility field.

The growth of a relatively small number of corporations to their present gigantic stature is the result of a number of different factors that have influenced the development of our modern economic structure. The adaptation of the corporate idea to the organization of private business not only provided the means whereby the expansion essential to the full realization of the economies of size could take place but also afforded a means of integration that made it possible for aggressive leadership to have its cake and eat it, too—as well as to take somebody else's cake. The corporation offered, at one and the same time, the opportunity for business leaders to finance giant enterprises while still retaining control of their affairs, to decentralize management and operations and thereby preserve the economies of size, and to spread into related fields of endeavor so as to mitigate the rigors of competition or eliminate it entirely.[8] The three main factors which have made this possible were (1) the right of one corporation to own stock in another corporation, (2) the right of a corporation to engage in almost any kind of business it wants to undertake, and (3) the right of an individual to own stock in any enterprise whose stock he can acquire.

A great deal of the blame for the problems that the large business corporation has created has been laid at the doors of state legislatures, which have granted extensive privileges in corporate charters without imposing corresponding responsibilities. The burden of this point of view is that the principal evils which have arisen from the use of the corporate device could have been prevented by corporation laws that imposed strict standards of incorporation, together with regular accountability of the corporation to the authorities which granted the charter. If, in addition, federal incorporation had been required of those enterprises carrying on a primarily or predominantly interstate business, the main loopholes would have been plugged.

There can be little argument concerning the abuses that have resulted from the charter-mongering activities of some states and from their consequent failure to impose anything resembling reasonable standards of incorporation and corporate responsibilities. Investors have been defrauded in scandalous fashion by inside manipulation and promotional activities. Omnibus charters, which allow the recipients to engage in literally any kind of business they see fit to undertake, have practically

[8]Louis B. Schwartz takes the position that "The logic of the situation calls for a public reexamination of the justification for these very largest multibillion dollar enterprises." *Antitrust Laws*, *op. cit.*, p. 128. Joel B. Dirlam says: "If the Congress wishes to make further statutory revisions aimed at deconcentration of existing centers of power, it must make a sharp break with traditional Sherman Act policy by specifying precisely the percentage or absolute limits for existing concentration. Only in this way would present levels of concentration be substantially reduced." *Administered Prices: A Compendium on Public Policy*, *op. cit.*, p. 131.

eliminated charter restrictions on the scope of corporate activities. The power to issue a variety of different kinds of stock without voting privilege has made it possible to concentrate control in the hands of a few individuals with small stake in an enterprise and, frequently, with little interest in its ultimate success. The lack of any meaningful minimum requirements for accounting and annual reports, either to stockholders or to the state, has made it possible for corporate officers to establish their own standards of accountability. Finally, the granting of charters which permit a corporation to own stock in any other corporation, or to be incorporated solely for that purpose, has given such scope to financial integration that, in the absence of other restraints, there is no limit to size or to the type of monopoly power that may be developed. These sources of abuse must be brought under control if the regulation of industry is to be successful.[9]

The story of the roles played by the holding company and intercorporate stock ownership in the growth of outright consolidations and integrated combinations has already been recounted. If corporations had not been granted the privilege of owning stocks, and if charters had confined corporate activities to a very narrow field of endeavor, the structure of industry would have been quite different. However, outright prohibition of intercorporate stock ownership, under all circumstances, or legislative refusal to grant the privilege, in the first instance, would not have been a practical approach. Furthermore, it could have been circumvented by such arrangements as community of interest or partnerships that performed the function of holding companies. Attempts, through charter provisions or legislation, to confine industrial corporations to a comparatively narrow field of endeavor would encounter analogous difficulties. It is practicable to have legislation confining railroad corporations to the task of railroad transportation; commercial banking affords a similar illustration. To define activities in the industrial field, however, in a similar and realistic fashion, is much more difficult. Vertical integration, in certain situations, also is certainly economical; but to specify those cases in general incorporation laws hardly seems to be feasible.

The need for thoroughgoing reform by the states of their incorporation laws and the administration of them is obvious; but this, of itself, would be quite inadequate for the present situation. Action on the federal level is also required. Apart from the difficulties involved in obtaining concerted state action to secure minimum uniform standards of incorporation, the states cannot control interstate commerce or take action to enforce federal antitrust laws. The necessity of regulating corporate activities, if our antitrust policy is to be made effective, makes federal

[9]The Securities and Exchange Commission has done much to eliminate corporate financial abuses, but it has had nothing to do with the relationship of corporate organization and antitrust.

legislation imperative. The scope of such control, its administration, and its specific implementation raise a number of important questions that deserve examination.

Federal control of all corporations whose activities bring them within the scope of interstate commerce would impose a burden of detail on the federal agency responsible for the administration that would endanger the success of the program at the outset. No matter what means were adopted to effect the regulation, the efforts of the federal authorities would be dissipated in supervising thousands of corporations that are of no real consequence as far as the major problems are concerned. There is real danger in overcentralization of control, and distinct merit in maintaining as much decentralization as possible. For these reasons, it would seem to be wise to limit federal control to the very large corporations, for it is with these that the real problem lies. Present information indicates that not more than 500 industrial corporations have assets totaling $50 million each or over.[10] This figure is commonly taken as marking the lower limit of the very large corporation. The number of enterprises falling within this category is certainly not too great for effective supervision. At the same time, this limit would give federal control of the industrial firms that created the problem of "bigness." If sales instead of assets were taken as the gauge of the very large corporation and $50 million were the dividing line, the number subject to federal control on this basis would be something over 500. This would certainly not be too large a number over which effective supervision by a federal agency could be exercised. Experience would demonstrate whether it was necessary to extend regulations to include smaller firms.

Federal control could be imposed in one of two ways. The first method would be to require all businesses over a specified size and engaging in interstate commerce to secure a federal charter. The second would be to require them to obtain a license from the federal administrative agency. There has been a great deal of discussion of the respective merits of these two possibilities. Many writers feel that federal incorporation is essential to a workable control of the corporation. Such a requirement, however, would raise many legal issues; and successful application would still require the services of an administrative commission. The alternative would be to set up federal legislation that would establish general standards which corporations would have to meet if they wished to engage in interstate commerce. This is analogous to the

[10]Railroads and other transportation companies and public utilities engaged in interstate commerce are excluded from this discussion because of the special regulatory procedures which apply to them. The same remarks are applicable to financial institutions such as banks and insurance companies. Corporations of this nature require special treatment and, therefore, need to be regulated separately from industrial concerns. The Fortune Directory of the 500 largest industrial corporations in the United States in 1962 shows 491 with assets of over $50 million. All had sales over $50 million; smallest sales total being $85,934,000.

procedure that obtained until 1944 in the field of insurance. An insurance company which was incorporated in one state had to meet the conditions specified by another state if it wished to do business there. The powers possessed by the Interstate Commerce Commission over railroad corporations, by the Securities and Exchange Commission over the public utility holding company, and by the Federal Reserve Board over banks which are members of the Federal Reserve System are also illustrative of what can be accomplished by federal legislation without federal incorporation. Regardless of the means by which federal control was exercised, corporations regulated by specific agencies such as the Interstate Commerce Commission, the Federal Power Commission, the Federal Reserve Board, and so forth should be excluded, because it is desirable to avoid as much overlapping of functions as possible, and because the control of the corporation needs to be integrated with the pattern of control for the industry.

It is not necessary in this treatment to go into all the details that legislation for federal control of the corporation should contain. A few items need special mention, however. The law should be written in the broad terms usually characteristic of statutes that are administered by commissions, so that a definite policy can be developed and adaptations made to meet specific situations. Consolidation, or merger in any form, of enterprises over the specified minimum should be permitted only with the consent of the commission. Whether consolidation of any of these firms with smaller ones should also require commission consent is a more debatable issue. Some restrictions are probably necessary. Possibly, consolidation could be allowed under such circumstances without requiring commission consent, provided, however, that the commission could prevent it if public interest demanded such disapproval. Intercorporate stock ownership, short of 100 per cent control, should require commission sanction, even when no question of direct competition is involved. The practice of fractional ownership has been used altogether too extensively to extend power and to form loosely knit federations that seriously impede the competitive process. To be effective, such a requirement would also necessitate commission control over the right of individuals to own stock in more than one of the large corporations. Community of interest presents too easy a means of evading the antitrust laws. What this really amounts to is that the holding company needs to be defined in terms of ownership rather than form of business organization. It should, therefore, include persons, as well as companies.[11] The example for this type of legislation has already been set by the Public Utility Holding Company Act of 1935.

Expansion, either vertical or horizontal, is dealt with only in part by the foregoing proposals. Most large enterprises in this country have

[11]See J. C. Bonbright and G. C. Means, *The Holding Company* (New York: McGraw-Hill Book Co., Inc., 1932), chap. i.

achieved their present stature with the aid of consolidation of one form or another. Many of them, however, have expanded into different fields of endeavor or acquired control over a series of processes and raw materials by internal growth. Much of this has been economical and is inherent in modern technology. It may also lead to as effective a monopoly position as absorption of independents. If the consolidation channel is closed, some form of limitation will have to be imposed on internal expansion. An upper limit to size does not seem to be practicable and would get at the problem only obliquely, if at all. The logic of the situation would seem to call for commission control over the types of activities that a particular corporation would be allowed to undertake; but it is difficult to know, at the present time, just where the line should be drawn.[12] It would probably be wise to confine immediate legislation to the more urgent requirements and to leave the formulation of policy on this matter for further experience and study to disclose whether any such over-all action is necessary and, if so, the precise direction that it should take.

Recent court decisions in the administration of the Celler-Kefauver amendment to the Clayton Act have indicated that severe barriers now exist to mergers between corporations that engage in the same or quite similar lines of production. However, this does not get at the issue of mergers between undertakings that are so thoroughly diverse as to fall completely outside of a reasonable interpretation of "any line of commerce." Diversification of this sort may bring under one corporate management and control: canned foods, magazines, soft drinks, steel, lumber, paint manufacturing, meat packing, and broadcasting. It may be contended that such conglomerate organizations do not reduce competition because the merger still leaves the same number of competitors. How they can add to competition is somewhat of a mystery, since they would seem to offer no advantages of economies of scale, specialization, or integration of functions, and if the testimony in the General Electric investigation means anything, they would only compound the problems of mangerial supervision and communication. Moreover, if "bigness" is a problem, and it certainly seems to be, this is one sure way to obtain it without apparently encountering difficulties with the law as it stands at the present time. To this writer, the objectives of the promoters of these enterprises is financial, and the building of corporate empires. This is not conducive to a healthy competitive economy. Careful consideration should be given to legislation which will limit each company to a functionally coherent group of business activities.[13]

[12]Restrictions of this type are in force in the field of transportation, but the line is much easier to draw in this case. The wisdom of the restrictions, however, is a matter of keen debate.

[13]See C. D. Edwards, *Big Business and the Policy of Competition* (Cleveland: The Press of Western Reserve University, 1956), chap. iv.

If the foregoing suggestions were adopted, federal control would have to be enforced through an administrative commission. The logical agency to perform this function would be the one entrusted with the task of enforcing antitrust laws. The Federal Trade Commission is the only one now in existence that might be in a position to discharge these responsibilities. Whether it would be able to do this satisfactorily without thoroughgoing reorganization will be dealt with in the next section.

THE PROBLEM OF ENFORCEMENT

Present Deficiencies in Enforcement

Substantive changes alone are inadequate to insure the success of the antitrust laws. It is now pretty generally agreed that the administrative procedure by which they are enforced is not geared to the task which it is called upon to perform. Present methods of enforcement suffer from two main weaknesses—namely, the division of authority for interpretation and application of the laws among the courts, the Department of Justice, and the Federal Trade Commission, and the reliance upon strictly judicial procedures for enforcing the Sherman Act. The joint responsibility of the Department of Justice and the Federal Trade Commission with respect to the Clayton Act makes for duplication of effort and possible conflict, while the Federal Trade Commission's expansion of the idea of unfair methods of competition into the area of Section 2 of the Sherman Act points up the fact that responsibility for enforcement of the antitrust laws is so diffused that a coherent public policy is scarcely possible.

Regulation in the industrial field has long since passed the stage where the task can be performed adequately by the courts. This was recognized before World War I and was one of the factors behind the passage of the Federal Trade Commission Act. The problem of regulation today is more than the negative one of prohibiting certain types of action; it requires the development of policy through the application of legislation to particular situations. The courts are not constituted, by temperament or procedure, to carry out this function. They are set up to interpret the law; and, although the law thereby develops as a result of application by the courts, the formulation of public policy in specific ways is not one of their primary functions. Furthermore, the procedure of the courtroom, the judicial practice of passing only on the issues at bar, the growth of the law by precedent, and the inability of the courts to embark upon investigations into the broader issues of policy make it impossible for them to develop any continuous process of regulation. A systematic and consistently formulated policy of industrial control calls for an administrative agency set up for that purpose.

From the standpoint of public policy, the subtleties of monopoly and restriction of competition are too great to be resolved satisfactorily in the courtroom. In modern industry, practically every firm possesses some degree of monopoly. Whether or not it is in keeping with public interest must be decided in each particular instance, seemingly, by a body charged with developing public policy. Monopoly and restraint of trade today are more comprehensive concepts than those envisaged either by the Sherman Act or by the court decisions enforcing it. It is rarely possible to speak of an industrial firm as being a monopoly, even though most of them possess monopoly power which, in some instances, is very extensive. The Sherman Act is, under present methods of enforcement, unable to deal with a wide range of these. Moreover, they are not all necessarily "bad" or "undesirable." The courts, however, are not the appropriate agencies to make this distinction. That is primarily a legislative function. It is not possible to frame legislation which is sufficiently inclusive to comprehend all of the practices which may be undesirable from the viewpoint of public interest. The answer, therefore, seems to lie in developing administrative agencies empowered to give specific content to the statutes in the light of changing conditions. This would make possible the formulation—in co-operation with industry itself, much of the time—of practices and procedures to be proscribed because of their undesirable effects on the operation of the market. The administrative agency, as an expert body, would also be in a position to recommend new legislation as experience disclosed the need for it.

Restriction of competition arising from agreements has, on the whole, been more satisfactorily adjudicated than that resulting from single combinations, although even here, the line between those practices which are considered to be restrictive and those which do not fall into this category has been drawn in uncertain and wavering fashion. The difficulty of establishing, to the satisfaction of a court, the existence of coercion, purpose to curtail production, or intent to enhance prices, or the fact that the necessary consequence of the arrangements leads to these results, either places too great a strain on the judicial process or leaves without benefit of careful examination a wide range of practices which may have an important bearing on public interest. Whether agreements among competitors or practices of trade associations—such as price publicity, for example—are in the public interest depends upon the specific circumstances. Again, as in the problem of consolidations and mergers, it is difficult to see how the issues can satisfactorily be resolved in the atmosphere of the courtroom.

The basic difficulty seems to be that the present laws make antitrust enforcement primarily a legal battle. The courts have probably been too lenient, especially in the interpretation and enforcement of the Sherman Act; and the cases show a definite lack of consistent approach. For this, the courts are not entirely to blame, since Congress has not seen fit to remedy the situation. The task of sifting facts essential to the enforcement of the laws has been placed upon the courts; and as a result, they have taken on many aspects of an administrative tribunal. This has saddled them with a burden which they have been unable adequately to discharge and for which they have neither the competence nor the staff. Extensive investigations and careful weighing of facts in the light of public policy are functions which need to be discharged by administrative agencies responsible to the legislature. Only in this way, it appears, will it be possible to develop a consistent and statesmanlike approach to the fundamental issues involved in the successful continuance of an economy based upon private enterprise.

Recent decisions by the Supreme Court, emphasizing market relevance and other such considerations in Sherman Act cases, point up the need for more effective means of fact finding and evaluation than can be obtained through direct court enforcement. The application of remedies to the situations found in the Alcoa, Paramount, and United Shoe Machinery cases call for the exercise of judgment at the public policy level that the courts should not be called upon to make. It may be true that remedies are not penalties and that the rights of the defendants should be protected, consistent with the requirements of sound public policy; but when a corporation has been found guilty of violating the law, the remedy must become the primary consideration. It is also true that the courts and the Department of Justice may seek the aid of the Federal Trade Commission on such matters, but they have not done so; and they are not likely to under present circumstances. Finally, the district courts are supposed to be the judges of fact in the cases before them; but the Supreme Court all too frequently substitutes its judgment for that of the lower courts, thereby undertaking to weigh the facts rather than confining its efforts to matters of law. Judge La Buy's evaluation of the facts of the Du Pont-General Motors case seems to be correct from a strictly legalistic point of view, but the verdict of the majority of the Supreme Court was in accord with sound public policy. Developments of this sort, however, could soon get us back to the unsatisfactory position of the United States Steel and International Harvester cases.[14]

Administrative Unification

The initial step in reorganizing the administrative procedure would be to unify enforcement of the antitrust laws by placing all of them under a single agency. The Antitrust Division would not be satisfactory for this because of the difficulties of direct enforcement through the courts that

[14]In *United States* v. *Singer Mfg. Co.*, 374 U.S. 174 (1964), the Supreme Court specifically stated in footnote 1 (p. 175) what dissenting judges have noted many times and what has now become a center of controversy, namely that the lower courts have been deprived of their primary function of ascertaining and evaluating the facts. "Whatever may have been the wisdom of the Expediting Act in providing direct appeals in antitrust cases at the time of its enactment in 1903, time has proven it unsatisfactory. . . . Direct appeals not only place a great burden on the Court, but also deprive us of the valuable assistance of the Courts of Appeals."

have just been discussed. The alternative, therefore, is to place all of antitrust under a single administrative agency. The principal changes in administration that this would call for would be to give it the initial responsibility of applying the Sherman Act and to eliminate the authority of the Department of Justice to carry cases under it and the Clayton Act directly to the courts.

The procedure that such a commission would employ to enforce the law would probably have to be patterned after the Interstate Commerce Commission and the leading public utility commissions. The commission would have to exercise extensive investigational functions and follow up its disciplinary actions.[15] It should be given the authority to take action on its own initiative and to sit as an administrative court to try cases brought before it.[16] The latter could be instituted by any interested parties. Because of the magnitude of the task and the desirability of placing the initiation of action on as broad a basis as possible, it would probably be wise to retain the Antitrust Division of the Department of Justice, giving it the power to prosecute cases before the commission, but depriving it of the right to take direct court action against alleged offenders or to enter into consent decrees. Of necessity, appeal could be had from the commission's decisions to the courts by any interested party. It is reasonable to expect that the courts would confine their attention, in such instances, rather strictly to matters of law, as they now do in cases involving the Interstate Commerce Commission or even the Federal Trade Commission. A clear-cut congressional mandate to the commission would carry great weight in bringing this about.

The adoption of the foregoing proposals would require a regrouping of administrative responsibilities along functional lines. There are good reasons, however, for using the Federal Trade Commission as the body to administer the antitrust laws. It already enforces all but the Sherman Act; and it has endeavored, with some success, to widen its scope to comprehend the broader phases of the antitrust problem. It has shown real competence in broad investigations and has accumulated a considerable fund of information on the pattern and operation of the industrial structure. It has gained a great deal of experience over the years of its existence and, as the result of a considerable amount of litigation, has made considerable progress in achieving a fairly clean-cut delineation of its functions and those of the courts. A new commission would have to start from scratch, and this would be a real disadvantage.

An attempt to turn the Federal Trade Commission into a full-fledged agency for the enforcement of antitrust would undoubtedly en-

[15]The present procedure, whereby only a limited number of "hand-picked" cases are brought to trial under the Sherman Act, is totally unsatisfactory.

[16]It would have no power, of course, to try cases under whatever criminal provisions the law retained. Where criminal matters were involved, the commission could refer them to the Department of Justice for prosecution.

counter considerable opposition. The legal profession, with its penchant for the courtroom and legal battles, on the one hand, and its dislike for enforcement procedures through administrative agencies, on the other, would oppose transferring the responsibility for the Sherman Act from the Antitrust Division.[17] Others would resist giving the authority to the Federal Trade Commission on the basis of its record to date. The relative ineptitude of the Commission, as compared with the Antitrust Division, in applying sections of the Clayton Act was pointed out earlier. The Commission has also failed to develop a body of "case" law in its own decisions; and too frequently, it has rendered decisions that were not supported by anything resembling an adequate marshaling of evidence.

If these shortcomings are inescapable in the present Commission, or if they constitute an insuperable political obstacle to the extension of its powers, then a new one is in order. This detail is not particularly consequential, because a rewriting of the law and a reallocation of functions would have to be made, in any case. What is important is that the administrative agency be given full authority and be saddled with the responsibilities commensurate with that authority. In addition, the quality and standing of the personnel should be in keeping with the new office. Only men capable of thoroughly judicious deliberations and with the appropriate training and experience should be appointed to the commission. This agency should be accorded the dignity and standing of a court. This does not mean that all the appointees should be from the legal profession, either lawyers or members of the bench; but some membership from the judiciary would be advantageous. Appointments should not be made as a reward for political services.

The functions of the Federal Trade Commission with regard to consumer protection, false advertising, and many other items connected with consumer protection should be administered by another agency. As was pointed out earlier in the appraisal of the Federal Trade Commission, the activities of the latter are too conglomerate and diversified. To establish a special bureau under the Commission to deal with consumer protection would perpetuate the scattering of efforts. It is well to remember that the economic limitations on the scale of operations are not confined to business. They are of equal applicability to governmental agencies.

[17]See Report of the Attorney General's National Committee, *Antitrust Laws, op. cit.*, chap. viii.

PART V

The Regulation of Transportation and Public Utilities

Chapter 21 THE TRANSPORT SYSTEM

INTRODUCTION

The role of transport in the life of every people and every country has been of such importance as to warrant special consideration and treatment by government throughout the ages. The role that it plays in the economic and political life of every country places it in a unique position among man's productive economic activities. In the final analysis, transportation involves all the movement of persons and things from one place to another. This may be in the plant or factory, in a store, on the farm, or at any other place, for that matter. It embraces not only movement for hire, but also that which a firm may perform for itself or that which an individual may undertake for himself.

The public aspects of transportation relate to those movements of persons or commodities from one place to another when some part of the facilities which are utilized are available for use by others than the owners, or are supplied for the use of people other than the owners. It is the public aspect of transport that bears directly upon the problems of public regulation. In this treatment, attention will be focused on the issues of national transport policy. The perplexing difficulties of urban transport and urban transport supply will be passed over, partly because of lack of space but also because they involve other complex urban economic problems that are not part of this book.

Reasons for Separate Treatment

Transportation calls for separate treatment because of its intimate relation to community life. In fact, the idea of community life is impossible without adequate means of transportation and communication. Throughout history, the body politic has found it necessary to participate in the supplying of transport facilities. Even in a country where the utmost possible development of private enterprise prevailed, public participation in supplying transport facilities would be necessary, particularly under modern conditions. It has never been possible to divorce transportation from community concern or interest, because it literally forms the physical framework within which a community is built and constitutes the spatial arteries that keep community life going. Transport routes are also decisive factors in the location of economic activity, thereby evoking public interest in the development and maintenance of them.

There is the further fact that transportation does not respond as readily or as completely to the forces of competition as manufacturing and many other activities. Even though part of the facilities of transport respond with ease, others yield readily to monopoly. Harbors are key points of entry for water transport; railway routes and highways are subject to limitations of terrain; even the seemingly limitless sky is already presenting serious problems of control at key points. The great cost of providing transport facilities, most particularly the harbors or ports and routes for inland transport, has imposed limitations which have restricted competition severely. As a consequence, regulation in some form has been characteristic of transport; and literally throughout its history, it has been subject to more public surveillance than any other of our production activities. In fact, it is in this field that our most comprehensive and varied experience in public regulation has been obtained.

The problems of public regulation of transport today have arisen, in part, from the complex nature of the modern transport structure. To understand these problems, it is necessary, therefore, to have a picture of the principal components of our national transportation plant, together with the functions performed by each and the relative importance of each in the transport structure. It is also necessary to recognize the sequence in the historical development of the different agencies, because it is out of this and the problems connected with this development that our present-day policies, and the assumptions upon which those policies are based, have arisen. Finally, although the different agencies have grown up at different times, they all remain as part of the current transport system; and while their relative positions have changed, they are all of greater absolute importance than at any previous time.

THE NATIONAL TRANSPORT SYSTEM

The national transport system of the United States consists of a network of railways, highways, airways and pipe lines, as well as an extensive system of inland waterways and coastwise and intercoastal water routes. (See Figures 5–9.) These five different modes or agencies of transport, for the most part, operate independently of each other. With relatively minor exceptions, there is no interagency ownership, each transport firm being confined to one particular agency. The five modes of transport are really five different industries, each performing unique services at the same time that each offers services that are quite readily substitutable for those of the others.

Railroads

The railroads constitute the backbone and core of every modern transport system. In the United States, they form the only nationwide system of mass transport, especially of freight. Well over 95 per cent of the total railroad freight tonnage is transported in carload lots, with the products of the mines making up more than half of the tonnage. The railroads are also the largest, for-hire, suppliers of urban and intracity passenger service. The railroad system of this country in 1963 consisted of about 215,000 miles of route, or over one quarter of the world's total mileage. The total estimated net investment in the railroads in 1963 was just over $30 billion. It should be noted that the railroads in this country own all the facilities they use in supplying their services and that they are almost completely privately owned.

Highways

The highway system of the United States consists of over 3 million miles of roads (outside of city streets), over 2 million miles of which are surfaced. Nearly 400,000 miles are of high-type surface. The primary interstate highway system, established by the Federal Aid Highway Act of 1956, calls for 41,000 miles of 2- and 4-lane highways, designed to link the principal cities of the nation by a single network. The total estimated cost of this network, to be incurred over the 15 years to 1972, is something over $50 billion, $37.3 billion of which is to be spent on city freeways, superhighways between cities, and state highways; of this $37.3 billion, $15 billion is to go to city freeways and belt routes. The city and urban problem has obviously become one of the most significant aspects of highway transport, for it mingles terminal and route traffic in a way unknown to the other means of transport.

The net depreciated investment (estimated) in all roads and streets in the United States at the present time amounts to some $60 billion; the estimated requirements for investment in highways and maintenance of them over the next 30 years is $297 billion. The Transportation Association of America has estimated that the total cost of highway transportation for both passenger and freight movement in the United States in 1962 was $85.3 billion. The net investment in highways and streets probably amounts to over $63 billion, which, together with some $75 billion for motor vehicles, gives a total of over $138 billion. This does not cover garages, service and filling stations, and so forth, all of which would have to be included in order to get a figure comparable to that of the railroads. Our system of motor transport is obviously very expensive.

The highway transport system is much more complex than the rail. Motor carriers consist of common carriers, contract carriers, non-regulated carriers for hire, and private carriers not for hire; there is only one kind of rail carrier—namely, the common carrier. Private motor carriers may perform commercial services for their owners, or they may be only for personal use or pleasure. Motor vehicles may be used for short- or long-distance traffic, although the bulk of them is used for short distances. In highway transport, ownership of the motive equipment is distinct from ownership of the roadway; and both of these are usually separate from the servicing facilities. In addition, the roadway facilities may be used by a multiplicity of operators; and none of them is limited to a particular route by the nature of the operation, although they may be so limited by law, particularly the common carrier. In passing, it may be noted that these contrasts between motor transport and rail transport are also true for water and air transport, which are similar in so many respects to motor transportation.

Waterways

Transport by water is the oldest form of bulk transport supply available to man. This confined man's commerce to navigable streams and other bodies of water until the development of the railroad, a circumstance which restricted the location of the major cities of the world to those which controlled key points on water routes or were the point of access to water routes. The domestic waterway system of the United States comprises, first of all, the Great Lakes, which constitute the major inland waterway route of this country, stretching at the present time from the head of Lake Superior to the lower end of Lake Erie at Buffalo, a distance of about 1,000 miles. With the completion of St. Lawrence waterway in 1959, a deep-sea route of 2,347 miles of waterway with a minimum channel of 27 feet from Duluth, Minnesota, to the Atlantic Ocean was created. The second part of our inland waterway system is the navigable rivers and canals, which supply some 2,700 miles of usable water routes, although much of this can accommodate vessels of only shallow draft. The principal river and canal system is the Mississippi, providing water transport from Kansas City, Chicago, and Pittsburgh to New Orleans. Mention should also be made of the New York Barge Canal from Buffalo to Albany, and the Columbia River from Idaho to the Pacific Ocean. The third part of the waterway system is the coastwise routes of the Atlantic, Gulf, and Pacific coasts, and the intercoastal route between the Atlantic and the Pacific via the Panama Canal.

These various routes accommodate mostly bulk traffic, especially coal, coke, lumber, and grain. All are toll-free at present, except the Panama Canal and the St. Lawrence Seaway. As in the case of motor carriers, the vehicle is separated from the surfaceway over which the carrier moves. The carriers are also of different types—mostly privately operated, some for hire, others not, and moving indiscriminately, as far as the route is concerned. No figures are available for the net depreciated investment in waterways of this country and the transport equipment which uses them.

Pipe Lines

Pipe lines constitute a highly specialized type of carrier confined almost entirely, at present, to the products of the oil fields, except for the long-distance transport of water supply. The pipe lines connected with the petroleum industry are of two types—namely, oil pipe lines and natural gas pipe lines. The petroleum pipe lines connect the major oil fields with the principal consuming centers where the refineries are located and with the ports from which the crude oil may be shipped. At present, there are some 123,000 miles of trunk lines and 62,000 miles of gathering lines in this country, varying in diameter from 4 to 26 inches. In addition, there are over 45,000 miles of refined oil or products lines measuring up to 36 inches in diameter. Most of the pipe lines are owned by the major oil companies and have been developed as an adjunct of the oil-refining business. A large number of them, however, are common carriers.

The interstate system of natural gas pipe lines connects principally the natural gas fields of the southwestern part of the United States to virtually all the cities in the country with a population of over 50,000 people. The natural gas lines own the gas which they transport, having purchased it in the field from producers, or having extracted it from their own wells. They do not offer direct competition with other means of transport; but their effect on the railroads, in particular, is severe because of the impact of natural gas transmission on the shipment and use of coal. The total pipe-line mileage of the country for both oil and natural gas has passed the 1 million mark.

Airways

The air transport system of the United States is composed of the airways, airport facilities, and the air transport equipment. The federal airways system consists of a network of lanes 10 miles wide along the most practical routes between cities over which regularly scheduled air transport operations take place. These routes, equipped with navigation aids and traffic-control facilities, now cover over 135,000 miles. They are toll-free. The airports may be privately or publicly owned; but the principal ones are publicly owned, the federal government, under the Federal Airport Act of 1946, contributing up to 50 per cent of the investment. For a project to be eligible for federal aid it must be included in the "national airport plan" which is revised annually by the Federal Aviation Agency.

The air transport service of the United States is supplied by 11 scheduled passenger trunk lines, 2 all-cargo lines, and 13 local service or feeder air lines, all of which are certified by the federal government through the Civil Aeronautics Board. There is also a considerable number of irregular or nonscheduled air carriers (35 in 1962), as well as private planes and those of the armed services. The commercial air transport facilities of the United States provide high-speed passenger service and transport air mail, air express, and some high-grade freight. The total net investment in air transport facilities in this country is not known;

but the Federal Aviation Agency estimated in 1961 that approximately $2.8 would be necessary for the major components for new acquisition and construction in the next eight years. From 1947 to 1959 the total programmed investment by federal and local governments was $1.1 billion. Total capital expenditure on the airways from 1935 to 1959 was approximately $550 million. The total net assets in the United States Scheduled Airline Industry was reported as just over $4 billion for 1962.[1]

Relative Importance of Agencies

The relative importance of the various agencies in the movement of intercity traffic in the United States is set forth in Table 3. It will be

TABLE 3

VOLUME OF INTERCITY TRAFFIC, PUBLIC AND PRIVATE, BY KINDS OF TRANSPORATION

Agency	Ton-Miles				Passenger-Miles			
	1961	1962	Percentage of Grand Total		1961	1962	Percentage of Grand Total	
			1961	1962			1961	1962
	Millions	*Millions*			*Millions*	*Millions*		
1. Railroads and electric railways, including express and mail	566,997	599,977	42.96	43.04	20,527	20,181	2.67	2.52
2. Motor vehicles:								
Motor carriers of passengers	....	....	....	....	19,703	21,279	2.56	2.66
Private automobile	....	....	....	....	692,000	719,680	89.97	89.81
Motor transportation of property	313,141	331,900	23.60	23.81	....	....	....	....
Total Motor Vehicle	313,141	331,900	23.60	23.81	711,703	740,959	92.53	92.46
3. Inland waterways, including Great Lakes	209,706	223,089	15.80	16.00	2,345	2,736	0.30	0.34
4. Pipelines (oil)	233,172	237,723	17.57	17.05	....	....	....	....
5. Airways (domestic revenue and pleasure and business flying, including express and mail)	895	1,182	0.067	0.085	34,599	37,491	4.50	4.68
Grand Total	1,326,911	1,393,871	100.00	100.00	769,174	801,367	100.00	100.00

SOURCE: Interstate Commerce Commission, *Seventy-Seventh Annual Report* (Washington, D.C.: U.S. Government Printing Office, 1963), p. 74. The water transport does not include most coastwise and intercoastal ton-miles, estimated by the Corps of Engineers, U.S. Army, at 317.4 billion for 1961.

seen that the railroads constitute the principal transport medium for the movement of freight today and the second largest carrier of passengers for hire. The private automobile, however, is the overwhelmingly predominant intercity carrier of passengers. The changing relative position of the railroads in the movement of freight is emphasized by comparing the figures for 1920 with those shown in Table 3. In 1920, the total volume

[1]Air Transport Association, *Air Transport Facts and Figures*, 1964, p. 31. A comprehensive compilation of transport statistics will be found in *Transportation, Facts and Figures* (annually) published by the Transportation Association of America, Washington, D.C.

of intercity freight traffic was 500 billion ton-miles. The railroads hauled 84 per cent of this, or about 420 billion ton-miles; inland waterways, 15 per cent, or 75 billion ton-miles; and motor vehicles, less than 1 per cent. An even greater contrast is afforded by the figures for passenger traffic, where the railroad position has declined drastically in absolute as well as relative terms. In 1920, the total volume of intercity passenger traffic was approximately 65 billion passenger-miles. It was estimated that 89 per cent of this was by public carriers, of which the railroads moved about 57 billion passenger-miles, or 85 per cent of the total. Intercity automobile and air transport was virtually nonexistent.

THE DEVELOPMENT OF THE AMERICAN TRANSPORT SYSTEM

Emergence of the Different Agencies

Early Transport. The story of the development of transport in the the United States is characterized by the predominance of water transportation down to the middle of the nineteenth century, the complete dominance of the railroad from then until 1920, and the rise of the newer components of the transport system in what may be called the transport revolution after World War I. Transport in this country was confined largely to local and coastal waterways down to the beginning of the nineteenth century. The need for internal communications after the revolution led to the construction of several thousands of miles of turnpike or toll roads. These were largely of local importance and were frequently aided by state subsidies. The federal government entered the picture with the construction of the Cumberland road between 1806 and 1838 at a cost of over $7 million. It extended from Cumberland, Maryland, to Vandalia, Illinois, and provided the only through overland route to the Middle West. The cost of transporting the goods over the turnpikes was somewhat less than over the ordinary roads, but it was still over $10 a ton per 100 miles; the cost per ton to ship goods from Europe was only $10.

Water Transport. At the same time that the toll roads were being constructed, two major developments in water transport took place, which opened up the Middle West and greatly reduced the costs of inland transport. The first of these developments was the successful trip up the Hudson from New York to Albany by Robert Fulton's steamboat, the "Clermont," in 1807. By 1817, regular service was established on the Ohio and Mississippi rivers. Traffic could move effectively both upstream and downstream, with the result that the Ohio and Mississippi rivers became the main arteries of commerce for the Midwest.

The second major development came with the construction of the Erie Canal from Albany, New York, to Buffalo in 1825. It was 364 miles long and cost about $7 million. It was such a complete success that it led to a veritable orgy of canal building by many states, especially Pennsylvania, Maryland, Ohio, and Indiana. The Erie Canal opened up the vast area around the Great Lakes to world markets. New York at once became the principal gateway of commerce to the outside world of this country, because the route through it from the interior was cheaper than any other in the country.

The Railroads. It was the invention of the steam engine and the development of the steam locomotive that made the railroad the prime agency of land transport. The success of George Stephenson's "Rocket" at the Rainhill trials in England not only stirred public interest in railroads in this country, but, more important, it led to the importation of English locomotives with their gauge of 4 feet, 8½ inches, which was destined to become the standard for American railroads. The first railroad common carrier to be constructed in this country was the Baltimore and Ohio, chartered in 1827 and first opened in 1830. This really marks the beginning of the railroad era in the United States.

The early stage of railroad development was one of experimentation with equipment and roadways. The initial lines were built as feeders to canals or routes to territories immediately adjacent to large cities. In 1842, a series of these lines were connected end to end to form a through route from Buffalo to New York with a gauge of 4 feet, 8½ inches. In 1853, continuous connections were made to Chicago. The period of experimentation with railroad building may be said to have ended by 1850, by which time the railroad had clearly established its position as the principal means of inland transport.

The enthusiasm and speculative fever aroused by the potentialities of railroad transport resulted in an enormous amount of private investment and public aid. Railroad mileage for the country increased from 9,021 miles in 1850 to 75,096 miles in 1875 and to 225,196 miles in 1905. The peak of railroad mileage in this country came in 1915, when it amounted to 264,378 miles. By 1860, the territory east of the Mississippi was well served with railroads, and a few crossings had been made to the territory farther west. In 1869, the first transcontinental railroad—from Council Bluffs, Iowa, to Sacramento, California—was completed with the joining of the Union Pacific and Central Pacific railroads at Promontory Point, Utah, just west of Ogden.

Judged by most standards, the supplying of the vast continental area of the United States with the most efficient type of mass land transport that has yet been made available was a phenomenal business and engineering accomplishment. This, however, was not without its accompanying problems. First of all, there were the excesses and abuses that seem invariably to emerge with the rise of a new industry in a new country. The extreme concept of *laissez faire* that prevailed at the time and the lack of grasp of many of the problems of the modern corporation led to financial excesses, fraud, and speculation that resulted in failures, heavy losses to investors, and an aroused public. The various governments—local, state, and federal—extended lavish aid of different kinds to encourage construction, which led to overexpansion, in addition to giving unscrupulous financiers and promoters almost unlimited opportunity to fleece the public and reap personal fortunes. These and other abuses, together with the emergence of the railroad monopoly of inland transport, soon led to the demand for public regulation—first of all, at the state level and, then, at the federal level.

The second problem connected with the development of the railroad arose from the nature of railroad economics. The railroad was the first of the modern industries that came to be characterized as "natural" monopolies. This meant that competition was a totally inadequate means of securing reasonable prices and of protecting the consumer. In addition, over-all competition was ruinous to competitors and resulted, inevitably, either in agreements to control it or in the emergence of a single firm without competitors. The monopoly position, heavy fixed costs, and unused capacity led to discrimination as an exercise of monopoly power and as a necessity for an economical pricing policy. These problems were an inescapable part of the economics of rail transport and would have required regulation—at least, as long as private ownership existed—without any of the abuses. Unfortunately, this was not understood, and the chief reason advanced in support of railroad regulation was the necessity of curbing the abuses and excesses. This still seems to be regarded as the principal basis of regulation, even today.

Rise of the New Transport Structure

The position of the railroad as the sole supplier of inland transport services, except for the somewhat limited role of water transport, came to an abrupt end with the new technological developments following World War I. This resulted in the revival of interest in inland waterways, the restoration of the highway to a new prominence with the growth of automotive transport, the rapid development of pipe-line transportation, and the emergence of a completely new means—namely the airplane. The effect of these changes was to turn transportation into one of the most competitive areas of economic activity in our whole productive structure, at least as far as the consumer is concerned.

Inland Waterways. The revival of interest in inland waterways at the turn of the century was the result of a number of factors. There was the general belief that waterways provided a natural route that was cheaper than the railroad. This was reinforced by the memories of and the nostalgia for the steamboat days on the Mississippi, coupled with the desire to secure federal aid for local advantage. The resentment against the railroads, together with their inability to supply transport to much of the country as cheaply as had been expected, led to support for alternative means. The administration of President Herbert Hoover undertook the vast Mississippi River development, in part, as a yardstick by which to measure the reasonableness of railroad freight rates, as well as a means of lowering them by competition. To further this program, Congress set up the Inland Waterways Corporation in 1924 to operate barges on the Mississippi and Warrior rivers to demonstrate the feasibility of commercial water transport in competition with the railroads. The congestion of railroad traffic resulting from the extraordinary one-way demands on facilities in World War I gave rise to pressure for waterways as a means of coping with the unusual demands of war. Finally, the desire to provide a deep-sea route from the Atlantic Ocean to the Great Lakes by canalizing the relatively short distance from Montreal to Lake Ontario and by enlarging the Welland Canal around Niagara Falls, coupled with the possibilities of power development that such a project offered, culminated in an agreement with Canada that commenced the joint development of the St. Lawrence in 1954. With the completion of this undertaking in 1959, the port cities of the Great Lakes have become deep-sea shipping centers.

Motor Transport. The automobile did not become a significant commercial factor in transportation until after World War I. By that time, Henry Ford had demonstrated the potentialities of mass production of automobiles such that the production of the Ford Company alone in 1920 was 1,074,336 cars. In 1921, Congress passed the first Federal Highway Act, providing for federal aid to highway building. The aid to the states, who were to match the federal funds in order to be eligible, was to be limited to 7 per cent of the total rural mileage in a state. This was the beginning of a nationwide system of interconnected highways.

The biggest relative impact of the automobile on passenger traffic movement took place between 1920 and 1930, for by the latter year, out of 196.3 billion intercity passenger-miles, private cars and busses accounted for 168 billion, or just over 85 per cent. It was during this same period, also, that the automobile came to the front in urban passenger transport, with the consequent difficulties for urban commercial facilities, especially street and interurban railways. The major impact of the motor vehicle on freight traffic came between 1930 and 1940. By the end of that period, railroad freight ton-mileage had declined to 62 per cent of the national total.

Air Transport. Air transport, like automobile transport, developed after World War I; but unlike the automobile, it has been confined almost entirely to mail and passenger transportation. Experimentation with air-mail service began in 1918; transcontinental air-mail service was undertaken in 1919; and in 1924, continuous day-and-night transcontinental service was established. Scheduled domestic air transport carried fewer than 6,000 revenue passengers in 1926; but by 1940, the total had risen to 2,802,781. The real growth in air passenger transport began after World War II and has increased to the point where it is now larger than

FIGURE 5

Major Rail Routes in the United States

FIGURE 6

The National System of Interstate and Defense Highways Status of Improvement
as of June 30, 1964

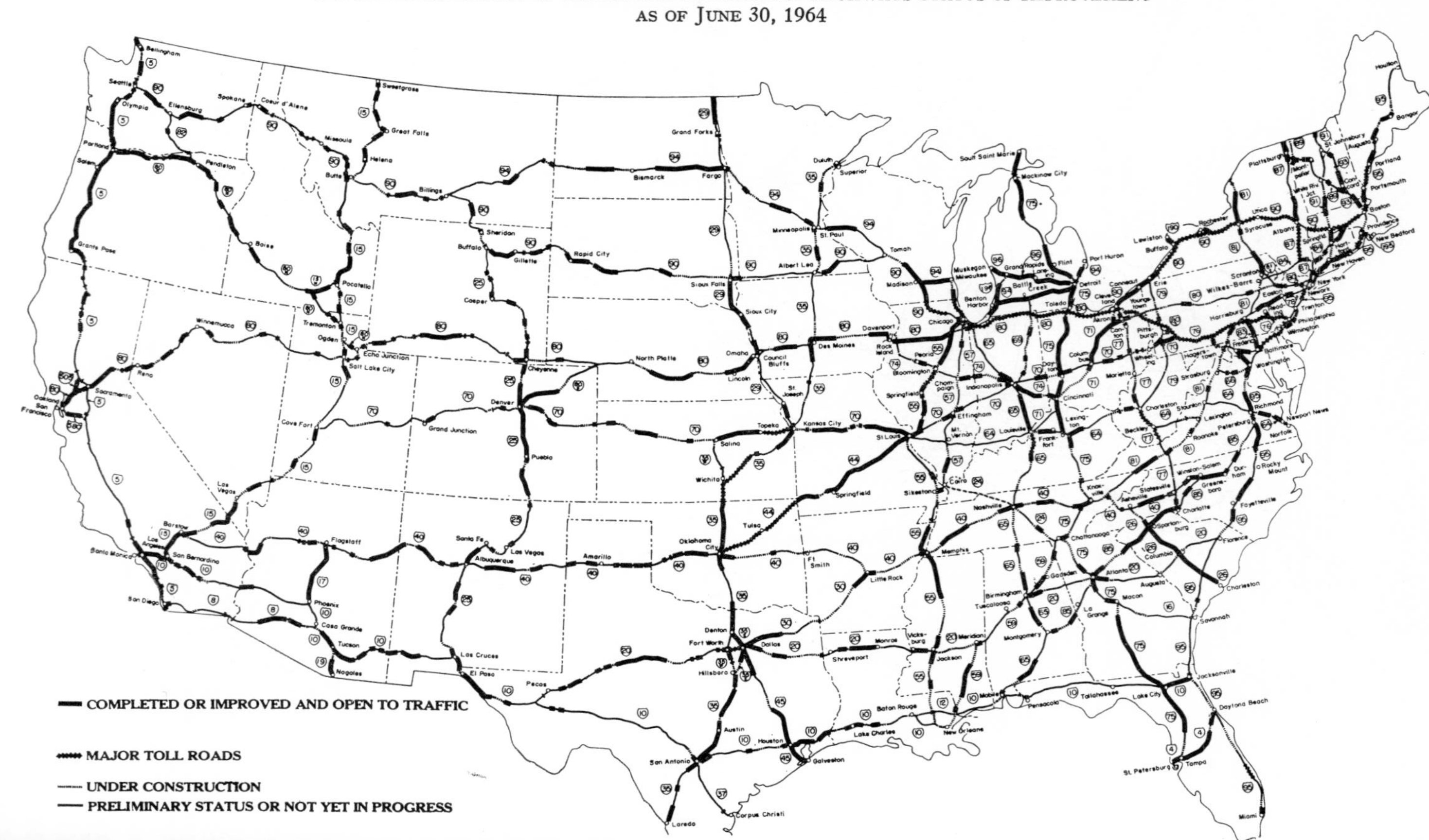

FIGURE 7

Inland Intercoastal Waterway System of the United States

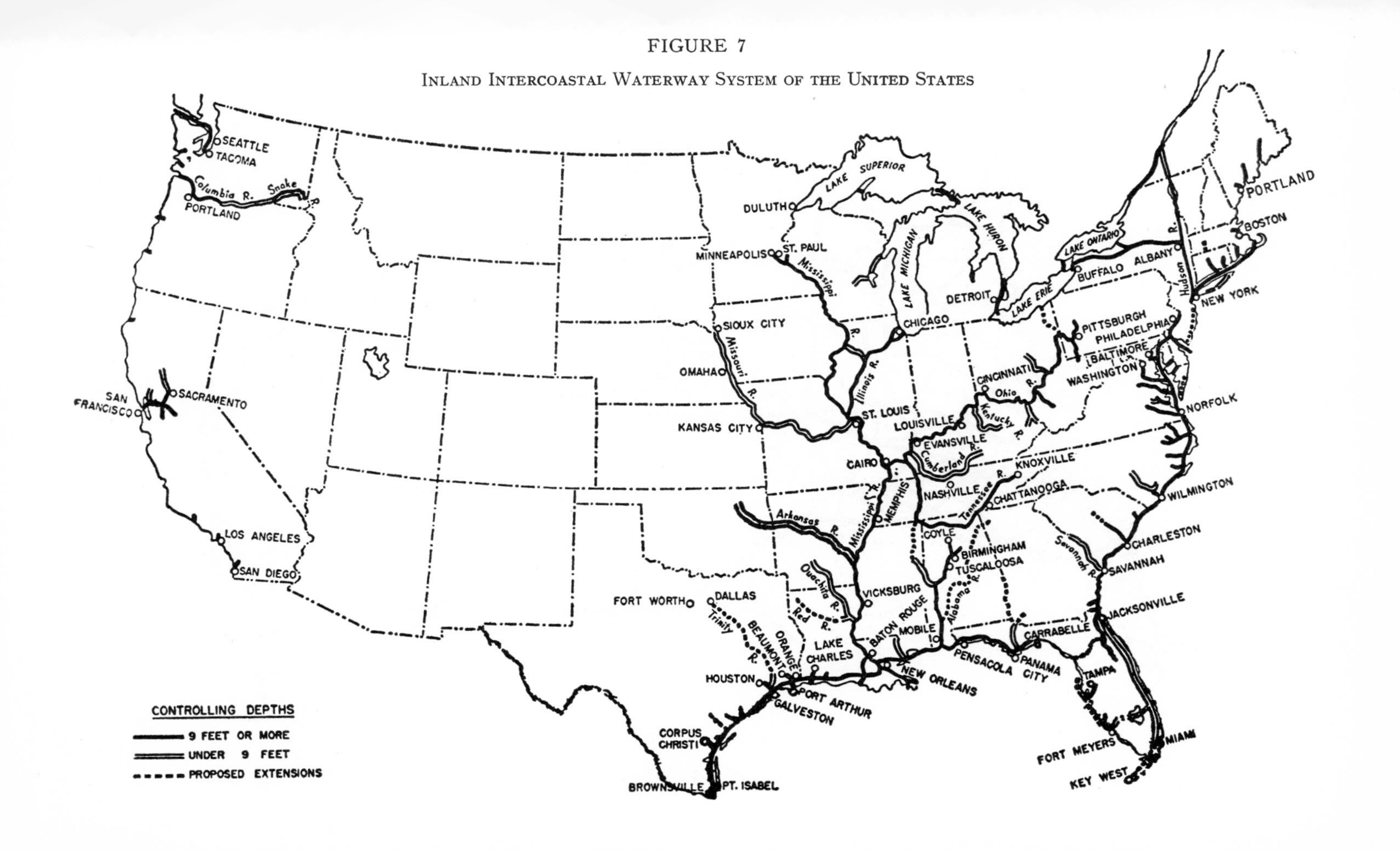

FIGURE 8

The Federal Airway System

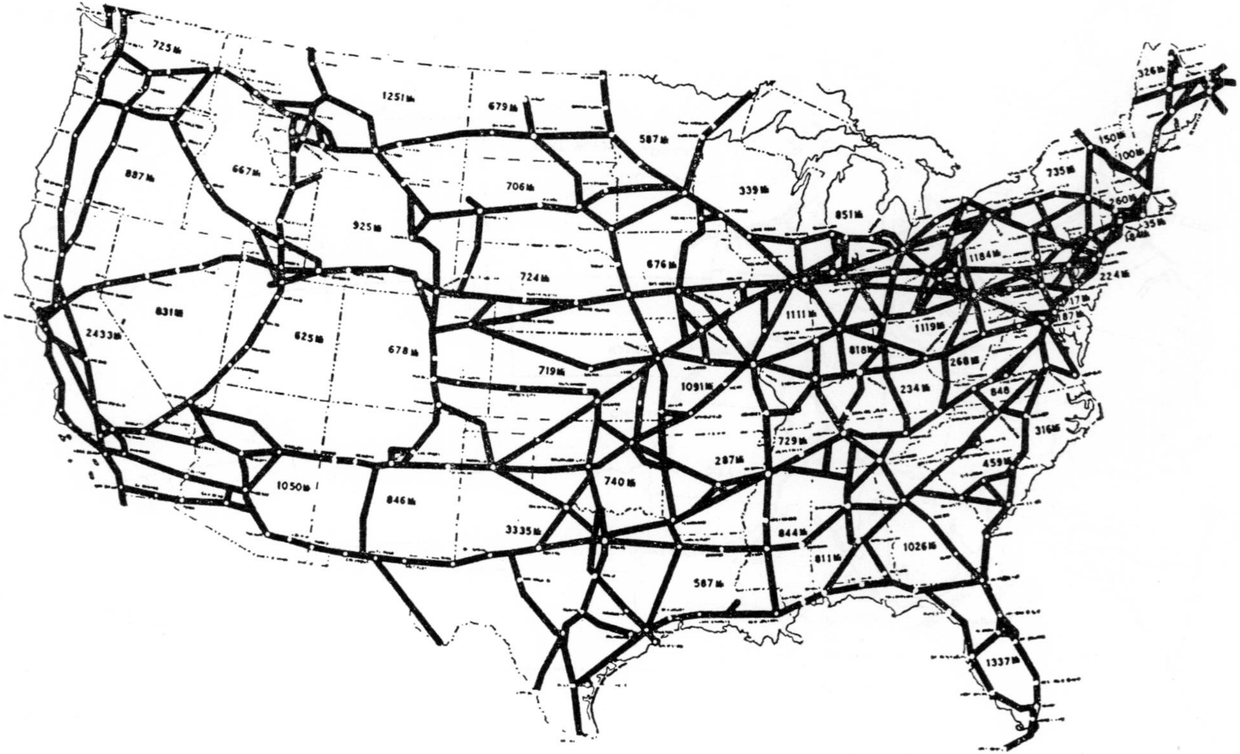

FIGURE 9

Invisible Network—A Million Miles of Pipe Line

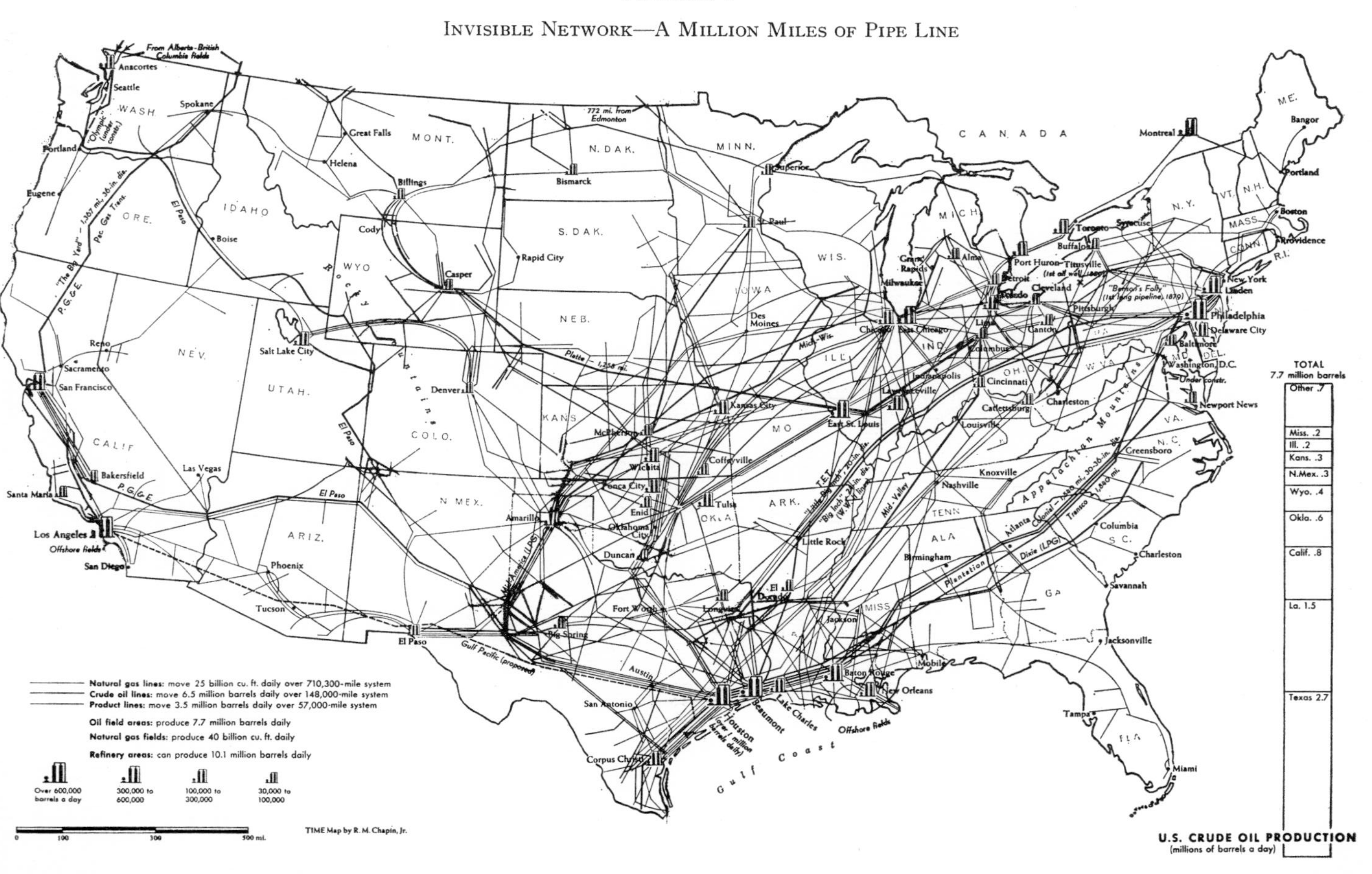

U.S. CRUDE OIL PRODUCTION (millions of barrels a day) — TOTAL 7.7 million barrels
Other .7
Miss. .2
Ill. .2
Kans. .3
N.Mex. .3
Wyo. .4
Okla. .6
Calif. .8
La. 1.5
Texas 2.7

that of the railroads. Coast-to-coast through flights today are made in less than 5 hours of flying time.

Pipe Lines. Pipe-line transportation of crude petroleum and its products is a highly specialized means of transport that does not serve the public in the general way that characterizes the operations of the other agencies of transport. Nor does it enter into national transport policy in the way the other modes do. The pipe lines are all privately owned and have not received public aid at any time. Many of the petroleum pipe lines transport only the products of their owners, and this is all that the natural gas lines do.

Pipe-line transport has been an important part of the petroleum industry from its beginning. It has become a significant component of the national transport structure since 1920, linking the vast petroleum fields of the Southwest with the big refinery centers of the East, and now even with the Pacific Coast. This development has added a great deal of new tonnage to the freight traffic of the country and has deprived the railroads of what was once a lucrative volume of traffic. The major problems of national policy connected with the oil pipe lines relate to the organization and structure of the oil industry. Some feel that pipe lines should be treated as part of the transport structure of the country and should be divorced from the petroleum industry. Others feel that pipeline transportation is so closely connected with production and refining that it would not be feasible to bring about this separation. So far, nothing has been done by way of legislation to resolve this problem. In the case of natural gas transmission lines, the gas which is transported is owned by the transmission lines which are regulated by the Federal Power Commission. This matter is dealt with in a later chapter.

The Effects of Changing Technology

The most obvious effect of changing technology in transport is improved transportation. It has rendered the movement of people and goods more regular and calculable, safer, more rapid, and cheaper. This has reduced the effect of space relationships, thereby making it easier for people to co-operate in activities involving spatial factors. The improvement in speed has reduced the cost of the time factor in the movement of people as well as goods. Improved transport has also widened the market and encouraged the division of labor and geographic specialization, thereby bringing about increased competition and a reduction of prices.

The foregoing consequences of improved transport differ from those arising from technological advances in other areas of production principally because of the bearing they have on spatial and time factors in the production process. There are other effects, however, which relate more directly to transport itself. One of these concerns the structure of transport. Only in the very generalized sense of a production activity that provides for the movement of people and goods can the various transport agencies be grouped together in the category of an industry. For firms to be so grouped, it is necessary that there be a rather high degree of homogeneity of product and similarity of economic structure or conditions of production.[2] Thus, railroads may be classified as an industry, because they have similar economic characteristics and offer essentially similar types of service. By the same token, the other agencies may be considered as separate industries. Over a considerable range, there is a good deal of ready—indeed, almost complete—substitutability of services among the different modes of transport; but they also offer services that are very distinct from each, some of them being scarcely substitutable at all. In other words, the suppliers of transportation manifest diverse economic characteristics with regard to costs, supply of services and facilities, and organizational structure. Prior to 1920, because of the predominant position of the railroads, it was possible to treat inland transport as an industry. The impact of the new technology, however, has converted inland transport into a group of industries with such markedly different characteristics as to have profound implications for national transportation policy. This question will be examined later on.

A second effect of changing technology on transport itself has been periodically to alter the position of the dominant type of carrier. At first, the dominant type was road transport, with the turnpike and slow-moving animal power. This was almost completely superseded by canals and inland waterways. From the middle of the nineteenth century down to 1920, the railroad took over; and water carriage was relegated to a minor role, except in specialized instances, especially the Great Lakes. Developments after World War I revived the old types of carriers, giving them new roles, brought the pipe lines into prominence, and established air transport. The railroads, measured by ton-miles of freight handled, are still the most important carrier, but they are no longer able to supply all the types of transport we need; they are now faced with ready substitutes for many of the services they alone used to provide.

A third effect is that "the transportation industry operates today in the general atmosphere of pervasive competition."[3] As far as the buyer of transport services is concerned, transportation over a wide range has no features of monopoly or even oligopoly. In fact, these are literally nonexistent in motor carriage and little in evidence in water transport. The structural characteristics of railroads have not changed; but on the supply side, the monopoly features have been so severely reduced as to render obsolete much of the regulation that was erected on the premise of monopoly.

[2]E. A. G. Robinson, *The Structure of Competitive Industry* (New York: Harcourt, Brace & Co., 1932), pp. 6–14.

[3]Report of the Presidential Advisory Committee on Transport Policy and Organization (Weeks Report), *Revision of Federal Transportation Policy* (Washington, D.C.: U.S. Government Printing Office, 1955), p. 2.

Changing technology has also had a profound effect on the issue of public ownership in transport. Public ownership played a prominent role in the development of transportation, even of the early railroads; but by the middle of the nineteenth century, the railroads in this country were almost all privately owned. Apart from public ownership of inland waterways, but not of the vessels on them, transport was provided by private ownership and operation. The issue of public ownership in the first quarter of this century centered on the railroads and, therefore, on the question of whether land transport should be supplied by the government or by private enterprise. This has now all been changed. Public ownership of a large part, at least, of the surface facilities for road transport is no longer avoidable; and this involves the bulk of the investment in the route facilities of land transport. At the same time, private operation of the greater part of the motor vehicles is apparently inevitable. In air transport, public ownership of the airways is unlikely to be put in private hands; and airports will most probably remain under public ownership, on the whole. Thus, we now have a mixed system of transport ownership and investment that, in all probability, will remain with us for a long time. It does not seem to be possible now to debate the issue of public versus private supply of land transport as a whole; both are likely to remain, with private and public interests alike having a major stake in the investment.

Changing technology has resulted in changing the role of the common carrier in supplying transport service. A common carrier is one who holds himself ready to serve all alike, without discrimination, at reasonable rates, under publicly specified conditions. The idea of a common carrier, arising from that of a "common calling," is an old one at common law; but it developed into its most comprehensive status with the railroad—so much so, that land carriage for hire came to be identified with the common carrier. The motor vehicle, in particular, has presented a new problem, because a great deal of its use is in private carriage and a considerable part is conducted under specific contract. Water transport lends itself only partly to common carriage. Air transport is mostly in the common carrier category; whether it will remain so depends upon technological developments. Thus, the effect of the technological changes has been to remove permanently a great deal of transport from the category of common carriage.[4] This has altered materially the position of common carriers, and it may be doubted that protection can be given them by extending the idea more completely to the noncommon carriers.

[4]It is estimated that about 67 per cent of the intercity freight ton-miles is regulated by the Interstate Commerce Commission; the remainder is not regulated by the ICC. This means that perhaps not more than half of this intercity freight is by common carrier. About 90 per cent of the intercity movement of people is by private automobile, which means that less than 10 per cent is by common carrier. See also J. C. Nelson, *Railroad Transportation and Public Policy* (Washington, D.C.: The Brookings Institution, 1959), pp. 134–38.

Indeed, it may be doubted that the concept even fits the bulk of motor carriage. A re-examination of this aspect of regulation is urgently needed, because it is by no means evident that the rules which applied in the days when the railroad was supreme are useful in the same way today.

PUBLIC OWNERSHIP AND PUBLIC AID

Public Ownership

Transport service is so important that providing it has been regarded almost as a responsibility, in some way or another, of the state. The urgent need for improved transport, together with the insufficient supply of private capital in the early days of the United States as a nation, led to proposals for extensive federal participation in the work of internal improvements. This gave rise to the famous Gallatin Report of 1808, which recommended that the federal government embark on an extensive scheme of highway and waterway developments. For the most part, however, public ownership and investment in these early facilities were confined to state and local governments. The transport vehicles were almost entirely privately owned.

There was some public ownership of railroads, too, at first. The state of Pennsylvania constructed two railroads; Illinois completed one; and Michigan, Georgia, and Virginia also undertook construction. Even today, the state of Georgia owns the Western Atlantic Railroad, although it is operated under private lease. State participation led to overexpansion and serious financial difficulties that brought about a collapse of state credit in many instances. This, together with the influence of the philosophy of *laissez faire*, brought an early end to public ownership in railroads. Not until after World War I did public ownership again become a prominent question. At first, this took the form of debate on the question of government ownership of railroads, which had spread rapidly throughout a large part of the world. Public ownership of this agency has meant ownership and operation of its entire transport plant.

In the period since 1920, the issue of public ownership of national transport facilities has taken on a different turn. The major change has been brought about by the development of motor transport. This is the result of a number of factors: (1) The ownership and operation of the motive equipment may readily be separated from the highway facilities—so much so, in fact, that it is literally impossible to combine them in any very extensive way. (2) Public ownership of the highways is unavoidable, for the most part. (3) The vehicles can move indiscriminately on highways and on the routes. This has important implications in pricing for transport services. In rail and pipe-line transport, pricing is used to control specific use of service, which means that prices can reflect both the quantity and the quality of the service supplied. This can be done for air and water transport also, although it is not the practice at the present time. Motor transport, so far, has been brought within this pattern only in a very limited way; and the prospects of extending it are not very great. The problem of precise pricing of the highway service to the operators of motor vehicles is one of the most difficult ones that has yet emerged in the field of transport because of the indiscriminate and largely undifferentiated use of the highway. A motor vehicle, with relatively few exceptions, pays as much per mile for the use of a dirt road as for a superhighway. The intermingling of private, for-hire, freight, and passenger traffic on roadway facilities, and the utilization of these facilities for both production and consumption purposes, have presented problems of measuring need for investment, pricing for the use of the services which the investment provides, and assessing the cost of the transport burden, which are the most complex that transport policy has ever faced. In addition, the individualization of transportation that characterizes highway traffic has undermined a significant part of our mass transport facilities, with the consequence that much of the transport supply has become more expensive than is commonly realized. This is because price, as the direct measuring rod of alternatives, and as a rationing device, has been dispensed with, to a large extent, in motor transport.

Public Aid

Public aid is now inextricably mixed with public ownership. Public aid was extended on an enormous scale to encourage railroad development in the nineteenth century. It took the form of donations of land, loans of government securities and cash, grants of right of way in the public domain and streets, subscriptions to railroad stocks and bonds, tax exemptions, and some other items. The most important of the public aids was the federal land grants, which amounted to some 215 million acres, of which title to some 131 million acres actually passed to the railroads. The latter, in return, granted the government special rates known as "land-grant rates." These were not terminated until 1945. Estimates of the total public aid vary rather widely, but the consensus is that the railroads, through *quid pro quo*'s, have repaid the value which they realized.[5] Professor Daggett points out that the present value of past public aid to railroads is negligible, either as a source of revenue or as a help in competition with other forms of transport.

Public aid to air, water, and highway transport, however, is in a different category. This is partly because aid to the railroads, at the time it was given, did not seriously affect other forms of transport or competition with them, since the other forms were virtually nonexistent, and partly because of the fact that current aid to the other forms takes place through the medium of public ownership of the fixed route or terminal facilities, which are then used by the many and varied private operators.

[5]See Stuart Daggett, *Principles of Inland Transportation* (4th ed.; New York: Harper & Brothers, 1955), pp. 740–41.

Governments supply inland waterways through river improvements and canalization. In addition, large amounts of public funds are spent on harbors. Practically all of the highway and street facilities are supplied by public funds, and the same remarks are true for airways and airports. This relieves the users from assuming the risks involved in the large investment in the fixed facilities, the obligation to meet interest charges, and so forth, and, in addition, gives them the benefit of lower interest costs resulting from reliance on government credit.

The method of providing public aid which obtains today raises many important questions, such as (1) the amount of public investment that should be made and how the requirements should be measured, (2) the bases of charging for the use of publicly provided facilities, (3) the items which should be included in calculating the full economic costs entailed in providing public transport facilities, (4) the effect of public aid on transport supply, and (5) the effect of public aid on railroads and the economical allocation of traffic. It is not possible to discuss these issues at length at this point; they will be dealt with later on. It should be noted, however, that they have arisen out of the breakdown of the mechanism of pricing as an effective guide to total necessary investment in transport because of (1) the way in which public aid is administered, (2) the difficulties accompanying the use of the pricing system as an effective rationing device in transport because of the technology of motor transport, (3) and the failure of public policy to require the various modes of transport to bear similar types of costs.

At the present time, no tolls are charged for the use of inland waterways or canals. Public aid excuses the users from meeting the costs of the investment in these facilities. The same remarks apply to the air routes and, to a considerable extent, to airports. Available information indicates that motor vehicle operators have not paid sums equal to the cost of public aid and that the deficit has been considerable.[6] The biggest deficits incurred on this score are in receipts of local rural units and urban areas for highways where general property taxes make up a significant portion of the total expenditures.[7]

So long as the total costs are not assessed on the users, the pricing mechanism is by-passed as a measure of economical investment allocation. Waterways and air routes could be constructed on the usual capitalistic basis, if we so desired, because control of use can easily be effected. Highway transport is another matter, however. It may be possible to assess aggregate road-route costs on the users; but even if this were so, there would still be the difficulty of charging the users on the basis of the costs incurred for each. So far, we have made little progress in arriving at those individual costs. Furthermore, we have not developed any workable

[6]*Ibid.*, p. 745.

[7]D. P. Locklin, *Economics of Transportation* (5th ed.; Homewood, Ill.: Richard D. Irwin, Inc., 1960), pp. 624–25.

device of general applicability whereby the user can be charged according to the quality of the facility he uses. Toll roads are an exception to this, but they are not in wide use and offer little prospect for urban traffic.

Finally, we do not yet seem to be willing to acknowledge that the costs which the users of water, air, and motor transport should cover are the same as those which the railroads have to bear. For example, railroads must pay taxes on their rights of way and terminals. No such comparable costs are assessed on public investment in the other agencies. This means that the buyers of rail transport services have to make contributions to the government not imposed on the users of the other modes. Whatever may be the arguments pro and con, it is obvious that choice of use among the modes does not entail similar or relatively equal cost considerations.

Public Aid versus Subsidy

At the present time, public aid to air, water, and motor transport is of such magnitude that a major shift in the allocation of traffic among the various agencies of transport would take place if the users were required to cover the costs of each mode in the same way. Whether this means that air, water, and motor transport are subsidized depends upon how one defines the term "subsidy." If it means direct payments to make up deficiencies in revenues so as to bring the latter up to a stipulated amount, then the only subsidized transport in this country today is air, where direct payments are made by the federal government to support it.[8] Operators in water and motor transport are not subsidized—in this sense, at least—but they do get aid in the form of facilities for which they do not pay in full. In view of the enormous investment being made in transportation in the United States today, this is a problem that needs to be given much more study and objective analysis than it has received to date.

THE ECONOMIC BASIS OF TRANSPORT

Transport and Location

The most important aspect of transportation as an economic activity lies in its role as a process in the production of goods and services. Its function is to bridge the time and space gaps separating producers and consumers. This is accomplished by the movement of goods made by the producer, in the case of freight transport, or by the movement of either the producer or the consumer in the case of passenger transport.[9] Trans-

[8]The total of these payments for 1963 was estimated at $86.07 million by the Civil Aeronautics Board. None of this subsidy went to the domestic trunk lines or to the transpacific and transatlantic airlines. Subsidy for *United States Certificated Air Carriers*, Civil Aeronautics Board, January, 1962, (mimeo).

[9]For a full discussion of this, see A. M. Milne, *The Economics of Inland Transport* (London: Sir Isaac Pitman & Sons, Ltd., 1955), chap. i.

portation is thus one of the most important aspects of the whole process of production. Its role in the location of industry, residence, and so forth is a matter of some debate; but it is recognized by all as being very decisive.[10] It appears to be the controlling factor in the location of many metropolitan centers as a result of the geographic factors that affect transport routes. Cities that are the crossroads of land routes or the meeting place of land and water routes become key points because of the transport factor alone. The rise of New York following the construction of the Erie Canal has already been noted as an illustration. In the same connection, the effect of transportation on the widening of markets and the furthering of division of labor makes it a key factor in long-term economic development.

The essential nature of transport to community life has, from early times, led government to participate in the supplying of transport facilities. As a consequence, the idea grew up that even though private enterprise supplied public transport, it was nevertheless performing a function of the state.[11] This imposes a special obligation on public transport agencies and gives them certain powers not possessed by other enterprises. Thus, public carriers may exercise the right of eminent domain, if necessary, to obtain the property they must have for the performance of their duties. This means that the carrier may acquire private property, such as land, at a fair price, even though the owner does not wish to sell it.

Public Carriage

When transport enterprises serve as public carriers, they assume a variety of obligations that are not imposed on private enterprise in general. The nature of the common carrier has already been discussed briefly. As early as the seventeenth century in England, transport came to be recognized as an industry affected with a public interest, which set it apart from those which were of purely private concern. This laid the constitutional foundation for the right of the state to regulate those activities so classified. The reason for this development, apparently, was that competition in transport always played a more or less limited role. Wharves and docks were key points for monopoly control in trade and commerce. Toll roads and canals were in a similar category. Later, when the railroad became the prime agency of transport, it was soon recognized that uncontrolled competition was ruinous. If private ownership was to direct businesses with such characteristics, it had to be regulated to insure adequate service and reasonable prices. Even today, the role of competition in transport is limited, although not in the simple fashion that obtained earlier. Highway construction cannot be left to competitive forces in the same way that is possible for steel plants; at the present time, private investment in highways is possible only to a limited extent, if

[10]Daggett, *op. cit.*, chap. xxii.
[11]*Olcott* v. *Supervisors*, 16 Wall 678 (1837).

at all. Similarly, competition in the construction of air routes and airports does not seem to be possible on a very extensive scale.

Need for Price Regulation

As a result of the limitations of competition in transportation, the problem of pricing has long presented unique features. The early common-law prescription that rates must be just and reasonable was incorporated into thoroughgoing regulation of railroad rates, because competition could not be relied upon to establish workable prices. Without public control, monopoly price was inescapable. Today, with the emergence of the newer agencies, especially the motor carrier, the pricing problem has taken on a new aspect. Monopoly pricing over a wide range no longer poses a threat, but price relationships among the agencies present new issues; and pricing for the use of highways is still an unresolved, if not an almost unrecognized, problem. In short, the pricing problems of transport are unique because of the economic structure of transport and because of the mixture of private and public ownership which seems to be inescapable.

THE POLITICAL BASIS OF TRANSPORT

Political Unity

Transport is also differentiated from much of the rest of economic productive activity because of its immediate connection with the political life of a country. It is because of this that transportation cannot be subject completely and directly to the full operation of the pricing system. Adequate transportation is essential to national unity. The centers of government must have continuous and relatively rapid communication with the people and the territories they govern. In the absence of economic inducements that are adequate for private enterprise to supply the necessary transport facilities, government must fill the gap. This was the reason for the early interest of the federal government in aiding the development of transportation in the United States. The states had to be provided with the physical basis of a unified country which they had lacked theretofore; transport routes had to be constructed for political reasons to secure access to the territory west of the Alleghenies. Later on, the federal government pushed the building of the first transcontinental railroad, in order to secure the western part of the continent for the Union and to bind California to the Union. In Canada, the Canadian Pacific Railway was constructed as part of the agreement by which British Columbia became part of the Dominion in 1873.

National Defense

Closely connected with political unity is the problem of national defense. This relationship has long been recognized by all governments.

In ancient times, it was the reason for the great system of roads throughout the Roman Empire. In some countries, military considerations were more important than economic ones in designing the system of railroads. This characterized railroad development, for example, in Germany. In the United States, one of the most important arguments used to support public investment in inland waterways was the needs of national defense. This consideration carried a good deal of weight in the decision to participate in the building of the St. Lawrence seaway; and during World War II, the national government constructed the Big Inch and Little Inch pipe lines to assist in carrying liquid petroleum products from the southwest to the eastern states. Recently, the requirements of national defense have been advanced as a major reason for the construction of a system of nationwide, interconnected superhighways. Similarly, the large current expenditures on air transport are based more on military and political considerations than on economic ones.

Thus, while it seems safe to say that the American transportation system has been shaped primarily by economic factors, political and military developments have played an important role. For this reason, transport policy cannot be examined in a purely economic setting. In fact, it can be examined in such a setting much less than much of the rest of economic enterprise. Public participation in the economic aspects of transport development and supply is unavoidable, because all of the decisions regarding them cannot be made on a purely economic basis, at least within the framework of the requirements of a private enterprise system. The economic features of transport preclude that possibility, and the political considerations that transportation entails likewise compel active and direct public participation.

AN ECONOMICAL SYSTEM OF TRANSPORT

Need for Cheap Transport

The Transportation Association of America has estimated that the nation's total freight costs for 1962 were $48.3 billions or 8.7 per cent of the Gross National Product, and that the total estimated cost of moving people was $60.2 billion or 10.9 per cent of the GNP; that is about 20 per cent of the GNP was for transportation.[12] It is almost axiomatic, therefore, to say that a country needs cheap transport and that it needs the cheapest possible transport system that will adequately meet the requirements of the country. This statement, however, literally means all things to all people and does not indicate what the essence of a cheap system of transport, in an economic sense, implies. The need for the cheapest possible transport system arises from three considerations:

[12]*Transportation Facts*, 1964, *op. cit.*, pp. 3–4. The figures do not include the cost of transporting natural gas or water.

1. As has already been pointed out, transportation is one of the large items, quantitatively, in the production process. As a matter of keeping production costs down with expanding markets, improvements in transport efficiency aid in increasing the productivity of industry and are one of the essential ingredients of improved productivity. In this respect, transport is in the same category as all other phases of productive activity; there is a constant striving to reduce the relative costs of the various processes of production.

2. The enormous total investment in transport facilities and the relatively large amount of our wealth—possibly about one quarter of the total—that is devoted to transport require that careful attention be given to ways and means of assuring that the investment is wisely made and that overexpansion is avoided as much as possible. This is once more becoming an acute problem because of the heavy demands that are being made for public investment in highways and because of the difficult problems of traffic congestion to which the automobile has given rise.

3. If transport is to be cheap, the allocation of economic resources to it must be in keeping with the efficiency principle, which means that those resources are being devoted to their most valuable use. The absolute amount of investment and expenditure in transportation is a significant matter in the final analysis only in so far as it relates to the problem of an economical allocation of resources. If the amount of resources in transport is the result of a rational allocation, a country has an economical system of transport, because—by economic criteria—it cannot afford any more and it has all it needs.

Cheap transport for a country and cheap transport for an individual or a firm are not necessarily the same thing. When an individual (or a firm) seeks cheap transportation or the cheapest means of transportation, he typically counts only the immediate prices or rates that he has to pay. These rates do not necessarily cover all the costs that are involved in supplying that transportation. The difference may be made up by subsidies, disguised costs, and taxes that are borne in large measure by others. Under such circumstances, cheap transport for the individual may actually be very expensive for the country. Whether this is so will depend upon whether the service that is being supplied is worth the total costs that are being incurred. Modern transport presents some very severe obstacles to ascertaining the full cost and even severer ones to gauging whether they are worthwhile. It is, in part, because of this difficulty that a good deal of confusion exists in public thinking, whereby cheap transport to the individual and cheap transport to the country are too frequently regarded as being the same thing.

Meaning of Cheap Transport

If a country is to have the cheapest transport commensurate with its needs or—in the words of Congress—"an adequate, economical, and efficient" transport system, it must measure its investment and costs of operation in terms of an efficient allocation of its economic resources. As has already been pointed out in this book, this means that consumers must be free to select the type of transport service they wish to employ, on the basis of the price they are willing to pay for it. That is, they must be permitted to select among the alternatives on the basis of the lowest relative rates. The various transport agencies which offer the alternatives will have to be allowed to seek the traffic on a competitive basis, so that the one that can profitably take the traffic at the lowest price is the one that will get it. This is the only way to secure an economical allocation of traffic whether the transport system is in private hands or whether it is entirely owned by the state. Furthermore, for economical price-cost relationships to exist among the agencies, it is necessary to see that all of them cover the full and similar costs of supplying the transport services. If there are reasons for differentiating among the agencies with regard to the cost burdens they must bear, those reasons will be of a political or some other nature, not economic.

An economical transport system means that there must be an economical allocation of traffic among the agencies and an economical investment in each mode. That is, the total investment in transportation should be such that the investment would not be worth more if made elsewhere and the investment made in one agency would not be worth more if it were made in another. This means that the benefits received from investment made in each agency of transportation should be worth more than if it were made in any other economic activity. This carries us back once more to the utilization of consumers' freedom of choice and the price mechanism as the gauge for economical investment. In other words, whether a transport system is economical depends on whether it can meet the competitive standards. If it cannot do so, it will not be economical, whatever else it may be.

The application of competitive standards to transportation is one of the most difficult tasks in economics. This is because of the technological structure of transport, the "mixed" system of ownership, and the political and social aspects. Unfortunately, this has been used too frequently as an excuse for justifying policies and expenditures that cannot meet the economic tests that are available, and as a basis for contentions that the diffused benefits of transport are such as to warrant abandoning the economic tests. The fact is that all costs of transport can be obtained with workable accuracy and that they can be assessed on users in the aggregate, if that is desired. It is the failure to use the measuring rods that are available that has led to the present transport dilemma in this country, with its railroad "crisis," highway "inadequacy," and metropolitan "congestion." Some of the complexities of transport costs and pricing are examined in the next chapter together with some of the implications for public policy.

Chapter 22 THE PRICING OF TRANSPORT SERVICES

INTRODUCTION

The economic principles which apply to the pricing of transport services are no different from those which apply to the pricing of the outputs of other industries. These principles have already been dealt with, and it is not necessary to repeat what was covered previously. The reason for separate treatment of the pricing of transport services arises from the complex problems that are connected with the application of the principles to transport.

First of all, it should be recalled that transportation is supplied by a group of industries that have diverse economic characteristics. Some of the agencies, as we shall see, are only partially competitive, at least within themselves, as the result of their economic structure; the others are capable of a high degree of competition. At the same time, the different modes of transport, over a rather wide range, offer services that are readily substitutable for each other, while each also has its own field of specialization.

Public policy, to date, has imposed limitations on competition in transportation by direct and continuous price fixing for common carriers, and by endeavoring to limit the number of enterprises in the various agencies that can offer service to the public. Thus, common carriers—be they railroad, motor, or any other—must secure certificates of public convenience and necessity which serve to protect the existing carrier unless it can be shown to the satisfaction of the appropriate public authority that an additional carrier is called for on the basis of public interest. This means that a convincing demonstration must be made on the part of the new applicant that public convenience will be served by the new addition and that it is necessary. In air, water, and motor transport, there are also contract carriers. Water and motor contract carriers must secure permits, but the restrictions on entry are considerably less severe than for common carriers. All of this is complicated by the fact that there is also a great deal of transport for hire that is not regulated at all in these same fields, either because of the nature of the transport or because of the commodities that are moved. Finally, there is a large amount of transport in these same fields, as well as pipe lines, that is private in nature—that is, it is not for hire. The movement of passengers by private car and the movement of freight by private truck are illustrations. Thus, the transport agencies supply public transport, private commercial transport, and private noncommercial transport, with a mixed use of public and private facilities, in a way that embraces public obligation, private discretion, competition, and monopoly found nowhere else in our industrial structure.

The regulation of transport prices has proceeded on the theory that public authority is called upon to fix the prices of an essential service supplied by monopoly or, at least, supplied by enterprises that enjoy a wide range of monopoly power. This puts transportation in a category apart from industry in general. It calls for an examination of the economic structure of transport upon which the theory was erected, but even more, especially at the present time, of the economic structures of the various agencies, to discern whether the theory fits the present situation or whether changed conditions have rendered obsolete the elaborate program of regulation that has been developed over the past century.

The regulation of monopoly price poses special and difficult problems, even in the simplest of situations. Most of the questions that arise in this connection will be examined in the discussion of public utilities. In these industries, the problem can be dealt with in literally isolated form, because each firm can be treated separately. Railroad transport exhibits many of the characteristics of the industries that are labeled public utilities and is subject to essentially the same legal rules. As a problem in monopoly, however, rail transport is considerably more complex because, first of all, monopoly has been less complete by virtue of competition among the railroads. Railroad rate regulation has therefore presented more difficult problems of monopoly price control than has public utility rate regulation. Today, with the rise of the newer modes of transport, application of the theory of monopoly price control to transport can no longer be undertaken on the assumption that it can be made to work by severely limiting competition or even eliminating it over a wide range. At the same time, the type of regulation that is imposed by the antitrust laws would, without any supplement, be inadequate for transport. Here is an area that falls between antitrust and public utility control in such a way as to give it a unique status in public policy.

Analysis of price policies and price control in transport in the United States has to be made in light of the ownership operation of transport facilities. It has already been pointed out that railroads own all the facilities they use and hence have to carry directly the burden of investment which this entails. Motor vehicles, even though they may pay for the highways they use, do not pay for them if they do not use them. Water and air transport do not pay for the "ways" in which they are used, even though these "ways" entail a large public investment. This makes for a difference in the cost characteristics of the operating companies and, therefore, in the costs which are the basis for decision making in the price policies of each. From a social point of view, the cost situations are essentially the same especially for rail, motor, and pipe-line transport; from a private point of view, they are radically different.

THE COST STRUCTURES OF THE AGENCIES OF TRANSPORT[1]

Railroads

Railroad costs, like those of most other firms, may be analyzed from the point of view of rate of output or from the point of view of traceability. Fixed and variable costs relate to the rate of output; joint or common costs, to traceability.

Fixed Costs. One of the distinguishing features of railroad costs is that a relatively large proportion of them are fixed for a particular period of time. Although it is axiomatic that all costs are variable in the long run, and that the impact of fixed costs is only for the short run, the short run in railroad transportation may be for a considerable period of time. Rights of way, roadbeds, and bridges may have a life of half a century or more. Locomotives, passenger cars, and freight cars are subject more to obsolescence than depreciation, which means that the investment in them is not a function of output; instead, it is a function of time. The dieselization of American railroads forced the retirement of a large volume of steam locomotives that showed little effect of wear when they were replaced. In other words, the plant facilities of railroads which give rise to a large part of the fixed costs last for a longer period of time than is true for most industries. Adjustments of total costs to output respond much more slowly to output than is the case for most productive activities.

Fixed costs for railroads are also large relative to total costs at any time. In fact, they always constitute the bulk of railroad costs for what may be termed the "short run." This is because the investment in the railroad plant is large relative to output for a given period. The relationship between investment and total income may be expressed in terms of capital turnover per annum. This is the ratio of capital investment to annual gross revenues from railroad services. The average annual turnover for railroad investment is about once every three years; that is, for an investment of $600 million, the average annual gross revenue will be about $200 million. By way of contrast, for the steel industry, the turnover is about once every one and one-half years; for petroleum, about once a year; and for large merchandising establishments, from 2 to 3 times a year. In fact, the only other industries that have a slow turnover like railroads are public utilities, in which it may range from 4 years for gas utilities to 10 years for hydroelectric plants.

It is difficult to state the precise proportion of total costs that is made up of fixed costs. In the first place, it will depend upon the rate of operations. Assuming the "normal" or average rate of operations that is

[1]For a more complete discussion of transport pricing, see D. F. Pegrum, *Transportation: Economics and Public Policy* (Homewood, Ill.; Richard D. Irwin, Inc., 1963), Part II.

used to calculate the rate of turnover, the fixed costs have rather commonly been estimated to constitute two thirds of the total. A study by the Cost Finding Section of the Interstate Commerce Commission[2] estimated that long-run rail operating costs were 20 to 30 per cent fixed, if investment was excluded. However, it concluded that only 50 to 70 per cent of rail investment was variable. Whatever the precise facts may be, it is obvious that fixed costs are a large part of railroad costs and therefore occupy a very prominent role in price-making decisions. As was pointed out in the section on pricing in this book, fixed costs are not "economic" costs in terms of price determination and therefore should not be taken into consideration when decisions are being made on rate of output or on the prices which should be charged for specific units of the output.

The relatively high fixed costs in railroad transport are the result of a number of factors that are characteristic of the industry. As has already been mentioned, investment is large, relative to annual output. This means that interest is a larger element of cost than for industries where the capital turnover is more rapid. Railroads must be able to retain and attract capital if they are to continue to serve, as well as to improve their service in competition with other agencies. A considerable part of railroad depreciation, especially if obsolescence is included under this heading, is independent of the volume of traffic. Much of the rolling stock becomes obsolete instead of wearing out, and a good deal of the railroad plant wears out because of weather and other factors, rather than use. Transportation expenses do not vary directly with the traffic. Minimum train crews and station and yard forces must be maintained, even through traffic varies widely; and motive equipment can be adapted only within limits to changing traffic volumes. Property taxes are a fixed cost, and state and local taxes based on the assessed valuation of the property are a significant item of railroad expense. Finally, as common carriers, railroads are required by law to maintain minimum train schedules on a regular basis, even though the traffic may not warrant them. Maintenance of unprofitable passenger service at the present time is a genuine source of difficulty for the railroads.

Variable Costs. Variable costs for railroads, as an average, are probably somewhat less than 50 per cent of total costs for the short run. These are the costs that are important in any particular time when pricing decisions are being made. Furthermore, this short run covers a considerable period of time, somewhat over five years. Thus, for railroads, the total costs which must be covered over time, if they are to continue in business successfully, are much greater than those above which it will pay to take traffic at any particular time rather than decline to do so.[3] It is this rather

[2]*Rail Freight Service Costs in the Various Rate Territories of the United States* (Senate Document No. 63, 78th Congress, 1st sess.) (Washington, D.C.: U.S. Government Printing Office, 1943), p. 75.

[3]The short run for pricing purposes must at least be as long as the period that is required to make changes in rates.

wide range between the total costs which must be covered over time if operations are to continue and the minimum to which prices may fall before traffic should be refused that makes it economically possible for railroad rates to fluctuate widely with varying volumes of traffic. In other words, the "economic" costs to be considered in railroad rate making for a given period are relatively less than those of enterprises with lower relative fixed costs. Unfortunately, it is not easy to ascertain with precision the range between the total costs that need to be covered and the minimum that must form the basis of decision for rate making.[4] Whatever the facts may be, it is clear that railroad pricing is subject to a wider range of variation over a considerable period of time with changing rates of output than is the case for most industries.

Joint and Common Costs. Cost-price relationships in railroad transport are also complicated by the presence of joint and common costs. The role that these play in this industry has been the subject of much debate.[5] On one point, at least, there seems to be complete agreement: When rail transport is supplied in one direction, it inevitably is supplied for the back haul. This is a case of true jointness. Professor Pigou contended that this was the only example of joint cost in rail transport, and many agree with him. Whether this is so depends partly on the definition of what constitutes a unit of railroad service. Pigou took the ton-mile as the unit and then insisted that the output was homogeneous. This, however, seems to be an oversimplification. If a railroad supplies service from A to C through B, it inescapably supplies service to B. The service to B is a different one from that which is rendered to C. Similarly, traffic may move at different times of the year. In other words, railroads are multiple-product firms in which provision of facilities for some places and at some times in one direction provides services for other places at other times and in the opposite direction. Furthermore, a ton-mile of freight of one commodity is not the same service as a ton-mile for another commodity, as evidenced by the differences in costs which may be incurred in supplying each. How much of railroad transport involves joint and common costs is not readily ascertainable, but they appear to loom larger than is commonly assumed by the regulatory authorities.

Cost Allocation. It is not possible to calculate the precise costs of performing each of the many services which railroads provide. In the first place, railroads are multiple-product enterprises. This means that there are joint and common costs; and, as was pointed out earlier, there is no rational method of allocating these costs. Any allocation that may be undertaken is arbitrary and serves no useful purpose.

[4]See D. P. Locklin, *Economics of Transportation*, (4th ed.; Homewood, Ill.: Richard D. Irwin, Inc., 1954), chap. 8; A. M. Milne, *The Economics of Inland Transport* (London: Sir Isaac Pitman & Sons, Ltd., 1955), chap. v; D. F. Pegrum, *loc. cit.*

[5]For a careful review of the literature on this subject and an extensive bibliography, see Locklin, "A Review of the Literature on Railway Rate Theory," *Quarterly Journal of Economics*, Vol. XLVII (February, 1933), pp. 167 f.

In the second place, railroads have large fixed costs. In so far as these are not joint, they could be allocated on an average basis among the units of output; but this would have meaning only after the volume of traffic had been ascertained, not before it had been moved. In other words, the fixed expense per unit of homogeneous traffic can be discovered only after the traffic has been obtained. What this means in terms of pricing has already been discussed—namely, that fixed costs are not "economic" costs for price-making decisions. As a consequence of fixed and joint costs in railroads, "average" cost is a meaningless term; and as a basis for decisions on the rates that should be charged, it is positively deceptive.

Cost determination is an essential part of railroad rate-making procedure. Much remains to be done by way of more precise cost finding for railroad traffic movements. The amount of joint costs, in all probability, can be obtained with considerably greater accuracy than is now the case; and the same remarks apply to fixed costs. No matter how "scientific" cost accounting becomes, however, it cannot allocate joint costs scientifit cally or fixed costs in advance. What is urgently needed at the presentime is better information on the minimum economic costs below which rates on particular items of traffic should not be permitted to go. The relationships of the rates above those minima should be based on market and policy considerations, not on cost.

Nature of Railroad Monopoly. During the railroad era, it came to be recognized that unregulated competition among railroads was an unworkable means of establishing satisfactory prices and that monopoly in some form or another was bound to emerge in the end. Monopoly and monopoly pricing was an inescapable feature of railroad transport because of the economic structure of the railroads. In other words, they were what has come to be known as "natural" monopolies.

The word "natural," as it is used in this connection, refers to the fact that monopoly emerges from the economic characteristics of the industry in question and that competition is forced to play a very subordinate role in the fixation of prices to be charged for the particular type of services offered. As one economist puts it, with reference to railroads: "Competition fails to establish a normal level of rates sufficiently remunerative to attract the additional investments of capital that recurrently become necessary."[6]

There are several reasons why monopoly is natural to certain industries. Capital has to be invested in amounts which are large relative to the market opportunities available for the goods or services that are to be produced. Capital costs, therefore, form a relatively large part of the total costs of production; and addition to the plant will involve a large proportionate increase in capital investment and will necessitate a large

[6]Eliot Jones, *Principles of Railway Transportation* (New York: Macmillan Co., 1925), p. 91.

prospective increase in the market. A railroad, for example, has to make large initial outlays to build a single-track line and acquire the necessary terminal facilities to operate it. When that plant is utilized to capacity, double-tracking will require a large additional investment, which cannot profitably be made unless there is prospect of a large increase in traffic. Expansion of this type entails difficult problems of market anticipation, because the facilities will have to be built well in advance of market opportunities. In the meantime, the traffic which is available will have to bear the burden of keeping the railroad in operation until the new traffic has been built up. If, instead of double-tracking, a new railroad were to be built, an almost complete duplication of facilities would be necessary; and the immediately available traffic would be inadequate to give either road a profit. In addition, the economies of scale which could be obtained by a fuller utilization of facilities by more continuous movement of traffic in both directions would be unavailable.

Then there is the fact that much of the investment that has been made is specialized, both as to functions and as to markets. Railroad tracks are only useful where they are laid and cannot readily be turned to other areas if the markets shift. In addition, they have little use except for supplying railroad transportation to a geographically fixed area.

Natural monopolies are also characterized by a concomitance of production and consumption. That is, the services must be consumed in direct conjunction with the production facilities. This results in the absence of what is known as "shopper's technique." The consumer cannot shop around, because no other supply is readily available to him. This is especially true of public utilities. The consumer is forced to take the services offered by a particular supplier. Otherwise, he must go without or move.

The facilities of two suppliers are not available to him, because it is too costly for both to supply the equipment necessary to be ready to serve. At the same time, producers can serve only those whom they are able to contact with their production facilities. The physical area served by the plant constitutes the limits of its market, and it cannot readily change those limits, because of the extreme immobility of its production facilities.

In other words, concomitance of production and consumption, together with relatively large amounts of investment in plant that is specialized both geographically and functionally, makes the presence of more than one producer in most markets impossible. Thus, direct competition is absent in most of the markets, and readily available alternatives or substitutes are not usually present. For these reasons, it has long been recognized that direct competition over the entire range of output of natural monopolies is an unsatisfactory way of trying to secure reasonable prices. As a consequence, monopoly in particular markets has been accorded public sanction and even protection.

The foregoing characteristics of rail transport have not changed under the impact of the growth of the newer agencies. What has changed is the alternatives that are available to consumers. Uncontrolled or over-all competition among railroads today would be an uneconomical as it ever was. The question of competition among railroads rests on very different grounds from the question of competition among motor carriers, water carriers, or air carriers. Whether these agencies should be dealt with in the same way as railroads will be discussed later.

Discrimination. The complexity of railroad costs, together with the monopoly features of railroad transportation, have created the exceedingly difficult problem of price discrimination. If all railroad costs were variable and directly associated with output, discrimination would be easy to detect. If railroads possessed no element of monopoly, they would be unable to practice price discrimination. However, railroads are multiple-product enterprises, as a consequence of which it is not possible to ascertain precise unit costs. At best, it is only possible to find the minimum "economic" cost below which a rate should not be permitted to go. In earlier years, the railroads enjoyed a good deal of monopoly power and hence were able to discriminate, no matter how that word is defined. At the present time, railroads do and must engage in differential charging, in the sense that rates will deviate from directly ascertainable costs and from average costs. How much this represents discrimination, in the monopoly sense, is a matter of conjecture. Whatever the facts may be, it is clear that they do engage in differential pricing, if that term can be applied to multiple-product pricing; and it is to this that the term "discrimination" commonly refers.

Discriminatory pricing in railroad rate making today is of two types—namely, discrimination among commodities and discrimination between places, or local discrimination. There is a wide range in the rates that are charged for transporting different commodities. The rate for hauling a ton of coal one mile is different from that for hauling a ton of steel, and both are less than that which is charged for hauling a ton of furniture. These differences may be explained on three grounds. First of all, there are differences in cost of service. Some articles require special and more expensive types of equipment than others, some are more bulky than others, and some entail greater liability and risk to the carrier. Rate differentials based on these cost differences do not constitute discrimination. Second, there is the element of joint and common costs. These must be covered by the traffic as a whole, and they cannot be attributed to any particular item of traffic. The market will have to be the gauge of the amount which the various commodities will contribute to these; and in so far as the market has competitive alternatives, the resulting differential pricing will not be discrimination, at least in any monopoly sense. Third, railroad pricing may also be based upon some monopoly powers. To the extent that this is so, some commodities may be required to bear charges that can be explained neither by assignable costs nor by joint costs. This will be true discrimination. How much of this exists in fact cannot be readily ascertained; and so long as a railroad is not making unreasonable profits in total, it is difficult to see how genuine discrimination exists. If the competitive alternatives to the buyers of transport services are such that the railroads can earn only a reasonable profit, then the differential charging will have to be explained on the basis of recouping unassignable costs in accordance with what the market will pay, and not on the basis of discrimination emerging from monopoly.

Local or place discrimination refers to differences in rates on a particular commodity that are unrelated to the distance that the commodity is hauled. If rates are based on cost, they will not be proportionate to cost, for two reasons: First, the terminal costs at each end will be the same, regardless of distance; and second, it costs more per mile to haul a commodity a short distance than a longer one, although the difference will diminish rather rapidly as the length of the haul increases and will disappear altogether over longer distances. Apart from these two qualifications, however, it is generally held that rates should vary with distance; and when this is not so, local or place discrimination is said to exist. This may take the form of equal rates for unequal distances, rates increasing with distance less rapidly than the cost of service justifies, or the charging of higher rates for shorter than for longer hauls over the same line in the same direction.

The problem of ascertaining whether place discrimination is being practiced is essentially the same as for any other form of discrimination. A railroad may haul freight from A to B and similar freight from A to C through B. If C is a place where there is water competition, the railroad may be forced to offer lower rates to C, in order to get the traffic that may move by water; and if there is unused capacity, it will pay the railroad to take the traffic, as long as the rate is higher than the costs that are directly attributable to that traffic. If the railroad is to stay in business, places like B will have to pay a higher rate under such circumstances. Whether this is discrimination—in the monopoly sense, at least—can be a matter of debate; the critical question really is whether such pricing is harmful, so that it should be limited or prohibited. If the railroad has unused capacity, if the lower rates to the more distant point make for more complete use of that capacity, and if the lower rates are compelled by another carrier that is carrying the traffic at its relevant costs, then the pricing is economical.[7] This is the situation that is commonly met at seaports which have the natural advantage of location and which, as a consequence, are able to secure more favorable rates. The intermediate

[7]See W. J. Baumol, *et al.*, "The Role of Cost in the Minimum Pricing of Railroad Services," *The Journal of Business of the University of Chicago*, Vol. XXXV, No. 4 (October, 1962), pp. 1–10.

point is not placed at a disadvantage by the pricing policy of the railroad, because the more distant point will get the favorable rates whether the railroad meets the competition or not. If, as a result of the practice, the railroad receives more than a fair profit in total, the remedy is to lower the higher intermediate rates, since these would be the source of the monopoly profit, not to raise the longer-haul rates. In other words, if unreasonable discrimination exists, the remedy is to lower the higher rates, not vice versa; and this is the corrective for any form of discriminatory pricing, because it is only from the higher prices that monopoly profits, if there are any, can be obtained. If, instead, public authority follows the policy of raising the lower rates, it is then protecting competitors, not protecting competition, which is presumably the objective of national policy; it is also not assisting in a greater utilization of capacity, which is the economical thing to do.

Ruinous Competition. Over-all competition between natural monopolies of the same type is ruinous. If two or more electrical utilities were allowed to compete for the business of every customer, it would be necessary for them to duplicate practically all of their facilities. This would result in continuous excess capacity, because all of the productive capacity of all of the companies could never by utilized at the same time. Because of the high proportion of fixed costs, each would endeavor to utilize its unused capacity by sales at prices that would only cover the extra or out-of-pocket costs. This would drive all prices down, so that none of the competitors would be able to cover its full costs. The end result of this would be the emergence of a single firm. It was the recognition of this fact that led to regulation under which public utilities have been recognized as monopolies and competition has been deliberately restricted by public authority. It should be noted, however, that competition between gas and electrical utilities is not ruinous. Over a wide range, each enjoys a monopoly, because the services are not readily substitutable. Where substitution is possible on a price basis, either one may be allowed to lower its rates so as to obtain business and utilize unused capacity. Many off-peak rates are sanctioned for the purpose of meeting competition.

Railroads are faced with the threat of ruinous competition, because they are natural monopolies. The problem has been more difficult to control in the railroad field because of the early competitive construction of them and also because of competing routes, competing markets, and competing areas of production. Even if all the railroads were under a single ownership a great deal of this competition would remain, and differential rate making would still be a vital issue. Problems of rate relationships among commodities and between places would present the same economic questions, because they emerge from the economic structure of railroads, not from the form of ownership.

Motor Carriers

Competitive Features. The development of the internal combustion engine has radically altered the technical and economic structure of transportation. It is no longer composed largely of natural monopolies. On the contrary, the economic features which characterize natural monopolies are almost completely lacking in the field of motor transport. The technical units are relatively small and may be very small. Operations may be started with a very small investment, and expansion may be achieved with very small increments of investment in direct and almost immediate response to the growth in traffic. Most of the facilities are not highly specialized or unalterably committed to a particular market or geographic area, and they can readily be shifted to any other market. Physically, the highways or routes are available to all who wish to use them. Alternative sources of supply can readily be made available to the buyer or consumer. There is no absence of shopper's technique; consumers may even supply their own facilities and do so a great deal of the time. Economic limitations on the additions to facilities are very slight, because small increases in traffic increase the need for additional equipment, at least within very narrow limits, and these additions may be made in small units. Existing facilities can be completely utilized except within narrow limits, and additional traffic can be accommodated only by acquiring additional motive power. This will not result in an appreciable lowering of the average total unit costs of output, since the additional output comes as a result of the incurrence of additional costs that are largely proportionate to output. Mr. Bonavia expresses this by saying: "When the internal combustion engine was sufficiently developed it became possible to enter the business of carrying goods with a very small initial investment, building up the business by reinvesting profits. The qualities necessary for success were largely similar to those required in the tramp shipping industry. The lorry, like the tramp steamer, often competes for freight under, it has been said, 'conditions of almost classical simplicity.' "[8]

Fixed and Variable Costs. Evidence supporting the foregoing evaluation of the economics of motor transport is afforded by studies which have been made of the cost characteristics of motor carrier operations. The Cost Section of the Bureau of Transport Economics and Statistics of the Interstate Commerce Commission has made some elaborate studies of cost behavior for both railroads and motor carriers.[9] These were made for the purpose of examining the relationships of fixed to variable costs

[8]M. R. Bonavia, *The Economics of Transport* (New York: Pitman Publishing Corp., 1947), p. 66.

[9]Interstate Commerce Commission, Bureau of Transport Economics and Statistics, *Explanation of the Development of Motor Carrier Costs* (Statement No. 4725) (Washington, D.C.: U.S. Government Printing Office, 1949), p. 103.

for different carriers and for varying conditions of operations. They endeavored to portray the basic principles underlying transportation costs and the relation of those costs to rate making.

The study on motor transport involved a wide sampling of the statistics available and an extensive analysis of operating costs under varying lengths of haul in different traffic densities. One analysis, based on data of Class I common carriers of general freight in the Central Region in 1943, involving an average haul of 300 to 349 miles, showed that, on the average, 93.6 per cent of the costs varied directly, and proportionately, with the traffic, while the remaining 6.4 per cent did not vary with the traffic; that is, they were fixed, regardless of traffic.[10]

The conclusion drawn for the study as a whole was that for Class I general commodity carriers, between 90 and 100 per cent of the operating expenses were directly proportional to output. This contrasted with long-run rail operating costs, which were estimated to be between 70 and 80 per cent variable if investment was excluded. But only 50 to 70 per cent of rail investment is variable, according to this study, which means that the variable expenses of railroads are a much lower proportion of total expenses, since railroads have a very heavy investment.

The contrast in the variability of costs between rail and motor carriers is explained by the fact that fixed costs are present in rail maintenance-of-way expenses and in the capital costs resulting from the investment in road property. The corresponding roadway costs for motor carriers are distributed on a "use" basis through gas taxes and license fees; and in so far as the motor carriers are concerned, they become proportional to the traffic carried.[11]

The operating ratios of rail and motor carriers reflect the same situation. Where fixed costs are high and the costs of capital a large part of the total, the operating ratio must be relatively low if the operations are to be profitable. If the fixed costs are low, the reverse will be true. In 1947, the operating ratio for Class I railroads was 78.27 per cent; in 1948, it was 77.26 per cent; while in 1941, it was only 68.53 per cent; in 1963 it was 77.95 per cent. The operating ratio for Class I motor carriers of property was 95.1 per cent in 1948 and 93.2 per cent in 1947. It averaged 96.4 per cent for the 8-year period from 1940 to 1947. It was 96.5 per cent for 1962.

Another test, which supports the two which have just been given, is afforded by the ratio of gross revenues from operations to the total capital investment, or the turnover of capital. The turnover of capital for railroads is about once every 3 years; or, to put it another way, the

[10]Interstate Commerce Commission, Bureau of Accounts and Cost Finding, *Explanation of Rail Cost Finding Principles and Procedures* (Statement No. 2–48) (Washington, D.C.: U.S. Government Printing Office, 1948), p. 88.

[11]Ford K. Edwards, "Cost Analysis in Transportation," *American Economic Review*, Vol. XXXVII, No. 2 (May, 1947), p. 453.

gross revenues from operations of railroads typically constitute, annually, about one third of the capital investment. The turnover for Class I motor carriers of general freight engaged in intercity service was approximately 3 times in 1948. Although individual carriers necessarily varied somewhat from this over-all picture, the variations from the average do not seem to have any correlation with the size of the individual carriers.[12]

Basis of Cost Features. The cost features of motor transport, and especially motor trucking transport, bring out clearly the fact that, as an industry, it possesses those economic features which characterize highly competitive industry. It does not have to provide its own highway, where the elements of fixed costs loom large. Instead, it is able to use the highways in which the investment is provided by public funds. The carrier's contribution to this investment, or the fixed costs arising therefrom, is made through various kinds of taxes, which are largely dependent upon the amount of use made of the highway by the individual carrier. In other words, from the standpoint of the carrier, the highway costs are variable costs. It is the state which has to take the responsibility for the fixed costs. Terminal costs are relatively low in motor transport and, in the main, have the same cost features for the individual carrier as do the highway costs, and for the same reasons.

The equipment is highly flexible, because it can be operated in relatively small units. Its mobility on the highway eliminates the necessity of rigid scheduling which the limitations of rail trackage impose on railroads. Then, too, the equipment can be moved from one highway to another with very few impediments. In other words, the equipment can follow the traffic. Finally, the small size of the operating units gives an extremely high degree of adaptability of plants to the volume of business or traffic.

Absence of Ruinous Competition. Competition among motor carriers cannot be ruinous. Ruinous competition, it should be emphasized, can arise only when fixed costs are a large part of the total costs of a firm, and when, as a consequence of the techniques of production, the consumer is unable to shop around. The essence of competition is that it provides the incentive to strive for profits and the compulsion to go somewhere else if they are not forthcoming. Reliance on competition keeps costs to the consuming public at the minimum necessary to attract the services for which it is willing to pay. There is no danger of rates rising above that level if competition is not restricted by public action. In other words, the cost structure of motor transport is such as to make it possible for competition to function as a fully effective force for establishing economical prices. In fact, obstacles placed in the way of such competitive pricing will redound only to the benefit of the protected carriers.

[12]This indicates severe limitations on economies of scale in motor transport. See M. J. Roberts, "Some Aspects of Motor Carrier Costs: Firm Size, Efficiency and Financial Health," *Land Economics*, Vol. XXXII, No. 3 (August, 1956), pp. 228–38.

It will be to the disadvantage of the consuming public and the carriers that are precluded from competing.

Other Carriers

The other carriers of our domestic transport system are not as important in the competitive picture as the rail and motor carriers; but they fit, in terms of their economic characteristics, into one of the two groups.

Pipe Lines. Pipe lines have cost characteristics similar to those of railroads—that is, they are natural monopolies with high fixed costs and specialized plants. The cost aspects upon which their pricing decisions are based are essentially the same as those of the railroads, but the pricing problems are simpler because of a greater homogeneity of services performed.

Water Carriers. The cost characteristics of domestic water transport are essentially the same as those of motor carriers, and for the same reasons. Ownership of the vessels can be separated from that of the waterways, canals, and terminals. Shipping costs are mostly variable; and the industry, therefore, is highly competitive in its structure. Discrimination is not a serious question or unavoidable, as in the case of railroads; and competition among water carriers is not a threat to consumer interests. It has been urged, on occasion, that competition has resulted in suicidal rate cutting, especially during the depression of the 1930's. This seems, however, to be a case of excess capacity, which it is the function of competition to eliminate. The carriers which cannot survive such competition have no economic justification to continue. In fact, concern for the survival of domestic water transportation has created the determination to protect it against competition from the railroads. This is certainly not a basis for price control in water transport, and the economics of water transport do not disclose why it is more necessary than for industry in general.

Air Transport. The economic characteristics of air transport are basically similar to those of motor transport, although the fixed costs may loom somewhat larger. In 1948, the scheduled air lines had an investment of 65 cents per dollar of gross income, which indicates a capital turnover of something like 1½ times a year. Because air transport costs are largely variable, there is no economic basis for natural monopoly or ruinous competition. Competition can function effectively as a regulator of prices.[13]

[13]Air transport is still largely in an experimental stage, with military considerations playing the primary role in the construction of aircraft, even for commercial purposes. Partly as a result of this, not much study has yet been given to the economic aspects of air transport. See R. E. Westmeyer, *Economics of Transportation* (New York: Prentice-Hall, Inc., 1952), chap. 29. See also H. D. Koontz, "Domestic Air Line Self-Sufficiency," *American Economic Review*, Vol. XLII, No. 1 (March, 1952), pp. 103–25; and discussion with J. P. Carter, *ibid.*, Vol. XLIII, No. 3 (June, 1953), pp. 368–77.

PRICING FOR TRANSPORT SERVICES

Today, public authority, through the various state and federal commissions, sets the prices which common carriers in all modes of transport may charge. The regulation of railroad rates developed after 1870, first of all, as a means of dealing with discrimination. This led to the control of maximum prices, to the exercise of the power to limit rate differentials, and, finally, to the fixing of minimum rates, which meant that precise rates came to be prescribed by public authority. The regulation of the rates of common carriers by water, motor, and air was not undertaken in any significant way anywhere until after 1920. Even then, the pattern that was followed was that which had been developed for the railroads.[14]

The General Level of Rates

The regulation of railroad rates developed on the theory that railroad transportation was an industry characterized by monopoly, which necessitated control of prices in the public interest. The original purpose was to protect the shipper against unreasonable rate differentials and exorbitant prices. Experience in imposing upper limits on railroad rates soon disclosed the fact that some measuring rod was necessary by which to gauge what that upper limit should be. The fixing of maxima on prices meant that the profits which a firm could earn were also limited. If private operation was to be successful, the profits had to be adequate for that purpose. In addition, the law of the land prevented public authority from limiting profits below what was fair and reasonable.

Thus, before particular prices can be set, it becomes necessary in some way to determine what the general level of rates should be. That is, it is necessary to ascertain the total revenue that is required before the specific prices which will yield that total revenue can be established. To do this means that total costs must be calculated, as well as the amount of the fair profit. To prevent profits from being siphoned off through costs, public authority must exercise contol over the costs which are to be covered and over the quality of the service which the costs are supposed to provide. Finally, a measuring rod must be developed as the basis for deciding what constitutes a fair profit.

The measuring rod for fair profit, first prescribed by the Supreme Court in the case of *Smyth* v. *Ames* (1898),[15] was comprised of some seven different items that had to be considered. Congress passed the Valuation Act of 1913, which instructed the Interstate Commerce Commission to make a valuation of all the railroads of the country on a basis that would meet the Court requirements. In the Transportation Act of 1920, Congress instructed the Commission to prescribe railroad rates that would

[14]The regulation of passenger fares is a relatively simple task and does not present any really complex problems of price control. It is not dealt with here.
[15]169 U.S. 466.

yield a fair return on the fair value for rate making which the Commission had determined, the fair return to be set between 5½ and 6 per cent, at the discretion of the Commission. The Emergency Transportation Act of 1933 repealed this provision and substituted in its place a rule of rate making whereby the Commission was to prescribe just and reasonable rates which gave consideration to the effect of rates on the movement of traffic, to the need for efficient railway transportation service, and to the need of revenues sufficient to supply such service. This very indefinite prescription is the legislative basis for controlling the general level of railroad rates today. Similar "standards" apply to the other common carriers; but because of the relative unimportance of fixed costs in motor transport, the Commission has endeavored to use the operating ratio as a guide to the general level of rates. The operating ratio is the ratio between operating expenses and operating revenues.

Factors Affecting Particular Rates

On the assumption that the general level of rates has been determined, the problem of rate making then becomes one of adjusting the rates on each commodity and for each haul, so as to provide the total revenue which the carrier needs. In determining what these rates should be, public authority must give consideration to cost of service, demand for service, and standards of public policy.

Cost of Service. The theory underlying price regulation is that the price for the services or commodities of regulated enterprises shall, as nearly as possible, be the same as they would be if thoroughgoing competition obtained. Cost of service therefore plays a primary role in the deliberations of public authority. The Interstate Commerce Commission proceeds on the initial assumption that each item of traffic should bear its fully allocated costs. This is what would happen if perfect competition obtained. First of all, therefore, each item of traffic is assessed with all the costs that are directly traceable to it. To these directly ascertainable costs is added a predetermined percentage of the nonallocable costs, which percentage may be arrived at on the assumption that each kind of traffic should contribute its proportionate share to the nonallocable costs, although this may be modified to account for some differences in conditions of haulage that are not reflected in the direct costs.

Even though one were to assume that all traffic should be priced on the basis of fully allocated costs, it is clear that it is impossible to give this term any meaning other than an arbitrary one. There is no means whereby nonallocable joint and fixed costs can be traced to particular items of traffic; and no formula, by the very nature of the problem, can be developed which can result in "scientific" rate making on a cost basis.

A strictly full-cost formula for rate making—even though, perchance, it yielded adequate total revenues—would nevertheless be arbitrary and would not, for this reason, result in the most economical utilization of transport facilities. If costs are to be used for rate making, with the latter purpose in view, traffic should be assessed with the costs that can be traced to it directly. The remaining costs should be recovered on the basis of what the market will yield, with due regard to limitation of monopoly profits, if that should be necessary.

Value of Service. Cost of service as the sole determinant of transport prices, especially railroad rates, breaks down because of the difficulties connected with ascertaining costs and because of the market situation which prevents the full utilization of the plant when price making ignores demand. Regulatory authorities recognize the influence of demand under the names of value of service, value of the commodity, or what the traffic will bear. In rate-making administration, at least, these three terms do not always mean precisely the same thing. Value of service is used as a means of apportioning nonallocable costs on the basis of what the market is willing to contribute, except that the limitation on such pricing is the total to which the carrier is entitled. As a consequence, the amount that each item is required to bear may be tempered by the judgment of the Commission rather than by the limitations of the market. Value of the commodity is supposed to reflect—in part, at least—differences in value of service, based on differences in the value of commodities, on the theory that commodities of higher value can and ought to pay higher rates than lower-valued commodities. Apart from the fact that commodities of higher value may entail higher costs of transport because of considerations such as greater carrier liability, there is no economic reason, at least, why they should bear a higher rate; and there is no a priori reason why they always can. "What the traffic will bear" is commonly taken to mean charging for each item of traffic what the market will pay. In this extreme form, it might lead to unreasonable monopoly profits. Where such is not the case, or where traffic is not contributing its "full share" to the nonallocable costs, what the traffic will bear is the same as value of service.

Standards of Public Policy. In fixing particular rates, commissions may also take into consideration the effect of rates on military policy, foreign trade, utilization of natural resources, industrial location, and so forth. These factors have had considerable influence on the distribution of the burden of covering the nonallocable costs and, therefore, on the shaping of the rate structures of the country. As long as it is assumed that total carrier revenues have to be limited, considerations of social policy have a place in rate making. They can have little place, however, in a competitive industry like motor transport; and their role in rail transport today is of dubious validity.

The Determination of Particular Rates

The determination of the charges which particular items of traffic should bear is a task that involves an enormous amount of sheer mechanics in price making and price regulation. Thousands of different commodities move among innumerable places within the country; and prices for these services, which are readily ascertainable by the employees of the transport companies and by the shippers, must be established. The pricing structure which has emerged has grown up over a long period of time and has been subject to rather continuous, although gradual, modification. It reflects the general considerations that have just been discussed and has become formalized in a number of different ways, most especially with regard to railroads.

Freight Classification. As a step in the process of pricing for particular services, railroads developed the practice of freight classification. The large number of commodities hauled were grouped into a limited number of classes or categories, on the basis of cost and value-of-service considerations. This procedure gave a "rating" for each commodity—first class, second class, and so forth—so that the first step in determining the charge to be made for shipping a commodity was to ascertain the class to which it was assigned. In 1952, a uniform classification for the United States was prescribed by the Interstate Commerce Commission, under which commodities fell into the same classes, no matter from what point or to what point they were shipped in this country. The classification merely established rate relationships in percentage terms, not in specific prices, among the groupings and between carload and less than carload rates. They reflected cost and value of service factors already discussed.

Although the classification now is uniform for the whole country, individual railroads or groups of railroads may be permitted to publish exceptions. This constitutes a recognition of the diversity of market conditions throughout the country. In addition to the exceptions, there are also commodity rates under which a shipment may be given special treatment apart from the classification. When a commodity rate is applicable, the price of shipment to be charged is given for that commodity between two specifically named points. Apparently, about 80 per cent of the railroad traffic of the country moves on commodity rates. The class-rate structure obviously applies only to a limited amount of railroad freight and to an even smaller percentage of freight by other carriers.

Freight Tariffs. The rates, or prices charged, for transporting the various commodities between specified points are published in the freight tariffs. For traffic which moves under freight classification, the tariff gives the price or rate on each classification from a particular station to every other station. Commodity tariffs give the rates on particular commodities from a particular station to every other station. Thus, every shipping point has a different set of tariffs, although they all have the same classifications.

Rate Systems. Until the adoption of uniform freight classification in 1952, much of the freight was classified differently in the three major territories of the country. In addition, there were a number of subterritories. Even today, there are subterritories for intrastate shipments; and commodity rates may also provide exceptions. The greater number of items shipped move in accordance with class rates, but the greater amount of the tonnage moves independently of them. In so far as the rate structures of the country can be characterized as rate systems, they consist of a uniform classification for the country for rate relationships of commodities, apart from the exceptions and what may be termed a number of "groups," as far as distance relationships are concerned.

A basic assumption of the Interstate Commerce Commission is that rates should increase with distance, due consideration being given to differences in terrain and so forth for different parts of the country. In 1952, the Commission established a uniform class-rate scale for the entire country except the Mountain-Pacific Territory, which embraces all of the eleven western states, excluding eastern Colorado. This endeavor to develop, out of a highly diversified situation, a uniform and unified approach to the distance factor in rate making has encountered difficulties similar to those of creating uniform classification. Competition of various kinds has precluded any uniform distance pattern for the movement of the bulk of the tonnage of railroad freight. Thus, different production centers located at different distances from common markets may compel an equalization of rates, if these centers are to be enabled to compete, and if the railroads serving them are to participate in the transportation. This may result in the blanketing of wide areas of origin or destination. California citrus fruit, for example, is shipped to all points east of the Mississippi at the same price, regardless of destination.

One of the most controversial aspects of the distance problem in railroad rate making relates to what is known as the long-and-short-haul principle. This states that a greater charge should not be made for a shorter haul than for a longer one where the shorter is included within the longer. The reason why railroads may wish to engage in pricing that contradicts this is, of course, that they will be better off to take the more distant traffic rather than forego it and that they cannot afford to lower their intermediate rates to the level of the more distant ones. When this is the result of competition which is beyond the control of the Interstate Commerce Commission, or where the higher-cost carrier has to meet the rate of a lower-cost carrier, relief from the long-and-short-haul restriction may be granted. The relief is afforded mostly to railroads because of the high variability of the costs of the other carriers, which prevents them from engaging in any appreciable distance differentiation. If railroads are granted such relief, the rates which are quoted must be reasonably compensatory—that is, they must cover (or more than cover) the additional expenses incurred, they must be no lower than necessary to meet existing competition, they must not threaten the extinction of legitimate water competition, and they must not impose an undue burden on the other traffic of the carrier to which the relief is granted.

One special problem of relief presents itself when railroads alone compete with each other between two points, with one carrier enjoying a shorter direct route and the other having a longer, roundabout route. In this situation, it has been the practice of the Commission to deny relief to the shorter road but permit the longer one to violate the long-and-short-haul principle under the conditions of reasonableness just set forth. If the revenues of the shorter road are high enough to give it a reasonable profit, it really has no basis of complaint; nor do the intermediate points on the longer road, since the added traffic is assisting in bearing part of the total cost. The terminal points can scarcely complain against the limitation on competition, because in the absence of regulation, it would probably be eliminated by combination or agreement.

Motor Carriers. Motor carriers rates are not as formalized as railroad rates and not as systematic, even for common carriers. This is because of the competitive nature of the business, predominance of short hauls, and the greater response to local conditions. In addition, a good deal of motor traffic moves under contract rates which provide for point-to-point charges, while the shipment of agricultural commodities is not subject to any regulation in interstate commerce.

Common carriers by motor have tended to base their rates on the railroad scale, although the levels of the two are not the same. Mileage scales are widely used, but they are not exactly in proportion to distance. It is common to group points of origin and destination. These groupings do not cover such wide areas as those of the railroads. Motor carriers also use a smaller spread of classes than the railroads. In addition, motor carriers are not subject to long-and-short-haul restrictions.

Other Carriers. Only a small fraction of water transportation is subject to common carrier regulation by the Interstate Commerce Commission. Class rates are patterned somewhat on railroad class rates, but are usually lower. Pipe-line rates are based primarily on distance. Minimum tender requirements have to be met by independent shippers. These may vary all the way from 100,000 barrels to the Texas rule of 500 barrels. Rates for freight by air are based on mileage, with application of the tapering principle. The scheduled air lines have a one-class system for class rates, but they also publish commodity rates. Rates are not graduated for volume up to 16,000 pounds for these lines.

Value of Service versus Cost of Service

Rate making for railroads is obviously an extremely complicated task. Railroads, as a public business, have not been allowed to adopt pricing practices and procedures that characterize private business, or the same practices and procedures that characterize most freight transport outside of railroads. Present competitive conditions are compelling a complete re-examination of public policy on this score. If existing policies of railroad rate regulation are to continue without major modification, it will be necessary to extend the pattern almost completely to the other agencies. There is little likelihood that this will be achieved now. The pervasive nature of present-day competition points in the direction of rate making taking on more and more the features of competitive pricing. This is likely to lead to a greater simplification of pricing procedures and less formalism of rate structures.

Recognition of this development has led many to argue that railroads must abandon value of service as a principle of pricing and turn more and more to cost of service. In so far as this means that rates based on the value of commodities rather than on the market for services are outmoded, this point of view is correct. In any other respect, however, it is wrong. The nature of railroad costs means that costs can be used only as minima. The precise rates will have to be made in accordance with demand considerations, and this is what "value of service" means. In other words, as rate making becomes more competitive, value of service will play a larger role than it has in the past. Cost of service, with large fixed and joint costs, can never be more than a minimum gauge.

CONCLUSIONS ON TRANSPORT PRICING

A Multiple Pricing Problem

The pricing problems of the various agencies of transport are not one, but many. Each mode has its own particular product and service, which may be priced more or less independently of those of the other agencies. The prices for these services will depend on the amount of intra-agency competition. In motor, water, and air transport, they will not, if market forces are permitted to operate freely, deviate significantly from fully allocated costs. In other words, differential pricing or price discrimination is not a serious problem in these areas of transport. In fact, apart from predatory practices, it cannot exist, except over a narrow range. Nor does monopoly pricing pose a problem for public policy except where competition is limited by public authority.

In railroad transport, intra-agency competition is necessarily limited, with the consequence that differential or discriminatory pricing can and should be practiced, if unused capacity exists and revenue requirements necessitate it. This may require some controls to prevent competition among railroads from becoming ruinous, as well as to prevent possible exploitation of the consumer.

Interagency Competition

If the different agencies were totally distinct from each other in the services they offered, or if they competed with each other only incidentally, no significant problem of interagency competition and pricing would emerge. This is not the case, however; and very extensive competition between rail carriers, on the one hand, and motor, water, and air carriers, on the other, has developed. Because of the different cost considerations that enter into price decisions for railroads and for these other carriers, there arises the question of the economical basis of competition among them. Only the railroads can resort to differential pricing to any significant extent in this competition. Should they be permitted to do so?

If traffic is to be shared by the different modes of transport according to their relative efficiencies for moving that traffic, then the apportioning of it must be made upon the basis of relative costs. Economical transport means that the agency which can move the traffic at the lowest cost should be allowed to take the business, if it wishes to do so. The costs which are the decisive ones in this connection are those that will be incurred if the traffic is taken and will not be incurred if it is refused. There is no difference "in principle" with regard to the costs which each agency should consider. All of the different modes of transport have costs which are independent of the volume of traffic they haul, and all have costs which vary with it. In other words, all of them can engage, economically, in differential pricing; but it is only with the railroads that this takes on any importance. Public policy which fails to give recognition to this fact is denying the public the use of the most economical type of transport. It is always in the interest of the economy to use the cheapest means for achieving a given objective. This is a cardinal principle of economics. Minimum rates, which attract traffic that increases the net revenue of the carrier that can get it, are in the public interest and are a necessary part of public policy which relies on competition. These rates are also a necessary part of public policy which aims at the most efficient utilization of economic resources. The fact that the minimum rates may be based on costs which are below "average" is not a relevant consideration. The important question is: "Will the net revenue of the firm be increased by obtaining the traffic?"

Differential Pricing and Efficiency

It is frequently urged that differential pricing by a carrier, with regard either to commodities or to places, results in prejudicial treatment to those commodities or places which are not accorded the lower rates. The fact is, however, that when this differential charging is the result of competition, it is because the carrier which grants the differential rates does so in order to get the traffic. If the carrier is not permitted to do this, the traffic will move by the carrier of another agency and so will get the benefits of the lower rates in any case. Thus, no matter what restrictions are placed upon the carrier which tries to get the traffic by economical differential pricing, it is not possible to protect the commodities or the communities against such charges. The only beneficiary of the policy which prevents carriers from engaging in this differential pricing is the carrier which is protected against losing the business to its more competent rival.

The objective of the transportation policy of this country, as stated by Congress, is to provide an adequate transport system at the lowest possible cost. The economic basis for achieving this is to permit and encourage traffic to move by the means which can haul it the most efficiently. The measure of efficiency for this purpose is the relative cost of haulage, the carrier which can afford to move the traffic at the lowest relative cost being the most efficient one. The costs which are relevant in this case are the "economic" costs. That is, they are those which will be incurred if traffic is taken and will not be there if the traffic is not taken. It is these costs which should set the minimum rates for any of the agencies. Any other basis for the allocation of traffic will impair the economic efficiency of the transport system of the country.[16]

[16]For a more extensive discussion of this question, see D. F. Pegrum, "The Special Problem of Inter-Agency Competition in Transport," *I.C.C. Practitioners' Journal* (December, 1956), pp. 307–14.

Chapter 23 THE REGULATION OF TRANSPORT

INTRODUCTION

The Basis of Regulation

From early times in English history, transportation had been subject to various regulations, because the supplying of transport services was what was known as a "common calling" and, under it, common carriers were required to serve all alike, at reasonable rates and without discrimination. There was also a recognition of the fact that the furnishing of transport facilities was, in many respects, a function of government. With the growth of private enterprise in transport, the theory developed that the agencies supplying transportation were performing governmental functions under grants of authority to do so. It was on this basis that private firms were accorded the right of eminent domain. In addition, legal theory also came to hold that when the owner of private property assumed the obligation to serve all who applied, he could not renounce his responsibilities without public consent, and he became subject to the special common-law rules for enterprises affected with a public interest.

Thus, the foundations for modern regulation were well established by the beginning of the nineteenth century, but it was not until the rise of the railroad to its prime position in inland transport that positive regulation began. It was the unique economic characteristics of railroads which brought this about. Had it not been for these characteristics, there is little reason to believe that regulation in transportation would have taken on anything resembling its present pattern.

Early Regulation

It was not until 1870 that any serious attempt was made to regulate the railroads in this country. Some early regulation had taken place through railway charters, which frequently contained schedules of maximum charges and, sometimes, of limitations of earnings to a percentage of capitalization. In some of the New England states, commissions had been created; but they had little power of control, being of the advisory type, with no authority over rates.

Reasons for the Development of Regulation

Positive regulation of railroads was the product of the granger movement, which began in 1867. This was really an agrarian manifestation of thoroughgoing discontent with economic conditions, of which antirailroad sentiment was but one phase. It was the result of the severe decline of agricultural prices following the Civil War, arising from previous inflation, overexpansion in agriculture, public land policy, and unfavorable foreign markets for grain. The railroads quickly became a focus of attention for this discontent, because they had failed to provide the low freight rates that had been expected. In addition, there was a great deal of discrimination in rate making, as well as an arrogant ignoring of the consumer. Finally, financial excesses and abuses, with heavy investor losses, together with much foreign ownership of stocks and bonds, aroused a great deal of local antagonism.

Railroad excesses and abuses were a legitimate basis of resentment and would have brought legislative reaction even in the absence of other factors. Even if these difficulties had not been present, however, regulation would have been inevitable because of the economic features of railroad transportation which have already been discussed. Furthermore, the comprehensive type of regulation that ultimately emerged would have been unavoidable, abuses or no abuses. Failure to understand the economic basis of regulation, together with the resentment which the railroads aroused, retarded seriously the development of a statesmanlike approach to the problems of railroad transportation. The carry-over in recent years of the early lack of understanding of the nature and sources of the problem has placed severe obstacles in the way of an economical resolution of the current transport dilemma.

STATE REGULATION

The Granger Laws

The initial steps for the positive regulation of railroads came when the states of Illinois, Iowa, Minnesota, and Wisconsin enacted what became known as the "Granger Laws" between 1871 and 1874. These laws had common objectives and very similar provisions, although they were not identical in their clauses. They all established maximum rate limits, Iowa prescribing rates for all distances up to 376 miles on various classes of freight and on specific commodities. Illinois and Minnesota, on the other hand, imposed the duty of prescribing maximum rates on regulatory commissions which were set up under their statutes. The various laws endeavored to deal with place discrimination by what were known as "prorata clauses," by which rates could not be higher for shorter than for longer hauls. This applied to any distance, no matter in what direction the traffic moved, or whether it was on a branch line or on the main line. An attempt was made to preserve competition by forbidding competing railroad lines to consolidate, and personal favoritism came in for some limitation with prohibitions against free railroad passes to public officials. Finally, the granger laws introduced the mandatory commission which, it was noted earlier,[1] was literally an American invention and one of this country's unique contributions to the development of the regulation of private industry. It was these commissions that formed the prototype of the Interstate Commerce Commission, which was to be set up shortly thereafter.

The granger laws enjoyed only limited direct success, and all of them except that of Illinois were repealed; for the remainder of the century, state regulation was quite ineffective. There were a number of reasons for the repeal of these laws. In the first place, both legal and administrative experience was lacking. As a consequence, in construction and application, there was insufficient adaptability. The maximum rate and distance provisions were too rigid, and the railroads frequently made the situation worse by taking full advantage of the maxima. Finally, economic conditions culminating in the panic of 1873 resulted in a rather thorough breakdown of the movement for regulation.

The results of the laws were not all negative in nature, however. A start had been made on the development of the idea of the mandatory commission, on the one hand; and, on the other, the unworkability of highly inflexible laws was clearly demonstrated. More important, however, was the fact that the testing of the granger laws in the courts established the unequivocal right of the states to regulate industries affected with a public interest and demonstrated clearly that the state could, through properly worked and administered legislation, develop very broad and comprehensive powers over private business.

Interpretation of the Granger Laws

It was to be expected that legislation as highly controversial and as novel as the granger laws would soon have to face the test of the courts; for here, the issue of purely private business versus that which had clearly recognized public responsibilities was squarely joined for the first time in this country. This question came before the Supreme Court in the granger cases, for which *Munn* v. *Illinois* (1877)[2] set the precedent. This case actually involved grain elevators in the city of Chicago, but the Court held that these were part of the transportation process and so came under the Illinois law. Three major questions were dealt with by the Court, although only the first of these has retained the scope given to it in the original decision.

1. *The Right to Regulate.* The legislation of the state of Illinois was, first of all, challenged on the ground that the fixing of minimum

[1]See Chapter 13.
[2]94 U.S. 113.

rates deprived the plaintiffs of property without due process of law and therefore violated the Fourteenth Amendment of the federal Constitution. The Supreme Court held that the state had the right to regulate an industry affected with a public interest and that certain activities had fallen into that category of common law for centuries. Transportation was such an activity. This ruling of the Court has been followed ever since, although the scope of the concept of an industry affected with a public interest has been broadened somewhat over the years since that time.[3]

2. *The Right of Judicial Review.* Even though the state did possess the right to regulate, the plaintiffs contended that such a power could not be exercised without limit. They argued that the owner of property was entitled to a reasonable compensation for its use and that what constituted a reasonable compensation was for the courts and not the legislature to decide. The Supreme Court rejected this idea, also, by stating that once the right to regulate had been established, the role of the courts had been exhausted. For protection against possible abuses of the exercise of legislative power, resort had to be to the polls, not to the courts.

This part of the decision did not stand for long. In *Stone* v. *Farmers' Loan and Trust Company* (1886),[4] the Court indicated that it believed that there were limitations on the control which legislatures could exercise, and that the courts would offer protection, when it said: "This power to regulate is not the power to destroy and limitation is not the equivalent of confiscation."[5] This point of view was definitely established in *Chicago, Milwaukee and St. Paul Railway Company* v. *Minnesota* (1890).[6] Under the Minnesota statute, the decisions of the state railroad commission as to reasonable rates were made final and conclusive. The Court held that the matter of reasonableness of rates was eminently a matter for judicial investigation. Subsequent cases affirmed this point of view;[7] thereafter, the controversy turned on the standards to be used for testing reasonableness.

3. *Power to Regulate Interstate Commerce.* A third point which was raised in the granger cases was the extent to which states could exercise jurisdiction over interstate commerce. At this time, there was no federal legislation whatsoever on this matter. In *Munn* v. *Illinois*, the Court found that the business of the warehouses was carried on exclusively within the state of Illinois. Their regulation was, therefore, a matter of domestic concern; and until Congress acted with reference to the interstate relations, the state could regulate them, even though in doing so, it indirectly affected interstate commerce.

[3]See Chapter 11.
[4]116 U.S. 307.
[5]*Ibid.*, p. 331
[6]134 U.S. 416
[7]See *Reagan* v. *Farmers' Loan and Trust Co.*, 154 U.S. 362 (1894)

The question remained, however, whether a state could regulate that part of a journey occurring within a state if the traffic moved beyond. This was the issue in *Wabash, St. Louis and Pacific Railway Company* v. *Illinois* (1886).[8] The law of the state of Illinois forbade violation of the long-and-short-haul principle. The Wabash Railway charged more for a shipment of goods from Gilman, Illinois, to New York than from Peoria, Illinois, the more distant point. The reason was severe competition at Peoria. The state of Illinois brought suit to prevent this. The Supreme Court held that this was commerce among the states and that, in such situations, the states were powerless to act.

Two other matters of importance to regulation were passed upon in the granger cases. At the time the granger laws were enacted, most of the railroad charters gave the railroads the right to fix their own rates. Because charters were contracts, the railroads argued that regulation was precluded. The Court ruled, however, that when the state had the right to regulate, the charter provisions did not carry with them the renunciation by the state of its own superior right of regulation, unless immunity from regulation was specifically and definitely conferred by the charter.

The other issue that arose had to do with the constitutionality of the mandatory commission as an instrument of regulation. It was contended that the powers conferred by the granger laws on the commissions constituted an unconstitutional delegation of legislative powers. The Court held that these commissions were administrative agencies, set up for the purpose of carrying out the will of the legislatures as expressed in the statutes. The commissions could not make laws, but they could administer the ones assigned to them by the legislatures.

State versus Federal Authority

The Wabash case definitely established the rule that when traffic fell exclusively within the category of what the Court ruled was interstate commerce, only the federal government could act. Two important issues, however, remained. The first was how far federal power could be extended under the concept of interstate commerce; and the second was whether, when federal authority had been established, the states could act if the federal government permitted them to do so.

The first of these issues emerged in the Minnesota rate cases, which involved the validity of certain intrastate rates prescribed by the Minnesota Commission.[9] The cities of Duluth, Minnesota, and Superior, Wisconsin, are adjacent to each other and compete for trade over a broad area in Minnesota. When the Commission ordered the railroads to reduce passenger fares and freight rates between points located entirely within Minnesota, the same railroads were forced by competition to do the same to Superior. The impact of the reduction affected rates over a wide

[8]118 U.S. 557.
[9]*Simpson* v. *Shepard*, 230 U.S. 352 (1913).

area, as far west as the Pacific Coast. The railroads protested the orders on the ground, among others, that they involved the regulation of interstate commerce. The Supreme Court held that in the absence of congressional legislation, the state might pass laws affecting local interests, even though interstate commerce was indirectly or incidentally burdened. The Court did point out, however, that the states could not under any guise impose direct burdens and indicated that Congress could act even where indirect effects existed, if it so desired.

The next year, in the Shreveport rate cases,[10] in a similar controversy, the authority of the federal government was definitely established. The Texas Commission maintained lower rates eastward from Dallas and Houston toward Shreveport, Louisiana, than the interstate rates westward from Shreveport to the same points. The Louisiana Commission complained to the Interstate Commerce Commission that the interstate railroad rates from Shreveport were unreasonable and discriminatory. The Interstate Commerce Commission agreed with Louisiana and established rates to eliminate the discrimination. The railroads contended that they could not be compelled to lower rates which were reasonable, and the state of Texas argued that Congress did not have the power to fix the intrastate charges of an interstate carrier. The Supreme Court held that the power of a state to prescribe intrastate rates could not be exercised in such a way as to defeat the legitimate exercise of federal control over interstate commerce. Congress, through the Interstate Commerce Commission, had seen fit to act and had the power to do so.

The final step in the growth of federal power came with the Wisconsin passenger fares case.[11] The state of Wisconsin prescribed a maximum fare of 2 cents per mile for carrying passengers solely in the state. When interstate fares were increased, the Wisconsin Commission refused to follow suit. The Interstate Commerce Commission ordered the railroads to raise these intrastate fares to the interstate level, on the ground that the intrastate fares constituted an undue burden on interstate commerce. The Supreme Court held that effective operation of the Interstate Commerce Act, as amended by the Transportation Act of 1920, required that state traffic pay a proportionate share of the cost of maintaining an adequate railroad system.

It seems to be clear, from the decisions of the Supreme Court, that federal authority over transportation can be extended almost without limit if it is necessary to do so in order to regulate interstate transport. The obverse of this is whether Congress can permit states to exercise control, even though this should affect interstate commerce indirectly. The implications of the foregoing decisions indicate that this can be done. So long as the congressional power is not exclusive, the states can act. In the

[10]*Houston, East and West Texas Railway Co.* v. *United States*, 234 U.S. 342 (1914)

[11]*Railroad Commission of Wisconsin* v. *Chicago, Burlington and Quincy Railroad Co.*, 257 U.S. 563 (1922).

regulation of motor transport, in particular, Congress has taken specific steps to limit the authority of the Interstate Commerce Commission, thereby reserving much motor carrier regulation to the states. It has taken similar steps with natural gas transmission.

FEDERAL REGULATION TO 1920

The Act to Regulate Commerce, 1887

After some years of investigation and debate, Congress responded to the need for the regulation of railroads at the federal level by the passage of the Act to Regulate Commerce of 1887. This initial legislation, which came to be known as the Interstate Commerce Act, became the basis of federal control over domestic transportation in interstate commerce. With the exception of air transport, which is under the Civil Aeronautics Board, all domestic interstate transport that is regulated by the federal government has been brought under the Interstate Commerce Commission by amendments to the original legislation.

Provisions of the Act. The act was made applicable to all common carriers by railroads engaged in interstate or foreign commerce. It did not apply to common carriers wholly by water, but it did include common carriers partly by water and partly by rail, where they were under common control or arrangement for continuous carriage or shipment.

1. *Reasonable Rates.* Section 1 required that all rates be just and reasonable, and provided that every unjust and unreasonable charge was unlawful. This was simply a statutory enactment of the long-standing common-law rule, although, prior to this enactment, there was no basis at the federal level for enforcing this rule.

2. *Personal Discrimination.* Section 2 prohibited personal discrimination by making it unlawful, directly or indirectly, for a carrier, by any device, to charge one person more than another for a like and contemporaneous service under substantially similar circumstances and conditions.

3. *Undue Preference or Prejudice.* Section 3 was really a blanket prohibition of undue or unreasonable preference or advantage of any form to any person, place, or kind of traffic. Thus, this was not a prohibition of preferential or differential treatment, but only a limitation to what might be considered just and reasonable.

4. *The Long-and-Short-Haul Clause.* This is the well-known Section 4 of the act, which prohibited a common carrier subject to the act from charging or receiving any greater compensation in the aggregate for transportation of passengers or of like kind of property, "under substantially similar circumstances and conditions," for a shorter than for a longer distance over the same line, in the same direction, the shorter being included within the longer distance. The Commission could grant exceptions in special cases.

5. *Publication of Rates.* Section 6 of the act stated that schedules of rates and fares were to be printed, made available for public inspection, and filed with the Commission. There was to be strict adherence to the published schedules and ten days' public notice was required before rates could be advanced.

6. *The Interstate Commerce Commission.* To administer the law, the act established an Interstate Commerce Commission, which was to consist of 5 members, appointed by the President, with the advice and consent of the Senate, for a

term of 6 years. Later on, this was changed to 11 members, appointed for a term of 7 years. The Commission was to be bipartisan in composition; and no commissioner could engage in any other business, vocation, or employment while holding office. Any commissioner could be removed for inefficiency, neglect of duty, or malfeasance in office by the President. There was no limitation on reappointment. By an amendment in 1889, the Commission was ordered to report directly to Congress, thereby assuming an independent status.

In order to enable it to carry out its responsibilities, the act gave the Commission the authority to inquire into the management of the business of common carriers. It could require the testimony of witnesses and the production of records on matters under investigation. It was empowered to order the preparation of annual reports and to prescribe a uniform system of accounts. Finally, it could undertake investigations upon complaint or on its own motion.

The act contained penalties for violation of its provisions, but these could be imposed only by the courts. The Commission could order those subject to the law to "cease and desist" from further violation; but if the respondent failed to obey the Commission's orders, it was necessary for the latter to appeal to the courts for enforcement. There was no penalty for failure to obey the Commission's orders; penalties were imposed only for violations of the law.

Judicial Interpretation. On the surface, the powers of the Interstate Commerce Commission under the new law were very comprehensive and adequate for the task of effective regulation. The law still had to pass the scrutiny of the courts, however, to discover its meaning. The result was that many difficulties appeared which had not been suspected. Much of the wording was anything but unambiguous; and in addition, the respective positions of the courts and the Commission in regulation remained to be worked out.

First of all, definite obstacles to enforcement appeared. Opposition arose over the power of the government to compel witnesses to testify. This was resolved by the passage of the Compulsory Testimony Act of 1893, which provided that no person should be prosecuted on account of any matter concerning which he might testify or produce evidence in a proceeding which alleged violation of the Act of 1887. The Commission also was handicapped by the fact that when it appealed to the courts to enforce its orders, the courts insisted on rehearing all the evidence and also permitted the carriers to introduce evidence not previously presented to the Commission. The Supreme Court, in 1896,[12] expressed disapproval of this practice; but further legislation was necessary to provide adequate remedies for the difficulty.

A second difficulty appeared in connection with the prescription of

[12]*Cincinnati, New Orleans and Texas Pacific Railway Co.* v. *Interstate Commerce Commission*, 162 U.S. 184 (1896).

reasonable rates. The Commission assumed that it had the authority to determine whether particular rates were unreasonable and, if it so found, it could prescribe reasonable maximum rates for the future. The issue came before the Supreme Court in the Maximum Freight Rate case of 1897.[13] The Court held that the power to designate rates for the future could not be implied from the provisions of the act of 1887, and that this power was not among those granted to the Commission by Congress. All the Commission could do was to pronounce a particular rate to be unreasonable, and then the dispute could start all over again on any lower rate established by the railroad.

The final blow to the Commission's rate-making powers came with the decision of the Supreme Court in the Alabama Midland case in 1897.[14] This dealt with the long-and-short-haul problem. The Commission ruled that competition between interstate railways at a distant point and the absence of like competition at a nearer point did not generally create such dissimilarity as to justify higher rates for the short haul. The Court held that competition at the more distant point constituted a dissimilarity of conditions sufficient to make Section 4 inapplicable. The Commission thus found itself virtually without authority over place discrimination.

Results of the Act. As a consequence of court interpretation of the Act of 1887, the Interstate Commerce Commission was stripped of all authority necessary to deal with the rate grievances that had led to the passage of the law. The legislation was not entirely ineffective, however. Publicity of rates had been secured, many of the grosser forms of discrimination had been eliminated, valuable statistical data had been accumulated, and experience in the pitfalls of the law had been acquired. Finally, and most important, the Interstate Commerce Commission had firmly established itself, so that Congress was ready to undertake steps to make it an effective enforcement agency. These came in a series of acts that were passed during the first decade of the twentieth century.

The Elkins Act, 1903

The need for strengthening the law relating to personal discrimination and rebating had become apparent even to the railroads themselves. The Elkins Act made the published tariff the only lawful one, and any departure from it was a punishable offense. The railroads, their agents, and their officers were liable in the event of violation of the law; and the recipients of rebates were liable, as well as the carriers which gave them. Finally, the courts were given jurisdiction to enjoin violations of the law.

[13]*Interstate Commerce Commission* v. *Cincinnati, New Orleans, and Texas Pacific Railway Co.*, 167 U.S. 479 (1897).

[14]*Interstate Commerce Commission* v. *Alabama Midland Railway Co.*, 168 U.S. 144 (1897).

The Hepburn Act, 1906

This legislation was the first positive step designed to give the Interstate Commerce Commission real authority over the railroads. It extended the Commission's jurisdiction to cover express and sleeping-car companies, switching companies, spurs, tracks, and terminal facilities of every kind, even to the extent of authority over the charge for switching services performed by industrial railways. Pipe lines for the transportation of any commodity (other than water or gas) were also made subject to the provisions of the law.

Recognizing that control over accounting was a fundamental basis for effective regulation, the Hepburn Act provided that detailed annual reports were to be rendered by all common carriers, under oath, three months after the close of each year. The Commission could require other reports and was to have access at all times to the accounts. The Commission was given the power, at its discretion, to prescribe the forms of all the accounts and records. It promptly proceeded to set up a uniform accounting system in accordance with these provisions.

The Hepburn Act provided that if, after full hearing and upon complaint, it was found that rates were unreasonable or otherwise unlawful, the Commission could prescribe maximum rates. The Commission could establish through routes and the maximum joint rates applicable thereto. Carriers could not engage in transportation until they had filed and published their rates, as required by law.

Many railroads owned coal mines and engaged in the production of other commodities, and this had led to a good deal of discrimination. By charging high rates on the commodities they produced, they could enjoy a distinct advantage over competitors who had to ship over the rail lines. To deal with this problem, Congress enacted the "commodities clause." This provided that no railroad should transport in interstate commerce any commodity other than timber and its manufactured products, produced by it, except such commodities as were necessary for its use in the conduct of its business as a common carrier. This is the clause which some people think should also be applied to petroleum pipe lines.

The Hepburn Act strengthened greatly the Commission's powers of enforcement. The orders of the Commission were to take effect within not less than thirty days from time of issuance; and if a carrier failed to comply, the Commission or any injured party might apply to the courts for an enforcement order. The penalty for disobeying an order of the Commission was $5,000 for each offense, and each day's violation constituted a separate offense. Moreover, the orders of the Commission were binding, unless suspended or set on one side by a court.

Judicial Interpretation. The interpretation of the Hepburn Act by the Supreme Court clearly demonstrated the fact that the Interstate Commerce Commission had become established as a full-fledged administrative tribunal and that the Court intended to support that position. A number of cases clearly attested to that fact, but the one that summarized it most completely was *Interstate Commerce Commission* v. *Union Pacific Railroad Company* (1912).[15] In its opinion, the Court said:

> In cases thus far decided, it has been settled that the orders of the Commission are final unless (1) beyond the power which it could constitutionally exercise; (2) beyond its statutory power; (3) based on a mistake of law. But questions of fact may be involved in the determination of questions of law, so that an order regular on its face may be set aside if it appears that (4) the rate is so low as to be confiscatory . . . ; or (5) if the Commission acted so arbitrarily and unjustly as to fix rates contrary to evidence . . . . In determining these mixed questions of law and fact, the court confines itself to the ultimate question as to whether the Commission acted within its power. It will not consider the expediency or wisdom of the order, or whether, on like testimony, it would have made a similar ruling . . . .[16]

The Mann-Elkins Act of 1910

This legislation extended the Commission's jurisdiction in two ways. First of all, it placed telegraph, telephone, and cable companies which were engaged in sending messages in interstate or international commerce under the Commission. Second, it gave the Commission further control of the railroad business.

Rate-Making Authority. The law empowered the Commission to suspend proposed changes in railroad rates by providing that when any new rate, fare, or classification was filed with the Commission, the latter should have the authority, either upon complaint or on its own initiative, to suspend the proposed changes for a period not exceeding 120 days, during which time it was to determine the lawfulness of the proposed changes. An additional suspension period of 6 months was permitted if the first period was insufficient to arrive at a conclusion. (At the present time, the total suspension period is 7 months.) The burden of the reasonableness of the new rates was on the railroad. To enable it to deal more effectively with rates, the Commission was also given control over freight classification.

Long-and-Short Haul. Commission authority over the long-and-short-haul clause was restored by the elimination of the phrase "under substantially similar circumstances and conditions." Henceforth, the long-and-short-haul prohibition was to apply under all conditions, unless the Commission specifically granted exceptions.

The Commerce Court. It was felt that a specialized transportation court should be established to expedite cases arising under the Interstate

[15]222 U.S. 541. See also *Interstate Commerce Commission* v. *Illinois Central Railroad Co.*, 215 U.S. 452 (1910); *Baltimore and Ohio Railroad Co.* v. *United States*, 215 U.S. 481 (1910); *Interstate Commerce Commission* v. *Chicago, Rock Island and Pacific Railway Co.*, 218 U.S. 89 (1910).

[16]*Interstate Commerce Commission* v. *Union Pacific Railroad Co.*, 222 U.S. 541, (1912) 547.

Commerce Act and to secure greater uniformity of decisions. The Commerce Court was to consist of 5 judges assigned to the Court by the Chief Justice of the United States for a period of 5 years. All cases were to go directly to it, with appeal only to the Supreme Court.

Unfortunately, the Commerce Court was short-lived. First of all, it interfered unduly with the orders of the Interstate Commerce Commission, contrary to the ruling of the Illinois Central case. Second, one of the members of the Court was found guilty of corruption. As a consequence, the Court was abolished by Congress in 1913.

The Panama Canal Act, 1912

The strategic position of the railroads with regard to inland transport meant that they could exercise effective control over water competition through ownership of carriers on competing water routes, ownership of water terminal facilities, and refusal to co-operate on through shipments requiring some rail haulage. Practices such as these were in contradiction to congressional policy for maintaining competition between rail and water carriers. The completion of the Panama Canal gave rise to some fears that the railroads might succeed in stifling water competition for transcontinental traffic. To meet this threat, Congress passed the Panama Canal Act of 1912. By this law, it became unlawful for any railroad to have any interest of any kind in a common carrier by water with which it competed or might compete, or in any vessel carrying freight or passengers. In the case of Panama Canal traffic, the prohibition was absolute. For other traffic by water, the Commission was authorized to permit the interrelations to continue, if it was of the opinion that they were being conducted in the interests of the public, and if water competition was not reduced or prevented thereby. As a result of this legislation, a thoroughgoing unscrambling of rail-water carrier relationships took place. In 1959 the Southern Pacific Company and the Illinois Central Railroad sought permission to acquire the J. I. Hay Company, a barge line on the Mississippi River, by joint ownership. The Commission refused to permit the acquisition.[17]

The Valuation Act of 1913

The main purpose of this legislation was to furnish the Commission with some standard by which to test the reasonableness of railway rates and the reasonableness of proposed changes in rates over which previous legislation had extended its jurisdiction. The Commission was directed to ascertain and report in detail as to each piece of property used and useful for common carrier purposes: the original cost to date, the cost of reproduction new, the cost of reproduction less depreciation, the methods by which these costs were obtained, and all other values and

[17]317 I.C.C. 3a (1962).

elements of value and the methods of valuation that were employed. When final valuations were ascertained, they were to be published and serve as prima-facie evidence of the value of the property in all proceedings arising under the Interstate Commerce Act.

The Transportation Act of 1920 (Esch-Cummins Act)

Background of the Legislation. For a number of reasons, the federal government decided to take over the operation of the railroads during this country's participation in World War I. When the war ended, it was decided, after much discussion, that the railroads should be returned to private ownership. Because of the discrepancy at that time between railroad income and expenses, some arrangements had to be made to facilitate the transition back to private ownership and operation. This alone called for congressional action, and the first part of the act of 1920 was concerned with the transfer.

There were more fundamental reasons than this, however, for the new legislation. The theory was that railroad transportation was a monopoly in which competition could function only in a limited fashion, and even this competition had to be subject to control. Regulation, to date, had been negative in nature and solely for the purpose of protecting the shipping public. It came to be recognized, however, that the control of private monopoly imposed positive responsibilities on public authority, if private enterprise in railroads was to continue. This required an extension of Commission authority over a number of items not theretofore under its jurisdiction, in addition to the provision of a legislative standard by which the reasonableness of the general rate level could be gauged.

The Rule of Rate Making. The Commission was to prescribe such rates as would permit the railroads as a whole to earn—under honest, efficient, and economical management—a fair return on the fair value of the railroad property held for and used in the service of transportation. Five and one-half per cent was set as the fair return for the first 2 years; after that, the Commission could raise the fair return up to 6 per cent if it saw fit. In 1922, the Commission set 5¾ per cent as the fair return. It should be noted that this was not a guarantee. The government was not responsible for making up any deficiency in the return, nor was the obligation cumulative. If a fair return was not earned in one year, there was no obligation to raise rates to make up for the past deficiency.

Because rates prescribed under the rule of rate making would give some carriers more than a fair return and leave others with inadequate revenues, Congress enacted the "recapture clause." This provided that one half the earnings of a carrier in any year in excess of 6 per cent of the value of the property should be paid to the Interstate Commerce Commission and placed by it in a railroad contingent fund. From this fund, the Commission might make loans to the weak lines for the purpose of meeting capital expenditures or of refunding security issues, provided that the loans were adequately secured. The interest rate on the loans was to be 6 per cent, a provision that rather effectively prevented the fund from being of any real use.

Two other provisions for rate making were also important. The Commission was given permission to prescribe minimum rates. This was felt to be necessary in order to prevent rate wars and to make control over discrimination more effective. The Commission was also given the power to prescribe the exact rate to be charged in lieu of a rate found to be unlawful, although it might set the maximum and the minimum, thereby giving railroad management a zone of discretion. The Commission's discretion over exceptions to the long-and-short-haul principle was also circumscribed somewhat, indicating congressional intent to protect water competition. The new amendment provided (1) that the rates on the long haul should be reasonable compensatory for the service performed and (2) that a lower rate to a more distant point might not be allowed on account of water competition not actually in existence.

Consolidations. The provisions in the act of 1920 relating to railroad consolidation were an integral part of the rule of rate making. The latter, of necessity, assumed an approximate equality of earning capacity of the various companies; and this could be achieved only if the railroads were consolidated into a limited number of systems of approximately equal earning capacity. This meant that an endeavor would have to be made to consolidate weak roads with strong ones. The law provided that the Commission was to adopt a plan of consolidation as soon as possible, in accordance with three conditions: (1) the preservation of competition, as fully as possible; (2) the maintenance of existing channels of trade and commerce, whenever practicable; and (3) the arrangement of the several systems so that the earning power of each would be approximately equal under uniform rates for competitive traffic. After a final plan was adopted by the Commission, no consolidations were to take place that did not conform to it. The Commission was powerless to compel consolidation, however.

Securities. Under the comprehensive plan of control envisaged by Congress, the regulation of railroad security issuance was necessary if effective rate control was to be exercised. The courts required consideration of the financial structure in fair-return proceedings. In addition, what constitutes a fair profit depends—in part, at least—upon the earnings a company needs in order to raise new capital. The control of the financial practices of a regulated monopoly is an integral and basic part of regulation. The act provided, therefore, that henceforth, it would be unlawful for any railroad to issue securities or to assume obligations with respect to securities issued by other persons, except upon authorization by the Commission. The latter was to approve applications only if it found the issue to be (1) for some lawful object within the corporate purposes, (2) compatible with the public interest, and (3) reasonably necessary for the rendition of the proper carrier service. Commission control was made exclusive, thereby making it unnecessary for the railroads to obtain the consent of state officials.

Service. The law gave the Commission extensive powers relating to quality and regularity of service, utilization of cars and locomotives, and so forth. It added an entirely new provision, whereby the Commission was given control over construction and abandonment of railroad mileage. Henceforth, no line was to be constructed until a certificate of public convenience and necessity had been secured from the Interstate Commerce Commission, nor could a line be abandoned without the sanction of the Commission. The primary objective of the regulation of extensions was to prevent overconstruction and the possibility of ruinous competition; the purpose in controlling abandonments was to protect needy communities from indiscriminate closing down of nonpaying branches. The theory obviously was that this was regulated monopoly and that competition could not be relied upon to check overexpansion or to maintain an adequate supply of service.[18]

FEDERAL REGULATION OF TRANSPORTATION SINCE 1920

Need for Further Legislation

The Transportation Act of 1920 was designed to fill out regulation of transport at the federal level so as to provide the Interstate Commerce Commission with completely adequate powers to make the private operation of railroads under regulation successful. If, in application, the subsequent regulations should prove to be unsuccessful, it was widely held that public ownership and operation would be the only solution. The basic assumptions upon which the act was built were (1) that the business of supplying inland transportation was essentially monopolistic in character, (2) that competition could be relied upon only incidentally as a regulatory device and that severe curbs had to be imposed upon it to prevent it from being ruinous, and (3) that economic conditions would be reasonably stable and that regulation would not have to adapt itself to widely fluctuating business activity.

In the course of the ensuing decade, the factual basis of these three assumptions was swept away by the impact of the technological change and the disastrous depression of the 1930's. The rule of rate making broke down for two reasons. First of all, the Supreme Court overruled the Interstate Commerce Commission in *St. Louis and O'Fallon Railway*

[18]The Transportation Act of 1920 also contained a section dealing with the settlement of labor disputes. This was not made an integral part of the program of regulation, however, and the Interstate Commerce Commission was not given any jurisdiction. Because of this, and also because public policy regarding labor in the transportation field and elsewhere raises issues that require special consideration before an adequate appraisal can be made, the labor provisions are not dealt with here.

Company v. *United States* (1929).[19] In this case, the Commission sought to recapture the excess earnings of the St. Louis and O'Fallon Railroad, calculated on the basis of the Commission's valuation. The Supreme Court held that the Interstate Commerce Commission had not followed the instructions of the Valuation Act, in that it had not given consideration to cost of reproduction in arriving at the final figures. Thus, as late as 1929, no basis had been established by which valuation for general rate level and recapture purposes could be ascertained. In the second place, the law—at least, as interpreted by the Commission—made no provision for averaging the fair return over a period of years. Thus, there was no way whereby the railroads could earn a fair return, on the average, if adverse business conditions cut into their revenues at any time. Added to this, the consolidation provisions, which were designed to assist in achieving the objectives of the rule of rate making, failed to accomplish that purpose. There was much disagreement over the plan which the Commission adopted; and in view of the fact that the Commission had no power to compel consolidations, none took place—at least, within the law.

The disastrous depression which began in 1929 would have placed a severe strain on any transport policy; but the railroads had been unable, in the period following World War I, to regain the financial strength that characterizes a strong and growing industry. How much our regulatory policy was to blame for this is a matter of considerable debate; but one thing is clear: The Interstate Commerce Commission did not develop a positive program that envisaged the possibility of severely adverse economic conditions. Furthermore, the regulatory program, as developed, placed extremely broad powers in the hands of the Commission without imposing upon it the corresponding accountability for any failure on its part. In fact, there were literally no standards by which the failure of regulation could be judged.

The clinching fact of all, of course, was the development of the newer agencies of transport. Within a period of about ten years, transportation became one of the most competitive areas of economic activity. The new technology provided the base for it; and government aid fostered on expansion that, in terms of total investment, was to dwarf the railroads. Under the most favorable circumstances, the transformation of transport would have been difficult to accomplish without severe repercussions. The economic conditions of the 1930's, World War II, and regulatory policies which assumed that there had been no change insured the emergence of a transport crisis.

Purpose of the Legislation

The period following 1920 has been the passage of a considerable amount of legislation dealing with transport. This legislation has had three primary purposes in mind. The first was to remedy what appeared to be the most obvious deficiencies of the existing law as it applied to

[19] 279 U.S. 461.

the railroads. This was done in the Emergency Act of 1933 and in the Transportation Act of 1940. The second purpose was to lay the basis for the development of an over-all national transportation policy. The first step in this direction was taken in the Emergency Act of 1933; and the second, in the Transportation Act of 1940. The third purpose of the legislation enacted after 1920 was to extend regulation, in the pattern of that which applied to the railroads, to the other agencies. This was done in the Motor Carrier Act of 1935, the Civil Aeronautics Act of 1938, and the Transportation Act of 1940.

Emergency Transportation Act, 1933

The immediate purpose of this legislation was to meet the emergency conditions which faced the railroad industry, but the law also contained some permanent amendments to the Interstate Commerce Act. The rule of rate making was changed by repealing the provisions of the act of 1920 and substituting the following:

> In the exercise of its power to prescribe just and reasonable rates the Commission shall give due consideration, among other factors, to the effect of rates on the movement of traffic; to the need, in the public interest, of adequate and efficient railway transportation service at the lowest cost consistent with the furnishing of such service; and to the need of revenues sufficient to enable the carriers, under honest, economical and efficient management, to provide such service.

At the same time, Congress repealed the recapture clause retroactively.

Although it has been said that this is a simplified and more flexible rule that the old one, it seems, in fact, to be no standard at all. Any commission charged with the responsibility of regulating private enterprise, on the assumption that private enterprise was to continue, could scarcely do otherwise than as instructed in the legislation; the carriers have little basis upon which they can argue that their rates are too low.

Because of the growth of the holding company, especially during the 1920's, and the use of it as a means of evading the consolidation provisions of the act of 1920, Congress amended that section of the law. The amendment provided that all combinations or unifications, irrespective of the way in which they were achieved, required the approval of the Interstate Commerce Commission. Combinations effected by holding companies were thus brought under the jurisdiction of the Commission.

The Co-ordinator, who had been appointed to administer the emergency provisions, was required to investigate and consider means for developing national policy in transport. He was to submit recommendations to Congress for further legislation that he considered necessary. These recommendations led to the extension of regulation to the other agencies of transport.

The Motor Carrier Act, 1935

In undertaking to provide for the regulation of motor transport, Congress indicated its intention that such regulation should preserve the inherent advantages of motor carriers, and that regulation should not be used as a device to protect the other modes from motor competition. Although, as has already been noted, the underlying theory of the legislation was that motor transport was to be regulated in the same pattern as the railroads, some differences had to be recognized. All motor carriage could not be brought under the rubric of "common carrier." One reason for this was that individuals and firms might provide their own transportation. Another was that the Supreme Court compelled a distinction between common carriers and other carriers for hire. California attempted to impose upon contract carriers the regulations which were applicable to common carriers. In *Frost & Frost Trucking Company* v. *Railroad Commission of California* (1926),[20] the Court took the position that a contract operator could not even indirectly be forced to assume the position of a common carrier. The operator had not held himself out to serve the public generally, and this was an obligation which could not be forced upon a person; it had to be assumed voluntarily.[21]

Types of Carriers. The law recognized three types of carriers: (1) common carriers, who were required to secure certificates of public convenience and necessity; (2) contract carriers, who had only to secure permits to operate (these are not as difficult to obtain as the certificates and impose less rigorous obligations); (3) private carriers, which are not-for-hire carriers engaged in supplying transport service for their owners. In addition to these three categories, there were a number of exceptions, notably exempt carriers which were permitted to haul agricultural products for hire in interstate commerce without any federal regulation.

Rates. The law gives the Commission the power to fix minimum and maximum rates for common carriers, as well as the precise rate. The same provisions for filing and adhering to published tariffs obtain as for railroads. The original act provided that contract carriers were required to file only minimum rates, below which they could not go. The Commission could control the minimum rates. Under a recent amendment, contract carriers must now file the actual rates that are charged;[22] but the Commission still has control only over the minimum. Motor carriers are not subject to the provisions of the long-and-short-haul section of the Interstate Commerce Act.

Consolidations. The Commission has authority over all consolidations, mergers, and other forms of control of motor carriers under its jurisdiction. Any unifications that are approved have to be "consistent with public interest."[23]

[20] 271 U.S. 583.

[21] See also *Michigan Public Utilities Commission* v. *Duke*, 266 U.S. 570 (1925); *Smith* v. *Cahoon*, 283 U.S. 533 (1931). Legislation which distinguished between common and contract carriers was upheld in *Stephenson* v. *Binford*, 287 U.S. 251 (1932).

[22] Public Law 85–124; 71 Stat. 343 (1957).

[23] Approval by the I.C.C. is not required if the number of vehicles is not more than twenty if a motor carrier is an applicant.

Securities. The issuance of securities by common and contract carriers is subject to the approval of the Commission. Because of the large number of small carriers in the industry, sanction is required only if the total of the securities to be issued, together with those already outstanding, exceeds $1 million.

Administration. Administration of the Motor Carrier Act was placed in the hands of the Interstate Commerce Commission, which created a special Motor Carrier Division of three commissioners to apply the law. Because of the large amount of intrastate transport by motor vehicle, the law provided for the establishment of joint boards when both federal and state interests are involved. These boards consist of a representative from each state commission affected and representatives of the Interstate Commerce Commission. In addition, the law recognized the importance of state control in the regulation of motor transport by prohibiting the Commission from prescribing or regulating intrastate rates for the purpose of removing discrimination against interstate commerce, or for any other purpose whatsoever. Thus, the Shreveport principle could not apply to motor carrier rates.

The Transportation Act of 1940

The enactment of the Transportation Act of 1940 was the result of lengthy consideration of the transportation problem during the 1930's. It was designed to provide a basis for the co-ordination of transport policy, to complete the extension of regulation to water carriers, and to provide for further investigation of transport as an aid to Congress in developing additional legislation.

National Transportation Policy. The act set forth, for the first time, a declaration of national policy for all carriers subject to the Interstate Commerce Commission. It read as follows:

> It is hereby declared to be the national transportation policy of the Congress to provide for fair and impartial regulation of all modes of transportation subject to the provisions of this Act, so administered as to recognize and preserve the inherent advantages of each; to promote safe, adequate, economical, and efficient service and foster sound economic conditions in transportation and among the several carriers; to encourage the establishment and maintenance of reasonable charges for transportation services, without unjust discriminations, undue preferences or advantages, or unfair or destructive competitive practices; to cooperate with the several States and the duly authorized officials thereof; and to encourage fair wages and equitable working conditions; . . . all to the end of developing, coordinating, and preserving a national transportation system by water, highway, and rail, as well as other means, adequate to meet the needs of the commerce of the United States, of the Postal Service, and of the national defense. All of the provisions of this Act shall be administered and enforced with a view of carrying out the above declaration of policy.

Unfortunately, the law did not spell out the meaning of the various phrases contained in this declaration. The result has been wide differences of opinion on the interpretation of such terms as "inherent advantages," "economical service," and so forth. Whatever the intent of Congress may have been, the declaration has not brought about any significant change in administration by the Interstate Commerce Commission. The declaration, nevertheless, has served to focus attention and discussion on some of the crucial issues of the current transport problem.

Consolidation. This act provided that railroad consolidations no longer needed to comply with a Commission-made plan. Henceforth, the Interstate Commerce Commission could sanction any proposed consolidation, provided that it was found to be "consistent with the public interest."

Board of Investigation and Research. This Board was to consist of 3 members, appointed by the President to make studies on (1) the relative economy and fitness of rail, motor, and water carriers, with the view of determining the service for which each was especially fitted or unfitted; (2) the extent to which rights of way or other transportation facilities had been provided with public funds for the use of each of the three types of carriers, without adequate compensation therefor; and (3) the extent to which taxes were imposed on the three modes of transport. The Board was also authorized to investigate any other matters relating to transportation which it might consider important for the improvement of transportation conditions or for the furtherance of the national transportation policy declared in the act. The Board was to have a life of 2 years. This was extended an additional 2 years, to 1944, by the President.

Land-Grant Rates. The Transportation Act of 1940 released the land-grant railroads from their obligations to transport mail and government traffic, other than military and naval property and personnel, at reduced rates. In 1945, Congress relieved these railroads of the obligation to transport even military and naval property and personnel at reduced rates. Thus, the rate concessions made by the railroads as a result of the land grants were finally extinguished.

Regulation of Water Transportation. The regulation of water carriers engaged in domestic transport had long been confused and divided. The Act of 1940 amended the Interstate Commerce Act so as to regulate water carriers subject to the Commission in essentially the same way that motor carriers are regulated. Contract carriers were also brought under the Interstate Commerce Commission. However, no provision was made for control of abandonments or security issues in either case.

The law recognized the distinction between common carriers, contract carriers, and private carriers, just as did the Motor Carrier Act. The similarity between water and motor transport was pointed out in the previous chapter of this book. The act, however, provided for so many exemptions from regulation that only a small percentage of all tonnage shipped by water is subject to regulation. The principal exemptions are

(1) commodities in bulk, when the cargo space of the vessel in which such commodities are transported is being used for the carrying of not more than three such commodities; (2) transportation of liquid cargo, in bulk, in tank vessels; (3) transportation by contract carriers when, by reason of the inherent nature of the commodities transported, their requirement of special equipment, or their shipment in bulk, is not actually and substantially competitive with any common carrier subject to the Interstate Commerce Act; and (4) private carriers and some other incidental exemptions. The Commission's actual authority over water transport in this country is obviously of a very limited nature.

The Transportation Act of 1958

The Transportation Act of 1958 was passed by Congress in response to what seemed to be a rapidly mounting railroad crisis arising from a decline in railroad traffic as a result of the business recession, together with the difficulties faced by the railroads in securing new capital. Recognition of the pressing need for overhauling national transport policy had led to moves in Congress to secure additional legislation,[24] but it was the force of circumstances which led to immediate congressional action. The resulting legislation was primarily of an emergency nature which, at most, can serve only as a stopgap pending a thorough revision of national policy.

The main provisions of the new law are as follows:[25]

1. The Interstate Commerce Commission is authorized to guarantee loans to railroads up to a total of $500 million outstanding at any time, to enable the railroads to finance capital investment in road and equipment for maintenance work. These loans are to be guaranteed only if the Commission finds that without the guaranty, the borrowing railroad will be unable to obtain the necessary funds on reasonable terms; that the term of the loan is not more than 15 years; and that there is reasonable assurance that the loan will be repaid within the time fixed for repayment. If the loan is for financing or refinancing expenditures for maintenance of property, the borrowing railroad cannot declare any dividends so long as any principal or interest remains unpaid. This provision of the law expired on June 30, 1963.

2. Upon petition of a carrier questioning the lawfulness of any intrastate rate, fare, or charge, the Commission is instructed forthwith to institute its own investigation and to give special expedition to the hearing and decision thereon, even though a state agency has not acted. In addition, the finding may be made without a separation of interstate and intrastate property, revenues, and expenditures, and without considering in totality the operations of any carrier or group or groups of carriers wholly within any state. This appears to be primarily congressional

[24]See Chapter 24 for a discussion of these developments.

affirmation of the authority it was assumed the Interstate Commerce Commission possessed, but which was placed in doubt as the result of two Supreme Court decisions.[26]

3. The Interstate Commerce Commission is given jurisdiction over the discontinuance or change of the operation or service of trains and railroad ferries. Where operations across state lines are subject to any state law or regulatory authority, the carrier may invoke the jurisdiction of the Commission by giving thirty days' notice of discontinuance of service. The service may then be abandoned, unless the Commission decides otherwise. If the operations are entirely within the boundaries of a state, a petition to discontinue may be filed with the Commission. After holding hearings in the state where the operations occur, the Commission may sanction discontinuance, if it finds that public convenience and necessity will permit it, and if it finds that continuance will constitute an unjust or undue burden on the interstate operations of the carrier.

4. The law, in effect, limits the exemption of motor carriers of agricultural commodities from regulation to those commodities now outside the jurisdiction of the Interstate Commerce Commission. This is designed to prevent further extension of exempt commodities by judicial action. Limitation on escape from the common or contract carrier category by private carriage has also been imposed by a more rigid and restricted definition of a private carrier.

5. The rule of rate making embodied in Section 15 (*a*) of the Interstate Commerce Act is amended by the following:

> In a proceeding involving competition between carriers of different modes of transportation subject to this Act, the Commission, in determining whether a rate is lower than a reasonable minimum rate, shall consider the facts and circumstances attending the movement of the traffic by the carrier or carriers to which the rate is applicable. Rates of a carrier shall not be held up to a particular level to protect the traffic of any other mode of transportation, giving due consideration to the objectives of the national transportation policy declared in this Act.

Just what the last phrase in the last sentence means, and what the effect of it on the declaration will be, remains to be seen; but the intent of the amendment seems to be that of prohibiting the use of the rate-making powers by the Commission to protect one mode of transport against "fair" competition by another mode. The amendment fails utterly, however, to give any instructions for the determination of the economic basis upon which interagency competitive rate making is to be based. The administration to date of this amendment to the rule of rate making has done literally nothing to clarify the meaning of the provision; nor has the Commission given any indication of substantial departure from average or fully-distributed costs of the so-called low-cost carrier

[25]Public Law 85–625 (1958).

[26]*Chicago, Milwaukee, St. Paul and Pacific Railroad Co.* v. *Illinois,* 356 U.S. 906 (1958); and *Public Service Commission of Utah* v. *United States,* 356 U.S. 421 (1958).

as the basis for minimum rates where intermodal competition is involved. The major departure from this is where the competition comes from motor carriers not under the jurisdiction of the Commission. Under the law, the Commission must give due consideration to the objectives set forth in the declaration of national transportation policy. This seems to have been interpreted by some members of the I.C.C. to require the continuance of "umbrella" rate making.[27] In addition, there is the dispute over the appropriate basis for calculating minimum rates for intermodal competition. So far, there has been no resolution of this problem, and it does not appear that one is likely if Congress does not see fit to act.[28]

THE FEDERAL AVIATION ACT, 1958

The regulation of air transportation falls into a somewhat different category from that of rail, motor, and water transportation in that policy regarding air transportation has involved both regulation and promotion. The same agency has had to deal with each of these, with the result that it has been engaged in economic regulation and the administration of subsidy and public aid at the same time. The regulation of air transportation has also been closely associated with public responsibility for technical developments in the industry. Consequently, there has been a considerable amount of mingling of control designed to promote aviation with the program of regulation. This has been accompanied by public participation in the development of airports and technical aids to navigation.

Initial participation of the federal government in air transportation was confined to promotional activities through air-mail contracts and aid in the construction of airports by the Civil Works Administration and the Federal Relief Administration during the depression of the 1930's. Positive regulation was undertaken at the federal level by the Civil Aeronautics Act of 1938, as modified by the Reorganization Act of 1939, and the executive orders of President Roosevelt in 1940. The pattern of regulation which was established was similar to that developed for railroads and motor carriers, but the administration was placed in the hands of a separate agency. The complex problems relating to the use of air space, together with conflict among the various agencies concerned with air navigation, resulted in the passage of the Federal Aviation Act of

[27]See *Commodities—Pan-Atlantic Steamship Corp.*, 313 I.C.C. 23 (1960), and 309 I.C.C. 587 (1960); *I.C.C.* v. *New York, New Haven and Hartford Railroad Co.*, 372 U.S. 744 (1963).

[28]See *Grain in Multiple-Car Shipments—River Crossings to the South*, 318 I.C.C. 641 (1963). The Southern Railway proposed to establish all rail grain rates on multiple-car lots on August 10, 1961. These rates were suspended until August 7, 1962. Division 2 of the I.C.C. acted favorably on the rates on January 21, 1963. The Commission, sitting as a whole, reversed the decision of Division 2, 321 I.C.C. 582. The rates had been suspended by court action until the Commission rendered its verdict on July 1, 1963. The Southern Railway has appealed the final decision of the Commission, and this now awaits action by the Supreme Court.

1958. This legislation continued the functions of the Civil Aeronautics Board as set forth in the earlier legislation. In addition, it created the Federal Aviation Agency to take over the functions of the Civil Aeronautics Administration that was set up in 1938.

The Civil Aeronautics Board

1. The Act established the Civil Aeronautics Board which is composed of five members appointed by the President, with the advice of the Senate, for a term of office of six years. The conditions of office are similar to those of the other federal regulatory commissions.

2. The Act provides that no air carrier shall engage in air transportation unless it receives a certificate of public convenience and necessity from the Board. However, the Board may grant exemption from this provision to any carrier not engaged in scheduled air transportation. All certificates authorizing United States nationals to engage in foreign air transportation, and all permits to foreign companies entering this country must receive the approval of the President of the United States.

3. The rule of rate making is similar to that contained in the Interstate Commerce Act. The rate-control powers of the Board are confined to common carriers engaged in domestic service, or between the United States and its possessions. It may prescribe minimum maximum or precise rates for the United States proper, but only minimum and/or maximum for overseas traffic. It has no power over rates to or from foreign countries. However, it has the authority with regard to these rates to eliminate unjust discrimination and to approve or disapprove agreements between carriers respecting fares and rates. It may suspend proposals for domestic rate changes for a period up to 180 days.

4. The Board has complete control over consolidations or mergers of common carriers by air and of the corporate relations with any other common carrier, or any manufacturer of aircraft. It has no power to compel consolidations; nor does it have any authority whatsoever over the issuance of securities by air carriers.

5. The Board had the responsibility of determining the fair and reasonable rates of compensation for the transportation of mail by aircraft. The rates thus established must be such as to give the carrier sufficient revenue from mail and other sources to develop an adequate air transport system. Since 1955, however, the Postmaster General has been required to pay only the amount to which the carriers are reasonably entitled for the services they perform in carrying the mail. The Board is required to make up, through direct subsidy, the difference between these payments and the total revenue required by the carriers.

6. It is the duty of the Board to investigate accidents and report the facts, and to make recommendations to the Administrator of the Federal Aviation Agency to prevent such accidents in the future.

The Federal Aviation Agency

The Federal Aviation Act of 1958 provided for a separate agency to exercise federal control over the physical facilities of civil aviation. This agency is under an Administrator appointed by the President with the advice of the Senate. He is answerable only to the President. He is in charge of the national airways system. He is instructed to develop long-range plans for air navigation and landing facilities and the allocation of federal aid for airport projects which conform to the National Airport Plan, which is also under his direction. In addition, he prescribes the rules and regulations designed to promote safety in air transport.

Administration of the Federal Aviation Act

The basic policy followed by the Civil Aeronautics Board on certification has been that of limiting competition among carriers, although this has not been followed consistently. No new trunk lines have been certified since 1938, but since 1955 increased competition among them on the more heavily traveled routes has been permitted, the tendency being to favor the weaker lines by granting access to the better routes. Certification of the local service or "feeder" lines has preserved their route monopoly, kept them independent of the trunk lines, and limited direct competition with the latter. At the same time the Board certified supplemental or irregular air lines to offer passenger service, limited, however, to 10 trips per month in the same direction between any pair of points. Upon recommendation of the CAB, Congress enacted legislation in 1962[29] which provided for authorization of charter service together with individual ticketed or waybilled operations for temporary periods where the services of the certified route carriers are inadequate. The Board was also authorized to permit individually ticketed and waybilled operations for a period not to exceed two years from the date of enactment of the legislation, to provide for a transition period for those carriers which had previously been engaged in such operations. The Board took immediate steps to put the provisions of the new law into effect. The scope of supplemental air transportation is now confined to plane-load charter operations.[30] No clear-cut policy has been developed on air freight, although the Board's attitude seems to be that of protecting the all-cargo carriers from competition of the trunk lines by limiting "blocked space" freight to the all-cargo carriers.[31]

Despite the fact that passenger transportation has been the most

[29]Public Law 87–528 (1962).

[30]Civil Aeronautics Board, *Annual Report*, 1963 (Washington D.C.: U.S. Government Printing Office, 1963) pp. 9–11.

[31]Shippers sign agreements to ship guaranteed amounts every week for a period of not less than 90 days. Lower rates are given in return for the guarantee.

significant areas of air transport development since the Board assumed its regulatory authority in 1938, and despite the fact that the regulation of air transportation has been predicated on the general theory of control that has governed public policy for transportation in this country, the Board has never developed or announced any general principles for the determination of passenger fares for air travel. It has been caught in the dilemma of applying an essentially public utility approach to regulation in the presence of a considerable amount of competition.[32] To this problem it has found no answer.

In implementing the policy of the Act on consolidations and mergers, the Board has dealt with four types of situations: (1) mergers involving only local service carriers; (2) mergers of local and trunk lines; (3) mergers of trunk lines; and (4) acquisitions by other air carriers. Policy on the merging of local service carriers generally seems to favor such consolidations if a stronger enterprise will emerge. Only one merger of a trunk line with a local carrier has been approved, and this involved the question of subsidy.[33] The only trunk-line merger so far approved was that of United Airlines with Capital Airlines when the latter was threatened with bankruptcy.[34] The Board's policy has virtually excluded surface carriers from air transportation.

With the exception of the separation of local service from trunk-line carriers, and the exclusion of other agencies from participation in air transportation, the actions of the Civil Aeronautics Board have been marked by indecision and inconsistency. Blame for this must be placed on both Congress and the Board. To date we have developed no clear-cut policy for air transport, and certainly not one in keeping with private competitive enterprise.

CONCLUSION

The foregoing discussion of the legislative basis of regulation of transport clearly establishes the fact that it is very thoroughgoing. The control of railroads is about as complete as can possibly be imposed on any private enterprise. The Commission's control over literally every phase of rail transport is such as to endow it with a large measure of managerial powers. The fact that its control over the other agencies is much less complete is because of technological conditions. Had it not been for these, it is reasonable to assume that all regulation of transport would have been as extensive as that of the railroads.

The organization and procedure of regulatory commissions has already been discussed in an earlier chapter. There is no need to repeat the

[32]Civil Aeronautics Board, *General Passenger Fare Investigation*, Docket No. 8008 (1960 mimeo), pp. 76–77.

[33]Civil Aeronautics Board, *Continental-Pioneer Acquisition Case*, Docket No. 6547 (1954).

[34]Civil Aeronautics Board, *United-Capital Merger Case*, Docket No. 11699 (1961).

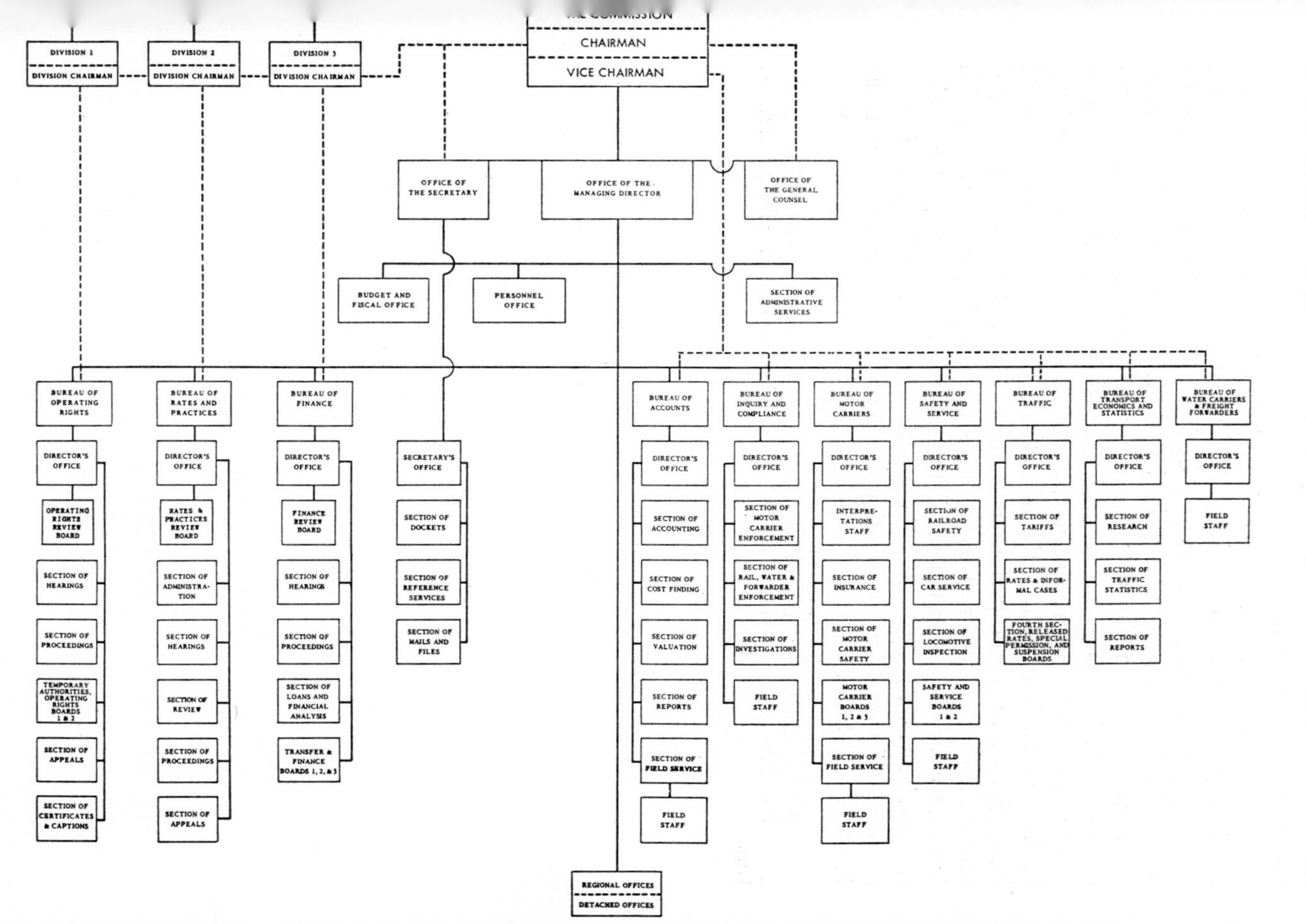

Reproduced from *Seventy-Seventh Annual Report* of the Interstate Commerce Commission (Washington, D.C.: Government Printing Office, 1964), p. 191.

remarks here. Figure 10 shows the general organization of the Interstate Commerce Commission.

The Interstate Commerce Commission is the most authoritative regulatory agency in this country. Whatever difficulties regulation and public policy in transportation may be faced with today, they cannot be ascribed to lack of scope and authority of the Commission.[35] These have been carried about as far as they can possibly go under a private enterprise system. The fact that air transport is under separate control does not seem to warrant any qualification of these remarks. There is little in the record to indicate that the Interstate Commerce Commission would have given any better performance than the Civil Aeronautics Board under the circumstances. The problems of regulating air transportation have been largely independent of those of the other transport agencies to date. The solution to current issues can scarcely come from the further extension of regulation in any significant way. The answer seems to lie in other directions.

[35]Perhaps an exception to this is found in the matter of consolidation where the authority of the Commission may possibly be impaired by conflict with the antitrust laws.

Chapter 24 THE NATIONAL TRANSPORT PROBLEM

INTRODUCTION

A Railroad Problem

For a period of approximately 75 years down to 1930, the transportation problem of the United States was the railroad problem. Today, nearly 30 years later, discussion of the current transportation crisis is still focused on the railroads. The issues are very different now, however, from what they were earlier. They can no longer be dealt with in isolation because of the total transformation of the transport structure which has taken place as the result of the dramatic developments in technology. While there is still a railroad problem, even it is more diversified than it was in the earlier period, and it is quite different in some respects. The railroad industry, as a whole, is suffering severely from lack of revenues, but the impact is spread very unevenly. About one quarter of the plant value in railroads earned over 6 per cent in 1955, and just over the same amount earned less than 3 per cent. For the passenger business as a whole, there was a 69 per cent deficit on a fully allocated cost basis, but apparently only about 31 per cent if the allocated expenses were not included. This deficit bore with particular severity on some lines with very heavy passenger and commuter obligations. This indicates that the perennial weak-and-strong road problem is even severer than it was earlier.[1] These divergencies suggest that remedies must be developed—in part, at least—for individual railroads and regions, rather than for the railroads as a whole. They also suggest that some of the remedies will have to be found within the industry. The entire solution does not lie in dealing with the new environment.

There is another main aspect to the railroad problem. That arises from the impact of the competition of the newer agencies for traffic which the railroads can haul. Until the rise of these newer agencies, part of the railroad problem was that of protecting water traffic from practices which would have eliminated it, even when such traffic was economically feasible. Today, the problem is literally reversed and has now become one of developing policies which will permit the railroads to get the

[1]Testimony of Merrill J. Roberts before the Smathers Committee (mimeographed), March 26, 1958.

traffic which they are economically fitted to take. Thus—in one aspect, at least—the railroad problem today is that of finding the role which the railroads ought to play in an economical system of modern transport.

A Transport Problem

The current transport problem is more than a matter of railroads, however. The elements of a modern transport system have already been described. Each of the agencies plays a vital and distinctive role in supplying the country's transport needs. But these agencies meet the needs under quite different circumstances and conditions. The economic structure of the railroads and pipe lines is that of natural monopolies; water, air, and motor carriers are strictly competitive in structure. As a consequence, each presents its own unique economic problems; yet, each offers transport services which, over a considerable range, are sufficiently similar to those supplied by the other modes to warrant characterizing them as immediately competitive. It is quite proper, therefore, to speak of the "transport problem" and thereby to approach it in a unified way, especially when dealing with the relative roles of the various agencies, the basis of competition among them, the issues of investment allocation, integration of the different types of carriers, and so forth. At the same time, it should be recognized that the unique problems and activities of each are such as to require separate and distinctive treatment which, in many instances, bears only indirectly or incidentally on the other agencies. From this point of view, the country faces not a transport problem but a series of problems. Public policy must face this fact, because an attempt to deal with the issues by uniform administrative and regulatory policies is likely to meet with little success.

Until recently, almost the sole attention to the national transport question was focused on the problem of regulation. As has already been pointed out, it developed as a means of controlling private enterprise in railroad transport to protect the consumer and in the public interest. Subsequent extension to the other agencies followed the same pattern. The theory was that transport was supplied by monopolists, that unregulated competition among them was ruinous, and that thoroughgoing regulation was necessary to protect the public interest. No attempt has been made, to date, on the part of the regulatory agencies or of Congress, to reconcile the theory with the facts nor to adapt the regulation of the various agencies to the totally different economic structures which they possess. Nor has any direct consideration been given to the question of reconciling the economic bases of pricing within the modes with pricing for the competitive traffic which they all seek. The theory has been that the bases of pricing should be uniform for all agencies, for competition within themselves as well as among each other. The framers of public policy apparently do not know what is meant by economic cost in price determination; and certainly, as yet, they have been unwilling to make any concessions to it on interagency competition.

Public Aid

Public aid has long been an issue in national transport policy, but it has taken on a very different perspective today. When aid was given the railroads, other agencies were not affected, whatever other results ensued therefrom; and moreover, the railroads were expected to return a *quid pro quo*, which they seemingly have done. In addition, it was an outright gift, after which the railroads were supposed to be fully self-supporting. Today, public aid does not fall into such a simple category. In the first place, public aid, for the most part, represents public investment in transport facilities which remain in public hands. In the second place, payment for the use of the public facilities presents an extremely complex problem. What should be included in calculating the total cost of supplying the facilities, how much should be imposed upon the direct users, and how the burden should be distributed among those users are all matters that national transport policy must resolve in some way. Whatever answers to these questions may be developed, public aid today in inextricably interwoven with competition in transport, the total supply of transport services, and the allocation of traffic among the agencies.

UNIQUENESS OF THE TRANSPORT PROBLEM

The formulation of a successful public policy for modern transport must recognize, at the outset, the uniqueness of the problem. This arises from two factors, both of which—in a significant way, at least—have emerged in the last quarter of a century: (1) Transport consists of a group of industries with highly diverse economic characteristics; and (2) there is now a high proportion of public investment in transport facilities, with the unavoidable use of them by private operators.

A Group of Industries

As has already been pointed out, transportation service is supplied by a group of industries, some of which are structurally in the category of natural monopolies and others thoroughly competitive in nature. Furthermore, a large amount of transport service is not for hire; it is supplied by the owners of the facilities for themselves. Much of it is readily substitutable for services which are sold for hire, and much of the for-hire traffic can move into the private category if for any reason the for-hire service is unsatisfactory. The regulation of railroads developed in the same pattern as the regulation of public utilities. Water, air, and motor transport lack the economic characteristics of public utilities. Even when they operate for hire, they do not fit the category; and when they serve their owners only, they cannot be brought under public regulation.

Antitrust Inadequate

Transport, however, cannot be put in the category of industry in general and subject only to the antitrust laws. The pricing of transportation for hire, no matter how effective competition may be, is more complex, and of necessity has to be more systematized, than industrial pricing. It is difficult to see how published rates, classification, and many other rules could be dispensed with, even under the most ideal conditions that could be obtained. Railroads still need to be regulated to prevent ruinous competition among them; and even if they were consolidated on a regional basis, this regulation could not be dispensed with. The problems of interagency ownership could scarcely be left to the jurisdiction of antitrust, because each situation is so individualized that public control is called for, no matter whether one assumes complete separation in principle or widespread integration. This is especially true in light of the Supreme Court's interpretation of the Celler-Kefauver amendment to the Clayton Act. The latter appears to be ill suited to the problem of mergers in transportation. Moreover, application of Section 2 of the Clayton Act (Robinson-Patman amendment) by the Federal Trade Commission to transport would seem to impose insuperable difficulties of regulation. To subject transportation solely to the antitrust laws would be to embark on uncharted seas with unknown consequences. The requirements of transport regulation today do not fit into the category of public utility control nor of antitrust.

Public Investment

Public investment in transportation today poses a unique problem, in that the investment decision for the supply of the "right of way" and terminal facilities for motor, water, and air transport must be made largely by public authority. Quantitatively, the most significant problem relates to highways, and this is precisely where the issues are most difficult. Reasonably adequate gauges for the proper amount of investment to be made are lacking, partly because all highway costs cannot very well be assessed directly on the users. Even if they could be, there would still be the problem of deciding what amount of costs should be imposed on the various kinds of users, and what differentials should be charged for the different highways and facilities that are used. These problems, of course, have to be resolved in a workable way; but the solutions that are adopted affect the total resources allocated to transportation and their distribution among the various agencies. The management of the public investment in transport, therefore, is an integral part of the national transport problem and program. To date, no attempt has been made to unify public investment policy in transportation, let alone integrate it with the private sector in the transport field.

REGULATION VERSUS ADMINISTRATION

The Function of Regulation

The formulation of a national transport policy today requires a distinction between regulation and administration. The function of regulation in transportation is to compensate for the deficiencies in competition, enforce the rules for competition, and protect the consumer against inadequate service. In carrying out these responsibilities, the regulatory authorities have to take public aid as datum. In fact, in so far as regulation is concerned, public aid, inequality of taxes, or other similar matters are of no consequence. A regulatory commission occupies much the same position as a judge in a horse race. He supervises the race and enforces the rules; he does not impose the handicap, if there is any, and the way the race is run is independent of the handicap. Regulation cannot deal with the inequalities of competition that arise out of the advantages or handicaps accorded to competitors by legislation. It can deal only with competitive relationships within the controlling conditions laid down by the law. The problems of regulation with which the commissions are required to deal are independent of such considerations as public aid, taxes, and so forth; and they would be of exactly the same type even though no differences of any kind arose from such factors. This means that regulation, at best, can deal with only part of the national transport problem.

The Function of Administration

The other part of the national transport problem is an administrative one. No matter what the policy of regulation may be, it cannot solve the investment problems if public investment in transport creates serious distortions in the allocation of investment among the agencies or results in aggregate overinvestment.

> Transport regulation, whether punitive or benevolent, is not an effective administrative vehicle for long-range transportation programming. In the first place, the supply and character of transport facilities and the recent technological factors affecting cost and service have not been determined primarily by regulatory processes but by public expenditures of billions of dollars for transport promotion. In the second place, the jurisdiction of federal regulatory agencies has of necessity been limited to only one segment of the transportation field, namely, the regulation of for-hire carriers in interstate commerce. The tremendous volumes of private transportation equipment and of intrastate and local for-hire transport services lie beyond the direct jurisdiction of federal regulation.[2]

The programming and long-range planning of public investment in transportation are administrative tasks that can be performed effectively only by the executive branch of the government. The development of a na-

[2]Dearing and Owen, *op. cit.*, p. 383.

tional transport policy for modern conditions needs a unified approach that only Congress can provide. The carrying-out of that policy involves two fundamentally separate considerations—namely, administration and regulation. To date, literally nothing has been done to unify the administrative aspects of the problem or, for that matter, even clearly to identify them.

SOME CURRENT ISSUES IN REGULATION

The most significant problem, from the standpoint of regulation of transportation, is that which relates to competition: the role which it can play and the basis upon which competition should be permitted to operate. For the most part, the economic questions which are involved here are no different in kind from those which apply to all industry, because all industry is faced with questions arising out of fixed, variable, specific, and common costs. The general issues to which these give rise were dealt with in the earlier chapters on pricing; their application to transportation was discussed in a previous chapter. There are some special features, however, which need to be pointed out in connection with the problems of regulation.

Inherent Advantages

Congress has emphasized its insistence on competition in transport by instructions to the Civil Aeronautics Board and the Interstate Commerce Commission to regulate in such a way as to preserve the inherent advantages of the carriers under their charge. In the Transportation Act of 1940, Congress issued a general statement of national policy which was to provide fair and impartial regulation of all modes of transportation, so administered as to preserve the inherent advantages of each. No definition of "inherent advantages" was given anywhere in the legislation, but it may be assumed that Congress had in mind the supplying of transport services by the carriers most economically able to do so. What this means calls for an examination of the concept of inherent advantages in economics.

Economical decisions are those that result in allocating resources to uses that satisfy those wants that we deem most important at the time the decisions are made. The price inducements resulting from these decisions draw productive resources into those activities that are most attractive, pricewise, and persuade them to leave those that are less so. Where this process is most completely effective, the resources are being used to their best possible advantage and are being put to the uses they are most capable of fulfilling. That is to say, they are being used according to their inherent advantages. Inherent advantages, therefore, may be conveniently described as those advantages which a producer possesses as a result of greater efficiency of operation, which make it possible for that producer to attract custom to his business at lower relative prices than those that a rival producer or supplier of alternatives can offer.[3]

The idea of inherent advantages is implicit in an economical allocation of resources and is therefore implicit in all competitive concepts. So much is this the case that the term is not even used in the general field of industry. Why, then, did it emerge in transport legislation and in the declaration of national transport policy? The answer seems to lie in the diverse economic characteristics of the industries that make up the field of transport and in the fact that monopoly and competitive situations are inextricably mixed in a way that is not found anywhere else in our industrial structure. The desire of Congress to preserve the inherent advantages of the different modes of transport arose out of its concern over the effects of competition among the various modes on each of them, especially the effects of railroad competition on the other agencies. Congress, however, did not recognize the difference in the economic characteristics of the various agencies. It assumed that they all needed to be treated alike. This led to the further assumption that there was no distinction between intra-agency and interagency competition. The difference between these two may be understood more clearly if the economic basis of public policy for motor transport and rail transport are discussed, before the interagency problem is examined. The regulatory problems of motor and rail transport exemplify the issues rather completely, because the other agencies fall into one of the two economic categories characterized by these; in addition, present-day issues—in this respect, at least—are most sharply focused on these two.

Regulatory Requirements for Motor Transport

The need for the regulation of motor transport rests on one of the two following conditions, or perhaps on both: (1) the necessity of regulation in order to assure consumer protection and (2) the necessity of regulation in order to prevent motor transport from subjecting the other agencies to destructive competition. The first of these two questions may be examined on the assumption that no other media of transport are in existence.

Is Regulation Necessary to Protect Consumers? The need for regulation to protect consumers against exploitation arises from deficiencies of competition. If an industry is competitive by virtue of its economic structure, the role of public policy is that of maintaining the environmental conditions of competition against predatory attempts to destroy them and against pressure groups seeking special privilege designed to

[3]For a more extended discussion of this, see D. F. Pegrum, "Why Inherent Advantages Are Important—and How to Obtain Them," in *Essays on Inherent Advantages of Railway Service* (New York: Simmons-Boardman Publishing Corp., 1954), pp. 9–12.

accord these groups advantages which they cannot acquire under the rigors of competition. Consumer protection, where competition obtains, does not require limitation of supply, the fixing of prices, or the control of profits. It rests on a different set of assumptions, which does not relate to the public control of prices or limitation of output. The consumer is interested in the lowest economic cost; this is what the competitive standard means and what competition will give him. The precise details of the regulation which is necessary under competition will vary from industry to industry. It may involve standards of quality, standards of service, financial responsibility, price discrimination, and so forth; but it does not require the fixing of relative prices or the control of profits. If the latter are included in a program of control, the advantages of competition are lost.

For an industry to be competitive, it is necessary that resources be both legally and economically mobile. To be legally mobile, it must be possible for them, as far as the law is concerned, to be free to move from one use to another and from one market to another. There must be freedom to move the physical facilities according to the wishes of the producers, or to convert them or divert them to other uses. Similarly, the decision for investment or disinvestment must be left to the enterprises. In other words, what is called freedom of entry, which also carries with it freedom of exit, is one of the fundamental requirements of a truly competitive structure. If this is denied by law, special privilege is accorded to an entrant into an industry or to an existing producer, which protects him to the extent that freedom of entry is limited against the pressures of competition. He is no longer faced with the threat of an alternative supplier of similar services who may wish to risk his resources in the belief that his venture may be successful.

In industries that possess a high degree of legal and economic mobility, little difficulty of relative over- or undersupply of facilities will occur, because inducements to ready response to changing conditions are always present. If, at any time, more services are available than can be disposed of at the prices which will take them off the market, losses will be suffered until contraction takes place. By the same token, however, undersupply will lead to higher prices until the needed additional facilities are made available. It is the function of competitive forces to maintain the balance. If they are prevented from doing so by private action, the evils of monopoly appear. If they are prevented from doing so by public policy, then the government is deliberately creating a monopoly situation. In such a case, either the monopolist will enjoy the advantages of the privileges thus bestowed, or governmental action designed to provide a substitute for the competition it has eliminated will have to be invoked. If competitive forces are restrained in their action by such a policy and the structure and conditions of the industry are primarily competitive, then the government is trying to play at competition with the necessary ingredients missing. The results are bound to be unsatisfactory, especially to the consumer.

As was pointed out in an earlier chapter, the economic structure of motor transport is that of a highly competitive industry. It possesses a ready adaptability of plant and facilities to changing market conditions, a high degree of geographic flexibility of plant and facilities, easily accessible alternative sources of supply of services to consumers, and an absence of economic characteristics that make competition a destructive force leading to the elimination of competitors and the emergence of monopoly. Competition can thrive if given the opportunity to do so by public policy which gives full weight to the economic characteristics of the industry. The consumer of motor transport services has alternatives that are not available in other forms of transportation and that are more closely related in type to ordinary commodities than to railroad or public utility services. The consumer, in the absence of public restrictions, can make his choice among a number of competitors. He may contract for services, hire equipment, or supply his own. These alternatives afford him protection against exploitation such as he enjoys in the area of competitive business. As far as the economics of motor transport is concerned, there seems to be no more foundation for the type of regulation that has been applied to railroads than there is for its application to business in general. Consumer protection and public policy do not require rate regulation so as to insure reasonable rates or stability of rates, nor do they require regulation of security issues in order to safeguard the financial stability of carriers. Restrictions on freedom of entry and rigid prescriptions of routes are likewise unnecessary. The only purpose they can serve is to protect existing carriers against competition and to aid them in maintaining possession of the field they have been afforded by public sanction.

It is an assumption of public policy today that a common carrier is entitled to some degree of protection against competition because of the obligations it assumes and is required to maintain, and that this protection should even limit the amount of competition which other common carriers should be permitted to offer. Because motor transport embraces a large number of suppliers who do not fall into the category of common carriers, it is necessary to draw a distinction between the latter and the former, so that those who are not common carriers are prevented from offering common carrier service. This, however, is not a sufficient reason for limiting the number of common carriers who wish to compete with each other. If a carrier wishes to offer common carrier service, presumably it thinks the business is worth while and wants to compete for it. There is no apparent reason why this should be denied when the structure of the industry is competitive; certainly, consumer protection is not furthered by a policy which imposes limitations on such competition. Nor is it necessary to restrict the competition of contract carriers if the objective of the policy is public interest or consumer protection. By the same token, present moves to reduce the role of exempt carriers seem to serve no useful public purpose. There is little evidence of protest from those who use these services. In fact, the avowed purpose of limiting the exemptions is to protect the regulated carriers. The economic justification for this warrants more careful study than it has received to date.

Is Regulation Necessary to Protect Interagency Competition? The second major question—namely, whether there is the necessity of regulating motor transport in order to prevent motors from subjecting other agencies to destructive competition—can be dealt with very briefly. If there is no threat of destructive or ruinous competition, then public policy in the interest of furthering an economical transport system should not impose limitations on motor carrier opportunities to participate in interagency competition. The need for protection of the other agencies against motor competition rests on the assumption that motor transport, by virtue of its economic structure, possesses some kind of advantage that makes it possible for it to resort to tactics designed to and able to kill off its rivals. If motor competition is not destructive within itself, however, it cannot be destructive to the other agencies. The relation of motor carrier costs to output precludes this, and so does competition among the motor carriers themselves. It is possible that motor carrier competition with railroads may be unfair because of the inadequacy of the charges imposed upon motor carriers for the use of the streets and the highways, but this is another matter. It is a problem of administration, not regulation, and it cannot be resolved by the latter. Motor carrier transport, therefore, does not need to be regulated because of its impact on interagency competition.

Limited Need for Regulation. In view of the nature of motor transport, it seems to be clear that the role of positive regulation is very limited. In fact, the requirements, in some respects, are less than those which the Federal Trade Commission faces in its administration of antitrust, because there is little threat of monopoly or monopoly problems in motor transportation. Nevertheless, regulation by an agency established to deal with transport seems to be in order because of the distinctive functions and obligations assumed by the suppliers of transport services. However, this regulation should be administered in the setting of a thoroughly competitive industry. This does not characterize public policy or its administration today.

The administrative aspects of motor carrier control are much more important than the regulatory. Highway investment, construction, finance, and the way that the costs arising from these should be met as a whole and assessed upon various users, are administrative, not regulatory, matters. Conditions imposed upon the privilege of using the highways, weights and loads for vehicles, safety measures, and so forth are also administrative details. The regulatory commission is not competent, by the nature of its organization or as the result of the major responsibilities which it must discharge, to handle these questions. The formulation and administration of national transport policy today needs to take full cognizance of this fact.[4]

Regulatory Requirements for Railroads

Defects of Current Regulation. The need for regulation of railroads, today, rests on the same two conditions that were examined in connection with motor transport. The difference is that rail transport needs to be regulated in a totally different way from motor transport, because it is not, in its economic structure, a competitive industry. If no other form of inland transport were available to the consuming public, the railroads would have to be regulated in the same basic pattern that was adopted in the Transportation Act of 1920 and for the same reasons that brought about the passage of that legislation. This is not to say that railroad regulation did not have its shortcomings, even on the assumption that technological conditions had not changed so rapidly. The Interstate Commerce Commission was given and assumed managerial functions that were far too extensive in scope to be compatible with responsible private enterprise. The regulation of rates was far too rigid for an economic environment characterized by instability. Requests for rate advances imposed too much of a burden on the carriers and entailed delays that resulted in irrecoverable losses of large amounts of revenue. Literally everybody was given the opportunity to oppose the carriers' requests, but only the railroads suffered the consequences. If the Interstate Commerce Commission made mistakes, the railroads paid the bill. The apathy arising from such a division of authority and responsibility has, in no small measure, contributed to the present difficulties of the railroads. Furthermore, rate regulation on the theory of average cost pricing prevented the development of a dynamic and market-oriented pricing program. Finally, the failure of public policy to bring about, by some means or another, a rational program of consolidation has perpetuated a condition of the weak-and-strong road problem, with its costly duplication of services, a

[4]For an extended discussion of issues in motor transport regulation, see Pegrum, "The Economic Basis of Public Policy for Motor Transport," *Land Economics*, Vol. XXVIII (August, 1952), pp. 245–63; Pegrum, "Effects of Regulation on Small Business in Motor Transport," *Hearings of Select Committee on Small Business* (Interstate Commerce Commission Administration of the Motor Carrier Act) (Washington, D.C.: U.S. Government Printing Office, 1956), pp. 465–70; Pegrum, *Transportation: Economics and Public Policy* (Homewood, Ill.: Richard D. Irwin Inc., 1963), chap. 14. James C. Nelson, "New Concepts in Transportation Regulation," in National Resources Planning Board, *Transportation and National Policy* (Washington, D.C.: U.S. Government Printing Office, 1942), Sec. VI. For a somewhat different point of view, see D. P. Locklin, *Economics of Transportation* (4th ed.; Homewood, Ill.: Richard D. Irwin, Inc., 1954), pp. 700–705.

continuously large amount of railroad insolvency, and ranges of individual earnings totally incompatible with either monopoly or competitive conditions.

Even had powerful rival agencies for traffic not emerged, railroad regulation would have required some rather drastic changes in order that successful private enterprise might remain. The development of the other means of transport has made the changes much more urgent than they would have been otherwise because of the pressure of the competition of substitute services. Whatever policies are adopted now, if they are to have any chance of success, must be geared to a condition of keen rivalry among the various agencies, especially rail and motor transport. The question remains, however, whether the railroads need to be regulated within themselves—that is, on an intra-agency basis—when external or interagency competition is so keen.

Need for Continued Regulation. Continued regulation of the railroads is a requirement of national policy for exactly the opposite reasons that reduced the necessity of regulating motor transport to the minimum controls set forth in the preceding section. The railroad industry is not competitive in its structure; there must be restriction of entry if ruinous competition is to be avoided; the greater part of the investment is not economically mobile; and consumers can shop around among railroads only to a limited extent. Discrimination cannot be avoided in railroad transport, at least as long as railroads remain self-supporting. If the weak-and-strong road problem were resolved by regional consolidation, these considerations would be even more pertinent.

The impact of the competition of other agencies on the railroads is such that the discretion which railroad management could exercise, if it were given the opportunity to do so, is very much less than it was before the new competition emerged. Whether railroad pricing will have to be almost totally market-oriented if the railroads are to get adequate revenues can be determined only by experimentation. It is quite possible, however, that some restrictions on pricing discretion would have to be imposed if a rational plan of consolidation was inaugurated, together with a program whereby the rival agencies bore the full cost of the facilities supplied to them, with those costs imposed on individual users in some way that bore a direct relation to the quality of facilities used and the quantity of use made of them. Finally, minimum price regulation in the case of railroads can scarcely be left entirely to private determination. The wide range of discretion which must be used in the economical pricing of railroad services would require public control in order to protect the consumer if there were no alternatives. With the interagency competition that now exists, some public control of minimum railroad rates seems necessary to prevent the possibility of predatory rate making.

The continuation of railroad regulation is warranted, then, by the nature of railroad economics; but the regulatory program needs to be reoriented so as to give full recognition to the defects of current regulation at the intra-agency level and to the impact of interagency competition.

Interagency Competition

The Problem of Interagency Competition. The problem of interagency competition in transport arises from the necessity of developing policy with regard to price competition among agencies possessing strikingly different economic characteristics. The importance of this problem lies in the fact that rates that are charged for the movement of traffic for which the carriers of two or more agencies may compete will determine who will haul the traffic. The task of the regulatory authorities is to establish or permit rates that will induce the traffic to move by the most economical means. If all the agencies fell into the category of industries with highly competitive economic structures, the minimum price which any of the competitors could afford to charge for any service would be close to the average cost of rendering it. In other words, differential pricing, or discrimination, would not produce any difficult problems. It is because railroads do not fit into this category that complicated issues of differential pricing do arise in transportation. The extent to which such pricing should be permitted as a means of securing traffic which might also be moved by other agencies is the special problem of intergency competition.

Basis of Interagency Rate Policy. From the standpoint of economics, any attempt to limit or eliminate differential pricing which is designed to increase (or has the effect of increasing) the use of economic resources is against public interest. Given the investment, or the technical necessities of a plant, prices for particular products or services that are below average costs are economically sound as long as they cover the costs that would not be incurred if such production did not take place. This assumes, of course, that the firm is better off at these prices than at any others that it could get for these services. That is, it assumes that the prices are market-oriented and are not quoted purely for predatory purposes. Minimum rates that attract traffic which increases the net revenue of the carrier that can get it are in the public interest and are a necessary part of public policy which relies on competition. These rates are also a necessary part of public policy which aims at the most efficient utilization of economic resources. The fact that the minimum rates may be based on costs which are below "average" is not a relevant consideration. The important question is: "Will the net revenue of the firm be increased by obtaining the traffic?"

Rate making on the above principles may be hard on some competitors. That, however, is the essence of competition. The purpose of public policy in an area where pervasive competition prevails is to preserve competition, not to sustain competitors. The competition must be fair, but fair competition has meaning only as it enables enterprises to succeed by the sale of their products to consumers who have alternative choices. This does not recognize survival by preying upon or devouring rivals; but it does make survival depend upon the ability to attract customers by superior service or lower prices, or both, in open market with rivals. The protection of competition demands the prevention of predatory pricing. When a seller is worse off by selling a product or service than he would be if he did not sell it, and knowingly does this to get business from a competitor, then he is engaged in predatory pricing. It is this sort of behavior in transport that the regulation of interagency competition should seek to prevent, and no other.

It is frequently urged that differential pricing by a carrier, with regard either to commodities or to places, results in prejudicial treatment to those commodities or places which are not accorded the lower rates. The fact is, however, that when this differential charging is the result of competition, it is because the carrier which grants the differential rates does so in order to get the traffic. If the carrier is not permitted to do this, the traffic will move by the carrier of another agency and so will get the benefits of the lower rates in any case. Thus, no matter what restrictions are placed upon the carrier which tries to get the traffic by economical differential pricing, it is not possible to protect the commodities or the communities against such charges. The only beneficiary of the policy which prevents carriers from engaging in this differential pricing is the carrier which is protected against losing the business to its more competent rival. This does not mean that such differential pricing should be limited to that which is necessary to meet the competition of a carrier of a rival agency. It will be to the interest of the carrier and the public for prices to go even lower, if by so doing, the net revenue is increased by virtue of the generation of traffic which will make for a fuller utilization of the carrier's plant.

Interagency competition and the economic basis of rate policy for such competition are not the result of private ownership of railroads; nor are they related to the problem of competition among railroads. They are independent of both. Even if the railroads were owned and operated as a single national system, thereby eliminating any intra-agency competition among them, the interagency problem would remain precisely the same as it is now. The cost structure of railroad transport would not be affected, and the basis for economical differential pricing would still be the same. The argument, therefore, that if policies for interagency pricing are to be developed on the basis of free and unhampered price competition, they should be extended throughout all the agencies on an intra-agency basis, is quite spurious. It is simply unrelated to the interagency problem. Policies for intra-agency competition in service and pricing should be dealt with on an individual agency basis.[5]

[5]For a more extended discussion of these issues, see Pegrum, "The Special Problem of Inter-Agency Competition in Transport," *I.C.C. Practitioners' Journal* (December,

Interagency Ownership

The problem of interagency ownership centers on the question of whether, in the interests of an efficient national transport system, ownership of the different modes should be kept in separate hands or whether the formation of transportation companies should be encouraged. At the present time, the ownership of one form of transportation by another, except in very limited cases, is generally either forbidden or made extremely difficult under existing statutes.

Advantages of Interagency Ownership. The essence of the argument in favor of transport companies is succinctly stated by the late Professor Daggett:

> Restrictions on multiple-type organizations tend to decrease the over-all efficiency of transport because they hamper the impartial assignment of machinery to the tasks which each unit can best perform. Technical knowledge can be employed by any management, and executive ability and experience is not monopolized by any group. But an organization with a broad outlook should be able to judge the possibilities of a given manner of providing service better than a management which is committed to a single method or to equipment of a single kind.[6]

Transport companies operating railroads, trucks and busses, ships, and airplanes could offer a complete service adapted to the needs of the customer at the customer's option. A complete integration and interchange of physical equipment could be employed; and presumably, the company would utilize the means of transport which was the most economical and which would give the consumer the benefit of the lowest costs.

Interagency Ownership and Competition. This argument assumes two things: (1) that there are genuine and real economies arising out of increased scale of operations and integration and (2) that the benefits to the consumer are competitively compelled. Although some economies from co-ordination and integration might be realized, there is no evidence that economies of scale would be achieved. The railroads would be the core of the organization; and if further economies of scale are available in transport, surely they should first be achieved by a rational program of consolidation which would eliminate many existing duplications. If the benefits to the consumer are to be competitively compelled, then it must be assumed that over-all competition among the companies will prevail. How this could obtain in the light of railroad economics is difficult to see. If the benefits to the consumer were not competitively compelled, they would have to be obtained by regulation. This would involve

---

1956), pp. 307–14; and "The Economic Basis of Regulation of Inter-Agency Competition in Transportation," in *Hearings on H.R. 6141* (House Subcommittee on Transportation, 84th Cong., 2nd sess.) (Washington, D.C.: U.S. Government Printing Office, 1956), Part III, pp. 1824–36.

[6]Stuart Daggett, *Principles of Inland Transportation* (4th ed.; New York: Harper & Bros., 1955), p. 562.

sacrificing the present possibilities of public benefit which interagency competition offers.

If the basic assumption of interagency relationships in transportation is that of competition, then ownership of carrier facilities should be kept in separate hands. At the present stage of the development of transportation, the extension of ownership of one type of carrier over another would mean integration around different railroads. It would result in the linking, by ownership, of a type of transport that is monopolistic in its structure with those that are competitive. If the competitive structure of motor transport were retained, railroad participation in the ownership of motor carriers would simply mean the entry into the motor carrier field of another competitor, whose prime interest would be that of keeping the railroad in business. It would not be possible to keep the affairs of the two businesses separate—at least, if economies of integration were to be obtained. It would therefore be difficult to prevent the railroads from using their size and monopoly powers in competing with other motor carriers.

The Problem of Geographic Organization. There is also the question of the areas which would be served by railroad-owned motor and other carriers. Railroads operate in rather precisely delineated geographical areas and are confined to the territories contacted by their roadbeds. Motor carriers crisscross railroad territories and operate in areas of different railroads. Extension into other territories is merely a matter of moving vehicles over other highways—assuming, of course, that this is permitted. If railroads were allowed to own motor carriers, except for such things as terminal and immediately ancillary services, would such ownership be confined to their own territories, and if so, would they be authorized to penetrate outside? It would be uneconomical to confine highway and air transport operations to the region served by the operating railroad. Yet, interagency ownership on any other basis which involves the railroads would present almost hopelessly complex issues because of the inescapable regional nature of railroads. It would appear, then, that interagency ownership points in the direction of regional transport monopolies. Such an arrangement runs counter to competitive developments and prevents the growth of policies designed to allocate traffic on the basis of relative efficiency. If regional monopolies were developed, the monopoly problem in transport would raise its head again on a wider scale than ever. Furthermore, they would be likely to present more problems of co-ordination than they would solve, particularly for traffic moving on an interregional basis. Interagency ownership, then, seems to offer no solution to present problems but, on the contrary, complicates them.[7]

[7]All of the issues that have been discussed in connection with interagency relations would become much more acute if the government were to take over the railroads. This requires too extensive an examination, however, to be pursued here.

The Independent Regulatory Commission

The conclusion was reached, in an earlier section, that continued regulation of transport is necessary in the public interest. For motor and water, the requirements are minimal as far as rates and other economic controls are concerned. Even if these were given up entirely, certification, interagency co-ordination of traffic, and integration for ancillary purposes, in the case of motor transport, would probably leave a considerable amount of activity that should be supervised by a commission rather than be left to some other agency of government. The same remarks apply to air transport, although public control of it relates overwhelmingly to technical and promotional matters. Even certification is as much a technical question as it is economic and may become more so, if limitations on operating rights of air carriers have to be imposed because of the problems of congestion of routes and the ensuing threat to safety of travel. Despite the growth of competition, positive regulation of the railroads will remain a necessity, although, as has been pointed out, it needs to be severely reduced and redirected from that which we now have. In other words, separate regulation of transport cannot be abandoned in favor of subjecting the carriers to the antitrust laws like other enterprises. If separate regulation were abolished, this would be the only alternative; complete exemption from any form of federal control is out of the question.

Unified Regulation versus Separate Commission. At the present time, federal regulation of domestic transport in the United States is almost entirely in the hands of the Interstate Commerce Commission and the Civil Aeronautics Board, if one excludes pipe-line transmission of natural gas. With the exception of air transport, the extension of regulation by the federal government has, in each instance, been assigned to the Interstate Commerce Commission. The regulation of air transport was given to the Civil Aeronautics Board, partly on the assumption that air transport faced different economic problems from the other agencies, and partly because of the technical and promotional aspects of air transport. There are those who feel that separate regulation of air transport is not compatible with a unified national transport policy and that the economic aspects of the Civil Aeronautics Board's regulatory functions should be transferred to the Interstate Commerce Commission. There are others who feel that the Commission has too much and too many diversified things to do already and that separate commissions for the various agencies would be more in keeping with current requirements. The answer to the questions raised by these divergent points of view turns, in part, upon the assumptions which are made with regard to the scope and character of the powers assigned to the regulatory authority.

At the present time, both the Interstate Commerce Commission and the Civil Aeronautics Board possess very extensive powers of positive control over the economic affairs of the companies coming under their jurisdiction. So far, Congress has not seen fit to reduce them. In addition, they both deal with a great many technical details of operation of carriers that only indirectly affect the economic regulation. The Interstate Commerce Commission, in particular, is engaged in an enormous amount of this work, including safety measures; if air transport were brought under its control, it is highly likely that such control would be unified, as it is over the other agencies. At present, this would merely add to the duties of the Commission and possibly make the interagency problem more complex than it is today.

If regulation is to continue on the same theory that governs it at the present time, and if the regulatory authorities are to continue to exercise as much control over managerial and technical matters as they do now, the case for separate commissions for the various modes is very strong. If public policy is to be predicated on competition among the agencies, regulation by a single commission presents serious difficulties. Transportation is not a homogeneous industry, and a uniform program for each type of transport is not the answer to today's issues. Regulation needs to be tailored to each mode. To place all the authority in the hands of a single commission is all too likely to result in a move toward a monopoly approach to transportation, especially when railroads occupy such a dominant position in the transport structure. The Interstate Commerce Commission can scarcely avoid being "railroad-minded" because of (1) the pre-eminence of the railroads, (2) the development of regulatory theory around the railroads, and (3) the theory of regulation which grew out of the unique economic characteristics of the railroads Separate commissions could focus their attention on each agency independently of each other. Each could deal with the problems of its own mode without the distractions of the conflicting claims of the others. Each would be compelled to recognize the competitive requirements of its own charge. Finally, the competitive pressure of independent and separate responsibility would serve as a stimulus to initiative, imagination, and adaptation that is sorely needed in transportation today. Competition is an excellent antidote to bureaucracy and vested interest.

A Transport Commission. If our national transport policy is reconstructed so as to make a clear-cut separation between regulation and administration, and if regulation is tailored to the various modes so as to give full recognition to their distinct economic characteristics, there is much to be said for a single transport commission. The task of regulating the economic aspects of air, water, and motor transport would be relatively small; railroad regulation, especially when shorn of all the technical operating controls that now occupy so much time of the Commission, would be a much less onerous task than it is today. Even if these changes were introduced, there would still be the necessity, however, of distinguishing clearly between the regulatory requirements of each mode.

At the same time, co-ordination among the modes is necessary for efficient transport, and some of this would probably have to continue to be provided by regulatory direction. These two requisites of successful regulation could be met by a federated transport commission. Each agency could be placed under a division possessing a large amount of autonomy, with commissioners in charge of each. Over the divisions could be a transport commission, consisting of the divisional commissioners and an independent chairman. Such a reconstruction of regulation would require some rather drastic changes in the present organization of transport regulation; but it would be simpler than the setting-up of separate commissions, and it probably could be built around the present Interstate Commerce Commission.

ADMINISTRATION AND THE FORMULATION OF PUBLIC POLICY

Federal Participation in Transport Supply

The federal government is engaged, on a large scale, in the provision and control of transportation facilities and services, apart from the direct regulation of the economic aspects of the activities of many of the suppliers of transport services. Federal action involves actual participation in rendering a wide variety of services, such as the administration of the federal-aid highway program, the operation of aids to air navigation and airport construction, the administration of air-line and merchant marine subsidies, the construction and sale of ocean vessels, and the financing and conducting of river and harbor developments and other promotional activities in the field of water transportation.

At the present time, the administrative tasks relating to federal participation in providing transportation services are scattered among a number of different federal agencies, both regulatory and executive. The Civil Aeronautics Board, the Federal Aviation Authority, the Bureau of Public Roads, the Interstate Commerce Commission, the Corps of Engineers (Department of the Army), the Federal Maritime Board, and the Coast Guard all have duties that really belong to the executive branch of the government. The activities of these various agencies are completely lacking in co-ordination and have no common spokesman in Congress. Some of them serve under the executive branch, while the Civil Aeronautics Board and the Interstate Commerce Commission are directly responsible to Congress. Thus, the federal government, in attempting to determine the volume and character of transportation services, divides this responsibility between promotional and regulatory agencies in such a way that there is no possibility of effective programming and no possibility of effective co-ordination of the different aspects of national policy.

Need for Unified Administration

The unification of administration of national transport policy is needed for at least five reasons:

First. The administrative tasks now delegated to so many of the agencies of the federal government are also frequently assigned to departments whose interest in transportation is only incidental to their main tasks. For example, programs for inland river improvement are formulated by the Corps of Army Engineers, with no general reference to transportation problems. Efficiency and economy in administration both call for a unification of the varied activities in a department whose interests and responsibilities are in transportation.

Second. The administrative tasks of the Interstate Commerce Commission, in particular, are so burdensome that it needs to be relieved of those that are not immediately connected with the functions of regulation. Effective regulation demands that the activities of the independent regulatory commission be confined to quasi-legislative and quasi-judicial matters. The administration of safety regulations for the various types of carriers, both public and private; conditions of use of highway, air, and water facilities; vehicle weights, and so forth are all technical matters, the enforcement of which dilutes the efforts of a regulatory commission. The responsibility for discharging so many executive functions poses a constant threat of transfer of the independent commission to the executive branch of the government. Removal of the purely administrative tasks would go far toward eliminating this threat and, in addition, would permit concentration on regulation.

Third. Today, public aid to transport and public investment in it are of such magnitude that they can no longer be left to haphazard programming and administration. The public stake in the investment and the impact of it on the transport structure are such as to demand immediate and careful study of the investment needs in transport, both the amount and the type. This involves the whole range of questions relating to the determination of the total costs to be assessed against public aid projects; decisions on the apportionment of costs among the numerous beneficiaries; and the structure, scale, and collection of user charges. All of these activities need to be co-ordinated with the programs of the various states, whose policies and decisions bear heavily on the national transport picture. If the federal government, for example, were to decide upon assessing user costs so as to equalize the competitive conditions of rail and highway transport, co-operation with the various states would be essential. Under present conditions, this it not possible, because responsibility for initiating and developing policy for this is no one person's or agency's duty at the federal level.

Fourth. There is also need for concentrating the executive functions with regard to transportation in a single department, in order to focus responsibility for transport policy. At the present time, no one person or organization is responsible for developing transport policy, and no one can answer to Congress or be answerable to Congress for failures in the policy. Instead, presentation to the legislative branch of the government is made by a number of competing and, all too frequently, conflicting groups.

Fifth. Transportation is of such importance to national defense that peacetime policies and programs cannot ignore the demands which national defense imposes on transport, especially in times of emergency. These were recognized by the establishment, in 1941, of the Office of Defense Transportation, which was placed directly under the President of the United States. The continuing problems of national defense today are such as to require that national transport policy should recognize them as among the factors which must be given consideration in the development of an adequate transportation system.

THE FORMULATION OF PUBLIC POLICY

Over the period in which the federal government has been engaged in regulating transportation, a large number of special commissions and study groups have been appointed to investigate and examine the transportation problem and to recommend revisions in transportation policy and administration.[8] Most of the studies have centered on the single form of transportation whose particular problem seemed to be critical at the time. This means that literally no attention has been paid to the complex issues of transportation as a whole. In addition, even more of them have failed to advance any generally acceptable basis for administrative reorganization, because—almost without exception—they have failed to distinguish between the functions and problems of regulation, on the one hand, and those of administration, on the other.

The full import of the impact of technological change on the transport structure was not grasped until after World War II. Recognition of the growing need for a thoroughgoing examination of the transportation problem in its postwar setting led President Eisenhower to appoint a Presidential Advisory Committee on Transport Policy and Organization in 1954 with instructions to make a comprehensive review of over-all transportation policies and problems, and to transmit recommendations regarding them for the President's consideration. The resulting report (known as the Weeks Report) marked a departure from previous ones by its emphasis on "pervasive" competition in modern transportation, although it did spell out the meaning and implications of the term.[9]

[8]For a description and evaluation of these over the fifteen years to 1949, see C. L. Dearing and W. Owen, *National Transportation Policy* (Washington, D.C.: Brookings Institution, 1949), pp. 381–87 and Appendix C. See also Pegrum, *Transportation: Economics and Public Policy*, *op. cit.*, chap. 20.

[9]Report of the Presidential Advisory Committee on Transport Policy and Organization, *Revision of Federal Transportation Policy*, (Washington, D.C.: U.S. Government Printing Office, 1955).

Since then a number of other reports have been issued, the Doyle Report being the latest and in many respects the most comprehensive; at least it is the largest.[10]

All of the reports since 1954 have placed considerable emphasis on the desirability of reducing governmental restraint on transport and of affording greater opportunity for the play of competitive forces. However, none of them have developed the economic premises upon which such an approach must be founded, nor have any of them explored the implications in terms of the limitations on and the functions of regulation under such circumstances. Curiously enough, all of them imply more positive regulation in many directions than now exists, by the suggestion that carriers be compelled to comply with rate regulation based on an ill-defined standard of cost orientation. Restrictions on competition are also proposed for the purpose of protecting the common carrier. There seems to be little understanding of the fact that competitively compelled rates will resolve the problems of cost-price relationships, and that all that is necessary, at most, is to prevent predatory practices and unreasonably high monopoly profits, if there is any possibility of obtaining them. None of the reports seems to grasp the fact that much of the field of transportation is not even amenable to regulation based on the theory of monopoly.

PRESIDENT KENNEDY'S MESSAGE

Recognition of the pressing problems that are burdening the transport system led President Kennedy to submit, on April 15, 1962, one of the most comprehensive messages on transportation ever transmitted by a chief executive to the Congress.[11] After a preamble and a statement on national transportation policy, the message was divided into four parts. Part I dealt with intercity transportation, Part II with urban transportation, Part III with international transportation, and Part IV with labor relations and research. Only the preamble and Part I will be dealt with here. The President stated that a chaotic patchwork of inconsistent and often obsolete legislation had evolved from piecemeal development, with the result that it had failed to keep pace with the changing structure. Commissions had been overburdened and management shackled in exercising its initiative. Less federal regulation and subsidization was necessary, therefore, for a healthy intercity framework. The basic objective of national policy must be to assure the availability of economical transportation services without waste or discrimination

[10]Preliminary Draft of a Report to the Senate Committee on Interstate and Foreign Commerce (87th Cong., 1st sess.) *National Transportation Policy* (Doyle Report) (Washington, D.C.: U.S. Government Printing Office, 1961).

[11]Message from the President of the United States April 5, 1962, House of Representatives Document No. 384 (87th Cong., 2d sess.), *The Transportation System of Our Nation* (Washington, D.C.: U.S. Government Printing Office, 1962). Reproduced in Pegrum: *Transportation: Economics and Public Policy, op. cit.*, Appendix I.

at the lowest economic cost. As a consequence, there had to be equal opportunity for all forms of transport and the users through greater reliance on the forces of competition, and an equalization of competitive conditions by imposition of the full cost of service upon the users. Common carriers should be aided by being given relief from the burdens of regulation that handicap them against unregulated competition.

The President then outlined a number of specific recommendations:

(1) That there be extended to all other carriers the exemptions from approval or prescription of minimum rates on bulk commodities, as applied to water carriers. The Interstate Commerce Commission's control over maximum railroad rates and prohibitions against discrimination were to be retained. Exemptions on agricultural and fishery products were to be extended to all carriers;

(2) That the 10 per cent transportation tax on intercity bus and railroad passenger transportation be repealed, but that a 5 per cent tax on air line tickets and freight bills be imposed, and that the 2-cents-per-gallon net tax on gasoline for air lines be retained and extended to jet fuels. A similar tax on all fuels for vessels on inland waterways was also proposed;

(3) That domestic trunk air carriers be made ineligible for subsidies in the future and that steps be taken to prepare a schedule for the termination of subsidies to the three certified helicopter services, together with a plan for sharp reduction of subsidies to the local service air lines;

(4) That a group of agency representatives be formed: (a) to formulate general administrative policies on mergers in each segment of the transportation industry, and (b) to assist the Department of Justice in developing a government position on each merger. The criteria for mergers were to be (i) maintenance of effective competition among the various forms of transportation, (ii) preservation of economical, efficient and adequate service to the public, and (iii) assistance to affected workers to make necessary adjustments.

Legislation was promptly introduced into Congress to put the recommendations into effect, but severe controversies among the agencies prevented any action being taken except for the repeal of the 10 per cent passenger tax for railroads and busses and the imposition of the 5 per cent air-line tax. President Johnson is now preparing new proposals for legislation by the 89th Congress which aim to place heavier reliance on competition in transportation. What the details of this will be have not yet been disclosed.

A Secretary of Transport

Even though the need for concentration of the executive aspects of transportation policy is recognized, there remains the question of whether this calls for a separate department with a Cabinet head or whether the responsibilities should be vested in some existing department.

The Hoover Commission proposed that most of these functions be assigned to the Department of Commerce. This seems to be an inadequate means of resolving the present difficulties. The task relating to national transport policy are so complicated, so diverse, and of such magnitude as to require the attention of a full-time Cabinet officer.[12] However, if the decision were made to concentrate responsibilities for transportation in the Department of Commerce, then, for this arrangement to be successful, it would have to be recognized that the major preoccupation of the Secretary would have to be with transportation. Most governments in other countries have long since acknowledged this by establishing separate departments which are headed by a cabinet officer. Such an officer in the United States would face a much bigger task than his counterpart in any foreign country.

[12]For a discussion of one possible organization of such a department, see Dearing and Owen, *op. cit.*, p. 391.

Chapter 25 THE REGULATION OF PUBLIC UTILITIES

INTRODUCTION

The Special Category of Public Utilities

The industries which make up the categories of transport and public utilities in many respects fall into a single grouping. So much is this so that some authors subject them to common treatment, and practically all put urban transit in the public utility group. There are definite reasons, however, for according separate treatment to those industries commonly labeled public utilities, excluding urban transport. The latter offers special problems today that have to be handled separately, but are most logically treated under transportation. The industries that fall into the category commonly labeled as public utilities are peculiar in their economic and technological structure, in that each can be confined in its economic activity to a specifically delimited geographic area, which confines both the producer and the consumer. Thus, it becomes possible to apply regulation to an individual enterprise with little threat of direct competition or substitute products to interfere with the regulatory process. In other words, public utilities present the unique situation of insulated and isolated monopolies, and afford an illustration of the problems of controlling monopoly under almost ideal situations. Even when they are publicly owned, the economic issues of management and administration are the same as when they are under private ownership.

Public utilities are so similar, in many respects, to rail transport that much that was dealt with in the previous chapters with regard to the railroads is applicable directly to them. The regulatory program with respect to public utilities is essentially the same as that which was set up for the railroads in 1920. Differences arise because of special conditions surrounding some of the services; but the major distinction emerges from the existence of more competition in the case of railroads, even before the rise of the newer agencies. If the railroads had been consolidated on a regional basis, the differences would have been negligible. Even now, pipe lines fall as readily into the category of public utilities as of transport, as far as their economic characteristics are concerned.

Public utilities, on the whole, are more a matter of local interest than much of transportation. This arises from the fact that they are intimately related to urban development; up to the present, they would have occupied an insignificant role apart from it and, in many instances, might not even have come into existence. As it is, they depend on urban life, and urban life depends on them. The result is that the states play a much larger role in regulation of public utilities than does the federal government. In fact, public utility regulation, as it directly affects sale to the consumer, is almost entirely a matter of state and local control.

The Institutional Features of Public Utilities

The peculiar problems of public utilities in the United States are almost entirely a matter of institutional arrangements. The economic features of these industries are the same here as they are in Canada, Great Britain, or Russia. The difference lies, first of all, in the different governmental structures of the countries. Canada and the United States have federal forms of government, which call for co-operation on many phases of control; Great Britain and Russia do not face those complications. In the United States, constitutional protections relating to property rights lead to a great deal of direct court participation in the process of regulation. In Great Britain and Canada, the function of the courts is limited to the interpretation of the statutes. No protection is available from the courts against the legislatures on the matter of property rights. On the other hand, where the utilities are in private hands, the regulatory authorities are faced with the same economic questions in determining fair prices for the services, standards of quality of service, amount of investment, and so forth. It is the institutional differences of the various countries that provide the principal basis for separate treatment in the various countries; but it is the economic features of public utilities which set them apart from other industries in any country.

The Public Utility Industries

The principal industries that are commonly thought of as public utilities and fall distinctly into the economic category of public utilities are water supply and sanitation, electric light and power, gas (natural and manufactured), and telephone and telegraph. It will be noted, with all of these industries—except, possibly, the telegraph service, at times—that the seller comes to the buyer, even to the point of installing facilities on the buyer's property. The services which are rendered or the commodities which are sold offer practically no storage opportunities for the buyer, and in only a limited way for the seller, and cannot be obtained by the buyer—except in a very restricted manner, on occasion—unless he is physically connected with the seller. In addition, the seller must maintain himself in a "readiness to serve" category at all times, under the conditions specified for the rendition of the service; otherwise, the buyer cannot make a purchase.

THE BASIS OF REGULATION

The Legal Basis

Public Interest. From a legal standpoint, an industry falls into the public utility category if the law of the land says so. The basis of the right of the state to regulate an industry was discussed earlier, and the details do not need to be repeated.[1] A few points that bear particularly on public utility regulation may be restated, although they differ little from what has already been said in connection with transportation. In its early development, at least, the concept of a public utility industry was that of one which was peculiarly affected with a public interest—that is, so intimately connected with public interest as to set it apart from most other economic activities. This very close connection with public interest arose from the dependence of the consumer upon the services of a particular firm. This might be because the consumer had to take the service of a particular enterprise, as in the case of electricity, or because he was unable to detach himself from a particular firm, without grave disadvantage, as in the business of insurance.

Down to the case of *Nebbia* v. *New York* (1934),[2] an industry affected with a public interest and a public utility were practically synonymous terms. In the Nebbia case, however, the Supreme Court held that there was no closed class or category of businesses affected with a public interest. By this decision, the Court broadened the scope of the legislative powers of price control and thereby created a distinction between an industry affected with a public interest and a public utility, the latter being a subcategory of the broader group of industries affected with a public interest. This, however, did not mean the passing of the public utility concept, as some have asserted,[3] but rather the sharpening of it into a more precise category, with more specific obligations than those activities which came under the general rubric of "affected with a public interest." The fact that the idea of "affected with a public interest" had been broadened did not mean that the obligations of public utilities had been lessened, nor did it mean that they had been extended to all industries falling into the category of those affected with a public interest.

Obligations. The obligations of public utilities are those of enterprises engaged in what were once known as "common callings." It was from this concept that the idea of a common carrier emerged. The common carrier and the public utility, in this respect, became one and the same thing. There are four basic duties which the enterprises falling into

[1]See Chapter 11.

[2]291 U.S. 502.

[3]See H. M. Gray, "The Passing of the Public Utility Concept," *Journal of Land and Public Utility Economics*, Vol. XVI, No. 1 (February, 1940), pp. 8–20.

these categories must discharge: (1) to serve all who request service, (2) to render adequate service, (3) to serve all at reasonable rates, and (4) to serve without discrimination. As the law has developed over time, the concept of a public utility has become that of a type of enterprise that is subject to a compulsory affixing of right and duties, on the one hand, with the voluntary procedure of entering into the public utility relationship, on the other. In other words, the public utility status is assumed voluntarily by an enterprise; but, once assumed, the obligations attaching thereto cannot be renounced without public consent. Although entry into the public utility industry is voluntary in terms of assuming the duties, it is usually necessary to receive public sanction to do so. However, if a business renders services of a public utility nature without sanction, public authority may compel it to get the necessary certification, or it may compel it to withdraw under threat of penalty. Once an enterprise has entered upon the public utility status, extension of service may be compelled by public authority but can be undertaken only with public consent. Abandonment of service also requires public sanction. It is this loss of freedom of action, once the status is assumed, that constitutes one of the unique features of a public utility. In the Nebbia case, the Supreme Court did not indicate that all enterprises that fell into the category of those "affected with a public interest" were at the same time subject to all the obligations of a public utility, or could be so subjected if the legislature wished to do it.

The Economic Basis

Natural Monopolies. In the final analysis, the real test of a public utility lies in its economic characteristics. It has been said that industries are not public utilities because they are regulated; but rather, they are regulated because they are public utilities. The unique consumer-producer relationship that leads to regulation arises from the existence of a natural monopoly supplying a particular product or service which is a necessity and for which no ready substitute is available.

Public utilities are natural monopolies, as far as their economic structure is concerned, for the same reasons as the railroads. The importance of fixed and specialized capital is greater in these industries than in any others; hydroelectric plants may have a capital turnover as low as once in fifteen years. The additional requirement of a natural monopoly —namely, the concomitance of production and consumption—is even more pronounced in the case of public utilities than in railroads, in that the consumer's facilities must be connected with those of the producer, thereby depriving him of any choice between one producer of a given service and another. This could not be altered, even though two different companies were allowed to operate in the same area, because the consumer could not be connected to more than one of them at the same time. The result is that each buyer, in fact, constitutes a separate market for each utility; and in the absence of restrictions, a utility could have a separate basis of charges for each and every buyer. In addition, with possibly minor exceptions, the commodities or services supplied cannot be stored by the consumer, as a consequence of which the supplier may be able to divide up even the market of an individual buyer into time segments. In other words, each buyer may, in fact, offer a multiple of markets. Monopoly, discrimination, and differential pricing are more difficult to solve in the case of public utilities than elsewhere, because there is very little opportunity to use the arbiter of competition in determining public utility prices.

Monopoly Pricing. Public utility services may be supplied by private or by public ownership. The problems of pricing are the same in both cases;[4] they are that of isolated and insulated monopoly. The need for regulation of private enterprise under the circumstances is obvious. In return for privilege of receiving permission to operate, it must submit to public control because of the unwillingness of the public to grant the privilege and then permit itself to be exploited by the beneficiary. The latter, no matter how benevolent he may be, is still a monopolist and must engage in monopoly pricing. Regulation is the substitute for the arbitrament of the market; the reconciliation of the interests of producer and consumer, which competition in the market achieves, is the task of regulation. When regulation is effective, the consumer can appeal to public authority for redress of his grievances; this is a privilege that does not usually exist under public ownership.

Control of Competition. Because public utilities are natural monopolies, competition must be controlled; otherwise, it would become ruinous; and because of their unique technological characteristics, it can be controlled. Public utilities can be confined strictly to a precisely defined geographic area. The producer cannot attract custom beyond that precisely defined area, and the consumer cannot patronize anyone else. He must take the service of the particular company that is in his area, go without the service, or move. Limitation of competition may be effected by a franchise, a permit, or a certificate of public convenience and necessity. The latter is quite commonly used by the independent regulatory commission. It grants permission to operate under the conditions specified in the certificate; in order to obtain one, the applicant must show that he is fit, willing, and able, and that public convenience and necessary require that it be granted to him. The certificate is not a guarantee, and it is not exclusive, although commissions commonly treat it as being so—at least, on the good behavior of the recipient; it is granted for an indeterminate period and may be revoked for good cause. In the absence of commission regulation, the franchise is commonly used as the

[4]For an illustration, see D. F. Pegrum, "The Public Corporation as a Regulatory Device," *Journal of Land and Public Utility Economics*, Vol. XVI, No. 3 (August, 1940), pp. 335–43.

means of limiting competition. It may also be used as a means of maintaining a degree of local control and as a supplement to the certificate; but where both are required, the franchise must first be acquired. This is the situation which obtains in California.

TYPES OF REGULATION

Early Regulation

The regulation of public utilities developed out of experience and necessity, just as it did for railroads. Because of the highly localized nature of utility services, early regulation emerged at the urban level and became a matter of state concern only at a considerably later date, when utilities began to expand beyond their local confines into larger systems frequently serving more than one urban center. Federal regulation did not appear until state control had developed into a mature and thoroughly comprehensive system in many states. For all practical purposes, federal regulation was of no consequence until the 1930's; whereas some states—such as California, Massachusetts, and Wisconsin—had commissions that enjoyed as much scope and were as authoritative as the Interstate Commerce Commission became under the Transportation Act of 1920, long before that act was passed.

Courts. The earliest type of public utility regulation was that imposed by the courts in settling disputes between consumers and producers on the basis of common-law obligations. This type of control was very elementary in nature and totally unable to grapple with the problems which the rising young industries presented, because the courts could take no initiative; they could act only on suit and only on the questions presented to them in the complaint.

Legislatures. As a means of prescribing somewhat more positive controls and remedies, various state legislatures passed laws under which rates and service conditions were prescribed by statute. These laws afforded literally no public protection, because they were unable to come to grips with the intricacies of public utility pricing, they afforded no control over competition, and they were implemented by no other means of enforcement than suit in the courts.

Regulation by Franchise

The especially local nature of public utility services and the failure of direct statutory control to provide a satisfactory means of regulation led municipalities, particularly larger cities in which the industries first developed, to undertake the task of regulation. In addition, the utilities, by the very nature of the services they offered, had to use streets and other public property; and for this, they had to secure special permission. This took the form of a franchise granted by a municipality, under authority conferred upon it by the state, permitting private parties to engage in the public utility business and to use public property for that purpose. The essential feature of franchise regulation was that control rested upon a contract between the city and the company, granting specific rights and privileges to, and imposing specific obligations upon, the company in supplying the public utility service.

Because of the binding nature of a franchise when it has been granted, and because it is the governing instrument of control when it is used for the purpose of regulation, it must be drawn up with meticulous attention to detail and with very careful consideration for the future. It will have to contain provisions regarding rate schedules, standards of service, accounts and reports, compensation (if any) for the use of city streets, and means for interpreting the provisions and adjusting disagreements. Early franchises typically contained very precise details of regulation and were of long duration, even for 99 years or more. The difficulties of long life and inflexibility led to two developments designed to correct the evils arising from these features. The first was to introduce provisions limiting the duration, and the second was to introduce arrangements to provide for flexibility in the rate structure.

Short-Term Franchises. The means of dealing with the problem of the duration of the franchise was to provide for a limited term—frequently, 50 years. This really did not meet the objections to the longer-life type; and in addition, it presented some other difficulties. Problems of capital financing might be aggravated because of the limited term of the franchise. If it had only 10 years to run, new long-term capital might be hard to raise because of uncertainty over conditions of renewal. This might lead to deterioration of service during periods of negotiation for a new franchise or might even lead to continued operation without a franchise, if agreement could not be reached.

Indeterminate Permit. To meet this problem, the indeterminate permit came into use. The essential feature of the indeterminate permit is the elimination of the fixed term and the substitution therefor of the privilege of continuous operation during good behavior. Usually, the permit empowers the municipality, in a manner prescribed by law, to purchase the properties of the utility at any time. The advantage of this type of franchise is that the company must, at all times, display acceptable good behavior. The disadvantage is that, to make this effective, the municipality must always be prepared to take over the properties. In addition, this type of franchise does nothing to cure the other inflexibilities. It is, however, a very useful and workable type when coupled with commission regulation.

Service-at-Cost Franchise. Attempts to deal with inflexibility with regard to rates and service standards have resulted in service-at-cost franchises and sliding-scale franchises. The typical service-at-cost franchise contains a number of principal features: (1) a grant of exclusive monopoly for a specified period, or terminable upon agreement; (2) detailed service standards, together with means of enforcement; (3) detailed classification of costs; (4) agreement upon the value of the property or the rate base to be used in ascertaining the fair return; (5) a stipulated rate of return on the agreed base, and an established schedule of rates to provide the return; (6) reserves for depreciation and contingencies; and (7) administrative arrangements for enforcing the terms of the franchise. The latter is necessary because of the details which have to be adapted to the changing conditions which are bound to occur from time to time; in addition, detailed supervision is necessary in order to be sure of compliance with the agreement. This type of franchise has much to commend it in the absence of effective commission regulation. To be effective, however, expert and careful public supervision must be provided. It encounters the difficulty that it is unworkable when applied to enterprises that extend beyond the boundary of a particular municipality because of the lack of coincidence of administrative authority with the scope of the enterprise.

The Sliding-Scale Franchise. The sliding-scale franchise is very similar to the service-at-cost form, except that it provides for an adjustment of rates inversely to the movement of the rate of return. The base rate of return is specified in the franchise; and a rate schedule, which is designed to yield that return, is established. If the return goes above that which is specified in the franchise, the rates are reduced; and if the return falls below the amount set forth in the franchise, the rates are raised. Thus, in the so-called "Washington Plan," the agreement stated that if earnings exceeded 7 per cent but were less than 8¼ per cent of the rate base, half the excess was to be used for reduction; if earnings fell between 8¼ and 9 per cent, 60 per cent was the measure of reduction; if earnings exceeded 9 per cent, 75 per cent was the measure. This type of franchise has its merits, in that it provides an incentive for reducing costs. It presents, however, the same type of administrative problems that the service-at-cost franchise poses.

Franchise regulation is still rather widely used, especially where "home rule" sentiment is strong, or where regulation by state commission is rather ineffective. In those states which have strong commissions, state regulation has generally superseded local regulation, especially on rates and finance. This has not eliminated the franchise even in these cases, however. For example, in California, utilities must secure franchises from the incorporated municipalities; and they must obtain the franchise before they can get a certificate of public convenience and necessity from the state commission. The franchises cannot cover rates and finance; but local municipalities may exercise control over service, if they wish to do so.

Regulation by Commission

State Regulation. Regulation by commission grew up to deal with public utility problems for the same reason that it developed for transportation. Most of the state commissions started out as agencies to deal with railroads and street railways. Their functions with regard to railroads diminished rather rapidly after the setbacks of the Granger movement and the rise of the Interstate Commerce Commission, but they were re-established on a more realistic basis with the rise of public utilities. In states such as California, Massachusetts, and Wisconsin, where the strong commissions rose to prominence, they were of the mandatory quasi-judicial, quasi-legislative type that became the first full-fledged regulatory agencies in the country. At the present time, they provide, except for interstate wire and radio communication, the only commission regulation of utilities at the consumer level. The federal government, with the exception just noted, regulates only at the wholesale level in interstate commerce. Thus, public utility regulation, in its direct relations with the consumer, is primarily a state and local matter.

Federal Regulations. The federal government first entered the field of public utility regulation through the Interstate Commerce Commission, which was given jurisdiction over telephone and telegraph companies by the Mann-Elkins Act of 1910. The Commission exercised its authority in only a perfunctory way, and federal regulation of communications did not commence seriously until the establishment of the Federal Communications Commission in 1934. The regulation of communication by wire was transferred to the control of this agency, which was also given jurisdiction over radio and television; but the control over these is primarily of a technical nature. Thus, the Federal Communications Commission is more than a public utility commission. In fact, the greater part of its time is occupied with problems concerning radio and television that are largely outside the public utility area. The regulation of interstate commerce in electricity and natural gas was placed under the jurisdiction of the Federal Power Commission by a series of enactments. This made the Federal Power Commission the only federal agency whose responsibilities fall entirely in the public utility category. The Securities and Exchange Commission was given jurisdiction over the public utility holding company in the fields of electricity and gas by the Public Utility Holding Company Act of 1935. The Commission's jurisdiction was confined to the control of the financial practices of these holding companies, and to the carrying-out of a program of corporate simplification and rational consolidation in electrical and gas holding company systems. Thus, federal jurisdiction in the field of public utilities is much more circumscribed than it is in transportation. What the future holds on this score will depend primarily on technical developments. The present tendency, however, is to confine federal regulation to strictly interstate matters and to make legislative provision for ending federal supervision at state boundaries.

The Courts. The courts play a more immediate and direct role in the regulation of public utilities than they do in other industries. The function of the courts in the general process of regulation was discussed in Chapter 11. All that needs to be noted here is that the detailed controls which the private utility status calls for and the fact that the regulation is supplied in such an individualized manner raise more questions of due process and the protections afforded by the Fifth and Fourteenth amendments than does the type of regulation that is applied under antitrust and transport legislation. Only in the public utility field today are the courts called upon to pass directly upon the issues of fair return and fair value, and for specific firms. If railroads were to be consolidated into regional monopolies, it is quite possible that they would have to be controlled in the same way as public utilities.

REGULATION BY STATE COMMISSIONS

Variations in State Commissions

At the present time, all of the states of the Union and the District of Columbia have some form of commission regulation. There is such a wide range in the legislative provisions regarding appointments, salaries, tenure of office, scope of jurisdiction, and so forth, however, that it is impossible to give any general description of them. In fact, some of the commissions cannot be put into the category of an independent regulatory commission, because in some instances, the commissioner or commissioners hold offices at the pleasure of the governor who appoints them; and they literally have to render decisions which accord with the way the governor wishes the law to be applied. On the other hand, in states like California, Massachusetts, and Wisconsin, the independent regulatory commission has developed into a regulatory body of the stature, competence, and integrity of anything that exists at the federal level. This may be attributed to the seriousness with which these states have grappled with the problems of regulation, of the thoroughgoing nature of the legislation, to the independence of the commissioners after they are appointed to office, and to the general support and respect accorded these commissions by the public and the utilities.

The California Public Utilities Commission

A brief description of the California Public Utilities Commission will serve to illustrate the nature of a strong state commission. It differs only in relatively unimportant details from those of Wisconsin and Massachusetts. The California Commission consists of 5 commissioners, appointed by the governor from the state at large for a term of 6 years. They may be removed from office, by a two-thirds vote of all the members of each house of the legislature, only for the dereliction of duty or corruption or incompetence. Any commissioner may be reappointed for another term. The commissioners elect one of their own members as president of the commission. No commissioner can have any official relation to, or any pecuniary interest whatsoever in, any enterprise over which the commission has jurisdiction.

The jurisdiction of the California Commission extends to every form of common and contract carrier; ancillary transport facilities, such as wharves, wharfingers, and warehouses; and all of the public utilities. Its jurisdiction, however, is restricted to those which are privately owned. It may hear cases on its own motion or upon complaint; it may determine what rates are just, reasonable, and sufficient; and it may compel the public utility concerned to abide by its findings. It may investigate rates or tolls whenever it wishes; and if they are found to be excessive or discriminatory, it may prescribe new ones. The Commission has supervisory power over the service rendered by enterprises under its jurisdiction,[5] and it is necessary for anyone carrying on a public utility business to secure a certificate of public convenience and necessity before undertaking operations.[6] Even when operating franchises are required by incorporated municipalities, a certificate must be obtained before the firm can render service. The Commission's jurisdiction over rates is exclusive, no other governing body having any authority whatsoever.

In order to facilitate the regulation of rates and to aid in determining what is a just and reasonable charge, the Commission is authorized to ascertain the value of the property of all enterprises under its jurisdiction, including any fact or element of value which, in its judgment, may or does have bearing on such value. The law, however, does not prescribe any method of ascertaining the value, the use to be made of the value, or what constitutes a reasonable return. The Commission can require that the enterprises follow a system of accounts, which must not be inconsistent with that prescribed by the Interstate Commerce Commission. Depreciation accounts; new construction; transfer, authorization, and issuance of stocks and stock certificates, bonds, notes, and other evidences of indebtedness; and consolidations are all to be handled according to regulations prescribed by the Commission. Finally, the law stipulates, among other things, that "the findings and conclusions of the Commission on questions of fact shall be final and shall not be subject to review"—except, of course, where constitutional rights are involved, in which case, appeal lies to the Supreme Court of the state of California or to the federal courts.[7]

One point of significance to consumers of public utility services is that the law specifically provides means whereby consumers may seek redress of grievances, without expense, through the Commission. The Commission may proceed upon complaint or on its own initiative, and

[5]Except that cities may elect to retain control.

[6]Except contract carriers.

[7]Public Utilities Act of the State of California, sec. 67. See also the Johnson Act, 48 Stat. 775 (1934), 28 U.S. Civil Code 41.

the ensuing proceedings may be formal or informal. A customer may complain to the Commission, which will then investigate and endeavor to resolve the matter. If the complaint warrants formal action, the Commission will undertake it. The orders are binding upon the utility after a specified date, unless enjoined or set aside by a court.

Appraisal of State Regulation

Appraisal of the effectiveness of regulation by state commissions may involve an evaluation of the regulatory commission in general as a device for dealing with the problems of monopoly in the field of privately owned public utilities, or it may be confined to a comparison of the relative effectiveness of state versus federal control. It is with the second matter that we are concerned here. State regulation has been subject to severe criticism on grounds of inadequacy, even in those areas where the control has not been limited by considerations of interstate commerce. Professor Clair Wilcox, for example,[8] concludes that state commissions have done little to control the quality of utility services, have manifested little interest in the structure of rates, have sought to control operating expenses in only a few states, and only in a few exceptions have endeavored to provide effective control over accounting systems. None has sought to maximize consumption by reducing rates to the lowest level that would yield a fair return. Rate cases are frequently long drawn out and expensive; when negotiation is substituted for litigation, the results are likely to be unsatisfactory. Most of the state commissions are too routine and too disinclined to formulate their policies or plan their programs in advance. The responsibilities for these failures of regulation cannot be charged to the commissions alone, according to Professor Wilcox, but must be shared by the courts, the legislatures, the executives, and the public at large.

All of this is a very severe indictment of state regulation, and a person in another country might readily conclude that state regulation is a farce that should be replaced in total by public ownership or federal control. On the assumption, however, that regulation of private utilities is to be one of the continuing means of dealing with the problems of these industries, regulation at the state level will have to continue to play the primary role in control of the local aspects of utility activities. Regulation by a federal commission in Washington, D.C. is not likely to be successful or acceptable—in part, at least—because the business transactions of most of the utilities are at the local level. More important, however, is the fact that the strong commissions are no more subject to the criticisms that have been detailed than are their federal counterparts. The Interstate Commerce Commission, the Federal Communication Commission, and the Federal Power Commission are all being subjected to severe ex-

[8]Clair Wilcox, *Public Policies Toward Business* (Homewood, Ill.: Richard D. Irwin, Inc., 1955), pp. 574–77.

amination. It is difficult to conclude that they can stand up better under severe scrutiny, on the grounds of more imaginative and aggressive policy, more effective scope of operations and enforcement of controls, greater integrity of personnel, and more success with the courts than the strong state commissions. Moreover, in the historical development of public utility regulation, the states have led the way, not the federal government. Regulation in a great many states certainly needs to be improved, but generalizations concerning deficiencies are difficult to make; and a composite picture derived from them is likely to present a characterization that is worse than the most ineffective one in the country. The development of regulation has not been even, of course; but the over-all results seem to be well expressed in the statement, "the effect has been to leave only a handful of state commissions conspicuously impotent; to round out the powers and facilities of the great bulk of commissions in a degree previously attained only by the more advanced, and to equip and empower a substantial number of commissions as completely as could be desired by the most enthusiastic proponent of commission regulation."[9]

FEDERAL REGULATION

The Federal Communications Commission

The Federal Communications Act, 1934. Regulation of communications by the federal government was first attempted under the Mann-Elkins Act of 1910, which gave the Interstate Commerce Commission jurisdiction over telephone, telegraph, and cable services in interstate and foreign commerce. In 1927, regulation of radio broadcasting was delegated to the Federal Radio Commission, which was charged with issuing licenses, assigning wave lengths, and some other duties of a technical nature. Finally, in 1934, Congress passed the Federal Communications Act, which abolished the Radio Commission and transferred its functions and those of the Interstate Commerce Commission over communications to the newly created Federal Communications Commission. Thus, this agency was assigned the task of regulating common carriers (or public utilities) in communications, as well as radio and television, which do not fall into this category on an economic basis and were not accorded the legal status under the statute.[10]

In its capacity as a public utility commission, the Federal Communications Commission is similar to other such agencies. It is composed of 7 members, appointed by the President of the United States with the consent of the Senate. The term of office is for 7 years, and they may be

[9]Ben W. Lewis, "Public Utilities," in L. S. Lyon, M. W. Watkins, and Victor Abramson, *Government and Economic Life* (Washington, D.C.: Brookings Institution, 1940), Vol. II, chap. xxi, p. 643.

[10]See *Federal Communication Commission* v. *Sanders Bros. Radio Station*, 309 U.S. 470 (1940).

reappointed. Not more than 4 members can belong to the same political party. The President is required to designate one of the commissioners as chairman. The orders of the Commission are binding when duly issued; and penalties are stipulated for failure to obey, unless relief is obtained in the courts.

The law prescribes that all charges, practices, classifications, and regulations shall be just and reasonable; schedules of charges must be filed in the usual manner, and the published rates are the only lawful ones. The Commission may fix maximum, minimum, and/or precise rates. Carriers subject to the act must file with the Commission copies of all contracts, agreements, or arrangements with other carriers. Interlocking directorates are forbidden, except as may be authorized by the Commission. The Commission is empowered to make valuations of the property of all companies under its jurisdiction, and the law sets forth a number of steps that may be taken to secure all information which the Commission thinks is pertinent to this end. Certificates of public convenience and necessity must be secured for the construction of a new line or the extension of an existing one. The law, however, contains provisions designed to prevent encroachment on state authority on this matter.

Although the act gives no control over security issues, it does give the Commission jurisdiction over the consolidation of telephone and telegraph companies. If, after public hearing, the Commission finds that the proposed consolidation complies with the law and is in the public interest, it may give its approval. It does not, however, have the power to compel consolidations.

The act contains special provisions to prevent encroachment on state authority. For example, the Commission does not have jurisdiction over local exchange service—even though a portion of this constitutes interstate or foreign commerce—in any case where such matters are subject to regulation by state commission or by local governmental authority. Co-operation between the Federal Communications Commission and state commissions may be obtained through joint boards, to be composed of members from the various states, as determined by the Commission. The Commission has endeavored continuously to co-operate with the state commissions on matters of uniform accounting and in making allocations between intrastate and interstate operations.

The Telephone Investigation. In 1935, the Federal Communications Commission was directed by a joint resolution of Congress to investigate the telephone industry. This turned out to be largely an inquiry into the affairs of the American Telephone and Telegraph Company, partly because this concern occupied such a preponderant position in the industry in this country. The report covered all phases of the telephone business, and no financial scandals or serious abuses were discovered.

Nevertheless, the conclusions reached were subject to a great deal of dispute, even within the Commission itself.[11]

The Commission reported that the concentration of by far the greater proportion of the telephone business in the hands of the Bell Telephone System, and the high degree of management unification and control attained by the Bell System, had made it necessary for both the users of the telephone service and the regulatory bodies to concern themselves largely with that unified and dominating agency. In other words, the Commission did not envisage any possibility of a group of independent and regional monopolies. Whether this issue will raise its head in the future remains to be seen, but the rapid and seemingly successful growth of the General Telephone Corporation in the years since World War II may demonstrate that a national monopoly is not necessary for efficiency or convenience.

American Telephone and Telegraph, through its manufacturing subsidiary, Western Electric, at the time of the investigation, accounted for 90 per cent of the nation's output of telephonic equipment. No agency has the power to regulate the Bell Telephone Laboratories or Western Electric, because these are manufacturing and research organizations which fall outside the public utility category. Because of the developments in the telephone industry, they bear a somewhat analogous relation to telephone service that pipe lines do to the oil industry. Yet, their charges to the subsidiary operating companies are important items of telephone operating costs, which, to a degree, can nullify the effectiveness of regulation. The Department of Justice filed an antitrust suit, in 1949, requesting that Western Electric be divorced from American Telephone and Telegraph and be split into three companies; that A. T. & T. be compelled to grant licenses to other manufacturers under its patents, at reasonable royalties; and that all manufacturers be required to make their sales by competitive bidding.[12] The Federal Communications Commission recommended only that it be authorized to prescribe cost accounting methods to be used by manufacturers of telephonic equipment. The suit was settled by a consent decree entered on January 24, 1956. Western Electric was enjoined from engaging in any business not of a character engaged in by it or its subsidiaries for companies of the Bell System; and American Telephone and Telegraph was enjoined from engaging in, other than through Western Electric, any business other than furnishing common carrier communications. Western Electric was ordered to maintain cost accounting methods for determining the cost to it of equipment

[11]Federal Communications Commission, *Report on the Investigation of the Telephone Industry in the United States* (House Document No. 340, 76th Congress, 1st sess.) (Washington, D.C.: U.S. Government Printing Office, 1939).

[12]*United States* v. *Western Electric Company*, District Court of the United States for the District of New Jersey, Civil Action No. 17–49, January 14, 1949.

sold to A. T. & T. and Bell operating companies. Finally, the patent-licensing system of Western Electric was revised so as to remove many of the restrictions imposed by that company; and, in addition, American Telephone and Telegraph was enjoined from receiving from Western Electric any payment of patent royalty "in respect of the manufacture, lease or sale of equipment by Western to the Bell Operating Companies."

The primary task of regulating telephone rates rests in the hands of state authorities. The Communications Commission has jurisdiction over interstate rates. The separation of facilities between intrastate and interstate business is made through complicated formulas involving elements of arbitrariness that are probably unavoidable under the circumstances.[13] The Communications Commission uses the fair return on fair value approach for interstate rates. The state commissions may pass judgment on the reasonableness of the charges made by the parent companies and subsidiaries, as for example, American Telephone and Telegraph Company and Western Electric for services and facilities supplied by them to the local companies, thereby bringing under state control costs that otherwise would escape supervision. The California Commission has recently applied this approach in a very comprehensive manner.[14]

Radio and Television. The Commission's jurisdiction over radio and television imposes a different duty upon it from that which it has to discharge as a public utility commission. Entry is rigidly controlled as a result of the technical aspects of broadcasting. This is because the number of channels which can operate in a given area is limited, and air space must therefore be allocated. This is largely a matter of enforcing traffic rules, since the broadcaster does not sell to the consumer, in consequence of which there are no rates to fix; support of the channels by the sale of advertising calls for no more regulation than does newspaper advertising at least so far as the rates and prices are concerned.

The purpose of the Communications Act with respect to radio and television is to maintain control by the United States over all the channels of interstate and foreign transmission. Broadcasters must obtain licenses from the Federal Communications Commission; and the Commission may classify stations, prescribe their services, assign their frequencies, determine their location, and fix their power. The Commission must endeavor to bring about efficient and equitable distribution of services among states and communities. It is empowered to inquire into the technical, financial, and moral responsibility of applicants and can issue licenses only for "public interest, convenience or necessity."

Although it is denied the power of censorship, the Commission is

[13]See P. J. Garfield and W. F. Lovejoy, *Public Utility Economics* (Englewood Cliffs, N.J.: Prentice-Hall, Inc., 1964), pp. 215–20.

[14]See Re: *Pacific Telephone and Telegraph Co.*, Decision No. 67369, June, 1964. The Commission's decision on rate reductions in this case is now on appeal to the California Supreme Court.

permitted to develop its own criteria of public interest in judging the public interest. It is, however, forbidden to interfere with the right of free speech. This does not mean that the air is free, since access to broadcasting cannot be demanded as a right; but broadcasters must give equal privileges to rival political candidates. In dealing with public interest, the law forbids the broadcasting of "any obscene, indecent or profane language" and "any advertisement of or information concerning any lottery, gift enterprise or similar scheme, offering prizes dependent in whole or in part upon lot or chance." Enforcement of this provision has proved very difficult because of the definition of the term "lottery." In a unanimous decision[15] in 1954, the Supreme Court held that the give-away shows were not lotteries, since nothing of value was contributed as a consideration by members of the audience, and stated that the Commission's rules had "overstepped the boundaries of interpretation." Finally, in order to maintain control of radio in the hands of the United States, licenses cannot be granted to aliens or foreigners in any form whatsoever; licenses for broadcasting stations must be renewed every three years; and licenses may be revoked for just cause. Revocation is such a severe penalty that it is used very sparingly.

In order to combat the threat of monopoly in the broadcasting industry, which it found to exist as a result of an investigation which it commenced in 1938, the Commission issued a set of rules in 1941. These new rules limited network contracts with stations to two years, permitted network affiliates to use programs from other stations, and enabled other stations to obtain network programs. The rules forbade networks to control the rates charged by their affiliates in competing for advertising business. The Commission also sought to compel the National Broadcasting Company to divest itself of one of its networks, either the Red or the Blue. In *National Broadcasting Company* v. *United States* (1943),[16] the Supreme Court upheld the Commission's contract regulations, saying that the act gave the Commission "not niggardly but expansive powers." In the meantime, the National Broadcasting Company sold the Blue Network, rather than contest a suit brought by the Antitrust Division. The Blue Network became the basis of the American Broadcasting Company, thereby giving the country four national networks: NBC, CBS, ABC, and Mutual. Only the first three comprise the networks in television.

The greater part of the effort and time of the Federal Communications Commission has been devoted to radio and television. Its policies have come under severe criticism, and charges of undue influence on members have also attracted public attention. The Commission has been attacked on grounds of inconsistency, as well as trying to exercise too much authority over programs. The quality of programs and the undue

[15] *Federal Communications Commission* v. *American Broadcasting Co.*, 347 U.S 284 (1954).

[16] 319 U.S. 190.

influence of advertising have aroused considerable opposition. Even the rivalry to forecast the outcome of elections and rush the results of voting before the polls are closed throughout the country has created demands for limitation on freedom of action. There is clear evidence of intense rivalry at the same time that the control by the national networks makes for a high degree of concentration.[17] Integration among the media of mass communication—newspapers, motion pictures, and broadcasting stations—also raises issues of compatibility with antitrust policies.

The impact of rapid technological change in broadcasting has presented the Commission with continuously changing problems of supervision. These are particularly complex under a system of private ownership where technological conditions prevent the application of a public utility type of control, yet where they also necessitate allocations of air space. The problem is also aggravated by limitations to the market approach because of inability to date to develop means of "rationing" the consumer through the price mechanism. If technology succeeds in resolving this problem in a satisfactory manner, the issues of control will be greatly simplified.[18]

The Federal Power Commission

Origins and Organization. The Federal Power Commission was created in June, 1920, as a compromise between those who desired private development of water-power sites on the public domain and those who wanted public development. The Federal Water Power Act of 1920 set up a commission consisting of the Secretaries of War, of the Interior, and of Agriculture, all of whom served ex officio. The work of the Commission was carried on by an executive secretary employed by the Commission and by personnel borrowed from three departments.

The ineffectiveness of this agency led to the reorganization of 1930 under an amendment to the Federal Water Power Act. This provided for an independent commission of 5 members, appointed by the President with the advice and approval of the Senate for 5-year terms. No more than 3 members could be from the same political party, and they could have no interest in power companies. It was to this agency that the duties of carrying out the provisions of the Federal Water Power Act, as amended by Title II of the Public Utility Act of 1935, and of the Natural Gas Act of 1938 were assigned.

The present Commission has three main responsibilities—namely,

[17]The Commission does not have direct control over the networks.

[18]For a more extensive discussion of these questions see: Report of the Network Study Committee of the Federal Communications Commission to the House Committee on Interstate Commerce (85th Cong., 2d sess.), *Network Broadcasting*, House Report No. 1297 (Washington, D.C.: U.S. Government Printing Office, 1958); J. H. Levin, "Workable Competition and Regulatory Policy in Television Broadcasting," *Land Economics*, Vol. XXXIV, No. 2, (May, 1958), pp. 101–12; C. Wilcox, *Public Policies Toward Business*, *op. cit.* (rev. ed.), chap. 25.

the licensing and supervision of power projects and water-power developments under the Federal Water Power Act, jurisdiction over interstate commerce in electrical energy and over utility companies engaged in such interstate commerce, and regulation of the transportation or sale of natural gas in interstate commerce. The Flood Control Act of 1938 instructed the Federal Power Commission to investigate the possibilities with respect to the generation of power at flood-control dams. The Commission also has various responsibilities with respect to contracts, rate schedules, and so forth under the Tennessee Valley Authority Act and the Bonneville Act.

Water-Power Development. The act of 1920 provided that power sites were to be leased to private or public interests for a period not to exceed fifty years. At the expiration of a lease to a private company, the Commission was empowered to recapture the site and equipment, or transfer them to state or municipal operation, or lease them to a private company. The law required the Commission to give consideration to the effect of the use of water for other purposes such as irrigation, navigation, and flood control, when it granted licenses. As a condition of the license, every public utility licensee had to agree to abide by such reasonable regulations as might be prescribed by the state in which it operated.

Each licensee which is a public utility is required to accept the regulation of rates and services by any duly constituted state authority. The Commission is given jurisdiction to regulate rates and services on transactions in interstate commerce, which would be beyond the control of any state authority, and to exercise similar control where no state authority exists, or where states having jurisdiction are unable to agree with regard to service, rates, or security issues of the licensee. The statute stipulates that value for rate making cannot be in excess of that which would be prescribed for the purchase price at which the United States might recapture the project. This must be the actual legitimate net investment in the property.

The scope of federal control over hydroelectric development was emphasized in *Appalachian Power Company* v. *United States* (1940).[19] Federal authority is limited to navigable waters and streams. The Court held that a lack of commercial traffic did not bar a conclusion of navigability; if a river is capable of improvements, it may be made navigable, and developments on nonnavigable tributaries to navigable streams are under the control of the Federal Power Commission.

Regulation of Electrical Utilities. Under Part II of the Public Utility Act of 1935, the Federal Power Commission is given authority to regulate the transmission of electrical energy in interstate commerce and the sale of electric energy at wholesale in interstate commerce, but the law does not apply to any other sale of electric energy; not does it deprive

[19]311 U.S. 377.

a state or state commission of lawful authority exercised over the exportation of hydroelectric energy which is transmitted across a state line. The Commission thus functions to supplement the control exercised by the state authorities; its sphere of usefulness lies in the control of those wholesale interstate rates that are beyond the reach of the states. In order to promote co-operation with the states, the Commission is empowered to refer problems common to two or more states to a joint board, which consists of one or more members, as determined by the Commission, from persons nominated by the appropriate state authority. Furthermore, the Federal Power Commission may confer with any state commission regarding any common regulatory problem.

The powers which the Commission exercises over the electrical utilities coming under its jurisdiction are similar to those possessed by the strong state commission and the Interstate Commerce Commission. Its authority extends to the supervision of accounting, control of rates and service, mergers and transfer of facilities, and the issuance of securities. Finally, it is empowered to make comprehensive investigations into virtually all phases of the generation, transmission, distribution, and sale of electrical energy throughout the United States and its possessions. The law also instructs it to divide the country into regional districts and to prepare plans for the voluntary interconnection and co-ordination of facilities.

The Natural Gas Act, 1938. Interstate transportation of natural gas dates back to the last 10 years of the nineteenth century; but it did not become of any real significance until about 1926, when the modern period of long-distance, high-pressure transmission began. By 1934, 23 per cent of the total output of natural gas in the United States moved in interstate commerce. Meanwhile, severe limitations on the powers of the states to control the price paid for imported gas had been imposed by the Supreme Court.[20] No one possessed any authority over the natural gas industry at either the producing or the receiving ends as far as the activities were clearly a matter of interstate commerce. Since most of the interstate transmission of lines delivered the gas right at the point of local distribution, state and local authorities were able to exercise little control over natural gas obtained from sources outside the state.

The Natural Gas Act was designed to provide for federal regulation of the natural gas industry in the area beyond state control. The Federal Power Commission was given control over natural gas companies. A natural gas company was defined as "a person engaged in the transmission of natural gas in interstate commerce, or the sale in interstate commerce of such gas for resale." Section 1 (*b*) of the Act provided that

> . . . this act shall apply to the transportation of natural gas in interstate commerce, to the sale of natural gas in interstate commerce, for resale for ultimate

[20] *Missouri* v. *Kansas Natural Gas Co.*, 265 U.S. 298 (1924).

public consumption, for domestic, commercial, industrial or any other use, and to natural-gas companies engaged in such transportation or sale, but shall not apply to any other transportation or sale of natural gas or to the local distribution of natural gas or to the production or gathering of natural gas.

Congress amended the Act in 1942 so as to give the Federal Power Commission control over the construction and extension of lines into unserved areas. The companies were required to obtain certificates of public convenience and necessity for all interstate construction, extensions, or acquisitions of natural gas lines.

The powers of the Commission over natural gas companies are very similar to those which it exercises over electrical utilities. It can fix just and reasonable rates, eliminate undue preferences, and maintain reasonable differences in rates, service, and facilities between localities and classes of wholesale customers. It can ascertain the actual legitimate cost of property, prescribe the accounting systems, and set the measurement of depreciation charges. It can also suspend rate increases for five months, if that is necessary to make adequate investigation. The Commission, however, has no authority to regulate the issuance of securities, mergers, consolidations, or purchases of property;[21] nor can it order interconnection of gas lines, even under emergency conditions. Finally, it can set rates only at wholesale for resale. Thus, it cannot set the charges which natural gas companies may make to industrial users, if the latter take service directly from the company.[22]

Interstate versus Intrastate Commerce. The failure of Congress to delineate with reasonable clarity the powers of the Federal Power Commission as they related to interstate commerce led to considerable litigation. In *Federal Power Commission* v. *East Ohio Gas Company* (1950),[23] the gas company contended that it was not subject to the jurisdiction of the Commission, because the company received all of its gas from other companies and transported gas itself only within the boundaries of Ohio. The majority of the Court held that the gas was in interstate commerce and that, because it moved in high-pressure lines of the company, it remained in interstate commerce. Mr. Justice Jackson dissented vigorously, on the ground that the Commission had exceeded the authority conferred upon it by the Natural Gas Act. Congress evidently agreed, because it amended the Act in 1954, whereby it exempted from federal regulation all natural gas companies engaged chiefly in intrastate operations. Separation of interstate and intrastate commerce could be effected at state borders.[24]

[21]See *United States* v. *El Paso Gas Co.*, 376 U.S. 651 (1964) for limitation of authority under Sec. 7 of the Clayton Act.

[22]These rates, however, may be regulated by the states. See *Panhandle Eastern Co.* v. *Public Service Commission of Indiana*, 332 U.S. 507 (1947).

[23]338 U.S. 464, See also *Natural Gas Co.* v. *Federal Power Commission*, 331 U.S. 682 (1947); *Panhandle Eastern Pipe Line Co.* v. *Michigan Public Service Commission*, 341 U.S. 329 (1951).

[24]Chap. 115, Public Law 323 (1954).

Federal Control of Production and Gathering. Another controversy arose over the meaning of Section 1 (*b*) of the Act as it related to control by the Federal Power Commission over production and gathering of natural gas. In *Colorado Interstate Gas Company* v. *Federal Power Commission* (1945),[25] the majority of the Court held that the Natural Gas Act "does not preclude the Commission from reflecting the production and gathering facilities of a natural gas company in the rate base and determining the expenses incident thereto for the purpose of determining reasonable rates subject to its jurisdiction." This meant that when a natural gas company owned production and gathering facilities, they were subject to the control of the Federal Power Commission. Congress responded to this decision by passing the Kerr Bill in March, 1950. This amended the law by exempting arm's-length sales of natural gas to natural gas companies. President Truman vetoed the bill.

The Commission then decided that it would undertake appropriate investigations where the sales of individual producers or gatherers had a material effect on interstate commerce, to determine whether these companies were natural gas companies within the meaning of the law. In August, 1951, the Commission rendered its opinion in the Phillips Petoleum investigation,[26] which it had commenced in 1948. The majority opinion held that Phillips Petroleum was engaged in the production and gathering of natural gas, which it sold in interstate commerce, but that it was not a natural gas company within the meaning of the law. This decision was appealed to the Supreme Court in *Phillips Petroleum Company* v. *State of Wisconsin* (1954).[27] The Court overturned the Commission's decision by declaring that the Commission had "jurisdiction over the rates of all wholesalers of natural gas in interstate commerce, whether by a pipeline company or not and whether occurring before, during or after transmission by an interstate pipeline company." Thus, practically all production and gathering that result in sales of gas that moves in interstate commerce are now subject to federal regulation. Congress promptly moved to restore the situation that prevailed prior to the Phillips decision; but President Eisenhower, on February 17, 1956, vetoed the bill because of alleged undue influence connected with its passage. Similar legislation is now before Congress, but the opposition of the consuming states is strong against it. At the bottom of the controversy is the problem of the price that should be allowed for the gas when it is delivered to the transmission lines. This will be dealt with in the next chapter.

The Securities and Exchange Commission

The Public Utility Holding Company. The holding company, as a device for effecting combinations, has had its most spectacular use in

[25] 324 U.S. 581.
[26] 90 P.U.R. (N.S.) 325 (1951).
[27] 347 U.S. 672.

the public utility field.[28] It developed because of its effectiveness in bringing about necessary and efficient combinations, as well as because of its unrivaled capacity to evade state regulation, to promote speculation, and to disguise fraud. It was during the 1920's that the holding company achieved such prominence in the electricity and natural gas industries. By 1932, the 3 largest holding companies in the electrical utility field controlled nearly half of the total electric energy generated by private utility companies; and the total supply controlled by 16 holding company systems amounted to about 80 per cent for the same year. In the natural gas field, 44 holding company groups controlled 66.4 per cent of the gas manufactured and 29.3 per cent of the natural gas produced in the United States in 1930. Most of the giant holding companies combined both gas and electrical properties.[29]

The growth of concentration in the hands of a relatively small number of utility holding companies, the speculative activities, and the financial excesses, together with the inability of regulation in most of the states to grapple with the holding company problem, led Congress to instruct the Federal Trade Commission to make a thoroughgoing investigation. The Commission concluded[30] that the public benefits that arose from the use of the holding company were manifest primarily in the stimulation of the development of public utility corporations, resulting in a rapid growth of widespread, improved, and economical services. The following advantages were frequently obtained:

1. Funds were secured which promoted more rapid extension and improvement for small utilities than would have been possible had they been independent units.
2. Combinations were hastened which gave the advantages of physical interconnection, large-scale production, and unified management.
3. Skilled management and expert engineering were concentrated on technical problems of production.
4. Service was improved and extended, consumption increased, and costs of production reduced, with a tendency toward lower rates.
5. Where management was wise and skillful, investors were able to obtain a diversity of risk and, at the same time, reap some of the profits of equity invested.

The principal disadvantages to the public were the following:

1. Intercorporate relations were sometimes extreme and resulted in dangerous structural forms.

[28]See Chapter 6.

[29]The Federal Trade Commission made an exhaustive investigation of the holding company in the gas and electrical utilities. The results of this were published in *Utility Corporations* (Senate Document No. 92, 70th Congress, 1st session). The hearings extended over a period of years and were published in some 80 parts, together with a *Summary Report*, Part 72*A* (Washington, D.C.: U.S. Government Printing Office, 1933). See also J. C. Bonbright and G. C. Means, *The Holding Company* (New York: McGraw-Hill Book Co., Inc., 1932), for a detailed account of the organization and activities of the most important holding company groups; and W. Z. Ripley, *Main Street and Wall Street* (Boston: Little, Brown & Co., 1927).

[30]Federal Trade Commission, *op. cit.*, pp. 800–882.

2. The holding companies were frequently an instrument of abuse in the exaction of excessive fees from the operating companies.

3. Capital structures were inflated, values of the subsidiaries' fixed property were frequently written up excessively, and the operating companies were placed under a constant pressure to produce earnings upon such inflated values.

4. Holding companies practiced many objectionable—and sometimes, very misleading or even fraudulent—methods of accounting.

5. Some companies sold to the general public large quantities of common stock and other securities which were highly inflated; on occasion, the sales of these were supported by market manipulation of the prices of securities.

6. Some utility empires assembled operating companies, under one control, far beyond any useful measure of public benefit; by pyramiding, a few individuals, with a minimum of investment, were able to control operations over vast areas of the country and the investments of millions of people.

7. Some holding company groups retained for themselves millions of dollars collected from some of their operating companies for federal income tax.

8. The depression resulted, in many cases, in severe financial setbacks, receivership, or bankruptcy, which, because of the pyramided arrangement, involved a huge loss to the investing public.

9. Interstate operations made it difficult for state regulatory commissions to control the operating companies under their jurisdiction.

The Public Utility Act, 1935. To deal with the holding company problem in the gas and electricity utilities, Congress passed the Public Utility Act of 1935, Title I—Control of Public Utility Holding Companies; only holding companies in gas and electricity were covered by the law. Enforcement of the law was placed in the hands of the Securities and Exchange Commission.

The act applied to holding companies, their subsidiaries, and their affiliates. A holding company was defined as any company which had the power to control the vote of 10 per cent or more of the outstanding voting securities of a public utility company; a subsidiary was a company, 10 per cent or more of whose outstanding voting securities were controlled by the holding company; 5 per cent was sufficient to make a company an affiliate. The word "company" was defined so as to include a person as well as all forms of business organization. The law excluded holding companies that were primarily intrastate in nature, and those that were only temporary or incidental holding companies.

All holding companies were required to register with the Securities and Exchange Commission by December 1, 1935, in order to do any interstate business and use the mails to issue or sell any securities, or to exercise any privileges with regard to voting. Common stock which was to be issued or sold was to have a par value and was to be without preference as to dividends. Compliance with state regulations was also required for security transactions. Officers and directors were required to file their stockholdings and make reports on changes. Any profits made by them as a result of holding stock for less than six months inured to the benefit of the holding company. Holding companies were forbidden to borrow from subsidiaries, and loans to subsidiaries had to receive SEC approval. Management contracts between affiliated companies were subject to SEC control, and management companies could not obtain profits from these contracts. The Commission could prescribe accounting systems and accounting practices for both management companies and holding companies.

The most important section of the act was the so-called "death sentence" clause. This provided that after January 1, 1938, holding companies were to be limited to a single, integrated public utility system and to such other business as was reasonably incidental, or economically necessary, to the operation of the system. The Commission's control over reorganization under this part of the act was thoroughly comprehensive. All the powers necessary to develop geographically integrated companies, eliminate all unnecessary holding companies, and bring about financial reorganization of the integrated firms were bestowed upon the Commission, which became virtually the sole judge of public policy on this matter.

Administration by the Securities and Exchange Commission. The drastic nature of the reorganization of corporate arrangements of gas and electrical utilities envisaged in the act of 1935 was bound to be met with challenge in the courts, and suits were soon forthcoming. The Electric Bond and Share Company refused to register. The Commission brought suit to enforce compliance, and its position was upheld by the Supreme Court.[31] The North American Company challenged reorganization, on the ground that the law exceeded congressional powers under the interstate commerce clause of the federal Constitution and violated the protections of the Fifth Amendment.[32] The American Power and Light Company contended that the law constituted an unconstitutional delegation of legislative power to the Commission, but the Court disagreed here[33] as in the North American case.

The Securities and Exchange Commission encouraged holding companies to exercise their own initiative in bringing about compliance with the law, and some companies undertook voluntary liquidation. In other cases, the Commission formulated the plan. The task of eliminating unnecessary holding companies was 85 per cent complete by 1952; but the formation of single, integrated public utility systems was more difficult and proceeded more slowly. The Commission has favored a compact system confined to a single area, with interconnected facilities and unified management. It has also favored the confining of activities to one industry. It has opposed the common control of gas and electricity; and in this, it is on sound ground, because it is difficult to demonstrate the

[31]*Electric Bond and Share Co.* v. *Securities and Exchange Commission,* 303 U.S. 419 (1938).

[32]*North American Co.* v. *Securities and Exchange Commission,* 327 U.S. 686 (1946). For a detailed description of the reorganization of this company, see *Business Week* (May 24, 1952), pp. 130–33.

[33]*American Power and Light Co.* v. *Securities and Exchange Commission,* 390 U.S. 90 (1946).

economies of scale which can result from combining the two. In addition, to the extent that gas and electricity are competitive, the advantages of competition can only be obtained by separation of ownership and management.[34] When a holding company is permitted to control more than one utility system, it must meet three conditions: (1) Such control must be needed to preserve substantial economies; (2) the systems must be contiguous; and (3) they must be small enough to permit local management, efficient operation, and effective regulation. The law also provided that other businesses could be retained by a holding company system if the Commission found them appropriate in the public interest or for the protection of investors or consumers and not detrimental to the proper functioning of integrated systems. Permission to retain other businesses has been granted in but a few instances, and then only in strict compliance with the intent of the law.

The sweeping reorganization of the electrical and gas utility industries has been a major accomplishment. More efficient operation has certainly ensued, and public utility enterprises now bear some relation to the regions they serve. The abuses, excesses, and financial debacles of the 1930's are no longer possible. The Commission is still working on the question of how utility facilities may be more economically combined and on divestiture of interests in companies for which final plans have not yet been worked out.[35] As of June 30, 1962, there were 25 holding companies registered under the Act. Of these, 19 were included in the 17 remaining active registered holding company systems, two of which each had one subsidiary holding company. In the 17 active systems there were 90 electric and/or gas utility subsidiaries, 40 nonutility subsidiaries, and 13 inactive companies, totaling 162 system companies with aggregate assets, less valuation reserves, amounting to $11,788,576,000. The Commission continues to supervise the financial activities of these companies and the issuance of securities by them.

CONCLUSION

Federal legislation was necessary to provide for the regulation of public utilities at the national level. The phenomenal growth of the industries in the public utility field in the period following World War I, their extension across state lines, and the development of the public utility holding company made it inevitable. The excesses that were experienced and the hostility that was generated by the depression probably made the legislation of the 1930's more thoroughgoing than it might have been otherwise. It does not seem possible to argue, however, that it was

[34]The SEC ruling does not apply to an integrated company under the control of a state commission. For example, the Pacific Gas and Electric Company in California supplies both electricity and natural gas to consumers over the wide area it serves within the state.

[35]Securities and Exchange Commission, *28th Annual Report*, (1962) (Washington, D.C.: U.S. Government Printing Office, 1963), Part VI.

too severe, for it merely erected at the federal level the type of control that many of the states already enjoyed. Furthermore, by scrupulously endeavoring to confine federal authority to interstate commerce, by denying the federal commissions the power to control the local prices charged to consumers, and by providing means for joint state-federal action, Congress made it possible for the states to regulate public utilities effectively, if they wanted to do so.

There are still some gaps in federal regulation, as has been indicated in previous sections. There is also some working at cross-purposes by federal commissions. The Securities and Exchange Commission and the Federal Communications Commission are engaged in both public utility and nonpublic utility tasks.[36] This cannot help but result in a diffusion of efforts because of the thoroughly different point of view that each involves. Public utility regulation is regulation of monopoly, and it is likely to remain in that category for a long time. A transference of the responsibility for all public utility regulation at the federal level to the Federal Power Commission—thereby making it a Federal Public Utility Commission—would unify and simplify federal control and, at the same time, make it easier to co-operate with the states.

[36]For a discussion of some of the problems connected with this divided responsibility of the Federal Communications Commission, see E. W. Clemens and L. W. Thatcher, "The Reorganization of the Federal Communications Commission," *Land Economics*, Vol. XXVII, No. 3 (August, 1951), pp. 213–24.

Chapter 26 PUBLIC UTILITY RATE MAKING

INTRODUCTION

The regulation of public utility rates is but one of a whole series of controls that must be imposed upon public utilities if limitations are to be placed on managerial discretion which the monopoly position affords. The economical allocation and utilization of resources requires that just enough of the right kind and amount of service shall be forthcoming at the time desired by the consumer, at prices that are no higher than necessary to achieve this result. This means that consumers would be receiving the desired services at the lowest possible or "reasonable" prices. If public utilities were subject to thoroughgoing competition, these conditions would be met; and even if they were subject to workable competition, they would be satisfied tolerably well. This is not the case, however; and so some substitute means has to be found to take the place of competition and provide the incentives and pressures which it supplies.

Cost-Plus Pricing

Theoretically, the objective of public utility regulation is to achieve the results that competition would yield; and theoretically, the cost-price relationships of competition are the ones that should be used. Unfortunately, the conditions that are necessary to the functioning of the competitive market are well-nigh totally absent. The consumer has literally no alternatives for the services. Regulation, therefore, turns to the cost side for the gauge for reasonable prices. However, the costs, which for competitive business are competitively determined, are only partially so for public utilities. The basing of rates on costs proceeds on the assumption that costs are readily and almost unequivocally ascertainable; whereas, in fact, this is not so. For example, in competitive industry, the presence of a relatively high or a relatively low return is taken to indicate either under- or overinvestment; but in public utilities, such a return suggests that rates need to be adjusted so as to bring the return into line. In competitive industry prices cannot be forced to adjust themselves to committed costs. In public utility regulation, this is what is done, and there seems to be little possibility of avoiding it.

As a basis for economical pricing, the cost-plus method has serious disadvantages; but if pricing by or for a monopoly is to be restricted below the full possibilities of exploitation, then the cost-plus approach must occupy a dominant role. This means that all phases of costs must be thoroughly supervised and controlled, and that standards of adequacy and quality of service must be established. The control of costs presents a particularly difficult problem, because the bulk of them are not subject to market determination at any particular time. Capital costs, including depreciation and return on investment, loom large in the public utility pricing process; yet, once they are committed, they are not subject to the forces of the market in a cost-plus approach. They are not economic costs to be considered in pricing; yet, they are treated that way in cost-plus pricing.

The monopolist resolves these problems by resort to the market and so preserves the same interplay of costs and prices, supply and demand, that obtain under competition, even though the compelling pressures for efficiency which competition imposes are lacking. Monopoly theory resolves the problem of cost-price relationships and price equilibrium by resort to the market. But economic theory, unfortunately, is able to resolve the problem of economical allocation of resources which monopoly presents only by introducing competition. This is not possible in public utilities. Therefore, regulation endeavors to curb the unrestricted exercise of monopoly powers. In so doing, it tries to resort to competitive standards in a situation in which the principal ingredients of market competition are lacking. This problem exists, however, whenever monopoly is present, be it under public or private ownership, unless full exploitation of monopoly power is permitted.

Marginal Cost Pricing

The difficulties connected with public utility pricing have given rise to the proposal that marginal cost pricing be used as the basis for pricing public utility services.[1] The premise upon which this proposal is based is that maximum satisfaction from the use of available resources

[1]For an extended discussion of the literature on the subject, see Nancy D. Ruggles, "The Welfare Basis of the Marginal Cost Pricing Principle," *Review of Economic Studies* (1940–50), pp. 20 f.; "Recent Developments in the Theory of Marginal Cost Pricing," *ibid.* (1949–50), pp. 107 f.; Harold Hotelling, "The General Welfare in Relation to Problems of Taxation and of Railway and Utility Rates," *Econometrica*, Vol. 6, No. 3 (July, 1938), pp. 242 f.; Robert W. Harbeson, "A Critique of Marginal Cost Pricing," *Land Economics*, Vol. XXXI, No. 1 (February, 1955), pp. 55 f.; Emory R. Troxel, "Incremental Cost Determination of Utility Prices," *Journal of Land and Public Utility Economics* (November, 1942), pp. 458 f.; (February, 1948), pp. 28 f.; and (August, 1943), pp. 292 f.; D. F. Pegrum, "Incremental Cost of Pricing—A Comment," *ibid.* (February, 1944), pp. 58 f.; J. Wiseman, "The Theory of Public Utility Price—An Empty Box," *Oxford Economic Papers* (New Series), Vol. 9, No. 1 (February, 1957), pp. 56–74.

is not achieved so long as individuals are willing to pay more for additional units of any commodity than the additional cost incurred in producing the additional units. Therefore, the output of commodities should be expanded in the short run until price is equal to short-run marginal cost and in the long run until price is equal to long-run marginal cost. If the technological and market conditions are such that a firm is operating under conditions of decreasing costs, marginal cost will be less than average total unit cost, so that a firm cannot adjust output so as to equate price and marginal cost without experiencing a loss. The theory advances the proposition that in industries of decreasing costs, or where there is excess capacity, pricing policies should aim at securing revenues that will cover only variable costs, in order to maximize the utilization of resources. That is, fixed costs are excluded from the burden to be borne by the purchasers of the services. This means that taxes must be used to cover the fixed costs. The justification advanced for this is that the consumer benefits achieved by full utilization of the resources are greater than the satisfactions given up by those upon whom the taxes are imposed. The assumption must also be made that the firms which are treated this way must be operating at full capacity, even in the short run; otherwise, full utilization of resources would not take place.

This proposal has been subject to very severe criticism, and space does not permit a careful evaluation of it here. However, it may be pointed out that this approach does not resolve the problem of the proper amount of initial investment to be made, because if investment is to be made through taxes, the short-run and long-run marginal costs to buyers, of the services become the same. In addition, the appropriate amount of investment to be made will depend on the market to be served, and the same scale of operations cannot be employed for different markets; yet, lower costs may be obtained from larger than from smaller markets on many occasions, although this is not always a matter of easy determination.

Public utility pricing has to be dealt with from the standpoint of the individual firm, not the industry; and the investment has to be made for what may be considered to be the appropriate market area for that firm. The economical scale of the enterprise will be that which yields the lowest cost for that market. If such a scale is attained, full utilization at that scale will require marginal cost pricing that will cover all costs. If demand at those prices exceeds supply, need for an increase in investment is indicated. If there is unused capacity, "discriminatory" pricing can be resorted to, so that those who will not pay more than the short-run marginal costs will not be denied the service. Unused capacity, at times, is characteristic of public utilities; and this means that differential pricing is economical pricing. It does not follow, however, that the lower prices need go down to short-run marginal costs; in fact, they should not do so if higher prices can be obtained that will utilize the resources; if they do, prices will not be fulfilling their rationing function. Marginal cost pricing for all services oversimplifies the peak-load problems. In addition, it ignores joint costs, of which all are not included in the fixed costs.

The coverage by taxes of those costs that are not recovered by the sale of services rests on the contention that the sacrifice of the taxpayers is offset by the gain to the consumers. This not only assumes that the loss of satisfactions of one person or group of persons and the gain of satisfactions to others are commensurable items, but also that taxes can be imposed in such a way as to avoid offsetting the very gains that marginal cost pricing is designed to secure. This merely pushes the problem back a step to that of devising a tax structure that will give the desired results. Until taxation becomes more precise in terms of welfare than it is at present, there is little prospect of solving this problem. The equating of gains to consumers against the losses of those called upon to bear the fixed costs would not present any problem if the consumers and taxpayers were identical, if their incomes were the same or inequalities were a matter of indifference, and if it were assumed that their desires for different goods and services were identical or reasonably similar. These are not the assumptions upon which a private enterprise economy is based. Differential or discriminatory pricing, used to cover all costs but controlled so as to prevent monopolistic exploitation as much as possible, at least gives the consumer more choice to allocate his purchasing power and guide the volume of his consumption accordingly. Taxation for providing services removes this choice and does not act as a direct means for rationing goods or services. This is one of the major problems that the provision of highways by taxation poses today.

THE GENERAL LEVEL OF RATES

The determination of what the general level of rates for a public utility should be involves questions of equity, economics, and expediency. Under competition, equity is resolved by the rules that are established; under regulated monopoly, rules must also be established as a matter of equity. These rules come through the action of those who initiate and administer regulation—namely, the legislatures, the commissions, and the courts. Public utilities have peculiar obligations; and in return, they receive certain rights and privileges. The economic problem is to promote the fullest possible utilization of the resources that have been economically allocated to the public utility business. Expediency enters the picture, because, as has been emphasized, precise economic gauges are not obtainable. Judgment must be exercised by public authority at all stages of the regulatory process, and this judgment must take into consideration the numerous conflicting interests and intangibles that are ever present. Because capital investment plays such a dominant role in public utility undertakings, the costs to which this gives rise, the determination of how that capital is to be measured or "valued" for rate-making purposes, and the return or "fair" profit which is to be allowed are focal points of the regulatory process.

Valuation of Rate Making

Three theories of valuation have been advanced for the amount of capital that is to be considered in the determination of reasonable rates —namely, market value, cost of reproduction, and what has come to be called prudent investment. The first two are really variants of the same thing, although they are arrived at in different ways.

Market Value. The market value of an income-producing property is dependent upon the net income which that property can be expected to yield. That is, it is the capitalized value of the expected net income. One method of ascertaining this value at any time is to find the market value of the outstanding securities. This will depend upon the income which the buyers expect to receive from these securities and the rate of return at which these buyers appraise that income. For example, if a security has a prospective earning of $10 a year and the rate of capitalization is 5 per cent, the capital value of the security will be $200. Another way of finding the value of a firm is to capitalize the net earnings at the going rate of return of such a business. If the total expected earnings are $10,000 a year and the rate is 5 per cent, the value of the firm will be $200,000. Whatever may be the precise technique that is used for ascertaining the value, the principle is the same—namely, capitalizing the expected net income at the appropriate rate of return.

This method, which is the correct way to ascertain economic value, cannot be used to determine what the base upon which fair profits are to be calculated should be, because it must assume that the earnings which are the object of control are known. Until these have been received, however, the economic value of the enterprise cannot be ascertained; and therefore, the economic or market value cannot be used to prescribe the fair profit that may be earned. In addition, net earnings are not a matter of revelation; they are the difference between the gross income and the costs of producing it. But these costs include, among other things, the costs arising from using up the capital, particularly depreciation and obsolescence. Some basis for calculating the proper amounts of these items must also be found; and obviously, that basis cannot be market value. In other words, market value is deficient on two counts: It fails to give a gauge for measuring fair profit which is independent of the earnings; and it fails to give a basis for calculating some of the most important items of cost, which must be known before net earnings can be discovered. Any firm must use some basis from which it calculates depreciation and obsolescence, and market value alone cannot serve as that base.

Cost of Reproduction. Cost of reproduction, as a method of determining the rate base, may mean one of three different things. It may mean what it would cost to reproduce an existing plant under original conditions; what it would cost to reproduce it under present conditions; or what it would cost to produce a substitute plant with the advantages of changed technology, which would afford the most modern services. The problem of prices also enters in, but it is usually assumed that current prices are to be used.

Calculating the cost to reproduce an existing plant under original conditions means primarily making an engineering estimate of what it would cost, under present-day prices, to reproduce the present facilities under the conditions which obtained at the time the plant was built. Such an estimate could have no possible relationship to reality in any way, because reproduction would not take place under such conditions. It would be ridiculous to assume the use of techniques as of the original time of construction, and to calculate the cost of reproducing nearly obsolete machinery would necessitate estimating what it would cost to produce the facilities to make that machinery. It would be like calculating what it would cost to produce a Model T Ford in a modern plant. Apart from creating a museum piece, nothing would be accomplished in doing it; and nothing would be accomplished in making the estimate. Much of the time, the estimate would involve calculating the reproduction cost of something that would not be reproduced. It would scarcely make sense to calculate the cost of reproducing many of the passenger coaches and railway stations still used by the railroads. In addition, nearly all of the facilities that are being "valued" are partially worn out. This may be accounted for by deducting depreciation, but depreciation calculated on the cost of reproduction would be as artificial as the initial evaluation.

Cost of reproduction under existing conditions is subject to even more criticism, in that much of the reproduction might not take place under existing conditions. For example, gas or water mains may be laid under streets now paved; if new facilities were to be constructed, an entirely different pattern might be developed. If many of our railroad routes were to be reconstructed today, they would be quite different with regard to grades, curves, and tunnels than they are now; and many of the huge passenger terminals would cease to exist.

The third meaning of cost of reproduction refers to the estimated cost of replacing an existing plant with the most up-to-date one that could be constructed under present conditions, with the needs of the future carefully in mind. Under strictly competitive conditions, this variant of cost of reproduction would be the equivalent of market value. It could be used as a measure of value, because it would equal the capitalized value of the prospective income. But it would not be independent of the prospective income, and so this would get us right back to the original problem. Market value and cost of reproduction are equal under strictly competitive conditions, because the forces on both sides of the market are freely adjustable to changing circumstances. Public utility property cannot be valued in terms of its alternative use, however, because most of it does not have an alternate use. It is the lack of this attribute that creates the problem in the first place. Even when there is an alternate use, it may not be possible to calculate the value. For example, the land values of railroad freight terminals cannot logically be ascertained on the basis of the value of adjacent lands. If the terminals were not there, the land values would be different; and what they would be may be impossible to calculate.

Finally, cost of reproduction at any particular time may not reflect value, even in nonpublic utility enterprises. For example, during the war, the value of houses was not reflected in what it would cost to reproduce them, in any of the three meanings of that term, because they could not be reproduced. Similarly, in times of severe depression, houses may be worth less than cost of reproduction because of the surplus. Cost of reproduction cannot reflect value in public utility enterprises at any time and, consequently, fails on the test of equity as well as a basis for rate making. The public is scarcely likely to sanction profits on modern equipment not in existence when the prices necessary to yield those profits may be coming from inferior property and services from which the prices may be obtained because of the presence of monopoly.

Apart from these considerations, cost of reproduction is impracticable. In other words, it fails to meet the test of expediency. It can be obtained only by extensive engineering appraisals, which are costly and time-consuming. They require years to complete in the case of large properties and lead to marked differences of opinion on amounts, because of the imponderables which must be evaluated. As a practical matter, they cannot be kept up to date; a new evaluation is needed every time an adjustment of the general level of rates is in order; but the process of making it is so slow that it would literally be out of date every time it is used.

Prudent Investment. The essence of the prudent investment method of determining the rate base is that it is based upon the amount of investment, wisely made, and used and useful in the public service, in a public utility plant. What this means is that the investment must be bona fide and in accordance with the judgment of prospective market conditions that sound business practice would dictate. The qualification of "prudent" is introduced to eliminate speculation and fraud, and to compel the exercise of good judgment. Thus, if the investment which a utility proposes to make is fully disclosed to a commission and receives the sanction of that body, it is regarded as being prudently and wisely made, even though subsequently it should be discovered that the initial estimates were in error because of unforeseen circumstances. The requirement that the investment be in property that is used and useful is designed to prevent property from entering into the rate base that performs no function in rendering public utility service. However, stand-by facilities that are not being used, but are useful and necessary, would be included in the investment.

Investment in property, whether tangible or intangible, can readily be ascertained if the accounts of the enterprise are maintained on that basis. When property is retired, the amount of investment that is thereby dispensed with, or written off, is a matter of record. When new property is acquired, that becomes a matter of record, too. For example, if a piece of property that cost $2,000 is retired and sold for $1,000, and a new item is acquired in its place for $4,000, this replacement will require $2,000 of new investment, the other $2,000 being derived from depreciation of $1,000 and sale of the original equipment for $1,000. Assuming that the transaction is properly carried out, the $4,000 will represent prudent investment; and it will also represent cost of reproduction new of the property at the time the transaction takes place. Because public utilities are continuously engaged in replacement, even prudent investment will reflect a considerable amount of current prices. These, however, will not be the result of artificial estimates but of actual transactions.

A great deal of the property of public utilities, excluding land, is in a state of being used up. The investment originally made in it has partially disappeared. It is the function of depreciation accounting to record this fact. At any particular time, the amount of depreciation that has actually taken place can only be estimated; and therefore, the calculation of the amount of the investment in any particular piece of property that has been used up can only be estimated. It may be understated, or it may be overstated; but this will not affect the rate base as a whole, because accounting for depreciation serves the purpose of maintaining the investment by deductions from earnings, which are thereby retained in some form of other assets in the business.[2]

If prudent investment is used as the basis for evaluation for rate-making purposes, the determination of the rate base becomes a matter of accounting. Ascertaining prudence, used and useful property, integrity of transactions, adequacy of service, and so forth are not solved by it. In fact, for prudent investment to be effective, these aspects of public utility operation must be carefully supervised. However, this is true under the other proposals for valuation. Prudent investment has the advantage, among others, of eliminating the valuation costs, delays, and

[2]This does not deal with the intricacies of depreciation policy with regard to adequacy of service or replacement. These are quite different matters, which involve other considerations. The effect of excessive depreciation charges at any time would be to make the cost of serving the public at that time higher to that extent. This would not alter the prudent investment of the firm as shown by the books, however. Therefore, the rate base and the net return would be unaffected. When the property was totally depreciated on the books, there would be no depreciation to enter into the cost of service, and the total revenue requirements would diminish accordingly; but the total investment in the firm would still be the same. Similarly, these remarks would apply, vice versa, to underdepreciation. The writing-off of intangibles is handled in an analogous fashion.

controversies, without adding to any of the other aspects of supervision which any method of control entails. The question of adequacy of earnings under it will be discussed later.

Prudent investment as a method of determining the rate base sometimes goes under the name of original cost to date, original cost plus additions, and betterments or historical cost. These are not necessarily the same thing; but in practice, that is what they amount to. Original cost to date means the amount actually invested in the property from the beginning. This takes into account property which has been retired as worn-out or obsolete, new investment made through the sale of securities, and earnings which have been retained in the business. If the records have been kept properly and the present property is used and useful, the amount shown will be the same as prudent investment. Because a good deal of utility investment was made before adequate regulation and control of accounting took place, it was necessary to make physical appraisals to determine the investment at the time of valuation. No matter how carefully it was done, it was still only an estimate. The California Commission dealt with the difficulty by what it called the historical cost method.[3] It established the estimated prudent investment as of the date of the appraisal; and then, with this as a starting point, it kept the valuation up to date through the accounting record of the changes in the property. It was necessary at all times, however, to include land in the rate base at market value because of the decision of the Supreme Court of the United States in the second Minnesota rate case.[4] The market value of land under this ruling was to be based upon the value of similar lands in the community. The method used by the California Commission is also sometimes called the split-inventory method because of the necessity of starting with an appraisal of the property before accurate accounting for maintaining the rate base can be introduced.

Fair Value and the Courts

When the Supreme Court of the United States reversed the position that it took in *Munn* v. *Illinois* and decided that appeal could be had to it against the action of legislatures and commissions when reasonable rates and the rate level were under consideration, it made the courts an immediate and integral part of the rate-making process. In theory, it was the function of the courts to see that rates were not set so low as to result in the taking of property without due process of law or confiscation, as it came to be called. Unfortunately, what the Court did, in fact, was to intervene in such a way that the Court measure of confiscation became the Commission measure of reasonableness, because the Court, in establishing the minimum below which rates could not legally be

[3]For a detailed discussion of this, see Pegrum, *Rate Theories and the California Railroad Commission* (Berkeley: University of California Press, 1932).

[4]*Simpson* v. *Shepard*, 230 U.S. 352 (1913).

compelled to go, embraced both equitable and economic considerations. Unfortunately also, the Court set no precise means for determining what the minimum should be, with the result that long-draw-out litigation has occupied the center of the regulatory stage. Fair value and fair return became the focal points of the controversy, the Court apparently believing that fair value and fair rate of return were independent variables for the determination of fair profit, and that each could be discovered by the application of principles derived from competitive economics.

Smyth v. *Ames* (1898).[5] This was the first decision of the Supreme Court to establish a judicial standard for public utility rate making. That standard, the Court stated, was a fair return on a fair value which was to be derived from the consideration of a number of different items which were enumerated by the Court. The case arose out of an order issued by the Board of Transportation of Nebraska, fixing maximum railroad freight rates. William Jennings Bryan, counsel for Nebraska, in defending the order, argued (1) that the states had a right to fix maximum rates, which should be interfered with by the courts only if such rates yielded an income so small as to leave nothing above operating expenses; and (2) that if the Court should pass upon the reasonableness of the profit allowed the railroads, the present value of the roads, as measured by the cost of reproduction, should be the basis upon which the profit should be computed. The cost-of-reproduction argument was advanced because the price level at the time much of the railroad property was constructed was considerably higher than it was in 1898, the price level at that time being only slightly above what it was in 1896, which was the low point in United States history. In addition, cost of reproduction was urged as a means of checking against the excesses that frequently took place in the earlier periods of construction and were manifest in the financial structures of the companies. In dealing with the arguments, Mr. Justice Harlan stated:

> The corporation may not be required to use its property for the benefit of the public without receiving just compensation for the services rendered by it. How such compensation may be ascertained, and what are the necessary elements in such an inquiry, will always be an embarrassing question. . . .
>
> We hold, however, that the basis of all calculations as to the basis of the reasonableness of rates to be charged by a corporation . . . must be the fair value of the property being used by it for the convenience of the public. And in order to ascertain that value, the original cost of construction, the amount expended in permanent improvements, the amount and market value of its bonds and stock, the present as compared with the original cost of construction, the probable earning capacity of the property under particular rates prescribed by statute and the sum required to meet operating expenses, are all matters for consideration, and are to be given such weight as may be just and right in each case. We do not say that there may not be other matters to be regarded in estimating the

[5]169 U.S. 466.

value of the property. What the company is entitled to ask is a fair return on the value of that which it employs for the public convenience. On the other hand, what the public is entitled to demand is that no more be exacted from it . . . than the services rendered by it are reasonably worth.[6]

Because of the facts of the case, the rates would have been invalid under any standard of reasonableness. It was not necessary, therefore, for the Court to make any definite finding on the fair value of the railroads, or even to give any intimation as to how the potpourri of irreconcilable and incommensurate statistical computations could be made to yield a single meaningful figure.

Litigation down to the end of World War I served to focus the whole controversy sharply on fair value. Operating costs dropped from the picture as an item to be considered in ascertaining fair value; earning capacity and value of stocks and bonds were rejected as valid factors.[7] Considerable weight came to be given to cost of reproduction as a means of arriving at the "reasonable value" of property; and the Court seemed to feel that cost of reproduction was a better measure than original cost, because it eliminated the excesses that had accompanied much of the original construction.[8] However, because property was not to be protected in its actual investment, recognition had to be given to the fair value, if this was more than its cost.[9] The results, at the time, were probably not far from a workable prudent investment figure; but the skyrocketing of prices as a result of World War I removed any relation that cost of reproduction might have had to prudent investment. In litigation that followed the end of World War I, the Court soon came to reflect the point of view expressed in the Minnesota rate cases. In *Southwestern Bell Telephone Company* v. *Public Service Commission of Missouri* (1923),[10] the Court unanimously agreed that the rates prescribed by the Missouri Commission were far too low by any standards, in that they did not accord any weight to the greatly enhanced costs of material, labor, and supplies. The majority held that weight should be given to cost of reproduction because of the greatly enhanced costs of construction of the post-World War I period over those of the prewar years. How much weight was to be given cost of reproduction was not indicated. In a minority opinion which concurred in the results but dissented from the reasoning, Mr. Justice Brandeis, supported by Mr. Justice Holmes, developed his famous and carefully reasoned presentation on behalf of prudent investment. And so the issue within the Court and before the commissions became sharply drawn.

[6]*Ibid.*, pp. 546 and 547.

[7]Minnesota rate cases, 230 U.S. 352 (1913); *Knoxville* v. *Knoxville Water Co.*, 212 U.S. 1 (1909).

[8]*San Diego Land and Town Co.* v. *Jasper*, 189 U.S. 439 (1903).

[9]Minnesota rate cases, 230 U.S. 352 (1913). See also *Willcox* v. *Consolidated Gas Co.*, 212 U.S. 19 (1909).

[10]262 U.S. 276; see also *Bluefield Waterworks and Improvement Co.* v. *Public Service Commission of West Virginia*, 262 U.S. 679 (1923).

McCardle et al. v. *Indianapolis Water Company* (1926).[11] Cost of reproduction as the most important factor to be considered in arriving at the rate base reached its highest point in this case. Said Mr. Justice Butler, speaking for the majority of the Court:

It must be determined whether the rates will yield . . . a reasonable rate of return on the value of the property at the time of the investigation and for a reasonable time in the immediate future. Undoubtedly the reasonable cost of a system of waterworks, well-planned and efficient for the public service, is good evidence of its value at the time of construction. And such actual cost will continue fairly well to measure the amount to be attributed to the physical elements of the property so long as there is no change in the level of applicable prices. And, as is indicated in the report of the commission, it is true that, if the trend of prices is not definitely upward or downward and it does not appear probable that there will be a substantial change of prices, then the present value of lands plus the present cost of constructing the plant, less depreciation, if any, is a fair measure of the present value of the property . . . . And it is clear that a level of prices higher than the average prevailing in the ten years ending with 1923 should be taken as the measure of value of the structural elements on and following the effective date of the order complained of.[12]

These quotations cannot be cited as proof positive that the highest court of the land required that the rate base be determined by the cost-of-reproduction method only; but the strong dissenting opinion written by Mr. Justice Brandeis, and subscribed to by Mr. Justice Holmes, indicated that they believed that the majority upheld the cost-of-reproduction theory. The language of the Court in the subsequent Baltimore Street Railway case supported this view. In the part of the opinion that dealt with the problem of depreciation, Mr. Justice Sutherland, speaking for the majority, said:

The allowance for annual depreciation made by the commission was based upon cost. The court of appeals held that this was erroneous and that it should have been based upon present value. The court's view of the matter was plainly right. . . . The utility "is entitled to see that from earnings the value of the property invested is kept unimpaired so that at the end of any given term of years the original investment remains what it was at the beginning" (*Knoxville* v. *Water Co.*, 212 U.S. 1, 13–14 [1909]).

This naturally calls for expenditures equal to the cost of the worn out equipment at the time of replacement; and this for all practical purposes means present value. It is the settled rule of this court that the rate base is present value and it would be wholly illogical to adopt a different rule for depreciation.[13]

Los Angeles Gas and Electric Corporation v. *Railroad Commission of California* (1933).[14] The turning point in emphasis upon cost of reproduction—or upon any particular formula, for that matter—in determin-

[11]272 U.S. 400.
[12]*Ibid.*, pp. 408, 410, and 412.
[13]*The United Railways and Electric Co. of Baltimore* v. *H. E. West et al.*, 280 U.S. 234 (1930) 254. For a similar interpretation by state courts, see *Waukesha Gas and Electric Co.* v. *Railroad Commission of Wisconsin*, 191 Wis. 565 (1927).
[14]289 U.S. 287.

ing the rate base for measuring confiscation, came in this case, which upheld the California Commission in the first forthright test of historical cost, the practical equivalent of prudent investment. This development may be attributed to four things: (1) The California Commission had established itself over a period of 20 years as one of the leading state commissions, and its rulings had not been challenged theretofore; (2) the Commission had been generous in its rate of return, so that it was difficult to contest the over-all result of fair return; (3) there was a growing tendency on the part of the Court to look with more favor on well-considered commission regulation; and (4) the price level was declining rapidly, and this dampened enthusiasm for cost of reproduction. The opinion of the Court foreshadowed developments that were to take place in World War II.

The Court pointed out that it did not sit as a board of revision but rather as an agency to enforce constitutional rights.

> The legislative discretion implied in the rate-making power extends to the entire legislative process, embracing the method used in reaching the legislative determination as well as that determination itself. We are not concerned with either, so long as constitutional limitations are not transgressed. . . . [The] question is whether the rates as fixed are confiscatory. And upon that question the complainant has the burden of proof. . . .
>
> In determining reasonable value for rate-making we have said that judicial ascertainment of value for the purpose of deciding whether rates are confiscatory "is not a matter of formulas, but there must be a reasonable judgment, having its basis in a consideration of all relevant facts."[15]

The Court found that, in determining the weight to be ascribed in this case to historical cost, the outstanding fact was that the development of the property had, for the most part, taken place in a recent period. Furthermore, the prices for labor and materials which were reflected in historical cost were higher than those which obtained in the later period to which the rates applied.

> It is the appropriate task of the Commission to determine the value of the property affected by the rate it fixes, as that of an integrated, operating enterprise, and it is the function of the Court in deciding whether rates are confiscatory not to lay down a formula, much less to prescribe an arbitrary allowance, but to examine the result of the legislative action in order to determine whether its total effect is to deny to the owner of the property a fair return for its use.[16]

Federal Power Commission v. *Hope Natural Gas Company* (1944).[17] The force of the opinion in the Los Angeles Gas and Electric case was emphasized by the Court in *Natural Gas Pipeline Company* v. *Federal Power Commission* (1942),[18] when it said:

> The Constitution does not bind rate-making bodies to the service of any formula or combination of formulas. Agencies to whom this legislative power

[15]*Ibid.*, p. 304–6.
[16]*Ibid.*, p. 314.
[17]320 U.S. 591.
[18]315 U.S. 575.

has been delegated are free . . . to make the pragmatic adjustments which may be called for by the particular circumstances. Once a fair hearing has been given, proper findings made, and other statutory requirements satisfied, the courts cannot intervene in the absence of a clear showing that the limits of due process have been overstepped.[19]

In the opinion of Mr. Justices Black, Douglas, and Murphy, this laid the ghost of *Smyth* v. *Ames* to rest.

The Natural Gas case itself, however, did not raise the issue of original versus reproduction cost. This matter came squarely before the Court in the Hope case.[20] The company argued for reproduction cost, while the Federal Power Commission stood by the original-cost basis of determining the rate base. The Court sustained the Commission's decision, but it did not espouse the prudent investment or any other basis of fair value. Mr. Justice Douglas, speaking for the Court, said:

It is not the theory but the impact of the rate order which counts. If the total effect of the rate order cannot be said to be unjust and unreasonable, judicial inquiry . . . is at an end. The fact that the method employed to reach the result may contain infirmities is not then important . . . . Rates which enable the company to operate successfully, to maintain its financial integrity, to attract capital, and to compensate its investors for the risks assumed [may be taken as a guide to reasonableness as far as the courts are concerned].[21]

It appears, under this doctrine of the "end result," that legislatures and commissions are now free to employ whatever method they see fit to determine the general level of rates. They are not bound by any formula or any set of rules. It is therefore more difficult for utilities to challenge commission decisions in the courts; but by the same token, it may be more difficult for commissions to be sure of their ground. The Court did not lay down a gauge by which confiscation could be measured; but quite possibly, a distinction can now be made between rates which are confiscatory and those which are reasonable from an economic point of view. It is with the latter that commissions must be concerned, especially in times of uncertainty. Severe economic stress might well bring the whole matter to the fore again.[22]

The Federal Power Commission and the Federal Communications Commission uses the actual or historical cost for determining the rate base. There is considerable variation in the practices of the different states. One group, including California, Massachusetts, and Wisconsin, use the prudent investment as the base. Another group uses fair value in which substantial recognition is accorded to cost of reproduction or

[19]*Ibid.*, p. 586.

[20]*Federal Power Commission* v. *Hope Natural Gas Co.*, 320 U.S. 591 (1944).

[21]*Ibid.*, p. 602.

[22]See also *Market Street Railway Co.* v. *Railroad Commission of California*, 324 U.S. 548 (1945); *Colorado Interstate Gas Co.* v. *Federal Power Commission*, 324 U.S. 581 (1945); *Panhandle Eastern Pipe Line Co.* v. *Federal Power Commission*, 324 U.S. 625 (1945).

current costs. In Ohio the governing statute requires the Commission to use cost of reproduction new less depreciation in determining the rate base. This has been used principally in telephone rate cases, because the Commission has direct jurisdiction over telephone rates, but serves only as an appellate body for other utilities whose rates are governed by local rate ordinances. To keep the task of valuation from getting completely out of hand, the Ohio Commission uses a system of index numbers to bring valuations up to date.[23]

Fair Return

The problem of fair return has always been an integral part of the problem of reasonable rates; yet, curiously enough, it has never been given the attention or promoted the controversy that has accompanied fair value. Slight reflection, however, will indicate that a change from a return of 6 per cent on a given base to 8 per cent is the equivalent of increasing the base 33⅓ per cent. The indifferent treatment that has been accorded fair return may be accounted for on three grounds: (1) that it is upon the value of property that firms are entitled to earn a reasonable profit, and the alternatives for investment are what determine the profit of competitive firms; (2) that returns on comparable business activities can be readily ascertained by observation; and (3) that the profits which a utility is permitted to earn are for it to disburse in accordance with its own judgment. In other words, financial structure is a matter of indifference in determining fair return and fair value. As a matter of fact, financial structure could not be given any serious consideration until cost of reproduction was dispensed with, because the two have no relation to each other.

It has become standard practice for commissions and courts alike to regard fair return as the income which is to be used as the payment to all of those who contribute capital to the enterprise. This fair return, therefore, is supposed to cover all interest costs, dividends, and whatever may be left over to go to surplus. Under the rulings of the courts, this fair return is what the firm is entitled to after corporate income taxes. The latter, for the purpose of calculating fair return, is an expense, just like all other taxes, to be covered before the return is ascertained. In addition, depreciation to the amount necessary to maintain the capital intact must also be provided for before the fair return is calculated. How the fair return is distributed among the suppliers of the firm's capital will depend upon the contractural arrangements with the security holders. Bondholders will be paid the interest specified in the indenture; preferred stockholders, the dividends stimulated in their stock certificates; and the common stockholders, the amount which is decided by management from

[23]For a detailed discussion of rate-base practices, see P. J. Garfield and W. F. Lovejoy, *op. cit.*, chap. 6.

what is left over after the other claims have been satisfied. Incidentally, it may be noted that bonuses to management are commonly an item which must be provided out of fair return, because they are not chargeable to expense.

Fair Return and the Courts. Over the years, the courts have sustained fair rates of return varying from 5½ to 8 per cent, depending on circumstances. Companies having well-established credit positions have frequently been accorded lower rates than others, and lower rates were upheld in the 1930's than were permitted earlier. In fact, Mr. Justice Butler stated, in the Indianapolis Water case, that he did not think that a fair return should be less than 7 per cent.

In *Bluefield Water Works and Improvement Company* v. *Public Service Commission of West Virginia* (1923),[24] the Supreme Court gave its most authoritative statement on fair return:

> What annual rate will constitute just compensation depends upon many circumstances and must be determined by the exercise of a fair and enlightened judgment, having regard to all relevant facts. A public utility is entitled to such rates as will permit it to earn a return on the value of the property which it employs for the convenience of the public equal to that generally being made at the same time and in the same general part of the country on investments and in other business undertakings which are attended by corresponding risks and uncertainties. . . . [It] has no constitutional right to profits such as are realized or anticipated in highly profitable enterprises or speculative ventures. The return should be reasonably sufficient to assure confidence in the financial soundness of the utility and should be adequate, under efficient and economical management, to maintain and support its credit and enable it to raise the money necessary for the proper discharge of its public duties. A rate of return may be reasonable at one time and become too high or too low by changes affecting opportunities for investment, the money market, and business conditions generally.[25]

This merely states the problem and does not specify any of the crucial measurements in concrete fashion. If it means what it says, it ignores either the problem of financial structure or the rate base. A rate of return based on this "formula" would have to be very high if the cost-of-reproduction rate base were much lower than the security obligations outstanding, or very low if the reverse were the case. The right amount would have to be ascertained by revelation, not by analysis.

Mr. Justice Douglas, in the Hope Natural Gas case, emphasized the ability of a company to attract new capital as the test:

> From the investor or company point of view it is important that there be enough revenue not only for operating expenses, but also for the capital costs of the business. These include service on the debt and dividends on the stock. By that standard the return to the equity owner should be commensurate with returns on investments in other enterprises having corresponding risks. That return, moreover, should be sufficient to assure confidence in the financial integrity of the enterprise, so as to maintain its credit and to attract capital. The condition

[24] 262 U.S., 679.
[25] *Ibid.* pp. 692–93.

under which more or less might be allowed is not important here. Nor is it important to this case to determine the various permissible ways in which any rate base on which the return is computed might be arrived at. For we are of the view that the end result in this case cannot be condemned under the act as unjust and unreasonable from the investor or company point of view.[26]

A comparison of these two statements, which were made twenty years apart by two judges having markedly different points of view, discloses the fact that as far as fair return is concerned, they both said the same thing. The difference lies in the concept of the rate base. This probably would make a difference in the end result, because Mr. Justice Butler was inclined to view some rate of return independent of the rate base as the correct one, while Mr. Justice Douglas is more likely to support the judgment of commissions. Nevertheless, apparently having dispensed with the rate-base controversy, the Court has shifted its position to financial requirements as the basis for measuring the legality of the fair return. If this is a correct interpretation of the position of the Court, it is necessary to establish what constitutes a sound financial structure before proceeding to deal with the fair return. This matter will be dealt with in the next section on the regulation of security issues.

When the rate of return is computed in accordance with the basis which was upheld by the Supreme Court in the Hope case, the rate base is divided into components derived from the capital structure. This method is known as the differentiated rate of return, because it arrives at the over-all or total rate of return from the components of the capital structure rather than from a flat rate arbitrarily assigned. The derivation of the differentiated rate of return may be illustrated by an example. Assume that of a total investment in a utility of $10 million, $5 million is raised by bonds at 4 per cent interest, $1 million by preferred stock at 5 per cent, $3 million by common stock, and $1 million from surplus or retained earnings. Interest on the bonds would be $200,000 and dividends on the preferred stock $50,000, giving a total of $250,000 of "contractural" payments. If 8 per cent were allowed on the common stock equity, another $320,000 would be required, bringing the fair return up to $570,000, or 5.7 per cent on the investment base. If the common stock equity were allowed 10 per cent, the total would be $650,000, or 6.5 per cent; if it were 6 per cent, the total would be $490,000, or 4.9 per cent. If a capital turnover of once in 5 years is assumed, the annual total revenues would be $2 million. The variation in the rate of return on the common stock equity between 6 and 10 per cent would be $160,000, or only 8 per cent of the total gross revenue.

Although there is no guarantee of a fair return to a utility, it is nevertheless necessary to recognize the fact that successful regulation must be able to give the highest assurance that interest on indebtedness will be covered regularly. Similarly, dividends on preferred stock will

[26] 320 U.S. 591 (1944) 603.

have to have a firm assurance of regular payment; or at least, commissions will have to see to it that they do not force rates so low as to jeopardize them. That is, interest and dividends on preferred stock are essentially in the same category as operating expenses as far as the necessary return is concerned, and they should be because of the protected position regulation is supposed to afford. This leaves only the common stock equity as the basis for calculating what amounts to the noncontractual requirements in the fair return.

The return on the common stock equity would have to provide, among other things, the necessary margin of safety over the bond and preferred stock requirements, because the common stock equity is supposed to supply this cushion. In addition, under the laws of many states, this is necessary if bonds and preferred stocks are to be legal investments for certain purposes, such as insurance companies and trust funds. A policy looking toward uniform dividends on common stock over the years would enhance the investment character of the firm. This would mean allowing earnings to rise above that dividend requirement in times of high business activity so as to provide a reserve that could be drawn on in lean times. This would necessitate keeping the reserve in a form that would be available when needed. If the return allowed on common stock equity were to be averaged in this way over a period of years, management would have to agree to co-operate with the regulatory authorities. Whether the return could be averaged as a matter of law has not been settled by the courts, but it certainly could be done on a *quid pro quo* basis by commissions. If companies were unwilling to co-operate, there would be no averaging of earnings.[27]

The determination of fair return on a differentiated basis of calculation would serve the purpose of "localizing" the problem of setting the rate. The common stock equity would be the only part involved. As already noted, great precision in setting it would not be very vital. This method, however, has been criticized on the same ground as any other prudent investment approach—namely, that it makes for too rigid a pattern of rates and fails to provide an adequate basis for response to changing price levels. On the other hand, there are those who feel that stability of rates is one of the major objectives of regulation. Prudent investment with a differentiated fair return may be used to provide for flexible rate levels or very stable ones. Stability or instability may be made a matter of policy and not a slave of formula. If cost of reproduction is used as the rate base, and depreciation and fair return are based on it, then instability, with fluctuations in price levels, is unavoidable.

[27]Mr. Justice Butler, in *Board of Public Utility Commissioners* v. *New York Telephone Co.*, 271 U.S. 23 (1926), held that earnings of one period could not be held below a fair return in order to compensate for excess above a fair return in a previous period. How the matter would be viewed today can only be a matter of conjecture, but the law would not preclude agreement by the company and a commission.

If the differentiated return, with prudent investment as the basis, is used, the element of instability from fluctuating price levels can be reduced to a minimum. At the same time, rate levels can be made to synchronize with the price level, if it is so desired, by at least as much as variations in the other elements of cost will allow. In addition, variations can be permitted in depreciation and the return on common stock equity. Accelerated depreciation in periods of higher prices would make it possible to adjust rates downward at subsequent times, thereby assisting in making rates more flexible. Regulatory authorities never seem to have understood that income may be received in one period for the benefit of a subsequent one and that such flexibility in rates as may be desired can be obtained without exploiting the consumer. If commissions would develop procedures such as these, much of the criticism of rigid rate levels would disappear; and a greater possibility of adaptation of regulation to changing conditions would be offered.[28]

REGULATION OF SECURITIES

Purposes of Regulation

The chief aim of security regulation, when it was first introduced, was to protect investors from financial abuses arising from fraud, excessive debts, and stocks issued without genuine value being received in return for them. There was some feeling that regulation of securities was necessary to protect consumers from receiving poor service from companies in financial difficulties. The connection between financial structure and fair return, however, was not generally grasped at first, because it was widely held that the capital structure of a firm did not affect the prices it charged.[29] While this may be true under competition, it cannot be true under regulation, for two reasons: (1) The courts, ever since *Smyth* v. *Ames*, have required that consideration be given to financial requirements in determining reasonable rates; and (2) if regulation is to be successful, it must be concerned with safeguarding the credit of utilities, because impaired credit inevitably leads to a deterioration in service.

Under the theory of regulation which seemed to obtain at least down to the Los Angeles Gas and Electric decision, fair value and fair return were largely independent of financial structure. How a utility raised its funds and disposed of its earnings was pretty much its own business. The regulation of securities was not an integral part of the process of setting reasonable rates. The Hope case apparently ended

[28]For an up-to-date treatment of the problem of fair return, see M. G. Glaeser, *Public Utilities in American Capitalism* (New York: Macmillan Co., 1957), chap. 28; also P. J. Garfield and W. F. Lovejoy, *op. cit.*, chap. 9.

[29]See *Report of the Railroad Securities Commission* (62nd Cong., 2d sess., House Document No. 256) (Washington, D.C.: U.S. Government Printing Office, 1911).

that, because if the end result is to be the test of reasonableness, the financial structure of a utility becomes the focal point of regulation. This was actually recognized by some state commissions many years earlier, the California Commission taking the position at the very outset that "the control over security issues and the disposition of their proceeds is the keystone of the entire arch of public utility regulation."[30]

Bases of Security Control

Effective regulation of the finances of a public utility enterprise requires that commissions have complete control over all aspects of the issuance of all securities. In California, it is necessary for a utility to secure Commission approval for the authorization of all forms of securities, including notes issued for a period of longer than twelve months, and then to secure approval when they are issued, as well as of the purposes for which they are issued. The company must account in detail for the way in which the proceeds are spent. The price at which the securities are sold must be sanctioned, together with the amount paid for marketing them.

The basis of valuation for rate control in California is historical cost, which is the estimate of the investment deemed necessary to erect a utility into a going concern plus investments actually made since the Commission made its first valuation. This is also the basis of valuation for purposes of determining capitalization. Stock dividends may be permitted only when a company has reinvested stockholders' money; but intercompany profits, past deficits, and discounts and premiums on securities cannot be capitalized. The Commission apparently does not have the power to fix the price which a utility may pay for property, but it achieves the same result by refusing to allow the purchaser to capitalize the price in excess of the valuation. Thus, consolidations are sanctioned only if the resulting capitalization does not exceed valuation.

The Commission also carefully scrutinizes financial structure. It regards bonds and preferred stocks as being in essentially the same category and has adopted the policy that these should be limited, in total, to 60 per cent of the valuation of the property. It is necessary for applicants to show that there are reasonable prospects for providing for fixed charges, as well as a margin for stockholder equities. Finally, although the Commission does not have complete control over reorganizations, it exercises a strong hand over reorganization expenses and takes the position that one reorganization is final. This means that the financial plan must be sound beyond question to be approved.

Because regulation began after many companies were in business, financial structures frequently did not conform to investment. The Com-

[30]For a detailed treatment of security regulation by the California Commission, see Pegrum, *Regulation of Public Utility Security Issues in California* (Berkeley: University of California Press, 1936).

mission could not compel readjustment to conform to its policies at the time; but whenever these companies have made application to issue new securities, the Commission has reviewed the entire financial structure and taken the necessary steps to bring the capitalization into line with valuation.

This brief description indicates the policies followed by the California Commission to make the financial structures of utilities correspond to their investment. In this way, security regulation has become an integral part of the process of determining reasonable rates. Some other state commissions, such as those of Wisconsin and Massachusetts, have followed similar principles. At the federal level, the Federal Power Commission and the Securities and Exchange Commission follow like policies for the utilities under their jurisdiction.

REGULATION OF COSTS AND SERVICE

Control of Costs

Prime attention in the determination of the general level of rates has been focused on fair return on fair value. This has not been without reason, because these two items may serve to control 50 per cent, or even more, of the total revenue to which the utility is entitled. For example, assume that a utility has an investment of $100 million, with a fair return of 6 per cent, a capital turnover of once in 5 years, and a depreciation rate of 4 per cent per annum. The total revenue would be $20 million; the fair return, $6 million; and the depreciation, $4 million. Fair return and depreciation, both dependent upon valuation, would absorb 50 per cent of the revenue. Depreciation is an operating cost; and including it, the costs of operation of the enterprise would amount to $14 million, or 70 per cent of the total revenue. Obviously, costs need to be thoroughly supervised if rate control is to be effective.

In so far as costs are market-determined, the only supervision that is necessary is to see that they are genuinely incurred and properly reported. A significant portion of them cannot be ascertained in this manner, however. Depreciation, as already noted, is just such an item. It is not necessary to discuss the appropriate rate, because that will depend upon circumstances. If investment is used as the basis for rates and security issues, a commission's major problem is to see that the depreciation is accounted for, so that investment is maintained and properties are retained in the rate base only at their depreciated value. If this is done and careful provision is made for obsolescence, there is little incentive for utilities to utilize poor equipment.

Other costs, such as service charges from affiliated companies, especially if these cannot be directly controlled by a commission, have frequently presented a real problem. The charges which were made by holding companies to their subsidiaries and by Western Electric to the affiliated Bell Telephone companies are illustrations. Salaries paid to top executives raise a difficult issue, because there is no very satisfactory measure of what constitutes fair compensation to them. Some commissions, like the one in California, have, on occasion, placed limits on the amount of these salaries that can be charged to expense. Wages and employee benefits are a matter of concern to commissions, too, because these may be pushed to the point of causing embarrassment to the utility and compelling monopoly prices to the consumer. The railroad labor problem is an illustration of the difficulties that can arise in regulated industries.[31] It does not seem that very much can be done by way of direct determination of these costs by commissions. Careful supervision of the accounting for them, however, detailed scrutinizing of them, and a public airing of them at rate hearings and on other occasions will ordinarily keep them within reasonable bounds. It is in the jurisdictions where utility regulation is weak that the difficulties arise.

Accounting

Strict control over accounting procedures is one of the most fundamental requirements of effective regulation. It is only through the accounts that the record of investment, expenses, and income can be obtained; and it is only by this means that publicity can be achieved. Where accounting is carefully supervised, very detailed reports are required, and these become a matter of public record. Even salaries of executives above a stipulated minimum, usually quite small, are open to public scrutiny. For the accounting records to be useful, they must be kept according to prescribed standards and subject to periodic check by public authority.

Control over accounting was accorded to the mandatory state commissions that were established shortly after the turn of the present century. It was generally required that these not be in conflict with the procedures established by federal agencies. The Interstate Commerce Commission established a uniform system of accounts for railroads under the Hepburn Act of 1906. The Federal Power Commission, the Federal Communications Commission, and the Securities and Exchange Commission all did the same thing for the utilities under their control.

Despite considerable similarity between the various state and federal systems of accounts, there was considerable divergence among them. As utilities spread beyond state boundaries, and with the development of federal regulation of interstate business, a movement to secure uniformity got underway. In November, 1936, the National Association of Railway and Utility Commissioners (NARUC) recommended that the states adopt new classifications of accounts for electric and manufactured gas utilities. It also approved the new classification for telephone utilities prescribed by the Federal Communications Commission. The Securities

[31]For a careful analysis of this, see F. H. Dixon, *Railroads and Government* (New York: Charles Scribner's Sons, 1922).

and Exchange Commission set up accounting procedures for holding companies and mutual service companies under its jurisdiction. The Federal Power Commission followed suit for electrical utilities in 1937 and for natural gas companies in 1940. Thus, national uniformity was achieved, as a practical matter, by the beginning of World War II, the differences remaining in the various state and federal systems being of a minor and largely technical nature.

Service

Control of rates necessarily involves control of service, because price, adequacy, and quality of service are mutually interdependent. Control of the quantity of service is achieved through the issuance of certificates of public convenience and necessity, which in many jurisdictions must be secured when a utility offers new services or makes extensions. Control is also exercised by some state commissions and by the federal commissions over extensions within the scope of existing certificates, if it is felt that a utility is tardy in supplying customers' needs. Similar control is applied to abandonment, public sanction being required before this can take place. A company cannot even go out of business completely without receiving permission from the appropriate public authority. A private utility, however, cannot be compelled to continue to operate at a loss; but public ownership may take over—if necessary, at a condemnation price—if continuation of the service is considered essential. Partial abandonment must also receive sanction; where some facilities can be operated only at a loss, commissions may insist on continuance of service, by permitting the deficiency to be recovered on other parts of the system.

Control of quality of service is mostly a matter of establishing technical standards of performance, such as continuity of service, limits of voltage variation, standards of heat content for gas, pressure for gas, and so forth. Where regulation is effective, a great deal has been done to control standards of service; but a good deal of credit should go to the aggressiveness and alertness of the utilities. The fact that commissions are ready to consider all complaints made by consumers may contribute appreciably to this.

PARTICULAR RATES

Principles of Particular Rates

The principles underlying the determination of particular rates for public utilities are essentially the same as those that apply to railroads. It is not necessary, therefore, to repeat the discussion on cost of service, value of service, discrimination, and so forth. There are some differences in conditions and procedures, however, which call for special consideration.

Public utility rate making does not have to contend with the amount of competition that characterizes the railroads. Differential pricing, because of competitive conditions, is not as important a factor in rate making; and interagency competition does not offer much of a problem. The consumer is connected directly and almost irrevocably with the producer. This makes it possible to charge the customer for the costs incurred in being ready at all times to serve him. Fixed and joint costs form an even higher proportion of total costs for public utilities, as a consequence of which discrimination or rate differentiation is actually a more important question than it is in the case of railroads.

The rate structures of public utilities vary widely from place to place among the same types of utilities, and even more widely among types. In some cases, attempts are made to relate rates directly to the amount of use and responsibility for rendering service; in others, there is, at best, only partial correspondence between the two. Electrical rates, for example, may be designed with a view to basing rates on the cost of being ready to serve the customer, the amount of energy the customer uses, and even the relation of the time of serving him to peak loads on the system. Telephone rates, on the other hand, are commonly the same for all who have the same type of service, for a given area, regardless of amount of use. This may also be true of water rates.

Scientific Rate Making

It is in the electrical and gas utilities that the most serious attempt has been made to develop "scientific" rate making. The refinement has gone so far as readily to create the impression that electrical rates can be based precisely on costs, and should be, in so far as market conditions will permit. In fact, deviations from cost under compulsion of market conditions are viewed as a sacrifice of "scientific" principles to the unavoidable but unfortunate exigencies of market pressures.

In order to simplify the pricing process, utility customers may be classified into groups. Some of the costs relating to these groups will be traceable to them, others will not be; in other words, there will be allocable and nonallocable costs. Those that can be traced directly belong to the group and should be assessed against the group. It is in connection with the other costs that the difficult problem arises. The treatment of these may be illustrated by the use of what is known as the "diversity factor." If the peak demands for service of different groups of customers come at different times, the total plant capacity that is required to meet these peaks is less than if they all came at once. Thus, if the total peak demands of three groups of customers amounts to 80 kilowatts, but the maximum demand that occurs at any one time is 40 kilowatts, the diversity factor is 2. This factor is used to reduce the demand charge assessed against the groups. The demand charge for which the users of the peak 40 kilowatts are assumed to be responsible is one half of the total capacity costs, even though the plant is being used to capacity at the time they are being served. In other words, those responsible for the peak demand are not responsible for bearing the total costs connected with it. Whatever else may be said for the "formula," it is not scientific; and it is not scientific because there is no scientific way of dividing joint costs. At best, it is arithmetic and, perchance, expedient. It is obviously a variant of average costs.

On the other hand, it does not follow that the peak load should carry all the capacity costs. The facilities are available to off-peak users; and they should contribute to them, too, if they can. Because the peak loads of electrical utilities are principally the result of the domestic load, it is frequently urged that the domestic consumer is undercharged because of the use of the diversity factor and that there is therefore a waste of electrical energy. In evaluating this argument, it should be recognized at the outset that the specific costs should be borne by the users responsible for them. The joint costs should be recovered as the market will permit.[32] There is no scientific way of allocating them.

Recovering joint costs according to what the market will provide might well give a utility more than a fair return. This raises the question of what rates should be reduced. The domestic consumer is in the position of having no alternatives, whereas the industrial consumer commonly does. Where these are really effective, economical pricing calls for charging the industrial consumer up to the amount that will lead him to seek the alternatives or else to the point that will maximize the revenue from him, if this is lower. If the total return to the utility on this basis is too high, the reduction should be given to the domestic consumer. The issue is not a matter of ethics but one of economics, and the industrial consumer may be the only one that offers a market gauge that can be used.

It is not possible here to go into the matter of setting rates within groups or classifications. Suffice it to say that economical and "scientific" rate making calls for assessing costs that are directly traceable on those for whom the costs are specifically incurred. The other costs, joint and common, cannot be allocated "scientifically" for the purpose of determining what prices ought to be. Recognition of this fact and the development of rate structures on this basis would give the only "scientific" rate

[32]Peak costs are not joint costs; they belong to the peak. But capacity costs are not all peak costs. The facilities that are used in common by peak and off-peak loads give rise to joint costs, and these are no more traceable to peak and off-peak services than are the joint costs incurred in producing beef and hides. Joint costs, on the whole, are ignored in public utility rate making. It does not seem to be recognized, for example, that electricity supplied after midnight is a different product from that which is supplied before and that these are joint products. This lack of recognition does not prevent commissions and utilities from resorting to differential pricing. They do not understand the economic basis of the differential pricing, however, and, as a consequence, regard it as a departure, which they feel should be resisted whenever possible, from "scientific" pricing.

structure that can be obtained.[33] Electrical and gas utilities have a better opportunity than most others to accomplish this, but they have done little toward it so far. Their main achievement in rate making, to date, has been a careful ascertaining and analysis of costs. This is the first step in economical public utility pricing. The next is to distinguish between those costs which are allocable and those which are not, leaving the contribution to the nonallocable ones to be determined by the market. Every commission in the country needs to learn this elementary lesson.

REGULATION OF NATURAL GAS RATES

Wholesale Rates

The regulation of natural gas rates by the Federal Power Commission has given rise to two major problems. Under the law, the Commission is charged with regulating the price of natural gas sold by the companies at wholesale for resale. This means that it can control the so-called "city gate" rates but not those which are sold directly to industrial users. The Commission has interpreted this to mean that in regulating natural gas companies, it can limit their earnings to a fair return. The sale of gas to industrial users increases the net earnings of companies. To deal with this problem, the Commission allocates costs and adjusts "city gate" rates so as to see that they do not yield any more than a fair return on the property used in supplying the gas at wholesale for resale.[34] This has been criticized on the ground that such a policy, in effect, overprices industrial gas by relieving residential customers of capacity costs properly chargeable to them if price is to be based on long-run marginal cost.[35] The problem again, of course, is that of joint costs. If domestic consumers pay for the costs incurred by the peak demands, the assessment of the joint costs becomes a matter of where the income can most conveniently be raised. Because industrial users have more opportunity for alternatives, it is difficult to see why they should not be charged up to those alternative prices, even if that means that industrial users carry practically all the joint costs. The higher prices to industrial users, if they can be obtained, will tend to reduce the consumption of gas for the so-called "inferior" uses, such as boiler fuel, and "conserve" it for the "superior" domestic use. Economical pricing does not mean allocating nontraceable costs by formula.

The companies justify low rates to industrial users on the ground that this makes for utilization of unused capacity. Just how significant

[33]See G. P. Watkins, *Electrical Rates* (New York: D. Van Nostrand Co., Inc., 1921).

[34]*Colorado Interstate Gas Co.* v. *Federal Power Commission*, 324 U.S. 581 (1945)

[35]See H. T. Koplin, "Conservation and Regulation: The Natural Gas Allocation Policy of the Federal Power Commission," *Yale Law Journal* (1955), pp. 855–60.

this is in lowering over-all costs is not quite clear. The Federal Power Commission seems to think that it is not very important for a load factor above 60 per cent.[36] If this is so, the very low rates accorded to industrial users scarcely seem to be in the public interest, because they do not assist in carrying much of the joint costs associated with pipe-line facilities. Nor is there much incentive to utilities to improve their earnings on this part of the business because of the over-all limitation on fair return. Some changes needs to be made in the legislation, so that rates on industrial sales can be integrated with the whole rate structure.

The Price for Field Gas

The second major problem in regulating natural gas is the price to be allowed the transmission companies for the gas when it enters the transmission lines. Some transmission lines produce all or part of the gas they transport, others buy their supply. In *Federal Power Commission* v. *Hope Natural Gas Company* (1944),[37] the Supreme Court upheld the Commission, which had included the natural gas reserves owned by the company in the rate base and used prudent investment as the basis of valuation. Mr. Justice Jackson, in his dissenting opinion, took the position that the rate-based method was valid for the transmission of natural gas, but was inapplicable to its production because of the totally different character of the latter. He argued that "gas is tangible, possessable and does have a market and a price in the field." The Commission, he contended, should therefore be left to fix the price of gas in the field, as one would fix maximum prices of oil or milk or coal or any other commodity. Thus, in Justice Jackson's opinion, natural gas companies took on a dual character. As far as transmission and distribution were concerned, they fell into the public utility category and could be regulated in the conventional way. In their production of natural gas, however, they did not fall into this pattern and should not be treated as so doing by the commissions and the courts.

In its investigation of the natural gas industry, the Federal Power Commission divided sharply on the issue of the price to be allowed for the natural gas. Two members held to the view that the price should be the "fair" field price, which could be readily ascertained, and that competition would be adequate to maintain reasonable prices. They believed that this should be applied to company-owned supplies, as well as to the gas sold by independents to the pipe lines. Two other members contended that the gas produced by the integrated companies should be regu-

[36]See Natural Gas Investigation, Federal Power Commission Docket G. 580 (Washington, D.C.: U.S. Government Printing Office, 1948); J. W. Ashley, *Some Economic Aspects of the California Natural Gas Industry* (Ph.D. thesis; Los Angeles: University of California, 1958).

[37]320 U.S. 591. See also *Colorado Interstate Gas Co.* v. *Federal Power Commission* 324 U.S. 581 (1945).

lated on the basis of prudent investment. It is not necessary to discuss the merits of the argument over the price to be allowed to integrated companies, because it was soon overshadowed by another development.

In *Phillips Petroleum Company* v. *State of Wisconsin* (1954),[38] the Supreme Court held that the Commission had "jurisdiction over the rates of all wholesales of natural gas in interstate commerce whether by a pipeline company or not and whether occurring before, during or after transmission by an interstate pipeline company." This meant that the production and gathering of natural gas in interstate commerce were subject to regulation. The Commission interpreted this to mean that its authority extended to all sales for resale, even at the wellhead in the field, if the product ultimately entered interstate commerce. In administering the law in light of the Phillips decision, the Federal Power Commission adopted the "fair field price" approach to valuing the gas; and it applied this principle to the integrated companies, as well as to the independents.

Adoption of the "fair field price" approach, however, did not end the controversy. The first challenge encountered by the Commission was in *City of Detroit* v. *Federal Power Commission* (1955)[39] The Court of Appeals held that the rate-base method was not the only one that might be used by the Commission, but at least it was necessary to use it as a point of departure. On remand, the Commission required the Panhandle Eastern Pipeline Company to adjust its rates so as to yield a 6 per cent return on its net investment in production and gathering. As matters now stand, natural gas produced by pipe-line companies rests on this basis. This is in conflict with the procedure for independent producers; reconciliation will undoubtedly have to take place when the problem of the independent producer is resolved.

The Commission proceeded to implement its fair field price policy as set forth in the Phillips Petroleum case by instituting area-wide rate investigations. In the meantime, it issued interim orders pending the determination of area prices. Its basic approach was set forth in an opinion and order on rates for Phillips Petroleum in 1960.[40] The Commission explicitly rejected the cost rate-base method because of the large number of independent producers with which it would have to deal, because of the impossibility of obtaining costs with reasonable accuracy, and because the cost rate-base method would almost always result in higher rates than those based on existing prices and applicable economic principles. In a statement of general policy[41] issued in connection with the Phillips decision, the Commission said:

[38]347 U.S. 672.

[39]230 Fed. (2d) 810; certiorari denied by the Supreme Court 352 U.S. 829 (1956).

[40]24 FPC 537 (1960).

[41]Federal Power Commission, *Statement of General Policy*, No. 61–1, September 18, 1960.

In arriving at the price levels for the various areas set forth in the appendix to this statement, we have considered all of the relevant facts available to us. Such consideration included cost information from all decided and pending cases, existing and historical price structures, volumes of production, trends in production, price trends in the various areas over a number of years, trends in exploration and development, trends in demands, and the available markets for the gas. Of necessity, we have not set forth the adjustments to these prices which must be made to take into account every possible provision of every contract which may affect the actual price, such as BTU adjustments, conditions of delivery, etc. The relevance of such adjustments to the basic contract price and the appropriate established price standard must be considered as each filing is made. As it becomes apparent that certain adjustments have general applicability in a specific area, the area price standard will be revised and set forth in greater detail with regard to the exact sale conditions to which the rate applies. We should, however, make it clear that these present price standards apply to pipeline quality gas as that term is generally understood in each area and, except for the Louisiana prices, are inclusive of all taxes.

Two price standards are set for each area. Initial prices in new contracts are, and in many cases by virtue of economic factors, must be higher than the prices contained in old contracts. For this reason, we have found it advisable to adopt two schedules of prices, one pertaining to initial prices in new contracts and one pertaining to escalated prices in existing contracts. It is anticipated that these differences in price levels will be reduced and eventually eliminated as subsequent experience brings about revisions in the prices in the various areas.

The decision of the Commission in the Phillips case was challenged in the courts, but the Supreme Court upheld the Commission by a 5-4 margin.[42] The majority recognized the difficulties of the Commission, taking the position that there was no single method that had to be followed, and that it is the result that is reached rather than the method employed that is controlling. The minority took the position that area pricing must include a showing that the individual producer will be able to recover his costs under the rates prescribed for the area. Investigation of area pricing for the Permian Basin resulted in an Examiner's report to the Commission on September 17, 1964. The recommended maximum rates per thousand cubic feet were different for gas-well gas, residue gas, and casing-head gas, and were higher in each instance for new gas than for old gas. What the Commission's decision on the Examiner's recommendations will be remains to be seen, but the issue is obviously far from settled, and extensive litigation appears to be in prospect unless Congress enacts legislation to exempt production and gathering from public utility regulation.[43] The imposition of greater limitations on the size of natural

[42] *Wisconsin* v. *Federal Power Commission*, 373 U.S. 294 (1963).

[43] For careful treatment of the problems connected with the regulation of the field prices of natural gas, see M. A. Adelman, "The Supply and Price of Natural Gas," *The Journal of Industrial Economics*, Supplement (Oxford: Basil Blackwell, 1962); P. W. MacAvoy, *Price Formation in Natural Gas Fields* (New Haven: Yale University Press, 1962); E. J. Neuner, *The Natural Gas Industry: Monopoly and Competition in the Field Markets* (Norman: University of Oklahoma Press, 1960); also P. J. Garfield and W. F. Lovejoy, *op. cit.*, chap. 15. See also the vigorous dissent of Mr. Justice Clark in *Wisconsin* v. *Federal Power Commission*, 373 U.S. 294 (1963).

gas pipe-line systems than is now the policy of the Commission would make for more effective competition in the purchase of gas. The decision of the Supreme Court in the El Paso Gas Company case[44] seems to be more realistic than was that of the Commission. Enhanced opportunity to penetrate different markets as illustrated by the application of Gulf Pacific Pipeline Company to serve certain customers in Southern California would also afford more competition without the threat of its becoming ruinous.

As was pointed out earlier in this chapter, a commission must supervise all costs that are incurred by a public utility. If these costs are competitively determined, it will accept them, provided they are genuine and properly accounted for. The controversy over the price for natural gas is still a bitter one, however. Some contend that it should be determined on the basis of prudent investment; some, that it should be a fair field price; and others, that the price to independent producers should be exempt from federal control altogether. Whatever may be the outcome of the present controversy, it is clear that if prudent investment is adopted as the basis for regulating the price, the Federal Power Commission will have to supervise the production of all natural gas. The separation of the costs of production of that which enters into interstate commerce from the other can be made only on an arbitrary basis. In addition, regulation of the oil companies would be inescapable, because much of the natural gas is produced in conjunction with oil. The task of regulating the oil and natural gas industries as public utilities is such as to offer little prospect of success.[45] These industries are competitive in structure and, to a large extent, in their behavior. The problems connected with regulating their prices would be far greater than those which are encountered in transportation; and this is an area for which we do not have a solution at present, despite seventy-five years of experience and experimentation. To the extent that monopoly presents a problem in petroleum and natural gas, it should be dealt with in other ways.

CONCLUSION

It was pointed out at the beginning of this chapter that the regulation of public utilities presented the simplest problem in thoroughgoing regulation, because the enterprises operate largely as isolated and insulated monopolies. Yet, even here, the issues are extremely complex. Where state and federal authorities have undertaken the task in a serious manner and have been given control over literally all phases of utility

[44]360 U.S. 651 (1964).

[45]For a discussion of these issues, see also Pegrum, "The Natural Gas Industry: An Appraisal of Public Policy," *Land Economics*, Vol. XXIX, No. 2 (May, 1953), pp. 168–81; Martin L. Lindahl, "Federal Regulation of Natural Gas Producers and Gatherers," *American Economic Review*, Vol. XLVI, No. 2 (May, 1956), pp. 532–44; Joel B. Dirlam, "Natural Gas: Cost, Conservation and Pricing," *ibid.*, Vol. XLVIII, No. 2 (May, 1958), pp. 491–501.

activities, the results have been fairly successful—in fact, one should say very successful, considering the imponderables that are always present. Nevertheless, the shortcomings are obvious; many of these are inherent in any type of control designed to secure the results of competitive efficiency when competition is absent. The task is unavoidable, because monopoly is unavoidable in public utilities. Public ownership faces the same type of problem, simply because it cannot eliminate the monopoly. The experience of public utility regulation should give pause to those who wish to extend this form of control to other areas of economic activity. Thoroughgoing regulation is difficult enough when applied to single monopolies; it is literally impossible when competition intrudes to any appreciable extent.

Chapter 27 PUBLIC OWNERSHIP OF UTILITIES

INTRODUCTION

Public ownership of public utilities in the United States occurs at the local, state, and federal levels. According to Professor Wilcox,[1] public ownership of all kinds in the United States in 1950 accounted for little more than 1 per cent of the nation's income; federal enterprises, for about three quarters of 1 per cent. This indicates that public ownership is not a significant part of the productive sector of the national economy. Whatever impact it has, however, is highly concentrated in a very few areas of economic activity.

The field of transport is one in which public ownership looms with particular significance, as has already been pointed out. So far, in this sector of the economy, ideological considerations have played a very small part in the development of public ownership. In the present transport system of the country, a large amount of public ownership is inescapable because of technology. At the same time, and for the same reason, a large amount of private ownership and operation is unavoidable. While ideological considerations may play some part in the development of future policies in transport, the most decisive influences will be economic and political. The influence that economic considerations will have will depend, to a considerable extent, upon the development of an understanding of the economic factors which must be weighed in arriving at decisions of public policy, and the dissemination of full information on them. The present plight of the railroads does not seem to be producing any ideological upsurge for government ownership; rather, it seems to be prompting a more thoroughgoing analysis of the causes of the dilemma. The effect of political influences on the outcome is difficult to predict. The arguments for public investment in highways, water transport, and air transport involve such diverse considerations as national defense, utilization of natural resources, and the inescapability of public investment in highways. In these areas of transport, the private operators and users of the publicly supplied facilities, as well as the manufacturers and agricultural interests that may get direct benefits from them, press for public investment, without too much regard for serious economic

[1]Clair Wilcox, *Public Policies Toward Business* (rev. ed.; Homewood, Ill.: Richard D. Irwin, Inc., 1960), p. 788.

considerations. If the ultimate outcome turns out to be public ownership of the railroads, it will not be the result of ideological considerations but of political and group pressures striving to maintain private enterprise in their own fields of endeavor, without being willing to meet competition on the basis of carrying full and equal costs, as a thriving private enterprise economy demands.[2]

Much of the foregoing discussion is applicable to public ownership in public utilities. Public ownership is found in telephone, gas, water, and electricity. It does not play much of a role in telephone and natural gas, nor is there any unavoidable public ownership in these fields. Telephone co-operatives may supply local telephone services, and municipalities may undertake the local distribution of gas acquired from private producers and transmission lines. These, however, do not pose any threats to private enterprise in their industries; nor do they present any particularly complex economic problems, because they are supported either by the rates charged or by taxes from the areas served by them. Whether the services are supplied on an economical basis can be determined only by examination of the individual situations; whether they should be is largely a matter of local decision.

It is in connection with water supply and electricity that the crucial issues of public ownership emerge. In many instances, the problem is one that is largely local in nature; in others, however, it is not. It is in reclamation, flood control, water supply, and hydroelectric power derived from navigable streams that the broader issues emerge. Public participation and public investment in these is unavoidable in many cases, especially where multiple-use projects are involved; and no amount of argument concerning the relative merits of public versus private ownership can escape that fact.

Public ownership, however, involves the allocation and utilization of economic resources just as much as does private ownership. The fact that public investment may supply services that are not directly vendible does not alter the situation; nor does it remove the necessity for recognizing and appraising all the costs that are involved, if economical decisions are to be made. If public ownership results in supplying nonvendible services, the price gauge for investment is not directly available; but if the full economic costs are known as much as possible, the decision makers will at least have the cost data to assist them in formulating their judgment. When vendible services are produced, the price gauge is available, as it is for privately owned utilities. This does not mean that the enterprises have to be operated at a profit; that may be a matter of

[2]One of the closest approximations to marginal cost pricing that we have today is probably in the field of motor transport. It does not present a very encouraging example of the way in which this pricing method works out in practice. Nor would it be easy to arrive at agreement as to how marginal cost pricing should be applied to the various users.

public decision; but if both sides of the market are fully known and disclosed, the decision can at least be made in light of all the facts.

FACTORS TO BE CONSIDERED IN PUBLIC OWNERSHIP

An evaluation of public ownership from the standpoint of economics requires that publicly owned utilities be subject to the criteria of economical allocation and utilization of resources.[3] This means that the economic resources devoted to publicly owned enterprises should find their most valuable use there rather than somewhere else. Theoretically, there is no distinction between the resource allocation problem of publicly owned utilities and that of the privately owned ones. Practically, there would be no difference if all the conditions which they both had to face were essentially the same. But all the conditions are not the same, because publicly owned utilities operate in a different "institutional" environment and do not have to meet the same kinds of obligations. Frequently, the differences are deliberately set up; but in some important instances, they are either ignored or unrecognized. If the differences are deliberately created with the alternatives clearly in mind, it cannot be said that they are irrational or uneconomical, even though they may not meet with universal approval or acceptance. It is a different matter if they are ignored or unrecognized. It is with the latter situations that we are concerned here.

Costs

The appropriate basis for calculating the costs of supplying the services of publicly owned utilities presents many of the same problems that are encountered with private utilities. In so far as regulation achieves results in the economical utilization of resources, it equates the necessary costs with the demands for services and satisfies the requirements of economic efficiency. Public ownership can do the same thing in essentially the same way, except that public management usually performs the function of both management and regulation, within the limits of the cost burdens imposed on it. The principal difference may lie in the costs which private and public ownership are required to meet.

Publicly owned enterprises are financed through public credit, normally supported—explicitly or implicitly—by the taxing power of the public owner. This results in a lower cost of capital, because all of the funds are borrowed, and because the risk is borne by the taxpayers. This may be deemed desirable in municipalities, where it may be assumed

[3]The issue of marginal cost pricing will not be raised here again. If it were valid as a principle of pricing, it would be applicable to all public utilities, as well as to many other industries. It does not dispense with the needs for ascertaining all costs if an economical evaluation is to be made. It therefore does not bear directly on the discussion of most of this section, which is concerned with bringing out the cost factors that need to be considered in public ownership. Marginal cost pricing is concerned with the way they should be recovered.

that in a very generalized way, the taxpayers and the consumers are the same people; but this assumption is not valid for regional power projects financed through federal credit supported by taxpayers in other regions. Furthermore, when public borrowing is literally strained to the limit, this places an additional burden on public credit that has serious fiscal implications. When the projects are not self-sustaining, this becomes of even greater significance. In either case, however, those who are receiving the services from enterprises dependent on public credit are not carrying the same burden of capital costs and risks, through the prices which they pay for the services, as those who are required to purchase from private concerns. This might not be of great consequence were it not related to two other considerations—namely, amortization and taxes.

Publicly owned enterprises are commonly required to amortize the bonds over a period of years, perhaps 20 or 50. Private companies do not ordinarily make such a provision. This amortization increases the cost of operation during the period in which it takes place. Whether such amortization is economically desirable is a debatable matter. It results in the creation of a public equity in the publicly owned utility out of rates charged to the consumer. This means that current consumers are supplying capital out of the prices they pay for the services. This is really the only way, under present forms of public ownership, that public enterprises can accumulate equity capital.[4] This capital, however, is not a free good, and it is not obtained through appeal to the financial market. There is no investor choice, and there is no market determination of resource allocation. When the equity is established, it becomes "costless" capital to the management. Apart from depreciation, this puts it in the category of an economic resource being used without payment for it by the users. To the extent that this is done, it results in an uneconomical use of resources. Public ownership is able to do this because the funds are raised through public channels. It could be counteracted, of course, by including an interest charge on this equity in the costs to be covered by the rates, but this is not the practice.

Taxes

Taxes paid by private utilities constitute a compulsory contribution to the support of local, state, and federal governments which is obtained from the consumers of their services through the rates which are

[4]The public corporation, as used in Great Britain for the Central Electricity Board, the London Passenger Transport Board, and the British Broadcasting Corporation, sold stock to raise capital. The stockholders were not permitted to vote, but the boards of directors were appointed through arrangements designed to prevent political interference. The directors were really public trustees, who were supposed to represent all the interests involved. There is nothing in this country comparable to this type of corporation. See D. F. Pegrum, "The Public Corporation as a Regulatory Device," *Journal of Land and Public Utility Economics*, Vol. XVI, No. 3 (August, 1940), pp. 334–43.

charged for them. Taxes on publicly owned enterprises vary widely, and precise comparison with private utilities can be made only in specific jurisdictions. In general, however, taxes paid by publicly owned enterprises are much lower than those paid by private utilities.[5] At present, publicly owned utilities are exempt from federal taxes, and most of them are exempt from state taxes. In addition, publicly owned utilities are not required to pay for franchises to the municipalities in which they operate. For publicly owned utilities to be taxed in the same way as privately owned ones, major changes in public policy would be required, together with constitutional amendments at the state and probably the federal levels.

The inequality of tax burdens on privately and publicly owned utilities means that consumers of the services of the publicly owned ones are not making the same contributions to the costs of government through the prices of the services they buy as are those supplied by private enterprises. Measurement of the difference in burdens of private and public ownership as the result of taxes requires the calculation of the tax equivalent in every way. This means that the real property owned, by whatever agency—local, state, or federal—should be subject to the same tax calculations as the private firms; franchise tax and corporate income tax equivalents should also be included. Whatever may be the merits of treating public and private ownership in different categories for tax purposes as a matter of public policy, tax equivalents must be included in comparing the economic aspects of public and private ownership.

Municipally owned utilities may render services to the municipality free of charge or at reduced rates. When this is done, these costs have to be calculated as an offset to tax benefits. They need to be precisely estimated, however. It would be much better for the charges to be made to the municipality, just as a private utility would do.

The Yardstick

Public ownership is often regarded as a means of establishing standards by which the efficiency of private ownership under regulation may be measured. When this is done, the rates charged by publicly owned utilities are compared with those of the private enterprises for similar types of service. Generally speaking, public rates are lower than private; but this, of itself, is not a valid measuring rod, for two reasons: (1) A comparison of rates is a legitimate basis for evaluating relative efficiencies only when the operating conditions are substantially the same. Two privately owned systems, for example, may have different rates without the conclusion being warranted that the one charging the lower rates is the more efficient of the two, unless evaluation of differences in operating conditions is made. If one of the two serves a heavily populated urban

[5]For a discussion of this, see P. J. Garfield and W. J. Lovejoy, *op. cit.*, pp. 388–91.

area with high density of traffic, while the other has a more sparsely populated metropolitan and rural region to supply, differences in rates may be the result of differences in operating conditions rather than in efficiency. (2) A comparison of rates, to have any meaning, must be based on the same cost considerations, as was pointed out in the previous section.

Public ownership and operation as a yardstick for privately owned utilities came into greatest prominence in connection with the Tennessee Valley Authority. According to Director David E. Lilienthal, Congress set up the public production of electricity in the TVA as a means of providing a "yardstick" by which the efficiency of private power companies and the effectiveness of regulation in the area could be measured. The yardstick idea had originally been advanced by President Herbert Hoover, who advocated an extensive system of inland waterways in the Midwest to provide, among other things, a yardstick by which to appraise the reasonableness of railroad rates. This was a totally invalid measuring rod, because no tolls were to be charged for the use of the waterways. The TVA as a yardstick for electrical rates was put on a more plausible basis, in that the electricity aspects of the project were to be covered by the rates charged and the production of power was to be assessed with "its share" of the joint costs. This alone would have invalidated the use of TVA rates as a yardstick, because the joint costs could be assigned only on an arbitrary basis. This meant that the costs were not comparable to those for electricity produced by steam plants or single-use projects.

Regional Development

Public ownership of utilities in the United States has come about in recent years through the development of regional projects on many of the important rivers of the country. When these undertakings are designed to serve a number of different uses, such as water supply, flood control, generation of electricity, and perhaps even navigation and recreation, they are not readily adaptable to private ownership. The extent to which all of these features, or a number of them, may be economically combined in one project is frequently a matter of vigorous debate. Ventures like the lower Colorado River development, the Columbia River project, or the St. Lawrence waterway can scarcely be constructed except as multiple-purpose enterprises. They require huge investments extending over many years under circumstances that make private ownership, in many instances, impracticable. They frequently involve a number of political jurisdictions that makes private ownership an ineffective means of dealing with the difficulties that arise. In addition, some of the purposes —for example, flood control—do not lend themselves to private enterprise. Public ownership, therefore, seems to be the most feasible method of securing co-ordinated and economical development of such regional projects. In other words, public ownership in some areas of the utility field seems to be almost as unavoidable as it is in some phases of transport.

An over-all economic appraisal of the advisability of some of these projects may be very difficult to make. If the products are directly vendible, such as is the case with water supply or electricity, costs and income can be compared and an evaluation made on that basis. When flood control is included, intangible benefits that are hard to evaluate in terms of the price calculus enter the picture.[6] Decisions on how much to invest in such enterprises necessitate the weighing of commercial and noncommercial factors. If these could be considered separately, evaluation would at least be simplified; but when they are part of a multiple-use project, only the separable costs can be ascertained for the various uses; the joint or common costs cannot be traced. Some basis, therefore, must be developed for handling these. If public authority decides to allocate them by some formula or by legislative fiat, then the costs of each of the various aspects of a project become ascertainable. When, under such circumstances, an economic appraisal of the results of each separate phase is made, it must be made in the light of the costs assigned. For example, if a multiple-use dam is constructed and 50 per cent of the investment in the dam is assigned to electricity, which is required to bear those costs out of its sales, the power authority may legitimately claim success if it meets these requirements. But the claim for success is valid only for the conditions laid down! Whether the conditions are reasonable from an economic or any other point of view is an entirely different matter. These considerations must be borne in mind when an evaluation is being made of the various regional projects in this country.

COSTS IN MULTIPLE-USE PROJECTS

The respective costs of providing the various services of multiple-purpose projects fall into two categories—namely, the separate and identifiable costs of each, and the joint or common costs applicable to all. It is with the joint costs that the difficulties arise.

Some writers, recognizing that these costs cannot be allocated except in some arbitrary fashion, and feeling that allocation by political action would be likely to prove futile, take the position that these costs should be treated as a general charge upon the public revenue in the same way as other social services. This, it is contended, is in harmony with the social nature of these undertakings.[7]

A variant of this point of view is the benefit-cost theory, which advocates allocating joint costs in accordance with the benefits to be derived from each function. This must not be taken to mean that each of the services rendered should be priced according to the market for it,

[6]For a critical evaluation of flood control programs and expenditures, see Walter M. Kollmorgen, "And Deliver Us from Big Dams," *Land Economics*, Vol. XXX, No. 4 (November, 1954), pp. 333–46.

[7]See H. M. Gray, "Joint Costs in Multiple-Purpose Projects," *American Economic Review*, Vol. XXV, No. 2 (June, 1935), pp. 224–35.

if there is a market. It means that all beneficiaries from the project, direct and indirect, should contribute to the joint costs. This requires a reduction of benefits to a common price denominator. The joint costs are then supposed to be divided among the various functions in proportion to the benefits received by each. The vendible services are expected to recover the joint costs assigned to them through the sale of the services; the remaining joint costs have to be recovered by taxes. The difficulty with this approach is that it is impossible to measure all the benefits in monetary terms. In practice, it resolves itself into an arbitrary assignment of a portion of joint costs to be borne out of taxes.

The most sophisticated theory for the allocation of joint costs was developed by the Tennessee Valley Authority. This was called the "alternative justifiable expenditure theory" or "alternative cost avoidance." This theory was based on the assumption that where multiple-purpose projects were possible, plants could be built for a single function at an ascertainable cost for each; or they could be built as a multiple-purpose project at a lower cost than the combined total of the separate plants. In applying this approach, the total investment for the multiple-purpose project was first ascertained. Then, the costs directly allocable to each function were deducted from this. The remainder was the joint costs which were to be divided. An estimate was then made of the cost of constructing separate navigation, flood control, and power projects. From each of these separate costs were deducted the direct costs assignable to each in the multiple-purpose plant. This gave what was called the "remaining alternative cost" of each function separately. The joint costs were then divided in proportion to these. To illustrate, suppose the separate remaining costs for each were estimated to be $30 million for navigation, $30 million for flood control, and $40 million for power, the total being $100 million. Navigation would be required to bear 30 per cent of the estimated joint costs of the multiple-use project; flood control, 30 per cent; and power, 40 per cent.

Two points should be noted in the evaluation of this theory. The Authority was required by Congress to make a division and assignment of costs. This method was certainly no worse than any other. The second point is that from the standpoint of economics, it was no better. It was arbitrary; and despite all the sophisticated calculations, it did not trace the joint costs; it merely assigned them and said what each of the three functions *should* bear. The estimated cost of each of these three types of services, constructed separately, could have been used as a measure of the maximum portion of the joint cost that each could economically have been expected to bear, because it would not have been economical to charge a service more under joint production than it would cost under separate output; but this did not provide a logical basis for allocating the joint costs in proportion to the separate costs.

Discussion of joint costs in multiple-purpose projects that are publicly owned seems to proceed on the assumption that these costs are different from similar costs in private enterprise and they they should therefore be handled in a different way. Just why they are not treated in the same way is not clear, at least as far as economic analysis and policy are concerned. If a multiple-purpose project is constructed to provide only vendible services—for example, water and power—the output of these two services can be sold in the market for what they will bring. The upper limit to the price for each could be set by the estimated cost of producing each separately. In the case of electricity, there would be the additional check of the estimated cost of producing it by steam; and either the hydroelectric or the steam costs could be used as the measuring rod, whichever was the lower. An economical gauge could thus be obtained for the upper limit of the investment in the facility. If the revenues received for selling the two products at what the market would bring should yield more than the total necessary to cover the costs, the price of the water could be lowered until the total revenue was that which was required. There might be other considerations which would justify giving electricity a somewhat lower rate than the alternative cost gauge would warrant; but if so, at least the amount of it would be known explicitly, and the validity of the reasons for it thereby could be subjected to some objective test.

Where multiple projects provide nonvendible functions such as flood control, the same considerations could apply. As much of the joint costs of the entire project as the market would yield could be returned by the sale of the vendible services. If these were unable to carry all of the joint costs, the difference would be ascertainable. If public policy still dictated that the project should be undertaken, at least the costs of supplying the nonvendible services could be ascertained by the market process rather than by arbitrary allocation. Some will contend that this means that the vendible services would be subsidizing the nonvendible ones, but this is no more valid than the assertion that beef subsidizes hides, or vice versa. If the project were of such a nature that the vendible part of the output was literally only a by-product of the nonvendible, the vendible services could still be sold for what the market would yield. The fact that these were not covering the joint costs would not mean that they were being "subsidized," unless one assumed that the nonvendible portions of the project were set up as a mere subterfuge for the purpose of providing services which could be sold.

MUNICIPAL OWNERSHIP

Municipal ownership of public utilities in the United States is confined largely to water supply and electricity. There are some municipal telephone systems in smaller cities. In 1953, gas manufacture and distribution were provided by 1.7 per cent of the cities with over 5,000 population reporting municipal ownership. Those reporting gas distribution only made up 2.7 per cent, and this was almost entirely natural gas. In the same year, 502 cities—or 20.6 per cent of those with population over 5,000 that rendered reports—owned and operated electrical utility systems; 290 of these—or 11.9 per cent of the reporting cities—engaged in both generation and distribution, the other 212—or 8.7 per cent—providing for distribution only. There were only 15 municipally owned plants in cities of over 100,000 population. Municipal ownership in electricity has declined in pronounced fashion from the peak of 2,581 municipal plants in 1922. The decline may be accounted for principally because of technological developments by which the economies of scale encourage the construction of plants and systems that can operate more efficiently when not confined to a single market. This disadvantage does not extend as severely to public ownership of the distribution system only, in which the economies of scale are not so pronounced.

The most extensive development of municipal ownership has been in water supply and distribution, in which 67.5 per cent of the cities with a population of over 5,000 were engaged in 1953, and an additional 6.2 per cent in water distribution only. Indianapolis was one of the large cities of the country whose water was supplied by a private utility. Water supply has generally been so closely connected with problems of sanitation and fire protection that public ownership has been looked upon as a convenient means of unifying these services for particular areas. It has also frequently avoided the troublesome problem of ascertaining the payment that would have to be made to a private firm for supplying fire and sanitation services.

The Los Angeles Municipal System

Los Angeles has the distinction of having developed the oldest and the largest municipally owned public utility in the United States. This utility supplies both water and electricity to the residents of the city of Los Angeles through the Department of Water and Power. In addition, the city participates as a member of the Metropolitan Water District, which transports water from the Colorado River to the Southern California coastal areas, to be distributed to the various member cities. The Department of Water and Power is a department of the corporation of the city of Los Angeles. It is under the direction of a general manager, who is selected by the Board of Water and Power Commissioners. There are 5 commissioners, who serve for 5 years and are answerable to the City Council. They are appointed by the mayor, subject to the approval of a majority vote of the Council, and are removable only under the same conditions.

Climatic conditions, including recurring periods of drought, led the citizens of Los Angeles to turn to public ownership as a means of resolving the local water problems by a more effective conservation of local sources and an extension of facilities to secure supplies from the mountain areas. The municipal water system was established in February, 1902. Steps were then taken to secure water rights in the High Sierras, some 250 miles north of Los Angeles. An aqueduct was constructed to transport the water to the city. This was completed in 1913. This source of water, together with supplies from rainfall impounded in the immediately surrounding mountains, provides the city of Los Angeles with about 86 per cent of the water which it uses today. The other 14 per cent is obtained from the Colorado River.

The power opportunities of the water supply from the High Sierras are large, because the source of the water is at elevations up to 8,000 feet while the outlet is at around 1,000 feet or less. The generation of hydroelectric power along the route of the aqueduct was undertaken as a by-product of supplying the water. The first installation of generating facilities was only 47 miles from Los Angeles. When the city finally acquired the electrical properties of the Los Angeles Gas and Electric Corporation in 1936, it came to supply, with minor exceptions, the entire city of Los Angeles with electrical energy. It obtained this from water power from the aqueduct, from steam plants in the area which it had acquired, and from contracts with the federal government for power generated at Hoover Dam on the Colorado River.

As already noted, 86 per cent of the water supply of the city of Los Angeles comes from facilities owned by the Department of Water and Power. The other 14 per cent is obtained from the Metropolitan Water District. This water is paid for in two ways. The Metropolitan Water District charges the city $25 an acre-foot for the water delivered to Los Angeles. In addition, the property owners of the city are assessed by the Metropolitan Water District for water district costs not covered by the sale of water. The share of these total costs to be borne by the taxpayers of Los Angeles is determined by the proportion that the assessed valuation of property in the city bears to the the total assessed valuation of property in the Metropolitan Water District. On this basis, the taxpayers of Los Angeles contribute, through taxes, some $7 million a year to the MWD. This does not appear in the operating statement of the water department as one of the costs of supplying water to Los Angeles; yet it amounts to about 40 per cent of the total costs of the department. The current cost per acre-foot of water being delivered to Los Angeles from the MWD is therefore about $225, and the average over the years has been somewhere around $1,000 an acre-foot.[8]

The Los Angeles Department of Water and Power has generally been regarded as an example of one of the outstanding illustrations of successful public ownership in the country. In comparing it with private ownership, however, certain facts should be borne in mind. Electricity

[8]A careful study of the Metropolitan Water District was made by J. W. Milliman as a Ph.D. thesis, University of California, Los Angeles.

generated by aqueduct power is treated as a by-product and does not pay a price for the falling energy. Secondly, while the Department of Power has transferred moneys at varying rates of gross revenue to the city treasury over the years, it has made no contribution to city tax collections and only a small contribution to *local* taxes on property owned outside the city. In 1952, the Southern California Edison Company paid over 26 per cent of its gross revenues in taxes, while the Los Angeles power system paid just over 4 per cent.[9] If to differences such as these are added the taxes paid for water received from the Metropolitan Water District, the results of the operations of the Los Angeles municipal system do not appear in such a favorable light as they are sometimes cast, nor do the financial results offer as convincing evidence of financial efficiency as is frequently contended. Under existing circumstances, it would not be a self-supporting system if all the costs of supplying Los Angeles with electricity and water had to be borne by it, to say nothing of taxes comparable to those assessed on private utilities.

The Metropolitan Water District

In 1927, the California State Legislature passed the Metropolitan Water District Act, by which an association of municipalities and other political areas, which did not need to be contiguous, could be organized as water districts. Under this legislation, the Metropolitan Water District of Southern California was set up, in 1928, by 13 cities in the Los Angeles area for the purpose of bringing Colorado River water to the Southern California coastal area. The MWD is a public corporation, governed by a board of directors made up of representatives appointed by the member cities. It can levy taxes for the purpose for which it was established, borrow money, acquire property, and sell water at wholesale.

The District began the planning and construction of the aqueduct from the Colorado River to the Southern California coastal plain in 1930. It contracted with the Secretary of the Interior of the United States for water supply, for which it agreed to pay 25 cents an acre-foot for water taken from the river, for power from Hoover Dam, and for half the power generated at Parker Dam. The power is for purposes of pumping the water from the river to destination. Parker Dam, 150 miles downstream from Hoover Dam, was constructed to form a reservoir from which the water could be pumped into the aqueduct. Payment for the water by the members of the District was on the basis already discussed for Los Angeles. Each member was given an allotment of water on an agreed basis but did not necessarily have to take it. The unused portion could be sold by the District to any other member. So far, for example, Los Angeles has taken only 5 per cent of its allotted share in any given year. Some of the members have been using more than their allotment. They, however

[9]See M. G. Glaeser, *Public Utilities in American Capitalism* (New York: Macmillan Co., 1957), p. 469.

can be required to adjust their purchases if other members wish to buy the full share to which they are entitled.

THE BOULDER CANYON PROJECT

The Colorado River Compact

The Federal Bureau of Reclamation, acting under the Federal Reclamation Act of 1902, began the first systematic study for the development of the Colorado River in 1904. Preliminary studies indicated that the favorable sites for power and water development were Black and Boulder canyons. Seven states had a vital interest in the utilization of the water and power of the river—namely, Wyoming, Utah, Nevada, Colorado, New Mexico, Arizona, and California. In 1921, Congress authorized a compact among the states comprising the Colorado basin. A commission was set up, with Secretary of Commerce Herbert Hoover as chairman. As a result, a Colorado River Compact was signed on November 24, 1922. This compact provided that the states in the upper basin above Lee's Ferry would guarantee the delivery, during each 10-year period, of a water supply of not less than 75 million acre-feet to the lower basin. Thus, the lower-basin states of Arizona, Nevada, and California were apportioned an average annual amount of 7.5 million acre-feet for beneficial use. The lower basin also acquired 1 million additional acre-feet from sources below Lee's Ferry.

The Boulder Canyon Project Act

Congress passed the Boulder Canyon Project Act in 1921. This legislation authorized the construction of Boulder (now named Hoover) Dam and power plant as well as the All-American Canal, which was to be used to irrigate the Coachella and Imperial Valleys. A maximum of $165 million was authorized for the dam and reservoir. Because of the danger that Arizona would not ratify the compact, California was required irrevocably and unconditionally to agree with the United States that its total annual consumptive use would not exceed 4.4 million acre-feet of the 7.5 million available from the upper basin, plus California's one-half share of the unapportioned surplus water. The Boulder Canyon Project Act finally became effective on June 25, 1929, but California's precise share of the water is still an unsettled matter.[10]

Financing the Colorado River Project. The act provided that construction of the dam could not begin until the Secretary of the Interior had secured contracts for the sale of water and power which would assure repayment of the cost of the dam to the Treasury in 50 years, with interest at 4 per cent on the unpaid balances. Repayment provisions were also applied to the All-American Canal, but the time limit was 40 years—

[10]For an extended analysis of the problem and the legal status as of the present time, see *Arizona* v. *California*, 373 U.S. 546 (1963).

without interest, however. Of the $165 million authorized expenditure, $25 million was applied to flood control. This was to be amortized frcm revenues from power after the other $140 million had been repaid, if it had not already been taken care of out of surplus revenues.

The Metropolitan Water District contracted for water delivery from Hoover Dam storage at 25 cents an acre-foot. The Imperial Irrigation District pays nothing for the water it receives from the All-American Canal, but it did agree to pay for its share of the investment in the irrigation facilities, in 40 annual interest-free installments.

Two considerations were involved in the power contracts. The first was that the dam was to be self-liquidating. The second was that the falling-energy cost at the dam could not be more, when added to costs of transmission, than the cost of energy at central stations in Los Angeles. The rate for firm power was consequently set at 1.63 mills per kilowatt hour; and secondary energy, at 0.5 mills. It was estimated that contracts for this energy at these prices plus the 25 cents an acre-foot for delivered water would cover the costs of the project. Subsequent adjustmnets in the interest rate and a lengthening of the period of amortization reduced the charge to 1.163 mills of firm energy, but the project is still self-liquidating

The city of Los Angeles and the Southern California Edison Company became the operating agents of the power facilities. They also supplied the transmission lines. Under the contract, the Metropolitan Water District was entitled to 36 per cent of the firm energy. Arizona and Nevada were each allotted 18 per cent of the firm power on an "if and when needed basis"; 4 per cent went to the cities of Pasadena, Burbank, and Glendale; 15 per cent, to the city of Los Angeles; and 9 per cent, to the Southern California Edison Company, the Los Angeles Gas and Electric Company, and the Southern Sierras Power Company. Because it was taken for granted that Arizona and Nevada would be able to use only a small amount of their firm power allotments for a long time, the city of Los Angeles and the private utilities each agreed to pay for one half the unused Arizona and Nevada energy.

There was no division of joint costs in the Boulder Canyon Project. The power rates were arrived at on a competitive (alternative cost) basis; the Metropolitan Water District agreed to make up the balance of the costs on the basis of 25 cents an acre-foot for delivered water. The project was set up on a self-liquidating basis, and the federal government will be paid back its principal with interest. There are no taxes on the federal part of the project equivalent to what a private company would have been required to pay had it undertaken to construct and operate the dam.[11]

[11]For a detailed examination of the Boulder Canyon project, see P. L. Kleinsorge, *The Boulder Canyon Project* (Stanford, Calif.: Stanford University Press, 1941).

THE COLUMBIA RIVER PROJECT

The Columbia River Basin

The Columbia River—together with its principal tributary, the Snake River—drains an area of 259,000 square miles, 39,000 of which are in Canada, where the headwaters of the Columbia itself are located. The river is some 750 miles in length in the United States, with a fall of 1,288 feet. It is tidal at the site of Bonneville Dam, which is located 140 miles from the Pacific Ocean. The Columbia is subject to extreme variations in flow, from 40,000 second-feet in the low days of winter to a high of 500,000 feet during the June peak. These were measured at Bonneville.

As early as 1925, Congress evidenced interest in the Columbia by authorizing a survey for the purpose of investigating the possibilities of development of the river for navigation, irrigation, flood control and power. The report, submitted in 1932, proposed a series of ten dams extending from Grand Coulee Dam, 94 miles northwest of Spokane, to Bonneville, 450 miles further downstream at tidewater. In the years since 1948, additional proposals for projects have been made with the view to developing the entire Columbia River basin for power purposes by both public and private agencies. However, no unified administration for control or planning has yet been established.

Bonneville Dam

The first dam in the entire project, which was constructed at Bonneville, was commenced in 1933. The first generating units were placed in operation in 1941. Bonneville Dam is a dual-purpose structure for navigation and hydroelectric power production. It has an installed generating capacity of 518,400 kilowatts and provides a navigable stream for ocean-going vessels as far as The Dalles, some 47 miles above the dam. Barge navigation is feasible to the upper reaches of the Snake River to Idaho and up the Columbia to Grand Coulee. Fish ladders were installed at Bonneville to enable the salmon to migrate up the Columbia to spawning grounds. The ultimate effect of these is still a matter of debate.

Under legislation passed in 1937, the administration of Bonneville was made a joint responsibility. The chief of engineers of the War Department was assigned the task of building and operating the power-generating and navigation facilities; the Bonneville power administrator, of marketing the electricity, together with the construction and maintenance of power lines. The administrator was made responsible to the Secretary of the Interior and was appointed by him. Under the law, the administrator could act only as a wholesaler of electric power. He was required (1) to encourage the widest possible use of all the electric energy that could be generated and marketed, (2) to prevent its monopolization by limited groups, and (3) to give preference and priorities to public bodies and co-operatives. He was authorized to establish schedules of wholesale electric rates, subject to the confirmation of the Federal Power Commission. These schedules were to be devised to permit the recovery of the cost of transmitting the electric energy, including the amortization of the capital investment over a reasonable period of years.

The capital investment, the costs of which were supposed to be covered by the rates, consisted of the investment in the generating and transmission facilities, together with such joint costs of the dam as were assigned to power by the Federal Power Commission. The law, however, stated that electric energy created from water power was an incident to and a by-product of the construction of the project. On this basis, the Federal Power Commission finally assigned 50 per cent of the joint costs to power, in the belief that this was as far as it could go. It was also probably influenced by the fact that on this basis of allocation, it estimated that the expected revenues would permit the amortization of all costs, including the assigned joint costs, over a fifty-year period. In passing, it should be noted that navigation on the river above the dam is negligible.

To promote the use of electricity on the widest possible basis, the administrator set a basic wholesale rate, available anywhere on the transmission system at $17.50 per kilowatt-year. The rates were available to public bodies, co-operatives, and private utilities for resale. All purchasing utilities were required to sell the energy at retail according to rate schedules established by the administrator. Beginning in 1940, with 142 miles of line, the transmission system underwent continuous expansion, so that, by 1953, it had grown to 5,707 miles of line and 145 substations. This provided for an interconnected electricity system throughout the Pacific Northwest of both privately and publicly owned utilities.

Grand Coulee

Construction of the Grand Coulee Dam as a second part of the Columbia River basin development was commenced in 1934 and completed in 1941. This is the largest in volume and the second highest of the masonry dams in the world, being second in height only to Hoover Dam. When this part of the undertaking is fully developed, it is expected that the Columbia Basin Reclamation Project will irrigate 1.2 million acres of land. The upper 80 feet of the reservoir capacity behind the dam can be used to regulate the river flow for the benefit of downstream power plants and navigation.

The joint costs of Grand Coulee are divided among the four purposes of the dam on the alternative justifiable expenditure basis, approximately 33 per cent going to power, 42 per cent to irrigation, 25 per cent to river regulation, and less than one half of 1 per cent to flood control and navigation. The marketing of the power from the dam is the responsibility of the Bonneville power administrator; this insures a uniform marketing policy for the whole basin development. The remainder of the Grand Coulee project is under the Bureau of Reclamation of the Department of the Interior. The development of the Columbia River basin shows no semblance of being a self-liquidating project at any time. The administrator turns the power revenues into the United States Treasury, and each of the agencies concerned with the operation of the Columbia project goes to Congress each year for appropriations to finance its operations.

THE TENNESSEE VALLEY PROJECT

The Tennessee Valley project represents the most comprehensive attempt at regional planning for natural resource utilization undertaken by the federal government in this country. The river watershed comprises an area of about 42,000 square miles with a population of about 3 million people. This area includes most of central and western Tennessee, northern Alabama, portions of North and South Carolina, Georgia, Virginia, West Virginia, Kentucky, and Mississippi. Some nagivation improvements were made on the Tennessee River in the nineteenth century, but the beginning of the present program really came with World War I. In 1916, Congress appropriated $20 million for the construction of a steam plant and the Wilson Dam at Muscle Shoals to produce nitrates for the manufacture of explosives. The Wilson Dam was completed in 1925 at a cost of $45 million, including the appurtenant power plant. No further development took place until 1933, and all of the facilities remained idle in the intervening period.

The Tennessee Valley Authority

In 1933, Congress created the Tennessee Valley Authority as an autonomous public corporation. It was to be governed by a board of directors consisting of 3 men, appointed by the President, with the advice and consent of the Senate, for a term of 9 years. Some 6 objectives of the project were set forth in the legislation. It was to provide for flood control; navigation; fertilizer production; soil erosion; hydroelectric power; and social, cultural, and economic development. According to the law, the primary purpose was flood control and navigation. The third purpose was to provide for the maximum generation of electric power, in so far as this was consistent with flood control and navigation.

The details of administration are under a general manager, who is appointed by and held responsible to the board of directors. The personnel is not subject to Civil Service. The Authority meets its operating costs from its commercial revenues; but it must obtain the approval of Congress for new construction, the Bureau of the Budget for its administrative expenses, and the Treasury for its borrowing.

In many respects, the most controversial part of the TVA program related to the generation and transmission of power. This brought it into direct conflict with private utilities, which led to litigation. In *Ashwander* v. *Tennessee Valley Authority* (1936),[12] the Supreme Court upheld the Authority's right to acquire transmission properties from the Alabama Power Company. The Court held that the construction and operation of Wilson Dam were a legitimate exercise of the government's war powers and the navigation features of the project were a legitimate exercise of federal powers under the Commerce Clause. The right of the TVA to engage in generating, transmitting, distributing, and selling electricity in competition with private companies was the issue at bar in *Tennessee Electric Power Company* v. *Tennessee Valley Authority* (1939).[13] The Court held that the private utilities had no legal standing to bring such a suit, because they had not been given monopolistic privileges by their charters or franchises. Then, in 1941, the state of Oklahoma sought to enjoin the construction of a federal dam and reservoir on the Red River.[14] The Court agreed that the project was part of a comprehensive flood control and navigation scheme of long standing and the matter was therefore one of congressional discretion. By these cases, the question of constitutionality was seemingly put to rest.

The TVA Power Program

Although the production of power was a matter of secondary importance, according to the law, it has been the most controversial aspect of the TVA undertaking and, in the eyes of the public, probably the most important. Under the act, the Tennessee Valley Authority was authorized to sell surplus power not used in its operations and to construct, purchase, or lease transmission facilities. In the sale of power, preference was to be given to states, municipalities, and co-operative organizations not run for profit. Power was also to be sold for the particular benefit of domestic and rural customers. To aid in developing this policy, the Authority was permitted to extend limited credit to public agencies to aid them in acquiring, improving, or operating distribution facilities and generating plants.

Almost at the outset, the Tennessee Valley Authority decided that, with very minor exceptions, it would not engage in the retail distribution of electrical energy. Accordingly, it entered into power contracts with municipalities and co-operatives. Under these contracts, which were for 20 years, electricity was sold under conditions whereby purchasers were required to adopt a standard schedule of resale rates designed to promote the consumption of electrical energy. Purchasers were required to distribute electricity without discrimination among customers of the same class, and without rebates or special concessions. Municipal purchasers were required to keep their books according to a uniform system pre-

[12]297 U.S. 288.
[13]306 U.S. 118.
[14]*Oklahoma* v. *Atkinson Co.*, 313 U.S. 508 (1941).

scribed by the Authority. The electrical utility of a municipality was to be run by a separate department, and municipalities were required to apply the revenues derived from the sale of electricity in a prescribed order of preference, starting with operating expenses. The TVA thus became a comprehensive regulatory commission for all municipal enterprises and co-operatives that entered into contracts with it. In 1955, there were 97 municipal power systems and 51 rural electrical co-operatives distributing TVA power. In 1955, over 60 per cent of TVA power came from steam plants, approximately 30 per cent from hydroelectric, and the remainder from purchases and interchange.

According to Professor Glaeser,[15] the rate of return on the average depreciated investment in power facilities in 1955 was 4¼ per cent, and the average return for the full 22 years of operation was 4 per cent per annum. The number of retail customers served by TVA distributors increased from 12,000 in 1934 to 1,388,000 in 1955, and the average annual home use grew from 600 kilowatt-hours to 5,240. In the same period, rural electrification in the valley increased from 15,000 farms to 400,000, and the rate of growth of use of electricity in the area was at least double that of the rest of the country.

The TVA is exempt from federal taxation, but it makes payments in lieu of taxes to the state and county governments in its operating area. The wholesale power contracts with local distributors require the latter to make payments in lieu of taxes to their respective local governments. Nevertheless, the total burden on gross revenues is considerably less than that of privately owned utilities.

In 1959, Congress amended the TVA Act to require payment to the Treasury of not less than $10 million in each of the first five years, following the legislation, $15 million in each of the next five years, and $20 million each year thereafter until a total of $1 billion has been repaid. The Authortiy was also required to pay a return on the government investment in power facilities at a rate equal to the Treasury's marketable debt for that year. The Authority may now issue bonds on notes up to $750 million a year to assist in financing its program. These obligations are not guaranteed by the federal government.[16] The new law also forbade the Authority to extend its operation more than five miles beyond its existing boundaries. At the present time, about 66 per cent of the generating capacity is from steam plants.

There is little doubt that the Tennessee Valley development has been a great boon to the area served. On the basis of the cost allocations, the power part of the project has met its obligations and provided a return of about 4 per cent. It has served to stimulate the use of electricity and has promoted experimentation in rate making. It has not returned to the

[15]Glaeser, *op. cit.*, pp. 560 f.
[16]Public Law 86–137 (1959).

various governments the equivalent in taxes which private utilities have to pay. Nor are the rates charged in the TVA area a valid yardstick for private utilities, for reasons given earlier in this chapter.

The project, as a whole, is not self-liquidating and was not intended to be. Joint costs are now divided 42 per cent to power, 27 per cent to navigation, and 31 per cent to flood control. Flood control benefits are difficult to evaluate, but the navigation costs are scarcely warranted by the results. If an attempt were made to impose tolls on the waterway, with the objective of covering the full costs involved in providing the navigation facilities, there is little likelihood that the traffic would be able to bear it. What the total evaluation of the project should be may be a matter of marked difference of opinion; but by the standards which private enterprise is required to meet in order to survive, the power and transportation aspects of the Tennessee Valley Authority cannot be judged an economic success.

RURAL ELECTRIFICATION

Electrification of rural areas developed very slowly, on the whole, until the mid 1930's. The National Electric Light Association, in 1923, undertook a program to explain and encourage the use of electrical equipment and appliances on the farm. Growth of use in agricultural areas, however, was hampered by the high costs of distribution arising from low density of customers except in areas such as the coastal region of Southern California, which was almost completely electrified by 1930. For a country as a whole, the number of electrified farms increased from 2.8 per cent in 1923 to 11.5 per cent in 1931; by 1954, approximately 90 per cent of the farmers had electricity in their homes. Much of the impetus to this growth came from the national power program of the federal government during the 1930's.

The Rural Electrification Act

The Rural Electrification Administration was set up in 1935 by executive order, under authority of the Emergency Relief Act. The administration was given permanent status the next year by the Rural Electrification Act. This legislation provided for a 10-year program. The Reconstruction Finance Corporation was authorized to loan $50 million for the first year, and Congress was to appropriate up to $40 million a year for the next 9 years. The money appropriated was to be loaned for the construction and operation of generating plants and transmission and distribution lines, for the purpose of furnishing electricity in rural areas to persons who were not receiving central station service. The act provided that preference should be given to the loan applications of public bodies and farm co-operatives. Originally, the maximum term for construction loans was 25 years; but the Pace Act, in 1944, increased the amortization period to 35 years and lowered the interest rate to 2 per cent. The initial legislation also empowered the administrator to make loans to finance wiring and plumbing and the purchase of appliances. The borrowing agencies were loaned the money at 2 per cent; the REA recommended that they charge the individual borrower an additional 2 per cent to cover handling charges. The administration of the program was in the hands of an administrator, appointed by the President with the approval of the Senate, for a 10-year term. The agency is now under the direction of the Department of Agriculture.

Farm Co-operatives

The general policy of the Rural Electrification Administration was to develop rural electrification through farm co-operatives. These were set up as corporations which sold their services only to the members, who were also the stockholders. The REA advanced money to the co-operatives to construct the capital equipment. It also furnished legal, financial, and operating advice, and thereby exercised considerable supervision over the co-operatives. Because the co-operatives were "nonprofit" organizations, in that they paid dividends only to the members who were also the customers, they were not subject to federal income and excess profits taxes, and were generally exempt from state income taxes.

One problem facing the co-operatives was that of securing electricity at low rates. The Administration claimed that the co-operatives could not be self-supporting unless rates of not more than 1.5 cents per kilowatt-hour were obtained. This was lower than the wholesale rates paid by municipal utilities. The private utilities objected to giving preferential treatment to the co-operatives. As a result, the REA adopted the policy of sponsoring the construction of generating plants.

In terms of providing electricity to rural areas, the Rural Electrification Administration has been a success. It has brought the price of electricity down to the point where most of the individual farmers can now afford it. The REA has also developed some technical improvements that have lowered local distribution costs where the load density was light. It forced private utilities into lower rural rates. This was brought about by the private utilities discriminating in favor of rural users, the urban consumer carrying the greater burden of the nonallocable costs. The REA program has not carried the costs, however, that private utilities are required to bear. It cannot be acclaimed as an economic success by the standards which have to be applied to them.[17]

THE ST. LAWRENCE WATERWAY

The Great Lakes and the St. Lawrence River provide the greatest system of inland waterways in the world, penetrating almost to the middle of the North American continent and providing a deep-sea channel

[17]In 1949 a program was undertaken to extend telephone service into rural areas, following the same pattern as that for electricity, and administered by the REA.

of 35 feet from Montreal to the Atlantic Ocean, almost 1,100 miles away. Steps have been undertaken to overcome some of the obstacles in the route between Montreal and Lake Superior ever since 1795. By 1914, improvements had turned this route into an interior waterway 2,300 miles in length, with a minimum channel from Montreal to Duluth of 14 feet in depth. In 1932, Canada enlarged the locks at the Welland Canal to a depth of 30 feet over the sills; and in 1943, the United States installed the MacArthur Locks at Sault Ste. Marie, with a depth of 31 feet over the sills. The most formidable remaining obstacles were in the 160 miles between Lake Ontario and Montreal.

Because the Great Lakes–St. Lawrence system is an international waterway with navigation and power aspects, joint development by the two countries came under consideration after 1909. In that year, the governments of the two countries signed a treaty which created an International Joint Commission as an administrative agency of the two governments. In the ensuing years, discussion concerning a dual-purpose project was carried on, but no action resulted therefrom. In July, 1948, separate applications were filed by the New York Power Authority and by the Hydroelectric Power Commission of Ontario for an order of approval of the joint project for developing power from the International Joint Commission. Simultaneously, the New York Power Authority applied to the Federal Power Commission for a license to carry out the American portion. The Federal Power Commission denied the application of the New York Power Authority, recommending federal construction of the entire project instead. Meanwhile, the Canadian government hinted that it might undertake an all-Canadian route if agreement could not be reached with the United States. In June, 1952, Canada and the United States submitted concurrent applications to the International Joint Commission for an order of approval of the power project. In July, 1953, the Federal Power Commission granted a license to the New York Power Authority to construct, in conjunction with the Ontario Hydroelectric Power Commission, the dams and necessary powerworks in the International Rapids section, as approved by the International Joint Commission. Congress responded to these developments by the passage of the Seaway Act in 1954. (See Figure 11.)

The Seaway Act of 1954

Navigation. Although the St. Lawrence project is a dual-purpose one, the legislation separates the navigation from the power production function. To deal with navigation, the Act created a public corporation known as the St. Lawrence Seaway Development Corporation, subject to the direction and supervision of the President or the head of such department as he might designate. President Eisenhower assigned the responsibility to the Secretary of Commerce in 1958. Management of the Corporation is in the hands of an administrator and a deputy administrator, who

FIGURE 11

JOINT UNITED STATES–CANADIAN ST. LAWRENCE SEAWAY

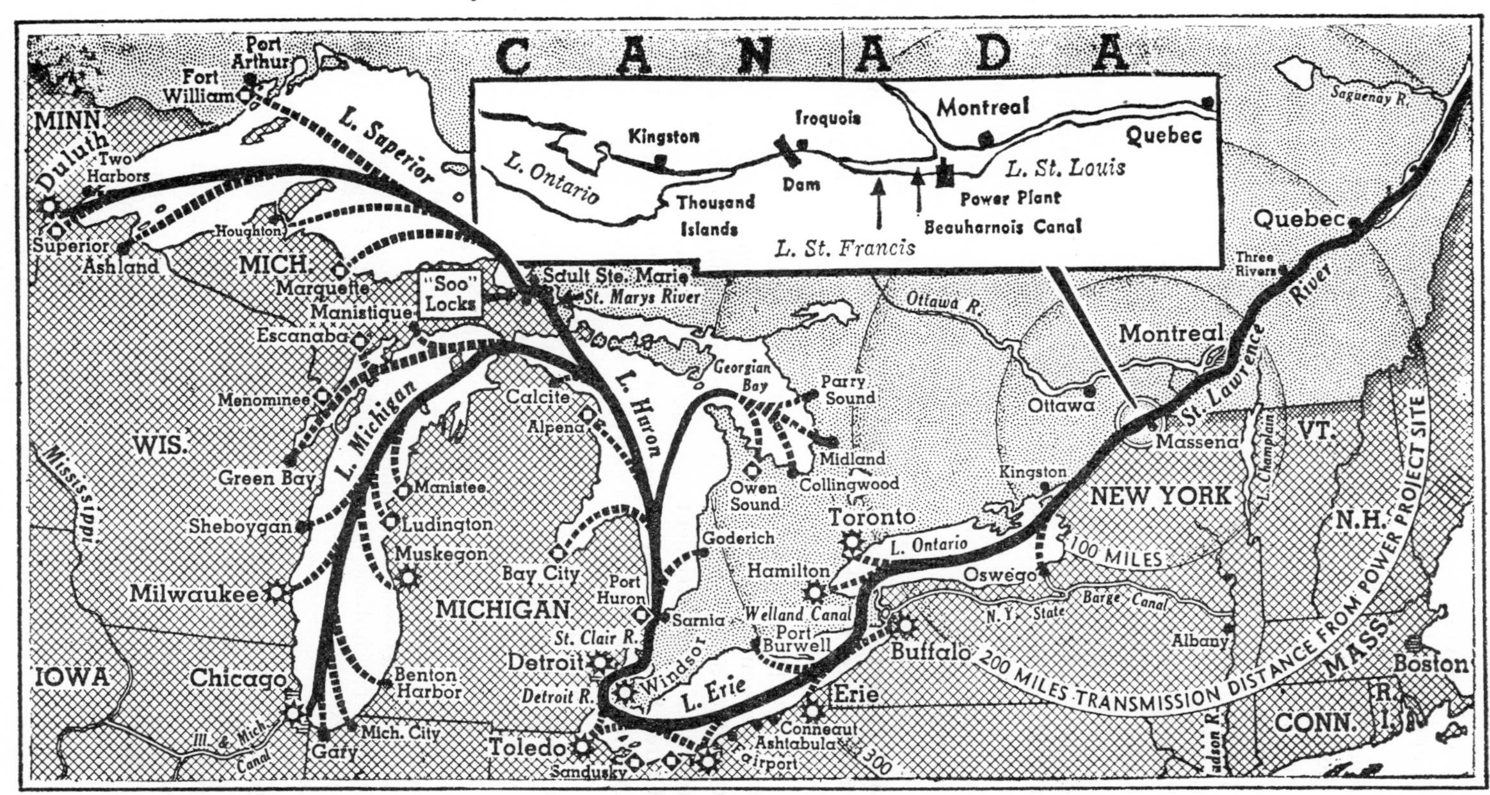

NOTE: Heavy line traces complete course of seaway. Inset map indicates section completed in 1958.

are to be advised by a board of five members. All of these officials are to be appointed by the President, with the advice and consent of the Senate.

The Corporation is authorized, in co-operation with the St. Lawrence Seaway Authority of Canada, to construct, operate, and maintain the single-stage navigation project in the International Rapids section and to do the necessary dredging in the Thousand Islands section. It is able to co-ordinate its activities with the New York Power Authority. The Corporation was directed to borrow $105 million through the sale of revenue bonds. The Army Engineers estimated the cost of the United States portion of the seaway construction at $88,074,000. The Canadian portion will cost $174,950,000, according to estimates.

The total investment of the United States government as of December 31, 1963, was $138.6 million, consisting of $122.6 million in bonds and $16 million in interest. Of the latter, $9,556,000 was deferred interest, the remainder being capitalized to give a total of $129 million in revenue bonds and capitalized interest.[18] The Corporation is authorized to borrow up to $140 million from the U.S. Treasury at interest rates fixed at the time of borrowing. These rates have ranged from 2⅜ to 4¼ per cent, and currently average 3.42 per cent. Some construction work is still taking place, but the Administrator estimates that the project is 98 per cent complete.

The project is supposed to be self-liquidating; and to this end, the Corporation was directed to negotiate an agreement with the appropriate Canadian agency on the tolls to be levied and an equitable division of revenues. If no agreement was reached, tolls were to be established for the United States portion of the Seaway. Five rules prescribe the basis for arriving at the tolls:

1. The rates shall be fair and reasonable, with consideration being given to the special character of bulk cargoes of raw materials.
2. Rates shall vary according to the character of the cargo.
3. Rates for vessel and ballast may be less than for passengers and cargo.
4. Rates shall be calculated so as to cover the costs of operating and maintaining the works of the Corporation, including depreciation, interest on obligations, and payments in lieu of taxes.
5. Rates shall be calculated with a view to providing sufficient revenue to amortize principal and debts and obligations of the Corporation over a period not to exceed fifty years.

The Corporation is not required to pay taxes equivalent to federal corporate income and excess profits taxes.

A schedule of tolls was drawn up for the opening of the Seaway in 1959. Under an agreement between the Corporation and the St. Lawrence Seaway Authority of Canada, the Secretary of Commerce established a Tolls Committee in January, 1963. The agreement also provided that after five complete seasons of navigation, and not later than July 1, 1964,

[18]St. Lawrence Seaway Development Corporation, *Annual Report*, 1963.

a report was to be made by the two Authorities to their respective governments on the sufficiency of the authorized tolls. There is little possibility that the agreed-upon tolls will meet the revenue requirements under the existing or currently prospective volume of traffic.

The Power Project

A 50-year license to construct, operate, and maintain the power facilities on the American side of the International Rapids was issued to the New York Power Authority. It was required to co-operate with the Army Engineers in constructing and improving navigation facilities associated with the power project and to furnish power, free of cost, for the operation and maintenance of the navigation facilities. All of the joint costs of the dual-purpose project were allocated to the power phase of the project.

Under the license, the Federal Power Commission is to determine the actual legitimate original cost of the initial project and any improvements thereon. The New York Power Authority is entitled to earn 6 per cent per annum on the net investment after the first 20 years of operation. Earnings above this 6 per cent are regarded as surplus, one half of which may be used to make up any deficiency in the stipulated return in the past or to establish amortization reserves to retire investment. The licensee must pay fees upon power output to reimburse the United States for costs of administration.[19]

Appraisal

The feasibility of the St. Lawrence project will have to wait the test of operation. If it fails to measure up to the estimates of self-liquidation, there will still be those that will insist that it was worth while and necessary. Whether power will be able to carry the obligations imposed upon it will depend upon the development of the market. Navigation, as far as the joint costs are concerned, is treated as a by-product. Its capacity to cover the direct costs incurred for it is a matter of serious doubt at the present time. In addition, large sums of money will have to be spent on harbor improvements before the advantages of deep-sea shipping can be realized by the Great Lakes ports.

One of the principal arguments for the seaway project was the problem of iron ore for the steel mills located around the Great Lakes. The depletion of the high-grade ores around Lake Superior has led to the search for other sources. Liberia, Venezuela, and Labrador seemed to be the important ones. The St. Lawrence project was therefore considered essential to the steel industry of the Great Lakes region. In addition, it was felt that a protected route for Labrador ore was vital to national

[19]A careful treatment of the St. Lawrence project is given by Professor Glaeser in "The St. Lawrence Seaway and Power Project," *Land Economics*, Vol. XXX, No. 4 (November, 1954), pp. 289–300; also *Public Utilities in American Capitalism*, chap. 30.

defense. Whatever may be the validity of the national defense argument, the contention that the Seaway is necessary for Midwest industry is valid only if that industry can pay for the costs of supplying the navigation facilities. However, now that it is constructed, tolls should be levied on the monopoly principle of maximizing revenue to obtain as much as possible up to the necessary amount. The burden of investment in transport in the United States today is of such magnitude that economy in utilization is a national necessity. Tolls so as to maximize traffic on the St. Lawrence, rather than revenue, will not contribute to this end.

CONCLUSION

Public ownership of utilities in the United States has been undertaken on a considerable scale and, as was pointed out earlier, seems to be unavoidable in some activities, especially in the regional developments and multiple-use projects undertaken by the federal government. None of the main publicly owned projects described in the foregoing sections are self-sustaining under the standards which private enterprise must meet. The Boulder Canyon project comes closest to meeting the test; but the Metropolitan Water District, which relies on Boulder Canyon, has fallen far short. This is not to say that these public projects should meet the private enterprise tests; but when assertions concerning their success are made, these assertions need to be supported by evidence other than the prices that are charged by the undertakings for their services, or the lower costs for other activities, such as water transport, that they make possible. The economic appraisal of the industrial functions of the projects needs to be based on the criteria used to measure the economical allocation and utilization of resources.

The major public projects which have been undertaken in this country have been able to rely heavily on special privilege. Their capital has been raised through channels supported by the public credit, and they have been relieved of the heavy tax burdens of private enterprise. In other words, these public undertakings are supported by the private enterprise sector of the economy. As far as the nonvendible functions of the projects are concerned, this is inescapable; but that is not so for the vendible functions. Certainly, the economic basis of public ownership does not offer a model for public ownership of all productive enterprise, because if this took place, it would be necessary to make the undertakings economically self-sustaining, as a whole, since there would be no private enterprise to call upon. Even public ownership of all utilities and the transport system of the country today would place a severe strain on the rest of the economy, if the present basis of public ownership and operation were applied without modification.

The operation of publicly owned enterprises in accordance with the standards of efficiency for economical allocation and utilization of resources calls for a separation of the industrial functions of public projects from the others. These industrial functions should then be subjected to the types of pressures and incentives common to the economic field. This would call for administrative changes in most of the undertakings and very probably would dim the enthusiasm for public ownership. At least, it would expose the issues more sharply than has been done to date.

Appendix I

Selections from the Antitrust Laws*

SHERMAN ACT[1]

SECTION 1.[2] Every contract, combination in the form of trust or otherwise, or conspiracy, in restraint of trade or commerce among the several States, or with foreign nations, is hereby declared to be illegal: *Provided*, That nothing herein contained shall render illegal, contracts or agreements prescribing minimum prices for the resale of a commodity which bears, the label or containers of which bears, the trade mark, brand, or name of the producer or distributor of such commodity and which is in free and open competition with commodities of the same general class produced or distributed by others, when contracts or agreements of that description are lawful as applied to intrastate transactions, under any statute, law, or public policy now or hereafter in effect in any State, Territory, or the District of Columbia in which such resale is to be made, or to which the commodity is to be transported for such resale, and the making of such contracts or agreements shall not be an unfair method of competition under section 5, as amended and supplemented, of the act entitled "An Act to create a Federal Trade Commission to define its powers and duties, and for other purposes," approved September 26, 1914: *Provided further*, That the preceding proviso shall not make lawful any contract or agreement, providing for the establishment or maintenance of minimum resale prices on any commodity herein involved, between manufacturers, or between producers, or between wholesalers, or between brokers, or between factors, or between retailers, or between persons, firms, or corporations in competition with each other. Every person who shall make any contract or engage in any combination or conspiracy hereby declared to be illegal shall be deemed guilty of a misdemeanor, and, on conviction thereof, shall be punished by fine not exceeding fifty thousand dollars,[3] or by imprisonment not exceeding one year, or by both said punishments, in the discretion of the court.

SEC. 2. Every person who shall monopolize, or attempt to monopolize, or combine or conspire with any other person or persons, to monopo-

*The Antitrust Laws, reproduced from a staff report to the Antitrust Subcommittee of the Committee on the Judiciary (House of Representatives, 85th Cong., 2d sess.) (Washington, D.C.: United States Government Printing Office, 1959).

[1]26 Stat. 209; 15 U.S.C. 1–7; Public, No. 190, 51st Cong. (1890).

[2]As amended by Miller-Tydings Act, 50 Stat. 693; 15 U.S.C. 1; Public, No. 314, 75th Cong. (1937).

[3]1955 Amendment, Act of July 7, 1955, amended section by substituting words "fifty thousand dollars" for the figure "$5,000" in the last sentence. 69 Stat. 282; 15 U.S.C. 1; Public Law 135, 84th Cong.

lize any part of the trade or commerce among the several States, or with foreign nations, shall be deemed guilty of a misdemeanor, and, on conviction thereof, shall be punished by fine not exceeding fifty thousand dollars,[4] or by imprisonment not exceeding one year, or by both said punishments, in the discretion of the court.

SEC. 3. Every contract, combination in form of trust or otherwise, or conspiracy, in restraint of trade or commerce in any Territory of the United States or of the District of Columbia, or in restraint of trade or commerce between any such Territory and another, or between any such Territory or Territories and any State or States or the District of Columbia, or with foreign nations, or between the District of Columbia and any State or States or foreign nations, is hereby declared illegal. Every person who shall make any such contract or engage in any such combination or conspiracy, shall be deemed guilty of a misdemeanor, and, on conviction thereof, shall be punished by fine not exceeding fifty thousand dollars,[5] or by imprisonment not exceeding one year, or by both said punishments, in the discretion of the court.

SEC. 4. The several district[6] courts of the United States are hereby invested with jurisdiction to prevent and restrain violations of this act; and it shall be the duty of the several district attorneys of the United States, in their respective districts, under the direction of the Attorney General, to institute proceedings in equity to prevent and restrain such violations. Such proceedings may be by way of petition setting forth the case and praying that such violation shall be enjoined or otherwise prohibited. When the parties complained of shall have been duly notified of such petition the court shall proceed, as soon as may be, to the hearing and determination of the case; and pending such petition and before final decree, the court may at any time make such temporary restraining order or prohibition as shall be deemed just in the premises.

SEC. 5. Whenever it shall appear to the court before which any proceeding under section four of this act may be pending, that the ends of justice require that other parties should be brought before the court, the court may cause them to be summoned, whether they reside in the district in which the court is held or not; and subpoenas to that end may be served in any district by the marshal thereof.

SEC. 6. Any property owned under any contract or by any combination, or pursuant to any conspiracy (and being the subject thereof) mentioned in section one of this act, and being in the course of trans-

[4]1955 Amendment, Act of July 7, 1955, amended section by substituting words "fifty thousand dollars" for words "five thousand dollars." 69 Stat. 282; 15 U.S.C. 1; Public Law 135, 84th Cong.

[5]1955 Amendment, Act of July 7, 1955, amended section by substituting words "fifty thousand dollars" for words "five thousand dollars." 69 Stat. 282; 15 U.S.C. 3; Public Law 135, 84th Cong.

[6]Act of March 3, 1911, 36 Stat. 1167, substituted "district" for "circuit" courts.

portation from one State to another, or to a foreign country, shall be forfeited to the United States, and may be seized and condemned by like proceedings as those provided by law for the forfeiture, seizure, and condemnation of property imported into the United States contrary to law.

SEC. 7.[7] Repealed.

SEC. 8. That the word "person," or "persons," wherever used in this act shall be deemed to include corporations and associations existing under or authorized by the laws of either the United States, the laws of any of the Territories, the laws of any State, or the laws of any foreign country.

CLAYTON ACT[8]

Be it enacted by the Senate and House of Representatives of the United States of America in Congress assembled, That "antitrust laws," as used herein, includes the Act entitled "An Act to protect trade and commerce against unlawful restraints and monopolies," approved July second, eighteen hundred and ninety; sections seventy-three to seventy-seven, inclusive, of an Act entitled "An Act to reduce taxation, to provide revenue for the Government, and for other purposes," of August twenty-seventh, eighteen hundred and ninety-four; an Act entitled "An Act to amend sections seventy-three and seventy-six of the Act of August twenty-seventh, eighteen hundred and ninety-four, entitled 'An Act to reduce taxation, to provide revenue for the Government, and for other purposes,' " approved February twelfth, nineteen hundred and thirteen; and also this Act.

"Commerce," as used herein, means trade or commerce among the several States and with foreign nations, or between the District of Columbia or any Territory of the United States and any State, Territory, or foreign nation, or between any insular possessions or other places under the jurisdiction of the United States, or between any such possession or place and any State or Territory of the United States or the District of Columbia or any foreign nation, or within the District of Columbia or any Territory or any insular possession or other place under the jurisdiction of the United States: *Provided,* That nothing in this Act contained shall apply to the Philippine Islands.

The word "person" or "persons" wherever used in this Act shall be deemed to include corporations and associations existing under or authorized by the laws of either the United States, the laws of any of the Territories, the laws of any State, or the laws of any foreign country.

[7]Repealed by Act of July 7, 1955, 69 Stat. 283; Public Law 137, 84th Cong. and superseded by Sec. 4, Clayton Act (15 U.S.C. 15). To become effective six months after enactment (July 7, 1955).

[8]38 Stat. 730; 15 U.S.C. 12 ff.; Public, No. 212, 63d Cong. (1914).

SEC. 2.[9] (*a*) That it shall be unlawful for any person engaged in commerce, in the course of such commerce, either directly or indirectly, to discriminate in price between different purchasers of commodities of like grade and quality, where either or any of the purchases involved in such discrimination are in commerce, where such commodities are sold for use, consumption, or resale within the United States or any Territory thereof or the District of Columbia or any insular possession or other place under the jurisdiction of the United States, and where the effect of such discrimination may be substantially to lessen competition or tend to create a monopoly in any line of commerce, to or injure, destroy, or prevent competition with any person who either grants or knowingly receives the benefit of such discrimination, or with customers of either of them: *Provided*, That nothing herein contained shall prevent differentials which make only due allowance for differences in the cost of manufacture, sale, or delivery resulting from the differing methods or quantities in which such commodities are to such purchasers sold or delivered: *Provided, however*, That the Federal Trade Commission may, after due investigation and hearing to all interested parties, fix and establish quantity limits, and revise the same as it finds necessary, as to particular commodities or classes of commodities, where it finds that available purchasers in greater quantities are so few as to render differentials on account thereof unjustly discriminatory or promotive of monopoly in any line of commerce; and the foregoing shall then not be construed to permit differentials based on differences in quantities greater than those so fixed and established: *And provided further*, That nothing herein contained shall prevent persons engaged in selling goods, wares, or merchandise in commerce from selecting their own customers in bona fide transactions and not in restraint of trade: *And provided further*, That nothing herein contained shall prevent price changes from time to time where in response to changing conditions affecting the market for or the marketability of the goods concerned, such as but not limited to actual or imminent deterioration of perishable goods, obsolescence of seasonal goods, distress sales under court process, or sales in good faith in discontinuance of business in the goods concerned.

(*b*) Upon proof being made, at any hearing on a complaint under this section, that there has been discrimination in price or services or facilities furnished, the burden of rebutting the prima facie case thus made by showing justification shall be upon the person charged with a violation of this section, and unless justification shall be affirmatively shown, the Commission is authorized to issue an order terminating the discrimination: *Provided, however*, That nothing herein contained shall prevent a seller rebutting the prima facie case thus made by showing

[9]As amended by Robinson-Patman Act, 49 Stat. 1526; 15 U.S.C. 13; Public, No. 692, 74th Cong. (1936).

that his lower price or the furnishing of services or facilities to any purchaser or purchasers was made in good faith to meet an equally low price of a competitor, or the services or facilities furnished by a competitor.

(*c*) That it shall be unlawful for any person engaged in commerce, in the course of such commerce, to pay or grant, or to receive or accept, anything of value as a commission, brokerage, or other compensation, or any allowance or discount in lieu thereof, except for services rendered in connection with the sale or purchase of goods, wares, or merchandise, either to the other party to such transaction or to an agent, respresentative, or other intermediary therein where such intermediary is acting in fact for or in behalf, or is subject to the direct or indirect control, of any party to such transaction other than the person by whom such compensation is so granted or paid.

(*d*) That it shall be unlawful for any person engaged in commerce to pay or contract for the payment of anything of value to or for the benefit of a customer of such person in the course of such commerce as compensation or in consideration for any services or facilities furnished by or through such customer in connection with the processing, handling, sale, or offering for sale of any products or commodities manufactured, sold, or offered for sale by such person, unless such payment or consideration is available on proportionally equal terms to all other customers competing in the distribution of such products or commodities.

(*e*) That it shall be unlawful for any person to discriminate in favor of one purchaser against another purchaser or purchasers of a commodity bought for resale, with or without processing, by contracting to furnish or furnishing, or by contributing to the furnishing of, any services or facilities connected with the processing, handling, sale, or offering for sale of such commodity so purchased upon terms not accorded to all purchasers on proportionally equal terms.

(*f*) That it shall be unlawful for any person engaged in commerce, in the course of such commerce, knowingly to induce or receive a discrimination in price which is prohibited by this section.

Sec. 3. That it shall be unlawful for any person engaged in commerce, in the course of such commerce, to lease or make a sale or contract for sale of goods, wares, merchandise, machinery, supplies, or other commodities, whether patented or unpatented, for use, consumption, or resale within the United States or any Territory thereof or the District of Columbia or any insular possession or other place under the jurisdiction of the United States, or fix a price charged therefor, or discount from, or rebate upon, such price, on the condition, agreement, or understanding that the lessee or purchaser thereof shall not use or deal in the goods, wares, merchandise, machinery, supplies, or other commodity of a competitor or competitors of the lessor or seller, where the effect of such lease, sale, or contract for sale or such condition, agreement, or understanding may be to substantially lessen competition or tend to create a monopoly in any line of commerce.

SEC. 4. That any person who shall be injured in this business or property by reason of anything forbidden in the antitrust laws may sue therefor in any district court of the United States in the district in which the defendant resides or is found or has an agent, without respect to the amount in controversy, and shall recover threefold the damages by him sustained, and the cost of suit, including a reasonable attorney's fee.

SEC. 4A.[10] Whenever the United States is hereafter injured in its business or property by reason of anything forbidden in the antitrust laws it may sue therefor in the United States district court for the district in which the defendant resides or is found or has an agent, without respect to the amount in controversy, and shall recover actual damages by it sustained and the cost of suit.

SEC. 4B.[11] Any action to enforce any cause of action under sections 4 or 4A shall be forever barred unless commenced within four years after the cause of action accrued. No cause of action barred under existing law on the effective date of this Act shall be revived by this Act.

SEC. 5. (*a*)[12] A final judgment or decree heretofore or hereafter rendered in any civil or criminal proceeding brought by or on behalf of the United States under the antitrust laws to the effect that a defendant has violated said laws shall be prima facie evidence against such defendant in any action or proceeding brought by any other party against such defendant under said laws or by the United States under section 4A, as to all matters respecting which said judgment or decree would be an estoppel as between the parties thereto: *Provided*, That this section shall not apply to consent judgments or decrees entered before any testimony has been taken or to judgments or decrees entered in actions under section 4A.

(*b*)[13] Whenever any civil or criminal proceeding is instituted by the United States to prevent, restrain, or punish violations of any of the antitrust laws, but not including an action under section 4A, the running of the statute of limitations in respect of every private right of action arising under said laws and based in whole or in part on any matter complained of in said proceeding shall be suspended during the pendency thereof and for one year thereafter: *Provided, however*, That whenever the running of the statute of limitations in respect of a cause of action arising under section 4 is suspended hereunder, any action to enforce such cause of action shall be forever barred unless commenced either within the period of suspension or within four years after the cause of action accrued.

SEC. 6. That the labor of a human being is not a commodity or

[10]As added July 7, 1955, sec. 1, 69 Stat. 282; 15 U.S.C. 15a, to become effective six months after enactment. Public Law 137, 84th Cong.

[11]*Ibid.*; 15 U.S.C. 15b.

[12]As amended July 7, 1955, sec. 2, 69 Stat. 283; 15 U.S.C. 16 (a); Public Law 137, 84th Cong.

[13]As amended July 7, 1955, sec. 2, 69 Stat. 283; 15 U.S.C. 16 (b); Public Law 137, 84th Cong.

article of commerce. Nothing contained in the antitrust laws shall be construed to forbid the existence and operation of labor, agricultural, or horticultural organizations, instituted for the purposes of mutual help, and not having capital stock or conducted for profits, or to forbid or restrain individual members of such organizations from lawfully carrying out the legitimate objects thereof; nor shall such organizations, or the members thereof, be held or construed to be illegal combinations or conspiracies in restraint of trade under the antitrust laws.

SEC. 7.[14] That no corporation engaged in commerce shall acquire, directly or indirectly, the whole or any part of the stock or other share capital and no corporation subject to the jurisdiction of the Federal Trade Commission shall acquire the whole or any part of the assets of another corporation engaged also in commerce, where in any line of commerce in any section of the country, the effect of such acquisition may be substantially to lessen competition, or to tend to create a monopoly.

No corporation shall acquire, directly or indirectly, the whole or any part of the stock or other share capital and no corporation subject to the jurisdiction of the Federal Trade Commission shall acquire the whole or any part of the assets of one or more corporations engaged in commerce, where in any line of commerce in any section of the country, the effect of such acquisition, of such stocks or assets, or of the use of such stock by the voting or granting of proxies or otherwise, may be substantially to lessen competition, or to tend to create a monopoly.

This section shall not apply to corporations purchasing such stock solely for investment and not using the same by voting or otherwise to bring about, or in attempting to bring about, the substantial lessening of competition. Nor shall anything contained in this section prevent a corporation engaged in commerce from causing the formation of subsidiary corporations for the actual carrying on of their immediate lawful business, or the natural and legitimate branches or extensions thereof, or from owning and holding all or a part of the stock of such subsidiary corporations, when the effect of such formation is not to substantially lessen competition.

Nor shall anything herein contained be construed to prohibit any common carrier subject to the laws to regulate commerce from aiding in the construction of branches or short lines so located as to become feeders to the main line of the company so aiding in such construction or from acquiring or owning all or any part of the stock of such branch lines, nor to prevent any such common carrier from acquiring and owning all or any part of the stock of a branch or short line constructed by an independent company where there is no substantial competition between the company owning the branch line so constructed and the company

[14]As amended by Celler-Kefauver Act, Dec. 29, 1950, 64 Stat. 1125; 15 U.S.C. 18; Public Law 899, 81st Cong.

owning the main line acquiring the property or an interest therein, nor to prevent such common carrier from extending any of its lines through the medium of the acquisition of stock or otherwise of any other common carrier where there is no substantial competition between the company extending its lines and the company whose stock, property, or an interest therein is so acquired.

Nothing contained in this section shall be held to affect or impair any right heretofore legally acquired: *Provided*, That nothing in this section shall be held or construed to authorize or make lawful anything heretofore prohibited or made illegal by the antitrust laws, nor to exempt any person from the penal provisions thereof or the civil remedies therein provided.

Nothing contained in this section shall apply to transactions duly consummated pursuant to authority given by the Civil Aeronautics Board, Federal Communications Commission, Federal Power Commission, Interstate Commerce Commission, the Securities and Exchange Commission in the exercise of its jurisdiction under section 10 of the Public Utility Holding Company Act of 1935, the United States Maritime Commission, or the Secretary of Agriculture under any statutory provision vesting such power in such Commission, Secretary, or Board.

SEC. 8.[15] No private banker or director, officer, or employee of any member bank of the Federal Reserve System or any branch thereof shall be at the same time a director, officer, or employee of any other bank, banking association, savings bank, or trust company organized under the National Bank Act or organized under the laws of any State or of the District of Columbia, or any branch thereof, except that the Board of Governors of the Federal Reserve System may by regulation permit such service as a director, officer, or employee of not more than one other such institution or branch thereof; but the foregoing prohibition shall not apply in the case of any one or more of the following or any branch thereof:

(1) A bank, banking association, savings bank, or trust company, more than 90 per centum of the stock of which is owned directly or indirectly by the United States or by any corporation of which the United States directly or indirectly owns more than 90 per centum of the stock.

(2) A bank, banking association, savings bank, or trust company which has been placed formally in liquidation or which is in the hands of a receiver, conservator, or other official exercising similar functions.

(3) A corporation, principally engaged in international or foreign banking or banking in a dependency or insular possession of the United States which has entered into an agreement with the Board of Governors of the Federal Reserve System pursuant to section 25 of the Federal Reserve Act.

[15]First three paragraphs as amended, August 23, 1935, 49 Stat. 717.

(4) A bank, banking association, savings bank, or trust company, more than 50 per centum of the common stock of which is owned directly or indirectly by persons who own directly or indirectly more than 50 per centum of the common stock of such member bank.

(5) A bank, banking association, savings bank, or trust company not located and having no branch in the same city, town, or village as that which such member bank or any branch thereof is located, or in any city, town, or village contiguous or adjacent thereto.

(6) A bank, banking association, savings bank, or trust company not engaged in a class or classes of business in which such member bank is engaged.

(7) A mutual savings bank having no capital stock.

Until February 1, 1939, nothing in this section shall prohibit any director, officer, or employee of any member bank of the Federal Reserve System, or any branch thereof, who is lawfully serving at the same time as a private banker or as a director, officer, or employee of any other bank, banking association, savings bank, or trust company, or any branch thereof, on the date of enactment of the Banking Act of 1935, from continuing such service.

The Board of Governors of the Federal Reserve System is authorized and directed to enforce compliance with this section, and to prescribe such rules and regulations as it deems necessary for that purpose.

That from and after two years from the date of the approval of this Act no person at the same time shall be a director in any two or more corporations, any one of which has capital, surplus, and undivided profits aggregating more than $1,000,000, engaged in whole or in part in commerce, other than banks, banking associations, trust companies, and common carriers subject to the Act to regulate commerce, approved February fourth, eighteen hundred and eighty-seven, if such corporations are or shall have been theretofore, by virtue of their business and location of operation, competitors, so that the elimination of competition by agreement between them would constitute a violation of any of the provisions of any of the antitrust laws. The eligibility of a director under the foregoing provision shall be determined by the aggregate amount of the capital, surplus, and undivided profits, exclusive of dividends declared but not paid to stockholders, at the end of the fiscal year of said corporation next preceding the election of directors; and when a director has been elected in accordance with the provisions of this Act, it shall be lawful for him to continue as such for one year thereafter.

When any person elected or chosen as a director or officer or selected as an employee of any bank or other corporation subject to the provisions of this Act is eligible at the time of his election or selection to act for such bank or other corporation in such capacity, his eligibility to act in such capacity shall not be affected, and he shall not become or be deemed amenable to any of the provisions hereof by reason of any change in the affairs of such bank or other corporation, from whatsoever cause, whether specifically excepted by any of the provisions hereof or not, until the expiration of one year from the date of his election or employment.

SEC. 11.[16] That authority to enforce compliance with sections 2, 3, 7, and 8 of this Act by the persons respectively subject thereto is hereby vested in the Interstate Commerce Commission where applicable to common carriers subject to the Interstate Commerce Act, as amended; in the Federal Communications Commission where applicable to common carriers engaged in wire or radio communication or radio transmission of energy; in the Civil Aeronautics Board where applicable to air carriers and foreign air carriers subject to the Civil Aeronautics Act of 1938; in the Federal Reserve Board where applicable to banks, banking associations, and trust companies; and in the Federal Trade Commission where applicable to all other character of commerce to be exercised as follows:

Whenever the Commission or Board vested with jurisdiction thereof shall have reason to believe that any person is violating or has violated any of the provisions of sections 2, 3, 7, and 8 of this Act, it shall issue and serve upon such person and the Attorney General a complaint stating its charges in that respect, and containing a notice of a hearing upon a day and at a place therein fixed at least thirty days after the service of said complaint. The person so complained of shall have the right to appear at the place and time so fixed and show cause why an order should not be entered by the Commission or Board requiring such person to cease and desist from the violation of the law so charged in said complaint. The Attorney General shall have the right to intervene and appear in said proceeding and any person may make application, and upon good cause shown may be allowed by the Commission or Board, to intervene and appear in said proceeding by counsel or in person. The testimony in any such proceeding shall be reduced to writing and filed in the office of the Commission or Board. If upon such hearing the Commission or Board, as the case may be, shall be of the opinion that any of the provisions of said sections have been or are being violated, it shall make a report in writing, in which it shall state its findings as to the facts, and shall issue and cause to be served on such person an order requiring such person to cease and desist from such violations, and divest itself of the stock, or other share capital, or assets, held or rid itself of the directors chosen contrary to the provisions of sections 7 and 8 of this Act, if any there be, in the manner and within the time fixed by said order. Until a transcript of the record in such hearing shall have been filed in a United States court of appeals, as hereinafter provided, the Com-

[16]As amended by Celler-Kefauver Act, Dec. 29, 1950, 64 Stat. 1126; 15 U.S.C. 21; Public Law 899, 81st Cong.

mission or Board may at any time, upon such notice, and in such manner as it shall deem proper, modify or set aside, in whole or in part, any report or any order made or issued by it under this section.

FEDERAL TRADE COMMISSION ACT[17]

SEC. 5. (*a*) (1)[18] Unfair methods of competition in commerce, and unfair or deceptive acts or practices in commerce, are hereby declared unlawful.

(2) Nothing contained in this Act or in any of the Antitrust Acts shall render unlawful any contracts or agreements prescribing minimum or stipulated prices, or requiring a vendee to enter into contracts or agreements prescribing minimum or stipulated prices, for the resale of a commodity which bears, or the label or container of which bears, the trade-mark, band, or name of the producer or distributor of such commodity and which is in free and open competition with commodities of the same general class produced or distributed by others, when contracts or agreements of that description are lawful as applied to intrastate transactions under any statute, law, or public policy now or hereafter in effect in any State, Territory, or the District of Columbia in which such resale is to be made, or to which the commodity is to be transported for such resale.

(3) Nothing contained in this Act or in any of the Antitrust Acts shall render unlawful the exercise or the enforcement of any right or right of action created by any statute, law, or public policy now or hereafter in effect in any State, Territory, or the District of Columbia, which in substance provides that willfully and knowingly advertising, offering for sale, or selling any commodity at less than the price or prices prescribed in such contracts or agreements whether the person so advertising, offering for sale, or selling is or is not a party to such a contract or agreement, is unfair competition and is actionable at the suit of any person damaged thereby.

(4) Neither the making of contracts or agreements as described in paragraph (2) of this subsection, nor the exercise or enforcement of any right or right of action as described in paragraph (3) of this subsection shall constitute an unlawful burden or restraint upon, or interference with, commerce.

(5) Nothing contained in paragraph (2) of this subsection shall make lawful contracts or agreements providing for the establishment or maintenance of minimum or stipulated resale prices on any commodity referred to in paragraph 2 of this subsection, between manufacturers, or between producers, or between wholesalers, or between brokers, or between factors, or between retailers, or between persons, firms, or corporations in competition with each other.

[17]38 Stat. 717; 15 U.S.C. 41 ff; Public, No. 203, 63d Cong. (1914).

[18]As amended by McGuire Act, July 14, 1952, sec. 2, 66 Stat. 632; 15 U.S.C. 45 (a); Public Law 542, 82d Cong.

(6)[19] The Commission is hereby empowered and directed to prevent persons, partnerships, or corporations, except banks, common carriers subject to the Acts to regulate commerce, air carriers and foreign air carriers subject to the Civil Aeronautics Act of 1938, and persons, partnerships, or corporations insofar as they are subject to the Packers and Stockyards Act, 1921, as amended, except as provided in section 406 (b) of said Act, from using unfair methods of competition in commerce and unfair or deceptive acts or practices in commerce.

(*b*)[20] Whenever the Commission shall have reason to believe that any such person, partnership, or corporation has been or is using any unfair method of competition or unfair or deceptive act or practice in commerce, and if it shall appear to the Commission that a proceeding by it in respect thereof would be to the interest of the public, it shall issue and serve upon such person, partnership, or corporation a complaint stating its charges in that respect and containing a notice of a hearing upon a day and at a place therein fixed at least thirty days after the service of said complaint. The person, partnership, or corporation so complained of shall have the right to appear at the place and time so fixed and show cause why an order should not be entered by the Commission requiring such person, partnership, or corporation to cease and desist from the violation of the law so charged in said complaint. Any person, partnership, or corporation may make application, and upon good cause shown may be allowed by the Commission to intervene and appear in said proceeding by counsel or in person. The testimony in any such proceeding shall be reduced to writing and filed in the office of the Commission. If upon such hearing the Commission shall be of the opinion that the method of competition or the act or practice in question is prohibited by this Act, it shall make a report in writing in which it shall state its findings as to the facts and shall issue and cause to be served on such person, partnership, or corporation an order requiring such person, partnership, or corporation to cease and desist from using such method of competition or such act or practice. Until the expiration of the time allowed for filing a petition for review, if no such petition has been duly filed within such time, or, if a petition for review has been filed within such time then until the record in the proceeding has been filed in a court of appeals of the United States, as hereinafter provided, the Commission may at any time, upon such notice and in such manner as it shall deem proper, modify or set aside, in whole or in part, any report or any order made or issued by it under this section. After the expiration of the time allowed for filing a petition for review, if no such petition has been duly filed within such time, the Commission may at any time, after notice and opportunity for hearing, reopen and alter, modify, or set aside, in whole or in part, any report or order made or issued by it under this section,

[19]As amended Sept. 2, 1958, 72 Stat. 1750; Public Law 85–909.

[20]As amended by Act of Aug. 28, 1958, sec. 3 (a), 72 Stat. 942; 15 U.S.C. 5 (b); Public Law 85–791.

whenever in the opinion of the Commission conditions of fact or of law have so changed as to require such action or if the public interest shall so require: *Provided, however,* That the said persons, partnership, or corporation may, within sixty days after service upon him or it of said report or order entered after such a reopening, obtain a review thereof in the appropriate court of appeals[21] of the United States, in the manner provided in subsection (c) of this section.

(c)[22] Any person, partnership, or corporation required by an order of the Commission to cease and desist from using any method of competition or act or practice may obtain a review of such order in the court of appeals of the United States, within any circuit where the method of competition or the act or practice in question was used or where such person, partnership, or corporation resides or carries on business, by filing in the court, within sixty days from the date of the service of such order, a written petition praying that the order of the Commission be set aside. A copy of such petition shall be forthwith transmitted by the clerk of the court to the Commission, and thereupon the Commission shall file in the court the record in the proceeding, as provided in section 2112 of title 28, United States Code. Upon such filing of the petition the court shall have jurisdiction of the proceeding and of the question determined therein concurrently with the Commission until the filing of the record and shall have power to make and enter a decree affirming, modifying, or setting aside the order of the Commission, and enforcing the same to the extent that such order is affirmed and to issue such writs as are ancillary to its jurisdiction or are necessary in its judgment to prevent injury to the public or to competitors pendente lite. The findings of the Commission as to the facts, if supported by evidence, shall be conclusive. To the extent that the order of the Commission is affirmed, the court shall thereupon issue its own order commanding obedience to the terms of such order of the Commission. If either party shall apply to the court for leave to adduce additional evidence, and shall show to the satisfaction of the court that such additional evidence is material and that there were reasonable grounds for the failure to adduce such evidence in the proceeding before the Commission, the court may order such additional evidence to be taken before the Commission and to be adduced upon the hearing in such manner and upon such terms and conditions as to the court may seem proper. The Commission may modify its findings as to the facts, or make new findings, by reason of the additional evidence so taken, and it shall file such modified or new findings, which, if supported by evidence, shall be conclusive, and its recommendation, if any, for the modification or setting aside of its original order, with the return

[21]Act of May 24, 1949, sec. 127, 63 Stat. 107; Public Law 72, 81st Cong., amended all laws in force on Sept. 1, 1948, in which reference is made to "circuit court of appeals" by substituting therefor the words "court of appeals."

[22]As amended by Act of Aug. 28, 1958, sec. 3 (b), 72 Stat. 942; 15 U.S.C. 5 (c).

of such additional evidence. The judgment and decree of the court shall be final, except that the same shall be subject to review by the Supreme Court upon certiorari, as provided in section 240 of the Judicial Code.[23]

(*d*)[24] Upon the filing of the record with it the jurisdiction of the court of appeals of the United States to affirm, enforce, modify, or set aside orders of the Commission shall be exclusive.

(*e*) Such proceedings in the court of appeals shall be given precedence over other cases pending therein, and shall be in every way expedited. No order of the Commission or judgment of court to enforce the same shall in anywise relieve or absolve any person, partnership, or corporation from any liability under the Antitrust Acts.

(*f*) Complaints, orders, and other processes of the Commission under this section may be served by anyone duly authorized by the Commission, either (*a*) by delivering a copy thereof to the person to be served, or to a member of the partnership to be served, or the president, secretary, or other executive officer or a director of the corporation to be served; or (*b*) by leaving a copy thereof at the residence or the principal office or place of business of such person, partnership, or corporation; or (*c*) by registering and mailing a copy thereof addressed to such person, partnership, or corporation at his or its residence or principal office or place of business. The verified return by the person so serving said complaint, order, or other process setting forth the manner of said service shall be proof of the same, and the return post office receipt for said complaint, order, or other process registered and mailed as aforesaid shall be proof of the service of the same.

(*g*) An order of the Commission to cease and desist shall become final

(1) Upon the expiration of the time allowed for filing a petition for review, if no such petition has been duly filed within such time; but the Commission may thereafter modify or set aside its order to the extent provided in the last sentence of subsection (b); or

(2) Upon the expiration of the time allowed for filing a petition for certiorari, if the order of the Commission has been affirmed, or the petition for review dismissed by the court of appeals, and no petition for certiorari has been duly filed; or

(3) Upon the denial of a petition for certiorari, if the order of the Commission has been affirmed or the petition for review dismissed by the court of appeals; or

(4) Upon the expiration of thirty days from the date of issuance of the mandate of the Supreme Court, if such Court directs that the order of the Commission be affirmed or the petition for review dismissed.

[23]Act of June 25, 1948, sec. 39, 62 Stat. 992; Public Law 773, 80th Cong., repealed sec. 240 of the Judicial Code. Sec. 1254 of Title 28, U.S. Code, contains similar provisions.

[24]As amended by Act of Aug. 28, 1958, sec. 3 (c), 72 Stat. 943; 15 U.S.C. 5 (d).

(*h*) If the Supreme Court directs that the order of the Commission be modified or set aside, the order of the Commission rendered in accordance with the mandate of the Supreme Court shall become final upon the expiration of thirty days from the time it was rendered, unless within such thirty days either party has instituted proceedings to have such order corrected to accord with the mandate, in which event the order of the Commission shall become final when so corrected.

(*i*) If the order of the Commission is modified or set aside by the court of appeals, and if (1) the time allowed for filing a petition for certiorari has expired and no such petition has been duly filed, or (2) the petition for certiorari has been denied, or (3) the decision of the court has been affirmed by the Supreme Court, then the order of the Commission rendered in accordance with the mandate of the court of appeals shall become final on the expiration of thirty days from the time such order of the Commission was rendered, unless within such thirty days either party has instituted proceedings to have such order corrected so that it will accord with the mandate, in which event the order of the Commission shall become final when so corrected.

(*j*) If the Supreme Court orders a rehearing; or if the case is remanded by the court of appeals to the Commission for a rehearing, and if (1) the time allowed for filing a petition for certiorari has expired, and no such petition has been duly filed, or (2) the petition for certiorari has been denied, or (3) the decision of the court has been affirmed by the Supreme Court, then the order of the Commission rendered upon such rehearing shall become final in the same manner as though no prior order of the Commission had been rendered.

(*k*) As used in this section the term "mandate," in case a mandate has been recalled prior to the expiration of thirty days from the date of issuance thereof, means the final mandate.

(*l*)[25] Any person, partnership, or corporation who violates an order of the Commission to cease and desist after it has become final, and while such order is in effect, shall forfeit and pay to the United States a civil penalty of not more than $5,000 for each violation, which shall accrue to the United States and may be recovered in a civil action brought by the United States. Each separate violation of such an order shall be a separate offense, except that in the case of a violation through continuing failure or neglect to obey a final order of the Commission each day of continuance of such failure or neglect shall be deemed a separate offense.

[25]As amended by Act of March 16, 1950, sec. 4 (c), 64 Stat. 21; 15 U.S.C. 5 (1); Public Law 459, 81st Cong.

Appendix II

Selected References for Further Reading

Bibliographical material on the public regulation of business, even for the United States alone in the area covered by this book, is enormous. It includes books; articles in both professional and trade publications; reports of local, state, and federal governments; legislative hearings and investigations; reports of agencies assigned to deal with the subject matter discussed in this text; decisions of courts and administrative bodies; special studies by legislative agencies, research foundations, and institutions established for the purpose of furthering economic investigation. There is a vast body of literature dealing with the technical, engineering, managerial, legal, administrative, political, marketing, financial, and geographical aspects of the various segments of our economic activity. The literature on other countries by both American and foreign authors is very large, much of it of direct relevance to problems in the United States. The following list of references is selected primarily from economic literature. It is intended to serve principally as an initial source of information for those who wish to pursue further study of the subject matter, as well as an immediate reference list to other material for those who wish to investigate a particular topic more intensively, or who seek other authors' points of view and exposition. The rather extensive footnote references in the various chapters refer to articles and other specific sources not included in this list of references. No attempt has been made to assemble anything resembling an adequate bibliography on any topic; this can be gathered according to the interests of a particular reader from sources identified below.

The following books give a broad coverage and contain extensive reading references at the end of each chapter: M. Anshen and F. D. Wormuth, *Private Enterprise and Public Policy* (New York: The Macmillan Co., 1954); J. M. Clark, *Social Control of Business* (2d ed.; New York: McGraw-Hill Book Co., Inc., 1939); M. E. Dimock, *Business and Government* (4th ed.; New York: Holt, Rinehart and Winston, 1961); H. Koontz and R. W. Gable, *Public Control of Economic Enterprise* (New York: McGraw-Hill Book Co., Inc., 1956); V. A. Mund, *Government and Business* (3d ed.; New York: Harper & Bros., 1960); D. S. Watson, *Economic Policy* (Boston: Houghton Mifflin Co., Inc., 1960); C. Wilcox, *Public Policies Toward Business* (rev. ed.; Homewood, Ill.: Richard D. Irwin, Inc., 1960). A comprehensive treatment is given in L. S. Lyon, M. W. Watkins, V. Agramson, *Government and Economic Life* (2 Vols.; Washington, D.C.: The Brookings Institution, 1939). A compilation of readings is contained in H. J. Levin, *Business Organization and Public Policy* (New York: Reinhart and Co., Inc., 1958); R. B. Heflebower and

G. W. Stocking, *Readings in Industrial Organization and Public Policy,* Vol. VIII (Homewood, Ill.: Richard D. Irwin, Inc., 1958).

The American Economic Association, *Index of Economic Journals* (Homewood, Ill.: Richard D. Irwin, Inc., 1886–1963) provides a complete index by subject and author of all publications in English since 1886 in the various economic journals. Comprehensive lists of current articles will be found quarterly in the *American Economic Review* and the *Economic Journal. The Encyclopedia of the Social Sciences* (Vols I-XV, 1935; New York: Macmillan Co.), contains a wealth of information on the social sciences.

READING SUGGESTIONS

Part I. The State and Economic Life

Brookings Lectures, Economics and Public Policy (Washington, D.C.: Brookings Institution, 1955); J. M. Clark, *Social Control of Business* (2d ed., New York: McGraw-Hill Book Co., Inc., 1939), chaps. ix, xxviii, xxx; H. Ellis (ed.), *A Survey of Contemporary Economics,* Vol. I (Homewood, Ill.; Richard D. Irwin, Inc., 1949), chaps. xii and xiii; M. Friedman, *Capitalism and Freedom* (Chicago: University of Chicago Press, 1962); J. K. Galbraith, *The Affluent Society* (Boston: Houghton Mifflin Co., 1958); J. Hackett and A. M. Hackett, *Economic Planning in France* (Cambridge: Harvard University Press, 1963); F. A. Hayek, *The Road to Serfdom* (Chicago: The University of Chicago Press, 1944); R. E. Kirk, *The Conservative Mind* (Chicago: Henry Regnery Co., 1953); B. E. Lippincott (ed.), *On the Economic Theory of Socialism* (Minneapolis: University of Minnesota Press, 1938); W. A. Orton, *The Liberal Tradition* (New Haven: Yale University Press, 1945); L. Robbins, *The Theory of Economic Policy* (London: Macmillan & Co., Ltd., 1953); W. Röpke, *A Humane Economy* (Chicago: Henry Regnery Co., 1960); G. H. Sabine, *A History of Political Theory* (rev. ed.; New York: Henry Holt & Co., Inc., 1950), chaps. xxxi, xxxii and xxxiv; J. Schumpeter, *Capitalism, Socialism and Democracy* (New York: Harper & Bros., 1942), chaps. xi, xvi, xxiii; H. C. Simons, *Economic Policy for a Free Society* (Chicago: University of Chicago Press, 1948); O. H. Taylor, *Economics and Liberalism* (Cambridge: Harvard University Press, 1955); D. S. Watson, *Economic Policy* (Boston: Houghton Mifflin Co., Inc., 1960), chaps. i–vi; B. Wooton, *Freedom under Planning* (Chapel Hill: University of North Carolina Press, 1945); D. M. Wright, *Democracy and Progress* (New York: Macmillan Co., 1948).

Part II. Institutional and Organizational Arrangements

W. Adams, *The Structure of American Industry* (3d ed.; New York: Macmillan Co., 1961), structure and price policies in different industries; B. A. Arneson, *Elements of Constitutional Law* (New York: Harper & Bros., 1928), an elementary treatise on the law of the American Constitution; J. S. Bain, *Industrial Organization* (New York: John Wiley & Sons, Inc., 1959), chaps. ii, iii, and iv; A. A. Berle and G. C. Means, *The Modern Corporation and Private Property* (New York: Macmillan Co., 1933), Books I, II, IV, a pioneer treatise on the modern corporation; Betty Bock, *Concentration Patterns in Manufacturing* (New York: National Industrial Conference Board, Inc., 1959); J. C. Bonbright and G. C. Means, *The Holding Company* (New York: McGraw-Hill Book Co., Inc., 1932), the most complete study of the holding company; A. R. Burns, *The Decline of Competition* (New York: McGraw-Hill Book Co., Inc., 1936); R. K. Carr, *The Supreme Court and Judicial Review* (New York: Farrar and Rinehart, Inc., 1942), an appraisal of the Supreme Court as a political agency; J. M. Clark, *Social Control of Business* (2d ed.; New York: McGraw-Hill Book Co., Inc., 1939), chaps. i–v; C. Edwards, *Maintaining Competition* (New York: McGraw-Hill Book Co., Inc., 1949), chap. iv; C. Edwards, *Big Business and the Policy of Competition* (Cleveland: The Press of Western Reserve University, 1956), the case for and against big business; H. Ellis (ed.), *A Survey of Contemporary Economics*, Vol. I (Homewood, Ill.; Richard D. Irwin, Inc., 1952), chap. iii on Concentration, chap. xiii on Capitalism; *Encyclopedia of the Social Sciences* (New York: Macmillan Co.), articles on Common Law, Contract, Capitalism, Equity, Civil Law, Corporations, Trusts; R. Heflebower and G. W. Stocking, *Readings in Industrial Organization and Public Policy* (Homewood, Ill.; Richard D. Irwin, Inc., 1958); J. Herling, *The Great Price Conspiracy* (Washington, D.C.: R. B. Luce Co., 1962), the General Electric price conspiracy; E. Jones, *The Trust Problem in the United States* (New York: Macmillan Co., 1929), chaps. i–iv on organization; A. D. H. Kaplan, *Big Enterprise in a Competitive Society* (Washington, D.C.: The Brookings Institution, 1954), a discussion of big business in the modern setting; R. H. Leftwich, *The Price System and Resource Allocation* (rev. ed.; New York: Holt, Rinehart & Winston, 1960), chaps. i and ii; R. Liefman, *Cartels, Trusts and Concerns* (New York: E. P. Dutton & Co., 1922), Introduction and chap. i; M. Lindahl and W. Carter, *Corporate Concentration and Public Policy* (3d ed.; Englewood Cliffs, N.J.: Prentice-Hall, Inc., 1959), chaps. i and ii on individualism; Part I, The Modern Corporation; Part II, Industry Studies; L. S. Lyon, M. W. Watkins, V. Abramson, *Government and Economic Life*, Vol. I (Washington, D.C.: The Brookings Institution, 1939), chaps. i, ii, iv on institutional and organizational arrangements; E. Mansfield (ed.), *Monopoly Power and Economic Performance* (New York: W. W. Norton & Co., Inc., 1964), Parts I, II, III; A. Marshall, *Principles of Economics* (8th ed.; London: Macmillan & Co., Ltd., 1922), Books I and II on fundamental notions in economics; E. S. Mason, *Economic Concentration and the Monopoly Problem* (Cambridge: Harvard University Press, 1957); E. S. Mason, *The Corporation and Modern Society* (Cambridge: Harvard University Press, 1959); J. P. Miller (ed.), *Competition, Cartels and Their Regulation* (Amsterdam: North-Holland Publishing Co., 1962); National Bureau of Economic Research, *Business Concentration and Price Policy* (Princeton: Princeton University Press, 1955), pp. 15–239; 331–61; J. U. Nef, *The United States and Civilization* (Chicago: University of Chicago Press, 1941); R. L. Nelson, *Merger Movements in American Industry* (Princeton: Princeton University Press, 1959); B. Schwartz, *American Constitutional Law* (London: The Cambridge University Press, 1955), a careful study of American constitutional law with a comparison with the British system; G. J. Stigler, *Five Lectures on Economic Problems* (London: Longmans, Green & Co., 1949); Temporary National Economic Committee, Mono. No. 18, *Trade Association Survey;* Mono. No. 21, *Competition and Monopoly in American Industry*; Mono. No. 29, *Distribution of Ownership in the 200 Largest Nonfinancial Corporations* (Washington, D.C.: United States Government Printing Office, 1940); C. S. Tippetts and S. Livermore, *Business Organization and Control* (2d ed.; New York: D. Van Nostrand Co., Inc., 1941), Part I, a detailed study of the various forms of business organization; H. C. Vatter, *The U.S. Economy in the 1950's* (New York: W. W. Norton & Co., Inc., 1963), a detailed study of economic change in the American economy from 1950 to 1960; M. W. Watkins, *Indus-*

trial Combinations and Public Policy (Boston: Houghton Mifflin Co., 1927), Part I on industrial organization; Part II, studies of particular combinations; S. Whitney, *Antitrust Policies*, Vol. I (New York: The Twentieth Century Fund, 1958), a detailed study of twenty industries.

Part III. The Pricing Process and Public Policy

Report of the Attorney General's National Committee, *Antitrust Laws* (Washington, D.C.: United States Government Printing Office, 1955), chap. vii on Economic Indicia of Competition and Monopoly; *Administrative Prices: A Compendium on Public Policy*, Subcommittee on Antitrust and Monopoly of the Committee on the Judiciary, United States Senate (88 Cong., 1st sess.) (Washington, D.C.; United States Government Printing Office, 1963), a series of articles on pricing policies; J. Bain, *Industrial Organization* (New York: John Wiley & Sons, Inc., 1959), chaps. ii, iv, and v; M. M. Bober, *Intermediate Price and Income Theory* (rev. ed.; New York: W. W. Norton & Co., Inc., 1962), chaps. v, vi on the theory of production; E. H. Chamberlin, *Theory of Monopolistic Competition* (6th ed.; Cambridge: Harvard University Press, 1950), especially Appendix B on economies of scale; J. M. Clark, *Competition as a Dynamic Process* (Washington, D.C.: The Brookings Institution, 1961), a comprehensive review of the competitive process; J. M. Clark, *Economics of Overhead Costs* (Chicago: University of Chicago Press, 1923), chaps. ii–vii, xi, xx, and xxi; J. Dean, *Managerial Economics* (New York: Prentice-Hall, Inc., 1951), chaps. ii, v, vii, and ix; Donald Dewey, *Monopoly in Economics and Law* (Chicago: Rand McNally & Co., 1959), chaps. i–viii; J. F. Due, *Intermediate Economic Theory* (rev. ed.; Homewood, Ill.: Richard D. Irwin, Inc., 1953), chaps. vii, viii, xi; C. D. Edwards, *Maintaining Competition* (New York: McGraw-Hill Book Co., Inc., 1949), chaps. v, vi; H. Ellis (ed.), *A Survey of Contemporary Economics*, Vol. I (Homewood, Ill.: Richard D. Irwin, Inc., 1948), chap. iv; E. Jones, *The Trust Problem in the United States* (New York: Macmillan Co., 1929), chap. xx; A. D. H. Kaplan, J. Dirlam, R. Lanzillotti, *Pricing in Big Business* (Washington, D.C.: The Brookings Institution, 1958); F. H. Knight, *Risk, Uncertainty and Profit* (London: London School of Economics, reprint No. 16, 1933), pp. xi–xxxii, and chaps. ii, iv, and vi; R. H. Leftwich, *The Price System and Resource Allocation* (rev. ed.; New York: Holt, Rinehart and Winston, 1960), chaps. vii and viii on production; M. Lindahl and W. Carter, *Corporate Concentration and Public Policy* (3d ed.; Englewood Cliffs, N.J.: Prentice-Hall, Inc., 1959), chaps. xvi and xvii on monopoly and oligopoly; L. S. Lyon, M. W. Watkins and V. Abramson, *Government and Economic Life*, Vol. II (Washington, D.C.: The Brookings Institution, 1939), chaps. xxiii–xxv, xxvii, and xxviii; H. J. Levin, *Business Organization and Public Policy* (New York: Rinehart & Co., Inc., 1958), Part I, secs. A–D; F. Machlup, *The Economics of Sellers Competition* (Baltimore: The Johns Hopkins Press, 1952); A. Marshall, *Principles of Economics* (8th ed.; London: Macmillan & Co., Ltd., 1922), Book V, demand, supply and value; D. H. MacGregor, *Industrial Combinations* (London: London School of Economics, reprint No. 1, 1935); National Bureau of Economic Research, *Cost Behavior and Price Policy* (New York, 1943); A. C. Pigou, *The Economics of Welfare* (3d ed.; London: Macmillan & Co., Ltd., 1929), chap. xvii on discriminating monopoly; A. Papandreaou and J. T. Wheeler, *Competition and Its Regulation* (New York: Prentice-Hall, Inc., 1954), chap. vi on price discrimination and the multiproduct firm; Joan Robinson, *Economics of Imperfect Competition* (London: Macmillan & Co., Ltd., 1934), chaps. xv and xvi on price discrimination; E. A. G. Robinson, *The Structure of Competitive Industry* (New York: Harcourt, Brace & Co., 1932); E. A. G. Robinson, *Monopoly* (New York: Pitman Publishing Corp., 1941); G. Stigler and K. Boulding (eds.), *Readings in Price Theory* (Homewood, Ill.: Richard D. Irwin, Inc., 1952), Part II on Costs and Returns; G. J. Stigler, *The Theory of Price* (New York: Macmillan Co., 1946); G. W. Stocking and M. W. Watkins, *Monopoly and Free Enterprise* (New York: The Twentieth Century Fund, 1951), chaps. iv–vii; Temporary National Economic Committee, Mono. No. 1, *Price Behavior and Business Policy;* Mono. No. 7, *Measurement of the Social Performance of Business;* Mono. No. 13, *Relative Efficiency of Large, Medium-Sized and Small-Scale Business;* Mono. No. 21, *Competition and Monopoly in American Business;* Mono. No. 32, *Economic Standards of Government Price Control* (Washington, D.C.: United States Government Printing Office, 1940); L. W. Weiss, *Economics and American Industry* (New York: John Wiley & Sons, 1961), pricing and structures of a selected group of industries.

Part IV. The Antitrust Laws

W. Adams and H. M. Gray, *Monopoly in America* (New York: Macmillan Co., 1955), the influence of government on the growth of monopoly; *Administered Prices: A Compendium on Public Policy,* article by J. P. Dirlam on the Celler-Kefauver Act; *Antitrust Bulletin* (1956–), articles on enforcement of antitrust; Report of the Attorney General's Committee, *Antitrust Laws,* a legal analysis of antitrust enforcement; M. H. Bernstein, *Regulating Business by Independent Commission* (Princeton: Princeton University Press, 1955), a critical evaluation of commissions; *Congress and the Monopoly Problem:* Fifty-six Years of Antitrust Development, Select Committee on Small Business, House of Representatives (85 Cong., 1st sess.), House Doc. 240 (Washington, D.C., United States Government Printing Office, 1957); J. B. Dirlam and A. E. Kahn, *Fair Competition* (Ithaca, N.Y.: Cornell University Press, 1954), an analysis of the new antitrust policy; Donald Dewey, *Monopoly in Economics and Law* (Chicago: Rand McNally & Co., 1959), chaps. ix–xvii; C. Edwards, *The Price Discrimination Law* (Washington, D.C.: The Brookings Institution, 1959), a detailed analysis of the enforcement of the Robinson-Patman Act; F. Fetter, *The Masquerade of Monopoly* (New York: Harcourt, Brace & Co., 1931), a caustic evaluation of antitrust enforcement; H. J. Friendly, *The Federal Administrative Agencies* (Cambridge: Harvard University Press, 1962); W. Gorter, *United States Shipping Policy* (New York: Harper & Bros., 1956); E. Hexner, *International Cartels* (Chapel Hill: University of North Carolina Press, 1945); J. W. Jenks and W. E. Clark, *The Trust Problem,* (5th rev. ed.; New York: Doubleday, Doran & Co., Inc., 1929); E. Jones, *The Trust Problem in the United States* (New York: Macmillan Co., 1929), a detailed study of the early trusts; C. Kaysen and D. F. Turner, *Antitrust Policy: A Legal and Economic Analysis* (Cambridge: Harvard University Press, 1959) contains detailed recommendations for revision of the antitrust laws; M. Lindahl and W. Carter, *Corporate Concentration and Public Policy* (3d ed.; Englewood Cliffs, N.J.: Prentice-Hall, Inc., 1959), chaps. xviii–xxv; L. S. Lyon, M. W. Watkins, and V. Abramson, *Government and Economic Life,* Vol. I (Washington, D.C.: The Brookings Institution, 1939), chaps. vi, x, xi; F. Machlup, *An Economic Review of the Patent System,* Study of the Subcommittee on Patents, Trademarks, and Copyrights (Committee on the Judiciary, U.S. Senate, 85th Cong., 2d. sess.) (Washington, D.C.: United States Government Printing Office, 1958); F. Machlup, *The Political Economy of Monopoly* (Baltimore: The Johns Hopkins Press, 1952); E. Mansfield (ed.), *Monopoly Power and Economic Performance*, Part III on the antitrust laws; D. D. Martin, *Mergers and the Clayton Act* (Berkeley and Los Angeles: The University of California, 1959), a detailed analysis of the development of Sec. 7; D. Marx, *International Shipping Cartels* (Princeton: Princeton University Press, 1953); L. Mason, *The Language of Dissent* (New York: The Long House, Inc., 1961), a scathing indictment of the policies of the Federal Trade Commission; M. S. Massel, *Competition and Monopoly: Legal and Economic Issues* (Washington, D.C.: The Brookings Institution, 1962), contains an exhaustive list of footnotes at the end of the book; J. P. Miller, *Unfair Competition* (Cambridge: Harvard University Press, 1941); J. P. Miller (ed.), *Competition, Cartels and Their Regulation* (Amsterdam: North-Holland Publishing Co., 1962); A. D. Neale, *The Antitrust Laws of the United States of America* (Cambridge: Harvard University Press, 1960), a comprehensive legal analysis by a Britisher; E. F. Penrose, *The Economics of the International Patent System* (Baltimore: The Johns Hopkins Press, 1951); H. Seager and C. A. Gulick, *Trust and Corporation Problems* (New York: Harper & Bros., 1929), a detailed analysis of trusts and the application of the antitrust laws; G. W. Stocking and M. W. Watkins, *Cartels in Action* (New York: The Twentieth Century Fund, 1946), case studies of international cartels; G. W. Stocking and M. W. Watkins, *Cartels or Competition* (New York: The Twentieth Century Fund, 1948), an analysis of the cartel problem; G. W. Stocking and M. W. Watkins, *Monopoly and Free Enterprise* (New York: The Twentieth Century Fund, 1951), monopoly and competition in the United States; H. F. Taggart, *Cost Justification* (Ann Arbor: University of Michigan Press, 1959), analysis of cost considerations under the Robinson-Patman Act; Temporary National Economic Committee, Mono. No. 16, *Antitrust in Action;* Mono. No. 31, *Patents and Free Enterprise;* Mono. No. 38, *Construction and Enforcement of the Antitrust Laws;* Mono. No. 42, *The Basing Point Problem, Final Report of the T.N.E.C.* (Washington, D.C.: United States Government Printing Office, 1941); H. Thorelli, *The Federal Antitrust Policy* (Baltimore: The Johns Hopkins Press, 1955), a thorough analysis of antitrust to 1904; U.S. Dept. of Commerce, Patent Office, *The Story of the American Patent System 1790–1940* (Washington, D.C.: United States Government Printing Office, 1940); M. W. Watkins, *Industrial Combinations and the Public Policy* (Boston: Houghton Mifflin Co., 1927), Part III; S. Whitney, *Antitrust Policies,* Vol. II (New York: The Twentieth Century Fund, 1958), analysis of leading antitrust cases and their consequences; C. Wilcox, *Public Policies Toward Business* (rev. ed.; Homewood, Ill.: Richard D. Irwin, Inc., 1960), Part II; J. G. Van Cise, *The Federal Antitrust Laws* (Washington, D.C.: American Enterprise Association, 1962), analysis of antitrust for the lay reader; J. G. Van Cise, *Understanding the Antitrust Laws* (New York: Practising Law Institute, 1963), analysis of the antitrust laws for practicing lawyers.

Part V. Regulation of Transportation and Public Utilities

General texts on Transportation:

T. C. Bigham and M. J. Roberts, *Transportation, Principles and Problems* (2d ed.; New York: McGraw-Hill Book Co., Inc., 1952), deals with all the agencies and contains extensive references at the end of each chapter; S. Daggett, *Principles of Inland Transportation* (4th ed.; New York: Harper & Bros., 1955), strong on geography and traffic, with extensive references at the end of each chapter; M. Fair and E. W. Williams, *Economics of Transportation* (rev. ed.; New York: Harper & Bros., 1959), deals comprehensively with both transport economics and traffic, contains extensive references; D. P. Locklin, *Economics of Transportation* (5th ed.; Homewood, Ill.: Richard D. Irwin, Inc., 1960), a comprehensive treatment of American transportation with extensive references at the end of each chapter; D. F. Pegrum, *Transportation: Economics and Public Policy* (Homewood, Ill.: Richard D. Irwin, Inc., 1963), emphasis on economic principles as applied to transportation and public policy with President Kennedy's Message in Appendix I and extensive references in Appendix II; R. E. Westmeyer, *Economics of Transportation* (New York: Prentice-Hall, Inc., 1952), covers all of the agencies.

General texts on Public Utilities:

I. R. Barnes, *The Economics of Public Utility Regulation* (New York: F. S. Crofts and Co., 1942), an exhaustive treatment of public utility regulation; E. W. Clemens, *Economics and Public Utilities* (New York: Appleton-Century-Crofts, Inc., 1950), covers all phases of public utilities; P. J. Garfield and W. F. Lovejoy, *Public Utility Economics* (Englewood Cliffs, N.J.: Prentice-Hall, Inc., 1964), careful treatment of rate regulation and rate making; M. G. Glaeser, *Public Utilities in American Capitalism* (New York: Macmillan Co., 1957), an institutional approach to public utility economics; E. Jones and T. C. Bigham, *Principles of Public Utilities* (New York: Macmillan Co., 1931), particularly good on valuation and rate of return; E. R. Troxel, *Economics of Public Utilities* (New York: Rinehart & Co., Inc., 1947), emphasis on theory and marginal cost pricing.

Other references:

M. A. Adelman, *The Supply and Price of Natural Gas* (Oxford: Basil Blackwell, 1962), particularly good on economies of scale and joint costs in petroleum and natural gas; J. C. Bonbright, *Principles of Public Utility Rates* (New York: Columbia University Press, 1955), the most complete treatment available on the subject; M. R. Bonavia, *The Economics of Transport* (new ed.; New York: Pitman Publishing Corp., 1947), concise coverage of all modes; J. M. Clark, *Social Control of Business* (2d ed.; New York: McGraw-Hill Book Co., Inc., 1939), Part III; M. Conant, *Railroad Consolidation and the Antitrust Laws* (Berkeley: Institute of Business and Economic Research, University of California, 1962); C. Dearing and W. Owen, *National Transportation Policy* (Washington, D.C.: The Brookings Institution, 1949), a study of transport policy for the Hoover Commission; K. T. Healy, *The Effects of Scale in the Railroad Industry* (Committee on Transportation, Yale University, 1961); E. Jones, *Principles of Railway Transportation* (New York: Macmillan Co., 1924), a thorough treatment of rail transport down to 1923; H. J. Levin, *Broadcast Regulation and Joint Ownership of Media* (New York: New York University Press, 1960); P. W. MacAvoy, *Price Formation in the Natural Gas Fields* (New Haven: Yale University Press, 1962), a careful examination of pricing problems in natural gas production; J. R. Meyer, M. J. Peck, J. Stenason, and C. Zwick, *The Economics of Competition in the Transportation Industries* (Cambridge: Harvard University Press, 1959), an examination of the role of competition in all the modes of transport; A. M. Milne, *The Economics of Inland Transport* (London: Sir Isaac Pitman & Sons, Ltd., 1955), especially chaps. iv, v, vi on transport pricing; *National Transportation Policy* (The Doyle Report), (87th Cong., 1st sess.) (Washington, D.C.: United States Government Printing Office, 1961), a comprehensive survey of transportation in the United States; J. C. Nelson, *Railroad Transportation and Public Policy* (Washington, D.C.:

The Brookings Institution, 1959), a thorough analysis of the railroad problem; A. C. Pigou, *Economics of Welfare* (3d ed.; London: Macmillan & Co., Ltd., 1929), chap. xviii on railroad rates; H. C. Pritchett, *The Tennessee Valley Authority* (Chapel Hill: University of North Carolina Press, 1943); J. S. Ransmeier, *The Tennessee Valley Authority* (Nashville: Vanderbilt University Press, 1942); E. W. Williams and D. Bluestone, *Rationale of Federal Transportation Policy* (U.S. Dept. of Commerce) (Washington, D.C.: United States Government Printing Office, 1960); C. Wilcox, *Public Policies Toward Business* (rev. ed.; Homewood, Ill.: Richard D. Irwin, Inc., 1960), Parts IV, V; Geo. W. Wilson, *Some Unsettled Questions in the Economics of Transportation* (Bloomington: Indiana University Press, 1962).

INDEX OF NAMES AND SUBJECTS

G

H

I

J

Z

INDEX OF CASES CITED

D

E

F

G

This book has been set in 10 point McKellar, leaded 2 points, and 9 point McKellar, leaded 1 point. Chapter numbers and titles are in 18 point Metro Medium. The size of the type page is 27 by 46½ picas.